Charles XII of Sweden

Charles XII in 1707, from a painting by J.D.Swartz

Charles XII
of
Sweden

R. M. Hatton

Weybright and Talley
New York

© 1968 by R. M. Hatton

Printed in Great Britain

Published in the United States by
WEYBRIGHT AND TALLEY, Inc.
3 East 54th Street,
New York, New York 10022.

Library of Congress Catalog Card No. 69–10605

Contents

Illustrations

The reproduction of these plates has been made possible by the kind permission of the owners or institutions to which the originals belong. The portrait reproduced on the jacket has not been published before and I am grateful to the owner, Vilhelm Assarsson, Esq., who permitted me to see it and to use it, and to His Excellency, Gunnar Hägglöf, Swedish ambassador in London for many years, who first brought it to my attention.

Maps and Plans

Maps and plans have been drawn by Surrey Art Designs, from plans and sketches provided by the author.

Preface

Charles XII of Sweden is one of those historical figures round whom discussion, lively enough in his own day, has never stopped. The riddle of his personality and the vast perspectives of European warfare into which his reign must be fitted have given rise to an endless balancing of cause and effect. Did he throw away Sweden's trans-Baltic empire in unjustified gambles on the battlefield, or did he – by nearly superhuman efforts of willpower and leadership – prop up the already shaky structure of that empire and prolong its existence beyond normal expectation? Was his death the only good service he ever did his country, or did the shot which ended his life on 30 November 1718 rob Sweden of her last chance to anchor the great power position securely? Was that shot fired by someone on the King's own side to rid Sweden of a ruler who did not want peace and whose power was coveted by others, or was it an enemy missile finding its mark (according to the philosophy of the individual commentator) by the accident of war, the chance of Fate or the will of God?

The reaction against the overcritical judgements of the King by nineteenth-century historians, the so-called 'old school' of Caroline historiography, produced in the early decades of the twentieth century the nearly equally oversimplified concept of the 'new school', in whose writings the King was for ever on the side of the angels. But though the historians of the 'new school' at times pushed their defence of Charles XII into the realms of *a priori* deductions, they laid the foundations of modern research and proved the unhistorical nature of many of the accusations of the 'old school'.

A widespread realization of the insufficiencies of the 'old' and 'new' schools alike sent Swedish historians, from the 1930s onwards, on a detailed search for objective truth; facets of the reign, aspects of policy, anything that could be factually demonstrated became the goal, and the reliability or otherwise of the documentary material available was minutely investigated. The sheer accumulation of monographs and scholarly articles published in the last thirty-five years demands and will eventually produce a Swedish biographical treatment in the light of modern research. So far none has been written, and there is no generally accepted picture of Charles XII, either among Swedish historians or among the Swedish educated reading public at large.

The obstacle to a biographical study of Charles XII, quite apart from the frightening amount of specialized work in many fields and languages to be mastered, is a psychological one. Swedish scholars who have had occasion in recent years to comment on the character of Charles XII – in works of reference, in general histories of Sweden or of Europe – are all agreed that the King's personality is complex and hard to grasp, obscured into the bargain by the propaganda of his own time, both Swedish and foreign. It has also become obvious that those who work in the field of Caroline research – unless they become adherents of either the 'old' or the 'new' school – are prone to that ambivalent emotional attitude towards Charles XII which Karl-Gustaf Hildebrand has so skilfully analysed in his historiography of the reign, finding traces of it even in writers who are commonly regarded as pure representatives of the wholly critical or the wholly admiring schools. Such self-knowledge exerts an inhibiting influence and prevents historians leaving the safe and factual field of their own specializations inside economic, cultural, military, diplomatic and administrative history for the hazards of a biography which demands commitment and speculation and where answers to the riddles both of Charles XII's life and death must be attempted.

The English do have a general picture of Charles XII. It is built up from two separate figures. One derives from the pamphlet warfare of the home front of Queen Anne's and George I's reigns. Tory and Whig, Jacobite and Hanoverian used oversimplified conceptions of the Swedish King as ammunition against their opponents. When that side won which had – for various reasons – produced a stereotype of a harsh, cruel and war-loving tyrant, Charles remained typecast for ever: so much so that Southey, nearly a century after the death of Charles XII, was tortured by nightmares in which that King and his inhumanity to Patkul were the central themes. The second figure was produced by Voltaire who – consciously editing the material at his disposal – in his *Histoire de Charles XII* of 1731 told the moral tale of a warrior-king whose very virtues made him incapable of being the wise leader of his nation. He did this so brilliantly that his portrait is etched indelibly on the European historical consciousness, while translations of the book into non-European languages have spread it far and wide: none of the *Remarques* or histories with which those who had known Charles XII, and did not quite recognize him in Voltaire's portrait, rushed into print could modify it.

In England Voltaire's conception of the King helped to tone down the cruelty inseparable from the pamphlet stereotype; but the undifferentiated war-lord image – the prototype for Geijer's 'our only illiterate warrior-king' of the nineteenth-century Swedish judgement – was fixed for ever when Johnson transposed Voltaire's moral tale into couplets of epigrammatic force in *The Vanity of Human Wishes*.

> On what foundation stands the warrior's pride,
> How just his hopes let Swedish Charles decide;

A frame of adamant, a soul of fire,
No dangers fright him, and no labours tire;
O'er love, o'er fear, extends his wide domain,
Unconquer'd lord of pleasure and of pain;
No joys to him pacific sceptres yield,
War sounds the trump, he rushes to the field;
Behold surrounding kings their powr's combine,
And one capitulate, and one resign;
Peace courts his hand, but spreads her charms in vain;
'Think nothing gain'd,' he cries, 'till nought remain,
On Moscow's walls till Gothic standards fly,
And all be mine beneath the Polar sky.'
The march begins in military state,
And nations on his eye suspended wait;
Stern Famine guards the solitary coast,
And Winter barricades the realms of Frost;
He comes, nor want nor cold his course delay, –
Hide, blushing Glory, hide Pultava's day:
The vanquish'd hero leave his broken bands,
And shows his miseries in distant lands;
Condemn'd a needy supplicant to wait,
While ladies interpose, and slaves debate.
But did not chance at length her error mend?
Did not subverted empire mark his end?
Did rival monarchs give the fatal wound?
Or hostile millions press him to the ground?
His fall was destined to a barren strand,
A petty fortress and a dubious hand;
He left the name, at which the world grew pale,
To point a moral, or adorn a tale.

Since 1749 several English biographies of Charles XII have appeared – larger in scope than Johnson's summary one of thirty-two lines. They are all worth reading, though the march of modern research has naturally left them behind. The one by R. Nisbet Bain of 1895 is a sober account, written in the spirit of the Swedish 'old school'; that by Oscar Browning of 1899 is a livelier story of a general who 'drank to the full of the joy of battle'; while that by Eveline Godley in 1928, *Charles XII of Sweden. A study of kingship*, though popular in tone, is influenced by the 'new school'. In 1960 a condensed version of the late Frans G. Bengtsson's two-volume Swedish biography from 1935 and 1936 was translated into German and English. The Swedish work, by a gifted poet, essayist and novelist, has had a deserved popular success: it is beautifully written and shows an impressive familiarity with the memoirs, war-diaries and letters of the Caroline period. A German three-volume history, *König Karl XII von Schweden*, by Otto Haintz, published between 1936 and 1958, is a scholarly study of the Great Northern War with strong emphasis

on the military and diplomatic aspects, though slightly vitiated by a somewhat
naïve, if sincere, belief that all would have gone well with Charles XII if only he
had allied himself with Prussia.

In my own work I have sometimes regretted that limitation I imposed on
myself by deciding that a one-volume work was all that I could ask my
students and the general public to accept: I have looked with some envy at the
five volumes in which Professor Braubach has so brilliantly covered the life of
Prinz Eugen of Savoy. But the memory of the advice of one of my late teachers,
Gustaaf Renier, has kept me to the narrower path: *Le mieux est l'ennemi
du bien.* To him and to the late Mark A. Thomson – also teacher and
friend – who first suggested that I might try to make the reign of Charles XII
'intelligible' to my own students, I look back in gratitude.

During my work in archives and libraries I have incurred other debts of
gratitude which it is a pleasure to acknowledge. The officials of the *Riksarkiv,*
the *Kungl. Krigsarkiv,* the Uppsala and Lund university libraries, *Kungl.
Biblioteket* and *Svensk Porträtt Galleri* in Stockholm have been most helpful,
as have those of the Public Record Office, the British Museum in London, the
Heinsius Archief at The Hague and the Huntington Library of California.
Swedish scholars of the Caroline period have given generously of their time
to 'talk shop', and I would wish particularly to mention Professors Karl-
Gustaf Hildebrand, Sven A. Nilsson, Jerker Rosén, Nils Strömböm, Dr B.
Kentrschynskyj and Dr G. Jonasson. The late Major-General Gustaf Petri
and the late director of the War Office archive, Dr Birger Steckzén, helped me
in so many ways, and Lieutenant-Colonel E. Bensow generously put at my
disposal maps which he had prepared for regimental histories. Among my own
colleagues, I have special obligations to those who supplemented my weak
Russian and my non-existent Polish: Dr I. de Madariaga, Dr M. S. Anderson
and Dr L. Lewitter. I owe much to discussions with the late B. H. Sumner and
to conversations with Professor A. N. Kurat of Ankara University. My debt
to European scholars working in the early eighteenth century will be seen
from the footnotes to my text, but I would wish to emphasize, for Russo-
Swedish relations, that to R. Wittram, V. Feygina, B. Shutoi and the late E.
Tarle; for Polish-Swedish relations that to J. Gierowski and the Polish and
Russian contributors to the collective work *Um die polnischen Krone,* published in 1961; for Swedish relations with the Habsburg state and the Empire
that to Otto Haintz, W. Holst, E. Hassinger and M. Braubach; and for
Swedish relations with Spain and the Jacobites that to S. Jägerskiöld and to
C. Nordmann in *La crise du Nord au début du XVIII* siècle published in
1962. The responsibility for all errors and misconceptions remains with me.

I must thank my college, the London School of Economics and Political
Science, for leave of absence for three terms spread over the years during
which this book has been one of my major research projects; the University
of London for two travel grants to enable me to visit Swedish archives and

libraries in the early stages of the work; and for a study-grant from the *Karolinska Förbundet* generously and unexpectedly offered through its then President, the late Professor Nils Ahnlund, to enable me to pay a visit to Sweden during my sabbatical leave in 1957. The secretarial staff of my college, and especially Miss Colette Ritchie, deserves praise for typing and re-typing successive versions of my manuscript. The interest and encouragement of my husband and family are beyond thanks.

Note on dates, distances, coinage and spelling

DATES Unless otherwise stated I use the Swedish style of the period covered. Up to 1700 this was the Julian calendar, the so-called old style (O.S.) in contrast to the Gregorian calendar, the new style (N.S.), adopted by most of the European countries but not by Sweden, England and Russia. Until 1700, old style was ten days behind new style; after 1700, it was eleven days behind. But in 1700 Sweden opted for a modified form of the Julian calendar in the hope of a gradual progress to the Gregorian one: they dropped leap-year of that year and thus remained ten days behind N.S. but at the same time one day ahead of O.S. In 1712 Charles XII decided this gave them the worst of both worlds and reverted to O.S. Double dating is given where this is essential for clarity's sake.

DISTANCES The continental mile in the late seventeenth and the early eighteenth century varied slightly from country to country, but differed markedly from the shorter English mile. Where distances are given, I have converted to modern metres, kilometres and miles.

COINAGE For an excellent summary of the Swedish coinage after Gustavus Adolphus in 1624 introduced a copper standard beside the silver one see F. Åmark, *Sveriges statsfinanser* (1964), Book I, 1 ff. For our purpose it is enough to know that in Charles XII's time the unit of account, the *riksdaler*, corresponded to the *Reichsthaler* of the Empire and equalled three Swedish *daler* silver mynt (indicated by dsm or ds), and six *daler* kopper mynt (indicated by dkm), while the expression 'barrel of gold' was a unit of account equalling 100,000 dsm.

SPELLING OF NAMES Where the name of a person or a place-name has an accepted English form (e.g. Charles for Karl, Stanislaus for Stanisław, Gothenburg for Göteborg, Scania for Skåne, Courland for Kurland) I have used this, since it would seem pedantic to do otherwise. For the rest, I have used the generally accepted contemporary spelling with the present spelling indicated in brackets in the index. Changes in territorial ownership since 1682–1718 may render some of the names used less acceptable to their present inhabitants, but my guiding principle – where there is no accepted contemporary spelling – has been to adopt that of the state to which the place belonged in the reign of Charles XII. I lay no claim to complete consistency. In one case I have deliberately adopted a nineteenth-century English spelling, namely Sleswig, to avoid the choice between the Danish Slesvig and the German Schleswig.

BOOK ONE

Charles XII and His Heritage

1

The Person and the Personality

We know what Charles XII looked like. We possess an abundance of authenticated portraits of him, professional and amateur,[1] where we can follow his physical development from infancy to the end of his life (we may add to these not only a portrait modelled from his dead face and for long believed to be a death-mask of him,* but also drawings and photographs of the remains of his embalmed corpse taken when his coffin was opened in 1917); we have a great many descriptions of him which were penned in his lifetime or put down after his death by people who had known him or had occasion to observe him. But since portraits and pen-portraits alike are stamped also with the personality of the artist and the recorder, and since the personality of the sitter was often difficult to pin down, we do not get complete agreement. 'No portrait that I ever saw of the King is like him', wrote a young Swedish student who in 1707 had an opportunity to watch Charles XII at close quarters, adding in partial explanation that the King was not easy to paint, his features even hard to recall once one was out of his presence.[2]

What is curious is that in the many portraits painted from life we can on the whole distinguish, irrespective of the individual artist, two types of face: on the one hand we find rounded contours and mobile features, which in youth at times give the impression of being unfinished; on the other we discover a face composed of taut, angular planes which frequently add up to a rather forbidding portrait. The difference between these two types cannot be one of the sitter's age, for though the second type is more commonly present in the post-1715 period, there are also examples of the rounder, more relaxed face till the end of Charles's life – and indeed the so-called 'death-mask' is of this type – while the angular face is to be found even among youthful portraits; nor does there seem to be a fully valid dividing-line between professional and amateur artists painting the King *ad vivum*. Both versions may be essentially true to life, expressing different facets of Charles XII's personality according to the mood of the sitter and the different response of the artist; but the presence of the *two* prevalent portrait types has created a specific problem.

When Gustavus IV in 1799 let Charles XII's coffin be opened, he was moved

* Cp. below, p. 505.

to do so mainly out of a desire to decide which portrait of the King was the one most true to life as far as could be judged from the embalmed physical remains. It was agreed by those present that one of the portraits painted towards the end of Charles XII's life, during the King's stay in Lund in 1717, by David von Krafft,* and kept in the Drottningholm collection, came closest to the impression received from the body:[3] a victory therefore for the angular type of portrait. But possibly an inconclusive victory, for it is not surprising that the dead and shrunken face, close to the underlying bone structure of the head, should lead observers to opt for the Krafft type of portrait; and it is curious and significant that when a drawing of the body was published in 1917, by an artist present at the opening of the coffin in that year, it was generally thought that Axel Sparre's portrait from 1712† (now in Gripsholm Castle) – one belonging to the more rounded type – fitted this 1917 impression best.[4] The real explanation of the two recurring types among the many differing portraits of Charles XII may well lie in two opposed 'schools' of conceptions of the King among artists and amateurs alike, while it is also possible that the ambivalent attitude found among those who have written about Charles XII's character and personality‡ finds its counterpart in the art of portraiture just in this problem of the two types of face.

Measurements taken and observations recorded at the various openings of Charles XII's coffin (there have been four in all, for the one in 1799 was preceded by one in 1746 and followed by one in 1859, the fourth and final one taking place in 1917) have helped to establish such facts about the King as his height, the extent of his limp caused by the accident of 1702, the state of his teeth, etc., while x-ray examination of his skeleton has enabled the injuries he suffered in life to be more surely ascertained and has even permitted discoveries of injuries he tried to hide when alive;[5] but the total impression of Charles XII received by those present at the openings would seem – to judge from the evidence available – to have been coloured by preconceived opinions of, or attitudes to, the King.[6] The portraits and even the conclusions drawn from the lifeless body of Charles XII must therefore be used with some caution.

The same is true of the descriptions found in private letters, in diplomatic reports, in diaries and in autobiographies or memoirs of those who had known, or just hastily glimpsed, Charles XII and who for one reason or another felt impelled to put down on paper, or to preserve in their memory and later convey by word of mouth, their impressions of the King's looks. Swedish officials, officers and travellers who joined Charles XII's army or visited his headquarters frequently attempted to describe the King in their letters home or in their diaries; foreign diplomats and soldiers, and onlookers of various kinds in the countries through which Charles XII passed, drew their pen-portraits of him in official reports, in private letters, and in chronicles and histories which they compiled; Swede and non-Swede often spoke of Charles

* See illustration facing p. 492.   † See illustration facing p. 205.   ‡ See above, p. xiv.

XII many years after they had met him, and their words were written down by others.

In factual matters the painted portraits do at times confirm the written evidence. The King's habitual pose, when listening to others in a relaxed frame of mind, with a 'half-smile' on his face so characteristic as to have been remarked upon by scores of contemporaries (what was the reason for it? – a willed effort to appear gracious to his subjects in accordance with his promise to his mother on her deathbed? – part of his technique for hiding his feelings? – just part of the pleasant if shy personality?) needs no verification from the portraits, though one unknown artist successfully perpetualizes this royal half-smile[7] while several of the well-known portraits hint at it. But it is curiously and nearly disturbingly illuminating, having read a Polish monk's observation from 1704 of the King's habit of opening the right eye wider than the left (showing a lot of white and producing a rather staring expression),[8] to come across the amateur portrait by Löwen from December 1703 which gives pictorial evidence to the same effect,[9] the right eye being distinctly larger and more staring than the left (possibly a sign of strain?). And a contemporary anonymous engraving has captured the King's habit, noticeable after his return from Turkey, of running his hand over his now balding pate.[10]

In the matter of physical likeness, Charles XII himself has been of the greatest help to the historian. He it was who insisted on realism in royal portraiture. His order to Johan David Swartz in 1706 that Major-General Creutz should be painted 'wrinkles and all'[11] was only an echo of the conditions he had laid down for portraits of himself as soon as he grew out of adolescence; smallpox scars were the order of the day when Swartz came to paint the King. The insistence on realistic portraits may well have been a protest against the richly allegorical royal portraiture practised at court when he was heir presumptive, for we know from his correspondence in later life that he preferred the direct approach and abhorred allegorical and literal allusions in other forms of art – in architecture for example. The realism and simplicity of the portraits of Charles XII after 1700 owe something also to habits he adopted as a soldier. The campaign portraits which were sent to Stockholm, at the demand of his sisters and his grandmother in the early years of the Great Northern War shocked the court: the 1701 miniature by Axel Sparre presented the King without a wig for the first time,[12] while the 1706 portrait from Saxony by Swartz* showed a royal skin far too tanned and marked by sun and wind and exertions of body and mind to coincide with the current taste of what was fitting in likenesses of crowned heads.[13] Charles XII himself was on the whole pleased with the results of the realistic portraits he demanded. He was not at all flattered in the painting by Sparre from Bender in 1712, in which his receding hair line and the plump face of the 'lazy dog-days' in Turkey (as he labelled those years in retrospect) are stressed in a manner which have caused some historians to classify this portrait† as a near

* See frontispiece. † See illustration facing p. 205.

caricature,[14] yet the King is known to have been 'marvellously pleased' with it and other Swedes in Bender considered it a true and pleasant portrait.[15]

Only once is there evidence of Charles's dissatisfaction with a portrait of himself; the painting which David Krafft made of him in Lund in the autumn of 1717 displeased the King so much on his first sight of the finished work that he slashed the face with a knife in Krafft's absence.[16] This, the most angular and harsh of all the portraits of Charles XII, giving an impression of cruelty and inhumanity, in spite of, or perhaps because of a vague smile that is nearly a sneer, must have touched the King on the raw to provoke so uncommon a reaction, to make one so noted for his self-control lose it. Even here, on reflection, Charles XII permitted the artist freedom from royal censorship; the full-length painting, done afresh by Krafft, was excellent in composition and execution and was much copied and used in Swedish embassies abroad and in official buildings at home during Charles XII's own lifetime. But the King's momentary anger and disappointment at the face which Krafft saw and depicted is illuminating: possibly some passing sorrow and unbelief at what life had made out of him and he of his own life, like that mingled sadness and annoyance that anyone in middle age may feel when faced with the results of a duty visit to the photographer. Certainly the angular and harsh face was not the one Charles XII wished to recognize as the reflection of his own personality.

II

From the various types of source material at our disposal, certain physical facts emerge clearly. Charles, fully-grown early in youth, was tall by contemporary standards, at least 1·75 metres (5ft. 9 in.), it has been estimated,[17] and looked taller because he was, except for brief periods of his life, very spare. The relative lack of exercise during his years in Turkey (1709–14), when foot injuries, several attacks of fever, and his general circumstances limited his freedom of action, made him put on weight; and Swedes who saw him in 1715 and 1716, after an interval of years, found the King plumper and also stiffer than before.[18] He was, after his return to the Swedish dominions in 1714, as active as before 1709, but the extreme suppleness of body which had enabled him to pick up a glove from the ground at the gallop was no longer his.[19] The uniform which Charles XII wore on the day of his death in 1718 has been preserved* and as it would fit only a slim man of his height, it has been deduced that the exertions of the King's two Norwegian campaigns and the frugality of his meals – he often dieted rigorously to rid himself of colds and other indispositions – made him lose weight again in the last two years of his life. His shoulders were broad, and his waist narrow: diplomats in pre-1700 Stockholm never failed to comment on the inability of the King to disguise himself at masked balls: however often he changed costume of an evening he was always recognized by his characteristic build.[20]

* Cp. below, p. 505.

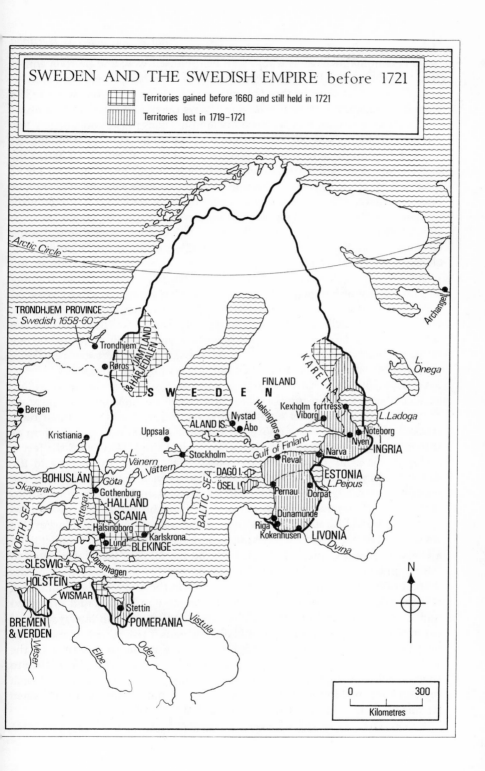

SWEDEN AND THE SWEDISH EMPIRE before 1721

Territories gained before 1660 and still held in 1721

Territories lost in 1719–1721

Arctic Circle

TRONDHJEM PROVINCE
~ Swedish 1658-60 ~

Trondhjem

Røros

JÄMTLAND & HÄRJEDALEN

S W E D E N

FINLAND

KARELIA

L. Onega

Archangel

Bergen

Kristiania

Uppsala

ÅLAND IS.

Nystad
Åbo

Hälsingfors

Kexholm fortress

Viborg

L. Ladoga

Nöteborg

Nyen

INGRIA

L.
Vänern

L. Vättern

Stockholm

Gulf of Finland

Narva

Reval

DAGÖ I.

ÖSEL I.

Pernau

Dorpat

L. Peipus

ESTONIA

BOHUSLÄN

Göta

Skagerak

Gothenburg

HALLAND

SCANIA

Kattegat

Hälsingborg

Lund

Karlskrona

BLEKINGE

BALTIC SEA

Dunamünde

Riga

Kokenhusen

LIVONIA

Dvina

NORTH SEA

SLESWIG

HOLSTEIN

Copenhagen

WISMAR

BREMEN
& VERDEN

Weser

Elbe

Stettin

POMERANIA

Oder

Vistula

N

0   300

Kilometres

On ceremonial occasions Charles XII held himself well, and he rode with a very straight back – he 'looked wonderful on horseback' everyone agreed – but when he was sunk in thought, either at table or when out walking, he tended to slouch. His movements were always quick and decisive; he walked fast, with long strides, hands clasped behind his back; his usual stance when talking or listening was one with the familiar half-smile on his face and his left hand resting on the hilt of his long sword: if, when out riding, he halted his horse to speak to someone, his hat was habitually put under his arm for as long as the interview lasted. His whole physical presence was one of energy, of bodily strength, of constant activity bordering on restlessness; he would walk up and down while reading a letter or pondering a reply; he would hurry to sign a letter before taking off his gloves – a habit which did not improve the elegance of his signature.[21] He would twiddle the button of a uniform or clergyman's gown, or pick at the lace cuffs of an officer,[22] while conversing with them. His health as a grown man was good; hard and conscious training and self-discipline had helped to develop a youth reckoned weak and cosseted by anxious parents and doctors into a physically tough and enduring man. He withstood the rigours of campaign-life surprisingly well; and though the courtiers and doctors and some of his officers deplored his disregard for his creature comforts and his tendency to take risks, his soldiers generally were proud of his hardihood and admired him for his physical courage.

Charles, like most men of his age and profession, was prone to riding accidents; horses often tumbled with him or fell on him, but only once, in 1702, did such an accident lead to any severe injury,* when his thigh bone cracked one hand's breadth above the knee and left him with a slight limp or stiffness which was quite noticeable when he was tired. He caught the fevers raging in his army off and on, but only once seriously (in Turkey in the summer of 1713, when he and his suite had been forcibly removed to the unhealthy marsh land round the castle of Timurtash. He had a tendency to slight stomach upsets in his youth and to bronchitis and catarrh both in youth and upon his return to Sweden from the warmer climate of Turkey. He was injured in battle several times; most seriously in 1709 when a bullet from a Cossack rifled gun pierced his left foot and the summer heat contributed to the wound fever which put him on the danger list and made the doctors despair of his life for three days. This wound was the one which kept him on a stretcher during the battle of Poltava; it was slow in healing and prevented him riding for several months; it also tended to open up in later years and cause him some discomfort. It would also seem as if the same foot received a new injury, the breaking of some bones in the ankle, at the time of the *Kalabalik*, the Bender fighting against his Turkish hosts in 1713. From time to time he suffered slight bullet- and sword-wounds. The most serious of such injuries happened in the Stresow battle on the island of Rügen in 1715, when he was hit in the chest, but the wound healed within four weeks.

* See below, p. 405, for a relatively severe but not permanent injury in May 1715.

He tended to make light of all injuries and illnesses, his own and those of his officers and men; mainly to set an example of courage and fortitude, but probably also from a rooted dislike of the doctoring and pampering of his youth. He developed his own régime to conquer illnesses which did not, like bullet wounds, need the surgeon's knife. As an adolescent he used to pour the medicines prescribed for his coughs and colds out of the window;[23] as a grown man his answer to fever and catarrh was a cutting down on food (he once starved himself for a week in the hope of getting rid of a troublesome cough),[24] and the kill-or-cure of exercise and fresh air. The cap which his sister Ulrika sent him in 1717 to help him keep warm and thus free from bronchitis he politely thanked her for, assuring her that he would treasure it as a keepsake since she had worked it with her own hands, but stating firmly that he had become too accustomed to wind and weather playing round his head ever to wear a wig or even a cap any more.[25]

Charles's putting aside of the wig in the autumn of 1700, during his first trans-Baltic campaign, was initially dictated by considerations of convenience in the field; but he never put it on again, except during one brief interlude in Saxony in 1707 when, on medical advice, he donned a wig to help him get rid of a chill, but was teased out of it pretty quickly when his officers pretended to believe he was smartening himself up to go a-courting.[26] He soon got so used both to going without a wig and to the conception of himself as – in the phrase of the time – 'wearing his own hair', that he felt it unnatural to use a wig. The change suited him in every way. It went with the personality he was consciously building up of the King who could easily be recognized by his soldiers from his wigless head and from the extreme simplicity of his uniform; the plain blue coat with brass buttons, the yellow waistcoat and the black taffeta cravat wound several times round his neck, worn with elkskin breeches – an outfit in telling contrast to the wigs and fine uniforms, often ordered by the King himself, of the officers of his suite and of his guards. Charles XII's one personal extravagance was the frequent replacement of his uniforms, but even this luxury was a near-necessity, since his clothes wore out quickly through the hard wear of active service.[27] In cold weather he put a cloak over his uniform; Mazepa presented him with a fur coat in 1708, and this was worn once or twice but was soon laid aside so that the King might share the hardship of the winter of 1708–9 with his men, who had neither fur coats nor fur-lined cloaks.[28] In Poland, if the winter was cold, Charles sometimes wore a cap of otterskin;[29] but his usual turned-up black hat (buttoned on the left), of the same model as those worn by his soldiers, was as often off his head as on, exposing his hair, cut short, dark blond in colour with a slightly auburn tinge, brushed upwards like a crown round his head.[30] The wind and sun of the King's open-air life bleached the hair; it tended to lose some of its colour as the years went by and became streaked with grey, and even white, especially over the ears. Always fine in texture, the hair began to recede relatively early, exposing that full, broad and domed forehead so characteristic of Charles XII from his late twenties onwards.

That forehead was balanced by a jutting nose inherited from his mother's family, a nose which in the more youthful portraits dominates the face too exclusively, but which in the mature face fits well into the general picture. The lips, rather pale in colour, were full and sensitive, the upper lip somewhat short. A small reddish birth mark can be distinguished on some portraits just below the left corner of the mouth;[31] a dimple or cleft in the strong chin becomes noticeable in later pictures but is not present in those of his early youth.[32] The skin was fine with a fresh colour until hardened and darkened by campaign life; slightly marked with the smallpox scars which Charles, as a boy of eleven, had welcomed with joy as producing a manly countenance. The best feature was his eyes, under finely formed eyebrows, deep blue, and generally admired for their brilliance, liveliness and intelligence.[33]

III

The total impression received from the face was one not of beauty, but of intelligence and energy and of a calmness achieved by self-control. It was a face not easy to read, schooled, like the King's temper, not to betray his feelings. Young Swedes serving in the Drabant corps – where the rank of a private equalled that of a lieutenant in the rest of the army – who had frequent opportunities to watch the King, admitted to a compatriot who visited them in the Saxony headquarters that they, after years of service, could not tell Charles XII's temper or mood from his looks.[34] Those who knew him at close quarters for many years could tell when he was angry; red patches appeared on his cheekbones, his lips curled upwards,[35] and he developed certain mannerisms of speech on occasions when he found it hard to keep a check on annoyance, such as repeating the phrase 'What do you say?' two or three times in a tone of voice which betrayed him.[36] His temper on the whole, however, was an even one; he was thought mild, generous and compassionate in personal relationships by all who knew him well, and in a revealing comment on his own character he once referred to the 'softness' of his inclinations and the slowness with which he was wrought to anger, finding it nearly impossible to say No to any one or to be angry with any one.[37] But for the 'choler' which the King showed in battle, his officers averred, they would have judged him of a phlegmatic disposition.[38]

This inborn easy-going temperament, regarded as a heritage from his mother, was allied in his nature to a strength of will inherited from both parents, though more easily perceived in his father, cultivated by the father's example in Charles XII's early teens, and tested and made ever stronger by the circumstances of his own reign as King of Sweden. Both these traits are commented on, consciously and unconsciously, by portrait painters and by those who described and discussed the King in words: they seem to have warred with each other and to have helped to produce varying impressions according to which had the upper hand at the time of observation. The King's face – his whole bearing, in fact – conveyed at times an impression of such mildness and simplicity of heart as to verge on stupidity at a superficial glance. Diplomats noted this with a spice of malice once or twice, particularly in his younger years;[39] Swedes, especially those who prided themselves on being accustomed to more polished society, allowed themselves to poke fun sometimes at their King's lack of elegance and presence. A second look, however, usually sufficed to discover both the intelligence and the will of steel, so that the awe and majesty emanating from the personality becomes as frequently commented upon as the mildness and the graciousness.

Here perhaps lies the answer to the riddle both of ambivalent judgements and different types in portraiture: the two sides of Charles xii's own character were observed not only according to the mood of the moment as far as the monarch is concerned, but also according to the capacity of the observer to grasp the essence of the personality composed of varying and warring strains. The young Swede who in half jocular, half impatient mood had likened Charles xii to one of his own peasant subjects in looks and behaviour, confessed, half mystified and half scared, that the feeling which the King inspired in him after constant and close observation ('This King, on whom I cannot enough feast my eyes') was one of 'venerandum mixed with horrendum'.[40] Other witnesses who observed Charles xii without knowing him well as a person also noted this streak of hardness which, particularly if the King was taking part in some public occasion, when he would take care to expose as little as possible of his inner self, transmitted itself to the observer as such an aura of power and ruthless determination that it sent premonitory shivers down the spine.[41]

That Charles had charm, especially in the day-to-day encounters with those who served him or who were otherwise thrown into close contact with him, is abundantly testified. He had a sense of humour which comes across to us down the years in many sayings of his, short and to the point, slightly cynical at times as he grew older, which spiced the often hard and humdrum life of the war years of those around him. In the same way, he himself preferred those serving him to be *lustigh*, of lively and reasonably cheerful disposition, able to make light of difficulties with quips and stories and wry jokes. To young observers at headquarters this was sometimes hidden: to them the King himself and his civil and military advisers looked serious, burdened with weighty business and much responsibility; but nearly all those who got close to the King shared a forceful, direct and basically optimistic temperament. Physical courage was part of their make-up, as of his; moral courage also, and a directness of approach in discussion of problems which suited Charles xii who, in his turn, allowed those in the inner circle – men like Rehnskiöld, Piper, Cederhielm in the early years, Feif, Meijerfelt, the Prince of Hesse, Görtz and others later on – astonishing freedom of expression and opinion.[42]

Those who had both physical and moral courage, but who had less in common with Charles XII in respect of temperament, men like Lewenhaupt, Hermelin and Horn, always remained at some distance, separated from the King by their more pessimistic attitude to life and to the problems before them. Even with them, as in general, outside ceremonial and formal diplomatic occasions, Charles XII behaved with such unselfconscious naturalness, with such a disregard for regal trappings or airs of any kind, that those used to a stricter court etiquette counted this the greater part of his charm: to talk to him, commented a diplomatic representative from Louis XIV in 1715, was to converse with a philosopher, not a king.*

It should be noted, however, that this emissary was a military man as well as a diplomat, for Charles XII always found it easier to unbend in the company of those who practised the same craft as himself: to the soldier and the administrator and the practical reformer he could talk easily and freely. This can be seen from records of conversations which have survived, and notably in the memoirs of Axel von Löwen, who visited Bender in 1712 for four or five weeks, having spent most of the years 1700 to 1711, on Charles XII's orders, serving on the allied side in the War of the Spanish Succession.[43] At that time, as also in the 1715–18 period, von Löwen had long talks with the King, discussing European views of Charles's generalship and policies. The letters of Casten Feif to Swedish officials,[44] on a wide range of administrative problems and Swedish domestic business in general for the years 1709–18, based on talks with the King, are equally informative.

Wherever there was a point of contact, Charles XII enjoyed the society of his fellow human beings. If contact was missing, or if he was preoccupied with problems which his military and civil leadership thrust upon him (in which case those who knew him well could guess his preoccupation from his behaviour and left him alone, while those who intruded at such moments through lack of perceptiveness or from ignorance, were apt to find that he did not answer them or, if they persisted, took refuge in flight) the King was reserved and silent, seeming shy, though shyness, once he had grown out of adolescence, was not typical of him. The point of contact between Charles XII and other people was often Sweden and all that word meant to him: memories of his own childhood and the circle of family, teachers, court officials and servants which made him keen to question men and women who brought news from home when he was far away; concern with the problems of the present and the possibilities of the future which made him attentive to the plans of reformers and inventors both Swedish and foreign. At other times the point of contact was more general; his quick mind and his mental alertness and curiosity made him keen to discuss the wonders of the world, the religious and philosophical problems of the intellectuals of his age; while his absorption in matters of taste expressed itself in a passionate interest in the cut of a uniform or an academic robe, in the wording of military regulations and the

* Cp. below ,p. 408.

Charles XI and his family, from a painting by D. Ehrenstrahl

ARX REGIA HOLMENSIS
versus Orientem

Stockholm Castle from the east, from an engraving by Erik Dahlberg

The gardens of Stockholm Castle, from an engraving by Erik Dahlberg

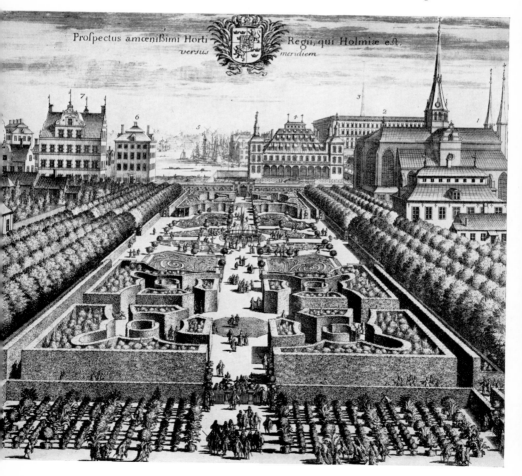

Prospectus amœnißimi Horti Regii, qui Holmiæ est, *versus meridiem*

purification of the Swedish language, in the building plans for Stockholm and in the voyages of cultural exploration to the Holy Land and to the Levant which he financed and encouraged and in whose rich rewards, in the form of drawings of places and people, he found much joy.

Charles XII seems to have shared his sisters' delight in music. His and Ulrika's personal friendship with the Düben family of court officials and musicians points that way; that his own interest went beyond accepting music as part of court festivities is seen from his servant Hultman's description of the concerts the King arranged in Turkey, 'nearly every day', by orchestras of more than thirty players with lutes, violas, oboes and 'every kind of instrument imaginable'. Hultman never forgot the 'pleasant, wonderful and beautiful music'.[45] We are on even surer ground when we approach the King's interest in literature, Scandinavian and foreign. His mother possessed a fine library and the teachers of his adolescence were well-read; he was brought up to appreciate French plays and European traditional stories as well as the sagas and the Bible, and the evidence we have of books carried on campaign by officers to be read, exchanged and discussed includes also those books that interested the King. He did not have much opportunity after 1700 to see plays performed, but he had enjoyed those put on by the French actors he called to Sweden before the war; he liked to read French 'when he had time', Nordberg noted from his own observation;[46] he read or listened to readings of the plays of Molière, Corneille and Racine, and took part in discussions of them when he had leisure in Turkey; he commented on Boileau (Nicolas Boileau-Despréaux) to Löwen during the siege of Stralsund. He carried Curtius's *Alexander* in his pocket as a young man and read the Bible every day of his life and became keenly interested in the linguistic and historical discussions connected with bible-studies after 1715. A concern with the Swedish language is noticeable long before this: he tried to find native words (often of dialect origin) for foreign expressions; he quoted poetry and phrases that struck him; he strove for clarity in official letters (though not always successfully in his own case); his private letters are forceful, direct and show a distinct gift for painting situations in words. The nineteenth-century Swedish judgement on him as 'our only illiterate warrior-king'[47] is certainly misguided, and his oft-quoted comment to his chaplain Rhyzelius in 1717, 'Better to travel than to ruin your eyes by excessive reading'[48], was in the nature of a pleasantry* to a clergyman known for walking long distances in Scania on shanks's pony.

Sometimes the point of contact was purely human and instinctive; the exchange of words with men on duty at night in times of danger, the mingled delight and exasperation of training young pupils, like Maximilian of Württemberg from 1702 to 1709 (whose companionship meant so much to him that he long mourned the loss of his 'best and truest friend')[49] and his nephew, Charles Frederick of Holstein-Gottorp, after 1715; the glance at a pretty girl (for though he pretended not to take much notice, he used to ask the name of

---

* In Swedish the quip has more punch: '*Thet är bätter at resa än mordläsa*'.

those who took his fancy, identifying them by a most minute description of looks and clothes, belying his air of indifference at the time of observation); the recognition of a face once seen; the return to a place once visited – symbolized most poignantly perhaps in his seeking out, on his 1718 campaign on the Swedish side of the Norwegian border, a farm where he had stayed before, finding his old chair, sitting for hours, rocking the cradle of the new baby, talking about those members of the family and neighbours whom he had met during previous visits.*

IV

Charles XII's position was all the same one of singular loneliness which could not but influence the development of his own personality and the attitude of contemporaries to him. He was born to absolutism, a burden heavy enough to shoulder even though adolescent inexperience and pride for a time made it seem easy; and the position of supreme responsibility both as military and civil war leader forced upon him by circumstances, only three years after his accession, increased both his loneliness and his vulnerability. It was a position for which he had been trained and one which he accepted with willingness – even alacrity, in the natural desire of youth to prove itself worthy of testing in the school of experience – but it was one which, in one sense, removed him from his subjects as leadership for the fate of Sweden became concentrated in the mind and will of an eighteen-year-old youth. He had advisers and teachers, particularly in the military field, but the final responsibility, just because so much was at stake for Sweden, had to be his – no one else was willing to take it on and he could not avoid it, even had he wanted to do so. The burden of office and of the war could therefore not help shaping and moulding the character of Charles XII: his obstinacy, at least in the opinions of the bureaucrats concerned with their own responsibility if anything should go wrong, e.g. if the King should die or defeat should come, increased – indeed, he had to be obstinate to get things done; his need to guard military plans and secrets imposed on him a strict discipline which made him taciturn and reserved in such matters and has not made it easy either for contemporaries or for posterity to uncover his own strategic ideas; his optimism, in public anyhow, became exaggerated so as to encourage the will of resistance in Sweden; while the very appeal to the dice of war which had been forced upon him encouraged in him a propensity – no doubt part of his inherited emotional make-up – to radical solutions. These, though carrying an element of risk, promised great benefits and more permanent solutions to Sweden's difficulties and he either could not or would not resist them.

In this manner, Charles XII, by the very task which office and circumstance put upon him, had to form himself into a war-leader whose character had to look simpler than it really was. The King who was frequently, both then and

* Cp. below, p. 477.

ater, thought unfeeling with his constant 'It does not matter' (*Det skadar inte*)* to the trials and tribulations of himself and others, had to control his softer sympathies so as not to unman others. To the seventeen-year-old volunteer whose toes had been frozen in the Christmas cold of 1708 he stressed the ways and means that would enable him to walk and ride again even if he lost 'half his foot'. To the colonel of the regiment he turned with a remark of pity for the injured's youth. The King who was by some contemporaries, and many historians, judged so little inclined to women as to be sexually abnormal, had to develop the control and philosophy of an ascetic to do what he regarded as his duty by example and precept for the army: 'I'll marry when peace comes.' The King who, to justify his policy with the cautious and pessimistically inclined, reiterated his 'We must take risks while luck is with us' (*Vi måste våga medan vi äro i lyckan*) provided himself with the reputation of one who took undue risks, much at variance with his meticulous and careful planning of campaigns. The King who half-jokingly, half-seriously cut across diplomatic negotiations which he suspected as being insincere and ill-intentioned with his 'The sword does not lie' (*Värjan ljuger inte*) helped to write his own epitaph as a militarist who despised the arts of diplomacy and peace, far removed from the real Charles XII that emerges from a study of the King as a negotiator.

It is necessary, therefore, to stress not only those characteristics of Charles XII which his position as an absolute ruler in time of war and crisis brought out and emphasized, but also to look behind the superficial and all-of-a-piece picture which is painted by these characteristics, exaggerated often for the sake of propaganda abroad, as well as by the King's own 'propaganda' with the Swedes. In a search for the half hidden or half suppressed traits of character, the surest help is a critical use of all the varied material at the historian's disposal. One must not utilize, e.g., Charles XII's own correspondence with his sister Ulrika Eleonora – the longest sequence of private letters from him preserved[50] – without taking into account (as some nineteenth-century historians failed to do)[51] that the early letters, the ones from which the King has been judged particularly unfeeling and needlessly optimistic, were written to a child, twelve years old when Charles left Sweden, whom he was anxious not to alarm. Quite naturally, in the years before 1709 he picked out for comment the humorous incidents of the campaigns and tried to make light of reverses. The tone of the correspondence becomes quite a different one after the loss of the elder sister, Hedvig Sophia, in 1709. Then Charles starts treating Ulrika as a grown-up, as his own representative and closest confidante in Sweden, to whom he is quite open about his plans and ideas.

Similarly, it will not do to convict Charles XII of personal cruelty – as has sometimes been done – on the basis of letters which he wrote to Rehnskiöld and Stenbock in Poland in the years 1703 and 1704 to encourage these two officers to be hard and firm in their policy of forcing into submission the

* Literally, 'It does no harm'.

Polish districts still holding out against the Swedes. These letters must be seen in their full context, against the background of intensive Polish guerrilla warfare that was imperilling the plans which Charles XII was attempting to push through as the ally of one section of the Polish nation at war with another section of the same nation, and also in the light of the routine phrasing – the convention of the military world of that age – of such letters.[52] Conversely, Charles XII's interpretations of Lewenhaupt's surrender at Perevolotjna must not be accepted as an objective statement, but must be examined in conjunction with other available material to ascertain whether Charles XII was deceiving himself, or even – as has been suggested – attempting to deceive others, on the reasons for the fateful surrender.*

In the same way, evidence about Charles XII given by contemporaries must be tested and graded for reliability. Some of those whose spoken or written words bearing on Charles XII have been preserved carry more weight with the historian than others. The fragments written down by Ulrika Eleonora quite a long time after her brother's death,[53] giving us a few stories from Charles XII's childhood based on family tradition, and some reminiscences from her own meetings with her brother in 1716 and 1718, are, in spite of the time which had elapsed between occurrence and record, more valuable than much of the diplomatic gossip from Stockholm about relationships inside the royal family written down during Charles XII's lifetime.[54] The considered opinions of those who had known Charles XII for long periods, men like Nicodemus Tessin the younger, 'the Italian of the North', who had seen the young King daily from 1697 to 1700, discussing European art and architecture with him, advising him on uniforms and court festivities, who had corresponded with him in Turkey at Charles's invitation (mainly on the subject of architecture) and continued the exchange of views ranging over a wide variety of administrative and financial problems after the King's return to the Swedish empire, who met Charles XII in person once more in 1718 over a period of three weeks and had long conversations with him,[55] naturally show a deeper understanding in their judgement on Charles XII than, shall we say, a foreign diplomat who had never been to Sweden, but who visited Charles XII's camp at Altranstädt for a day in 1707 and whose pen-portrait,[56] valuable in itself as a lightning sketch, but by no means profound as a summing up of the King's character, became well known to posterity through its being printed in Lamberty's *Mémoires*.

Sometimes an outsider, a foreigner, scores a bull's-eye. One of the liveliest impressions of Charles XII from 1708 is the one conveyed in conversation by an old Polish noblewoman in 1807, based on her vivid memory of four days the King spent on her father's estate† when she herself was a girl of eleven.[57] Her parents' advice to 'mark this Prince well, for he is a great man like Stefan Batory or John Sobieski' etched everything she noticed about Charles XII's

---

* See below, p. 303.

† This has been identified by August Quennerstedt as at Korolny in Lithuania; the lady was Pani Onjuchowska, her young relative Thaddeuz Bulgarin.

looks and behaviour on her mind. What is remarkable is not only that her memories ring true when tested against other independent evidence, but that the picture she evoked so long afterwards has all the delightful freshness of a child's observation of a visiting important guest. We listen in with her to the consultations between the family cook and the King's adjutant on the kind of food Charles XII preferred; we follow her in the garden where she and her sister, struck by the contrast between the slim royal figure and his high boots, large gloves and outsize sword, had a fit of the giggles, as little girls are prone to at the seemingly ridiculous and inexplicable garb of strangers; we sit at table and watch with her and hear the King's compliment to her mother on the apples from the garden; in short, we are transported across the centuries to share some quiet days (which were all the same full of planning and preparation of which the girl knew little) during Charles XII's 'Russian campaign'.

Often the very abundance of material and the consistency of interest in Charles XII permit interesting comparisons of judgements by one and the same person from widely different periods. In the 1760s, the young tutor to the sons of a Swedish district governor (*landshövding*) once the secretary of Charles XII, wrote down the snippets about the late King which fell from his employer's lips at the dinner-table talk of Nils Reuterholm and his guests;[58] by good fortune we can compare these not only with Nils Reuterholm's own memoirs, written down in his old age, where they deal with Charles XII,[59] but also with his letters to a close friend written when he was actually serving in the chancery-in-the-field, in 1705 and 1706:[60] the composite picture of the King which is thus built up is far more valuable than that conveyed by any one of the three separate parts of the Reuterholm evidence.

The historian can afford to neglect nothing. What seems insignificant at first glance frequently turns out to be deeply interesting and illuminating or, taken in conjunction with other information, may help to correct too facile or preconceived an impression. An officer, escaped from Russia where he had been a prisoner since 1709, rejoined Charles XII at Stralsund in 1715; much later in life he put down (in his *merit* report, his record of service) the story of his reception by the King: in his faithful rendering of Charles's exact words we can catch the accents of the King's mannerisms of speech so well that we seem to hear his very intonation.[61] A letter written by a quartermaster on duty that night in November 1714 when Charles XII himself turned up in Stralsund after his long ride from Turkey, casually mentions the fact that the King had grown quite a heavy beard during his travels,* and thus helps to settle an early twentieth-century controversy concerning Charles XII's supposed hermaphroditism.[62] A chance remark by someone in attendance at headquarters in Norway in 1718 solves – in a prosaic enough way – the mystery of what papers Charles XII burnt on the last day of his life and thus helps to kill the legend that the King had a premonition of his own death (or even that he went out

---

* See below, p. 389.

that Sunday night seeking death) and therefore took care to get rid of papers he did not want to be read by others: the documents related neither to secret negotiations nor to personal affairs, they were simply an informant's letter warning Charles XII of plots and opposition plans forming against him, his Norwegian venture and his policy in general, and were burned according to the King's 'invariable habit of destroying such papers'.*

V

This last was a characteristic enough gesture, for though Charles XII had a share of that suspicion so characteristic of his father in his make-up, he was, all witnesses agree, unwilling to act on unsubstantiated, or even substantiated if one-sided, evidence and was loyal to his subordinates. If orders were followed, many military men and civil officials have testified, one could be sure of the King's support even if the orders had been oral and things had gone wrong. There are many instances of Charles XII standing up for those being criticized or blamed, finding points in their favour. Quite apart from a temperamental bias in the direction of wanting to think well of people, a promise he had made his mother on her deathbed never to judge his subjects out of hand but always to hear both sides of a story was thought by contemporaries to influence him;[63] his consciousness (as seen in his correspondence with Tessin) of the Swedish besetting sin of talking ill of others,† and his conviction that only by setting an example of *not* listening to such gossip could this national weakness be conquered, certainly also reinforced this trait.[64] He had to work, not only within the framework of his own character and inheritance, but also within the limits of Swedish society and Swedish character and problems. To avoid offending needlessly the bureaucratic hierarchy he preferred the indirect approach in official matters, the suggestion sent through someone else ('as from yourself') and the conscious example which in its turn set rigid bounds for his personal behaviour. His care for his job, his willingness to take pains and make sacrifices, his demand that others should be willing, when necessary, to do the same, became therefore – through circumstances more than anything else – the dominating motive of his life.

* See below, pp. 471, 487.
† King Stanislaus, when a refugee in Sweden, commented on this trait to Tessin: R. Josephson, *Tessin I*, I, p. 169.

2

The Family

Prince Charles of Sweden was born on 17 June 1682 at Stockholm Castle,* the first son born to King Charles XI in his marriage to the Danish Princess Ulrika Eleonora. The engagement of his parents had been entered into when they were both nineteen years of age in 1675 as part of a conscious policy, urged by influential men in both Sweden and Denmark, to put a stop to the age-old enmity between their two countries or at least to prevent the war-party in Copenhagen from making use of the opportunity of the European struggles, ranged for and against Louis XIV of France, to attempt a reconquest of provinces lost to Sweden between 1643 and 1660.[1] Less than three months after the publication of the engagement, however, the hopes built on it were shattered; Sweden's reluctant involvement in hostilities against Brandenburg, as a result of her alliance and subsidy-treaty with France, proved too much of a temptation for Ulrika's brother, Christian V, and in September 1675 Denmark declared war on Sweden. The marriage of Charles and Ulrika was officially postponed, but it was generally assumed that it would never take place, especially as the war between the two countries proved long and bitter. Charles XI, after a youth in which – though he had been declared of age in 1672 and was from then on nominally the ruling monarch – the senators and particularly those of their number who had acted as regents during his minority had held the reins of government firmly in their own hands, came to manhood and responsibility during the hard-fought battles with the Danish invasion army; it was believed that he would not relish the idea of marrying into the enemy nation.[2] In the humiliation and resentment which followed in Denmark upon news of the Danish defeat at Lund in December 1676 Ulrika Eleonora was for her part pressed to denounce her engagement with Charles XI. This she refused to do. She was devout by nature and upbringing and regarded herself as bound by her word; she spent the war-years working for the welfare of the Swedish prisoners-of-war in Denmark[3] and praying for the restoration of peace between her own people and those she looked upon as her future countrymen.

When that peace came, in September 1679, the victorious Swedish King –

* See illustration facing p. 13.

for though the basis of the peace was the restoration of the *status quo ante belli*, Sweden had successfully fought off Danish attempts to regain a foothold on the Swedish peninsula – showed that he also was willing to honour his engagement to Ulrika. He was reserved in personal matters and he kept quiet on his motives. He may have felt, since he was a deeply religious man, as bound by his word as did the pious Danish Princess; conversations with his brother-officers in the war certainly show a strict and orthodox view of sexual morality and marriage.[4] He may also have been influenced by reports of Ulrika's goodness of nature and physical beauty – though eulogies in such matters were commonplace when royal marriages were negotiated and were usually found to be much exaggerated[5] – but also by the manifest evidence of her loyalty and devotion to Sweden during the war.

The need for an heir made an early marriage essential in any case, and several factors, apart from Charles XI's personal feelings, whatever they may have been, worked in favour of the Danish union. The men on whom Charles XI had learnt to rely during the war-years, those who, like the senator Johan Gyllenstierna and the two Wachtmeister brothers, fellow-officers and boon-companions, had shared and fanned his resentment at the policy which the majority of the regents and the senators, and even the high nobility as a class, had pursued since 1660,* favoured the Danish marriage. They hoped through it to achieve a policy of peaceful coexistence with Denmark in which Sweden might ultimately become the mentor and controller of Danish foreign policy. They looked upon Denmark, where the absolutist form of government had been introduced in 1660, as a model for Sweden since they intended, with the willing cooperation of Charles XI, to increase the powers of the Crown.

Sweden's great-power position had been built up in the sixteenth and seventeenth centuries with the help of the nobility, high and low, and with the expertise, energy and capital of non-Swedes who were speedily rewarded by ennoblement. Rewards or repayment of loans to the nobility as a whole, and particularly the high nobility, had been given in the form of Crown land – theoretically as a mortgage but in practice hardly distinguishable from out-right cession – to the extent that by 1654 the Crown had hardly any income from land. Conversely, the nobility controlled 63 per cent of Sweden's soil, having absorbed nearly all of the 28·5 per cent of the Crown† and having encroached also on the 50 per cent at which the peasant holdings‡ were estimated in the early sixteenth century so that these now stood at 27 per cent. Only by a dynamic and drastic policy of change, including the resumption of Crown land and other income alienated to the nobility in former reigns, the

---

* Their view of this policy as vacillating, selfish and ultimately dangerous for the state since it had failed either to prevent or prepare for the war with Brandenburg and Denmark in 1675, was of course a subjective one and the difficulties under which the regency government laboured have been stressed by modern Swedish historians.

† Derived largely from Gustavus Vasa's confiscation of Church land at the time of the Reformation.

‡ Peasant proprietors who paid taxes to the Crown and therefore had the right to be represented in the the Diet, were known as tax-peasants.

reform-party argued, would it be possible to establish the Swedish state on a sound financial footing which would allow for adequate defence of the Swedish trans-Baltic possessions without the ties of foreign subsidy-treaties (of the kind which had brought Sweden into the late war on the French side at a time when no specifically Swedish interests were threatened); only by an increase in royal power amounting to the introduction of absolutism, they further argued, could the necessary changes be forced upon the majority of the high nobles who had successfully nipped in the bud all previous plans for a 'reduction' (as the resumption was generally called, even by foreign diplomats, who adapted the Swedish word *reduktion*)[6] of Crown land.

The marriage between Charles and Ulrika was unpopular with those senators who felt power slipping from their grasp. They justified their dislike of it by stressing that never had there been any Danish marriage 'happy for Sweden', but they knew in their hearts that their dislike was rooted in fear that this particular Danish marriage was part of a policy which threatened their political and economic supremacy. They understood both the aims and the means of the reform programme advocated by their opponents; but they pretended to see only selfish motives in the 'young Heads' who, they intimated to foreign diplomats, had won Charles XI to their side by unfair methods so that they now 'wholly possess'd' him.[7] There was little that these dissatisfied senators and noblemen could do to prevent either the marriage or the new policy. Their leader, the once all-powerful Magnus Gabriel de la Gardie, was 'almost crushed',[8] and the three non-noble Estates of the Swedish Diet (those of Clergy, Burghers and Peasants) were solidly behind the reformers, while the First Estate, the House of Nobility, was divided since the issues at stake went beyond friction between noble and non-noble Estates and concerned the very foundations of Sweden's great-power position.

Opposition to the Danish marriage came also, however, from a more powerful quarter; from Charles XI's mother, Hedvig Eleonora of Holstein-Gottorp, and her intimate advisers who feared that the proposed connexion might bring with it cooperation with Denmark of a kind which would imperil the fortunes of the family from which she sprang.[9] The Swedish alliance, dynastic and political, had become the mainstay of the Dukes of Holstein-Gottorp in their struggles with the Crown of Denmark. These struggles centred round an interpretation of the relationship of the ducal parts of the two duchies Sleswig and Holstein with the royal parts of the same duchies. Until the early sixteenth century Sleswig and Holstein had in their entirety been possessions of the Crown of Denmark (though the latter duchy was held as a fief from the Emperor and formed part of the Holy Roman Empire); since that time gifts of land intended to serve as appanages for younger members of the Danish royal house had by inheritance all devolved on the ducal house of Holstein-Gottorp so that in Sleswig and Holstein royal and ducal districts were scattered up and down the duchies without seeming rhyme or reason, while some (the so-called 'unions') were jointly held and administered.[10] This situation was fraught with strategic and legal complexities, and the aim of the Danish Crown was to reincorporate the lost parts, and in particular those of Sleswig, by exchange or by conquest, in the meantime limiting the rights and privileges of the Holstein-Gottorp family in the duchies as strictly as possible.

Here, however, Sweden proved the stumbling-block to Danish ambitions. Swedish statesmen had realized in the 1640s that through the Dukes of Holstein-Gottorp they could checkmate Denmark on her southern frontier, gaining as it were a back-door entry to Jutland and the Danish isles. For this reason they insisted, as part of the peace terms imposed on Denmark in the mid-seventeenth century, on Danish recognition of Holstein-Gottorp sovereignty over their lands in Sleswig and Holstein and backed the Dukes to the hilt in any controversy over the interpretation of that sovereignty. Charles X, King of Sweden between 1654 and 1660, chose a bride from the house of Holstein-Gottorp to cement the political with a dynastic alliance. The Swedish alliance can, in retrospect, be seen as a limitation on Holstein-Gottorp freedom of action – it prevented, for instance, negotiations between the ducal house and Denmark which might have led to exchanges of territory and reconciliation – but to most seventeenth-century members of the Holstein-Gottorp family, and certainly to Hedvig Eleonora, it seemed the very corner-stone of the security of a small state living in perpetual dread of Danish attack.

However, those who urged Charles XI's marriage to Ulrika Eleonora had no intention of sacrificing the Holstein alliance so useful to Sweden; though hope of a pacific relationship, not only between Sweden and Denmark, but also between Denmark and Holstein-Gottorp, was entertained.[11] To calm his mother's fears Charles XI, who was devoted to her and always showed her the greatest respect, insisted on separating the negotiations for his marriage to Ulrika as much as possible from the political negotiations, those of peace and alliance, which took place with Denmark in 1679 and 1680. The bitter memories of the war, the hostility of the majority of senators and high nobles, the fear and uneasiness of his mother, all help to explain the very private ceremony and the very modest festivities which solemnized and accompanied the marriage between Charles and Ulrika on 6 May 1680 at the estate of Skottorp in Halland, though the shyness and reserve typical of the King in personal matters also played their part.[12]

II

Charles XI, who had a hot temper, was once heard to rebuke Ulrika who had angered him (by pleading for less ruthlessness in the application of the resumption-policy, a subject on which the King himself suffered pangs of conscience at times), that he had taken himself a wife to bear him children, not to give him advice on matters of state.[13] Their union certainly proved fruitful: seven children were born to them in the first seven years and nine months of their marriage.[14] The first baby, born in June 1681, was a daughter and was christened Hedvig Sophia. Both the parents and the people at large, who had shown tremendous interest at the prospect of an heir to the throne, had hoped for a boy. Foreign diplomats, caught up in the general speculation and gossip and conscious of the real importance of the succession being secured at a time when the King was at loggerheads with much of the nobility, had commented with the directness of the age on the progress of the pregnancy and the precautions taken against miscarriage after the Queen's public entry in Stockholm in November 1680 and her coronation in December. As the time for the birth drew nearer, bulletins on Ulrika's health were included on most post-days. 'The Queen', the English envoy Warwick reported in the spring of 1681 when he informed his court of various visits the King and the Dowager Queen had paid to residences outside Stockholm, 'is forbid any excursion for feare of her great belly, she expecting now in June'.[15] 'The Queen is so big now', he related in the early summer, 'that she cannot well dress herselfe* but with Inconveniencey so she sees company no more'.[16] The joy of an heir – for daughters as well as sons could succeed, though sons took precedence – mixed with some disappointment at the birth of a mere girl is mirrored in Warwick's letter of 27 June to the English Secretary of State for the North, the Earl of Conway:

> My business today must be to tell your Lordship the Queen being happily brought to bed, to the great Content of the whole Court, which was on Sunday last at ten in the Evening, her Majesty falling in Labour about ten at Noone, the great Gunns of the Towne and Castle went of, and the accustomed ringeing in these Cases, and when all this was don, it is but a Girle, I should have sayd a Princesse. The Queen cryed when the King came and told him she had done her work ill, seeing it was not a Prince. His Majesty anwered, Courage, we'l have a Prince (if it be that your desire) by this time Twelve Months.[17]

We do not know from whom the envoy had received this report of the conversation at the Queen's bedside, but the King's words, affectionate, proud and fondly teasing, ring true and fit what we know and can deduce about the relationship between him and his wife.

The prophecy about a Prince before another year was out came true. Even opportunities for conception were noted in the diplomatic correspondence as soon as Ulrika was 'perfectly well recovered' after Hedvig Sophia's birth,[18] and Charles XI had returned from his summer tour of inspection of regiments. 'The Queen, poor Lady', Warwick commented on 7 September, 'after long expectations and many disappointments got the King here last night, so that I hope we may keep him here some time now, that Love and business may best advance.'[19] As soon as it became known that Ulrika was with child again, news of the progress of her pregnancy became part of the diplomatic reportage of court news. Hopes for a boy were more openly expressed in Sweden than in the previous year and were reflected in Warwick's letters to London.

---

* That is, dress formally for court functions.

The Queen is now so neere her time that she seldom dresses herself [he wrote on 26 April 1682], so that the great Expectations here is a young Prince.

The Queen stirs not [ran the report of 3 May], for we expect her crying out now daily So the Prayers and Healths are not wanting for a young Prince.

We shall not have to wait much longer [was the comment by the post on 8 June], for 3 days are now past beyond her Majesty's reckoning. So that a young Prince is duly prayed for, and every moment expected.[20]

On 17 June came the great news. Warwick wrote on that day to the Earl of Conway, with an opening allusion to England's own succession problem:

My lord, I hope the Dutchess* may suddenly give the same newes to Europe (I am sure I wish it) as Sueden can, the birth of a young Prince who came into this cold Climatt this morning at three quarters past six, her Majesty being in Labour but an hour and a halfe. All publick Ministers were with the King this morning and I suppose everybody gave him the formall Compliments of such occasions, at which his Majesty seemed pleased enough.[21]

Charles XI's feelings of happiness, gratitude and paternal pride in having a son and heir were obvious to all at court and can be read into the final sentence of the entry he made in his diary for the day of the birth:

The 17th, which was on Saturday morning at a quarter to seven, My Wife was delivered and bore a son, God be eternally thanked and praised, he who helped her, may he soon restore her to her former health. My son Carel was born in the morning at a quarter to seven.[22]

There were joyful celebrations in Stockholm throughout the day; the toasts to the Prince were many and it was said that few went sober to bed that Saturday night.[23]

With the birth of a prince many Swedes had hoped to see the traditional name of the Vasa family, Gustavus (Gustav, or Gustaf, in its Swedish form), revived with its memories not only of the founder of the dynasty but also of the great Gustavus Adolphus. Charles was not a particularly popular name for a King, since, as Queen Christina's correspondent from Stockholm wrote her:

On avoit icy fait reflexion sur ce que tous les Roys de Suede du dit nom ont este en peu austeres et rigoureux.[24]

This reason was not given to Charles XI, though the name Gustavus was proposed to him. The King preferred, however, to perpetuate the name of his father and grandfather, conscious of his own Palatinate-Zweibrücken branch of the Vasa dynasty which had become the ruling house of Sweden on Queen Christina's abdication in 1654. *Carolus*† was therefore the name given to the prince at the private baptism which, according to Swedish custom, was made as soon as possible after the birth itself and repeated at the public and solemn

---

* i.e., the future Queen Anne.

† 'Karl' in modern Swedish, but in the seventeenth century 'Carl'. The variant 'Carel' (indicating pronunciation) is used in Charles XI's almanac entries.

christening ceremony which took place on 12 July.[25] This was attended with some festivities: the guards took up positions round the Palace, the cannon were fired, and wine and sweetmeats were offered to guests in the Queen's apartment.

The choice of godparents had been a subject of discussion at court and among diplomats. It was assumed that the Swedes 'had mind enough to have had Crowned heads', but since it was difficult to avoid 'Ugly Jealousies' at home and abroad, in the end only relatives of the young Prince were named as godfathers and godmothers. The Danish and Holstein dynastic connexions were nicely balanced: Prince George of Denmark was one of the godfathers, the other two being the Duke of Holstein and the Prince-Bishop of Eutin. Queen Christina – holding court in Rome – and the Queen of Denmark headed the list of godmothers, whose numbers were completed by the Princess Landgrave of Hesse and the Princess Dorothy of Holstein.[26]

III

Many strains mingled in the family heritage of the new-born Prince. The Vasa dynasty had produced an unusually high proportion of exceptionally gifted men and women since the founder of the house, Gustavus Vasa, had put the seal on Sweden's successful breakaway from the Scandinavian dynastic union of the late Middle Ages by having himself elected King of Sweden in 1523: intellectuals of the calibre of Eric xiv and Queen Christina, far-seeing administrators who also possessed a genius for political leadership such as Gustavus Vasa himself and Gustavus Adolphus. Circumstances, in Sweden itself and in Europe at large, tended to put emphasis on and develop the martial qualities of the dynasty. The struggle against Denmark to maintain the independence achieved and the border-skirmishes with Russia from Finland (a Grand Duchy governed from Sweden since the early Middle Ages) were intensified once the weakness of the Order of the Sword made the east-Baltic sea and littoral a battle-ground for the rival ambitions of Russia, Denmark, Sweden and Poland. The fight for power and succession among the sons and grandsons of Gustavus Vasa merged with the conflict between Lutheranism and Catholicism when the Catholic Vasa, Sigismund, King of Poland, was dispossessed. This conflict in its turn became part of the many religious, strategic, and economic and European issues fought out in Germany during the Thirty Years War. Domestic problems – the factions and groupings resulting from contested succession as well as the struggle for power between ruler and mighty subjects – also moulded the scions of the Vasa house, deepening the suspicious strain typical of nearly all of them and putting their quick and autocratic minds under considerable strain. Some of them succumbed when dangers in Sweden's external situation or private griefs and problems put an added burden on them: Eric xiv became temporarily insane, Charles ix suffered a stroke, Queen Christina abdicated.

They were as a family passionate, choleric, emotionally highly strung, and they all – in spite of their basic optimism – knew periods of despair and depression. A love of power for its own sake and ruthlessness and persistence in achieving desired objectives also characterize the dynasty as a whole; dynamic energy, a capacity for hard and sustained work and great ambitions for Sweden are equally distinguishing traits expressing themselves not only in the firm organization of all branches of the state administration and in the furthering of the economic and cultural life of the nation but also in bold and aggressive plans for Swedish expansion. The most successful Vasas, and certainly the most popular both with contemporaries and with posterity, were those who possessed the largest measure of those gifts which fate and heredity measured out to the Vasas in less constant quantities: the ability to handle people by the exercise, consciously or intuitively, of psychological insight; the eloquence which could, by the choice of the right words, strike chords from the very essence of the Swedish temperament; the realization of the dictum that politics is the art of the possible. In these respects Gustavus Vasa and his grandson, Gustavus Adolphus, were the most fortunate ones: the founder of the dynasty, despite his ambitions for Sweden, was realistic enough to relinquish attempted conquests when he had no quick success, while his weathering of the frequent and violent domestic crises of his long reign can be explained in terms of his well-planned propaganda by word of mouth and by letter and proclamation (by which he managed to a remarkable degree to project both the weight and the charm of his personality) no less than by his more obvious attributes of ability, energy and ruthlessness.

The one son of the marriage of Gustavus Vasa and Catherine of Saxony-Lauenburg, and the two of his marriage to the Swedish noblewoman Margareta Eriksdotter of the Leijonhufvud family, while all inheriting the ambitions and the drive of their father, lacked in various ways some of the balance of his character and personality: Eric XIV frequently attempted to put into operation plans which, though logically and theoretically well-conceived, failed to assess the prevailing situation, whether at home or abroad, realistically enough; John III, intellectually and artistically nearly as gifted as his elder half-brother and his equal in respect of grandiose schemes for Swedish expansion, was by temperament a much less dominating ruler than the two previous Vasa Kings; Charles IX, with a capacity for practical kingship reminiscent of that of his father, never achieved popularity, his ruthlessness and love of power being too undisguised, except with the peasants who formed the major part of the Swedish population and who approved of Charles's hard ways with the nobility. His eldest son,* however, Gustavus Adolphus – who had to take over the government when only seventeen years of age at a time of crisis both in domestic and foreign affairs – possessed in the fullest measure those gifts which facilitated smooth Swedish acceptance, by all classes, of royal

---

* Of his (second) marriage with Christina of Holstein, the only outstandingly intelligent and capable Queen in the elder Vasa line.

leadership: wonderfully eloquent in debate and speech, adept at working with others, able to reconcile, by personal charm and timely concessions, the High nobility to the dynasty; while in the handling of Sweden's external problems he was sustained not only by his own brilliance as a general and by favourable political circumstances, but also by a fine civilian collaborator, Axel Oxenstierna who knew how to keep Gustavus's bolder flights of fancy under control and to pour oil on troubled waters by skilful diplomacy.

The last ruler descended directly in the Vasa line, Queen Christina, was probably less handicapped by traits of character inherited from her mother than is often assumed, but she was at a disadvantage by coming into personal power only after a long regency (she was six years old at the time of her father's death in 1632) which had permitted the high nobility to entrench themselves at the expense of the Crown. With typical Vasa energy, intelligence and shrewdness she found ways to restore the balance once she herself took over the reins of government, but jeopardized it by her decision never to marry and produce that heir of her own body which the country at large wished for.[27] It needed all her ruthless skill, using existing friction and tension between the nobility and the non-noble Estates, to force the House of Nobles to accept her cousin, Charles Gustavus, as the rightful heir and successor in such a manner that the power implicit in hereditary monarchy as opposed to elective monarchy was maintained. Once this had been achieved, Christina took a step which she had for some time contemplated, namely, abdication in favour of her cousin. Her motives have been much debated, but it would seem that the decisive ones were her wish to enter the Catholic Church (which she assumed to be more liberal than she found it), and her fear of childbirth.

Charles Gustavus, crowned as Charles X,[28] was the son of Catherine, Gustavus Adolphus's half-sister, in her marriage to John Casimir of Pfalz-Zweibrücken-Kleeberg of the Palatinate house of Wittelsbach. He had been born and brought up in Sweden, where his parents were living as refugees from the Thirty Years War; Christina and he had indeed spent their childhood years under the same roof, since his mother took charge of the girl-Queen after 1632. A brief engagement between Charles and Christina, broken by the latter, made him ambitious for the throne, to which he was in any case the nearest heir. The 'German' characteristics of the King, his son and grandson, all bearing the name *Carolus*, have been much exaggerated: those historians who have postulated a complete change from a specifically 'Swedish' to a typically 'German' temperament and mentality[29] have oversimplified the picture and ignored both previous German marriages of the Vasas and the vitality of Vasa characteristics in the cognatic as in the agnatic line of descent.

The Wittelsbach family to which John Casimir belonged (he was a distant cousin of the Elector Palatine) was an old and distinguished one. It brought added intelligence and a serious and conscientious devotion to duty, typical of the Calvinist religion which the family as a whole had embraced, to its union with the Vasas. The political sacrifice of that religion on the part of John

Casimir for his son, so that Calvinism should not rob Charles Gustavus of his chance to succession in Lutheran Sweden, may account for the somewhat cynical attitude of Charles X to religious issues,[30] but the religious temperament noticeable both in Charles IX and in Christina was reinforced by the heritage from the Wittelsbachs and helps to explain the deep and enduring religious faith of Charles XI and Charles XII. Similarly, the rather introvert natures, emotional but reserved, of Charles XI and Charles XII, and their devotion to work for its own or duty's sake rather than as a consequence of the more direct Vasa lust for power, may be interpreted as manifestations of Wittelsbach traits. The extreme secrecy with which both Charles X and Charles XII surrounded their military plans seems, on the other hand, to have been the product as much of similar circumstances – both rulers being in supreme and personal command of armies fighting simultaneously on several fronts – as proof of a hereditary propensity towards secrecy.

It might be held that part of the Wittelsbach heritage passed on to Charles XII was a lust for travel, a desire to be on the move. John Casimir's years of wandering from university to university, from country to country as a young man find their parallels in the peregrinations of Charles Gustavus before his accession and possibly even in his wide-sweeping campaigns as a warrior-king; in Charles XI's travels all over Sweden, on constant rounds of inspection, on manœuvres for mere pleasure as when he went north to Lapland; in Charles XII's intense interest in seeing the world for himself and in absorbing new places through the reports and drawings of other travellers. When Charles XII was a small boy he expressed the wish for a brother who could stay at home to rule the kingdom so that he himself might travel* all over the world;[31] when he was a virtual prisoner of circumstances in Turkey he organized and financed voyages of intellectual and geographical exploration into Asia Minor and to the Holy Land; when circumstances tied him to southern Scandinavia between 1716 and 1718 he encouraged and helped de la Motraye's journey to Lapland.[32]

In physical characteristics the new line made itself felt at once. Charles X as a type differs strongly from the Vasa one.[33] The Vasa men had been tall and broad, on the whole slim in relation to their build, fair of hair, skin and beard: Charles X was short and dark and grew fat long before middle age. The domed forehead of the Vasa's changed and became lower, sloping at a different angle; the eyes – still blue – were set under heavier lids; the Palatinate jaw with its forward-jutting lower lip made its appearance. But though unlike his mother's forebears in looks, Charles X, born in Sweden, educated and brought up as a Swede of the royal family with the Vasa traditions inculcated at an early age, proved himself a typical Vasa in character, though possibly with an exaggerated propensity to the kind of radical solutions of Sweden's problems which had earlier appealed to Eric XIV and John III and which were to exert their fascination also on Charles X's son and grandson. But he was more strongly

* Frequently misquoted as 'fight'.

aggressive than either predecessors or successors.[34] In his short reign – six years only – he attempted to solve, at one and the same time, Sweden's problems with respect to Denmark–Norway, Russia and Poland, aiming at bold and definitive consolidations of eastern and western frontiers. He combined such efforts, for good measure, with an economic challenge to the nation that dominated Baltic trade, the Dutch, whom the Swedes both admired and envied. The complications which issued from these four objectives simultaneously pursued tested Charles x's military and diplomatic gifts to the full and probably overstrained them; but success was achieved for at least one of his aims – possibly the most fundamental one – that of obtaining those frontiers against Denmark and Norway which could be regarded as the natural ones on the peninsula.

Charles XII modelled himself very consciously upon the example of his father and sought parallels to his own task preferably in Gustavus Adolphus when he spoke of Sweden's past history; but the reign and the problems of the wars of his grandfather, Charles x, must have intruded on his consciousness. There were traits in Charles x's character – such as the breaking of the treaty with Denmark in 1658 – of which Charles XII could not approve, either by upbringing or personal inclination, and the aggressive nature of his grandfather's wars went against the grain of his father's teaching. Yet the position which Charles x faced by choice, war on several fronts, was in the military sense not so different from the one Charles XII had to meet when a powerful anti-Swedish coalition attacked him in 1700.

Charles x was, for Charles XII, one in the line of ancestors, dead, glorious, whose memories were kept alive by trophies and mementoes of various kinds, by busts and portraits, and in the case of his paternal grandfather more particularly by the journal from his years of youthful travels which Ulrika Eleonora had copied and gave to her son as a New Year present when he was seven years old.[35] Charles x's wife, however, Hedvig Eleonora of Holstein-Gottorp, who survived both her husband and her son (and nearly her grandson also, since she died at the age of seventy-nine in 1715) was very much part of Charles XII's everyday life, the paternal grandmother whose opinion and advice counted for much in the family relationship; a link with the past more concrete and real than the letters and news which arrived from Queen Christina, his godmother, until she died in Rome in 1689.

Hedvig Eleonora had been married to Charles x in the very year of his accession, 1654. It would have been impolitic for Charles Gustavus to have taken a wife while the Queen to whom he had once been engaged was still reigning and might yet change her mind; now it was imperative for the continuation of the dynasty of the cognatic Vasa branch that the King should have an heir. The Holstein-Gottorp princess, eighteen at this time, was thought to be healthy and likely to produce a child quickly, while Charles had already proved his fertility through an illegitimate son born in 1647.[36] The royal bride was neither good looking nor possessed of much charm, and the choice had fallen on her, from a number of suitable princesses of as much presumed fecundity, out of political considerations, to cement that connexion with the house of Holstein-Gottorp which was already looked upon as an important bastion in the defence of Sweden's gains from the Thirty Years War period both in Germany and on the Scandinavian peninsula.*

One son, named Charles after his father, was born of the marriage in 1655. As the boy grew up, it became clear that Hedvig Eleonora had passed on to him some of the physical characteristics of her family, notably the receding chin, the heavy-looking eyes and a rather petulant expression. The Oldenburg strain introduced into the Swedish dynasty through Hedvig Eleonora has also been held responsible for the fact that Charles XI, when measured against his predecessors, was markedly their inferior in intelligence. The Oldenburgs, from whom the Holstein-Gottorp family stemmed, were certainly not the equals of the Vasas or the Wittelsbachs in intellectual equipment, but the limitations of Charles XI can be accounted for as much by lack of a formal education and rigorous training of his mind in childhood and youth as by maternal heritage.

And Hedvig Eleonora herself was far from stupid. She was not, it is clear, interested in or fitted for affairs of state in their aspect of a steady daily toil; but she was a knowledgeable and passionate supporter of the arts: her chief occupation during the long years of widowhood was building and restoring palaces – she built Drottningholm and Strömsholm, she improved on Gripsholm and Ulriksdal – furnishing them, laying out gardens, and collecting paintings and sculptures and *objets d'art* of many kinds. There is much evidence of her excellent taste and of her ability to draw foreign craftsmen and artists to Sweden. Her partiality for Holstein-Gottorp, her haughtiness of demeanour, her lust for power were facets of her personality which have been frequently commented upon and chiefly by her political enemies, the diplomats from Denmark accredited to her son's court; but there were also other sides to her nature. She was good at personal relationships; she made a success of her short-lived marriage, accompanying her husband – like Swedish queens before her – on campaign; she was generous and even magnanimous, as shown in her kindness to and care for Charles x's illegitimate son; her real and passionate concern was with the health and welfare of her own boy who was left fatherless in 1660.

IV

Charles XI, proclaimed King when only five years of age, was not a robust child. To strengthen his weak constitution became the chief objective of the upbringing he received from Hedvig Eleonora: the emphasis was therefore on sport and games in the open air, with a minimum of attention given to study and instruction in a scholarly manner. His health improved, he became a

---

* It was to become even more essential after the expansion at the expense of Denmark–Norway which took place during the reign of Charles x.

tough and intrepid horseman and a good shot; but in the council-chamber he remained shy and uncertain of himself even after the formal regency of the five high officials of the Realm had come to an end when he reached the age of eighteen.

His childhood and youth suffered from lack of paternal influence in forming him for the task ahead; the role which his father had by his last will and testament allotted to his own brother, Duke Adolf John, by making the Duke as well as Hedvig Eleonora members of the regency, had been nullified by the decision of the Swedish nobility, anxious to profit by the minority of the King and to ward off in particular the resumption of Crown lands begun by Charles x, to set aside the will and exclude Charles xi's uncle from the regency. Religious instruction and moral precepts were given and found a receptive temperament. Charles xi grew up pious but not smug, God-fearing, and God-loving, anxious to be honest and straightforward, willing to conform to the Church's and his mother's standards of ethics and sexual morality. Conversely, hardly any theoretical or practical training for the job of kingship was offered, since the regents were only too anxious to keep Charles xi inactive in matters of state and Hedvig Eleonora had no real grasp of affairs and was in any case more concerned with the physical well-being of her son.

The war of 1675 and in particular the invasion of Sweden by a Danish army tested the stuff that the young King was made of. He was found to have his full share of Vasa energy and to be as determined and strong-willed as any of his predecessors, with a deep-rooted sense of responsibility for the fate of the country. He learnt to pick men for advisers whose mental capacity he respected and who, in their various ways, had more experience of government than himself and on whom he felt he could rely to work more selflessly for the good of Sweden than he thought the regents had done. With them he planned the strengthening of the power of the Crown and the restoration of the great-power position so nearly lost during the war and the European peace negotiations that followed. These advisers, men like Johan Gyllenstierna and Erik Lindschöld on the civil side, and Field-Marshal Rutger von Ascheberg on whom he looked as a father,[37] were his superiors in intellect and in knowledge of the world, but the moral leadership was his because of the initiative he had forced himself to take and the military gambles he had risked in the desperately dangerous early stages of the war. The war experience hardened him and brought out that capacity for ruthless and logical pursuit of aims which, boldly conceived or accepted, made the 1680s and '90s the years of reform amounting to a revolution from above in Sweden. He continued reserved in behaviour, but the hot Vasa temperament simmered below the surface and could not always be kept under control: he could go wild with anger when provoked and, never quick with his tongue, was then tempted to use whatever came to hand, his sword or his stick or his bare fists. It was the war years that caused Charles xi's awareness of the dilemmas inherent in Sweden's great-power position and drew him into the leadership of the movement for reform and reconstruction.

Sweden had been able to throw back the Danish army from the Scandinavian peninsula by her own efforts, but her navy had been much inferior to that of Denmark–Norway and her resources had not proved sufficient to prevent her provinces in the Empire being overrun by her enemies: Swedish Pomerania by Brandenburg and Denmark in cooperation, Bremen-Verden by Denmark supported by the Netherlands. These possessions (with the exception of a strip of land on the eastern bank of the Oder which had to be sacrificed to Brandenburg) were returned thanks to French help in the field and at the conference-table, though the mutual jealousies of Denmark, the Netherlands and the North German princes in respect of Bremen and Verden also facilitated the restoration of Swedish control of those areas. But the way in which Louis xiv handled the peace settlement, dictating not only the peace of St Germain with Brandenburg without Swedish participation but also that of Fontainebleau between Sweden and Denmark in a similar fashion, created in Sweden and more particularly in Charles xi himself a feeling of humiliating dependence, of near vassalage, which left a bad taste in the mouth. The gratitude which might be expected towards France, which had after all obtained from Denmark just what the Swedish delegates to the Nijmegen peace congress had demanded, the restoration of the *status quo*, was obscured by the resentment at Louis xiv's high-handed methods and by indignation that the preferential treatment of Dutch commerce in Swedish ports, secured by treaty in 1659, had not been ended.

Independence from foreign tutelage in war and peace now became one of the central aims of Charles xi's reform programme. Such independence could only be achieved by the tackling of a problem at home which had begged solution since 1648 or even earlier: how could Sweden finance her great-power position? how could she pay for the troops which were needed to defend her empire? how could she create a large enough navy? Axel Oxenstierna and the Swedish high nobility had pinned their hopes on the customs-dues and tolls levied at the Baltic river-mouths controlled by Sweden; but these – especially after 1635 when the West-Prussian ports had to be returned – had proved insufficient for the purpose, and it was to supply this deficiency that the regents of Charles xi's minority had accepted those subsidies from France which eventually brought Sweden into the war on Louis xiv's side in 1675.

Another method of raising the necessary money had, however, been urged by the non-noble Estates and by some noble advisers of the Crown since the 1640s: to make the nobility pay a larger share of taxation, or, alternatively, to resume sufficient Crown land to balance a defence budget. During Charles x's brief reign beginnings had been made in 'reduction' but his death in 1660 brought it to a stop.[38] On Charles xi's attainment of his royal majority some slight activity was resumed at the instigation of the non-noble Estates, who hoped for the King's vigorous cooperation to weaken the power and curtail the privileges of the high nobility, but the war of 1675 (like the wars of Charles x's own reign) effectively paralysed any resumption, since good relations with the First Estate were essential to the war effort.

The means whereby the Crown could restore its power and independence in domestic and foreign affairs had, however, been sufficiently indicated, and with the return of peace a far more radical resumption-policy became the kernel round which the reform movement was built. It was held that the income already enjoyed from alienated Crown land had long since compensated for services rendered or loans tendered, and a committee (the so-called *reduktionskommission*) was empowered to scrutinize title-deeds and documents to decide the extent of any individual family's indebtedness to the Crown.* Parallel with the work of the committee went an inquiry, called a 'retrospect' by foreign diplomats, by a special commission into the government of the regents, and those who were found guilty of malpractices in economic and financial matters were punished with heavy fines.[39] On the proceeds of reduction and retrospect a permanent budget was set up, in which the income of the Crown from customs and tolls formed the only other large entry on the credit-side; but the combined annual yield in money and in kind was sufficient to allow for the foundation and upkeep of an adequate army, navy and administrative machine.

The role which the nobility played in the life of the nation was not basically changed by the resumption which touched none of the many privileges of nobles of all ranks, such as their exemption from tax on their manors and exemption from military service for their servants and farm-labourers. Ennoblement of commoners remained the usual and coveted channel of promotion in the service of the King, in the armed forces as well as in the bureaucracy. The formation of large manorial estates was helped rather than hindered by the equivalent-principle applied by the cameralists when putting the resumption into practice; but the general uncertainty introduced into land ownership by the long legal scrutinies of old title-deeds and the many opportunities offered to those who had cash resources to amass land cheaply created great bitterness.

The ex-regents, or their heirs, struck simultaneously by the resumption and by the fines levied on some of them by the retrospect, were of course hardest hit financially; but irrespective of the size of the repayment to the Crown very few families were able to take the loss of land and of income, to which they had become accustomed over generations, with equanimity. Charles XI and his advisers, some of whom were justly accused of extending their own holdings in land in the unsettled years of the resumption, were hated and cursed, and foreign envoys reported home on the dangers of dissatisfaction. Duncombe wrote from Stockholm to Whitehall in 1689 in a heavily cyphered passage (only three words being left *en clair*): '*For as a secrett be it* spoken, *these people*

---

* Once this indebtedness was established, equivalents in cash or land were accepted commensurate with the debt.

are so sensible of the miseries the reduction hath brought *them to that I know not whether they will long be patient under them and I wish it were not true that tho the King hath got all their lands he hath lost all their affections.'*[40]

Rumours of imminent revolution which were spread all over Europe and widely believed proved false, just as stories which gained currency about the sorry plight of individual noblemen ('Count Oxenstierna cannot afford to eat meat'[41] is typical of many) were grossly exaggerated. Before long, noblemen who had suffered by the resumption made use of the career opportunities which the expanded army, navy and bureaucracy offered,[42] and the royal absolutism which had been introduced to force reform through was accepted as in tune with the times, though a feeling that it was 'un-Swedish' persisted among the nobility and helps to explain the opposition which formed against it towards the end of the reign of Charles XII.*

V

The hard but absorbing task of reorganization and reconstruction filled the days and the years of Charles XI's life from 1678–9 onwards.[43] The working out of amounts due to the Crown was the work of cameralist experts; but the King was ceaselessly active in the fields where he himself had experience, particularly in the creation and training of the army. Into this life of dedicated toil his marriage to Ulrika Eleonora brought the sweetness of love and of family-life for twelve years that passed only too quickly. The King enjoyed the open-air exercise of mock-battles, the hunt for bears and wolves and hares; he took a passionate interest in the building of churches, noting progress and plans in his diary; but his deepest joys and sorrows came to him through the affection and love that ripened between him and his wife. His was an emotional and affectionate nature, but a reserved one also, and there were some at court who failed to notice the strong bonds between the royal couple and were surprised at the inconsolable grief of the King when Ulrika died. Then all became aware of how much she had meant to him, though many had guessed it earlier. 'Need I wear my heart upon my sleeve', was Charles's retort to those who had misinterpreted their relationship and had fastened on the occasional difficulties between Holstein-Gottorp mother and Danish wife (in which the King seemed always to take his mother's part) and on the rare but real differences of opinion (as on the question of Erik Lindschöld's governorship of Prince Charles).† These had noted the uxoriousness of the King, but failed to see the engagement of his emotions.

Ulrika Eleonora possessed a temperament and a personality which made her generally loved, a 'dove of peace' she was often called, sent from Denmark to Sweden to heal the wounds of many wars. Her looks are said to have caused the King a momentary disappointment at their first meeting, but they were, to judge from portraits and descriptions of her (including those of

---

* See below, pp. 519–520.   † Ibid., pp. 45–46.

er political enemies), on the whole very pleasing. She was fair of hair and blue-eyed, with the high rounded forehead which both Charles XII and Ulrika Eleonora, the daughter called after her, inherited. Her nose was a trifle long, but she held herself well and had a good figure. Her intelligence was well above the Oldenburg average, and she had received a careful education. She delighted in reading in several languages, as her library still kept at the summer residence of Karlberg testifies; she was interested in the arts and had some talent for drawing and painting. She was devout and serious-minded, but happy by disposition and generous both with her time, her money and her efforts on behalf of others.

Her warmheartedness, her open and direct nature seemed to establish bonds of sympathy with everyone she met. Even diplomats, with whom her acquaintance was no more than superficial, felt the goodness and charm that radiated from her. She made a deep impression on the English envoy Duncombe who stayed in Sweden for three years between 1689 and 1691. 'I cannot,' the envoy's secretary wrote on one occasion, 'I believe the Envoy himself cannot express, how much Veneration this incomparable Princess raised in him.'[44] She had the gift of making her children happy. They lost her early, but her memory stayed with them, and so did the standards she had tried to teach them. They reminded each other of what she had said and done, and even the thought of her touched some spring of emotion so that they, just like their father, could hardly speak of her without bursting into tears. Hedvig Sophia, the 'glad princess', jolly and pert, cried when her mother's favourite hymn was sung;[45] Charles XII and Ulrika Eleonora meeting as grown-ups who had not seen each other for seventeen years spoke of the mother and of the promises they had made her and could hardly speak for the tears choking them.

Charles XI never recovered from losing her. He confessed to his mother on his own death-bed, four years later, that he had not spent a truly happy day since his wife died.[46] To have left such a gap in the family circle, and to have left such happy memories, Ulrika Eleonora must indeed have been an 'incomparable Princess'.

3

The Childhood of a Prince

The Stockholm in which Prince Charles was born, the capital of the state he was expected to govern if God granted him a long enough life, was by far the largest town in the whole Swedish empire, and haughty travellers from Europe sometimes said it was the only real town in Sweden itself. It had grown and expanded with the great-power position: in 1620 it had only 10,000 inhabitants, by 1674 it had 55,000,[1] quite a sizeable proportion out of the 1½ million people living in Sweden or even out of the total population of the empire, estimated at between 2½ to 3 million. Stockholm was a lively town. There were fewer sailors and shipwrights about in Prince Charles's boyhood than there had been, for in 1680 the main fleet was moved from Stockholm to a newly built naval station in the south, Karlskrona, as the war of 1675 had shown the need for naval defence to be concentrated nearer the centre of the empire; but there were many more soldiers, for Charles XI made Stockholm a garrison town and stationed the Lifeguards, the Drabant corps, the very nucleus of the new army, in and near the Castle. Stockholm was also a busy commercial port, where ships from many lands, but principally from England and the Netherlands, sailed in to fetch Swedish iron and copper and Finnish tar; there were shipbuilding yards and repair-shops both for Swedish merchant vessels and for the detachment of the navy that was still kept in Stockholm waters. There was the bustle and hustle of the market-place, for here iron and copper were weighed and inspected, imports from abroad sold, exchanged, warehoused, bargained over; here lived the foreign factors; here was the Bank and the merchant houses. Above all, Stockholm was the centre of the court and the administration and since the two were for all practical purposes synonymous the court was indeed the hub round which Stockholm increasingly revolved. In the old days kings and court had moved from royal castle to castle, eating their way from one stored magazine to another and administering the country as they went along; but from Queen Christina's time the court and the colleges of the civil service became permanently based in Stockholm while the meetings of the Four Estates of the Realm in the Diet or *Riksdag* were only exceptionally held outside Stockholm.

The capital was a beautiful town as well as a busy one.[2] It had expanded too quickly, encroaching on the islands of the archipelago and the countryside, to allow for detailed planning and there was a lack of symmetry which offended the perfectionists.[3] But the setting was magnificent, the copper spires of churches and copper roofs of big buildings could be seen from far away and when one got closer there were – apart from the dominating Royal Castle – many imposing palaces and houses,[4] the town-residences of the nobility who in the time when they 'built with German money' (a polite euphemism for loot or gain from the Thirty Years War) had not only begun to construct wonderful palaces or manor-houses on their country estates but had also started to compete with each other in erecting sumptuous town headquarters for their families. In this they had been encouraged by Axel Oxenstierna, who wanted to make Stockholm a capital worthy of a great power and desired also to entice the nobility into the administrative machine. By the time Prince Charles was born these palaces were complete in all their splendour and the nobility as a class had become servants of the state, either in the bureaucracy or in the armed forces, to such an extent that the noble landowner who only managed his estate was hard to find. Indeed these noblemen had no right to refuse to serve the Crown. The ties with the countryside remained strong, however, and the love of country life deeply rooted, even if the day-to-day care of the estate had to be left to capable wives, relatives or bailiffs: the noble adminis-trator tended to escape to his country house as frequently and for as long periods as duties in the capital permitted. The King's departure from Stock-holm, whether on business or pleasure, was usually the signal for 'everyone' to leave town so that foreign diplomats complained it was useless for them to remain: they could find no one with whom to discuss affairs, and often began a round of visits of estates.

Life in Stockholm surprised visitors by its luxury and by its close contact with European tastes and trends in fashions and art.[5] They commented on the treasures in sculpture, paintings and books brought to Sweden from Europe; on the beauty and refinement of interior decorations and furnishings; on the number of carriages and servants; on the fact that Italian scent and French and English fashionable goods could so easily be obtained. There was obviously an element of conspicuous consumption in all this, but even the most carping critic of a nation that in its exuberance laid claim to an 'antiquity in learning' (which was not accepted) admitted its love of beautiful things for their own sake and the lively interchange of ideas, by travel, by correspon-dence and by reading, among the educated Swedes who formed such a large part of the Stockholm population. The links with the Continent had been tied fast in the early seventeenth century, when the expansion had been most vigorous, for not only had the Swedes then, principally through service in the army, been pitchforked into Poland and Germany, but a great many foreigners had been drawn to Sweden and had eventually settled there: Netherlanders (South and North), French and German mining-experts, financiers and indus-trialists to make use of the opportunities which offered; Scottish professional

soldiers and German professional administrators who wanted to better themselves; political and religious refugees prepared to behave discreetly in a
country known for its Lutheran orthodoxy. The foreign element had also
been increased by German-speaking subjects from the Baltic provinces or
from the new Swedish possessions in the Empire who for one reason or other
decided to make their homes in Sweden itself.

When rich, or successful in the armed forces or in the administration, the
foreign settlers were soon absorbed into the Swedish nobility by marriage or
by ennoblement for services rendered: of all Swedish noble families registered
by 1700, more than one half was of non-Swedish descent on the paternal side
and an even higher proportion on the maternal side. Consequently, the
Swedish nobility was as German or foreign by blood as some historians have
wanted to label the dynasty of the Palatinate-Zweibrücken Vasa branch; but
it felt itself as Swedish as the dynasty and shared that typical pride in Sweden
and its achievements which blossomed into the great 'Gothic' movement in
literature and history-writing, an attempt to match the glorious present with
an equally glorious past when the Goths, whose direct descendants the Swedes
believed (or made themselves believe) they were, held sway over Europe.[6]

The Swedes of European descent usually maintained family and trade connexions with their countries of origin; and young Swedes, whether of the high
or the lesser nobility (and even those who aspired to serve the Crown in ways
which those of noble rank usually might ignore) spent the most impressionable
years of their youth abroad: through service in the continental armies and
navies (including that of England) to gain experience, through grand tours
which usually took in parts of Germany, the Netherlands, France and
England if their parents could afford the expense (less fortunate young men
still made the tours, but as companions or tutors), through unpaid secretary-
ships at Swedish embassies abroad, or – if their bent was artistic or scientific –
through royal or high-noble patronage which subsidized studies abroad,
particularly in Italy and France. The most common ladder of social nobility
upwards came when the gifted son of a peasant was sent to Uppsala University to study (usually theology) and when his sons in their turn received
educations which fitted them for administrative office, or when a merchant
became rich enough (usually in combination with shipping ventures) to have
his daughters marry well.*

Seen against this background the close contact of Stockholm and of the
Swedish nobility with Europe becomes less surprising. Some of the original
treasure, whether a valuable manuscript or a piece of sculpture, may have been
cheaply acquired (or looted) in the wars; but collections were added to through
ordinary commercial transactions with cash that was not always easy to raise.
Many families mortgaged their estates to send their sons to Europe, to indulge
their collectors' instincts or passions, or even to keep up with the changing

---

* The outstanding example is the Stockholm burgher Olof Hansson, one of whose daughters
married Count Piper, another Arvid Horn, and a third Meijerfelt.

fashions in furniture and clothes: to replace oak with walnut, to buy the new bureaux, the new English chairs, the French gilt furniture, the Chinese porcelain and Dutch Delft ware, the Italian and German glass, the carpets and gobelins, the silver and gold wallpapers derived from Spanish patterns, the expensive linen and silver for table and toilet, the rich materials, the watches and jewellery, even the expensive toys from Leipzig and Nürnberg for the amusement of the children. 'He has ruined himself in the building and furnishing of his house', is not an infrequent observance made in respect of Swedish noblemen of 1680s,[7] though the 'ruin' is usually metaphorically meant. Another common cause for running into debt was too liberal a hospitality, whether abroad when representing one's country, or at home where the Swedes had a reputation with foreign visitors for showy excess. The large banquets, the breaking of glass against wall or floor (which was polite custom and not always a sign of drunkenness), may to some extent have misled the foreign observer of Swedish seventeenth-century life. Tradition in the north, as in other agricultural societies, demanded the choicest food for guests and big spreads for special occasions, such as marriages and funerals. The complementary trait, that of simplicity in everyday living, was probably missed by the important visitor from abroad or the diplomat whom the Swedes were anxious to impress.

One feature of Stockholm life could not be denied in spite of the town's European atmosphere and outlook: its very physical distance from the Continent. It lay far to the north, possibly too far to the north in an empire where communications were quick by sea and slow by land. The winter climate was vile and foreigners suffered from it (it was difficult to make a middle-aged diplomat who had already served in Sweden go back, and the appeals, to be recalled before winter, 'because my Body will bear this Climate no longer',[8] were often penned by those who felt they had done their turn); but those born to it took it in their stride even when they had lived abroad in milder airs. Their whole mode of life could cope with the cold and with the biting winds; their winter diet and clothing was adjusted to it, their houses had warm stoves, there were baths, both private and public, usually of the sauna type, which helped to keep them fit. What some found difficult to overcome was the feeling of isolation, of being far from the centre of things in Europe. Those who had been abroad kept alive by correspondence their contacts with the places where they had studied (whether in Italy or England) or served as officers and diplomats (whether in France, the Netherlands or the Germanies). Real longing was felt by those who had never travelled but yet thirsted for a sight of the world: Charles's sisters Hedvig Sophia and Ulrika in their teens walked in the royal garden* with a Danish diplomat and his wife and asked a hundred questions about 'the south'.[9]

Travel south was quicker in winter, when sledges could make use of the snowy roads and frozen lakes; in summer, with coach and carriage, along

* See illustration facing p. 13.

dusty roads, from two and a half to three weeks was the usual time from Stockholm to Gothenburg. The post took one week under favourable conditions to reach the Swedish German possessions, more to the East Baltic provinces.

II

Tradition has it that mysterious signs appeared in the sky over Stockholm the Saturday morning Prince Charles was born: storms raged, presaging the stormy reign to come, comets flared, foretelling his meteoric rise and fall. None of these did in fact happen, they are part of the legends which grow to satisfy the popular instinct for dramatic emphasis in the birth as in the death of heroes. Care must be taken also with stories told of Prince Charles's childhood, for if the memories were not recorded till the Prince had become King – and even more when he was already the late King – they easily become selective, picking out traits which fit the mature personality. We possess, however, much factual material which illustrates his childhood; many entries in his father's diaries; instructions for his teaching and the reports on his progress as a pupil; some of his exercise-books and drawings; a few letters he wrote and the fragment of a diary he kept during an illness. We can add to this contemporary news of him in letters and reports which, though they may have to be scrutinized for veracity, bias or source, cannot possibly be coloured by hindsight.

His childhood must have been a happy one. The central security, that of being wanted and loved by his parents, was his, as the firstborn son so essential for the continuation of the dynasty. He also had more of his parents' company and care than would be usual in European royal circles, since Charles XI and Ulrika liked a simple life with little ceremony and their greatest delight was to spend their free time with the children. The King took his meals with the Queen and the Dowager-Queen, and Hedvig Sophia and Charles were allowed to eat with them and accompany them on journeys and outings from a very early age. The Queen supervised all the details of their upbringing, chose nursemaids and servants with the greatest care. She was convinced that her children could not but be influenced by the character of those in attendance on them and laid down that only God-fearing, honest, respectful and calm people should be employed. She herself was with them as much as possible. 'The Queen keeps to her own apartments, looking after her children', is a recurring theme in contemporary reports from court.[10]

The first portrait of the infant Charles,* by Ehrenstrahl, the Rome-trained German painter whom the King's mother had made her protégé and to whom we owe so many drawings and paintings of the royal family in the 1680s and '90s, was done when the Prince was less than a year old.[11] It shows a happy and smiling child, beating a drum with evident enjoyment at the noise he is making.

* See illustration facing p. 45.

There is so much life in the face and in the pose that the trappings of a regal portrait in the baroque style hardly detract from the impression that this is a private record for the family album: the curly-headed fair baby with the laughing blue eyes is obviously adored by parents and grandmother and all in the family service and who is possibly going to be a little spoilt and get his own way too much.

But not long after this portrait was made tragedy and grief came into the family life of Charles XI and Ulrika in such overflowing measure that it must have made a deep impression even on young Hedvig Sophia and Prince Charles. Two more boys had been born to the royal couple in quick succession after Charles; Gustav in 1683, Ulrik in 1684. Gustav was a charming child of so sweet a disposition that people later argued he would have made a more popular king, 'generous and mild'.[12] Ulrik was the Queen-Dowager's favourite, probably because she took charge of him as an infant[13] when the Queen was ill, or possibly just exhausted. She had started another pregnancy very quickly after the birth of Ulrik and she always found the winters so trying.

The spring of 1685 came with unseasonable weather and an epidemic of fevers. Prince Gustav was taken ill and died in April; the parents were beside themselves with grief however much they tried to resign themselves to God's will. 'I never knew it hurt so much to lose a child', Charles XI wrote to a close friend.[14] In May Ulrik caught the same illness and suffered so much that the end, though dreaded, had to be accepted with relief.[15] In July Prince Charles went down with measles. The Queen kept him in her 'innermost chamber', nursing him herself, afraid to let him out of her sight even though he was not considered dangerously ill.[16] In September the new baby, another boy, was born and christened Frederick. He was welcomed in sad joy as God's gift to soften the cruel losses of the spring, but lived only a few weeks.[17] Yet another son, Charles Gustavus, was lost in infancy: born in December 1686 he died in February 1687.[18]

Both parents found it hard to accept the deaths of four of their children, and the grandmother was inconsolable at the loss of Ulrik. The King sought relief and forgetfulness in hard work; the Queen, whose activities were more physically circumscribed, became ill: she suffered from toothache, from coughs and fevers, from abdominal and rheumatic pains and above all from 'a heavy mind'. A Hanoverian doctor of some repute, Dr Pardisius, was called to Stockholm and suggested more exercise and fresh air; and the new royal physician, young Urban Hjärne, was of the same opinion.[19] The palace of Karlberg, a short distance from the capital was now bought for her by her husband. This delightful and intimate palace, built for Magnus de la Gardie by the French architect Jean de Vallée, became the favourite of Ulrika and the two children, whom she could now hardly bear to part with for even short periods. Karlberg was near enough to Stockholm to allow the King, when working in the capital during the day, to ride over and join the family in the late afternoon.[20] Most of the year 1687 the Queen spent quietly, often confined to bed with one illness or other, pale and listless when up and about, waiting for the birth of another child. She and her husband hardly dared hope that they would be allowed to keep the girl, born to them in January 1688. The formal christening of Ulrika Eleonora, called after the Queen, took place quietly and not till the the child seemed likely to survive was there real improvement in the Queen's health. Then she recovered her will to live. Acceptance of the loss of the four sons was symbolized by two paintings she commissioned from Ehrenstrahl and whose grouping she planned herself; one showed Gustav, Ulrik, Frederick and Charles Gustavus in the heavens while she herself contemplated a paper on which was written '*Dein Willie geschehe*';[21] the other depicted her with the surviving children by her side and those she had lost tumbling together on a cloud.*

The spiritual crisis through which the Queen passed to reach the stage when she could publicly proclaim 'Thy will be done' was one which deepened her religious devotion and her concern for the lot of the unfortunate: money was given to the poor in memory of her lost sons; from her own dowry and from the generous allowance which the King gave her she supported families and individuals who had suffered from the 'reduction'; she founded orphanages which she also hoped would serve as centres for introducing such arts as that of the weaving of tapestries in Sweden; she sent gifted young people abroad to study, and showed in all manner of ways that she was trying to forget her own grief in serving others. But her real solace came in the care for the moral and physical well-being and the happiness of the three children whom God had spared them; here she and Charles XI met and cooperated and sometimes clashed as they were both persons of deep convictions, though Ulrika had the easier temperament and was willing to submit to her husband with a good grace as long as no principle was at stake.

One field where difficulties sometimes arose was in the relationship with the Dowager-Queen. Hedvig Eleonora had a high opinion of the respect due to her as an ex-regent of Sweden, and to counteract her fears of political use being made of her son's Danish marriage she insisted that her rank should remain higher than that of her daughter-in-law. Her name was mentioned before that of the Queen in prayers for the royal family, foreign diplomats made their visits first to her, then to the Queen, her staff, given equality of rank took precedence over that of the Queen. Ulrika did not resent this; she was as convinced as her husband of the need to obey the command about honouring thy father and mother. The households of the two Queens frequently made trouble, however, and complaints and gossip and intrigues became the order of the day in a way which was much resented by both the King and the Queen. Ulrika had brought with her from Denmark a lady-in-waiting, Miss Marschalck, whose friendship with the Queen and supposed influence was much resented by the Dowager-Queen's staff;[22] Ulrika for her

---

* See illustration facing p. 44.

rt was made aware of occasional attempts to take her down a peg or two
hich hurt enough to make her mention them, or hint at them, in letters to her
other, the King of Denmark–Norway, or in conversations with Danish
plomats.[23]

But the struggle for prestige was in the main one that concerned the court
nd the diplomats – the Danes being particularly involved, though they on the
hole realized the wisdom of Ulrika being submissive to her mother-in-law[24]
more than the family. The Queen and the Dowager-Queen shared an interest
the arts, in news from abroad, in card-games (which were a favourite pas-
me at court) and above all in the royal children. The one family row known
have involved both the Queens came when Charles XI took offence at an
nplied but probably unintentional lack of respect for his mother. Hedvig
ophia and Prince Charles had been dressed up, to amuse the family, as
ummer and winter'. Prince Charles's costume included a cap, probably a
now-ball', which could not easily be removed without ruining the effect.
Vhen his son appeared in the Dowager-Queen's presence with covered head,
he King flared up, tore the cap from the boy's head and vented his temper in
ard words on the ladies-in-waiting responsible for the entertainment.[25]
Jlrika tried with some success to act as a conciliator; but there was at this
ime – towards the end of 1688 – just enough political tension between his wife
nd his mother to explain Charles XI's seemingly irrational outburst.

It was a time of intense friction between Christian V of Denmark and the
Duke of Holstein-Gottorp. In 1684 the King of Denmark had forcibly
occupied the ducal parts of Sleswig and, thanks mainly to Swedish diplomatic
upport, a congress had been called at Altona in 1687* to mediate between
he two parties. The Duke's wife, Ulrika's favourite sister Frederikke Amalie,
nd their son, the young Frederick of Holstein-Gottorp, had arrived in Stock-
olm for a prolonged visit partly because of the Duchess's natural desire to
remove herself, a Danish princess, from the turmoil. As tension mounted
between Sweden and Denmark, Charles XI threatening to make good Swedish
guarantees of Holstein-Gottorp rights unless the congress came to a speedy
decision, the Stockholm court divided into 'Holstein-Gottorp' and 'Danish'
factions which could not but create some ill-feeling between Ulrika and her
mother-in-law. Rumours flew thick and fast. The King, it was said, had been
considering the future of the dynasty. In the event of his own death, Ulrika
would be excluded from the regency for Prince Charles while the Dowager-
Queen would be included; a marriage was being planned between Frederick
and Hedvig Sophia and, in the event of Prince Charles's death, Frederick
would become the King of Sweden. The possibility that war might break out
between Denmark and Sweden as a result of the crisis was in itself enough to
worry Ulrika, and there is some evidence that she found the Dowager-Queen's
open partisanship for the Holstein cause hard to bear. 'The more I give in to

---

* The mediators, apart from Sweden, were William III of England, the States General and the
two dukes of Lüneburg.

the Dowager-Queen, the more I try to please her by being kind and conside▸
ate to the Prince of Holstein-Gottorp,' such was the gist of the Queen'
complaints, 'the more she tries to humble me'.[26]

The situation was delicate and difficult, and every incident, particularly th
one connected with Prince Charles's costume, was magnified out of all propor
tion by gossip and interpreted as a break between the royal couple. Th
marriage was happy, those in the know insisted, whatever the relationshiⱼ
between the Queen and the Dowager-Queen. In an attempt to stop speculatioⱼ
and gossip about the family's private affairs Charles xi issued strict order
against the carrying of tales. Everyone became very secretive all of a sudden
diplomats complained, daring to talk only of wind and weather, and o
nothing more 'confidential' at court than the royal dogs.[27]

III

A personal disagreement between husband and wife had, however, arisen
about the same time as the political tension between Denmark and Holstein-
Gottorp tended to disrupt the family peace. This difference, on a point of
principle, became a real test of the strength of their love. In the autumn of
1688 and the spring of 1689, observers noticed that there was something
wrong: some knew what issue was at stake, but not the root-cause of the
problem, which was the education of Prince Charles now that he was rapidly
nearing the end of that period of life which the age reckoned as infancy and
early childhood.*

Until the Prince reached the age of six the King and Queen had been able
to cooperate harmoniously in the upbringing of the heir to the throne. Ulrika
approved of her husband's insistence on fresh air and exercise: Charles was
taught to ride as soon as he could keep his seat on a horse, and on his fourth
birthday he was able to inspect a guard drawn up in his honour, riding right
round the detachment on a pony with a leading-rein; skating and sledge-
riding were winter-pursuits; rowing, sailing and running about in the orchards
those of the summer. Charles xi for his part was happy to leave the early
instruction of the children to the Queen, and Prince Charles's first lessons
were given to him by his mother. Every morning and evening he was taught
his prayers kneeling in her room; she told him Bible stories and illustrated
them from her collection of copper engravings.

The Queen also chose Prince Charles's first teacher, Norcopensis, the
Uppsala professor of *Eloquentiae*, during a visit which she and her children
paid to the university in July 1686. The castle of that city had been given her
as a present by her husband: she sometimes visited it to see how the restoration she had ordered was progressing, but on this occasion she came for the
express purpose of hearing a sermon preached by the teacher-elect. Tradition
has it that Prince Charles was allowed to pick his own tutor, the four-year-old

---

* See below, p. 521, for a contemporary division into the four ages of life.

Ulrika Eleonora and her children, from a painting by D. Ehrenstrahl

Prince Charles in 16.
from a painting by
D. Ehrenstrahl

Prince Charles on
horseback,
from a sketch by
D. Ehrenstrahl

•lding out his hand first to Norcopensis, one of the three professors con-
lered for the post; but the kindly scholar, devout and with a reputation for
·mplete indifference to fashionable and worldly life, was certainly the
ueen's choice.[28] Norcopensis, already fifty-three at this time, had a way with
.ildren and soon became a favourite both with the Prince and with the royal
·mily; he was ennobled in 1687 and as Nordenhielm remained responsible,
·til his death in 1694, for Prince Charles's general education. Under his
.idance the Prince began to read and write and to start his study of languages
.d history. Charles's signature, obviously modelled on that of his father,
·mained curiously identical to Charles XI's *Carolus* all his life.[29] The first
·ters which have survived are two from 1688, one to his godmother,
ueen Christina, sending his New Year greetings, and the other to Admiral
·achtmeister, thanking him for the present of a model ship.[30]

The King, content with the Queen's choice of teacher, took a hand in laying
·own the curriculum once the first steps of reading and writing had been
·astered, and the instructions given to Nordenhielm in December 1688 were
·nned by Charles XI himself.[31] The Prince, they stressed, must be brought up
· a God-fearing spirit, and must for that purpose study the Bible;* for the
·st he must begin to learn about Sweden's constitution and her armed forces
·d the principles of fortification and artillery. Of bodily skills, fencing and
·ding must be encouraged. Religious instruction was also provided by the
·ell-known theologian Bishop Erik Benzelius. Each morning after prayer and
·reakfast Charles spent an hour with the bishop, having a chapter of the Bible
·xplained to him and going through also the texts for the next sermon in
·lottskyrkan. Before long Charles had to write summaries of sermons he
·ttended and these have survived for the years 1688 to 1692. The Bible studies
·ere also made to fit in with his linguistic studies as he grew older, the text
·eing read not only in Swedish and German but in Latin and Greek.

Before this time, however, the harmony between the royal parents over the
·rince's education had been disturbed. The King wanted to appoint as the
·oy's governor Count Erik Lindschöld, a trusted friend since his service dur-
·ng the war of 1675–9 as secretary in the Chancery-in-the-field. He was a
·ouncillor, a quick-witted and experienced official who could teach the
·rown-Prince affairs of state; he was also an outstanding humanist, interested
·n education and had in his youth, as tutor to Charles X's illegitimate son,
·ravelled widely in Europe. The Queen, however, opposed the choice of Lind-
·chöld. He was reckoned of the Holstein-Gottorp party and those who heard
·f the disagreement between the royal couple put her distrust and dislike of
·im down to this account; and there may well have been some truth in the
·ears ascribed to her that he might turn the Crown-Prince against Denmark.[32]

---

* It has been argued that prolonged preoccupation with the Old Testament gave Charles an
·xaggerated belief in Jehovah, the jealous God who demanded an eye for an eye and a tooth for a
·ooth; but quite apart from the fact that study of the Old Testament was typical of the age, there
· evidence that the Christian virtues of mildness and justice tempered with mercy were equally
·tressed in Charles's religious education.

C

But the real and deeper reason for her opposition was that she found Lin schöld too worldly and not devout enough to be entrusted with her son upbringing; she had a horror of her children coming into close contact, whi young and impressionable, with people who did not measure up to the stan ards she hoped they would attain in adult life. Possibly there was also som thing irrational about her dislike of Lindschöld, a question of person antipathy; for no grave fault of character has ever been laid at his door contemporaries, even his enemies, saw him as a true servant of the King wh refrained from feathering his own nest and resisted all temptation to accep gratifications from abroad: a fairly common failing among Swedish statesme in spite of Charles XI's intense disapproval of it.*

The King had his way. Lindschöld† was made governor for the Prince an the strain which the Queen's opposition had caused was smoothed over wit the help of the royal chaplain Wiraenius. Ulrika's disapproval and oppositio can, however, be seen to have forced something of a compromise. Lindschö never became part of the family circle, in the way Nordenhielm was part of i and the knowledge that he was *persona non grata* with the Queen had restraining effect on Lindschöld himself and on his governorship of Princ Charles.[33] If the King had intended by his appointment to begin the Prince' worldly education and to give him a better preparation for politics at hom and abroad than he himself had received, he was checkmated twice over: firs by the Queen's lack of cooperation, secondly by death, since Lindschöld die suddenly in 1691, only forty-six years old. 'In him I have lost a servant wh meant well both for me and for my son', was Charles XI's farewell tribute t him.[34]

As successor to Lindschöld the King appointed Nils Gyldenstolpe,‡ agai an experienced and travelled man of affairs, again one who was reckoned o the French party, again one who was not popular with the Queen. Gylden stolpe was as worldly as Lindschöld and more liable to criticism on mora grounds.[35] He had, however, less time than his predecessor to spare for th Prince, being second-in-command of the Chancery, and Nordenhieln remained influential. When the latter died in 1694,[36] another Chancery officia was picked by the King to succeed him. He was Thomas Polus, good at Lati and very knowledgeable in foreign affairs (the only one who really understand politics in the Empire was the contemporary verdict of European diplomats i Stockholm on him). However, he found himself so busy with his norma duties in the Chancery where he was Secretary of State that it becam necessary to appoint an assistant teacher, young Gustaf Cronhielm, o whom fell most of the responsibility in the years 1695–7. Cronhielm was a admirable choice; gifted, independent,¶ travelled – a man who was to mak

---

* For a discussion of this problem see Hatton, 'Gratifications and foreign policy', *William II. and Louis XIV*, edd. R. M. Hatton and J. S. Bromley, pp. 68–94.

† See illustration facing p. 76.

‡ See illustration facing p. 76.

¶ For his moral courage in opposing Charles XII being declared of age, see below, p. 75.

s reputation as chairman of the commission which codified Sweden's laws. The consistency of Charles XI's choice of teachers for his son among those ith experience of affairs of state and with knowledge of Europe is significant: seems to point to a masculine and realistic drive to prepare the son for the orld and the task awaiting him, even at the expense of the Queen's maternal id devout desire to keep the Prince young and inside the circle of approved timates of a religious temperament.

IV

he appointment of Lindschöld was but the beginning of the process whereby rince Charles, at six and a half years of age, was 'taken away from the omen'. From New Year 1689 he was given his own apartments, his own aff and servants, his own regiment, Prince Charles's Lifeguards. This did not nply in any sense a separation from his mother and his sister – the close imily life of shared prayers, shared meals and shared amusements went on ist as before – but it did signify a stage in the process of growing up. It was so the passport to the world where the father's company and training began) play a larger part than before. Prince Charles now went along on some of ie hunting-trips of the King and the proud father noted the son's successes in is diary: in September 1690 he bagged three deer at Kungsör, the simple iyal residence that was hardly more than a hunting-lodge; in the severe inter of 1692 he killed a wolf on an island in the Stockholm archipelago.[37] he Prince was also allowed to accompany the father more than previously on is own, and he particularly enjoyed inspections and other trips that meant ding. Nordberg – Charles XII's first Swedish biographer – heard from those ho had known the King as a boy that he did not bother about food or sleep s long as he could be on horseback.[38]

Charles XI's influence, together with that of Lindschöld is also noticeable in ie new and fuller teaching instructions which were drawn up in 1690.[39] These ere based on those set up for Charles XI himself when he was a child (some-mes sentences were copied word for word from the older set) and were as omprehensive and ambitious as plans for the education of princes tended to e, on paper, all over Europe. But some new and individual conceptions of eaching are worth stressing. In the section dealing with Latin, for instance, was laid down that the Prince should not start with the study of grammar as n end in itself; he should first be encouraged to read the more entertaining iieces, such as the fables of Aesop and the letters of Cicero; from Cornelius Jepos and Livy he might learn geography and history as well as Latin; Caesar ould be used to interest him in military life – he should be made to feel, it was mphasized, that he himself marched with Caesar. In the comments on history eaching a similar approach can be discerned: maps should be used, the con-iexion between the languages studied and the history of Europe should be itilized. Stress was also laid on character-building; the object of the education

should be a prince who learnt independence, clear thinking and decisive actio
and books such as Cicero's *De Officiis* and Theophrastus's *Characters* we
recommended for this purpose. A detailed book-list was indeed given for a
subjects, ranging from Luther's *Cathecism* and the synopsis of it by Hafe
reffer (much used in Swedish schools at this time) to readings in politic
science by Aristotle, Lipsius and Grotius.

The full programme laid down in 1690 was not carried out in its entiret
partly because it had been drawn up to cover Prince Charles's education till I
should reach eighteen years of age and his whole life was changed by Charl
XI's death before the boy was fifteen. The general plan was that Prince Charl
should be at his lessons from 8 to 11 in the morning; that he should have fr
time from 11 till 2, and that his studies should continue in the afternoo
from 2 to 6. It is clear that in practice the formal afternoon tuition was ofte
skipped, especially in the early years. This was to allow for recreation whic
as the instructions had emphasized, was also desirable, to permit expeditio
of various kinds which were after all also part of the Prince's education, t
watch cannon being cast, ships being launched, regiments being inspected, t
teach him his share in the royal duty of entertaining visitors, the welcome on
as well as those found dull and boring.[40]

Thanks to exercise books, diary fragments and teachers' reports, we ca
judge how much of the detailed curriculum laid down in 1690 had bee
covered before Charles XI died. The religious instruction had proceede
according to plan; Benzelius had compiled a *Brevarium* to be used by his roya
pupil and the history of the Church had also been covered. Latin had pro
gressed well. By February 1692 Cornelius Nepos had been completed, by 169
Livy, Justinus and Curtius also – for Quintus Curtius's biography of Alex
ander, the Prince seems to have conceived a particular liking: this was th
book which in a small pocket edition went with him on all his campaigns, an
from which he was once heard to quote, *Memini me Alexandrum non merce
torem.** With the help of Glaser's *Epistolae* the Prince had by 1697 learnt t
write Latin well enough 'not to need much correction of late'; and his know
ledge of Latin, if not perfect, remained good enough for him to conduc
negotiations in Poland in that language and to listen to lectures in Latin wit
ease between 1716 and 1718. His instruction in Greek was rudimentary; bu
his modern languages were good.

German came easily to him, being so much used at court during foreig
visits and with diplomats (it used to be said in England that a knowledge o
'High-Dutch' was essential for any diplomat going to Stockholm)[41] that i
later years he felt 'at home' as soon as he crossed from Poland into Germany
He spoke and wrote German with facility throughout his life: his correspon
dence with both his brothers-in-law, Frederick of Holstein-Gottorp and
Frederick of Hesse, was always in German.[42] A special teacher was engaged
for French and both his governors, Lindschöld as well as Gyldenstolpe, wer

* See below, p. 226.

ancophiles and encouraged him to read French. Gyldenstolpe used Péré-xe's *Vie du roy Henri le Grand*, which was required reading for Louis XIV as a hild to train him in the French royal tradition, for much the same purpose Prince Charles's case; and we know that his pupil conceived a lasting admira-on for Henry IV.[43] Lindschöld, who much admired Barclay's novel *Argenis* nd its model picture of an absolute king, had it translated into French so that he Prince might read it. During and after adolescence, Charles continued nd widened his reading in French to include the plays of Corneille, Molière nd Racine; but though he read with ease,* he did not have nor seek much ractice in speaking French until after 1709. The difficulty of admitting rance's pretensions that a national language, as distinct from the universally ccepted Latin, should have preeminence in diplomatic intercourse was nainly to blame for this; rather than submit Charles let interpreters translate is Swedish – to be honoured as much as Louis XIV's French – for diplomats om France. Charles XI employed a teacher of Italian for his daughters, and nere is some evidence that Prince Charles also obtained a smattering of talian, useful in later life in Turkey where this language still held first place n diplomatic intercourse. Charles must have had a certain facility for picking p languages, since contemporaries claimed that during his campaigns he earnt some Polish and Turkish, and that he spoke some Finnish in which e had taken instruction from an officer of that country.[44]

Charles XII's inclination towards mathematics was strongly pronounced ven in childhood. When he was given his own staff at New Year 1689 a rilliant officer of Scottish descent, Karl Magnus Stuart,† was one of them. tuart had served as a musketeer in Charles XI's army, had been a pupil of the reat Swedish fortification expert Erik Dahlberg‡ and now became Prince Charles's teacher in the history and art of war, and in mathematics. Every Vednesday and Saturday morning from 1691 onwards, fortification was on he time-table and soon became the Prince's favourite lesson; in his exercise-ooks the drawings of animals become fewer while those of soldiers and forts ncrease. Dahlberg's battle-plans and topographical engravings were used to liscuss tactics, strategy and history; all the battles of Charles's father and randfather were gone over in detail again and again, and those of Gustavus Adolphus's reign also. As an adult, Charles XII could reconstruct Charles X's attle of Warsaw and Gustavus Adolphus's battle of Lützen from memory, ointing out the positions of the regiments involved and going through all tages of these past appeals to the dice of war. The military writers of the day, uthorities such as de Pagan and Ruysenstein were used, but the study of

---

* Cederhielm, a Chancery official, commented in a letter to his brother of 18 July 1708 that the King's command of French was so perfect that he was able to spot mistakes in construction by quite skilled linguists.

† See illustration facing p. 76.

‡ This hero from Charles X's wars was an artist of importance (it is through him that we know he palaces and views of seventeenth-century Sweden best); he was successively Governor-General of Bremen and Verden and Livonia; cp. below pp. 63, 85, 102.

topography and of generalship from historical examples was more promine
in the curriculum. Mathematics, as the very basis of a future commander-i
chief's training, was naturally strongly emphasized and the mathematic
working out of tactical problems loomed large in the tasks set the Prince I
Stuart. But quite apart from competence in solving such problems, Charl
early showed a keen delight in mathematics as an intellectual exercise. This I
always retained, so much so that as an adult he pronounced anyone witho
mathematics as but half a person.*

History, as well as forming part of military studies, was taught also as
subject in its own right. Pufendorf, Swedish historiographer royal since 16;
and Queen Ulrika Eleonora's secretary between 1682 and 1686, wrote tw
history books which were used as textbooks for the Prince. The one entitle
An Introduction to the History of the States of Europe, the favourite reading
Rehnskiöld on campaign, was available in Swedish even before Charles
birth; and the so-called *Continuation* (published in German in 1686, translate
into Swedish in 1688) which in reality was a history of Sweden, was muc
read and underlined by the Prince as a schoolboy.[45]

The one subject catered for on paper which seems to have been compara
tively neglected in practice, since teaching of it had been planned for when th
Prince should be between fifteen and eighteen years of age, was that
advanced philosophy and political science. We know that Cronhielm trans
lated Erasmus's *Institutio Principes Christiani* into Swedish for his pupil's us
in 1695, its Latin being presumably thought too difficult for a boy of thirteen
but the more ambitious books listed in the plan do not seem to have bee
studied in any detail. In the Lund period of 1716–18 Charles XII put pen t
paper on philosophical problems which discussions with visitors to his head
quarters and his own attendance at the 'Academy' had prompted him t
ponder,† an incident which shows that Charles was not as indifferent t
theoretical speculation on the nature of life and morals as has sometimes bee
thought. Against the background of Charles XII's early teaching and upbring
ing such indifference would indeed have been strange. The inculcation o
ethical principles had permeated his lessons from the very earliest days whe
Nordenhielm was given charge of the Prince's education. On the practica
side this was expressed even by the earliest phrases chosen for the young pupi
to copy (*Vincere aut mori: Si Deus pro nobis, quis contra nobis*), and th
emphasis on reasoned thinking started as soon as possible and was attempte
through written dialogues between teacher and pupil. Those from the perio
April 1687 to December 1688 have survived and give us an insight into th
ideas of kingship which they were intended to transmit and into the metho
whereby the boy was being encouraged to examine moral principles. These
dialogues were based on conversations between Nordenhielm and the Princ
as to right and wrong behaviour. In the actual exercise the teacher takes the
part of the devil's advocate, putting forward unjust and morally unsound

* See below, p. 430.   † ibid., pp. 430–1.

ews, leaving the Prince to argue against him and to find reasons both for the ght action and for the right argument. The final sentence is usually a brief cknowledgement of the teacher giving in, 'The Prince gained the better of e'.

Historians used to argue that the pattern of these dialogues must have fosred Charles's obstinacy and selfrighteousness.[46] This is perhaps to take the x year old's victory in the battle of wits too seriously (did Nordenhielm's omment mean much more than the 'star' or 'flower' mark of distinction hich twentieth-century children, at least my own generation, received for ood work in the early school years?) and to ignore the evidence of conceptual inking which the dialogues offer. They were means to develop at an early age e Prince's logical and analytical powers and were intended also to impress n him a code of morals which stressed the need for a king to love justice, to onour his word and to accept adversity as well as good fortune in a spirit of umility before God.

4

The Heir Apparent

From the time when his formal tuition started Prince Charles began to realiz
his own position within the family and the Swedish empire. It was brough
home to him that he would one day succeed his father as King of Sweden an
that he would then play an important and responsible part in the life of th
nation. For a small and high-spirited boy the prospect of future power wa
perhaps easiest to grasp; once when Cronhielm threatened to report him t
the King for having punched him in the nose, Prince Charles retorted that
he dared to do so he would make sure he got his own back 'when I am king'
Those in charge of the Prince, parents and teachers, did their best to impres
upon him the duties which would be his and attempted to give him a philo
sophy of kingship that would help him. Both Nordenhielm and Linschöl
explained to him that he would become King through no virtue of his own, hi
royal birth was an act of God, a good gift which he must treasure and do hi
best to deserve; but while Nordenhielm tended to lay emphasis on what th
Prince could do to train himself to become a just and wise ruler, Lindschöl
tried to impress upon him the need to listen to the advice of older and mor
experienced men. Charles XI, being less articulate and more practical b
nature, tried to show by his own example what it meant to be King: he was u
at five in the morning, worked when in Stockholm in Council and committee
from eight to one, and saw experts and deputations in his cabinet in the after
noon.[2] When he was out with the army or on tours of inspection he was als
at work from morning to night,[3] simply dressed – *Gråkappan* was one of hi
nicknames, after his plain grey mantle – content with simple fare. Ulrika
with her gift for getting into direct contact with her children, concentrated he
advice round brief maxims of conduct: be generous and mild to your subject
when you become king; do not believe those that carry tales; always hear bot
sides of a quarrel; keep your word.

All his teachers agreed that Charles was an intelligent child with a receptiv
mind. His strong will was evident to all who knew him; so was his obstinac
once he considered himself in the right. He took his mother's teachings t
heart, because he adored her and was anxious to please her and also becaus
he had inherited enough of her temperament to make her moral standard

ppeal to him. Even Ulrika could not always move him from a position which
e adopted in the light of her maxims as he understood them. Charles's
oungest sister, when she was Queen of Sweden wrote down a childhood
cident which illustrates this:[4] it must have taken place before the Prince was
x years old since he was still in the charge of a nursemaid. This maid, engaged
o a lieutenant, wanted to slip out and say goodnight to her sweetheart and left
rince Charles alone in his room, making him promise her faithfully that he
ould not stir from the chair in which he was sitting while she was away. The
ueen arrived to fetch the Prince for divine service earlier than expected and
as surprised and annoyed at Charles's reiterated, but unexplained, refusal to
ome with her. The mystery and the promise were not revealed till the maid
ame back. Ulrika Eleonora was four years younger than her brother and can
ardly have remembered this incident, but it must have become part of the
amily lore and was the story with which she chose to begin her reminiscences
f her brother. Her intention was to emphasize how early in life he began to
nsist on keeping his word once given – a characteristic of his throughout his
fe – but the story also hints at a secretive strain,* a shyness or unwillingness
o give reasons for personal actions which was very pronounced in his father
nd which in Charles XII, though tempered by the greater openness and frank-
ess of nature possessed by his mother, was noticeable above and beyond the
ecrecy necessitated in matters of policy and military matters.

A certain head-strong and dare-devil attitude of the young Prince in physical
natters worried those in charge of him. At a time when Gyldenstolpe was his
governor (so that the Prince must have been at least eight years old) but absent
vith Charles XI at Kungsör, Queen Ulrika's lady-in-waiting, Miss Marschalck,
vrote in some despair to the governor about some escapade of the Prince's in
a wonderful mixture of German and French: '*La faute du prince besteht, dass
alle klagen, dass er kein Gehör gibt, zu dem habe Ihre Maj:t heute remarquirt
qu'il se picqait de gloire dass er solche Ausstehen könne et bien loin de témoigner
à la reine, dass ihm leid were, dass er mutwillig unvorsichtig gewesen, hat er ein
sonderliche Freude marquiret das er in solche Gefahr gewesen, dass alle darüber
ein verschrecken.*'[6] Whatever the Prince had done (climbed a tree, run away on
some little trip of exploration alone, taken out a boat without permission or
crossed the ice when it was not judged safe: in the absence of any date we can
only guess wildly at the cause of the commotion) it is clear from this letter that
those who felt responsible for his safety found him far from docile. It is not
easy to decide, because of the lack of any clear indication where the Queen's
quoted opinion ends and Miss Marschalck's begins, whether Prince Charles's
mother was advising the court to pay less attention to the boy's small experiments in independence and defiance and thus lessen his delight in them, or
whether she shared to the full the views expressed by Miss Marschalck. The
Queen was certainly more concerned than anyone else lest Charles should

---

* '*C'est un prince fort caché*', was to be the French ambassador d'Avaux's comment on
Charles XII.[5]

injure himself or fall ill. The Prince was not considered robust by nature, both he and his youngest sister were 'chesty', and a constant guard was kept over their health. The fear of losing any more children was never absent from the minds of the royal parents, the slightest indisposition of Prince Charles, the first-born and only surviving son caused great uneasiness: every cold and cough and bit of fever was commented on at court and in the diplomatic correspondence. This impedes any real assessment of the health of the royal children, but concern and anxiety are genuine enough. Charles, both at the time and when discussing his childhood as an adult, considered himself to much fussed over and mollycoddled.[7]

He sometimes managed to bully or cajole his way past the sentence of being 'kept indoors'. We can observe his methods in a diary he kept for some weeks in 1690 (started off by a desire, or command, to commit to paper the story of the first launching of a ship he had ever witnessed, the armed merchantman *Princeps Carolus*).[8] Here he recounts on 14 March how he was nearly left behind when the family went to Karlberg for the day since he had a cold and his governor wanted him to stay in Stockholm. The doctors were sent for to decide the matter on Miss Marschalck's suggestion (she must have had a soft spot for the Prince after all, or she might have wanted to score off Lindschöld) and Charles – keen not to miss the treat of a trip – broke into the consultation with an indignant exclamation that the doctors could not know their job if they intended to keep him in for the sake of a mere cold in the nose and won his point by making the Queen and the rest of the party laugh. There were, however, some illnesses which could not be laughed away: a fairly serious fever in 1689 which at first was thought to be smallpox,[9] and a longish illness in 1692, the double tertian ague.

During convalescence from this the boy began another journal[10] in which he lists the day's happenings: news he has heard from visitors, the comments of the doctors on the pattern of his fever-attacks (he was obviously quite impressed when their prognosis was right and the fever did return at the time they had forecast), descriptions of his presents. Behind the simple and matter-of-fact reporting of the nine-year-old we sense the relief of the relatives and court at his recovery and their concern to keep him happy and amused. Stuart brings letters and draws pikemen and musketeers for him to copy, as the Prince enjoyed illustrating whatever he saw or read about; Count Wrede's son calls with a model of the Salberg silver mine. His mother thinks of a new and interesting present nearly every day: money to have his watch repaired: red crystal glasses (one to drink out of, one fluted and filled with *L'eau d'Hongrie*), a gold and emerald decorated statuette of a Turk which could be opened to disclose a hiding-place for a small box, a knife, and – meriting the longest entry – the gold medal which commemorated Charles XI's election as a Knight of the Order of the Garter in 1671 which was brought to him on loan that he might study it. With the return of health and regular work the journal was discontinued. Some writing of essays in the 'disputation' form had already

een done while the Prince was confined to his own room; and after 18 April,
hen he notes that he has begun 'to study seriously' with Nordenhielm once
ore, there is only one further entry, of a jolly wedding held at the castle on
9 May. Life was obviously more tempting than journal-writing: there is a
onging to be out of doors in the entry for 15 April that he had seen from a
indow a man walking with 'a horse and some dogs'.

II

Charles XI's love of dogs and horses made Prince Charles used to and fond of
these dumb companions. Dogs were always welcome presents in the royal
household: get some 'Beare dogs, Bulldogs, and Irish greyhounds', was the
advice of an English diplomat asked to suggest a suitable gift for the King of
Sweden in 1689, 'a Dog and a bitch of eache sorte and of ye fiercest and young-
st that are not errant puppies'.[11] Horses the King cared even more for and
had paintings made of all his favourites.[12] When valuable horses from abroad
arrived, bought or given by other rulers as presents of politeness, such as the
Spanish horses in 1694 or those sent by William III in 1695, all the family was
taken to admire them.[13] The King followed the Prince's progress on horseback closely; he was given a good riding-master, Gösta Hård, and Ehrenstrahl in one of his lively sketches has captured the interest and pride on the
faces of the royal family – parents, grandmother and the two sisters – while
watching from a box Charles as a nine-year-old showing his paces on a lively
mount.* The Prince is splendidly dressed for the occasion in feathered hat,
full-bottomed wig and brocade coat, and has a fine sword at his side.

These elaborate dressage shows, in imitation of the French carousels, were
staged when royal relatives visited Sweden from abroad. Such visits were filled
with festivities of many kinds, on a more magnificent scale than the outings
and parties of everyday existence. In the ordinary daily round Prince Charles
had few friends of his own age. The sons of trusted officials came to visit at
times† but neither these nor the pages of his own staff could mix on terms of
equality with him, as an invisible cordon was drawn round the royal children
by their very position rather than by any conscious insistence on ceremonial
respect. The elder sister, Hedvig Sophia, was thus Charles's only constant
companion. She was lively and full of fun and known as 'the happy Princess'.
She was pretty and had learnt to hide a physical defect (she was born with
thumbs which had double top joints)[14] so well that it was hardly noticeable.
She was bright and grew up accomplished in singing and playing music. She
was darker than the two other children, more like the father's side of the
family and was, for that reason possibly, a favourite with the grandmother.
The younger sister, Ulrika Eleonora, was too young to share the amusements
and interests of the two elder ones; in Charles XI's diaries we can note how

* See illustration facing p. 45.
† We know, for instance, that Edvard Gyldenstolpe, the eldest son of his governor, did so.

'Prince Charles and Princess Hedvig' are thrown together when outings an treats are recorded, and it is 'my sister and I' in the Prince's own journals an letters.

The circle was widened, however, when royal visitors arrived; and one cousin in particular spent so much time in Sweden that he was one of the famil circle for years. Frederick, the son of Duke Christian Albrecht of Holstein Gottorp and the Queen's beloved sister, Frederikke Amalie, came to Stock holm for a visit with his mother in November 1687 and stayed till July 1690 he and his mother came back once more in the autumn of 1691 and remaine in Sweden till October 1693. These visits were connected with the trouble situation between Holstein-Gottorp and Denmark but they gave the roya family much private happiness. The Duchess of Holstein-Gottorp was ga company for the Queen and had indeed come partly for the purpose of cheer ing her up. Frederick, some six years the senior of Prince Charles, provided the King with young company to take along for rides of inspections and fo hunts at a time when his own son was tied to his lessons for a good part of th day. For the two elder royal children, cousin Frederick brought fun and a change in routine, though his teasing was at times hard to bear. The painting by Ehrenstrahl from 1687 of Hedvig and Charles dancing, dressed in Roman costume, is evidence of the efforts to provide more sophisticated amusement than the usual ones.*

During the second Holstein visit a masked ball of great magnificence was given in February 1692; the Queen planned it on the lines of a continental *Wirtschaft* party, to represent the meeting of travellers from many lands at an inn. Ninety guests marched in festive procession from the Queen's apartments to the big drawing room where seven hundred candles flared, 125 different courses of food were served, and twenty-eight pyramids of sweetmeats were set up. Prince Charles was dressed as a Muscovite, and though he and the other children (even Ulrika was present) were not allowed to stay up and dance and play cards till six in the morning, like most of the grown-up guests they had a fine time.[16] Charles XI was known as moderate in drinking and his example was followed by all at the ball. 'It lasted with feasting and dancing from 8 at night till 6 or 7 the next morning,' ran the report of one diplomat, 'the King tarrying all the while, and ended without any other excess besides that of Mirth'.[17]

III

The Queen had appeared as a spectator only at the masked ball. Her health was giving increasing grounds for worry.[18] The doctors had advised a visit abroad to seek a cure at one of the famous spas as early as 1690, for they con-

---

* Of these the English resident wrote in 1691 to a correspondent in Berlin who had regaled him with gay news from that capital: 'Our divertisements at court are different from yours, here the diversion of the Court Assemblys go no higher than Prison Bays, Drop hanckerchiefs and the like Sports, which you must be well acquainted with in the Countrey pastimes in England, to understand.'[15]

ssed themselves unable to help. The King urged her to go, her suite was
icked and other arrangements made, but Ulrika finally decided that she
ould not bear to be parted from her children and that she would commit her-
elf to God: if he wanted her to get better, she would regain her health at home
s well as abroad.[19] She felt needed at home, the King was prone to riding
ccidents, the children were frequently confined to bed. As if to prove her
ght, Charles XI went down with fever just a few weeks after she had made up
er mind to stay and Prince Charles and Hedvig caught the measles some
months later.[20] Her husband and her children soon recovered, but there was
o improvement in her own health. She was up and about most of the time,
naring family life from a chair or a seat in the garden, playing cards with the
Dowager-Queen; but her 'old troubles' kept plaguing her, pains in her limbs
nd abdomen so that she could not walk and had often to be carried about;
n bad days she had to take to her bed. A growing conviction that she would
ever see her family in Denmark again made her tearful when she spoke about
er relatives there on the other side of the Sound.[21]

The summer of 1693 brought a great deal of sickness to Sweden; the heat
vas at first intense, the hottest for a century it was said, then the weather
urned comparatively cold and people began to go down in an epidemic of
evers. The Queen moved to Karlberg to get better air. There she became
eriously ill. Her husband tried to persuade himself that she would recover
rom this bout of weakness as from so many others, that it was but temporary,
lue to the weather and a mistakenly diagnosed pregnancy. But he was alarmed
nough not to move from her side, nursing her with 'incredible tendresse';
ifting her in and out of bed, comforting her at night when she woke in agony
nd convulsions.[22] When the doctors told him that death was imminent, the
children were brought in to make their farewells. Ulrika made Prince Charles
promise her solemnly that he would always take care of his sisters and that he
vould conduct himself when he became King according to the principles
he had taught him.[23] The next evening on 26 July she died, thirty-six years
old.

The shock was great both for husband and children. Charles XI fainted and
nad to be bled. Prince Charles went down with a fever. The sorrow of those
who had served and loved Ulrika hung like a pall over Karlberg and spread
over the country with the sad news. Everything was dressed in black, the
furniture in the houses, the carriages, the guards. The King walked about in
the late Queen's room, cried whenever her name was mentioned and said
when he had to leave for Stockholm, 'Here I leave one half of my heart.'[24]
Hedvig Eleonora seems to have been less affected than most. She was heard to
speak about the need for the King to remarry, though she did not dare to
mention it to him at this stage.[25]

When the time came for a remarriage to be openly urged by Hedvig
Eleonora her son refused to consider it.[26] There were feelers from abroad in the
same direction, including one from Württemberg, where the negotiator held a

brief both for a daughter of the house and for her widowed mother, arguin
that if Charles XI wanted a young wife and more heirs to secure the successior
he ought to choose the former, but if he preferred a middle-aged stepmothe
for his own children, the latter would do very well.[27] The King who even thre
months after Ulrika's death, could not hear her spoken about without burs
ing into tears, made it clear to the diplomats as to his mother that he would nc
remarry. 'When Prince Charles is eighteen I will marry him off and that wi
take care of the succession,' he answered, 'for my part I could never get
mother for my children half as good as the one I lost.'[28]

I V

The King's comfort was the company of Ulrika's children. In them he foun
living mementoes of his dead wife. He asked that a painting of her as a sma
girl should be sent to him from Copenhagen so that he could verify if littl
Ulrika Eleonora was as like her mother as he was told by those who ha
known his wife as a child.[29] He took the three with him for outings when ther
was an opportunity. One summer's day in 1696 he rowed them round a
island in the archipelago;[30] but it was naturally enough Prince Charles wh
became his most constant companion and charge, going with him both o
army manœuvres and on fishing and hunting-trips. The open-air life improvec
the Prince's health and he weathered further illnesses relatively easily. H
went down with a fever which laid all the royal children and Hedvig Eleonora
low in May 1694,[31] and before the grandmother had recovered the Princ
caught smallpox. There was some initial anxiety when it looked as if the po
would 'turn inwards' and the old Queen let herself be carried to his room tha
she might be near him; but when it became clear that the attack was a mild
one, the illness was counted a blessing as it would now render him protected
for the future.[32] The Prince himself was quite proud of the scars left on his
face, they made him look 'more manly, he thought.[33]

Prince Charles's share in his father's duties and pleasures can be charted
from Charles XI's diary entries after 1693. Every success as a shot is noted: in
February 1694 Prince Charles shot his first bear;[34] in the same month he
managed to hit a fox running at full speed; in September 1695 he hit a doe
at ninety-six paces; in December he joined his father and his officer-friends
on a regular hunt. The supplementation of his theoretical military training
looms even larger: he took part in mock battles, led by officers who had
gained experience abroad; he came along on winter inspections when at
least once the mode of transport was sledges drawn by reindeer; he was at
his father's side when he drilled Guards regiments in the summer of 1696;[35]
he examined the new lavette invented by Stuart and watched the casting of
cannon; he saw ships launched, sailed with the men-of-war and for the rest
of his life could recall nautical terms for every part of ships and their rigging.

He grew very like his father in mannerisms and in habits. He did not look

ke his father but began to talk like him, brief, to the point, with a certain
ry flavour born of the need to set an example, to minimize danger, to guard
gainst premature commitments. To anyone familiar with Charles xii and
is sayings as an adult it is quite illuminating to come across Charles xi in
692, trying to parry a Dutch diplomat's insistence that Sweden must guard
gainst the danger from France. It was raining at the time. Charles xi went
o the window of the audience-room, opened it, laughed and commented,
Gentlemen, as long as it does not rain mill-stones we have nothing to fear.'[36]
Charles xi's desire to come and go without fuss and notice is another habit
which Charles xii took over. The head-shaking concern with which courtiers
nd diplomats noted in 1684 that the King had ridden home alone, on a
ost-horse at that, and been at the castle two hours before even the guard
new of his return[37] is repeated often enough in Charles xii's reign.

In these, as in other traits, inherited characteristics as well as a conscious
modelling must have been at work. Charles xii lost both mother and father
o early that the natural rebellion of adolescence was in his case never directed
against his parents. His grandmother and the 'old men' in the administration
were made to feel some of the revulsion which young people usually entertain,
or a time, of the principles and conduct of their elders: but having lost his
mother when he was eleven and his father when he was fourteen, Charles
venerated their memories in a pre-adolescent state of innocence. He was
imbued with the desire to follow their example and obey the maxims and
standards they had impressed on him. Any objective appraisal of the parents
as human beings in the round, a process whereby most adolescents learn to
come to terms with the world and its need for compromise, was denied him.
This may in part account for that lack of psychological insight into the
motives of men and the faulty assessment of the endurance and quality of
others which Charles xii showed at times when a grown man. The understanding of human character is helped by the sad but salutary experience of
measuring beloved parents against their own standards and learning to
recognize in oneself family weaknesses as well as family virtues. As it was,
Charles xii had to learn in a harder school. Harder for him than for one not
born to be an absolute King, since his position in Sweden isolated him to such
an extent that the necessary stage of disillusionment was postponed till he
discovered in warfare abroad that the moral standards he had been taught as a
child were not those practised by other crowned heads when *raison d'état*
was involved.

Charles xi certainly attempted to prepare his son for the business of government by explaining and by having politics explained to him. When Thomas
Polus of the Chancery was made his preceptor after Nordenhielm's death
it was expressly stated that he should introduce the Prince to affairs of state;[38]
but the level at which one can discuss such matters with a thirteen- or fourteen-
year-old differs very much from that at which one can talk with a boy of
seventeen or eighteen, and above all the interpretation of motives, declared

or hidden, made by the younger party in such a discussion must vary significantly with age. We do not know the words in which Charles XI touched upon matters of importance at home and abroad to his son between 1695 and 1697 but we do know (from hints in diplomatic correspondence and in the memoirs of men at court, from the reports of the King's oral instructions to Prince Charles on his death-bed and from deductions about the written instruction which the King dictated for his son to be read by him and destroyed when he succeeded to the throne) that he had begun to take his son into his confidence in questions of policy.

One problem which had to be faced was the future marriages of the royal children. Ever since the first Holstein visit to the Swedish court in 1687 there had been rumours that the elder Princess, Hedvig Sophia, was to be engaged to her cousin Frederick (who succeeded his father in December 1694) to cement the Holstein-Gottorp ties with Sweden. Presents exchanged were often interpreted as the betrothal having taken place.[39] The old Queen was known to be in favour of the marriage (she 'has given her hand to the Duke that it will come to pass' it was said in 1692); Queen Ulrika herself was rumoured to be against it.[40] At the same time a Danish marriage for Prince Charles had been suggested to 'balance matters' and to please Queen Ulrika; her brother the King of Denmark had a daughter, Sophia, who would be suitable from the point of view of age, though five years older than the Prince.[41] Speculation on Hedvig's engagement became more intense from 1695 onwards when she had reached the age of fourteen. The King agreed that the Holstein marriage would be suitable, but he considered the Princess too young, and did not want to bind her till she should come to *annos discretionis* and even then only if she did not object to Frederick as a husband.[42]

The marriage was eagerly sought by Frederick as a further strengthening of his position *vis-à-vis* Denmark, since his Danish uncle had not shown himself anxious to carry out the terms agreed at Altona. Indeed, Danish acceptance of the Altona Agreement of 1689 – a restoration of the Holstein-Gottorp lands and rights as they had been before 1684 – had only been gained because the King of Denmark feared a Swedish invasion if he did not comply,[43] while the Anglo-Dutch guarantee had been given in the hope of securing Charles XI's entry into the Nine Years War against France as a *quid pro quo*.[44] A war-policy was, however, anathema to Charles XI for several reasons. He was unwilling to jeopardize his reform work at home. Then, the virtual union of the two Maritime Powers under William III's leadership from 1688 onwards brought about a situation different from the one of 1681 and 1683 when Sweden had shown herself willing to participate in some restraint on Louis XIV, at least of a diplomatic kind.[45] Europe was no longer faced with one monarch aiming at too preponderant an influence; Europe was divided into two big blocs, the combined naval power of England and the Dutch Republic being conceived as a political danger to Sweden, possibly more so than Louis XIV.

This was one reason why Swedish policy was prevaricating during the years 1689 to 1697: Charles XI and his advisers, whichever side they favoured (for there were among them adherents both of a 'French party' and of an 'Allied group'), wanted to remain neutral as long as possible, reserving Sweden's strength for intervention at a decisive moment, to act, in the phraseology of the time, as a 'balancing power' in Europe.[46] If this were done, she might obtain the position of an armed mediator, which could yield gains of territory or valuable guarantees for her Baltic possessions. Neutrality offered advantages and Swedish shipping enjoyed a boom period. The merchant fleet grew rapidly, and there were hopes of realizing the ambition from Charles x's reign: to transfer a sizeable share of Dutch and English Baltic trade permanently to Sweden.[47] The exploitation of Swedish resources and opportunities became the responsibility of the College of Commerce, headed by Count Fabian Wrede (the man who presented Prince Charles with the model of the silver mine in 1692);* a forceful exponent of economic ideas which had grown with Swedish expansion in the eastern Baltic into a regular theory of empire.

Such ideas had indeed been a powerful impetus behind the earliest expansion.[48] The need to guard Finland against Muscovite raids and the urgency to answer appeals for help from the Order of the Sword before Denmark got too firm a footing in the East Baltic had pushed the Swedes east and south of the Gulf of Finland into Karelia, Ingria, Estonia and Livonia. But the prospect of controlling the trade of Viborg, Narva, Reval and Riga had also acted as a spur. The East Baltic provinces were rich in valuable exports, in grain and masts in particular; but it was also hoped to channel an ever increasing proportion of Russian and Polish trade to Europe (trade in flax and hemp and furs and tallow as well as in grain) through the Swedish Baltic ports so that dues and tolls in cash would swell the coffers of Sweden. Such hopes had been only partly fulfilled, even though Karelia, Ingria, Estonia and Livonia had become Swedish and indeed formed the nucleus of the Swedish empire. Russian and Polish trade had showed a regrettable tendency to avoid the Swedish net; the Russian via Archangel, the Polish over the Courland and East and West Prussian ports. The question of extending the Swedish Baltic littoral, as well as of rectifying the frontier with Russia so that Archangel should fall on the Swedish side of the border, were prospects which were discussed in Sweden. No one advocated a war of aggression to obtain these glittering prizes, but they were desiderata to be remembered if a favourable situation should develop in the future. In the meantime ambitions for the Swedish Baltic ports crystallized in schemes for attracting traffic to them from far away, from Persia, India and China, along routes which had long ago been used to carry valuable eastern goods to Europe,[49] while efforts were made both to increase European trade to the Baltic provinces and to expand the Swedish merchant fleet so that naval stores could be carried to customers in Swedish ships.

* See above, p. 54.

The principal motive for such expansion of trade and shipping, as behind the hope for extension of the Swedish Baltic littoral, was one of obtaining ready cash. Increased money income was less necessary after Charles XI's reforms than earlier, but the nobility (who hoped to lessen the need for the full force of the 'reduction') and the King were at one in regarding the Baltic provinces as the money-spinner of the empire, its very life-blood. The German provinces, by contrast, though their position astride river-mouths served economic as well as strategic purposes, had never paid their way. Swedish Pomerania with Stettin and Stralsund, Wismar further west in the Baltic and Bremen and Verden on the North Sea commanded the Oder, the Elbe and the Weser much as the East Baltic provinces commanded the Dvina and the Peipus–Ladoga lake and river systems. The Empire had many alternative ports, and the important town of Bremen was not a Swedish possession, though the Swedes had expected it to become theirs in 1648 and it was the prize most desired as a reward from an armed mediation between Habsburg and Bourbon.

The Swedish provinces in the Empire were indeed strategic bastions rather than economically or constitutionally integrated parts of the empire,* expensive but necessary strongholds on the Continent. As long as the threat from the Catholic Vasas of Poland had existed, they had been essential as out-posts from which the danger to the religious and dynastic settlement of Sweden could be defended; but even with the force of the Counter-Reformation spent, the Habsburg drive to the north halted and the Polish Vasas no longer kings of Poland, the Swedish possessions in the Empire were regarded as vitally important. They were the ones that made Sweden a European power; through them she had a voice in the Diet of the Empire, through them (for their garrisons could easily be reinforced from Sweden in times of European tension) she was a military force to be reckoned with not only in the Lower Saxony Circle but in European great-power politics, within striking distance of Austria, France and the Netherlands; through them she could exert pressure on Brandenburg, always jealous of Swedish Pomerania and worried about Swedish intentions in Courland and Poland.

Even more essential was the role of the German provinces for Sweden's restraint on Denmark. Bremen and Verden, Wismar and Stralsund taken in conjunction with the Holstein-Gottorp alliance contained Denmark from the south and prevented her attempting to regain the western and southern coastal districts on the Scandinavian peninsula, Bohus, Halland, Scania and Blekinge, except at times when she had strong military allies. These peninsular Swedish conquests, with their access to Kattegat and Skagerak and the open North Sea, as well as their command of the eastern shore of the Sound, were so vital to the Swedish state as to be the very heart of the empire. No reconciliation with Denmark could be contemplated which jeopardized this

---

* In the East Baltic provinces Charles XI could introduce Swedish absolutism; in the German ones he was obliged by the terms of the 1648 peace to respect the constitutional and social pattern of that date.

coastline and, *mutatis mutandis,* no reconciliation with Denmark which sacrificed the Holstein position and alliance could be entertained.

The neutrality of Sweden in the Nine Years War endangered, however, the possessions and sovereign rights of the Duke of Holstein-Gottorp. The Maritime Powers, disappointed with Charles xi's dilatoriness and with Swedish treachery (as they labelled the neutrality policy),[50] felt no strong urge to uphold the Swedish interpretation of the Duke's rights, and the King of Denmark at least pretended to believe (in order to test Swedish reaction) that Charles xi on his own would not come to the help of the Duke. In 1696 Sweden's standing with the Maritime Powers was at its lowest ebb. It was in this year that a Dutch diplomat, disillusioned, disheartened and disgusted with what he regarded as Swedish double-dealing, wrote home, '*Je vous assure, que je perde patience icy avec des gens si terrible*' and felt tempted to leave Sweden out of the allied diplomatic system altogether. In that case he prophesied the Swedes would soon be chased out of Livonia, Bremen and Pomerania and be obliged to withdraw to '*leur rochers, bois et montagnes.*'[51] Christian v of Denmark, well informed of Sweden's unpopularity, sent troops into Duke Frederick's territories and razed the fortresses which had been built there to force him to desist in his claim to the *jus armorum* of a sovereign. The Duke was in no mood to take this lying down. Dahlberg, the Governor-General in Bremen – just on the point of being moved to the same position in Livonia – considered him too rash and too firm on his rights, fearing that hostilities might develop which would involve Sweden,[52] but Danish taunts that the Duke would get no more than good words and offers of mediation from Sweden made Charles xi see red. He swore, possibly with an emphasis that was meant to reach the King of Denmark (as it duly did), that he was determined to succour the Duke with his full military might.[53] A stormy period in Danish–Swedish relations could be forecast with certainty; whether it would be possible to ride the storm, as in 1688–9, only time would show.

The prospect of war with Denmark over Holstein-Gottorp was worrying to a King who loved the memory of his Danish Queen and who understood Danish well. It is worth stressing that neither Charles xi nor Charles xii shared the popular hatred of the Danes which had its foundation in the ruthless burning and ravaging of the Swedish countryside during the Northern War of 1563 when the Danes from their provinces on the Scandinavian peninsula invaded Sweden; nor that distrust which found expression in the common saying that 'A Swede will not trust a Dane till hair grow in the palm of his hand'. That his worry contributed to or aggravated that cancer of the stomach* which we now know caused his death[54] is a proposition which modern medical opinion might well endorse.

Charles xi had not felt well since Ulrika died.[55] He himself attributed it

---

* Cancer has been diagnosed from the drawings and notes at the autopsy which Charles xi decreed from his death-bed.

to his sorrow and grief ('I have not had one happy day since the Queen died').[56] Contemporaries thought that blows of fortune, quite apart from the Holstein troubles, had something to do with the King's low spirits. The Livonian nobility was restive under the introduction of absolutism, arguing that since theirs was not a conquered country, their ancestors having called in the Swedes of their own free will, their Estates had the right to veto any change in the government.[57] The harvests which had been so plentiful throughout the 1680s and early 1690s failed in 1695 and 1696 so that the price of grain rocketed and famine and sickness induced by malnutrition spread in Finland as in Sweden in the winter of 1696–7. There had not been such suffering and such a rise in the number of deaths for a century and a quarter. 'The Queen must have taken all her blessings away with her'[58] was a common saying.

Slowly it became evident, however, though no one dared speak openly about it, that the King was not only unhappy, he was physically very ill. He suffered terribly from pains in the stomach and became thin as a skeleton. Some nobles who hated him for the resumption of the Crown lands saw this as God's well deserved punishment: his body wasted because he had stolen what was not his. The foremost medical experts of the time, Swedish and foreign, were consulted and various remedies tried which brought temporary relief; but by March 1697 Charles XI was preparing himself for death and pitying his mother who would be left with the care of his three children.[59]

He would have liked to live long enough to be present at the confirmation of Prince Charles, the symbol of his heir's entry into responsible Christian life. Benzelius, now Bishop of Strängnäs, had been called to Stockholm in the New Year of 1697 to prepare the Prince for his confirmation. The King asked the bishop to instruct and test his charge most particularly in the articles wherein the Roman and the Lutheran Church differed: he felt his son's future responsibility as head of the Swedish Lutheran State Church weighing on his mind. He hoped that he and his boy might celebrate communion together,[60] but on 2 April, when Prince Charles's confirmation and first communion took place in Slottskyrkan, the King's death struggle had already begun. His sufferings over several weeks had been frightening to watch, but they had been patiently and even heroically borne. He liked to have his mother with him and old and trusted servants. He saw his chaplain and confessor Wallin and also Wallenstedt, the president of the High Court, and dictated to him his last will and testament in the form of instructions for his son when he should come of age. On 3 April he bade farewell to his children. He kept Prince Charles at his bedside for two hours to give him his final blessing and advice. No one was ever told what father said to son during this conversation, and of the promises the future king made the dying one, we know only of one.* It was rumoured that the gist of Charles XI's last words to his heir was that he wished him to fear God, to love his subjects

* See below, p. 90.

and not listen to the advice of those who were out for their own gain,[61] but the injunctions were probably more specific and detailed.

Two days later Charles XI died, only forty-two years old. Even so he reached the highest age of any of the Swedish Vasa kings: they ruled a country where in the line of duty they were equally exposed to the risk of death in battle or an early grave through overwork and tension induced by their attempts to cope with 'problems of the peace' which defied solution.

BOOK TWO

The Young King

1

Sovereign Ruler

It had not been the intention of Charles XI that his son should exercise personal government at too young an age. Eighteen would seem to have been the ideal age in his opinion, but with the Swedish situation so uncertain in many ways, both at home and abroad, he had refrained from laying down in his will, or even in his death-bed instructions, an actual date by which Charles XII should become King in fact as well as in name by being declared of age. In Sweden, the legal age for full responsibility for one's actions at that time was fifteen, but past royal tradition for taking over the reins of office varied between seventeen (Gustavus Adolphus and Charles XI) and eighteen (Christina) and the constitution of 1604 gave eighteen as the age when a monarch ceased to be regarded as a minor. Possibly Charles XI in his will (made in 1682 after the birth of his first son and altered in 1693 after Queen Ulrika's death) wanted to emphasize the power of the Crown by not tying himself or his successor to any particular year, for there were theorists of the absolutist party who argued that sixteen or even fifteen was a more fitting age than the 'old-fashioned' eighteen.[1]

Practical reasons may have prompted the lack of precise instructions on this point (which at first seems so surprising) from Charles XI's death-bed. He was shrewd enough to realize that just as Denmark might attempt to profit from the situation arising from his death while Prince Charles was still a mere boy in respect of Holstein, so the dispossessed nobility in Sweden might try to undo absolutism and all it stood for. In these circumstances it would be unwise to make a rigid decision, there would have to be freedom of action for those servants of Sweden and the absolutist régime whom he trusted. For his own part he certainly regarded Prince Charles as a child. *Anni discretionis*, when the King spoke about them in relation to the seventeen-year-old Hedvig Sophia, were 'years ahead in the future',* and he must have hoped that the regency government which he devised for the interim between his own death and his son's legal majority would be allowed to function undisturbed till the ideal age of eighteen had been attained.

Six regents were named in Charles XI's will. The Queen-Grandmother, to

* See above, p. 60.

emphasize the preeminence of the royal family in an age of absolutism, was
to preside over the regency and possess two votes in all deliberations. The five
other regents, each with one vote, were all Counts, Royal Councillors, and
experienced administrators: Lars Wallenstedt, the President of the High
Court, had been in the King's confidence for years and was respected for his
integrity and devotion to the Crown; Bengt Oxenstierna, the President of the
Chancery, was a more controversial figure, but he had an unrivalled knowledge of foreign affairs and was on excellent terms with the Dowager-Queen;
Fabian Wrede, head of the Exchequer and College of Commerce, was the
acknowledged expert on economic policy and the 'best cameralist Sweden
possessed',[2] though hardly a popular man, brusque and haughty; Nils
Gyldenstolpe, Oxenstierna's second-in-command at the Chancery was close
to the royal family as Prince Charles's governor; Nils Gyllenstierna, a brother
of the famous Johan, was one of the King's comrades-in-arms from the
Danish War and now a governor of Pomerania. To mark the break with
former practice – in the pre-absolutist days the five highest officials of the
state, the *riksdrots* and the heads of the (then) four colleges had *ex officio*
been members of any regency – Charles XI expressly ordered that four of the
five non-royal regents should as a regent control a branch of the administration not his own while remaining in his non-regent capacity head of his
college and responsible for it to the regency. In this way the country was made
to realize that the regents were named by royal grace and not by virtue of
their office. The system had the further advantage that no individual regent
would become too powerful and thus be tempted to lead a coup against
absolutism.

That there was a powerful and fairly well organized group of malcontents
who hoped to use the opportunity of Charles XI's death is certainly true.
Behind the exaggerated rumours of conspiracies which diplomats reported
home in good faith, conditioned as they were to believe from the grumbles
and curses and wild threats of many noblemen when absolutism and the
'reduction' was being discussed that 'revolution' would be instantaneous when
Charles XI died,[3] there are some hard facts. A small number of dissatisfied
men[4] deliberated together on the best means whereby they could get back
land lost to the Crown by the resumption, or at least to stop the process not
yet completed. Count Nils Bielke, a personal friend of the late King, who
had recently been accused of malpractices in his governorship of Wismar and
for that reason suspended from office, was in contact both with this group
and with diplomats, principally those of Denmark, with whom the 'restless
ones' discussed possible tactics. There was talk of 'bringing in the neighbours'
to force the Crown to concessions; oaths that Scania would be well sacrificed
if only the nobility could get its estates back – even protestations that the
loss of some provinces abroad might be a real gain for Sweden since they
had ever involved the country in expense and war; but within a short time
even the extremists calmed down and agreed among themselves that the

sensible and honourable way would be to act not by open rebellion but by grasping the political initiative.[5] Custom decreed that the Estates would have to be called for the King's funeral; and such a meeting would afford opportunities for the airing of grievances and for political action.

The regents were aware of the meetings of the malcontents, and Wallenstedt's argument that under an absolute régime the Estates need not be called for Charles XI's funeral may be explained by his desire to rob the opponents of absolutism of their chance to imperil, if not to destroy, the work of reform. There was enough inflammable material to hand in the capital already. The Royal Castle had been severely damaged by fire* while the King's body lay in state, an accident which, though later proved to be due to the negligence of some of the fireguards,[6] caused some mass-hysteria; the long winter of 1697, which never seemed to give way to spring, made it difficult to speed up the importation of cereals to alleviate the miseries among the poorer people caused by the bad harvest of 1696. But to forbid the Estates to attend the King's funeral was not a practicable proposition. It smacked of defeatism, of disrespect to the late King, and the Estates were duly invited and a Diet called for 5 November, the date fixed for Charles XI's funeral.

The only means to check the 'restless ones' would seem to lie in a strong emphasis on absolutism as the legal form of government, coupled with a reminder which might be read as a threat that Charles XII would soon prove himself a firm ruler of his father's type. In a manifesto which the regents printed three days after Charles XI's death they put the following words into Charles XII's mouth: 'We who through the grace of God have reached the years when we can soon, in God's name, think of entering Ourselves upon the government and management of Our hereditary Kingdom'.[7] The absolutist party, no less than the malcontents, was preparing for action.

II

Various reasons made the regents reluctant to act without the express approval of the boy for whom they were to take decisions. The memory of the 'retrospect' which Charles XI had instituted into the conduct of the regents of his own minority was the strongest inhibitive factor. The punishment meted out in fines was vividly remembered. For good measure they were reminded in the late King's will that they would be responsible to Charles XII when he reached his majority for their actions. A concern to train Charles XII in affairs of state may have occasioned his regular attendance at the meetings of the regency[8] but it was the spectre of another *förmyndarräfst*† which made the regents take care to ascertain his views on every subject under discussion and to enter in their protocol, 'The King was pleased to concur

* The church which Charles XI and Ulrika had loved so much was destroyed and so was Tessin's fine new wing.
† The Swedish name for the process of the 'retrospect'.

in this' or 'The King graciously expressed his agreement with that' decisions were usually put off if the King did not express any opinion of his own.[9]

Disagreements between the regents, both on personal grounds and on questions of foreign policy, also tended to have a paralysing effect. Wallenstedt and Oxenstierna could not abide each other, and Oxenstierna was generally suspected by his fellow-regents of bringing the risk of war with Denmark closer through encouraging the Duke of Holstein-Gottorp, a policy which they assumed he followed in order to curry favour with the Queen-Grandmother.[10] The regents were divided in their sympathies abroad; though they agreed on the main lines of Swedish foreign policy, they differed on the means of pursuing them. Charles XI had been successful in avoiding commitment in the Nine Years War, and his neutrality policy had brought the much desired mediation: Sweden had been asked, just a few days before his death, to preside at the peace congress of Ryswick. But the success was a superficial one; the belligerents, equally disgusted with Sweden's pursuit of selfish ends, were at one in denying her any real influence on the peace negotiations and any gain from the Congress, unless she became at the last moment an arbiter through mediation and commitment to one side or the other during the Congress.[11]

Here the regents split. Most were pro-French in the sense that they could see no willingness among the Allies to reward Sweden and therefore favoured closer cooperation with Louis XIV; but Oxenstierna hoped at this moment when commitment to the Allies might not cost much in men or ships to make real gains by taking a stand against France. Oxenstierna's vote with the two votes of the Dowager-Queen exactly equalled the three votes of Wrede, Wallenstedt and Gyllenstierna. Gyldenstolpe, though he leaned to the French party, tended to sit on the fence out of regard for his prospects with the Dowager-Queen if and when he should succeed Oxenstierna – an old man of sixty-eight – at the Chancery. This 'balance' was perhaps what Charles XI had intended,[12] but it made for a negative foreign policy which disgusted each individual regent as he contemplated opportunities lost which might never return. Oxenstierna in particular, whose whole interest was concentrated on European affairs, despaired of working with the regency and his thoughts began to circle round the advantage of a single person whom he might influence, a King in full power.

Similar considerations were at work in the minds of the other regents. They feared that Oxenstierna, backed by the Queen-Grandmother, and possibly also – in a moment of crisis – by Gyldenstolpe, would prove too strong for them; and argued that from the point of view of Sweden's foreign policy it might be safer to have Charles XII, before whom matters could be argued out openly and fully in private, in control. They had been struck during the regency meetings by the young King's intelligence, his sensible questions, his obvious determination to come to grips with problems, and by his serious and responsible attitude to whatever subject was under discussion.[13]

The subjects which the regents had been able to discuss and to deal with had, however, been confined to practical matters of some urgency in home affairs: here they were not as suspicious of each other nor as reluctant to commit themselves as in foreign policy or in the big issues on the domestic political front – the threat to absolutism and the land settlement which were too delicate matters to talk over at meetings for which a protocol was kept. They acted, in perfect agreement and with speed, to alleviate the distress caused by the failure of the harvest; they continued Charles XI's policy of distributing bread to the poor of the capital twice a week, they sent flour and seedcorn to the districts round Mälaren which had been so hard hit that bark and straw had to be mixed in the bread and where even farm-owners died from illnesses caused by malnutrition; they curtailed the right to distil spirits so as to conserve grain; they gave tax-relief to compensate farmers for losses sustained; and when ships bringing cereals from the trans-Baltic provinces were frozen in the waters outside Stockholm as late as May 1697, they sent troops to break the ice and help get the ships unloaded.[14] By the middle of the month the flow of exaggerated stories of starvation-deaths and riots not only in the capital, but all over the country, stopped. The situation became calm once more: 'The famine is much abated here, and most of the Provinces has suffer'd less than had been reported', Whitehall was told.[15]

The regents had also acted vigorously to cope with dislocation caused by the burning of the Royal Castle on 7 May. The central administration (which had its offices in the castle) had managed to save most of their archives and rooms were found for the various Colleges in noblemen's palaces. The Chancery moved into that of Bengt Oxenstierna and there the regency also met to order on 8 May an enquiry into the cause of the fire and a speedy rebuilding of the castle. Tessin's plans for a Royal Palace, grandiose and impressive in its classical proportions (more 'regulated and imposing' to the taste of contemporaries than the old castle, which had consisted of so many buildings from different periods)[16] were completed and accepted by mid-June and work started at once. To house the royal family till the new palace should be ready – for on the scale on which it was planned[17] the building of it would take at least six years* – the Wrangel palace was bought and renamed *Kungshuset* (i.e. the King's House).† This palace had been empty for some years, having been damaged by a fire in 1693, and it was urgently necessary that various structural changes, as well as redecoration, should be carried out before the Estates met for Charles XI's funeral: a big state-room for the solemn opening and closing of the Diet had first priority. The Queen-Grandmother stayed with the royal family at Karlberg while

---

* In spite of the fact that Tessin, an admirer of mechanization, was known as an architect who could do with his machines and four men 'the work of 40'. In the event work proceeded slowly after war broke out, came to a full stop in 1720 and the palace was not completed till 1754.

† See illustration facing p. 77.

work on *Kungshuset* was in progress and took a lively interest in making
it a worthy setting for the new King: treasures salvaged from the castle were
moved into it, and Tessin's ever fertile genius and the craftsmanship of
his pupils was exploited. When refashioning was complete, the temporary
royal home was much admired: those with a practical bent praised the
modern plumbing; others waxed enthusiastic over the impressive reception
rooms.[18]

III

With the approach of the Diet political tension had grown. The group of
trusted servants of Charles XI, those who believed in the reform-work as the
only means of keeping Sweden's great-power position, or who feared the
selfishness of the high nobility as a class, began to band together as closely
as the 'restless ones'. These, for their part, hoped to use the meeting to bring
the resumption of Crown land to a stop and to reverse policy by the return
to the nobility of land resumed in excess of the moderate reduction decreed
in the reign of Charles x,* little caring whether in the process they undid the
reforms of Charles XI. The men who in the autumn months of 1697 prepared
to defend the absolutist bureaucratic state created in the late King's time were
also motivated by the struggle for power. They were in office and intended
to remain in office both for national and personal reasons. They were the
exponents not only of reform but of the right of the Crown to pick its servants
from whatever rank could produce brains and ability, in opposition to the too
narrow recruitment wanted by the high nobility. These were some of the
issues at stake for the 'abolutist' party. The prominent men in this group
(e.g. Wallenstedt, Wrede, Gyldenstolpe and Gyllenstierna), though powerful
and enjoying rank which put them into the high nobility class, were new men
for the most part. Behind them were others who were still in the lower ranks
of nobility but on their way up, men like Thomas Polus and Karl Piper,
both Secretaries of State in the Chancery, both increasingly in Charles XI's
confidence during the last few years of his life.

A further cross-current was occasioned by the resentment which the
Council, as a body, raised against the regency: the regents seemed full of their
own importance and the Council felt relegated to a less significant role than
in Charles XI's lifetime. The dissatisfaction of those Councillors who were
not regents might therefore serve as a spring-board for those malcontents
of the high nobility who wanted the Council restored to its old position when
as 'the Senate' it had been the equal if not the superior of the Crown. This
programme was admittedly one advocated by a minority group within the
opposition, since the majority of the malcontents would be satisfied if only
the resumption of Crown lands could be stopped and/or reversed. Those in
favour of return to 'Senate' government would have to reckon with a bitter

* The so called 'quarter-reduction', the *fjärdepartrsreduktion*.

ght not only with the 'absolutists' in the Council and the administration,
ut also with the three non-noble Estates, always suspicious of the designs
f the high nobility, and as concerned to keep the reforms of the 1680s as
vere the bureaucrats and theorists of Caroline absolutism.

Into this charged atmosphere the magic formula of declaring Charles XII
f age during the *Riksdag* was released. We may never be able to say with
ertainty who started the campaign for the boy-king's majority. If we followed
nly official sources, such as the protocol of the various Estates at the Diet,
ve would be misled into believing that there was no real campaign, that
he whole thing was spontaneous and unanimous. The Speaker of the First
Estate, Nils Gripenhielm, on 8 November expressed a wish that 'God give
he King was governing for himself'; this cry was taken up by the whole
Estate, present in unusually large numbers – eighty-five of the nobility of
he first class being present* or represented through a plenipotentiary of the
nead of the family, twenty of the second class and 362 of the third class – and
t was unanimously decided to petition Charles XII to take upon himself the
ourden of government. The other Estates, when informed, asked to be
oined with the First Estate in the appeal. The Council and the regency, when
consulted, agreed and the issue was settled at 6 o'clock the same evening when
a deputation of the Four Estates called upon the King with their petition
and received his acceptance of their proposal.[19]

Much of the spontaneity, haphazardness and unanimity disappears when
events are studied more closely and from other sources than the official ones.
The explanation generally accepted is, however, that there was broad concurrence by all parties in the desirability of the step once it had been urged
by the First Estate. This Estate, so runs the argument, hoped for amelioration
of the 'reduction' programme, trusting to Charles's generosity or
inexperience; the Third and Fourth Estates agreed because they were royalists
to a man; the Second Estate, that of the Clergy, which alone asked for some
little time to consider the issue, was too cautious to oppose the other three;
and the regents were quite willing to lay down the burden of office with its
dreaded prospect of future inquiry and fines. The only voice raised against the
proposal was that of Cronhielm, the King's teacher, who considered his
charge too young to assume the responsibilities of office.[20]

In recent years new theories have been put forward. T. T. Höjer in 1942
postulated a link between Charles XII and the Speaker of the First Estate,
Gripenhielm,† and suggested that there was some truth in Voltaire's contention (derived from conversations with the Swedish diplomat Gedda) that
Charles XII wanted to be declared of age and took steps in that direction
himself. According to Höjer, therefore, Charles XII knew of the movement in
favour of his being declared of age and, possibly advised by Piper or the
Wachtmeister brothers, worked through Gripenhielm to make use of the

---

* Twenty-three counts, sixty-two barons.

† His father had been Charles XI's teacher; his son had been one of Charles XII's pages when he
was Prince Charles.

meeting of the Estates to gain his wish: so far from the burden of kingshi
being laid on Charles XII's shoulders, Charles XII himself and a royalist part
round him grabbed the chance as soon as it came their way.[21] G. Jonasso
has recently put Oxenstierna and his concern for his own 'system' in foreig
policy into the centre of the discussion – according to his reading of th
material the Chancellor used the Queen-Grandmother's Holstein-Gottor
inclinations to gain his first ally and hoped that Charles XII, in charge of th
government, would prove his second.[22]

My own interpretation of the happenings between 3 May when the Estate
were called and 8 November differs in emphasis somewhat both from Höje
and Jonasson, in that I have come to the conclusion that Charles XII's person
role must have been less active than Höjer assumed, but more active tha
Jonasson allows. By July there was undoubtedly agitation that the King ough
to take on the government himself when the Estates met, though it is impos
sible to say how this started. It could have come from those who wanted t
checkmate the regency; it could have been initiated by the opposition group
as a first step to create friction between the King and the regents and thu
produce a situation favourable for action by the malcontents in November
What seems certain is that it was fastened upon by the 'absolutist' grou
as the best way to deal with the danger from the malcontents: if Charles wer
declared of age, they felt confident they could ride the storm of the Diet an
outwit the stratagems of those of the First Estate who wanted to undo th
reforms and the land-settlement. There was a significant rumour from
3 November that Wallenstedt, Wrede, Gyldenstolpe and Gyllenstierna
wanted to see the King declared of age *before** the Estates should sugges
such a step, indicative (at least) of a belief in their desire to take the initiative
if possible.[23] Piper's name is not mentioned among those who favoured the
change till after it had taken place, but this can be explained by his being les
in the public eye than the regents: as one of the strong men in the absolutis
group he must have been consulted, and tradition has it that his role was a
important one.[24]

Charles XII's own position is illuminated for me by two remarks, separated
in time but bearing on the same problem. During the preliminary discussions
Wrede suggested to the Queen-Grandmother that the King ought to be asked
for his opinion, to which Hedvig Eleonora answered that he was in no position
to refuse, especially as he was now over fifteen years of age.[25] Some time
afterwards, at a moment of exasperation, Charles XII turned on his advisers of
the absolutist party with the taunt that they had persuaded him, for the sake
of the country, to go against his dead father's wishes and take over the
government younger than Charles XI had intended.[26]

It seems to me therefore that Charles XII was the tool, a willing one but
still a tool, of the absolutist group rather than the initiator of his own
majority. And this group, in its turn, was alarmed by the danger which

* italicized here.

Count Erik Lindschöld, 1690,
from a painting by D. Ehrenstrahl

Friherre Carl Magnus Stuart,
from a painting after D. von Krafft

Count Nils Gyldenstolpe,
from a painting by M. Mytens

Nikodemus Tessin,
from a painting by G. Desmarées

Carlberg Palace, from an engraving by Erik Dahlberg

The Wrangel Palace, the 'Royal House' after 1694, from an engraving by Erik
Dahlberg

Palatium Illustrissimi Comitis   CAROLI GUSTAVI WRANGELII
R.ni L.ti Marschi, quod Holmiæ   est, et vergit ad Lacum Meler.

they sensed to the work of Charles XI and were willing to go along with those opposition groups which had misguided ideas as to the advantages to be reaped by the First Estate from Charles XII being declared a major. They must have known of Louis XIV's majority at the same age in somewhat similar circumstances and – if they could have known of it – would have concurred in the sentence Louis put into his memoirs for the guidance of his son: 'It is not good for a King to be declared of age as young as fourteen, but sometimes it is necessary to prevent greater dangers.'[27]

IV

The means whereby the opposition could be foiled was not without its own danger: for while the economic and bureaucratic character of Charles XI's Sweden would be maintained, the effect of absolute power on a boy of fifteen could only be guessed at. Necessity made for optimism. The absolutist party had to deal with the nearest and most fundamental problem and give hostages to fortune as far as the King's future behaviour was concerned. There were already some signs they found disquieting in his attitude to the Queen-Grandmother and his governor, Gyldenstolpe. The young King clearly felt more in charge of his own life, more determined to direct it along his own lines, particularly in being able to harden and toughen himself with exercise without being prevented from taking risks. He had the physically courageous youngster's desire to test himself, to dare, and became irritated at the complaints when, as happened on occasion, he fell with his horse when out riding. For him it was enough that both he and the horse were unharmed, and even a matter for pride that he kept his seat, so that '*lappri*' (i.e., rubbish), a word which was becoming a favourite of his, was his unfeeling retort to those who had eyes only for the needs of the monarchy and not for those of the growing boy. He flaunted his new-found independence by staying late at Karlberg, coming back to Stockholm and a distraught grandmother at 1 o'clock in the morning without a word of apology; like many another adolescent before and after, when reprimanded he reduced the grown-up, so sincerely and tenderly concerned, to impotent fury by the simple expedient of silence: 'He says nothing, smiles a little and walks away.'[28]

All this, however, was on the personal level; in application to business and in taking advice and instruction in the day-to-day routine of government he seemed intelligent, sensible and even pliable, eager to learn. His looks were approved of as well; he had grown into a tall lad and though slightly shy with strangers made a good impression by his regal bearing and his handsome open face. It was hoped that he would combine the best qualities of both parents: the virtues of the father without his choleric temper; the intelligence and sweetness of the mother without her excessive dependence on the Church. He favoured his mother's side in looks, so much so that those who had hated Charles XI for his policies' sake triumphantly diagnosed that all the 'Palatinate

D

temper and emportement' would be buried underground with the body o
Charles XI, leaving them a good and benign ruler.[29]

Though the issue of regency versus personal government had been decide
by 8 November, it was agreed that the regents should continue in power til
after Charles XI's funeral on 24 November. It was also laid down that Charle
XII's coronation, fixed for mid-December, should take place in Stockholm
and not in Uppsala as customary. These decisions were sensible from th
practical point of view and suited the purposes of the absolutists. Th
Estates had turned up in force for Charles XI's funeral. Apart from th
unusually high number of noblemen present,* the Second Estate had sen
seventy-one bishops and clergymen and the Third Estate, that of the Burghers
was represented by 114 delegates. To these must be added an unknow
number of members of the Fourth Estate.[30] It would be an expensive busines
for all those who came from outside the capital to be recalled for a coronatio
ceremony if they were allowed to disperse after the funeral and the closin
session of the Diet. A speedy coronation ceremony was desired by all wh
hoped to gain any advantage from the King being declared of age; it woul
set the seal on Charles XII's ability to act alone but – it was hoped by th
various groups – rightly advised. The decision to continue the regency for a
long as the Diet was sitting did, however, suit the policy of the absolutis
group best; it tended to paralyse their opponents, for though the regent
could be regarded as powerless with so few weeks of their tenure left, th
King was not a legitimate object for political pressure till after the regent
had laid down their office.

Charles XI had decreed that his funeral was to be a simple one; bu
5 November saw an impressive if sombre ceremony. Storkyrkan on Riddar
holmen was dressed in black, the Garter was the only decoration on his coffi
apart from the regalia, the Councillors wore black mantles instead of thei
usual purple ones. Tessin had been in charge to make everything dignifie
and worthy of the memory of the late King in the eyes of his family. Th
snow which carpeted the streets through which the procession wound its wa
was felt to add solemnity since the sound of the carriage wheels was hushed.[3]

For funerals there were many precedents – not least the last sad one o
1693 – but for Charles XII's coronation there were none: he was the firs
Swedish ruler *born* to absolutism. Theorists agreed, as did the King himsel
that this must be marked by changes which would impress on the natio
the very essence of the new form of government. The opportunity might als
be taken to shorten the coronation service, which was oppressively long an
hard to bear for those who had begun to feel their years (even in its new an
shortened form it lasted nearly seven hours and caused Bengt Oxenstiern
to collapse).[32] The one order which we know originated with Charles XI
personally was his decision that out of respect for his father's memor
everyone should be dressed in black, himself included, though he woul

* See above, p. 75.

have to wear the purple coronation mantle, as much part of the ceremony as the crown and sceptre. This order covered both 13 December, when the oath of fealty would be given, and the following day when the religious service would take place. The other changes made have usually been laid as squarely at the King's door; but it seems improbable that they were anything but the result of consultations between the King and his advisers.

Possibly the impetus towards some of them came from the sealed instructions for Charles XII from his father which were handed to him by the Queen-Grandmother on 25 November, the day when the Diet was formally closed and the regency passed its powers and duties to the King. At this ceremony Charles XII thanked his grandmother formally for her work, kissed her hand and the hem of her skirt; he then thanked the regency as a body in a speech which was answered by the oldest regent, Bengt Oxenstierna. The instructions were those which had been dictated by Charles XI on his death-bed to Wallenstedt. Charles XII read and presumably destroyed them on Charles XI's order, since they have not been found in the archives. Reports of what they had contained did, in part, leak out.* These throw no light on any guidance by the late King for the first absolutist coronation, but they do insist that the instructions advised Charles XII what men to trust, and thus lend support to the supposition that the young King did not on his own initiative decide what changes should be made in the usual ceremonies.

The first break with tradition came as a shock for the vast majority of those present at the coronation and brought home the reality of absolutism more than anything that happened afterwards. On 13 December, when every member of the formally dismissed but not dispersed Diet gathered to take their oath of fealty to the new King, the King gave no oath in return: the *Kungsförsäkran*, so deeply rooted in Swedish constitutional life, had been quietly dropped. The non-noble Estates who had been more than willing parties to the introduction of absolutism had aimed at the practical advantages to be derived from it – the solution of the defence problem and the weakening of the overpowerful nobility. The theoretical justification for absolutism as a political creed had not interested the majority of them, nor had the symbols by which the contents of absolutism might be conveyed and secured. Now, with the non-delivery of the royal oath, a relic of promises made in return for elective kingship, the enormity of the changes embarked on hit them. The bleak day and the fact that the ceremony took place in the open courtyard of the former Wrangel palace,† helped to depress the participants; they had to stand for five hours in snow and sleet and biting wind while each individual paid his homage and vowed fidelity to Charles XII.

The changes connected with the religious ceremony had been more widely discussed and had met with opposition from the Queen-Grandmother.[33] She was not devout by temperament, but at her age (she was sixty-one at this

---

* Cp. below, pp. 83, 87.

† Since *Kungshuset* had no room large enough to hold them all and permit the ceremonial rites at one and the same time.

time) any major change in traditional ceremony seemed a bad omen. Some
of the extreme absolutists, e.g., Wallenstedt, had argued that just as it was no
longer fitting that the absolute King of Sweden should give an oath to the
Estates promising to observe the conditions they laid down for him, so it was
no longer necessary or even desirable from the point of view of absolutist
theory that Charles XII should have a coronation at all. But they admitted
that it might be expedient in practice lest the enemies of absolutism should
use the absence of the ceremony to argue that Charles was not the 'crowned
King of Sweden' with all the subtle power of that attribute. A compromise
solution was achieved whereby Charles XII, to symbolize that he was an
absolute King, should place the crown on his own head before he proceeded
to Storkyrkan where the anointment would be performed by the Archbishop
in conformity with the biblical expression 'anointed by God'. The King was,
however, to remove and replace the crown at the anointment rite. In the
procession to and from the church the King alone was to ride on horse-back
while Councillors and noblemen (contrary to ancient custom) had to walk
with the rest of the assembled dignitaries.[34]

Visitors came for the big day: on 14 December, the King's maternal aunt
the Duchess of Holstein, brought her daughter and one of her younger sons
from Kiel;[35] a personal representative of his maternal uncle King Christian of
Denmark came from Copenhagen.[36] Tessin did his best to make the setting
and the procession impressive in spite of the funeral black. A canopy was
carried over the King during the procession. The choir of the church was
dressed in purple and the royal ladies were present in spite of the Queen-
Grandmother's threat that she would rather remain at home than watch
such a new-fangled coronation. They left early to be at the church when the
King and the procession arrived and were therefore not witnesses to the
mishap when Charles, the crown already on his head, mounted his horse to
begin the procession ride; the crown slipped from his head and was caught
by the Chamberlain, Count Jan Stenbock, standing by his side. In retrospect
this loss of the crown, and the Archbishop's accidental dropping of the horn
of anointment in the church, have been interpreted as portents of the loose
hold which Charles XII and absolutism proved to have over Sweden. At the
time these signs of nervousness or tension* were remarked upon, but it was
the 'Noveltys' (i.e. the omission of the royal oath and the King's placing the
crown on his own head) which were 'variously descanted upon and fill a
great many people with Superstitions and other fears'.[37]

Charles bore himself well during the long service, looking pale but composed. The return procession in the bitterly cold weather, which the royal
ladies, who had left the church before the King, observed from Oxenstierna's
palace, went smoothly while the guns of the capital gave a four-fold salute.
At night the scene became more festive when the whole of Stockholm was

---

* Or possibly, in Charles's case, lack of rehearsal in mounting a horse with such unusual
headgear?

illuminated' and the Estates 'entertained with a splendid supper at Charles XII's charge'.[38]

Charles was now, in the term contemporaries used for absolutism, a sovereign King. He was known to be devout. He had spent hours in lonely prayer after his father's death, particularly, it had been noted, at times of decision. When he had received the deputation from the Estates on 8 November, he – though he must already have been committed to the absolutists – went into his own room and remained kneeling for an hour before he returned with his answer; and he prepared himself for the coronation service by withdrawing into prayer and solitude.[39] Upbringing, the example of both parents, the appeal of both mother and father from their death-beds for him to fear God urged him towards religious practices. Charles XI's last instructions to him, it was confidently reported, began with an injunction for Charles XII to keep his peace with God above all.[40]

He was known to be generous by nature, in contrast to his father who though he could dip deep into his pocket for those he loved was parsimonious by temperament. Those around Charles XII noticed already in the summer of 1697 what pleasure it gave him to be able to empty his purse into the hands of an old soldier he met, or to hide money-presents in the pockets of friends and servants in the fond hope no one would guess they came from the King.[41] He was known to be a hard worker. As soon as the regents had laid down their offices, he had, in the words of a foreign diplomat, 'begun to take cognizance and give orders about all matters, with the same assiduity and constant application that has been taught Him by his Father's Example, being every Morning up by 5 o'clock and in continual occupation the greatest part of the day'.[42] He was known to be open and friendly in personal contact – again a legacy from his mother's side – but observers remarked on a change in him from the moment when he took over personal responsibility on 25 November 1697: the need to guard his tongue, the need to keep his own counsel in a world of clashing temperaments, differing points of view and rival schools of thought even among those who formed the absolutist group, was already creating the reserve and the cool mask behind which Charles XII had to learn to live.

2

The Adolescent

A period of confusion and suspense followed the coronation while Stockholm – and Europe – waited to find out what kind of king Charles XII would prove to be and which of the many groups and individuals fighting for influence round him would gain the day. It was noticed that the full Council was not called (though Charles had attended its meetings during the regency period), and from the King's habit of working with individuals in private sessions it was assumed that he might designate a 'Secret Council or Cabinet' of five or six persons to advise him in the government of the country.[1] From the people he consulted, as from the ones he avoided when affairs had to be discussed, deductions were made about Charles XI's sealed instructions. It was said that the late King had warned his son to keep aloof from Bielke while investigations took place into his governorship of Swedish Pomerania, that he had advised him not to trust Wrede too fully in matters where money was concerned; that he had put him on his guard against those that had 'French stomachs'.[2]

It was obvious that Wallenstedt and Piper had been recommended by Charles XI; these were the men the new King seemed to trust most. He saw the higher officials of the Chancery most days, both those concerned with domestic and with foreign affairs – Oxenstierna, Gyldenstolpe, Polus, Åkerhielm, Piper and Bergenhielm were those of most experience and influence – but proof of the special position of two of them, Polus and Piper, came when they were created Counts and made members of the Council early in January 1698. Their promotion had something of the same touch of stage-management that Charles XI had enjoyed: a surprised Stockholm learnt the news when two extra ducal chairs were put out for the Sunday service.[3] Polus, who was the Queen-Grandmother's secretary as well as a Secretary of State in the Chancery, was not an ambitious man; he was a clever expert in foreign affairs but had the reputation of being 'lazy' or 'unambitious' outside his own particular sphere;[4] Piper on the other hand, just fifty against Polus's sixty-four, had tremendous drive, possessed an ambitious wife* and his field was that which interested the King most, that of domestic affairs.[5]

* See above, p. 38*.

Apart from the chosen few, Charles XII tended to be inaccessible. When Oxenstierna arrived with dispatches for the King to read, he was reminded of the regulations which laid down that these should first be read and commented on in the Chancery.[6] Wrede, one of the Councillors whom Charles frequently consulted, tried to get into the King's cabinet when orders had been given to the guard at the door that no one should disturb Charles: he was told to desist and wait for the King to call him.[7] There was greater secrecy about Charles's comings and goings and the people he saw at court than in his father's time. After morning prayers it was customary that those who wanted to talk to the King gave in their names, but whereas in Charles XI's days the door had been left open and it was possible to catch the King coming out from prayers, Charles XII worshipped behind closed doors and went to his room unseen. He would sometimes admit those who put their names down, but not regularly enough to make it worth while attending court on the off-chance of a word with the King. The men in his confidence, Wallenstedt and Piper, were also known as 'little given to conversation' about affairs of state.[8]

In these circumstances one had to judge by actions, not words. Already on 30 November, just a few days after the regency had come to an end, a whole series of royal commands had been issued which emphasized the royal initiative in many fields: Colleges were ordered to begin new projects or to speed up the completion of old ones; provincial governors were recommended to put the finishing touches to *indelingsverket*, Charles XI's masterpiece for the financing of the army; measures were taken to prevent, since the harvest of 1697 had also proved a bad one, the recurrence of the grain famine of 1696–7; the committee set up in 1687 to codify Sweden's laws was asked to speed up its labours and the bishops were advised to complete their revision of the translation of the Bible.[9]

The First Estate used the twentieth anniversary of the battle of Lund to suggest that the nobility which had served Sweden so well in 1677 would welcome a reversal of the resumption policy, but on 28 January 1698 a petition to that purpose was answered forcefully if not diplomatically: the reduction 'would never be undone' and the King must regard the efforts of the nobility as attacks and artifices against a policy which all Estates had agreed to for the good of Sweden.

There were other indications that the King and his advisers would bear harder on the nobility than Charles XI had done in matters outside the resumption. The privileges of the nobility of 1617 were not confirmed and already by New Year 1698 various regulations intended to whittle down some of the pride of the nobility were promulgated: the difference in rank between noble and non-noble members of the High Court was abolished, so was the *forum privilegatum* of the nobility in cases punishable by death. Appointments of non-nobles to important posts were added straws that showed which way the wind was blowing ('*il n'y aura guère d'employ pour les gens de qualité durant cette regne*', one of the Bonde family complained).[10] Piper with his supposed hatred of the high-born was blamed, but the attitude of Charles XII towards

rank and merit remained a consistent one since the day when he underlined
a sentence in one of his school books to indicate his agreement with the sentiment of Magnus Ladulås who 'paid greater regard to the virtues of foreigners
than to the mere rank and name of his own compatriots'.[11] It is probably best
illustrated in the mature Charles by the well-known discussion in Poland in
1706 about a young nobleman who ought, in the opinion of some, to be made
an officer without having first served as a private, in view of his family connexions. Rank, answered Charles, had nothing to do with merit; if the young
man was any good, he would become a better officer by sharing for a time the
lot of the common soldier with its guard duties and foot-slogging: then he
would learn to know the problems of his men and be able to care for them
when promoted.[12]

The nobility's plan for throwing itself on the King's mercy in the matter of
the reduction – a polite way of saying that they hoped to bring him round to
their way of thinking – had misfired. The absolutists who had thus maintained
the base for Charles XI's reforms were anxious to make the position clear also
in the political field. A chance to impress upon the country that public
criticism of the régime would not be tolerated came when a clergyman from
Dalecarlia, Boëthius by name, in sermon and in print attacked absolutism as
a form of government alien to Swedish tradition. The Estates, he argued, had
acted illegally during Charles XI's reign when they transferred to the Crown
the sovereign powers which were theirs under the constitution of 1604. As for
the young 'absolute' Charles XII, he referred his listeners and readers to the
biblical prophecy of the misfortunes which would befall kingdoms whose
rulers were children. Boëthius was condemned to imprisonment for life to
restrain like-minded critics from voicing their opinions: that his punishment
was meant as a warning to others and did not stem from any personal vindic-
tiveness on Charles XII's part (as has sometimes been argued) is obvious from
the fact that not only was his sentence cut to ten years by the exercise of the
royal mercy, but the King was willing – on a petition from Boëthius's wife – to
set him free after six months, a freedom which the clergyman refused on the
grounds that he did not want to owe his liberty to the intervention of any mere
female, even his wife.[13]

The mitigation of the sentence (to say nothing of the offer of complete
liberty) did not, however, receive the publicity accorded, quite consciously, to
the original punishment, and the severity served its purpose: there were no
more public attacks on the absolutist form of government and on the early
declaration of the King's majority. There were many who admitted in private
that they would have preferred the regents to remain in office for another
year,[14] and Cronhielm, the King's teacher, who had shown considerable moral
courage at a time when everyone was clamouring for, or admitting the necessity of, Charles XII being declared of age,* never changed his mind about the
undesirability of the step.

* See above, pp. 75–7.

It is impossible to say for certain who was behind the action, taken immediately upon Charles's assuming power, against the Reformed Church. The
Swedish clergy had always been strongly orthodox Lutherans ('such a rigid
Religion as Calvinism is not tolerated here, it is considered worse than
Popery', an Englishman in holy orders commented);[15] but Charles XI had
not been too strict where foreign subjects were concerned and had allowed
them to worship 'by connivance'. Now it came as a shock that the chapel of
the French Reformed Church was shut and that Dutch subjects were forbidden
to visit the private chapel of the resident of the States General.* In later life,
Charles XII was tolerant, respecting for instance the Catholicism of Poland
while attempting to obtain tolerable conditions for Polish Protestants. He
also showed considerable sympathy for the Pietist movement which was so
abhorred by the Swedish clergy, but we have no evidence on which to base
any conjecture as to whether he was either indifferent to or in favour of the
orthodoxy of the measures of January 1698 discriminating against foreign
Calvinists.

Charles XII's strong interest in measures of military preparedness which
were put into effect shortly after his declaration of age is, however, demonstrable. The naval base of Karlskrona was completed; the defences of the two
southern strongholds of Sweden, Karlsten and Kalmar, were improved, and
modernization of the fortifications on the outer perimeter of the empire was
begun under the supervision of Stuart and Dahlberg: the fortresses of Nöteborg, of Narva and Riga in the east and of Stade in Germany were first put
in hand.

This work on the defences of Sweden was carried out in the spirit and along
the lines of Charles XI's reorganization rather than motivated by any sudden
fear that Sweden might be involved in war on a European scale in the immediate future. There was no desire to commit Sweden, beyond pacific mediation
at the Congress of Ryswick. The activity in naval and military affairs which
began with Charles XII's assumption of power certainly led the diplomats
accredited to Sweden to believe that such commitment might take place. 'This
new Government', reported the English resident, 'pretends to look abroad
with more concern than was done in the last Reign'.[16] It soon became clear,
however, that the policy of accepting, and even seeking, alliances with all the
great powers which now began was in reality a continuation of Charles XI's
policy of neutrality and independence translated to peace-time conditions: a
policy of friendly alliances without commitment except if strong gains could
be made for Sweden; indeed, part of the traditional policy of seeking renewal
of existing guarantees on the accession of a new king.

An alliance with the States General was first concluded in January 1698, but
the treaty was innocuous enough to make the Dutch (who had hoped for
Swedish help at the Congress of Ryswick) feel cheated. They took comfort in a

---

* Members of the Anglican Church were treated with greater leniency and allowed to worship
at the English envoy's home since that Church was considered closer to the Lutheran.

clause which promised a future closer alliance between Sweden and the Mari
time Powers;[17] but in spite of great efforts by Dutch and English diplomats
and of those Swedish statesmen who favoured commitment to England an
the Netherlands, Charles XII personally insisted on having a treaty with Franc
signed first according to the policy which he and his advisers favoured of no
offending any one great power. The treaty with the States General and tw
equally non-commital treaties with Hanover* and Brandenburg being signe
before the treaty with Louis XIV would, it was argued, prevent offence bein
given to the 'allied' side; while the French treaty, signed in June 1698, befor
the promised engagement with the Maritime Powers *en bloc*, should similarl
keep France contented that the honours of prestige and influence remaine
even.

The French–Swedish treaty created much anxiety among allied diplomats
and there was relief when they procured a copy of it and found it as much o
'un grand rien'[18] as the Dutch treaty. Louis XIV was no more satisfied than th
States General with the contents of his treaty, but each party congratulate
itself on not having been left out of the Swedish policy of renewal of friendl
alliances on the accession of a new king. Negotiations also took place for
Swedish treaty with the Emperor Leopold; but here insuperable difficultie
emerged. The Swedes were willing to take on the duty which such a treat
would bring of renewed commitment to send auxiliaries to the Emperor if h
were involved in war once more, but against such a charge they wanted to se
a Swedish gain.† A guarantee of Livonia was ardently desired and persistent
though unsuccessful, efforts to obtain it began in January 1698.

II

The outstanding problem in foreign policy, the pressing one which absorbec
the real attention of Swedish statesmen of influence, was the relationship with
Denmark and with Holstein. This problem became entangled in an issue
which affected Charles XII personally, that of his own marriage, which be
came the centre of diplomatic and court gossip, of speculation, intrigues and
party-recruitment from the moment he became a sovereign.

There had been much talk while Charles XI was alive of a future marriage
between Charles and his cousin Sophia of Denmark as a complement and
balance to the one expected between Hedvig Sophia and the Duke of Holstein-
Gottorp.‡ It was important for Denmark to continue the dynastic alliance
policy begun in 1680, and though the King of Denmark had no sons of an age
to suit Hedvig Sophia there was little Prince Carl who might do for Ulrika

---

* The Electorate of Hanover had in 1692 been created from the territories of the Lüneberg
Dukes, Georg Ludwig of Hanover and Georg Wilhelm of Celle; though the actual transference o
Celle to Hanover did not take place until the death of its Duke (who had no sons) in 1704.

† Charles XI had allowed Sweden's treaty with Leopold to lapse during the Nine Years War and
used every stratagem to avoid or nullify his obligations before the date of expiry.

‡ See above, p. 60.

Eleonora and, above all, there was Sophia,* rather older than Charles but
so like him in looks 'she might have been his sister'.[19] Charles XI was supposed
on his death-bed to have expressed himself in favour of the marriage between
the two cousins, 'to avoid war' between Sweden and Denmark,[20] and
Baron Jens Juel, a Danish Councillor experienced in Swedish conditions and
politics from earlier missions to Stockholm, was charged with negotiating the
marriage if at all possible, or failing that an engagement.

To assist him Juel had Danish diplomats who had lived in Sweden for years
and who had good contacts at court dating from the time of Queen Ulrika
Eleonora. They knew the Swedish ladies who used to be the companions of
that Queen and who were now in charge of the young Princesses; and also Dr
Urban Hjärne, who had been the Queen's medical adviser and who was responsible for the physical welfare of her children. Some minor contacts, maids
and servants, were rewarded with money or presents by the Danes for information received, reports of conversations, of moods, of quarrels; but the most
important channels of influence were pro-Danish because they hoped for
peace and amity between the two countries or because they revered the
memory of Charles XI's Danish wife. 'God give us yet another one like her',
was a frequently expressed hope. The Danish diplomats, and especially Juel
himself, also had valuable contacts among the politicians. While the Diet was
sitting, for instance, Juel found delegates who were willing, either from political conviction or personal friendliness (helped by lavish hospitality and even
by money-presents) to give him information by which he checked the news
given him from his court contacts.[21]

The Danes were not the only starters in the marriage-race. The Württemberg representative who had so eagerly pressed either mother or daughter of
the ducal house which he served on Charles XI, was not slow in suggesting the
younger of the two ladies for Charles XII.[22] The Duchess of Holstein was
known to favour a marriage between her daughter Maria Elisabeth and
Charles XII and the young lady was thrown into the King's company as much
as possible; a relative from the house of Bavaria-Wolfenbüttel arrived with
her daughter to be discreetly paraded; Berlin sent a portrait of a suitable
Hohenzollern bride though it was realized that her Calvinist religion might
make her less welcome in Sweden than one of the Lutheran faith.[23]

If Charles was at first embarrassed and bored by the talk of marriage-plans
for himself, Hedvig Sophia was elated but uneasy at the suit which her aunt
and grandmother pressed on her on behalf of the Duke of Holstein-Gottorp.
She sought her brother's advice and felt rather annoyed that he restricted himself to repeating his father's words: she was to be left free to decide. Neither of
them seems particularly to have liked Frederick and his '*fierté insupportable*':[24]
what if she should not be happy with him? But when she passed other possible
suitors in review, who was there really for her to marry except cousin Frederick? A king's daughter, she ought not to accept anyone of lesser rank than a

* See illustration facing p. 108 for Sophia as grown-up.

reigning duke. Inquiries had been made by the Emperor Leopold if she migh marry his son, but though she longed to see Europe, she could not possibl become the bride of the Archduke Joseph who was a Catholic. William I now a widower, was thought too old.[25] Who else was there for her to marry a suitable age and religion? Did her brother want her to become an old maid It was all very well for him to leave the decision to her; he ought to give he brotherly advice, beyond the bald comfort of assuring her that 'all would b well'.[26] The Queen-Grandmother and the Duchess of Holstein did not find easy to discuss Hedvig's marriage with Charles XII. They met at dinner an supper, but the young King knew how to avoid topics of conversation h found unwelcome. He often took refuge in flight, leaving the table early an escaping to his study or to the offices of Piper or Wrede.[27] Hedvig Eleonor complained with tears that neither he nor Hedvig Sophia took the slightes notice of what she wanted.[28]

The ladies therefore had recourse to go-betweens. Oxenstierna, less sure o himself with the new King than with the old, did not like to broach the delicat subject but used his brothers-in-law, the Wachtmeisters, with their easier an more direct approach (their *bouffonnerie* as political enemies labelled it)[29] t attempt to influence Charles in favour of his sister's marriage to the Duke. The knowledge that his father had been anxious for a dynastic alliance t strengthen the political Holstein connexion must have weighed heavily wit Charles XII – and he may well have had direct instructions from his father o this point[31] – but what evidence we possess points to Hedvig Sophia makin up her own mind. She was eager for married status and adult life, happy at th prospect of going abroad to milder climates and more sophisticated festivities In April the Duke himself arrived in Stockholm with a suite of thirty-fou cavaliers, and a few days later he and Hedvig exchanged rings and gifts t signify their engagement. With the decision made and herself pledged throug the ring which she gave the Duke – the most valuable ring in Sweden (origin ally a present from Louis XIV to Magnus de la Gardie) which Charles XI ha given to Ulrika Eleonora as an engagement ring[32] – the Princess burst int tears. Charles XII patted her cheek and comforted her as best he could: 'Do no be unhappy', were the words those close enough heard him say to her, 'yo shall never lack for anything as long as I live.'[33]

We do not know how much a feeling of duty had contributed to Hedvig Sophia's decision. She must have been conscious of her grandmother's an her aunt's wishes and of the traditional dynastic and political alliance wit Holstein-Gottorp: but if she had wanted to refuse Frederick she would undoubtedly have got her brother's support. With her seniority of a year, which had counted so much in childhood, she was used to exercising contro and influence in their relationship, so much so that observers credited he with ascendancy over the young King even in political matters.[34]

With Hedvig Sophia's marriage a certainty – Tessin was hard at work o the plans for a summer wedding[35] – attention became concentrated on the ossibility of the King following her example. Danish efforts to score a uccess to counterbalance that of Holstein were redoubled. At the meeting of he Diet, the non-noble Estates, always concerned with the continuity of the uccession as a means to keep the nobility in check, had (not unassisted by Danish promptings) petitioned Charles XII to think of marriage and the need o produce an heir and the name of Sophia of Denmark had been mentioned, coupled with the memory of his own mother, that good Danish princess.[36]

Charles XII was himself at first unpleasantly surprised at the petitions of the Estates, though he thanked the various deputations for their concern for him and his house and promised to consider their suggestion. He had been rushed into his majority and his coronation: was he to be rushed into marriage also and lose some of the freedom of action he had only just gained? His father's advice had been to marry at eighteen or even as late as twenty.[37] For a boy of fifteen who was busy and physically active and not particularly disturbed – as far as can be assessed from our evidence – by sexual curiosity there seemed no hurry. There were, however, people in his immediate surroundings who made it their business to encourage what natural and awakening interest he did possess; some because they favoured a particular marriage-alliance and others because they believed that Charles XII would not live long and they were concerned with the succession in the direct line rather than with the boy who happened to be king.

Everything he said or did which might have a bearing on his likes or dislikes where women were concerned was minutely reported and discussed; his doctor, courtiers and servants frequently brought conversation round to the topic of sex and marriage and the individual candidates who were being considered as suitable wives for him. There was great joy in the anti-Holstein camp when it was noted that the young Princess of Holstein-Gottorp did not appeal to him, and his admission, when pressed by Bielke, that he could never fall in love with a girl 'ugly as Satan and with such a devilish big mouth', was gleefully repeated.[38] Since Maria Elisabeth was short, it was immediately concluded that Charles XII preferred those *'qui ont une belle taille, et qui sont un peu longues'*.[39] Painters were kept busy improving on portraits which various courts were submitting, or arranging to let the King see, as if by accident, those of princesses who might appeal to him more. The one of Sophia which Juel had brought over was considered too unflattering to be presented ('she looks like a peasant-girl')[40] and while the Danish diplomats waited for a miniature to come from Copenhagen, Ehrenstrahl was asked to remedy matters by an embellished copy or some skilful overpainting.

Though the elaborate plans made for Charles XII's discovery of the improved portrait in Ehrenstrahl's studio miscarried,[41] Sophia seemed all the same to draw ahead in the marriage stakes, much to the delight of the Danish diplomats. The young King showed himself as indifferent to the Bavaria-Wolfenbüttel female relative as he had to the Holstein-Gottorp one; the Württemberg candidate was out of the running once she had been reported 'sickly';[42] the Brandenburg princess was ruled out on account of her Calvinism. Charles himself brought forward this objection when marriage to her was discussed, revealing that he had promised the late King on his death-bed never to marry anyone outside the Lutheran religion.[43] A match with a king's daughter would be more prestigious, many argued at court, than with a princess from a minor German court. There were only two Lutheran kings in Europe – the King of Sweden and the King of Denmark–Norway. What could be more fitting, the protagonists of Sophia Hedvig asked, than the marriage of Charles XII to the daughter of Christian V of Denmark?[44] A Danish dynastic alliance, it was stressed, would be a sensible move politically. One Holstein marriage, that of Hedvig Sophia to Duke Frederick, was enough. It would serve to restrain Denmark from rash actions against Holstein-Gottorp, Sweden's ally. But a second Holstein marriage, if Charles XII wed Maria Elisabeth, would be a gratuituous insult to King Christian and might have dire results,[45] whereas no surer means to establish friendly relations could be thought of than a union between the King of Sweden and Sophia.[46] Had not the peace between the neighbours in recent years been helped by Charles XI's Danish marriage?

Sophia's name began to be frequently coupled with exhortations to marry directed at Charles by those who for various reasons were keen to secure the succession.[47] Marriage, it was argued, would improve the King's health: his colic, his weak chest and his toothache would all be cured by a queen to warm and comfort him.[48] His doctor even discussed with Danish diplomats the advisability of secretly administering aphrodisiacs to the King to turn his thoughts towards marriage. The problem was how to induce him to swallow such a concoction? Charles XII invariably threw bottles of medicine out of the window now he was his own master and no aphrodisiac was known to the plotters which would be effective if smuggled into the only medicament the King could sometimes be prevailed upon to apply: an ointment for his chest.[49] Marriage was suggested as a cure for boredom as well as a duty to the nation; the delights of the marriage-bed were broadly hinted at ('better than anything else in the whole world');[50] and the subject of sex and marriage was one that was pursued in conversation even when Charles showed himself 'as fleet as a hare' in attempting to avoid it.[51]

There is no doubt that such talk offended both his modesty and his pride. He returned noncommittal answers from the 'I don't believe I am of an age yet for marriage' to his doctor (only to be told he was mature enough physically for the married state)[52] to his vaguer, 'That will be some time yet' to courtiers who asked him when he intended to marry; but naturally enough his thoughts, given the constant stimulus of open and veiled hints, began to circle round women and marriage. It was noted that he showed a greater leaning towards female company and that he was rather attracted to one of the ladies at court, the wife of the conductor of the royal music, Düben. She was small and neat and vivacious; Charles XII's admiration for her was open enough to make some believe that Düben's career in the King's service was furthered by his wife's *affaire* with Charles XII. Years later it was confidently stated that she had been the King's mistress when he was the young and relatively carefree monarch of the pre-war period.[53] Contemporary evidence, however, makes it clear that the parties at which Charles XII met the lady* were very respectable, and that the teasing and fooling and dancing which took place were of a kind which even those who wished it otherwise could only label innocent.[54]

Charles XII's liking for Mrs Düben served, however, to make him ponder his own problem in relation to marriage and to be freer in discussion on the topic with some of his own entourage. He made it clear that he would like to make his own choice and stressed how galling and unmanly he found it to be chased by those who wanted to sell him marriage.[55] That he took the romantic view of love, typical of his own age-group, we can see from his comments on a court-case that came before him on the bench of the Court of Appeal at this time. A young couple had been accused of marrying without the permission of the girl's parents. The special difficulties in the case arose not only from the fact that she was of a socially higher family than the husband, a common soldier, but also from the circumstances that they had found no clergyman willing to marry them and had therefore let a non-commissioned officer perform the marriage service. Charles XII argued strongly that the difference in rank did not matter since the two loved each other: the marriage was in his opinion valid even without benefit of clergy since 'the Testament had been read' over the couple.[56]

For himself he seemed to have begun to hope for similar true love. He wished – as he often said outright later in life – to have a marriage based on love and not on political expediency. He felt drawn towards his cousin Sophia, and when in September 1698 he accompanied Hedvig and Frederick of Holstein-Gottorp to the south of Sweden† he sent one of his pages to the Danish court at Kronborg Castle to give him a confidential report on the Princess. What he heard pleased him. He began to tease the page who came back full of praise for Sophia's beauty and goodness that he had been sent to report objectively, not to fall in love. Safe in his first-hand information Charles was heard to retort to someone who doubted Sophia's piety: 'Forgive me, I know better', adding – it seems as if to cover up a possible indiscretion – 'and, anyhow, no one in our family inclines to disbelief'.[57] From now on the prospect of Sophia as a bride for Charles was much talked of in the inner circle at court, the King being particularly open with his sister Ulla and with Miss Lewenhaupt, one of the ladies-in-waiting whose intelligence and wit he had learnt to respect. The cousinship, the knowledge that Sophia was like his mother in looks and temperament counted. Yet he was in two minds. He did not like the fact that Sophia was his senior by five years. He confessed his longing for a wife to come home to after the day's work was over, but also his fear that a queen older than himself might not respect him and might regard him as a

---

* These were frequently at the home of Count Piper's father-in-law.
† See below, p. 94–5.

mere child. Always he came back, in any conversation touching on marriage and himself, to his own youth: better to wait a few years.

This was also the advice of his seniors at court who spoke to the Danish diplomats about the match. Piper and Wrede, Rehnskiöld and the Queen-Grandmother came out in favour of the marriage once they realized Charles XII's inclination towards Sophia;[58] but political considerations dictated caution.*

Before Charles XII had reached the age at which his father considered he ought to marry, a Danish bride had been rendered inaccessible through the outbreak of the Great Northern War: the King of Denmark–Norway went to war with Sweden when Charles was just seventeen and a half, and though the Swedes tried hard, as soon as peace was restored after the brief campaign of 1700, to reopen the marriage negotiations they had no success: Frederick IV was biding his time to rejoin the coalition against Charles and did so in 1709.[59] It seems likely, given Charles XII's temperament and the example of his parents, that some romantic ideal of waiting for Sophia as Charles XI and Ulrika Eleonora had waited for each other remained at the back of his mind, at least down to 1709 or 1710. He postponed marriage 'till after the war', and no word of criticism or hatred for the Danes beyond references to the 'mistakes' or 'illusions' of his 'brother Denmark' was ever heard from him. Certainly Ulrika assumed that he would marry Sophia 'after the war'.

Two portraits of Sophia as a young woman now in Frederiksberg Castle, one a miniature,† are utterly delightful. They show the family likeness and radiate intelligence and charm which seems to come from the sitter as much as from the artist. One can only feel sorry that Charles never was able to marry (as Ulrika said) 'his Sophia'. Perhaps Sophia, who knew of Charles XII's interest in her – his portrait had been presented to the Danish court and the visit of his page, though secret, had been noted – felt equally drawn to the pattern laid down by Charles XI of Sweden and Ulrika Eleonora of Denmark. She never married, either in Charles XII's lifetime or after his death and devoted herself to good works.

III

The tensions which the marriage speculations created in the young King intensified both the moodiness of adolescence and the inclination to take violent physical exercise and risks. The concern of the doctors for his health, the rumours which were bandied about on the need to safeguard the succession because of his constitutional weakness worried him because he was too inexperienced to realize that they were in part propaganda in favour of an early marriage. He believed at times that he might not have long to live and at other times expressed himself so fed up with life that he would gladly die.[60]

---

* See below, pp. 104–5.   † See illustration facing p. 108.

He was left with a distaste for civilian doctors* and medicine and a determination to cure himself by toughening his body.

This was one reason for his hard riding; but the long rides at great speeds must also have satisfied that urge to get away from it all which all adolescents feel at times, to drive away problems, acknowledged and unacknowledged ones, in exercise absorbing all energies and all conscious thought. He took to his horse when lakes and roads were frozen and sensible people would travel by sledge, and rode for hours at a stretch, till his horse stumbled, worn out, and the King himself was too exhausted to dismount and had to wait till his companion caught up with him and helped him to his feet. The older generation commented that the boy-King was trying to show by such mad rides that he possessed a force and vigour which were not his.[61] He tried to taunt his page and an officer of his guard into crossing a small arm of the sea by jumping with him from icefloe to icefloe on horseback and he let his horse swim him across only when he had become convinced that the ice would not bear him.[62] But he accepted correction from those he respected and did not regard as unduly given to fuss.[63]

Worse was to come with the Duke of Holstein's visit in April 1698. Frederick brought with him a party of high-spirited young cavaliers, and Charles, flattered by the attention of the older man and his friends and eager to measure up to his duties as a host, fell in with all kinds of pranks which shocked the staid court. Even when allowance has been made for exaggeration in the reports of them,† a residue remains which makes the contemporary talk of the King's *délire* understandable.[64] In the months before the Holstein marriage windows were shot to bits in *Kungshuset* and in other places; chairs and other furniture were thrown from palace-windows to smash in the courtyard below; hares were chased round the big gallery of *Kungshuset*; young men, half drunk, came back from a day's hunt late at night with noise and laughter which woke up the sleeping burghers of Stockholm. Those who went to their windows to look out were particularly scandalized to see that most of the riders had their shirt-tails flapping. It was with some relief that the King was seen to be properly dressed. Sports which were popular on the Continent, but not usual in Sweden, such as the baiting of wolves, bears, and steers, took place once or twice and were transformed by second-hand reports into orgies of decapitating animals till the King's room was spattered with blood. Traditional Swedish sports, relatively unknown on the Continent,‡ such as the capture of live bears by means of wooden sticks and nets, were put on for the visitors: not really dangerous, Charles XII commented later in life, when you know how it is done.[65] Gallops for wagers were also common and speeds were achieved

---

* His relationship with the surgeons of the army was always good; for his enlightened ideas on hygiene in the army to prevent sickness, see below, p. 158 and note 11.

† They were grossly distorted from a desire to discredit the unpopular Duke of Holstein-Gottorp.

‡ They therefore earned Charles XII a reputation abroad for incredible carelessness of life and limb.

which made the anti-Holstein faction murmur that the Duke was trying to kill Charles XII so that he might succeed to the Swedish throne.

Charles XII's generosity to his sister on her marriage was interpreted as yet another sign of a lack of balance in the King during his 'mad period'. He was known to be open-handed, *jusqu'à prodigalité* as the French ambassador put it,[66] and the Swedes very much resented the amount of jewellery and money which left the country with Hedvig Sophia. A dispassionate examination reveals, however, that Charles was bound by his father's will to provide his sisters on their marriage with two hundred thousand *riksdaler* worth of dowry in cash or in valuables or in any combination of the two. Hedvig Sophia received the full amount in money since it was argued that furniture and clothes and everything she might need could be bought more cheaply, and at a saving in transport, from Hamburg. As for jewellery and gold and silver from the royal collections, both the Queen-Grandmother and Charles XII showed themselves generous towards their beloved Hedvig. The young King's pride as well as his affection was involved: Queen Christina's valuable ring, redeemed from a pawnbroker in Amsterdam by Charles XI in 1681, and a precious set of pearls were among two of the many presents which the new Duchess of Holstein-Gottorp received from her brother.[67] Apart from his sister's dowry Charles XII's personal expenditure in money was on a scale very similar to that of his father: Charles XI used seventy thousand *riksdaler* for his own civil list in the last two years of his reign; Charles XII in the two years 1698 and 1699 (which included expenditure on entertainment of many foreign visitors) used 74,450 *riksdaler*.

IV

Everyone, including the Queen-Grandmother herself, was relieved when the time had come for the visitors to leave Stockholm in August. The marriage of Hedvig Sophia and Frederick at Karlberg on 4 June 1699 had been a private and pleasant ceremony; the little chapel beautifully decorated by Tessin; the company after dinner dancing simple country dances to the accompaniment of song and fiddles. But the duty of amusing the large Holstein party at a time when preparations* for Charles XII's *Eriksgata* – the traditional tour by which Swedish kings presented themselves to the nation and received its homage – occupied the court, tended to become onerous.

Once everything was ready, spirits lifted and the royal family and court set out in a holiday mood. The oldest member of the party was the Queen-Grandmother and Ulrika Eleonora the youngest. We can follow the happenings and incidents of the journey not only from the reports which Düben sent through his wife to Juel, the Danish ambassador, but also from the letters which Ulrika, then ten years old, sent to her tutor in Stockholm.[68] The King used to ride ahead of the main party to see that the quarters for the night were worthy

---

* Their scale can be seen from the need to collect 1,500 horses for the journey south.

of his family and visitors; there were occasional hunts and several sightseeing trips not so much to break the monotony of the journey as to give relief from the physical hardship of those who travelled by carriage and who were sometimes blue and black from the jostlings they received along the less good roads. In the first week of September they reached Karlskrona and inspected the base. Here the royal party split up: the Duke and Duchess of Holstein sailed for Kiel, Charles accompanying their ship three miles out to sea; the Queen-Grandmother and the young Princess went north by slow stages while the King visited Scania and the port of Gothenburg. By early October Charles XII caught up with his grandmother and sister and all three travelled home to Stockholm by easy stages, visiting the castles of Strömsholm and Ulriksdal on the way.

In Stockholm there was much speculation on how Charles XII would settle down, robbed of, or freed from, the excitements of the past half-year. He could not be said to have neglected his duties even during the 'mad months' of April to August; he had always been up early in the morning attending to affairs of state and had shown great interest both in his work on the Court of Appeal and in his training as a military leader; but the memory of the *délire* with its seeming irresponsibility and its silly pranks worried advisers as well as observers. There would seem to be three alternatives open for him, speculation ran in Stockholm at the time of his return: as a crowned king who had made his *Eriksgata* he could continue in the bad ways of the *délire*,* he could take refuge in 'hardness' or 'melancholy', or he could regret his past follies and 'go into himself' again.[69]

* There had been one or two disquieting incidents during the royal progress: on one occasion in Kalmar the King and a party of Holstein cavaliers had ridden their horses into the room where the Queen-Grandmother was sitting at her card-playing and given her the fright of her life.

3

The Reins of Office

It was with relief that Stockholm noted quiet and seemly behaviour in the King who came back to the capital in October 1698. He spent more time at his devotions morning and night, his secretary saw him reading the Bible and religious books, he busied himself regularly with domestic affairs in the morning and with foreign ones in the afternoon, calling Councillors and College experts to the room he kept for work. It was not easy for the world at large to find out the actual business afoot, King and advisers keeping their by now customary silence on 'affairs'.[1] What Charles XII did with his spare time was more easily ascertained. He wrote frequently to Hedvig Sophia, whom he missed very much, and he relied more than before on little Ulrika for company.[2] He saw a lot of Tessin. They had first come into closer contact when the plans for the new royal palace had been discussed in 1697; Charles had admired the model which the architect, commissioned by Christian V, had made for a Copenhagen palace,* and had shown himself anxious that the Stockholm palace should not be on less grand a scale: Tessin mentioned in a letter to the Swedish diplomatic representative in Paris, Cronström, that Charles XII showed a real interest in architecture as well as an inclination towards magnificence.[3] Their real intimacy dated, however, from the summer of 1698 when the King, with Tessin as his guide, had visited the Swedish gobelin works. A small colony of French artists had been busy since 1693 on the production of tapestries commemorating the victories of Charles XI in his war of 1675–8. Charles XII suggested that the tapestry designs should be engraved on copper to command a larger circle of admirers and a Dutch engraver was called to Sweden for this purpose and to help with the engravings for Dahlberg's magnificent record of Swedish towns, castles, palaces and manor-houses, *Suecia Antiqua et Hodierna*.

After Charles XII's return from the south he and Tessin had 'a thousand talks'. The King visited the architect's studio most days. He was fascinated by his collection of copper engravings; he heard of the art treasures of Europe and the court-life of France; he began to make plans for the embellishment of

* The building of it, because of the outbreak of the war between Sweden and Denmark, was not supervised by Tessin.

Stockholm as a capital and for a livelier court. The balls, the masks, the costumes and theatres of Versailles were taken as models and adapted to Swedish circumstances, Cronström in Paris being given constant commissions for 'coloured drawings': the request for some 'of the uniforms of the French royal guards' may have been dictated by curiosity about 'ceremonial' magnificence, but one suspects it was also prompted by Charles XII's continued interest in military dress and liveries.[4]

Now the twelve months period of mourning was coming to an end, liveries for the King's household were made to a new design,[5] and a French dancing-master, Ducroi, was engaged to teach the royal pages the fashionable steps.[6] Singers and dancers performed, and negotiations were successfully concluded with a certain Mr Rosidor from Metz to bring his company of French actors to Stockholm to perform twice weekly for the royal family and guests on a stage built in *Kungshuset*, with permission for public performances at Rosidor's own discretion.[7] Italian statues, including two huge stone lions intended for the entrance of the new palace, were ordered and a statue of Charles XI* was planned for its court.[8] The King's gardener, Hårleman, was sent to the Netherlands and France for fresh inspiration. In all this an aesthetic awakening is discernible, beyond the concern that Stockholm should be able to hold its own among the capitals of Europe.

The love of drawings and engravings and the interest in architecture remained with Charles XII all his life; he kept up a correspondence with Tessin throughout the years when the Great Northern War kept him away from Sweden, he liked watching artists and draughtsmen at work when he could; the loss he most mourned at the *Kalabalik* of Bender was a chest which contained some of the drawings made for him by the Swedish expedition to the Holy Land and the Levant. His personal taste also started to take form during these sessions with Tessin. He began to find out what he liked and why and to have the courage of his opinions, and from this time we can trace his concern that the shape and designs of material objects should satisfy a personal conception which he held as to the rightness of it. We note it first in relation to uniforms and his own style of dress, then in portraiture, later in silverware for table and church and in all that surrounded him during his war-years on the move. Finally, during the relative leisure of his years in Turkey he is able to defend, against his old teacher, Tessin, personal and radical views on the role of sculpture in decoration and to discuss with him architecture and town-planning in an independent manner. 'The King does not pretend to be an architect', Feif (his Secretary of State at this period) wrote to Tessin, but frequent sketches from the royal hand – of palace buildings and ordinary dwelling houses, of sailing ships and galleys – accompanied the letters from Turkey to Stockholm.[9] During the busy period of reorganization from 1715–18 Charles XII found time, and indeed this was his chief relaxation, to impress his now fully developed taste on material objects. His work with Tessin, both

---

* For Charles XII's discussion on the placing of this statue, never executed, see below, pp. 433–4.

poring over plans for buildings to come in a happier future, he liked to keep secret lest he should give offence by such seemingly irresponsible pastimes when money was tight; but he openly and confidently decided or designed himself the accoutrements and belongings of his new army and his new bureaucracy, from the standards of the regiments to the badges of the couriers of the Chancery.*

In 1698–9 most of his activity in the sphere of design was imitative. The carousels given in May and June 1699[10] were more elaborate and elegant than those of his father's time and clearly modelled on those of Versailles; the new theatre, the one for public performances, being built was similarly French-inspired. The King's new interests matured him, and when Hedvig Sophia and her husband returned to Sweden in the late summer of 1699 there was no recurrence of the 'mad months'. Another reason for this was that Charles had the upper hand in his relationship with Frederick: the Duke and his wife (though invited to Sweden) were in effect political refugees who had come to plead for Swedish help in face of Danish invasion (thought to be imminent) of Holstein-Gottorp land. This, however, was kept a secret for as long as possible and their visit was in public treated as a family reunion which offered opportunities for festivities.

Charles XII was happy at the thought of seeing his sister after nearly a year's parting, whatever the circumstances. He went south to meet the ducal couple at Ystad and accompanied them all the way back to Stockholm.† Here a magnificent entry had been prepared. The new state coach was used and a dignified King sat inside with his guests in contrast to earlier comings and goings of the Holstein connexions: in 1697 he had acted as driver for his aunt Frederikke's sledge;[11] in 1698 he had been the courier who had hurried ahead to see to lodgings for the night. Masked balls and firework-displays followed,[12] and on 5 August the French players gave their first performance.[13] More ordinary entertainment included drinking and gambling on a moderate scale. We know that at this time Charles XII played cards for money and drank wine. On 23 September his page noted the King's loss of twenty-nine ducats to Rehnskiöld;[14] and Charles himself mentioned in a letter to his sister Ulrika from Kungsör, where he and the Duke had gone hunting at New Year, that they had both drunk her health to wish her all happiness for 1700.[15]

On at least one occasion during this period Charles XII had more to drink than his grandmother thought wise for him. We do not know if he was one of those who helped to make a captive bear drunk by giving it too much Spanish wine on 8 August 1699 (the only occurrence reminiscent of the coarse amusements of the *délire* period, and one which was much criticized since the bear in its drunken state fell out of a palace window and was killed);[16] but some time later in 1699 or early in 1700 the King, thirsty after hunting, drank enough to make Hedvig Eleonora upbraid him for slurred speech, slovenly

* See below, p. 434.

† The journey served also other purposes; his interest in Scania was advertised and fortifications were inspected.

dress and generally objectionable behaviour.[17] The reaction of this more mature and independent Charles was not the defiance of the younger boy: he felt ashamed and vowed never to touch intoxicating liquor or wine again. Having given this promise he stuck to it. On two later occasions only do we know that he swallowed strong drink: once in 1709, when the doctors gave him some to deaden the shock of cutting into his foot;[18] once in the *Kalabalik* of 1713 when 'a large glass of wine' was used to slake thirst after the drinking water had gone.* Charles XII's abstinence became one of his most commented-on traits of behaviour. He was soon known all over Europe as the monarch who drank nothing stronger than *petite bière*, and that so weak and watery that it was not much better than the 'pure element'.[19]

II

Behind the festivities, behind the relaxation of hobbies, Charles XII from the autumn of 1698 was taking the reins of office firmly into his own hands. The domestic situation had been mastered by a united absolutist party at a time when the King was too inexperienced to be more than a willing tool in the hands of the advisers his father had bid him trust. Now the foreign situation, where the absolutists were themselves divided and where his principal helper, Count Piper, felt out of his depth, was becoming threatening enough to put the main burden of responsibility on the young King himself.

In this there was nothing new. Charles XI had established a system whereby the Council and the high officials of the Chancery debated and prepared foreign policy issues, while he read, listened and discussed, reserving the ultimate decision for himself after consultation with individuals whom he trusted. This system continued practically unchanged, though with a brief break about the time of Charles XII's declaration of age, when the Council was hardly ever called (except to sit as a judicial body) since the King's advisers feared subversive activity on the part of individual councillors against absolutism. Some modifications were noted. Charles XI used to work in his own apartments, quite informally, and was usually accessible to members from the College of Chancery, whose offices were within the castle precincts, and others who wanted to see him. In particular the President of the Chancery, Count Bengt Oxenstierna, had got into the habit of seeing the King in private or to join in any consultation which was taking place in Charles XI's room – whose door was often left ajar – when he happened to be passing. The sympathy which existed between Oxenstierna and the Queen-Grandmother was one reason for the liberties which the President of the Chancery permitted himself: he could always rely on Hedvig Eleonora to mollify the King if he should take offence.[20] Charles XII, probably because he was as yet unsure of himself, was as inaccessible to casual callers among officials and councillors as to casual callers among courtiers. He moved his papers to a special study, where the door was

* See below, p. 360†.

kept firmly shut, opening only for those who had been specifically called for consultation.[21] He was usually 'gracious' to Oxenstierna,[22] but he treated him as head of the Chancery rather than as an intimate adviser and ignored the Queen-Grandmother's hints that the President ought to continue in the special position which he had held in the last reign. Indeed, Hedvig Eleonora was heard to complain that her grandson refused to discuss matters of state with her and was more obstinate than her son had ever been.[23]

One reason why Charles XII was wary of Oxenstierna in the early months of his personal rule was the knowledge that the President was a 'Holsteiner' – a pensioner of the ducal family to boot[24] – so that Oxenstierna's political opponents could represent him as a dangerous adviser who might tempt Charles XII into unwise promises to the Duke of Holstein-Gottorp, promises which might make that young man too stiff in his relations with Denmark. The chief advice which Charles XI had left his son in respect of foreign policy – all reports of the secret instructions agree – was that he must avoid being involved in war, 'unless you are dragged into it by the hair'.[25] A premature and provocative support of Holstein at a time when Charles XII's cousin, Frederick IV of Denmark–Norway, was negotiating for a Swedish alliance and marriage connexion, would be unwise.

But in the relationship between Oxenstierna and Charles XII there existed some tension and unease quite apart from the King's not wanting to expose himself to pressure in favour of Holstein. The mannerisms of the older generation may have got on the nerves of the youngster.* The soft-spoken, secretive and rather sanctimonius President of the Chancery was not a person for whom the King felt any sympathy. He was once irritated enough by Oxenstierna's talk of 'sacrificing a happy existence outside Stockholm for the call of duty' to ask why the President, if he so much preferred life in the country, did not stay there?[27] Oxenstierna cleverly tried to play the game according to the young King's rules. He recognized the special position of Piper (whom he found 'cold and disrespectful')[28] in home affairs, and relied on his own wealth of experience in foreign affairs to be brought to bear through College and Council. And as the Queen-Grandmother could no longer be used as an informal direct link with the King in affairs of state, Oxenstierna found other means of putting his advice privately before the King:[29] first through his brothers-in-law, the Wachtmeisters (who were helped by that aura of personal friendship with Charles XI which still clung to them and by their expertise in military and, especially, naval affairs), and also, increasingly, through his son-in-law, the army officer Magnus Stenbock, of a generation closer to that of Charles XII.

The younger army men, those who had served abroad with the armies of William III and Louis XIV, were coming into their own as the foreign situation became more serious and complex. Karl Gustaf Rehnskiöld, who had been made governor-general of Scania in 1698, had been permitted to quit his post

* There is a report from 1699 that Charles XII, in a mood of disgust, bemoaned to his sister Ulrika the habits of their grandmother, 'the old one who nods and spits'.[26]

or the time being and accompany Charles XII back to Stockholm after the *Eriksgata* of that year and was often closeted with Stuart and Arvid Horn, the captain of the crack Drabant corps, the cavalry lifeguards which served as a school for the training of officers for the whole army as well as an élite corps. This corps was limited to picked men. An ordinary private had lieutenant's rank and pay; the officers were similarly upgraded and paid above their actual rank. In the tough training of the drabants Charles XII increasingly took part and was thus groomed for military leadership. Frequently Horn and the King would lead opposite sides in mock battles. In one of these, where both parties were riding without saddles and attempting to score off the 'enemy' with hazel twigs as mock swords, the King accidentally hit an abscess on Horn's cheek. The pain was intense enought to make Horn faint, inflammation of the wound set in – it was hot summer weather – and the captain had to take to his bed for some weeks. Charles, full of remorse, visited him every day, presented him with two thousand *daler* and promised to pay his surgeon if ever he became wounded on active service. On another occasion – a naval exercise – when the big firehoses of Stockholm were used as cannon while smaller hoses played the part of muskets, Horn managed to escape from the King's ship, where he had been held as prisoner-of-war, in a small dinghy. Accurate aim with the hoses sank Horn's little craft, but he refused to give himself up and calmly swam round and round the royal ship much to the mingled annoyance and admiration of all aboard. Charles XII wanted to know if swimming was difficult and Horn, with a teasing echo of words which were often on the King's own lips, answered 'Not at all, as long as one is not afraid.' Charles jumped into the water, but found that 'courage alone was not enough' and had to be towed ashore by the captain of the drabants.

Horn's grandson, who published these reminiscences in the late eighteenth century, deplored that his grandfather (who had played a significant political role in Sweden after the death of Charles XII)* should have had to waste his time on such 'Gothic amusements' to please the King.[30] The commando training element in these amusements is, however, clear enough, and the two stories which Arvid Horn put on paper in his old age are interesting for the light they throw on the methods used in that training.† We have other evidence of the toughening process the Drabant corps and the King underwent. In the winter of 1699–1700 races on toboggans down icy hills were not without danger. Horn and Hård, the King's riding master, were among those taking part and Hård broke a rib on one occasion. Storming of forts, snowballs being used for cannon-balls, also formed part of the mock-battle exercises which sometimes sent Charles XII back to Stockholm with grazes and bruises.[31] Drill for the army as a whole was intensified. Bayonets and flint-muskets were ordered as European novelties in equipment and tactical ideas were tested and adapted to Swedish conditions.[32] The military forces were augmented. Charles XI's

---

* For this see Hatton, *New Cambridge Modern History*, VII, pp. 351ff.
† Horn wrote them down because he felt they illuminated various facets of Charles XII's personality.

army of sixty-five thousand men was raised to seventy-seven thousand, an
the eleven thousand men who manned the fleet at the time of Charles XI'
death were brought up to sixteen thousand. The fleet itself was enlarged s
that by 1699, it comprised forty of the line and eight frigates with 2,800 gun
in all.[33] A strong navy was essential for the defence of the trans-Balti
provinces and nearly half the Swedish army was tied down by garrison dutie
in the empire. On these garrison towns the defence of the empire rested in th
first instance and to put their fortifications into line with the post-Vauba
concepts of strong defence money was needed. Such money was levied in th
autumn of 1699 without any reference to the Estates, in conformity wit
powers granted to Charles XI and his successors 'in times of danger'.

III

The danger envisaged was from Denmark, but a secondary threat seeme
possible also from Russia. In May 1697 Christian V of Denmark – emboldene
by the death of Charles XI – had sent his troops into Holstein-Gottorp terri
tory in Sleswig to raze the forts built by the Duke in accordance with the *ju*
armorum which he claimed, with Sweden's support, was part and parcel of th
sovereignty accorded him in the treaties of the 1650s. The guarantors o
Altona met at Pinneberg to attempt an agreed interpretation of the Duke'
sovereignty, but met with stubborn Danish resistance to the *jus armorum*
Moreover, there were signs that Denmark was attempting to gain Russia
support to balance the Swedish championship of the ducal cause. In the sprin
of 1697 a Danish diplomat, Heintz, was sent to Moscow on a mission which
caused uneasiness in Stockholm since the nearest precedent for it was one o
1675, just before Denmark declared war on Sweden. By the time Heintz
reached the Russian capital, Tsar Peter had left on his European journey; bu
news of feelers for an anti-Swedish alliance which Heintz put out even in the
Tsar's absence,[34] rumours of Danish efforts to get in touch with Peter during
his travels, and reports of anti-Swedish expressions by the Tsar and his entourage were persistent enough to increase the misgivings of officials and officers.[35]

Dahlberg, the governor-general of Livonia, in Stockholm for Charles XI's
funeral, had predicted Russian attempts to achieve a foothold on the Baltic
before long;[36] Lillieroot was told that Peter in Amsterdam had been pretty
open on his intentions to set about getting one as soon as he had 'finished with
the Turk';[37] Oxenstierna admitted in the Council he feared that 'a reorganized
Russia' would not be content to respect the Teusina and Stolbova peace-
makings which had given Sweden Ingria and the Kexholm province of
Finland.[38]

Russia and Denmark had been in agreement over the Polish election of
1696–7,[39] both favouring the candidature of Augustus of Saxony as King of
the Polish-Lithuanian Commonwealth on the death of John III Sobieski.*

* Though Russian requests that Denmark close the Sound against the Prince of Conti,
Augustus's rival, were refused.

obieski's eldest son James appealed to Charles XI for support,[40] but Sweden
adopted a strictly neutral position as the Chancery was anxious not to offend
Louis XIV (known to sympathize with Augustus's rival, the Prince of Conti)
while the Congress of Ryswick was in progress. For similar reasons Russian
feelers for a closure of the Sound against Conti, escorted by the famous Jean
Bart and a French squadron, were ignored.

The success of Augustus was contested, but definite, since Conti was elected
but not crowned, while the Elector achieved election and coronation. The
Polish situation did not create any apprehension in Sweden. There was some
disappointment on account of the Electors' change to Catholicism; but there
was also a family tie in that Charles XII and Augustus were cousins on their
mother's side. Moreover Augustus expressed his willingness to negotiate a
treaty to guarantee Sweden's territorial possessions and uphold the Swedish
interpretation of the Duke of Holstein-Gottorp's sovereign rights. His offer
was eagerly accepted and it was the ensuing negotiations, cleverly pursued
with many signs of sincerity from Augustus's side, which blinded experienced
Swedish statemen and diplomats to what was really happening. They knew
that Augustus was in touch with his Danish uncle and in June 1698 Mauritz
Vellingk, Swedish governor-general of Bremen and Verden, got hold of a copy
of a treaty signed between Augustus and Christian V in March.[41] The secret
articles of the treaty, those with a clear anti-Swedish bias, aiming at a coalition
of Denmark, Saxony and Russia to attack Sweden before Charles XII's régime
should be safely established, were not discovered. The treaty in itself roused
enough suspicion to make Stockholm send Mauritz Vellingk himself, regarded
as a perspicacious man and a skilled diplomat, to the court of Augustus
wherever he should be, in Dresden or in Warsaw, to test his sincerity.*
Vellingk, however, was completely taken in by Augustus's friendliness and did
not discover the double diplomacy in which, though the Polish-Lithuanian
Commonwealth had no official part, individual members of it were involved.
Wachschlager knew something about the desire of some in the Republic to
work against Sweden, but Vellingk's optimistic reports were given greater
credence.[42]

Augustus had several reasons for participating in an anti-Swedish coalition.
He was ambitious for his dynasty and would have liked to convert the elective
kingship of the Republic into an hereditary one and to exploit the country's
potential power by changes in its constitution and administration along
absolutist lines. The Polish-Lithuanian Commonwealth (the *Rzeczpospolita*)
was vast in extent, with a population estimated at 9–11 million – a giant
compared with the Swedish empire of $2\frac{1}{2}$–3 million. It had, however, ceased to
play a role in European politics commensurate with its size and population.
This was due in the main to the permanent checks on the royal power exercised
by the magnates who resisted reform. The country was indeed split among

* The Swedish diplomat accredited to the Republic, the German-born Wachschlager, though
knowledgeable on Polish affairs, was not held well-connected enough to gain access to high Saxon
officials.

family connexions, ruling as princes over vast tracts and intolerant of an
central authority. The independent existence of Lithuania apart from th
dynastic union was recognized inside the *Rzeczpospolita* by the existence c
two Crown armies and two sets of officials: one for Lithuania, one for Polanc
At this time the mighty Lithuanian family of Sapieha was indeed refusin
to recognize Augustus as their King, carrying on actual warfare again:
him with the ultimate aim – since their own candidate, the French Princ
Conti had not been accepted by the Republic – of achieving an independer
Lithuania under a Sapieha dynasty. In this situation a conquest of Swedis
Livonia by Augustus would have many advantages. The Commonwealth wa
proud, conscious of its glorious past and resentful of past losses of territory t
Sweden and to Russia, but unwilling to take the initiative for reconquest an
indeed unable to reach agreement on any one policy since family jealousie
and competition for office and dignities rendered any unanimous actio
impossible. If Swedish Livonia were conquered by Saxon arms, Augustu
would be in a position to make several profitable deals: he might win over th
Sapiehas to his cause, making them accept this gain as an equivalent fo
reconquest of land lost to Russia; he might – and this was uppermost in hi
mind – hand over the booty to the Republic against the bestowal of hereditar
kingship on his family, with all the possibilities for reform of the country an
its reinstatement as a great power which that implied.[43]

These plans remained hidden, for the moment, to Swedes who accepted a
their face value Augustus's offers of a Saxo-Polish guarantee for Swedisl
Livonia and favourable consideration of the Duke of Holstein-Gottorp's case
Behind this façade of friendliness the threads of the anti-Swedish coalitio
were firmly tied. Such double diplomacy was of course no novel experience
but the Swedish Chancery, though on its guard at times, failed to discern a
motive for Augustan enmity and eagerly grasped the opportunity to gain the
Livonia guarantee and support for Holstein: the Polish ambassador whe
visited Stockholm was given valuable bronze cannon to take back to the
King-Elector; the common interests of Saxony and Sweden as Protestan
powers in the Empire and of Poland and Sweden as neighbours of a Muscov
bent on expansion were emphasized.[44]

In the case of Denmark past experience suggested wariness; the marriag
negotiations, though sincerely meant from the Danish side, were suspect jus
because history offered a disturbing precedent. Those Danes who favoured a
peaceful relationship with Sweden and negotiated the engagement of Charle:
XI and Ulrika in good faith in 1675 had not been successful in staving off the
war of 1676: other Danes had used the negotiations as a shield behind whicl
they prepared for war against Sweden. Charles XII's advisers were therefore
suspicious of the Danish offers of partners for the King and for Ulrika Eleon
ora. The Princess's case was easy to postpone. She was still a child and it
would in any case be inadvisable to make arrangement for her until Charles
should be married and have produced children of his own. A handle might be

iven to the anti-absolutists if Charles should die without heir and with both sters married, for the old constitution stressed the preferential right of an nmarried princess over a married one. The real struggle came in the negotia- ons for a marriage, or an engagement, which the Danes were prepared to ettle for as the Swedish attitude hardened, between Charles XII and Sophia.

Here even those influential Swedes who expressed themselves in principle in avour of a Danish marriage for the King, men like Piper, Wallenstedt, Stuart, Lehnskiöld and Wrede, all urged postponement. They gave all kinds of easons: Charles was too young for marriage; he had, they felt sure, inherited he passionate and uxorious nature of his father and would 'wear out his ealth and strength on the marriage bed'. He was too self-willed for an engage- nent; once the engagement was announced, they were convinced, he would nsist on a speedy marriage with the same dangerous and deplorable results.[45]

In reality these well-meaning advisers were worried about being cheated by he Danes; unwilling to take the risks of recommending the marriage to iophia until Danish intentions were clearer. Only time would show what were he purposes of Christian V's overtures (and later Frederick IV's) to Tsar Peter nd what were his real intentions towards the Duke of Holstein-Gottorp. ihould he attack the Duke on his own, an attack which implied an attempt to veaken Sweden's southern defences, he could be dealt with, with or without he help of the other Altona guarantors. Should he obtain the cooperation of ['sar Peter to make an attack on the Baltic provinces, the situation might rove more serious and contingency plans were completed for handling such imultaneous eastern and southern attacks, coupled – as they might be – with ı Danish invasion from the west, on Scania.

Such a situation was not to develop immediately. Peter was still at war with Turkey, and was known to be working hard, if unsuccessfully, to keep the War of the Holy League in being. One counter-measure of the Swedish Chan- :ery was to encourage the Turks – via Polish diplomats – to carry on the war vith Peter even when the Emperor Leopold and the Republic of Venice made peace.[46] Another was the splendid embassy which left Stockholm for Moscow n July 1699[47] to announce the accession of Charles XII and ask for the renewal of ancient treaties according to custom. Its splendour was meant to mollify Peter for the slight which the Tsar complained of when he had stopped in Riga *ncognito*, on his way to Europe in 1697. Three important and experienced officials were chosen: the Court-chamberlain, Bergenhielm, regarded as the Russian expert of the Chancery, Lindhielm, the governor-general of Viborg province, well versed in Finno-Russian relations, and Eosander (von Göthe) who had visited Russia several times before. To help them they had secretaries and interpreters and also the long-established Swedish resident in Moscow, Kniper, with his useful connexions. Behind the official mission and the cere- monial handing over of a portrait of Charles XII on horseback, lay the real task of establishing friendly relations to prevent Danish–Russian cooperation against Sweden.

All seemed to go well. Tsar Peter was pleasant and made no objection to th renewal of the treaties with Sweden. He did refuse to kiss the cross at th ceremony of the signature, but they accepted his explanation that this wa unnecessary, 'having been performed already at my accession'. With the wi dom of hindsight we can distinguish the implied mental reservation by whic the Tsar regarded the renewal as null and void since he had not kissed th cross; the Swedish embassy may well have thought him too 'modern' to obe 'ancient' customs – in any case they could hardly insist, since they feare Danish competition in Moscow.

There were other signs of the times which strike the observer who knows th course of events, but which were not correctly interpreted or singled out by th Swedes. Patkul, a Livonian nobleman and a Swedish subject, who in 1694 ha been sentenced to death as leader of a movement to resist the introduction c absolutism in Livonia but had escaped abroad, turned up in Moscow. H travelled under an assumed name in the company of a Saxon diplomat, vo Carlowitz, and he was seen visiting Heintz.

Unbeknown to the Swedes Patkul had already been extensively used as go-between in the anti-Swedish negotiations of the King of Denmark and th Saxon Elector. As a Livonian patriot he was passionately anxious to assist i the formation of any alliance against Sweden which might bring with i independence for Livonia and a restoration of the power of the local nobility He realized, however, that a protectorate under one of Sweden's enemie might be a necessary temporary measure. Indeed, to promote the prospect o war against Charles he exaggerated to Augustus the willingness and readines of the Livonian nobility to rise in armed revolt the moment hostilities brok out, and hid his ultimate aim of independence. Patkul had been present at th meeting at Rawa in the summer of 1698, when (after secret talks between thei emissaries in the Netherlands and in Vienna) Tsar Peter and Augustus met t discuss a joint attack on the Swedish empire. They shared a disappointmen that the Emperor Leopold who had his eyes turned west – focused on th Spanish Succession issue – was determined to end the War of the Holy Leagu against Turkey. Augustus, who as King of Poland had inherited John Sobi eski's share in that war, had hoped to regain the ancient Polish territory o Moldavia, which would have served his purposes in the Republic as well a Livonia. Peter, though still desperately keen to reach the Black Sea, was con vinced that he must take the opportunity of Dano-Saxon plans for an anti Swedish coalition to pursue Russian objectives on the Baltic. Such a chance if let slip, might never return.

Patkul had been the messenger between Augustus and the new Danisl King, Frederick IV, when Christian V's death in August 1699 had made i necessary to confirm the treaty of March 1698. By September 1699 a new an expanded treaty was signed. The alliance was now specifically offensive. Tim and place for the attack on Sweden was settled: Augustus was to invad Livonia in January or February 1700, Frederick to march into Holstein at th

time time and to follow this up with an invasion of southern Sweden once the
sar and the King-Elector were keeping Charles XII busy in the east Baltic. In
his way the Swedish forces would be split and success for all three members of
the coalition would be more likely. It was to clarify the Tsar's position, and in
articular to tie him down to a date by which he would obtain an armistice (if
not a peace) with Turkey, that von Carlowitz and Patkul came to Moscow.
When the latter was accidentally recognized by one of the Swedes in the
apital, inquiries were made. The 'official' Russian story that Patkul had come
the Tsar's dominions to throw himself on his mercy and serve him in the
ar against the Turks was believed; and as von Carlowitz went out of his way
help the Swedish embassy in various ways* the collaboration between the
axon diplomat and Patkul remained unsuspected, as did their negotiations
ith Tsar Peter.

Three days after the Swedish embassy left Moscow in November 1699 a
reaty guaranteeing a Russian attack on Ingria for the year 1700 was signed
etween Augustus and Peter though the Tsar refused to name a specific date.
t only remained for the King of Denmark to adhere to this treaty by a separate act. In January 1700 Frederick IV's signature was put to such a document
nd the diplomatic forging of the anti-Swedish coalition was complete.[48] The
ice of war would soon roll.

V

acking detailed information about what was happening, deceived and out-
vitted by clever diplomatic feints at times, the Swedish uneasiness was yet
persistent enough to counsel a bold counter-stroke against Denmark in the
ater summer of 1699. This was the announcement, immediately on Charles
xII's entry into Stockholm with the Duke and Duchess of Holstein-Gottorp,
hat Swedish forces in Wismar and Bremen-Verden would be strongly rein-
orced and that the Duke (who had already on his marriage been given the
itle of *generalissimus†* of the Swedish army in the Empire) would be able to
all upon these troops to help him rebuild the fortresses razed by the King of
Denmark. The new regiments for Germany embarked hurriedly in October to
get across the Baltic before winter storms and ice made communications
lifficult.

The challenge to Frederick IV was obvious and the guarantors of Altona
night take umbrage. Stockholm Councillors and Chancery officials main-
ained to foreign diplomats that the decision was the King's personal one,
agreed with the Duke during their journey from Ystad to Sweden, quite
unknown to either College or Council.[49] For this reason historians (who are

---

* He was particularly useful in smoothing out trouble which arose between the Russians and
he Swedes after a party brawl.
† Actual control of the use of these forces remained, however, with Charles XII. See below,
p. 397–8, for a similar *generalissimus* position for Ulrika Eleonora's husband.

sometimes apt to take diplomatic explanations at their face-value), have fr
quently assumed that nothing more than a dynastic or family concern, or eve
a mere whim of Charles XII's, was behind the move, and the countersignatu
of Piper has been ignored. Many have argued that the action was so provocati
that posterity can fairly put the blame for the outbreak of the Great Norther
War on Charles XII's shoulders. Had he been more pacific and more respo
sible, had he refrained from supporting the Duke of Holstein-Gottorp s
openly, runs the argument, the war might have been prevented.[50]

There was certainly an element of gamble in the counter-stroke: as in a
diplomatic moves and counter-moves in an atmosphere of tension. But it w
not decided on for personal reasons and there is evidence to support the co
tention that it was a planned move which would serve to clarify the situatio
and make the conflict with Denmark break out – if it had to – at a time whic
suited Sweden: before Tsar Peter would be free from his southern war an
while Augustus, if he felt bound by the March 1698 treaty to help Frederic
IV, might not be too firmly established in Poland.[51] The only alternative, t
sacrifice the Holstein-Gottorp position, was held to be unacceptable by a
Swedish statesmen. The treaty of friendship signed between Christian V an
Charles XII in December 1698 had said nothing of the Holstein-Gottorp prob
lem just because it was such a vital one for both parties: neither felt able t
compromise in a matter so important to their respective national interests. Th
negotiations for the marriage of Sophia and Charles XII had made no progres
because of the lack of willingness, on both sides, to bring into the open the
firm adherence to committed and incompatible traditional policies ove
Holstein-Gottorp. Such a marriage, if Denmark accepted the *status quo* i
respect of Holstein-Gottorp, would be welcome from the Swedish point o
view. But the *status quo* was unacceptable to Christian V and to Frederick IV
The 1683 will of Christian V had *inter alia* bequeathed to his successors th
'sacred duties' of the absorption of ducal lands in Sleswig and Holstein an
the reconquest of the peninsular provinces lost by Denmark–Norway t
Sweden. Once it became clear that Charles XII and his advisers were not willin
to compromise on the sovereign rights of the Duke of Holstein-Gottorp, or a
d'Avaux put it, pay the price for the marriage by sacrificing the Alton
treaty,[52] war was decided on. The marriage negotiations were continued i
Stockholm by Danish diplomats who were not always fully in the picture, as
screen for negotiations with Augustus and Tsar Peter and as a means to exer
pressure on prospective allies in the anti-Swedish coalition.

The war of nerves between Sweden and Denmark over Holstein-Gottor
had been continuous since 1684. The invitation to the ducal couple to vis
Sweden in 1699 was, in part, motivated by fear that Frederick would give in t
Danish pressure and thus, in the long run, prejudice Swedish interests.[53] Wit
the Duke in Stockholm, Swedish initiative had free play and the decision t
challenge Denmark was taken. That this policy might lead to war was possible
but by no means certain. Only strong measures during the Congress of Alton

Frederik IV, Duke of Holstein-Gottorp
with his wife Hedvig Sophia, from a
painting by D. von Krafft

Princess Sophia Hedvig of Denmark,
from a miniature by an unknown painter

Field-Marshal Carl Gustaf Rehnskiöld,
from a painting by D. von Krafft

Count Arvid Horn,
from a painting by D. von Kraff

Count Magnus Stenbock,
from a painting by J. D. Swartz

Count Axel Sparre, from a painting
attributed to David Richter the elder

ıd forced Denmark to climb down. Similar tactics might, it was hoped,
ıcceed once more. Charles XI had achieved a Treaty of Altona which, if it
ıd not solved the Holstein-Gottorp problem, had at least obtained great-
ıwer guarantors for the *status quo*. Perhaps a Treaty of Pinneberg would
ıfine and guarantee the Duke's sovereignty in accordance with Sweden's
ıterpretation of it?

Charles XII's share in the counter-stroke is difficult to estimate. It is certain
ıat it would not have been made without his concurrence. He had studied the
ıreign situation – in so far as it was known – with his advisers, and the fear of
ıncerted Danish and Russian action at some future date, when Tsar Peter
ıould be free from his war with the Porte, was one which officials and officers
ıd discussed with him. Since the move was a military one, with diplomatic as
ıell as strategic implications, it seems most likely that Rehnskiöld and
ıuart,* the two officers working on plans to resist attacks on the Swedish
ınpire, were more directly responsible than the Chancery officials in advising
ıe King on the desirability and the timing of the Swedish measure.

* In the summer of 1698 Stuart had carried out a tour of inspection of the fortresses destroyed
˘ the King of Denmark.

E

4

On the Brink of War

Only time would show the outcome of the unequivocal Swedish support of t[ ]
Duke of Holstein-Gottorp in the defence of the Altona *status quo* and t[ ]
Swedish empire. Ever since the initiation of the alliance with Sweden [ ]
Charles x's reign, the ducal house had had some four or five hundred Swedi[ ]
soldiers and some officers, particularly expert engineers, on loan, and [ ]
Hedvig Sophia's marriage to Duke Frederick a Swedish battalion had be[ ]
designated as the Duchess's lifeguard and stationed on ducal territory. But t[ ]
march of two Swedish regiments – 2,400 men – in the autumn of 1699 into t[ ]
lands of the Duke,[1] ostentatiously helping in the work of rebuilding the raz[ ]
forts, was military support on a different scale altogether, particularly in vie[ ]
of the Swedish reinforcements for Wismar which amounted to double t[ ]
number of men detailed for the Holstein-Gottorp task. Foreign observe[ ]
thought that war between Sweden and Denmark over the Duke's rights w[ ]
imminent. The Austrian minister predicted that Danish troops would be se[ ]
in to raze the rebuilt forts, that an armed clash with Swedish troops wou[ ]
follow and that a general war would then result.[2] By December 16[ ]
Charles xii was rumoured to have picked the thirty horses he intended for h[ ]
personal use in the coming campaign.[3]

Diplomats also commented on the calmness and even indifference of t[ ]
people in general at the prospect of war;[4] but the Swedish people had liv[ ]
with the Holstein-Gottorp crisis for a long time and optimistically hoped th[ ]
things would be patched up without war. The hopes of official circles, and [ ]
the King himself, were that the gamble might come off and war be avert[ ]
through Frederick iv's climbing down and acquiescing in the Duke's right [ ]
maintain fortresses wherever he pleased on his own land. If the Danish Ki[ ]
did not, war would have to come since the Holstein position could not [ ]
sacrificed without endangering the Swedish conception of imperial securit[ ]
but it would not be welcomed except in so far as a war with Denmark, if it h[ ]
to be fought, would be more acceptable while the Tsar was still preoccupi[ ]
with the Turks.

War as such was not wished for. There were still unfinished odds and en[ ]
of the work of reform begun in Charles xi's time: the resumption of Crow[ ]

nds was not quite complete; regiments stationed in remoter districts had not
t been practised in the new drills and tactics; recourse to war was always
sky, however much one might feel sustained by being the defender of the
atus quo and not the disturber of the peace. Charles XII himself, and the
hole generation of his army and civil service advisers, had been brought up
i the teachings of Pufendorf and his rules of just and unjust wars. Pufendorf's
osition at the Swedish court during Charles's childhood, as secretary to
ueen Ulrika and as historiographer royal until his departure in 1686,[5] had
rved to render his influence particularly direct and impressive. His history of
e European nations and their 'interests' rightly or unwisely pursued – with
amples to drive home the lesson – was widely read: it had been Prince
harles's textbook in European history and Rehnskiöld always carried a copy
˜ it on campaigns.[6] Pufendorf's treatises on war and peace were also well
town and quotations from them were frequently on the lips of Chancery
ficials.[7] In Charles's own case its categorical division of wars into just and
njust ones had been reinforced by Charles XI's injunction never to have
course to arms unless he was absolutely forced into war for the sake of
weden's vital interests. Some remarks of Charles XII on this subject have
irvived from the Diet of 1697 when his conversation with some officers
irned on the possibility of his ever leading Swedish troops in battle: however
uch he would like the opportunity of being at the head of a Swedish army, as
s father and grandfather before him, the fifteen-year-old confessed, he had
onceived 'a perfect horror' at the mere prospect of an aggressive war.[8] To
xplain the Northern War, as has sometimes been done, as due to the 'war-
st' of Charles XII and his desire to shine as a commander seems therefore ill-
ounded. Nor is the charge that Charles entered into the struggle with Den-
iark for personal or dynastic reasons out of friendship for Duke Frederick
isy to sustain.

Charles XII was friendly and attentive to the Duke of Holstein-Gottorp for
is sister's sake – for she, like all the children of Charles XI and Ulrika, was
motional and passionate by nature and became greatly attached to her hus-
and in spite of her relative indifference to him before marriage.* But there is
vidence which suggests that Charles XII was less partial to Frederick. The
Ling and the Duke were too different in outlook and nature for them to have
ie kind of personal friendship diplomatic observers, judging superficially,
stimated as the ascendancy of the older man over the younger one, the Duke
eing the 'favourite' of the King and able to dictate to him in matters of
olicy.[9] The Duke was indolent by nature and enjoyed his comforts – traits
hich Rehnskiöld who had been in attendance on Frederick of Holstein-
Jottorp when they both served as volunteers under William III[10] had dis-
overed. In addition, Frederick had already given Charles XII's beloved sister
ome cause for heart-ache by his affairs with other women, affairs which the

* Much in the same way, Ulrika Eleonora fell head over heels in love with Frederick of Hesse
ho married her in 1718 for political reasons, see below, pp. 400, 512.

Queen-Grandmother tried to conceal from the King lest he should becon
'cold' with the Duke.[11] The arrogance of the Duke, his teasing and conde
cending tone with his cousins during the reign of Charles XI, had left son
irritation and resentment. He terrified little Ulrika Eleonora so that she nev
forgot it with his teasing threats that Charles XII would marry her off to th
barbarian Aleksey, the son of Tsar Peter of Muscovy.[12]

The strongest proof of Charles XII's desire to avoid war can be found in tl
negotiations for a treaty between Sweden and the Maritime Powers whic
began in earnest in the autumn of 1699. A triple alliance had been conten
plated ever since the renewal of treaties between Sweden and the Dutc
Republic in February 1698, but the Swedes had been in no hurry, unwilling
commit themselves, as William III and the Grand Pensionary Heinsius desire
to a guarantee of the Peace of the Pyrenees as well as of the Peace of Ryswic
since that would jeopardize the balancing policy of Sweden. Now, howeve
in order to produce a united front among the Altona guarantors and thus pe
suade Denmark to stick to the Altona treaty, Sweden began to make conce
sions to the Maritime Powers. Officials and diplomats worked to ascertain th
lowest possible price for a renewed Anglo-Dutch guarantee of the Altona treat

This time, remembering Charles XI's 'ingratitude' after the Altona treat
William and Heinsius determined to drive a hard bargain and to tie Swede
firmly to their side in case they ever had to fight France again. Charles XII w
forced to guarantee all parts of the Ryswick settlement which affected the tw
Maritime Powers. His diplomats were hard put to avoid a guarantee of th
Peace of the Pyrenees, which would have extended their liabilities even beyon
the Spanish Netherlands, and were grateful to be permitted to leave the claus
relating to the Emperor Leopold in the Ryswick Treaty on one side.* Even s
Charles XII and Sweden had been driven off the path of non-commitmen
They were now bound to come to the military aid of the Maritime Powers
Louis XIV should attempt to invade the Spanish Netherlands or to suppo
the Stuart cause: no light sacrifice at a time when in spite of negotiations fo
partition treaties to divide the Spanish heritage serious doubts existed whethe
such treaties would be honoured by all parties concerned on the death c
Carlos II. Louis was known to have agreed with William III and the State
General on a first partition treaty; and a second treaty, necessitated by th
death of the Electoral Prince of Bavaria – the heir-designate to Spain in th
first treaty – was in progress of negotiation. There was, however, pessimism a
The Hague and in London in respect of the Emperor's willingness to accep
the terms being laid down and suspicion remained as to Louis XIV's 'firmnes
should a crisis develop through Leopold's intransigence.

To have mortgaged Sweden's freedom of action in advance, to hav
accepted commitment to the anti-French cause, was against the policy lai
down in Charles XI's time and still aimed at by Charles XII and all his advisers

---

* Their arguments (that they were receiving no compensatory guarantee from Leopold an
that Charles XII could not be brought to condone clause 4 with its promotion of the Catholi
interest in the Empire) carried the day eventually.

rere seemed no other way out of the dilemma since Danish efforts to split e guarantors of Altona and thus isolate Charles XII and the Duke enabled 'illiam and Heinsius to call the tune.[13] On 10 and 13 January 1700,* the vedish treaties with England and the Dutch Republic were signed, embody- g the reciprocal guarantees. The English minister at Stockholm congratu- ted Whitehall with near-incredulity and put the emphasis on the right spot: t is the necessities of the Holstein affairs which overbore all other consider- ions.'[14] The reluctance to pay the price was, however, strong. Commitment advance on European questions was a bitter precautionary medicine to vallow, even for the sake of the Holstein alliance within the Swedish defence 'stem, and Charles XII hesitated till the last minute whether to refuse ratifica- on or not. There was obviously a strong hope, shared by the King and some . least of his advisers, that the crisis might blow over, that the show of force, upled with the mere news of the signature of Sweden's treaties, might achieve e desired result and prevent war. Not till after the news of Frederick IV aving marched his army into the Duke of Holstein-Gottorp's Sleswig ossessions reached Stockholm on 20 March did Charles XII sign the tifications of his treaties with the Maritime Powers.[15]

II

he march of the regiments to their embarkation points for Germany in the utumn of 1699 proved a good test of the way in which the mobilization of the hole army would work, should this become necessary. Charles XII himself sited all four of them either at their local points of rendezvous or during eir march south. Each regiment was scheduled to cover three Swedish miles day, resting every third day, along routes which would permit a steady rarch with no competition between them for roads or lodgings. The indivi- ual soldier, on receiving his marching orders, left the small homestead where e was maintained by a given group of farmers – a *rota* – who provided him 'ith house and land, with uniform and boots as well as with pay, to join the 49 soldiers from the same or neighbouring parishes who formed the unit alled a *korporalskap* after the non-commissioned officer in charge. Two of rese units then merged at a prearranged place to form a company (*kompani*) :d by a lieutenant; four companies converged along their different routes to rake up a battalion (*battalion*) under a captain; finally the two battalions 'hich made up the regiment met at the appointed time at a given rendezvous, sually the largest town in the county or province from which the regiment ook its name. Here the colonel took charge. Non-commissioned and com- rissioned officers lived on 'crown-farms' within the county. The local ties etween soldiers, officers and district were strong,† building on the age-old :adition, far older than the Swedish sixteenth-century state, of men from the

---

* That with England was of 9 January (O.S.), that with the States General of 24 January (N.S.).
† Both infantry and cavalry regiments had a double complement of officers below colonel's rank ɔ that replacement of casualties should not even temporarily break the local bonds.

same valley joining in the defence of home and farm. The company met on
a month for exercises; the regiments once a year for a fortnight for more i
tense training. Cavalry regiments were, after Charles XI's reforms, recruit
in the same way as the infantry regiments, but since the equipment of
cavalryman with his horse was more expensive than the fitting out of a foo
soldier, larger farms, or bigger groups of small farms, were held responsib
for a cavalryman each. The basic unit of the cavalry regiment, the squadro
(*skvadron*) was slightly smaller than the *korporalskap* – 100 to 125 men to th
150 of the infantry basic unit – so that a cavalry regiment on full streng
counted 800 to 1,000 men as against the 1,200 of an infantry regiment.

At the regimental meeting-place equipment and arms were inspected an
the administration of the regiment sprang into life: the commissariat colle
ing and distributing the food, each company having three covered carts for th
transportation of stores; the field-hospital service with the regimental surgeo
his three assistants (*Gesellen*) and other helpers and his wagon with the b
chests full of instruments and smaller ones full of medicines; the *audit*
branch, with its responsibility for correspondence and contact with the centr
authorities, sending in the necessary reports as to men and equipment, bei
the ever-watchful eye of the army organization. The colonel was in charge
all operational correspondence, in close contact with the high command b
letter or oral orders from the King.[16]

The experience of Charles XI and his officers, particularly the able Rutg
von Ascheberg, a veteran (like Dahlberg) of the wars of Charles X, who ro
to the rank of field-marshal, and passed on his experience to Rehnskiöl
whom he himself picked as his successor, had moulded the new army
absolutist Sweden. With the genius for practical administration which wa
typical of the bureaucracy of the great-power period everything had been for
seen, everything had been arranged and fitted into a master-plan so that th
army could be maintained at a reasonable cost, be mobilized speedily an
made to function efficiently. Sweden needed, they estimated, in peacetime
mobile army of some thirty-six thousand men raised and maintained by th
largest social group of the country, the peasants, to set beside the paid troop
about 23,500 in number, who garrisoned the ninety forts and castles of th
empire. This compared well with the standing armies of other powers at th
period; Denmark was estimated as having twenty-five thousand and Brander
burg and Saxony thirty thousand each. In wartime it was obvious that th
mobile army would have to be increased to enable Sweden to put larger force
in the field and though this was not publicized arrangements existed whereb
recruits could be found inside the framework of *indelingsverket*. The peasa
rota already had the duty, if its soldier became a casualty or too old or unfit t
serve, to replace him; in war-time new regiments could be formed by a give
number of *rota* units combining to raise a soldier (the so-called *tremannings* c
fjärdemannings regiments, depending on whether three or four units joined
again with the usual obligation to replace him if need be.

Because of their basic nature of local levies, as compared with the standing
ercenary armies of the Continent, mobilization in Sweden could never be as
eedy as, for instance, in Denmark or in the German states. The very nature
d size of the country also played its part. Cleverly chosen march-routes,
tensive training and timing cut mobilization time down, but even so it was
timated that from the day the order to march reached the colonel of the
giment a whole month was necessary for the regiment to collect at its rendez-
us, while the time needed to march to embarkation points in the south
ried, with distance, from four to five weeks. A further factor to be reckoned
ith was the need to transport armies across waters which frequently froze in
e winter. Winter was often the best time for campaigns in north and north-
st Europe, the time when marshes and rivers could be crossed easily, but
oops had to be got to the other side of the Baltic or the Gulf of Finland
hile the sea was navigable.

Sweden had not been unaffected by the minor revolution in tactics and drills
cessitated in all European armies towards the end of the seventeenth century
cause of the improvement in fire-arms (principally by the introduction of
ntlocks as opposed to wheel-locks) and the adoption of the bayonet instead
the pike. The Swedish army did not abandon its pikemen, as did many con-
nental armies, but the flintlock and the bayonet were also introduced (the
ntlock, because of the difficulty of manufacture in sufficient numbers, rather
ore slowly than the bayonet). The greater speed in firing necessitated modi-
ations of methods of defence and attack. Once the experts with their mathe-
atical calculations had evolved the necessary changes, both in the evolutions
the cavalry and in the different groupings in depth and line for the infantry,
w drills were put on paper and exercised when company and regiment were
gether.

The experimental work, the testing and discarding or retaining of ideas
om abroad, took place in the 1680s and early '90s; the battalion larger than
x hundred men was rejected, the adoption of *chevaux de frise** in defence
as discontinued as not suitable to Swedish conditions or temperament, but
e pattern of firing called *plutoner* and *maroner* had been adopted. From 1695
nwards the new drills and regulations were committed from drafts, which had
ndergone many changes during practice periods, to print, signalling the end
f the phase of modification and adaptation. The regulations for the cavalry
ere printed in 1695–7, those for the infantry were not quite ready at the time
f the outbreak of the Great Northern War and were completed by Charles
I and Stenbock in the winter-quarters of 1700–1, going into print in 1701.

The basis of Swedish tactics remained the attack with *armes blanches*,† the
ld steel of the sword, the pike, the bayonet. There was a deliberate sacrifice
f fire-power both for infantry and cavalry. When in battle-formation on a

---

* In Sweden these were known as 'Spanish (or Flemish) riders'.
† The Swedish term is *blanka vapen*; such an attack was in Swedish often characterized as one
'*gå-på*' (literally, 'go-on').

line of four rows, the two backmost rows fired once at forty metres distanfrom the enemy, the two front ones 'when they saw the white of their eyes
then attack proper with the 'cold steel' began. The soldiers were taught to di
regard enemy fire with the help of a religiously inspired fatalism ('God woul
not let one be killed till one's appointed hour had come'). Their own contemp
for fire-power, which was at this period inaccurate and consumed time i
reloading, gave Swedish tactics their strong dynamic impetus. Constant prac
tise in marching and wheeling, the drums beating out the orders, had speede
up infantry movements and made the foot-soldier a pliable instrument for th
brains of those who planned the battles; constant practice in the change c
front within the square of the cavalry-line, where the officers were so statione
that they always formed the front line whichever way the square faced, ha
given the Swedish cavalry a speed and cohesion unrivalled on the Contine
at this time.[17]

Of the four regiments which marched south in September 1699 to reinforc
Swedish forces in Germany, two were infantry, the other two cavalry. To sav
shipping-space and time, and possibly also to impress on Europe the lack c
aggressive intent, no horses were taken along. On the 5th of October the troop
embarked in sixteen warships* though they had to wait till the 18th before
good wind carried them across the Baltic. On the 19th they sighted Rügen, th
island guarding Swedish Pomerania, and on the 21st they landed at Peene
münde. They were put under the command of Nils Gyllenstierna, who – in th
absence of the suspended Bielke – controlled all Swedish forces in the Empire
those in Pomerania as well as those in Bremen-Verden. Most of these wer
garrison troops, but with the newly arrived four regiments Gyllenstiern
disposed of a mobile army of seven thousand men.

III

Coupled with the show of force and with the gaining of allies to impress th
King of Denmark with the gravity of the situation, went a peace-offensiv
waged through the Prince of Holstein-Gottorp himself. While Charles x
insisted that the Duke's *jus armorum* was 'very clear and evident', and that h
himself had 'every right' to send troops to his German provinces and would g
to war with anyone that interfered with the ships transporting the four regi
ments,[18] the Duke expressed his perfect willingness to submit his quarrel wit
Frederick IV to the mediators at Pinneberg once more. He promised to sto
work on his fortifications if negotiations were restarted on the sole conditio
that Frederick IV should not demand the withdrawal of the five hundre
'permanent' Swedish troops engaged on the rebuilding.[19] For a while ther
seemed some probability that peace would be restored. The conference a
Pinneberg reopened and though Frederick IV moved an army of twent
thousand into the royal parts of Sleswig and Holstein as soon as the Swedis

* Twelve of the line and four frigates.

einforcements landed in Germany, this army did not violate the ducal parts.
n reality Frederick IV had already made up his mind and was indeed, as we
now and some contemporaries guessed from more or less well-informed
eports (Heinsius being among those best informed via the commander-in-
nief of the Danish forces),[20] committed to the anti-Swedish coalition he him-
elf had initiated. He had no intention of listening to those powers that
oreached up Peace and Moderation',[21] but was delaying his attack till
ugustus had declared himself by an invasion of Livonia so that Sweden's
orces would have to be split from the very onset of hostilities.

There had been some hope that the King-Elector would mount his offensive
y New Year 1700. One of the necessary preparations for the war against
weden was a pacification, however temporary, with the Sapieha family and
thers in Lithuania who had opposed Augustus's cause; and the terms of this
acification, which stipulated withdrawal of Augustus's Saxon troops from
Lithuania, were signed in December.* Saxon troops had indeed been pouring
nto Lithuania on the excuse of the disturbances there so as to use the area as a
ase from which to mount the offensive on Sweden and, logically, the invasion
f Livonia should have followed immediately on the December treaty with
apieha. Negotiations were, however, also proceeding with the Elector of
Brandenburg, for an agreement to allow Saxon troops transit when needed
ver Brandenburg territory, while denying permission for Swedish soldiers
rom Pomerania to cross Brandenburg soil, and these took longer than expec-
ed. The anti-Swedish coalition had hoped to bring Brandenburg actively on
heir side as a founder-member of the alliance, but the Elector, for various
easons,[22] wanted to delay committing himself though he was keen to obtain
wedish Pomerania. Against Augustus's promise to support him in his efforts
o become 'King in Prussia', he agreed in January 1700 to sign a convention
lenying transit through his lands to Swedish troops while granting it to Saxon
roops. Brandenburg's 'neutrality' weighted in favour of Saxony freed
Augustus from fear of a Swedish attack over Brandenburg territory either on
axony or in the rear of the Saxon army marching on Livonia.

On 11 February (N.S.) Augustus and his army of fourteen thousand
narched out of the Saxon camp in Lithuania and into Swedish–Livonian
erritory without a declaration of war. The King-Elector had hoped for quick
ains, and especially that Riga would fall into his lap by the very surprise of
is attack and by the immediate rising of the Livonian nobility. The watchful-
ess of Dahlberg and the improved defences of Riga foiled such plans. The
mall fort of Kobron, opposite Riga, but on the southern side of the Dvina
iver, was taken and Dünamünde, slightly larger but with a garrison of only a
ew hundred men, at the mouth of the river was besieged and had to capitulate
n 14 March. Patkul tried to exploit the discontent of the nobility with
wedish absolutism, and proclamations declaring a war of liberation against

* From now on, unrest in Courland was made the ostensible reason for the continued presence
of Saxon troops.

Sweden were issued but had little effect since even those who sympathize
with Patkul wanted to see the outcome of the war. The main Saxon arm
remained temporarily fairly passive, however, waiting both for the revolt t
take effect and for siege artillery to be brought up so that Riga itself could b
invested.[23]

As soon as Augustus had crossed the frontier a messenger was sent b
Dahlberg to bring the news with all speed to Stockholm. A quick direct pass
age by sea was impossible at that time of the year and the officer chosen as
dispatch-rider went by land, through Livonia, Estonia and Ingria – round th
Gulf of Finland – traversing southern Finland, hurrying along the long curv
of the Bothnian Sea since the water was frozen but not solid enough to carr
horse and rider. He arrived at Kungsör where Charles XII was hunting on
March. The French ambassador, Guiscard, who was of the royal party tha
day, has recorded the King's calm and confident reply, 'We shall soon mak
Augustus return the way he came.'[24] The shock was all the same considerable
The '*mouvement*' in Livonia has taken everyone by surprise, the Danish diplo
mat reported twenty-four hours after the news had been made public. Th
successful double dealing of the Elector-King stood revealed and once th
veil had been rent the connexion between Augustus and Frederick IV of Den
mark was obvious. Here they reckon war has already begun, the report t
Copenhagen continued, and 'all' think that our King is behind it.[25] Charle
XII was certainly of that opinion. 'It is strange', he said on the 9th, 'that bot
my cousins want war. So be it. We have a just cause, and God will help us.'[2
The King's calmness is, in part, explicable by the assurance that preparation
were in hand to meet at least the Danish challenge. In December 1699 th
colonels of all regiments had received orders to keep themselves in readines
to mobilize, waiting only for the final word of command, and preparations o
all kinds were evident enough for an English diplomat's report to Whitehal
on 2 December to read:

> This Court is taken up with Comedys and other divertisements as if there wer
> nothing else on hand; yet neither are more weighty matters neglected, especially th
> preparatives for a War, which are making in diligence, both for the Sea and Lan
> service, as farr as the Season will permitt; so that if the Duke of Holstein's fforts b
> attacq'd, we expect no other than that this King will immediately repair to th
> ffrontiers towards Denmark, and fall on the Danes some where or other malgré al
> the inconveniences and difficultys of a war expedition.[27]

There was, however, no desire to jump the gun: Frederick IV would have to
commit an overt act of hostility either against the Duke of Holstein-Gottorp
– in which case Sweden would act as guarantor of the Treaty of Altona in the
sure expectation of receiving support from the Maritime Powers, or against
Sweden herself – in which case she would defend herself and would be entitled
to some help under her treaties with the Maritime Powers. On 20 March news
of the Danish army's march into the ducal parts of Sleswig and Holstein

:ached Stockholm, Frederick IV having put himself at the head of his troops
ad given orders to move as soon as he had been informed of Augustus's entry
.to Livonia. By occupying the whole of Holstein he intended to seal off the
.wedish troops in Germany from Denmark, leaving minor detachments to
:al with the forts of the Duke of Holstein-Gottorp in Sleswig and the rela-
vely few Holstein and Swedish soldiers in both Duchies. By the end of
1arch the forts were razed and the storming of Tønning, the Duke's most
nportant fortified town,* was prepared.

The Dano-Saxon cooperation had ruined Swedish plans of forcing Frederick
ᵥ to move before Russia could come to his help: he had sprung an unexpected
nd closer ally, Augustus, on them. That Tsar Peter would remain neutral for
ɔng was disbelieved, though he sent protestations of friendship and gave
otice of his intention to establish a permanent mission to Stockholm as a
:turn compliment for the Swedish embassy of 1699.[28] It was politic to res-
ond politely,[29] but there was little doubt that Sweden would soon be put to
1e test on three fronts – that her great-power position would be challenged
nd even her form of government, for Tsar Peter had at Rawa expressed a
esire, which now was repeated abroad, for the abolition of the Swedish
1onarchy and the transformation of the country into a republic, 'for
.epublics were less dangerous to their neighbours'.[30]

IV

Vhile Sweden was still on the brink of war and the full extent of the coalition
1ad not yet been revealed, the young King spent a good deal of his time on
1on-military affairs. Here, as in the preparations to meet the foreign crisis – in
o far as it was realized – he relied on the advisers whom Charles XI had
ecommended to him, and was obviously not independent, though absolute.
\ll witnesses among those who had the job of training him for the fuller
ndependence that he would inevitably exercise later – given the intelligence
ınd the temperament they discerned in him – agree that he was more deeply
nterested in civil domestic affairs than in foreign relations.[31] 'He would have
nade a good ruler, if the war had not come,' is a verdict heard often enough
:ven from the Swedes who came to disapprove of the way Charles XII used his
ıbsolutist powers in his maturity.

Because of the King's youth and inexperience it is difficult to assess his real
;hare of policy-making, civil and military, in the pre-war years. That he was
.earning to exercise his own judgement is obvious; but that he was kept on a
:elatively tight string by the absolutist party – in the interests of the reforms of
:he 1680s – is equally clear. His advisers warned him against being taken in by
people with an axe to grind ('selfish interests', it was usually labelled) and
preached that he could not 'submitt his affaires to the deliberation of others
without some diminution of his supreme power'[32] since they feared that he,

---

* The garrison there was commanded by a Swedish officer.

being still impressionable and malleable, would come under the influence o men outside their own group. Indeed, a foreign observer closer to the Oxen stierna than to the Piper 'faction' judged the King in these pre-war years 'ver easily persuaded that every body designs to take advantage of his Youth' though he also found him without 'reservedness in consulting others'.[33]

The attempt to separate Charles xii's decisions in policy-making from tha of the 'in-group' among his advisers seems, to me at least, neither feasible no profitable: they were members of a team united by feeling of responsibility fo the welfare of the country at a difficult time. Care must therefore be taken i attributing to Charles's achievements or views on specific problems which ma belong to men more mature than he. It would be tempting, for instance, to se a sign of the King's tolerance in religious matters (provable in later years)* i the decision to help Calvinists affected by the Emperor Leopold's concession to Louis xiv at Ryswick through the 4th article of that treaty.[34] Swedish law would not permit Calvinists seeking new homes to settle in Sweden itself, bu Charles xii gave permission for them to enter Sweden's German province and also his own independently inherited principality of Zweibrücken. Money was collected all over Sweden and in all Swedish dependencies to help Calvin ist refugees. We can certainly trace a concern in Sweden (as elsewhere in the Protestant countries at this time) that a second Counter-Reformation was i progress, from the King's orders to Oxenstierna to discuss with the Danish diplomat Sehested ways and means for Lutherans and Calvinists to cooperate against Catholic proselytizing and the spread of papal authority.[35] But we are not entitled to assume that the initiative implied in this order and in the actions to help the religious refugees originated with Charles. The most we can say is that these measures must have had his approval.

We possess, however, one source which permits us to assess some of Charles xii's personal attitudes and opinions between 1697 and 1700, namely the pro tocols of the Council as a Court of Appeal.[36] The King presided *ex-officio* and his exchanges of views with other members of the Court are noted verbatim. When read right through they exhibit characteristics which a study of his later years prove to have become constant and must therefore have been facets of his personality already formed.

The concern for the person involved in a case is striking: the King is always asking for information which will bring out facts helpful to the accused, and is worried lest injustice shall follow from the judgement pronounced. The strict and abstract sense of duty with which Charles xii is usually credited by histor ians is here seen shot through with compassion: better to allow a guilty man to escape than to punish an innocent one is his advice in cases where he has any doubt about the prosecution having made good its charge. His promise to his mother 'to be good to his subjects' may be held responsible for this; but it also fits in with his own analysis of his inborn 'softness'.

An interest in the position of women in society and in women's biological

* See below, pp. 431–2.

unctions is also evident. On one occasion prompted by the case under dis-
ussion the King asked for information about the development of the foetus
according to medical and scientific opinion of the time. The pregnancy of his
elder sister* may have made him curious, or the frequent notice he had been
given of the country's need for 'heirs of his own body'; but his mature delight
in scientific information of all kinds is also indicated. Where women in general
are concerned the King seems to have a more feminist attitude that the older
members of the Court: explicable no doubt by his attachment to mother and
sisters and to the fact that his youth had so far protected him from receiving
any blows of fate through the female sex. In cases where love and marriage
entered into the picture, Charles stood up for young lovers who defied parents
putting obstacles in their way for reasons of differences in wealth or rank.†
His view was youthful and romantic: the benefit of clergy was not essential to
make a union legal. On the other hand, he was much harsher than the other
members of the Court in cases of adultery.[37] Without the mellowness of time
and experience to make him show compassion, in such cases he wanted to
inflict the full severity of the law for transgressions against the code of the
Bible and of the Church. He desisted when told that the penalties he urged had
not been inflicted for generations; but could not resist a parting shot that the
letter of the law, and not custom, was 'right'.

A conviction that the ordinary Swedish peasant was the solid foundation on
which the prosperity of the state was built finds expression in many of his comments, and he favoured the system whereby tenants of Crown land could, on
payment of a sum of money, transform themselves into tax-paying peasants
with right of representation in the Fourth Estate. This conviction was
strengthened in maturity and led to significant reforms in the principles by
which taxation was levied and dues paid.‡

In the cases so far discussed (however briefly and inadequately) Charles XII
as a young man emerges as one who held views and attitudes typical of what
we now think of as the 'Early Enlightenment'; the stress on the rights, as well
as the duties, of the individual; the criticism of accepted social demarcation
lines; the interest in 'modern' knowledge. That he reasoned in an 'enlightened'
way is, I think, clear from a case in February 1699 when the request of the
Dorpat High Court for permission to use torture against prisoners suspected
of high treason was debated. The King refused to agree to the request. He
postulated that an innocent man might be tempted to confess during torture,
momentarily desiring death and the end of pain above all else and argued that
it would be morally wrong to condemn to death a self-confessed traitor whose
confession had been extorted by torture. In time, he added, God would show
who was the guilty one.

The abhorrence of torture and the disbelief in its efficacy was fairly widespread among the educated classes in Sweden at this time and we must beware

---

* Hedvig Sophia gave birth to a son in April 1700.   † See above, p. 91.
‡ See below, pp. 343–4, 346–7, 469–70.

of thinking of Charles xii as 'ahead of his time' in this respect, though son members of the Court of Appeal – before concurring with the King – suggeste that the deterrent of torture might be justified for the specific crime Dorp had in mind. Charles had been brought into contact from early years with m who applied reasoned and critical analysis: Urban Hjärne, the court physicia managed – beside his considerable achievements in the scientific field – to p an end to the legal persecution of witches in Sweden.

The death-penalty was not questioned by Charles xii for serious crime such as murder, either before 1700 or later; in the interests of military disci line he had it strictly enforced to prevent looting or desertion and, in spite remonstrances against his decision, he let the death-sentence on Patkul fro his father's time be carried out in 1708. He had compounded the high treas for which Charles xi had sentenced him; now he must be made an example lest the contagion spread, as must Paijkull, a Swedish Baltic subject who ha taken service with Augustus.*

But that Charles's attitude over which crimes did and did not deserve th death-penalty differed, in at least one case, from that of Swedish authorities shown in 1713 when his personality was mature and had acquired its characte istic touch of irony. General Lybeker had been sentenced to death on thre separate counts for his failure to defend Finland against Tsar Peter. Th judgements were transmitted to Charles xii in Turkey. He waxed gently sa castic on the three lives poor Lybeker must be supposed to have and inquire about the three enormous crimes. He agreed that 'self-interest' was a 'capita offence and that 'neglect of duty' was a bad thing; but as for criticism of th King this charge made Charles smile: 'If all those who criticize me suffered th death penalty, there would not be many left alive in Sweden.'[38] The Kin guessed that bad luck and lack of support from home might have somethin to do with Lybeker's failure and as he had served well in earlier years he wa pardoned and permitted to retire to his estates.

* Cp. below, pp. 217–18.

BOOK THREE

The Great Northern War

1

The Danish Campaign

The effect of war – even the defensive war which on 6 March 1700 Sweden knew herself fated to fight – on the young King's personality was one which worried his civilian advisers. With Charles XII on campaign, there would be less room for the free play of forces round him than in the orderly and regulated routine of peacetime existence. He would of course take along a skeleton staff, a Chancery-in-the-field, and the contact with the Chancery in Stockholm would be maintained; but some of the experts on foreign affairs – and in particular Oxenstierna – were too old to go on campaign and was there not a danger that the military men would make him despise 'pen-pushers' in general? And might not Charles XII himself diminish Sweden's prospects of obtaining a speedy peace? It had become clear during the Holstein-Gottorp crisis that he was – as his father had been – proud and jealous of the reputation of Sweden. When would-be mediators put forward their suggestions, he had been quick to resent them if couched in too hard and authoritative terms. Chancery officials who used the King, as did officials in every country in relation to their own master, as a lever in policy (as an excuse for inaction or as a scapegoat for unpopular decisions) stressed to foreign diplomats that they must take Charles's youthful rashness and wilfulness into account. He had to be 'managed'. They must put their points as 'friendly and easy as possible, that it may not look like constraint; which of all others is not the way to gain the King's complyance to anything whatever.'[1] The 'undiplomatic' emphasis in the last part of that sentence hints that officials also found it necessary to move a little warily at times; and there was – and remained – genuine worry among even the younger men of the Chancery, Cederhielm for instance, that Charles XII, with his a streak of obstinacy, might acquire a penchant for military *gloire* and become more difficult to manage as a result of the war.[2] His higher intelligence, when compared with his father, rendered him potentially more independent of advisers. Absolutism was too recent in Sweden for the central core of it, the sovereignty of the ruler, to have taken root to the extent of the bureaucracy contemplating a king on whom they were dependent: Swedish officials were very safe in their posts and wanted the power that went with the job.

Officialdom, as advisers, found the prospect of war unsettling irrespective of the way it might or might not mould the King's character. Among the pious, the attitude of the Church – preached from pulpits throughout the Great Northern War – was accepted; any war, even a just war, was a punishment from God for sin; the gift of peace would not come till the Swedish people turned away from sin. But in the worldly sense the war raised problems in respect of Sweden's economic and strategic positions over which men of influence differed. All accepted that Sweden was a satiated power and that she ought never to embark on war to widen the frontiers achieved by 1648 and 1660. But if war were forced on her then, according to the ideas of the time, compensation (*satisfactio*) could be claimed from those who had begun unjust hostilities. The concept of 'just compensation' for the victim of attack – if he managed to resist aggression – was generally accepted; where men differed was in what areas compensation could most profitably be obtained and to what pitch they thought it sensible – if God gave victory – that Swedish demands should be tuned.

A few were for getting out of the war as soon as possible, accepting money compensation for expenses incurred. But most looked forward to territorial extension in areas in which they held particular official and private interests. Those concerned with Sweden's position in the Empire wanted to secure communications at sea and visualized Bornholm, which had been held for some brief years during Charles x's reign, being ceded by Denmark to Sweden. Those interested in trade and shipping pointed to the Norwegian district of Trondhjem (Swedish between 1654 and 1660) with its fruitful valley and access to the North Sea. Possession of it would facilitate control of the barren but contested areas of the far north of the peninsula, an area in which Denmark, Norway and Sweden had long manœuvred (and at times fought) for supremacy. Some even pondered if the whole of Norway might be incorporated with Sweden. Many had their eyes on Baltic trade. With Augustus an obvious aggressor after 14 February 1700, and the knowledge that Poland must be at least conniving at his attack, compensation in that area might be, if not the rich West Prussian ports in Sweden's temporary possession between 1629 and 1635, then possibly Courland, to rid Sweden of a rising competitor in trade.[3]

Russia excited even more speculation. That Tsar Peter was a member of the Dano-Saxon league was now taken for granted since the happenings in Moscow during the great embassy of 1699 could be looked at with hindsight. Indeed, already in April 1700 reports of imminent Russian attack were so strong in the Baltic provinces that the authorities of Ingria and Estonia dared not risk sending troops south to help Dahlberg in Livonia: rumour had it from various places on the frontier that the invasion by Kalmucks and Tartars as well as Russian regular troops, and the ravaging of the countryside, had already begun.[4] And if the Tsar did attack unjustly, then future compensation – again if God gave strength in defence – might be exacted in ways which benefited both strategy and commerce: the eastern frontier might be pushed further back to put Ladoga on the Swedish side of the border; while in the far north the Kola peninsula might be gained, including the port of Archangel, so that one gap in the imperial economic defence might be stopped.

None of these speculations amounted to hard and fast plans; but those who discussed them reminded each other that though Charles XI had advised his son to avoid war 'until he was dragged in by the hair', he had in the same breath told him that if war was forced upon him he must 'wage it with the full power of Sweden.'[5] Surely here was a pointer to the late King's planning for *satisfactio*: he had been tough enough in his 1696 demands for entry into the Nine Years War on the allied side: security for Holstein-Gottorp, the town of Bremen and the disputed territory of Hadeln in Lauenburg for Sweden, as well as a guarantee for Sweden's Baltic provinces had been his price.* Might not the late King have listed in his secret instructions to his son what compensation for unjust attack or attacks he regarded as most desirable?

On the latter point we have no information. But that the speculations of of those whose thoughts played round *satisfactio* were, to some extent anyhow, shared by or approved of by Charles XII is demonstrable by the Swedish attempt, as soon as Tsar Peter declared war, to take Archangel by surprise[6] and by the implications of Charles's 'grand design' for a more permanent solution of Sweden's eastern frontier problem.†

II

In the early months of the war those who hoped to circumscribe the war effort took comfort from the fact that neither Augustus nor Frederick IV had declared formal war on Sweden when they began hostilities on 14 February and 11 March respectively. Could perhaps the transgression in Livonia be looked upon as a minor and isolated border dispute? And could not Danish action be referred to the Pinneberg conference, so that Sweden confined her response to cooperation with her fellow-guarantors of Altona? This line of thought was in effect the one adopted, though contingency planning for defence against a possible Russian attack had to be made. Nor could the threat to Riga be taken as lightly by the College of War as some of the Chancery assumed.

Military planning in the period of crisis before hostilities opened had been based on a two-front defence against Denmark and Russia, in which the nearer enemy, Frederick IV, would have to be dealt with first while the eastern enemy was kept at bay by minor border fortifications and the strongly fortified towns of Narva, Reval and Riga. Russian forces might not be prevented from swarming into Ingria, or even Estonia and Livonia; but imperial defence rested on the theory that the garrisons would hold out – if necessary as isolated islands in a sea of enemy troops which would be brought to battle and chased out when strong operational forces arrived from Sweden.

* For these terms see Hatton, 'Gratifications and foreign policy', *William III and Louis XIV*, pp. 90 and 91.

† See below, pp. 167 and 458.

This general plan could be adapted against Frederick and his unexpecte(
ally Augustus. Charles XII said as much to the French ambassador on 9 Marcl
when he – having commented on the coincidence of both his cousins wantin{
to wage war against him* – continued, 'I will first deal with the one, after tha'
will be time enough to talk to the other.'[7] But since Tsar Peter's intention{
were also suspect (though this was kept from foreign diplomats), the Swedisl
East Baltic provinces needed strengthening: orders were given to Finnisl
regiments to march to the help of Ingria, Estonia and Livonia.[8]

In view of the probable double danger in the east, Swedish reaction to Denmark's opening of hostilities was extremely circumspect. There was no doub*
in Stockholm that the occupation of Holstein-Gottorp territory was but a preliminary, should it meet no opposition, to the invasion of Sweden proper,
from Denmark into Scania and from Norway into Bohuslän and Järmtland.
Danish sources confirm this. Frederick IV's policy was based on the assumption that Charles XII would be the only Altona guarantor to offer immediate
military resistance to his occupation of Holstein-Gottorp land, and that by
the time other guarantors were ready or able to move – if at all – stage two of
the operations would be well under way: the Swedish troops in Germany
would have been beaten and the Danish reconquest of the peninsular provinces would proceed rapidly, aided by that splitting of Swedish forces which
his allies Augustus and Tsar Peter would dictate. The Maritime Powers could
not, even if they decided to help, send squadrons to the Sound until the late
spring and the Saxon army would keep Hanover quiet. English and Dutch
warnings in 1699 that they would send a joint fleet to the Baltic to act against
the party judged the aggressor in the Holstein-Gottorp crisis – warnings which
were solemnly repeated in January 1700 (after the signature of their treaties
with Sweden)† – were not taken seriously in Copenhagen. This was in part due
to the reliance which Frederick IV placed in Louis XIV's diplomatic help.
France was courting Denmark and it was confidently predicted that Louis –
who in his turn was assumed to be courted by the Maritime Powers for the
sake of his adherence to the second partition treaty – would know how to
immobilize London and The Hague.[9]

Sweden (and Charles XII), which had bought Anglo-Dutch renewed guarantee for Holstein-Gottorp so dearly, did not intend to throw the one desirable
fruit of the January treaties away. Gyllenstierna with his seven thousand men
was no match for the twenty-thousand-strong army of Frederick IV even if the
ducal troops, amounting to some five thousand if those lent by Sweden were
included, acted with him. The Stockholm decision was therefore to wait for
the fellow-guarantors to act, for Dutch and Hanoverian troops to strengthen
the Swedish–Holstein army at Denmark's back door, and for an Anglo-Dutch
fleet to reinforce the Swedish one. The Danish navy was only slightly larger
than Sweden's new navy, but it had a finer tradition and was justifiably proud
of the experience and skill of the men from Denmark–Norway who officered

* See above, p. 118.   † ibid., p. 112.

nd manned it. By geographical position the Swedes were less of a seafaring ation and were looked upon with some contempt by Danes and Norwegians: wedish sailors were but 'farmhands dipped in salt water'.[10] Swedish naval fficers had for the most part served in navies abroad and had varied and good xperience; but there was speculation in diplomatic circles as to how the fleet vould acquit itself now its sailors counted far more Swedes than in the pre-eform days when it was not considered 'fitt for service without a mixture of etter [sailors] which upon any expedition used to be levied at Hamburg, Lübeck, etc.'.[11]

The naval reorganization of the 1680s and '90s had aimed at a guaranteed upply of some fourteen thousand sailors recruited in much the same way as he army, but from the coastal population of fishermen and merchant-navy rews.[12] The building of the fleet and the upkeep of the ships, as well as the alaries of officers and skeleton crews, were in theory paid for from income llocated for the purpose in the fixed state budget laid down after the reduc-ion and the retrospect; but experience in the Great Northern War was to how that the navy always needed more cash than was easy to come by. It was ealized that Swedish sailors were not 'of the best' if compared to those of the ig naval powers,[13] but it was hoped they would improve and be fit for more han transport duties within the Baltic. Swedish merchant shipping had ncreased by leaps and bounds during the Nine Years War* and needed, in imes of European warfare, convoy-protection in the North Sea and the Bay of Biscay and even within the Mediterranean.[14] For this reason, and also with an ye to possible conflict with Denmark–Norway, the ships of the Swedish fleet ended to be large. Of the fifty men-of-war Sweden had in the year 1700, hirty-eight were ships of the line and only twelve frigates.

Small detachments in Stockholm and Gothenburg secured the capital and the vestern approaches, but the largest part of the navy was based on Karlskrona. From Karlskrona the southern part of the peninsula could be defended and all parts of the empire could be speedily reached: with fair wind and weather in wo to three days, though in the stormy conditions of spring and autumn it night take up to a fortnight to sail to any individual port. There was no perma-nent naval station in Finland – a fact which has been much criticized by modern Finnish historians who have blamed many of the misfortunes of the Great Northern War on this omission[15] – since little need for a separate naval establishment in the eastern Baltic was felt. The Brandenburg and Polish navies vere negligible and Russia had no access to the Baltic. Small Swedish squad-ons, such as those used on Lake Peipus and at the mouth of the Neva during he early stages of the war, were easily built or detached from the frigate-fleet. The navy itself could be added to, not only by new building, but by the use of nerchant-ships which, according to ancient Swedish custom, were favoured by customs regulations in direct proportion to their usefulness as armed

* It then reached its highest total (three hundred ships fit for long voyages) of the great-power period.

men-of-war in time of need.[16] It was hoped, however, that such stop-gap measures as the use of merchant-ships could be avoided now the permanent navy had been built, allowing the mercantile marine to carry on, even in war-time, its valuable trade.

The new navy was a source of pride, and was not to be risked lightly. There was comfort in the thought that an Anglo-Dutch squadron would arrive in the spring and there was no intention of taking risks till it was close enough for junction. It was decided that Sweden would refrain from action, either by land or sea, against the King of Denmark until she could act with her fellow-guarantors. In the meantime Swedish statesmen took care to emphasize Charles XII's willingness to come to terms with Denmark in respect of the Holstein-Gottorp troubles. Piper told Guiscard that the King, as well as the whole Council, would welcome Louis XIV's help in re-establishing peaceful conditions between Duke Frederick and King Frederick.[17] The main Swedish diplomatic efforts were, however, directed towards speeding up action by the guarantors: the Maritime Powers were reminded of the commitments Charles XII had accepted by ratifying the January treaties; with Hanover, persistent Danish refusal to acknowledge the electoral title was exploited.

III

Behind the shield of joint action by the Altona guarantors Swedish military and diplomatic planners hoped to achieve the goal of inflicting a decisive defeat on the Danish navy. If Frederick IV's fleet could be brought to battle against the overwhelming odds of the Anglo-Dutch squadron joined to the Swedish main fleet, Sweden would achieve operational control of the Baltic for long enough to permit her to turn towards the enemies in the east without fear of Danish–Norwegian attack in the rear. Time was to show that the Maritime Powers had no intention of being used in this way,* which would in effect upset that balance between the two Scandinavian powers which it was in their interest to preserve; and it was realized in Sweden that a measure of luck would be needed to bring off the coup.

In the meantime, preparations for the summer campaign, both with Frederick IV and Augustus in mind, went ahead. Swedish subjects serving abroad were called home[18] and the army was mobilized. Ten thousand troops were stationed along the Norwegian border to guard against invasion and sixteen thousand were concentrated in the south of Sweden so that they could be brought into play either against Denmark or against the Elector-King. Army expenses were on the whole defrayed by the so-called *durchgård*, a traditional levy for food and lodging during the march of an expeditionary corps to the theatre of action; but ready cash to complete the fitting out of the navy was hard to find. Concessions were made to the nobility in the hope that the First Estate would lend money to the Crown, Charles being persuaded to

* See below, pp. 134ff.

old over the outstanding resumption cases. Loans at six per cent proved luggish but Piper and Wrede, 'to encourage the credit', put up 10,600 *daler* vhich saved the day.[19]

Preparations were also made for the King's move south. Silver and linen, lorses and dogs and servants were chosen and sent ahead. Decisions were nade on which officials should go with Charles and which should stay in tockholm. Oxenstierna, Wallenstedt and Wrede were entrusted with the .dministration in the capital, while Piper, Polus, Åkerhielm and Cederhielm ravelled south to form the nucleus of the Chancery-in-the-field. A regular orrespondence was arranged between Oxenstierna and Rehnskiöld – to be ead by the King – for contact between the head of the Chancery and the ommander-in-chief. The Council was not given any special powers, so as not o revive the pre-absolutist tradition of its taking charge at home when the ing went to war, but a committee of the Council was constituted as a defence-commission' with special responsibility for keeping up the strength of he army. The Colleges were given more scope than in peacetime. Local and provincial governors were asked to direct all letters to the respective Colleges nd not to the King so that officials could sift what matters needed to be for-varded to headquarters. The *Statskontor* was given powers of anticipation of ncome to defray expenses of the armed forces. Swedish diplomats were ordered to correspond both with Charles XII and with the Stockholm Chan-ery, but decisions in matters of foreign policy were, without exception, to be eserved for the King.

On 14 April, early in the morning, Charles quietly left Stockholm,[20] having aid goodbye to his grandmother and sisters the night before. The Duke of Holstein-Gottorp travelled with him, en route for the army in Germany. On he way south they received news that Hedvig Sophia's child – a boy – had peen born and christened Charles Frederick.* The King's letter of congratu-ation to his elder sister has been lost; but that to Ulla, now twelve years old, complimenting her on her dignity as an aunt opens the series of letters which lave survived from him for the war years.[21]

That these years should prove as long as they did and that he should never see either his favourite sister Hedvig or his grandmother again probably did lot occur to Charles. Older people could not help contemplating what would lappen if Charles should be killed in battle. The Queen-Grandmother was leard to thank God 'for the prince in the cradle if anything should happen o the King',[22] and the beginnings of a division into parties for a succession-truggle can already be discerned. The uncertainty which absolutism had prought to old constitutional arrangements affected the issue. According to pre-absolutist law women could inherit the crown, an elder daughter having preferential right over a younger one if both were unmarried. Absolutism, it vas argued by some, had implicitly changed the situation in favour of a male

---

* The Duke paid a visit to Stockholm to see his wife and child before embarking on 23 May at Gothenburg for Germany.

succession, and the respective claims of Hedvig Sophia, her son, and Ulrika
Eleonora were debated. Both sisters were ambitious. When Hedvig Sophia
was widowed in 1702, she refrained from remarriage mainly because her
advisers insisted that this might prejudice her chances if – God forbid –
Charles should die;[23] and Ulrika Eleonora, after her elder sister's death in
1708, was careful not to accept Frederick of Hesse as a suitor without Charles'
permission lest the prospects of her nephew should rise and her own fall.* I
was agreed that Charles, an absolute king, could lay down binding rules for
the succession, but he – devoted to both sisters and (when he got to know him)
to his nephew – refused to choose between them and shelved the problem
behind repeated references to marriage and heirs of his own body 'when peace
comes'.

     In the pre-1715 period the succession-issue affected the households of the
different members of the royal family and officials with an eye to their future
careers more than the royal family. Ulrika as an adolescent found speculation
about what would happen on her brother's death offensive and answered
hotly that she was only too happy to forget any right she might possess in the
hope that Charles would come home safe from the war and marry 'his
Sophia'.[24] As for the King, it was years before he began to be willing to admit
even to himself that any succession issue existed. He was strongly attached to
home and family; news from Stockholm, letters and portraits from the family
became increasingly important to him as the war went on and on and his
longing for emotional security concentrated on his affection for his sisters.

IV

The arrival of the Anglo-Dutch squadron was fixed for the end of May.
Frederick IV, convinced at last that it would materialize, tried to come to
grips with the Swedish navy before that date but it stayed snug in harbour and
Danish attempts to take Gothenburg and thus cut Charles's communication
with the west were unsuccessful. The military position also became alarming
when Frederick IV learnt that Dutch troops were on their way to join the
Swedes in Germany and when Hanoverian troops – emboldened by this –
began to cooperate with Gyllenstierna. To improve his chances, the Danish
King decided to storm Tønning before the Dutch arrived. On 19 May he
moved into the outwork of the fortress. This became, however, the signal for
the Swedes and Hanoverians to cross the Elbe into Holstein, and when his
attack was beaten off on 22 May Frederick found it best to give up the siege
and march to meet the forces of the guarantor powers now commanded by the
Elector of Hanover in person and amounting to near twenty thousand in all.
News that the Anglo-Dutch fleet had sailed reached Frederick about the same
time.

     Danish expectations of having to deal with Sweden alone had not succeeded

* See below, p. 371.

'he Tsar's attempts to restrain the Dutch had failed, Brandenburg had
:mained inactive (in spite of tempting offers of a share in the coming partition
f Sweden) since Augustus produced no victories in Livonia, and William III
ireatened to invade Cleve if the Elector should feel tempted to make common
ause with the anti-Swedish coalition. Swedish success was not, however, in
iverse proportion to Danish failure. The guarantors intended to remain in
rm control to prevent Sweden from using the situation to her own advantage.
'hey did this by completely ignoring – to the point of pretending incredulity –
he coalition against Charles XII in all negotiations with Sweden. Heinsius and
>tanhope, in conferences with Lillieroot at The Hague, found him 'very hasty
o engage us directly in a warre'[25] and learnt their lesson. They went out of
heir way to stress to the Emperor, the Tsar and the Elector of Brandenburg
hat they were not acting as warring parties but as guarantors of Altona to
estore the Duke of Holstein-Gottorp to the lands Frederick of Denmark had
aken from him. Even this they intended to do by diplomatic pressure rather
han by military action. The situation in Holstein settled down to marches and
ounter-marches to lend emphasis to the many offers of mediation which were
ent to the King of Denmark from Leopold, from Louis XIV and from the
;uarantors themselves. Charles XII left the Duke of Holstein-Gottorp – now
vith the army – free to accept or reject any peace offers made to him; but the
lisinclination of the guarantors for action did not bode well for Swedish
>lans to knock Denmark out of the coalition under the Altona umbrella.

The Maritime Powers were sincere enough in wishing to restore peace in
he North, but they, naturally enough, looked at the situation from the point
>f view of their own interests and preoccupations. Their main objective was to
ind a solution for the Holstein-Gottorp problems permanent enough not to
enflame' either the Empire or Scandinavia should the Spanish succession
>roblem lead to war. If peace were not maintained in Germany, Louis XIV
night prove intractable on the death of Carlos II; if Sweden were not free of
he Holstein-Gottorp incubus the Maritime Powers could not call on the
uid pro quo arranged in the treaties of January 1700. Both Denmark and
;weden would have to be restrained: Frederick IV by a direct confrontation
ind Charles XII by a strictly limited cooperation.

This Charles experienced when the squadron of the Maritime Powers –
hirteen Dutch men-of-war and twelve English – arrived on 9 June off Gothen-
>urg and had by the 16th moved '3 or 4 leagues short of the Sound', where
hey waited for the Swedes to join them.[26] Charles XII, with Piper and Rehn-
,kiöld, on board the flagship *Kung Carl* left Karlskrona on 16 June with thirty-
:ight of the line carrying in all 2,700 guns. But junction of the three fleets
>roved too difficult. The Swedes soon gave up their attempts to persuade Sir
George Rooke and Philippe Almonde to accept Wachtmeister as a joint com-
nander: the fact that he was the highest ranking officer and his King's 'Master
>f the Baltic'[27] was politely ignored lest Charles XII take control of the opera-
ions. Independent command with cooperation by consultation was the most

that could be achieved; but even after this had been agreed contrary winds
unexpected storms followed by dead calms, slowed down the Swedish progress
while a cleverly chosen station by the Danish commander across the broad
channel* of the Sound kept the guarantors apart. The Swedish fleet had hoped
to meet with the Danish one – forty ships strong – on their way from Karl
skrona to the Sound and risk a battle, but Admiral Juel had withdrawn and
put himself between the Swedes and their allies in such a manner that whoever
attacked him would do so under unfavourable conditions. Tempers began to
fray all round. Almonde complained of lack of information about draughts
and soundings; the English minister, John Robinson, hurrying by land and
sea from one fleet to another to smooth matters over, found the English 'more
than enough apprehensive' that the 'Spanish pace' at which the Swedes had
proceeded would 'spoil all' and the Swedes 'at first not much more content
with us than we with them'.[28]

Charles XII cut the Gordian knot by ordering Wachtmeister to take the
greater part† of the Swedish fleet through the shallow and treacherous
Flintrännan (the Flatts), close to the Swedish shore to effect a junction without using the main channel of the Sound. Wachtmeister was naturally reluctant to risk so many ships,[29] but things went well on 3–4 July and Charles XII's
letter of thanks to his admiral was warm and heartfelt.

With the junction achieved on the 7th, the difference in approach to Denmark between the Anglo-Dutch squadron (ordered to avoid 'a general rupture') and the Swedes (keen to come to grips with the Danish navy) came into
the open. The Maritime Powers intended to use their naval force to exert
pressure on Frederick IV by a demonstration of guarantor solidarity while
counselling delay and patience to the Swedes. Juel, for his part, withdrew to
Copenhagen harbour, helped by wind from a quarter which permitted him to
retire safely and then changed to prevent a Swedish pursuit. Some half-
hearted bombing of the Danish fleet in port took place on 14 and 17 July but
the Swedes failed to persuade their fellow-guarantors to attack Juel's ships.[30]

V

The Swedish high command had to think of alternative measures and in their
consultations with Rooke and Almonde put forward the idea of a Swedish
landing on Zealand, protected by the joint fleets: this would exert pressure on
Denmark from the north, reinforcing that from the guarantor army in the
south. Such a move might also, the Swedes argued in private, be used to ruin
the Danish fleet. Zealand had but five thousand troops left for its defence, and
a march on the Danish capital might encircle Juel's fleet from land and sea.
The plan, devised by Rehnskiöld and Stuart and discussed with Charles XII,

---

* Kongsdypet in Danish, Kungsdjupet in Swedish.

† The largest ships had to be left behind and some detachments had already been made for
other duties. Of those that used Flintrännan, five touched bottom but were refloated.

proved acceptable to the Maritime Powers since Frederick – hoping for spectacular success by Augustus and eagerly awaiting a Russian diversion – was
adroitly avoiding coming to heel. He protested his willingness to reopen the
Pinneberg conferences and hinted at recognition of the Ninth Electorate, but
he could not be pinned down. A descent on Zealand would also have the
advantage of preventing Swedish reinforcements in Holstein with their
attendant danger of increased tension in the Empire.

Preparations for the Swedish landing were speedily made; Stuart reconnoitred and Rehnskiöld collected the invasion force in Landskrona. Charles
XII, who had intended to join the army in Holstein if the naval battle he hoped
for had ensued, decided to take part in the venture. It was originally timed for
21 July but a storm caused delay. Stuart, up at 3 o'clock in the morning on
the 22nd to gauge wind and weather, found the King – keyed up like any
young soldier at the prospect of action stations – pacing the harbour wall. A
sensible man, he gave Charles work to do; the two went to Stuart's room to
study the plans for the descent once more.[31] On the 23rd the wind abated,
though it was still of gale force, and the first four thousand troops were
embarked in pouring rain. Robinson, who came along to wish Charles 'a good
voyage and happy success' found him busy, as he had been 'from 5 in the
morning' and was to continue 'till 11–12 at night', helping to get the soldiers
to their allotted ships.[32]

The next morning, at 7 o'clock, the transports sailed for their rendezvous,
near the isle of Ven, with a detachment of the combined fleets to escort them
to the coast of Zealand and protect their landing with its guns. Stuart's plan
depended for its success on a feint to draw Danish troops away from the spot
he had chosen for the landing at Humlebæk. The coastline was well protected
by fortifications and against the five thousand troops stationed on Zealand the
Swedes, because of the improvised nature of the descent, could only land four
thousand men at a time. Moreover, the Swedish preparations had been visible
from the church-towers and windmills of Denmark so that an invasion was
expected. Rooke was doubtful of success,[33] but Stuart's scheme unfolded as
planned. After spending the stormy night of 24 July uncomfortably at anchor
off Ven, the troops were moved in a feint against Rungsted, south of Humlebæk, and then swiftly put ashore, at a point where they were opposed by only
eight hundred men. The main force of the combined fleets bottled Juel's
ships up in Copenhagen and the guns of the detachment sent with the transports kept the Danish army positions under fire as arranged. Stuart's eye for
suitable terrain had picked on a spot where the steep banks rising from a
narrow beach made it difficult for the defenders to take proper aim at the
landing-craft so that the Swedes could wade ashore without exposing themselves to enemy fire. Danish reinforcements from Rungsted were delayed,
as expected, by a river obstacle. Swedish losses were therefore small. Stuart
himself was wounded but continued in command till the bridgehead was
secured.

When Charles XII's turn came to land he found that the right wing where h
had been placed had no real fighting to do, since the left wing, led by Rehn
skiöld, had already overcome the brunt of the resistance. The King's teacher
kept an eye on their pupil, both to ensure his safety and to observe his bearin
under fire, and were well pleased with him. Stuart noted in his journal of th
operation:

> His Royal Majesty himself animated and spoke to the soldiers with an incompar
> able charm, showed also an exceptionally great Conduite in correcting everythin
> which he noticed getting into disorder, and wanted later always to be among th
> first, wherefore also His Majesty jumped into the water before the Eschalou
> touched bottom, and then all the others followed him.[34]

In Swedish propaganda full use was made of Charles XII's acquitting him
self well in his first action. In a 'relation' speedily made available to foreig
diplomats the victory was attributed to:

> the heroic Courage of His Majesty alone, not only in overcoming so many difficulty
> of contrary Winds and Currents and other disappointments, but in his rangeing an
> animating His Troops with the conduct of an old General, and lastly his incompar
> able valour, having Himself led on the first Battalion of the right Wing withou
> any other concern, save only that He was not on the left, where there was mor
> opposition.[35]

Behind this flowery language and the exaggeration in attributing the whol
success of the landing to an eighteen-year-old in his first action, there was
kernel of truth: the King's strong support for Stuart's plan, his willingness t
take risks and his making light of difficulties had been valuable, and the sym
bolic unity of command which his presence gave was important for morale.

The impact of the Zealand landing on Frederick IV was strong enough t
ruin the real objective of it as seen by the Swedish military command. By
August more than ten thousand Swedish troops, including cavalry, had bee
landed at the bridgehead, and artillery and ammunition had also been brough
across the Sound. Danish forces on Zealand had withdrawn to Copenhagen
The Swedes considered a storming of the Danish capital too risky,* and
estimated that they could bring about its surrender by bombardment from th
sea and land. Their blockade – effective since 29 July – was already keeping
the town short of food. Even if the Danes, caught between the Swedish army
and the combined navies, should destroy their fleet rather than letting it fall
into Swedish hands, the goal would have been reached.

On 11 August the Swedish army was on the point of marching on Copenhagen when a messenger arrived from Georg Ludwig of Hanover with the
news that Frederick was willing to make peace, and Charles was requested to
stop hostilities and prepare for immediate evacuation of Zealand. The Danish
king, fearing for his capital and even more for his fleet, had indeed promised
to recognize Georg Ludwig as Elector, the ultimate union of the Lüneburg

* Memories of Charles X's failure were a potent deterrent.

territories, and the restoration of the Duke of Holstein-Gottorp to his possessions. These promises paved the way for a conference at Travendal and by the time Charles XII received the Elector's message peace had indeed been signed, on 8 August, between Frederick IV of Denmark–Norway and Frederick IV, Duke of Holstein-Gottorp, whereby the King undertook to evacuate ducal land, to allow the contested *jus armorum* and to pay a compensation of two hundred and sixty thousand *rigsdaler* for damage suffered and loss of income sustained during the occupation. The treaty of Travendal, signed also by the Altona powers, guaranteed this settlement and contained the significant clause (the so-called 'amnesty' clause) that Frederick IV promised not to act 'like an enemy' towards either Sweden or the House of Lüneburg, nor help their enemies. At the insistence of the Swedish negotiator, a special act was also signed by the guarantors to the effect that they understood Frederick as pledging his word not to help Augustus of Saxony-Poland in his war against Charles XII[36] – though some of those present, being unaware of the real situation, found the special act unnecessary and inexplicable: what possible connexion could there be between the Holstein-Gottorp problem and Augustus's invasion of Livonia?

The chagrin of being cheated of the fruit of their planning was obvious in Charles XII's headquarters on 11 August. The Maritime Powers had already foiled Swedish hopes of levying Sound dues during the temporary occupation of Zealand, having countered arguments that this would only be to take a leaf out of Frederick IV's book (he was using the Duke of Holstein-Gottorp's revenues in ducal Sleswig) with the threat of withdrawing their squadrons. To allow Swedish pretensions in this respect seemed too dangerous a precedent and might encourage Swedish ambitions. 'They had to yield to us', Robinson tersely summed up the outcome of talks on the Sound dues between the naval commanders, himself and Åkerhielm.[37]

A tug-of-war broke out between the Chancery officials and Charles XII (presumably backed by military advisers, though we lack specific information on this point) as soon as the message of 11 August arrived.[38] The King was for continuing the march on Copenhagen and beginning the siege of it till certain news should arrive of the peace having been signed: after all, the Elector's letter spoke of promises, not of hard facts. Civilian advisers were doubtful as to the wisdom of this; but reluctantly agreed that Charles had a point. On 13 August, however, with the army on its way, an express arrived from the Duke of Holstein-Gottorp to say that peace was signed: so did one from Rooke to Wachtmeister (present at headquarters) giving the chief points of the treaty of Travendal. The Swedish admiral was asked to tell his King that now that the objective of the guarantors had been gained the Anglo-Dutch fleets would return home, though they were willing to help escort the Swedish army back to Scania if Charles XII stopped his march on Copenhagen and immediately began preparations for re-embarkation.

It was obvious that the plan to catch the Danish fleet had foundered, but

Charles was reluctant to call the march off till he had received a copy of th
Travendal treaty and judged whether Frederick IV had really been forced ou
of the anti-Swedish coalition. Sweden's security was at stake and he ought nc
to take the risk, though the Duke of Holstein-Gottorp might have bee
satisfied, of Sweden being left with a war on two fronts. The Chancer
officials argued that Sweden could not afford to fall out with the Maritim
Powers whatever the contents of the Peace of Travendal – a view they sincerel
held and in which they had become strengthened during their abortive nego
tiations over the Sound dues. They played on strings which they knew woul
touch the King. He would, they told him, stand before Europe as an aggresso
if he continued the march and the peace was found to satisfy the Duke's pre
tensions. If, on the other hand, he voluntarily abstained from achieving
great gain for Sweden he would prove himself a man of honour, leaving Zea
land the moment he was told the Duke's wrongs had been righted. The reaso
given for the Zealand descent was the achievement of this objective: mus
Sweden show herself guilty of ulterior motives? They reminded him that ther
was an urgent need to deal with Augustus who had made a direct attack o
the Swedish empire. Surely Frederick had now learnt his lesson in Sleswi
and would not proceed to invade Scania the moment the Swedes turne
their backs?[39]

The gist of these arguments was accepted by Charles XII. Wachtmeiste
sided with the Chancery group, Stuart was in Sweden 'nursing his Con
tusion',[40] and – presumably – Rehnskiöld and the King decided that nothin
could be gained by being too stiff. On the 13th therefore Piper informed th
Danish authorities in Copenhagen that the Swedes would evacuate Zealand
Frederick IV having made peace with the Duke of Holstein-Gottorp; Rehn
skiöld went to Scania to collect transport-ships; and the Gothenburg expedi
tion intended for the relief of Tønning was countermanded.[41] The next day
copies of the Treaty of Travendal and of the special act reached Charles x
and, to everyone's relief, the amnesty-clause was found to give no loophole fo
continued Danish cooperation with Augustus.

The need to put pressure on Charles XII on 13 August has often beer
adduced as evidence of the King's dangerous rashness and obstinacy from th
very opening of the Great Northern War. Charles's prudence in not abandon
ing prematurely or lightly one method of knocking Denmark out of the wa
before another had been examined deserves, however, some recognition. He
knew the military problems of defence better than the Chancery officials; he
was familiar with the Stuart–Rehnskiöld plan for destruction of the Danish
navy and/or defeat of the Danish army before turning towards Augustus; and
he was well versed through studies of past history in the Swedish tradition o
how to cope with a war on two fronts: 'It has always been the Maxime here i
such cases, to end matters first with Denmark.'[42] Equally commendable wa
his decision to accept the advice of those he realized were better qualified thar
himself to judge the impact of Swedish actions on foreign observers.

It must have been with some relief that Charles studied the documents he
eceived on 14 August. These offered an alternative way of restraining
'rederick IV, less sure than a naval or military defeat, but yet an alternative
vhich could be made to work. The guarantee of the signatories gave some
ecurity that Denmark–Norway would not attack Sweden in the near future.
juarantees of that nature were never foolproof; having them put into effect
lways cost something. Charles had recently experienced this himself by the
bligations Sweden had to take on to make the guarantors of the Treaty of
ltona move.* Unless the fortunes of war smiled on Charles XII, no guarantees
ould in the long run restrain Frederick IV. But in the short run, Sweden's
escent on Zealand, made possible by the cooperation of the Anglo-Dutch
quadron and the 'Altona' army, had achieved a breathing-space. If this were
tilized to the full, Augustus of Saxony might be forced to make peace and
Denmark would be robbed of any ally.

* See above, pp. 112–13.

2

Narva

Once Charles XII had found the Travendal peace acceptable, speedy removal o
the Swedish army from Zealand was essential. Not only would it be dangerou
to delay its return to Sweden beyond the departure of the English and Dutc
squadrons – for with numerical superiority in ships once more, who coul
guarantee that Frederick IV might not be tempted to attack the Swedis
fleet? – but it was urgently necessary to free soldiers and transport-ships for
major operation intended to dislodge Augustus from Livonia before winte
storms and ice should render large-scale reinforcements of Swedis
forces in the Baltic provinces or Germany impossible. There was a fain
hope also that speed in transporting troops from Sweden to the trans
Baltic Swedish territories might act as a restraining influence on Peter o
Russia.

The Tsar had made a thirty-year armistice with Turkey at the end of July,
news of which became known in Scandinavia at about the time of the Traven
dal peace, but the Russian action against Sweden which this was thought t
forebode might be prevented if Charles XII were able to mount his counter
attack against Augustus before the campaign season of 1700 was over
Absolute certainty about the Tsar's intentions was impossible; the Russia
envoy, Chilkov, who arrived in Sweden in the summer of 1700 and followe
Charles XII to Zealand to present his credentials, gave assurances of friendshi
and offered his congratulations on the successful descent. He was receive
with all possible goodwill so that the Tsar might find no excuse to break o
relations. That the very day of Chilkov's audience, 20 August, was the one o
which Tsar Peter in Moscow issued his declaration of war on Charles XII di
not become known in Sweden till much later.[2]

The evacuation of Zealand was spurred on both by the Danish governmen
and by the commanders of the Anglo-Dutch squadrons. The former was kee
to get rid of unbidden guests;[3] the latter were anxious to reach home port
before bad weather set in. Both helped Charles by providing transport-ship
and Rooke and Almonde gave cover in case of Danish treachery.[4] By 2.
August every Swedish soldier was on his own side of the Sound, the Kin
having been one of the last to cross. On 28 August the Swedish fleet left fo

arlskrona and the following day the men-of-war of the Maritime Powers set
il for home 'with a very good gale of wind'.[5]
A burning question for the Swedish high command throughout the summer
onths[6] had been where to direct their counter-attack on Augustus. It was
nerally accepted that more troops must be sent to the Baltic provinces, if
ıly as a precaution against Russian hostilities; but there were arguments in
vour of a suggestion put forward* that the main attack on Augustus should
: made in Saxony. Augustus had invaded Livonia with Saxon troops and the
epublic of Poland was emphatic in its disassociation from the aggression of
e King-Elector, though most Swedes, including Bengt Oxenstierna, doubted
all Poles were as innocent as they protested in this matter.[7] It would there-
re be logical and natural, as well as tempting, to force Augustus to withdraw
s Saxons from Livonia by using the Swedish troops in Pomerania and
emen-Verden as the nucleus of an army whose objective would be an
vasion of Saxony. The Swedish forces in Germany had been reinforced
ıring the summer to such an extent that even if six thousand were left on
.rrison duties, ten thousand were immediately available for this purpose;
ith further strengthening from the Zealand army an operational force cap-
ole of coping with Augustus could be created. An important consideration
favour of this plan was that a march into Augustus's Electorate would move
e war from Swedish territory into enemy land, freeing Livonia from the
ospect of becoming a main battlefield. A Swedish invasion of Saxony
eant crossing Brandenburg territory, but it was argued that its Elector had
rmitted Saxon troops the liberty of transit and that he was not likely to
oject forcibly to a Swedish march provided strict discipline was kept. That
harles XII's army was capable of such discipline had been demonstrated
ıring the Zealand campaign. Observers had commented on the absolute and
.ccessful control of the soldiers in their relationships to the civil population
ıd had even concluded that: 'The strict discipline observ'd in Seeland, and
e great tenderness shown towards those Inhabitants has incommoded the
ıedish Troops not a little, and returned them worse than they went, though
ot to any such degree as can render them unfit for the farther Service they
e design'd to do.'[8]
Speculation as to this 'farther Service' was ripe in Europe. The diplomats
ho waited for Charles XII in Hälsingborg and followed him to Kristianstad
ıd Karlshamn eagerly picked upon rumours or preparations from which
ey could give their principals ideas about the destination of the troops which
ere preparing for embarkation in south-east Sweden.
Charles XII was personally attracted to the Saxony invasion plan, regarding
as 'the promptest means whereby the King of Poland can be brought to
ason', and orders which would permit the plan to be put into effect, either
a main attack or as a diversion to facilitate Swedish operations in Livonia,

---

* Mauritz Vellingk seems to have been the first to have put this suggestion on paper; the Duke
Holstein-Gottorp supported it: see G. Jonasson, *Karl XIII och hans rådgivare*, p. 168.

F

were sent to Gyllenstierna in Germany soon after Charles's return to Swede
The prospect of action against Saxony was, however, strenuously opposed
the Maritime Powers.[10] From their point of view it would throw away t
fruit of the relatively expensive labour to settle the Holstein-Gottorp issue
pacified Europe.

The overriding interest of William III and the States General was stal
conditions until the Spanish succession issue had been settled. Carlos
death was expected and the second Anglo-Dutch partition treaty with Lo
XIV had prepared a scheme whereby the Spanish heritage could be so divid
that the balance of power in Europe would be maintained;* but neither Spa
nor the Emperor Leopold favoured partition and neither William nor Lo
could be certain of being able to control either Madrid or Vienna. Indee
Leopold who resisted the thought of partition did so in the belief (proved
be justified) that if war should break out between him and Louis, the Maritir
Powers would – sooner or later – be brought to fight on his side agair
France. The Emperor's refusal to accede to the second partition treaty did n
at this stage particularly worry William III,† who tended to fret more abc
the detrimental effect which hostilities anywhere in the Empire might have
French loyalty to the treaty. Saxo-Swedish warfare on Imperial soil w
anathema to William, therefore, because he regarded it as likely to encoura
Louis XIV, in the event of Carlos's death during such armed conflict, to ask f
higher terms than those laid down in the second partition treaty.

There was yet a further danger implied. If war should break out over t
Spanish succession issue William had to reckon with the involvement of t
Maritime Powers and must look to Germany, the normal recruiting grou
for auxiliary troops to be subsidized or hired with English and Dutch mon
Memories of the Thirty Years War were still strong: what German prin
could be expected to send his soldiers out of his own land if a Swedish arn
was fighting on Imperial soil? It was thus imperative for William III a
Heinsius to dissuade Charles XII from any invasion of Saxony. They could p
on the gratitude of Sweden for the naval help of Rooke and Almonde. Th
could also play on Swedish fears that they might, in certain circumstanc
not honour their guarantees of Travendal.

Gratitude was on the whole uppermost in Swedish minds, for quite ap
from the support in the Holstein-Gottorp issue, William and Heinsius w
showing goodwill towards Sweden by promising, under the general h
clause stipulated in the January treaties, to send quantities of cloth for u
forms, gunpowder and other necessities to help Sweden in the strug
against Augustus. At Rooke's farewell visit to Charles XII in his Zealand hea
quarters, the admiral had been received with great cordiality and Swed

* For this, and the fate of the treaty after Carlos's death in November 1700, see Hatt
'Louis XIV and his fellow-monarchs', *Louis XIV* (ed. J.Rule).

† See Hatton, loc. cit., for the assumption of William and Heinsius that the will of Ca
would leave the whole of Spain to one of Leopold's sons and that the partition treaty would
used to wring enough concessions from the Emperor to prevent Louis going to war.

...ops had staged a ceremonial march-past in his honour. Robinson, on return to Stockholm in September, reported the praises which every one ...ped upon him for the services of William III,[11] and the desire of Sweden for ...ther help according to the treaty of 1700: 'Equivalents in money would ...ommodate this count more than Troops.'[12] Though the collaboration of ...: joint fleets had at times been difficult owing to the disparate aims of ...eden and her fellow-guarantors, there was no denying that without the ...p of the Maritime Powers and the consequent immobilization of the ...nish army the Zealand descent would not have been possible, while the ...arantee of England and the States General of Travendal formed the very ...sis for any operation against Augustus in the autumn of 1700.

The positive attitude of the Maritime Powers compared favourably with ...t of Louis XIV whose ambassador, Guiscard, had scuttled between Scania ...d Copenhagen in a way which put the Swedes 'out of humour' during the ...mmer.[13] French disinclination to do anything effective to honour the ...arantee of the Peace of Oliva of 1660, which Augustus had infringed by his ...asion of Livonia was contrasted with the help offered under the January ...aties from London and The Hague. A Swedish suggestion that Louis XIV ...ght cooperate in the proposed Saxony invasion as guarantor of Oliva was ...ended to test French reaction and demonstrated that France did not intend ...go beyond offers of mediation.[14]

II

...e uncompromising neutrality of France compared with the willingness of ...: Maritime Powers to honour their treaty obligations influenced Swedish ...iberations on the coming operations. It was obvious that Charles XII could ...t in the circumstances afford to ignore the wishes of William III and Heinsius ...o pressed strongly for abandonment of the Saxony project; and though no ...cific promise was made that Sweden would for all future abstain from an ...asion of Saxony, the Maritime Powers were assured that in view of their ...ections Charles XII would direct his counter-attack on Augustus to ...onia.[15]

There were, however, other considerations which pulled in the same direc-...n. Denmark and Brandenburg let it be known that they would not stand ...y by if the Saxon Electorate were invaded. More significantly, news arrived ...m Ingria that a Russian attack was imminent: Tsar Peter's troops were ...rching towards its borders in such numbers that there could no longer be ...y doubt of his warlike intentions.[16] Before the end of September the Russian ...laration of war was known in Charles XII's headquarters in Karlshamn. ...o enemies in the East Baltic provinces must relegate the Saxony project to ...ere diversion irrespective of the attitude of the Maritime Powers:* every

---

See below, pp. 194 ff., however, for periods when the Anglo-Dutch veto of a Saxony invasion of greater significance.

Swedish soldier who could be embarked before the onset of the winter w
needed to help defend Ingria and Livonia from the double onslaught of Pe
and Augustus.

The Tsar motivated his attack by 'indignities and humiliation' which he h
suffered in Riga when he stayed there for some days en route for his Europe
travels. His accusations made Dahlberg indignant: the Tsar had insisted
1697 that his incognito be respected and as much ceremony and civility h
been shown to the Russian party as was compatible with this request. H
could you treat the Tsar according to his proper rank when he amused hims
by playing the role of a footman during dinner – stationing himself behind t
chair of one of his entourage and waiting on him? The only cause for co
plaint that Dahlberg could think of was that the Swedes had not shown pleas
when some of the Russians made drawings and measurements of the n
fortifications.[17]

In retrospect few historians would deny that the Tsar's complaint was bu
cover or a rationalization,[18] an attempt to convert what contemporar
regarded as an unjust war to a just one. Peter was genuinely convinced that
was morally entitled to take back land which his predecessors had held, ev
if – as in the case of Ingria – such possession had been short-lived. Since
had not kissed the cross at the renewal of the Suedo-Russian treaties in 16
he could argue that he had shown his non-recognition of documents wh
made Karelia and Ingria part of the Swedish empire and was therefore fr
from observance of the treaties in question: a piece of sophistry not untypi
of the age. In the eyes of Charles XII, Tsar Peter was certainly a straig
forward and honest enemy since he – in contrast to Frederick IV and Augus
– did issue a formal declaration of war.[19] Even when Frederick William
Prussia and Georg Ludwig of Hanover (at a time when he is better known
George I of Britain) joined the anti-Swedish coalition, they did not displ
Peter in this particular table of ranks: though these two eventually decla
war, they had previously appropriated Swedish territory under the guise
friendship.

The defence against Augustus had moved in fits and starts during the spr
and summer of 1700, conforming too much to the pattern of Augustu
attack (which in its turn waxed and waned with European conjunctures)
please the Swedish high command and Charles XII himself. Dahlberg h
saved Riga from a surprise attack in February; Major-General Maidel
May defeated a major part of the Saxon army and forced them to retire acr
the Dvina; the Livonian nobility remained loyal or at least quiescent,[20]
General Otto Vellingk, ordered to retake the fort of Dünamünde, plead
(with some justification) difficulties which prevented him from doing so a
received a letter from Charles XII which is perhaps the first (to my knowled
of those rockets which became as typical of the King's contacts with
officers as his letters of thanks and praise when courage and determinat
had been shown, whatever the issue of the action. The contents of the let

ay well have been inspired by others, but the tone is unmistakably that of
arles: the sentences rather more involved than in later years, but the mean-
g crystal clear. 'It is good to exercise caution,' so the letter ended, 'but not to
ch an extent that all [opportunities] become lost which might have had
ccessful issues if one had not used too much prudence.'[21]
Vellingk's diffidence gave Augustus an opportunity for a second attempt on
ga: in mid-July the King-Elector moved seventeen thousand men over the
er and began a siege of the town while Vellingk retired north. The situation
s potentially dangerous since the Livonian Estates, having forsworn the
bellion which Patkul strove to organize after the Maidel victory, might be
ble to change their minds if a Saxon success followed. The news of Traven-
l halted Augustus's military operations however. He was shrewd, as well as
acious, and earned a reputation for double-dealing second to none among
e European rulers of his time.[22] Now, while with his right hand he sent
gent messages to Tsar Peter for succour, with his left he dispatched equally
gent appeals to Louis xiv to procure him an armistice with Charles xii; and
ile he thought it prudent to stop the bombardment of Riga and withdraw to
e southern bank of the Dvina once more, he took care to strengthen not
ly Dünamünde, but also the forts of Kokenhusen and Kobron which would
ep his lines of communication with his Russian ally open.[23]
The Saxon withdrawal from Riga did not become known to Charles xii till
himself landed at Pernau on 6 October; but the mediation offers of Louis
v were put before him before he left Sweden. These offers sparked off a
bate on the conduct of foreign policy in which the majority of the Chancery
ficials, both at the King's headquarters and in Stockholm, deplored the
ethods adopted by Charles xii. The beginning of this debate can be traced
ck to the moment when the King returned from Zealand and found himself
rsued by foreign diplomats: a Hanover representative wanted his explicit
arantee for the Danish recognition of the Ninth Electorate implied in the
eaty of Travendal; a Brandenburg emissary, uneasy at the rumours of a
vedish invasion of Saxony, offered his master's good offices with Augustus;
envoy from Leopold of Habsburg solicited Swedish support against the
cond partition treaty powers; while the French ambassador and those of the
aritime Powers urged Charles xii's accession to the second partition treaty.
he complaint of the Chancery men was that the King did not sufficiently
plore the possibilities which these various overtures offered and that he left
em insufficient instructions and/or power to act in his place with any pros-
ct of success. The Emperor's envoy was sent to negotiate with the Stock-
lm Chancery, but Oxenstierna felt handicapped and humiliated by having
talk in general terms only.[24] Even worse, the King was far too open and
rect: he told Guiscard that Sweden could not possibly join the signatories of
e second partition treaty as the Emperor was against the whole scheme and,
ain, Oxenstierna was discomfited when the Frenchman reported this to him
Stockholm.[25]

Charles XII's advisers on foreign affairs were at one with him in thinking inconceivable that Sweden would at this time, when she had trouble enou on her hands, commit herself in any line-up for the as yet hypothetical war the Spanish succession; but they felt alarmed at the King's failure to obser the conventions of their craft whereby negotiations were sometimes start not for their own sake but because suggestions followed up, overtu: returned, might yield results in the future, or at the very least provide use information about the intentions and plans of other powers. They argued th Charles XII's directness and brevity might waste valuable opportunities in t diplomatic struggle for the allegiance of the non-committed states in t Spanish issue. The expected behaviour, the normal one, in these circumstan — however deeply a ruler were engaged with problems of national or dynas importance – would be to negotiate with both sides in order to test and wei advantages which might come his way. In this respect the conduct of August of Saxony-Poland was to them more praiseworthy than that of their own rul Charles's preoccupation with the military preparations, urgent though the were, was regarded as excessive. Polus found it at times difficult to gain t King's ear for memoranda from Stockholm and on at least one occasion was firmly bowed out of the room before he got properly into the stride of l *exposé*.[26] Even Rehnskiöld in his correspondence with Oxenstierna deplor the King's lack of interest in the European vistas opening up.[27]

Charles XII's reaction to the French mediation offers high-lighted the diff ing attitudes of King and Chancery. Charles immediately accepted the offi of Louis XIV in the most civil and graceful manner, but to the Chancery seemed to put an obstacle in the way of peace by insisting that Augustus wo have to evacuate Swedish Livonia before an armistice were signed. This w tantamount to saying (so the civilian argument went) that he did not wa peace: one could not expect Augustus lightly to give up what land he h taken – was it not better to accept an armistice first to get negotiations start lest the King of Sweden be depicted as warlike and intractable?[28]

This debate has left great tracks in the historiography of the period. T letters in which the Chancery officials expressed their views both to Char XII and among themselves have been widely quoted and superimposed on t whole of the reign of the King so that we get too undifferentiated a picture o ruler who preferred the sword to the pen and despised diplomacy. There obviously some truth in this in so far as the attitude of the soldier tends differ (though one can think of exceptions)* from that of the diplomat. E two modifying factors must be taken into account. Firstly, the King's you and inexperience; Charles had to learn in the field of diplomacy as in oth fields of his job and it was only by degrees that he learnt to take the whi European situation into account. Secondly, Charles XII, responsible for m tary and foreign policy, is usually found to have a short-term military obj tive in view at times when the Chancery officials find him particularly annoyi

---

* One exception in the period is Marlborough.

intractable. In this particular instance, Charles suspected that Augustus's
ill to peace was dictated by a desire to delay the Swedish trans-Baltic expedi-
on till the season forbade it. Negotiations for an armistice were better post-
oned, he thought, and probably the high command thought so too, till the
my from Sweden stood in Livonia when the cards would no longer be
acked in favour of an enemy with greater military resources at hand. As
on as Charles xii had landed in Estonia, with Guiscard close at his heels,
gotiations began in earnest and Charles – having learnt that Riga was safe –
oved quite willing to proceed to an armistice while the Livonian forts of
unamünde, Kokenhusen and Kobron remained in Augustus's hands. This is
plicable not by any mysterious change of heart, nor by a conversion induced
the sermons of the Chancery men, but because he was now in a position to
gotiate with Augustus on roughly equal terms. He was influenced also by a
w short-term military need: negotiations with Augustus would enable him
concentrate Swedish forces against Tsar Peter.

Charles's failing in his early years in respect of the Chancery lay in his lack
real contact with its officials. He asked for their opinions, he read or listened
reports sent in, but he did not explain at any length the reasons for his own
cisions, and in particular he was quiet on the way military necessity
fluenced political decisions. The secrecy needed in any military operation to
eserve the necessary element of surprise may help to account for this, but
narles's failure to put all those who felt entitled to be in his confidence com-
etely into the picture must carry most of the blame. This trait in the King's
aracter was judged by one Chancery official who served in a subordinate
pacity, but with good opportunity to observe him and his methods between
03 and 1707 (for some time as his private secretary), to be the outcome of a
ur to be proved in the wrong. Charles, Reuterholm thought, liked to keep
iet about his motives and to hide his reasoning till the success or otherwise
any one line of policy could be seen.[29] It seems more likely, however, to stem
om Charles's lack of insight into the psychology of the men who served him
advisers in foreign policy, for these, when they learnt to demand explana-
ns and to force discussions on the King, found him quite ready to debate
e relative merits of different ways of approaching a problem though without
ejudice to his own final decision.[30] Similarly Charles xii in maturity proved
ady to discuss his actions in retrospect and to admit failures and false steps,
ving the reasons which had made him decide on this or that policy at the
ne.* But left to himself it does not seem as if the King would ever have
alized the need of his civil advisers on foreign policy to relieve tension and
hten responsibilities of which they were deeply conscious by informal give
d take in discussions before he made up his own mind. Certainly in the
tumn of 1700 neither the young King nor the officials had as yet found a
dus vivendi in this respect.

Yet another point must be taken into account when weighing evidence on

* See below, pp. 373–4.

disagreements or differences between Charles XII and his advisers, not only
the autumn of 1700, but up to 1709. The officials, in their letters and in the
reports, always had an eye to the future, more so than in their private discu
sions with the King. Charles XII, as several of them testified after his deat
allowed them the greatest liberties in discussion and never harboured a
resentment at views opposed to those he himself held when honestly present
or pressed: there was no need to dissimulate with him. But in war it was on
to be expected that the King might die suddenly, and, in view of the unsettl
succession, officials felt a need to insure themselves against being made scap
goats in the struggle between rival candidates for the throne or against bei
held responsible by reason of their advice to a late ruler by inquiries institut
either by the successful candidate or by the Estates, if absolutism should n
survive Charles. In times of crisis, therefore, and in times of decision, offici
tended to emphasize Charles XII's sole responsibility for the course adopt
and to set down their objections and fears on paper as a form of insurance f
the future. It is essential not to use the letters from such periods, when ever
thing seemed to hang in the balance, without comparing them with the lette
of the same officials when the policy decided on had led to success.

III

By 1 October the military preparations were far enough advanced for Char
XII to set sail from Karlshamn for the Baltic provinces. Transports were on
available for five thousand men in the first instance, but it was intended th
the ships should return, weather permitting, for a second load of troops.
keep Augustus guessing as to the destination of the reinforcements, nothi
had been said publicly about the abandonment of the Saxony project; but t
plan was for landing the army roughly halfway between the Saxon and t
Russian threats to the East Baltic provinces, to join up with Otto Vellingk a
his army and to decide the military campaign in the light of the circumstanc
prevailing on the spot.

Six ships of the line protected the transport-fleet. The King sailed on boa
one of these, the *Wästmanland*, with those carrying the drabants and t
Chancery-in-the-field officials in close contact.[31] The south-westerly win
served the Swedes well at first and gave them a speedy passage to within sig
of the Courland coast, but storms from the 3rd onwards scattered the fle
Charles XII shared the seasickness of the landlubbers as ships had to ride o
the storm at anchor; some transports were lost with many casualties in hors
while others were forced to return to Sweden, their task unaccomplished. C
the 6th the King landed just south of Estonia, the rendezvous to which art
lery and money for the pursuit of the war had already been sent.[32] Char
XII used the yacht *Sophia** – the one he had used also in the Zealand landin
– to take him ashore from the *Wästmanland*.

* The choice may have had some emotional significance; cp. above, pp. 91–2 and belo
pp. 209, 377–8.

The mayor and council of Pernau received the King on the quay, the guns
of the fort saluted him and muskets were fired in the town square while he
walked to his lodgings; but the atmosphere of the town was subdued and the
Swedes were conscious of Estonian fears of the enemy and dislike at the
prospect of becoming a battlefield. Intelligence reports had put the Russian
army at eighty thousand strong and some of them were already on Estonian
soil. Rumours that Russian prisoners were found to be women dressed as
men were industriously spread, to bring hope 'that this army will not prove as
formidable as it is strong in numbers', but without much success. All but two
of the professors at Dorpat Academy fled, setting a bad example to the
students, and the people in general made a 'scared' impression.[33] A thick fog
on the 7th delayed disembarkation of the troops which had arrived with the
King, but on the 8th, after the arrival of Rehnskiöld and Wachtmeister, dispositions were made for sending some troops to Narva, to give succour to the
Swedish garrison under Henning Horn besieged by some forty thousand
Russians since mid-September, while the King and most of the newly arrived
troops prepared to join Vellingk and attack Augustus.

Charles XII and Rehnskiöld made a quick visit to Vellingk, stationed some
ten miles to the south, on the 11th, and the news he had for them changed
their plans. Augustus had become alarmed at the Tsar's concentration on his
own attack on Ingria without regard to appeals for assistance in Livonia.
Fearing that Charles might either attack Saxony or occupy Courland, Augustus had put his army into winter quarters in Courland, himself retiring to
Warsaw and proclaiming once more his willingness for peace. Pursuit of the
Saxons into Courland might be a waste of time in view of the danger from
the Russians in Ingria. The roads south, though free from enemies, were
'indescribably'[34] bad and deep in mud at that time of the year, and there was
little food to be had in the Riga region, Vellingk's and Augustus's armies
having made heavy demands on southern Livonia.

Augustus quiescent, though still in command of Dünamünde, Kobron and
Kokenhusen, and willing to negotiate was no immediate threat and Charles
lent a ready ear to the proposals of Guiscard and Welz who (after visits to
Stockholm and deliberations with Chancery officials and the Duke of
Holstein-Gottorp) arrived at Reval in mid-November. Welz's demand, as the
price for imperial mediation, that Swedish troops should help Leopold oppose
the second partition treaty made Vienna's offices unacceptable; but Guiscard's suggestions were welcomed, not only because France was an ally of the
Maritime Powers through the partition treaty and there was thus no possibility that Sweden might offend the English and the Dutch – with whom she
was negotiating for help in money and other war-necessities – but also because
Guiscard showed himself sensible of the justice of the Swedish claim for
eventual return of the forts still in Saxon hands. Restitution, the French diplomat argued, could be arranged for before ratification of a peace treaty and he
himself thought it fair to insist that Augustus should be made to return the

forts in the state in which they had been before the outbreak of hostilities a
not razed to the ground as the King-Elector had put forward in his tentati
peace terms.[35]

Charles felt somewhat handicapped in his negotiations with Guisca
through the absence of any senior Chancery official expert in diplomac
Åkerhielm, who had been so active in Scania and Zealand, had been l
behind in Stockholm to assist Oxenstierna, and Polus had suffered a stro
soon after his arrival in Pernau. Piper, who accompanied the Chancery-i
the-field as the King's chief adviser on domestic affairs and link with t
Stockholm colleagues dealing with these matters, now had to take over t
duties in foreign affairs meant to be carried by Polus: a fortuitous circu
stance thus made him so prominent an adviser that observers began to ta
of him as a *premier ministre* or head of the Chancery-in-the-field. His ra
alone, a Councillor and a Count, as well as the King's great reliance on hi
served to make him keep this position even after a replacement for Polus
the shape of the professor of *eloquentiae* at Dorpat Academy, Otto Hermeli
joined headquarters in 1702.[36] Contact between Piper and the Stockholm Cha
cery was kept through correspondence with Oxenstierna and Åkerhielm till the
deaths, within a short space of time, in 1702; and also through the correspo
dence of Cederhielm, the third-in-command of the Chancery-in-the-field, wi
his prospective father-in-law, Åkerhielm, till 1702 and with his friend Samu
Barck and his brother Josias, both working in the College of the Chancer

Already before Guiscard's arrival and the start of negotiations wi
Augustus, the decision had been taken to turn all Swedish forces that cou
be spared against the Russians. It seemed inconceivable that the Kin
Elector could quickly remount an offensive in the south of Livonia and t
opportunity must be used to remove the threat to Narva and to drive Ts
Peter's forces out of Ingria and Estonia. Orders were given for all Swedi
regiments of foot and horse to collect in Wesenberg. It was estimated th
eight thousand cavalry and seven thousand infantry might be there before t
end of November. Magazines of food for six weeks and clothes, such as glov
and fur cloaks necessary for a winter campaign, were also gathered ther
Henning Horn was told by a message from the King that help would l
coming: 'We shall soon be with you and dislodge the enemy', ran the letter
15 October,[37] and (if the attempt against the Russians at Narva shou
succeed) a further offensive was planned against the border provinces
Pskov and Novgorod to force Tsar Peter to withdraw from Swedish territor
To those who asked the King where he intended to make his winter quarte
he answered that none would be necessary, as the army would be on t
move.[38]

IV

Tsar Peter did not intend to make it easy for Charles XII to relieve Narv
The Russian army, though not reckoned experienced by European standard

inted troops which had seen action against the Turks, and many foreign
icers of repute were serving with the Tsar, notably du Croy from the
anish Netherlands, a veteran of the war against the Porte, and the Saxon
n Hallart, sent by Augustus to help in the campaign. By the end of October
: Russian artillery had arrived, bombardment had started and it was
>ected that Narva would fall before the end of November. Sheremetev was
it with five thousand men to destroy the Swedish magazines in Wesenberg,
d though Vellingk's troops were able to stop him east of that town, he laid
ste all land between Wesenberg and Narva to delay the Swedish march
d ensure Narva's fall.

There were those at the headquarters of Charles XII who argued that the
cumstances were too adverse to risk the relief of Narva and the battle with
: huge Russian army which this would entail. The roads were bad, the
lages and their stores burnt, illness had begun to spread among the troops,
>d was difficult even in Wesenberg, there were gaps in the equipment, and
>rale was not high. Charles XII retorted that too much was already at stake
him not to risk the hazard of a battle: the loss of Narva would mean the
oding of Ingria, Estonia and Livonia by Russian troops. He was heartened
the fact that Sheremetev had been made to retreat by Swedes far fewer in
mber than the Russians and used this to drive home his point that Swedish
>ops by tradition had always had to fight Russians who were much superior
numbers but who could yet be beaten. He took part in reconnaissance trips,
visited and inspected the regiments and tried to strengthen the morale by
ting his own optimism and reliance on God's help be known. Dispositions
re made which publicized a belief in victory meant to be catching. A regi-
:nt that did not arrive at Wesenberg by the time the King was ready to
gin the march to Narva was ordered, not to hurry after the main army, but
station itself near lake Peipus in order to prevent the Russians, 'when
iten', getting their siege artillery to safety across the lake.[39] Charles's
:rgy and example brought about an improvement in the spirits of the men;
t even those officers who were convinced of the need to risk the relief of
irva were by no means confident of the outcome. 'If the King succeeds',
ote Rehnskiöld on the eve of the march, 'there never was any one who had
triumph over such obstacles.'[40]

On 13 November the march began. The army, not more than eleven thou-
1d men,[41] had to make its way over roads soft after autumn rains, across
untry ravaged and burnt by the Russians. Food was scarce, fodder for the
rses were lacking, men, hungry and cold, had to sleep in the open. The
:mory of it burnt deep. Diarists and letter-writers agreed that the exhaustion
luced by marching through mire to halfway up the leg was the worst.[42]

A much needed encouragement came on the 17th, when Charles XII with an
vance-guard of four hundred men, caused Sheremetev with a force of five
ousand to leave the Pyhäjöggi pass. The Russian commander, it is now
own, had orders not to get involved in a fight with the main Swedish army,

and the latest Russian and Swedish authorities agree that he retreated acco
ing to plan rather than that – as earlier Swedish writers assumed – he suffe
a significant defeat and failed to check Charles XII's advance at a place v
suited for defence. But to the tired Swedes in November 1700 the Russ
rear-guard's fight, sustained just long enough to permit the main force
retire, was a successful skirmish, if not a battle, and the booty in guns a
other equipment was welcome. A pass which could have cost the Swedes d
in men had been taken with hardly any loss of life. The road to Narva v
free. Significant for army morale was the part Charles XII had played. It v
the first action in which the King had commanded independently without
presence of one of his military teachers. Maidel was there; but Charles
took command, chose his ground well so that the fire of the Russian guns w
over the heads of the Swedes and showed himself a leader of promise. T
news spread round the army and helped to create confidence that the K
was a chip off the Vasa block.

By 19 November the Swedish army was within a mile and a half of Nar
near enough for a prearranged series of shots to tell Horn that help was ne
The Russians, though warned by Sheremetev of Charles XII's advance, did i
expect any sudden attack by the Swedes, but anticipated a slow build-up
forces on both sides and a battle some time in the future. Tsar Peter left
army on the night of 17–18 November to organize reinforcements, and
Croy was given command of the army besieging Narva. This army was co
tained within a large fortified camp on the southern side of the town and v
protected by a wall nine feet high, a ditch six feet wide and 140 cannon. T
Swedes' plan was for speedy action: they were not well enough supplied
afford to wait. On the 20th in the morning, marching in columns, they ca
out of a wood – which had to some extent hidden them from the Russian vi
– and took up battle positions to invite a Russian attack. None came. T
fortified camp would have to be stormed. Rehnskiöld set up guns on a sli
rise to protect the Swedes while carrying out a brief reconnaissance and t
necessary preparations, such as the making of *fascines** for the crossing of t
ditch.

Just as the Swedish lines began their attack at 2 o'clock a snow-sto
reduced visibility, hindering the defenders more than the attackers, since
blew straight into their faces. The impetus of the Swedish attack gained fro
this, within fifteen minutes the Swedes were inside the entrenchment and t
battle proper was joined. Rehnskiöld himself commanded the left wi
where the King was stationed, surrounded by his drabants under Hor
Vellingk was in charge of the right wing. The Russian right was the first
give way: so many thousands fled towards the river to escape that the brid
broke under the weight of them; others defended themselves till dark in
improvised strong-point made up of hundreds of wagons. By dawn the co
mander of the Russian left, seeing himself encircled, stopped fighting. T

* These bundles of twigs and brush are known as *askiner* in Swedish military terminology.

mber of prisoners taken was such that Charles XII had no possibility of eping them or feeding them; those that had fought bravely were allowed to ep their arms, the rest had to lay theirs down. All privates were permitted leave for home: from 4 in the morning of the 21st till far into the next day a ntinuous stream of Russians left the camp to march east. The high-ranking ficers were detained. The non-Russian ones were soon freed without ransom, it the Russian ones were sent to Sweden in the hope that cartel arrangements uld be made which would release Swedish prisoners, military and civilian, Russia.

Swedish losses in dead and wounded were estimated at two thousand, some which had been incurred when Swede fought Swede unwittingly in the dark a time when the right wing had orders to go to the aid of the left. Russian sualties were thought to be between eight and ten thousand.[43] In the battle ere had been little distinction on the Swedish side between military and vilian: Count Piper had at one time led a cavalry-charge, Cederhielm had lped to round up prisoners.[44] Horn and Stenbock had shown conspicuous llantry and were both promoted major-generals the day after the battle, hen Charles XII went into Narva for a service of thanks in its main church. he victory, 'if anything human had a share in it', was Rehnskiöld's and the ing's: Rehnskiöld's plan of attack, though not favoured by everyone in the igh command before the battle, proved him, as Stenbock wrote, 'a real eneral', and Charles XII's 'firm and unbending resolution' both to risk battle nd to let Rehnskiöld fight it according to his own plan had made that eneralship possible.[45] Moreover, the King's bearing in this his first big attle had confirmed the promise he had shown in Zealand and at Pyhäjöggi: e had been one of the first over the entrenchment, he had been cool and esourceful in moments of danger and had led both cavalry and infantry ttacks in the action with success. The official relations of the battle, '*l'action 1 plus hardie, la plus heureuse, & la mieux conduite du monde*', exaggerated in vays that seem intolerable and even ridiculous when they insisted that Charles XII had 'himself alone with incomparable Courage and prudent com- 1and led and conducted the whole Glorious action',[46] but those who wrote hem probably chose one way of expressing their relief at a victory against reat odds. Another way was chosen, we learn from Russian sources, by ome of the soldiers, particularly the Finnish regiments, who got drunk on Russian stores of spirits and wine.[47]

The men to whom the glory of Narva, a battle whose renown has stood the est of time, is due are Rehnskiöld and, behind the scenes, Stuart.[48] But Narva did mark a stage in Charles XII's emergence from tutelage: he was given ractical responsibility as well as a share in strategic planning. The fact that e had exposed himself to danger was deplored in Sweden – the bullet found n his neckerchief* after the battle was widely commented on[49] – yet there was

* Posse, who was close to the King during stages of the battle, tells of another bullet which did ot penetrate the sodden cloth of the royal uniform: this officer often comments in letters to his rother, 1702–8, on the way in which rain-soaked uniforms tend to minimize the danger from shot.

no other way for him to learn the art of soldiering. Some part of him, the s
and grandson of great soldiers, seemed anyhow to glory in the danger: the
who served under him noticed that though they would have called his te
perament phlegmatic in everyday life he showed the 'choleric' side of
ancestors in battle.[50]

3

The Crossing of the Dvina

he victory at Narva improved the Swedish position greatly. The magazines
of food and ammunition which the Russians had collected in their fortified
camp were welcome additions to the meagre Swedish stores; and the army
moved into the Russian tents as soon as Tsar Peter's soldiers left for home.
The fine new artillery, at least 140 cannon and field-guns, was the principal
booty. Standards and other insignia which spelt victory large were sent to
Stockholm where the news of the battle became known early in December. A
great victory celebration, with illuminations that were much admired, took
place in February 1701.[1] Fame came to Charles[2] and to Swedish arms.
Memories of the Thirty Years War were revived as the news of the prompt
dispatch of the Russian enemy spread over Europe.

But a happening in a corner of Europe far removed from Narva had on 1
November (N.S.) altered the conjunctures in Charles XII's disfavour. On that
day Carlos II of Spain died and his last will and testament was found to
nominate Louis XIV's grandson, the Duke of Anjou, to be his sole heir – with
the proviso that if Louis refused to accept the will in its entirety the whole of
the Spanish heritage was to be offered to Austrian Habsburgs. The dilemma
for Louis XIV and his advisers was terrible and crucial. When acceptance was
decided on, tension naturally enough developed between Louis XIV and his
partners of the partition treaty. The French king was faced, between 1700 and
1702, with a problem not dissimilar to the one which Holstein-Gottorp had
posed for Sweden between 1697 and 1699. Only if Louis agreed to a partitioning of Spain could he hope to make William III and the Dutch Republic accept
the Bourbon candidature;[3] but if he did so the Spanish Council would proceed to offer the whole of the inheritance to Vienna. Leopold would be sure to
accept for his second son and the safety of France would be jeopardized since
Leopold had refused to give assurances that an Austrian Habsburg who ruled
Spain and its empire would be barred from inheriting the Austrian Habsburg
dominions.[4] The spectre of the encirclement of France as in the days of
Charles V loomed on the horizon. For the Maritime Powers the reality of an
overmighty France in Europe and a skilful exploiter of the Spanish dominions overseas seemed already a reality, and helped on its way by fortuitous

circumstances as well as by mistakes and misjudgements on Louis XIV's part
the War of the Spanish Succession was born. Actual hostilities between th
Martime Powers and France did not break out till 1702, though war w
decided on shortly after Leopold had sent his troops into the Italia
peninsula to claim Spanish Milan as an escheated fief of the Empire in th
summer of 1701.

Long before this, indeed from the moment Louis had chosen the will
Carlos II instead of sticking to the partition treaty, French fear of retaliatic
from the Maritime Powers had dominated Versailles's foreign policy. N
where were the effects more speedily apparent than in Louis XIV's attitude
Charles XII's war. Until the will was known Guiscard had worked hard
obtain an armistice between Augustus and Sweden. After the will, on th
mere supposition that trouble might break out between France and Willia
III, Guiscard's orders were reversed: it would now be in the French interest
keep the war going lest Augustus or Charles (or both) be gained by the Mar
time Powers against France. The Swedes discovered, immediately after th
battle of Narva, that they could no longer reckon on French help to obtai
that security – whether in the form of an armistice or a peace – which wou
make it feasible to continue the campaign against Russia as planned.*

The powers which either objected to Carlos's will or resented Louis XIV
setting aside of the partition treaty were not slow to renew their offers o
mediation; but the price of Leopold's offices was opposition to Louis XIV
and when a Dutch diplomat, Haersolte van Cranenburg, arrived at the Swec
ish headquarters in June 1701 his price was only slightly less stiff. William
tried hard to find an English diplomat with military experience to atten
Charles XII in the field from December 1700 onwards,[6] but had in the end t
settle for John Robinson – in holy orders, but with the advantage of havin
lived long in Sweden and knowing Swedish well – who, for one reason an
another, did not leave Stockholm for Charles's headquarters till early in 170
But even if an English representative of William's had joined Welz and Haer
solte with the Swedish army at an earlier date, it does not seem possible tha
this could have affected the issue. For the favourable opportunity for Sweden
when Augustus was inclined to give up his war against Charles XII, since both
Frederick IV and Tsar Peter had been beaten, disappeared into thin air befor
the smoke cleared over the battlefield of Narva. By the time the mediatior
offer of the Maritime Powers got into its stride the general situation, with
France and the Emperor bidding in earnest for Augustus's support, had
turned to Saxony's advantage. Both the King-Elector and the Tsar found
their second winds, and Frederick IV began to watch for an opportunity to rid
himself of the shackles of the Travendal treaty.

The alignment of the European states into pro-French and anti-French
which began in late November 1700 could not but complicate the Swedish
position. In the widening split between France and the Maritime Powers

* See above, p. 149–50.

Sweden found herself driven, by her need of international loans as well as by her feeling of gratitude for past help, but most of all by her need to have the Travendal treaty guaranteed, to reaffirm the bonds of January 1700 and tie them even closer. By the treaty of 1700 she was only obliged to render help to the Maritime Powers if they were attacked; by that of February 1702 Charles XII promised military help – on the same scale – 'as soon as his own war would permit him to do so', whether his allies' war was defensive or offensive.[7] But having declared war on France the Maritime Powers naturally enough began to think of Charles XII as selfish and self-centred when his help did not materialize: why did he not make an end to his own war and join the common cause? Each side was too immersed in its own gigantic struggle to really grasp the problems of the other. The Maritime Powers underestimated the obstacles towards peace in the east and were too free with accusations that Sweden went France's errands – 'whether she knew it or not'; Charles XII was incapable of looking at the European situation from the point of view of the Maritime Powers and felt increasingly betrayed by the Dutch and, after 1709, by the English.[8]

Swedish historians have stressed that the War of the Spanish Succession gave Charles XII and his advisers freedom of action after 1702 to attempt their radical solutions of Sweden's eastern problems. But until 1706 such freedom was largely illusory, for the war of the Maritime Powers limited and conditioned Charles XII's policies. Concern for the reaction of Great Britain and the Dutch Republic, the one sheet-anchor that held Frederick of Denmark down, made it impossible for Charles XII to undertake any operation against Augustus in Saxony. Not till the autumn of 1706, when the Allies had gained such victories over France that they could not claim that Charles was knifing them in the back by his entry into Germany, did such an invasion take place. It immediately knocked Augustus out of the war. Freedom of action against the Saxon elector might have shortened the long years of Charles's war in Poland and released Swedish forces against Russia in the period 1702–6. After 1706 such freedom existed, but it was one that had been gained by Charles's calculated risk in moving into the Empire.

II

The French negotiations with Augustus of Saxony for an armistice with Charles XII had helped to secure the Swedish flank during the Narva offensive. The change of French policy robbed Sweden of that support and necessitated a choice of front and a settling of priorities as between Augustus and Tsar Peter: who was the most formidable enemy? against whom should Charles XII turn first? A winter campaign by the whole Swedish army after Narva might have enabled Charles XII to inflict a more decisive defeat on Tsar Peter; but large-scale pursuit of the Russians into Russia – an invasion of Russia proper – proved impossible at that time. Discussions, taking into account

both military considerations and political advice by Swedes who had escaped
from Moscow, had indicated the desirability of a speedy follow-up of the
Narva success and plans were drawn up for a campaign directed against the
heart of Russia to be carried out as soon as the roads hardened with winter.[9]

These plans had, however, to be pared down considerably. More and more
Swedish soldiers fell ill; infectious diseases which had raged in the Russian
camp spread like wild-fire among the Swedes after they settled into the former
Russian quarters.[10] The memory of the many deaths from illness in the winter
of 1700–1 left Charles XII determined to avoid the unhealthiness of enclosed
camp-life for his army for ever afterwards.[11] It was impossible to get recruits
and reinforcements from Sweden until spring. Equipment and money needed
attention as well and for all these reasons the main army was moved into
winter quarters in Livonia and Estonia. Charles XII established headquarters
at Lais, some miles north of Dorpat, to fight the sickness, to drill and
train for the next year's campaigns. Minor detachments under experienced
officers were ordered to test Russian defences in the border districts: Cronhjort with five hundred men was sent north to guard Ingria and to take the
Pskov province if possible; when this was found to be held strongly by forty
thousand Russians, Stenbock was ordered to attack the Russian stronghold of
Gdov – an attack which failed – while Spens and Schlippenbach were detailed
to destroy Petschory, another stronghold which like Gdov was used as a base
for Russian ravaging of Estonia: in this they were partly successful in that the
town and the magazines were burnt but the fortified monastery remained
intact.

It was clear that Tsar Peter did not intend to let the reverse of Narva stop
him. He proved his determination by his melting down of Russian church
bells to provide new cannon, his taxation demands on the Russian people,
above all his treaty with Augustus in February 1701, when the two met at
Birsen with various advisers and experts, notable among whom was Patkul,
to discuss plans for the summer campaign. Augustus, courted by both Louis
XIV and the Emperor, and already secretly committed to Leopold in return
for a guarantee of his Polish crown, was able to impose stiff terms on the Tsar.
The Birsen treaty was a virtual *Diktat* by the one member of the anti-Swedish
coalition who had not yet suffered a major defeat at the hands of Charles XII.
The Tsar had to agree that Estonia and Livonia would fall to the King-
Elector's share when the Baltic empire of Sweden was partitioned, and to bind
himself to furnish heavy subsidies and an auxiliary army of fourteen to
twenty thousand men to help Augustus make his conquests. Ingria alone was
reserved for Russia.[12]

The terms of the Birsen treaty were communicated to the Swedes by Polish
patriots who felt incensed at Augustus's cooperation with Russia. These
men, among them the commander of the Crown army, Jabłonowski and his
son-in-law Rafał Leszczyński – an experienced official and diplomat who
had represented Poland at the Porte – wanted cooperation with Charles XII

THE POLISH–LITHUANIAN COMMONWEALTH AND WESTERN RUSSIA

SWEDEN

BALTIC SEA

Narva ✕ INGRIA
ESTONIA
Gdov
L. Peipus
Pskov

LIVONIA

COURLAND Riga
Mitau

Volga

RUSSIA

Moscow

Kaluga

Oka

Tula

Dvina

SAMOGITIA

WEST PRUSSIA
DANZIG

EAST PRUSSIA

BRANDENBURG-PRUSSIA

Heilsberg

GREAT POLAND
Warta
Fraustadt ✕ Kalisz
Rawicz ✕
Kliszow ✕ LITTLE POLAND

SAXONY

SILESIA

AUSTRIA
Vienna

Budapest

Vilna
Smorgonie ✕
LITHUANIA

Grodno
Thorn ✕ Pultusk
BLACK RUSSIA

Niemen

Vistula
POLAND
Warsaw
Posen

Bug

Holovzin
✕

Beresina

Pripet

Smolensk
Tatarsk
Mohilev
✕ Liesnaja

Drut

Sozh

Brtansk

Briansk

Mglin

Lost to Russia 1667

Starodub

Desna

Don

P O L A N D

VOLHYNIA

Cracow

Lemberg
RED RUSSIA

GALICIA

Prut

MOLDAVIA

Kiev
UKRAINE

Baturin

Sula

Veprik

Vorskla

Kharkov

Psiol

Poltava
Perevolotjna

ZAPOROZHIAN

Dnieper

Sich

COSSACKS

PODOLIA

Bender Ochakov

Perikop

KHANATE OF CRIMEA

WALLACHIA

Danube

O T T O M A N

ADRIATIC SEA

NAPLES

Adrianople
Constantinople

E M P I R E

BLACK SEA

N

MOREA
(Venetian)

0	400

Kilometres

in order to regain the lands which the Commonwealth had lost to Russia by 1667, the *avulsa imperii* of Smolensk, Kiev and the Ukraine, which succeeding kings on their election had to swear to reconquer. Leszczyński had plans for a combined attack on Russia by Swedes, Poles, Turks and Tartars, since the Porte was known to desire the reconquest of Azov. The Sapieha family might become allies of this group of patriots since their short-lived understanding with Augustus had already broken down: though the Sapieha ambitions were somewhat disturbing, the family tended to be anti-Russian.

There was yet another group – more numerous than the two already mentioned – that objected to Augustus's collaboration with Tsar Peter, but this group, led by the cardinal *primas*, Prince Radziejowski, neither wished to go to war with Russia, nor to cooperate with Swedes or Turks. Its quarrel with Augustus was on the grounds of domestic issues since it resisted that strengthening of the royal power with the help of lesser magnates which the King-Elector was now known to favour. Success in war, the men who composed the group argued, would make Augustus stronger in relation to the *Rzeczpospolita Polska*. If Augustus had had a speedy success in February 1700 they might have gone along with his expansionist policy, but now they decided to petition him to make peace with Sweden and remove his troops from Polish territory. This group was the one whose objectives were hardest to fathom for the Swedes, and its ambivalent attitude in years to come – now using Sweden against Augustus, now putting obstacles in the path of Sweden's policies – became a mire in which it was hard indeed to find firm footing.

Augustus, from other accounts received at Lais, was not taking the opposition groups inside the Commonwealth seriously.[13] He had his guarantees of the Polish crown from the Emperor and from the Hohenzollern dynasty; he had his Birsen treaty which gave men and money; he had the prospect of Denmark coming into the war once more if Sweden suffered reverses in the 1701 campaign[14] and felt confident that he could win victories against Charles XII speedily enough to permit him to handle the Polish situation. He was considerably helped already by opposition to the Sapieha family which he used to foment civil war inside Lithuania. Wiśniowecki, the commander of the Lithuanian Crown army newly appointed by him, the Ogiński family connexion, and other groups known as the 'United Families', took the field against the Sapiehas in December 1700.

The strengthening of Augustus's position meant that for the Swedes the Saxon enemy became increasingly more important. During the winter the Russians kept inside Russia, cordoned off by the Swedish garrison posts strung out in the east, but the Saxons raided southern Livonia from their base in Courland. Whatever peaceful intentions and willingness to negotiate Augustus expressed to the Emperor and the Maritime Powers, he was determined on an intense campaign against the Swedish army in 1701 and the main lines of his plan were well known to those in Lais who had to decide the next step.

Ideally Charles XII should have been able to mount simultaneous strong attacks on Tsar Peter and Augustus in 1701. But the strength of the army, even when the recruits expected from Sweden in the spring were taken into account, would be no more than twenty-four thousand, so this would be impossible to achieve. Any splitting of the operational army – certainly less than that number and possibly no higher than eighteen thousand – would weaken its impact. On the other hand, speed in achieving success against both enemies was desirable, and plan of campaign number 1 postulated a solution which it has only recently been possible to analyse, thanks to some marching-orders of the day (the so called march-*seddel*, i.e. ticket) which have come to light during the researches of G. Jonasson.[15] When these orders, giving the detailed planning for the march and the billeting of the regiments of the main army for an attack on Russia, are seen not to have been stopped till October 1701, it becomes obvious that the hitherto accepted idea that the Swedes made an early choice to attack Augustus while contenting themselves with holding operations against the Tsar must be abandoned. This view was deduced from the facts that the army accepted battle with the Saxons for the Dvina and then moved on, crossing to Courland, leaving minor forces – dispatched earlier in the campaign towards the borders of Russia – to cope on the north and east of the front.[16] The newly published marching-orders, which go far beyond a date when they can be assumed to serve only the purpose of a feint, permit a clearer reconstruction of Swedish military planning.

Feints there would have to be, to keep the strong Saxons guessing as to the place where the Swedes would challenge them to battle; but what headquarters planned was a crossing of the Dvina and a fight with the Saxons which would, it was hoped, be victorious enough to enable them to push on to Courland with minor forces, leaving the main army to take up the struggle with Tsar Peter in the dry late-summer weather which gave as good campaign conditions as in mid-winter when roads became passable because they were frozen. The objective of this plan number 1, though it has no number or name in contemporary records, was to meet Sweden's enemies outside the Swedish empire, to move the battlefields away from the Baltic provinces, to 'get some air' to use the contemporary phrase of military planners of all nations, so that their own population should not suffer the destruction of home and crops and the epidemics that so often came with armies on the march.

III

There was sickness enough in the Swedish army when this plan was worked out at the headquarters at Lais by Stuart and Rehnskiöld. Charles XII was put in the picture, as was their wont, by discussions of plans set up for the purposes of his strategic training, and no doubt – though we have no information about this – the steps to be taken if Augustus was not decisively defeated were considered, since in that case a choice might be forced upon the Swedish army between the Saxon and the Russian as the main opponent for the second stage of the campaign. The fevers which were taking their toll of soldiers in their winter quarters had spread also to Lais: in Charles's own suite his doctor, his chaplain and one of his gentlemen-in-waiting died.[17]

The King was saddened by the waste of soldiers' lives through sickness, and it was for the express purpose of preventing him from brooding over the harsher aspects of campaign life (so several witnesses inform us)[18] that those with talents in the arts and for entertainment organized festivities from time to time. The gifted Stenbock[19] conducted an orchestra playing music composed by himself on 28 January – which was Charles's saint's day – and ballet and theatrical performances were given from time to time. In his letters home Charles concentrated on the lighter side of the war: he mentioned their traditional celebration of Christmas and gave news of officers and officials known to the royal family; to little Ulla he described a peasant wedding he had seen and pretended that war was a *lustigh lek*, a jolly game of chasing the enemy which translated into modern idiom might be rendered as cops and robbers.[20] Letters from home were equally light in tone. Hedvig Sophia tried to hide anxiety both for husband and brother behind tales of court ladies forming a company of their own, having uniforms designed for them and choosing herself for their lieutenant: 'God help the Russians if we come over to help you, or perhaps God help us.'[21]

Work filled most of the time. Apart from the poring over maps which strategic planning and the setting up of march-routes and 'tickets' involved, drill regulations were finalized for the infantry and committed to print, mock battles were fought (including an attack on a snow fortress) to train the soldiers, and the shortcomings of many kinds which the hurried and improvised campaign of the autumn of 1700 had revealed were remedied.[22]

The Swedish crossing of the Dvina was carefully prepared. In April Dahlberg, still in his governor-general's residence at Riga, was asked to construct a pontoon bridge strong enough for the cavalry to use, which could be floated into position at the last moment and thus help preserve the element of surprise. He was further asked to cooperate with Stuart in devising plans to baffle the Saxon enemy and protect the Swedes till they were safely across the river. Troops would be left at Dorpat and Neuheusen to protect Estonia and northern Livonia from invasion; and stronger forces under Horn, Cronhjort and Schlippenbach were detailed towards Pskov and Gdov to test whether these Russian districts might prove easier to capture than during the brief operations of the immediate post-Narva period. If they were successful, this would 'give air' to the Baltic provinces in the north and east and move the war into those Russian border-territories which the Swedes regarded as suitable compensation when peace was negotiated.

The campaign proper could not be started till the roads were in a reasonable state after the spring thaw, till grass grew for the horses, and till the reinforcements from Sweden arrived. In May ten thousand soldiers arrived at

Reval and the regiments already in the Baltic provinces were ordered to break up from their winter quarters. On 17 June, the King's nineteenth birthday, the main army destined for battle with Augustus and his Russian auxiliaries in stage one of the operations began its march south from the Dorpat region. The main road to Riga – over Wolk, Wolmar, Wenden – was taken, but at Wenden the army turned in the direction of Kokenhusen, as if to make an all-out effort to retake this fort. This was done to divert some of the enemy forces to that place. Three miles from Kokenhusen, however, on 3 July, the Swedes wheeled left and hurried in forced marches to Riga where everything was in readiness for the crossing, the King himself having inspected the technical preparations and taken part in reconnaissance trips on 4 and 6 July.[23] Steinau, the Saxon general in command of Augustus's army (the King-Elector was in Warsaw), expected a Swedish attempt to cross the Dvina, but he had of necessity to string his army of nine thousand Saxons along the broad front of the river till he was sure of the place chosen by Charles XII. Only some of the ten thousand Russian auxiliaries had as yet joined him; he had felt obliged to send reinforcements in the direction of Kokenhusen; and he was further misled by a Swedish feint, on the night before the crossing, whereby troops marched down-river, away from Riga, as if the main attack would be made on Dünamünde. When the Swedes began their crossing in the dawn of 9 July, therefore, it took time for Steinau to collect a sizable army to meet them.

The battle of wits to achieve surprise had gone in favour of the Swedes. The protective measures taken against Saxon fire during the crossing also proved remarkably effective. A smoke-screen was laid to prevent accurate aim, the local boats requisitioned by Dahlberg for the transport moved behind a screen of small boats piled high with bales of hay to absorb Saxon cannon balls and musket bullets, the transport-ships themselves had been given rectangular leather 'sails' to repel bullets, while the wooden landing-stages rigged in the bows of some boats also served as shields for soldiers and horses since they were fixed in an upright position till the moment of disembarkation. The guns of Riga fort and those of armed merchant-men accompanying the transport played on the enemy batteries and continued to do so throughout the battle on the far beach with such accuracy that Steinau attributed much of the Swedish success to skilled use of this artillery. One vital part of the assault plan failed, however: the pontoon bridge, ingeniously constructed in sections and meant to be floated across the six hundred-metre-broad Dvina with the force of the stream, could not be assembled and launched in time, a strong north-westerly wind upsetting the calculations of the experts. This failure prevented the cavalry from playing their proper share in the second stage of the battle.

The first stage, the actual crossing of the infantry with minor detachments of cavalry – some six thousand in all – and the establishment of a bridgehead on the other side, was completely successful. The attempts of the Saxons to force the Swedes back, first under the command of the Livonian Paijkull and then, as soon as he arrived, of General Steinau himself, were beaten off and after a hard fight, lasting several hours, a Saxon council of war decided on retreat. The second stage, the Swedish pursuit of the Saxons to force them to accept a second and decisive battle, 'to ruin the enemy's army' as Dahlberg phrased the objective of the day,[24] could not be put into effect because of the delay in getting the Swedish cavalry across. Rehnskiöld and Vellingk, as soon as it became clear that the pontoon bridge had failed, improvised measures to speed men and horses across by boat, but not enough cavalry had joined the infantry by the time the Saxons broke off the fight and left the battlefield.

The Dvina crossing marked a new stage in Charles XII's development as a commander. His role was more independent than at Narva. The King had, as for the Zealand descent and the Narva battle, taken the closest interest in the battle plan and familiarized himself with all parts of it; but he had allotted himself more responsibility than formerly in the actual battle. Rehnskiöld and Stuart, who had hitherto always been close at hand, were both on the Riga side of the river during the early part of the battle; the King, with Lieutenant-General Liewen, was in command of the assault infantry. Liewen was an experienced officer and to him Charles entrusted the tactical leadership in the lodgement area; but the King showed quick initiative in adapting the plan outlined before the crossing to the changing situation which he and Liewen met as battle was joined and Charles was outstandingly successful in controlling and encouraging the troops during the battle. He had obviously made up his mind that his days of apprenticeship must be drawing to their close, and his role – as he conceived it – was not as a commander away from the dust and sweat and blood of the battle but at the head of his soldiers, leading them.

Much later in his career he discoursed with a Swedish officer* who had served with the allied armies in the War of the Spanish Succession on the reasons for this decision. It would not do for him, who led 'ordinary' Swedes and not mercenary soldiers, Charles XII explained, to follow the example of those of the western commanders who made up their plan of battle and then watched it unfold from a position overlooking the battlefield, ready to intervene with orders to subordinate officers. The Swedes were not particularly warlike by temperament. 'Phlegmatic', the King said of them (as they of him in daily life) and since they went to war only to protect their country, it was necessary for him to take an active part in the actual fighting. He had to show that he was ready to risk as much as they did, their lives, to achieve cohesion and thrust in the attack. He did not think one method of command better than the other, but his way, he argued, was essential for a Swedish king in his circumstances.[25]

Charles XII's religious belief that the time and hour of his death was in God's hand reinforced his decision to exercise command by leadership and example. He derived strength from the conviction (and also used it to brush aside appeals not to risk his own life) that one could not escape one's fate:

* Cp. below, pp. 321 and 373ff, for Charles's talks with Axel von Löwen.

rovidence was in control, not the enemy sword or bullet. Charles XII's expres-
ons of religiously coloured fatalism in this respect can be matched by those
f most of his fellow-officers, and meet us again and again in diaries and letters
f the period. The King and his officers tried to encourage among the soldiers
similar attitude.[26] Each regiment had its pastor and chaplains who, as well
s acting as welfare-officers in general and facilitating contact with home and
amilies, helped to build up the morale of the soldiers by preaching reliance on
od's almighty providence. The dedication of the Swedish army to the
ervice of God before battle by prayers and singing of the hymns familiar
rom home and childhood served, if only in the second place, a military as
vell as a religious purpose.[27]

More consciously directed towards the strengthening of morale in attack
vas the King's reward of gallantry and valour in action. His correspondence
vith subordinate commanders from 1701 onwards offers evidence of the
mportance he attached to this means of developing the offensive spirit of the
urmy. Normally promotion went by seniority; exceptional merit in action or
nitiative otherwise displayed, the King argued, should be made the oppor-
unity for signal promotion, 'so that others may see the effect of it'.[28]

The spirit of the army was in these various ways being moulded and
ashioned to make it an instrument of policy. Already at the Dvina battle the
steadiness of the Swedish infantry under Saxon fire and the way in which the
uttack was pressed home by the Swedes *aux armes blanches* – in total dis-
egard of the musket bullets of the enemy – was noted with astonishment by
he experienced Saxon troops. Towards the end of the battle the numbers of
nen opposed to each other were roughly equal, but in the first and vital stage
of gaining a foothold and widening it the Swedes had been much inferior and
1ad yet been able to throw the Saxons back.[29]

IV

The victory over the Saxons at the Dvina crossing made an even greater
mpression on Europe than had the victory over the Russians at Narva just
because of the greater reputation of Augustus's troops. From the Swedish
point of view, however, the Saxons – who had, all agreed, 'fought very
bravely'[30] – by getting away had cheated them of the decisive victory which
had been hoped for in plan number 1. The pursuit of Steinau in the hope of
forcing him to accept battle once more was begun, but had to be called off, at
least temporarily, after one mile. The Swedish infantry was exhausted, and –
more significantly – the Swedish cavalry was not present in sufficient numbers
to make pursuit effective. With disappointment in their hearts and on their
lips Charles XII, Rehnskiöld and Stuart (both of whom had got across the
Dvina in time to take part in the later stages of the battle) had to reconcile
themselves to the prospect of letting Steinau get away. Losses on both sides
had been relatively light: the Swedes had five hundred dead and wounded, the

Saxons some eight hundred (both Steinau and Paijkull were known to b
among the wounded) and seven hundred Saxons had been taken prisoner.
A diminution of Augustus's forces by fifteen hundred was not good enoug
for Swedish strategic purposes: once it was rested and collected, the arm
would have to find the Saxons once more and fight another day.

There was some uncertainty as to Steinau's route of escape. Conflictin
reports were received: he had moved east into Polish Livonia to join up wit
the Russians in the Pskov province, said some; he had gone into wester
Courland to safeguard his communications with Saxony, said others. I
reality Steinau had moved due south in the direction of Kowno. The Swede
would not dare, it was assumed, to pursue him into Poland proper. But this
as well as Steinau's later move into West Prussia en route for Saxony, wa
not known with any certainty at Swedish headquarters till the end of July. I
any case it was important for Charles XII, in accordance with the overall plan
to make sure of Courland and to drive the Saxons out of the Swedish Livon
ian forts. Kokenhusen and Kobron the enemy left of their own accord after
news of the Dvina crossing; a detachment of troops and a small squadron o
ships were sent to besiege, blockade and storm Dünamünde, where th
Saxons held out till December. Another minor force was given the task o
occupying Mitau, the Courland capital. Charles XII and the main army pro
ceeded to take Bauske, important from the point of view of communications
and Birsen. Swedish troops replaced the Saxon garrison there and began work
on the improvement of the fortifications.

It was at this stage that some modifications had to be made to the original
plan for the year's campaign.[32] With the Saxon army virtually intact, action
on any large scale against Tsar Peter would have to be postponed till Sweden's
relationship with Augustus and the Polish Commonwealth could be clarified.
That the high command still intended only postponement and not abandonment is clear from the detailed costing of food for men and horses, the march-
routes fixed, the camp-sites and lodgings arranged between Dahlberg at Riga
and Stuart at headquarters – these visualize a move by the whole army from
Courland to the Russian border country at Pskov with magazines established
on the Peipus.[33]

Meanwhile it was sensible to move the operational army into Courland for
some time and this was done in the last week of July and the early part of
August. From the strategic point of view Courland was the best place to
intercept the Saxon army if it should try to link up with the Russians; yet it
was near enough to permit support to be sent to the Swedish troops in the
Baltic provinces if these should be attacked by Russian forces stronger than
they could cope with. Here the main army could be housed and fed without
being a burden to the Swedish provinces. Since the young Duke's uncle had
permitted Augustus to use Courland as a base, it was just – by accepted
standards of the time – that he should do the same for Augustus's enemy.
The occupation was thus to be made to serve Swedish economic needs, to

et 'the war pay for the war', but measures were also taken which point to the
ong-term plan of a possible incorporation of Courland in the Swedish
mpire. The tolls of the ports of Libau and Windau were levied according to
he Riga scale and were used by the Swedish Crown, as was the ducal income
(the Duke himself having fled to Warsaw) from customary taxation of all
kinds; contributions were also levied – though on a moderate scale – to defray
he cost of maintaining the army. An oath of loyalty to Charles XII was
demanded of all Courland officials, prayers for the Swedish King were
ordered in the churches, surveyors from the Baltic provinces were sent for to
map the country and to make agricultural surveys on the Swedish pattern, the
contents of archives and libraries were removed to Riga.[34]

Many of these changes could not be kept secret and served to incite suspicion among seafaring and trading nations that Sweden intended to extend
her empire in the Baltic. A small Swedish expedition to Archangel in the
winter of 1700–1, intended to take that port by surprise, met with no success,
but it had already made the Maritime Powers aware of Swedish aggressive
commercial intentions. The Swedes for their part contended that Dutch
spies had betrayed the plan to the Russians and were responsible for the
failure.[35] The Courland occupation, and particularly those aspects of it
which seemed to forebode a permanent incorporation of that duchy with the
Swedish empire, gave rise to outspoken criticism by England, the States
General and Prussia. In order to mollify Sweden's western allies – for at this
time Lillieroot at The Hague was negotiating a treaty with the Maritime
Powers[36] – great emphasis was placed by Swedish diplomats on the temporary
and military nature of the occupation, though without any firm assurance
being given which would tie Sweden's hand in the future. In the event,
Swedish occupation was a fact between 1701 and 1709 (interrupted by temporary Russian control in 1706 and 1707) and did much to foment those suspicions of Charles XII as the would-be architect of a *dominium maris Baltici*
which complicated Swedish relations with the Maritime Powers and Prussia
throughout the Great Northern War.

V

The Swedish presence in Courland put the various groups in the Commonwealth into agitation and competition in spite of the efforts of the 'neutralist'
party under Cardinal Radziejowski to compose matters. The cardinal and
those who thought like him wanted to prevent the Sapiehas calling for Charles
XII's help to fight the Saxon army on Polish soil, and thus bringing the Swedes
into the Commonwealth, while at the same time they hoped to use the proximity of the Swedes to gain concessions from Augustus and the reform party.
Their ultimate objective was to force the King-Elector to withdraw his Saxon
troops for ever from the Commonwealth and to give up his plans for curtail-
ing the power of the magnates. Radziejowski therefore gladly fell in with

Augustus's suggestion that he, as *primas*, should write to Charles XII to extract a promise that the Swedes would not enter the territory of the neutral Republic.

This letter, which was delivered to the King on 25 July 1701 was not the only one to arrive from Polish parties. The patriot group round Jabłonowski and Rafał Leszczyński was in lively contact with Swedish headquarters and so was the eldest of the three Sobieski brothers who lived in Silesia in a castle put at their disposal by the Emperor Leopold after James's unsuccessful contention for the Polish crown in 1697. James had ever since that date tried to interest Sweden in his cause though he was careful not to suggest more on paper than Swedish protection for his estates and for those of his supporters if the war should move to the Commonwealth. But the idea of Augustus' dethronement and the possibility of James Sobieski replacing him was aired by men of the Chancery:[37] Oxenstierna had suggested to Charles XII as early as August 1700 that Sobieski might raise a Polish revolt against the Saxon Elector and by February 1701 the Chancellor told the King how 'useful' Augustus's dethronement would be;[38] Åkerhielm also held that dethronement discussions would help the Swedes by weakening the Republic. Piper concurred; and Wachschlager, who from Imperial soil kept up his contacts in Poland, gave advice along similar lines.

The King was against secret encouragement to revolution,[39] but he accepted the dethronement idea in principle if the Poles themselves would work for it by a letter to the Chancery of 28 May 1701 he proposed that 'the Republic might be told that if she wants to get rid of her present king, We will help her to achieve that purpose.'[40] This stand was not at all welcome to the officials either in Sweden or with Charles in the field. They realized the need to rob Augustus of his Polish base, as he had been robbed of the Courland one; but they wanted the Poles to sort out – and if necessary fight out – their own troubles and counselled caution in negotiations with Polish parties and groups. Those in the King's vicinity desired a non-committal answer to the cardinal's July letter.

From the point of view of the war effort, however, it was essential to promote a speedy decision in Poland so that a winter campaign against Russia might be launched. Preparations for such a venture were prepared – as a substitute for the late summer one and indeed as a mere postponement of it – during July and August, and show that Charles XII intended to undertake it with twenty thousand troops. On 30 July, therefore, in his answer to Radziejowski, Charles XII came into the open with his demand that the Poles should dethrone Augustus, assuring the cardinal that he would postpone his pursuit of his Saxon enemy on to the Polish soil where he had found shelter till he should hear from the cardinal again.[41]

Charles XII miscalculated the effect of his letter. In particular he had not bargained for the cardinal's making it public knowledge in preparation for the Diet of December 1701. Before long he was to admit that if he had realized hat Radziejowski would do this, he would not have put the dethronement uggestion on paper.[42] His miscalculation in the summer of 1701 proceeded 'rom an underestimation of the neutralist party and a correspondingly too)ptimistic assessment of the strength of the patriot groups and of the Sobieski ;upporters.

It is clear, however, that even if he had made a better judgement his basic military dilemma would have remained and driven him along similar paths. -Ie could not turn against Russia with the Saxon army undefeated; he knew)f Danish negotiations to make common cause with Augustus if he did so. -rederick IV felt tied by Travendal in inverted ratio to the Maritime Powers')reoccupation with the Spanish succession; yet that very preoccupation made :hese powers more adamant that Charles XII should not hit at Augustus in >axony. The Polish situation somehow had to be turned to Sweden's advan-:age. It did not seem likely that Augustus (safe both in Russian and Danish sympathy and support) might be persuaded by the Polish patriots to make :ommon cause with the Swedes against Tsar Peter. The dethronement of Augustus, which in the King's view had the blessing of the Chancery and which was advocated by many Poles, seemed therefore the logical step, to be followed by the election of a Polish king – James Sobieski was the candidate everybody had in mind[43] – willing to cooperate with the Polish patriot group and with Charles XII: thus alone security for the flank of the Swedish army during its Russian campaign could be gained. Even if military Suedo-Polish cooperation did not follow, benevolent neutrality would be assured.

The argument of some Swedish officials, and many historians who have dealt with the period, that Charles XII's demand for the dethronement of Augustus damaged Sweden's cause[44] is a perfectly valid one; but the further argument of these historians that without this demand the Polish situation would have developed in Sweden's favour cannot be tested and does not seem to be well founded. There is indeed something to be said for the opposite view: that the Poles themselves were too divided to take any decisive step[45] and that Charles's demand was the only way to procure action commensurate with Swedish needs.

4

Involvement in Poland

The Polish answer to Charles XII's demand for the dethronement of Augustus was much slower in arriving than the Swedish King had expected, and the waiting time – from the end of July till mid-October – was hard to take in view of the need for military action. The position in the East Baltic provinces see-sawed. In September Schlippenbach gained a victory over a strong Russian force which tried to test Swedish opposition to a junction between the Tsar's forces and those of Augustus. This victory seemed at first sight to make the winter campaign against Russia less urgent, but a bare month later Schlippenbach was defeated by Russian troops far superior to his own in number.[1] This served to rub in the dilemma of the Swedish high command in Courland: how could they move against the Tsar till Sweden's relationship to Poland was clarified? And how could that relationship be clarified till the Diet – put off till December by Augustus's efforts – met?

Here the Swedish lack of real information about Cardinal Radziejowski's intentions handicapped them. They did not realize that he was one of those who had been party to Augustus's negotiations with Moscow in June 1699 to which he had given at least half-hearted support in the hope that Poland, without much sacrifice, might benefit from the easy victory which the anti-Swedish coalition promised.[2] Augustus might have his eye on Swedish Livonia as a bargaining counter to be used with the Commonwealth, but many Poles looked in the same direction and were prepared to put forward claims to Livonia older than those of the conquest which Augustus planned. The cardinal and those who thought like him were therefore prepared to go along with the King-Elector till the time seemed ripe to enter the ranks of Charles XII's enemies officially. The failure of Augustus's attack, had, however, convinced them that real as opposed to ostensible neutrality was the only sensible policy. At the same time they intended to use the proximity of the Swedish army to gain concessions from Augustus and by the late autumn of 1701 they prevailed on him to withdraw his Saxon troops from Polish soil. This removal would, they hoped, rob Charles XII of any excuse to bring the war into Poland, though they wished to keep him close by that they might exact further safeguards from Augustus for Polish traditional liberties.

Radziejowski was important enough for the Swedes to make them treat him with the utmost delicacy. By his very position he would, if the dethronement policy succeeded, be the virtual ruler of the Commonwealth during the interregnum between Augustus's deposition and the election of a new king. Charles XII had to refrain from hurrying him or pressing him for an answer. Desiring a move, indeed needing action to promote the interests of Sweden, Charles began to feel a prisoner in Courland. The autumn weather grew cold. The soldiers were billeted in houses or built earthen huts to keep warm. Charles stayed in his tent, which was heated by glowing cannon balls on particularly cold nights. He stayed 'because he liked it', it was said;[3] but a contributory reason was that he could not bear to move into winter quarters and thus advertise his acceptance of the slowing up of Sweden's pursuit of those who had attacked her.

Charles's life in Courland settled down into a daily routine which was observed by the diplomats who flocked to headquarters in competition for Sweden's commitment in the Spanish succession issue. They commented upon the pattern of his days and weeks and speculated on the personality of the King, picturing him as he seemed to them and to those Swedes in the camp willing to discuss him.[4] Other evidence, such as portraits of Charles XII, which were painted at this time, confirm physical changes and changes in habits which had taken place in the year he had been away from home. He had left off his wig, a fact which, noted in Stockholm from a miniature sent home, caused alarm to the women at court, convinced as they were that the innovation would render him susceptible to colds.[5] He had simplified his uniform, modelling it on that of the ordinary soldier, wearing grey or blue – never red, it was said, since he regarded that as the colour of his Danish and Saxon enemies and would not permit his officers to wear it.[6] His breeches were of elkskin and his waistcoat either of leather or cloth. Pictorial evidence shows that he sometimes wore a metal breastplate and in cold weather a fur collar or fur lining to his jacket.[7] His plain hat caused comment. The '*méchant bonnet de peau*' which the Dutch envoy saw him wearing throughout his visit at headquarters from 1701 to 1702 seemed so old and worn that he well believed the rumour it was the very one which Charles had worn at the battle of Narva.[8] The black taffeta scarf which the King preferred to the usual officer's cravat of fine lace similarly struck foreign observers as odd and they tended – now and later – to put down the extreme simplicity of Charles's uniform as indifference to his own appearance.[9] His wearing of high boots throughout waking hours, and the fact that he only wore gloves when riding, were also commented on.[10] The quality of the King's clothes was good, however, and considerable attention given to material and fit. He had, as he once told a traveller, left his 'night-cap, his night-gown, his shoes and his slippers' behind in Stockholm when he went to war;[11] but the linen for his shirt was of the finest quality and so were his white cotton stockings.[12]

There was deliberate choice in the type of uniform Charles XII evolved f
himself. There may have been a family preference for simple styles in clothe
Queen Christina in her youth and Charles XI in his maturity had shown simila
inclinations. Charles's personal taste certainly developed into an avoidance
unnecessary decoration and fussy detail, with a pronounced preference f
clear and bold lines over the whole range of design. In architecture, in silv
and glassware for private or ceremonial use, in coins and medals or any oth
object on which his advice was sought or his wishes expressed this is easy
observe. But in respect of his own uniform, we are probably justified in assum
ing that a desire to signal his own presence to the soldiers played a part thoug
the King may initially not have been consciously aware of his own motiv
Simply dressed, without a wig, he was the figure which could easily be picke
out among the more gaudily dressed, be-wigged officers who surrounde
him.[13]

Charles's table was considered as simple and strange as his clothes b
foreign observers:[14] only seven courses were served at dinner, except o
very special occasions, and though wine was offered to the officers and officia
who dined with the King, he himself drank neither wine nor strong liquor.
His mealtimes were not even regular; they depended on the duties of the day
inspection rides, drills, and exercises of various kinds, administrative wor
and those mathematical calculations which formed part of his continue
training as a tactical commander but which also appealed to him on inte
lectual grounds: he was seen to fill sheets with figures and with battle form
tions. He was known to be satisfied with a piece of bread and a glass of beer i
some peasant's modest home for his midday meal. He had a good appeti
throughout his life ('He could eat', said one of his unwilling Norwegian hos
during the 1716 campaign),[16] particularly for bread, bacon and game, fc
salad stuff like cress, parsley and spinach, for fruit like apples, orange
lemons, melons, cherries and pears; but he was already schooling himself t
go without when necessary and experimenting with that fasting when he ha
colds or fevers which became one of his pet remedies for minor ailments.[17]

He was also teaching himself to do with little sleep. Family traits ma
suggest an explanation here also: Queen Christina, for instance, had bee
able to manage with far less sleep than normal, and his own father had been
habitually early riser. But again, necessity was the deciding factor. In th
campaign life which became his lot, ability to work and fight after only thre
or four hours' rest at night was an asset in times of crisis though he preferre
five to six hours. Indifference to creature comforts was part of the same régim
of training: a straw mattress was often chosen in preference to a soft be
when sleeping away from headquarters[18] to accustom himself to times whe
no bed at all should be available. That Charles learnt to sleep when and ho
he could is amply documented – by a camp-fire in the Polish woods,[1]

---

* Recent investigation of the royal accounts have shown that expenditure on food, wine an
luxuries was quite heavy.[15]

Friherre Axel Gyllenkrook,
from a painting by G. Schröder

Count Adam Ludvig Lewenhaupt,
from a painting by D. von Krafft

Friherre Carl Cronstedt,
from a painting by J. H. Scheffel

Frederick of Hesse (later Frederick I of Sweden),
from a painting by an unknown artist

Count Karl Piper,
from a painting by D. Ehrenstrahl

Olof Hermelin of the Chancery-in-the-
from a painting by Ludvig Weyant

Josias Cederhielm of the Chancery-in-the-field,
from a painting by Lucas von Breda

Friherre Casten Feif,
from a painting attributed to Starb

wrapped in his cape on a river-bank,[20] stretched out on a 'bed' of Norwegian spruce branches.[21] When short of sleep he cat-napped voluntarily, or even against his will when he sat down to the talk of fellow-officers or to listen to a sermon. His chaplain biographer who knew him on campaign from 1703–9 could not find it in his heart to criticize him for nodding during long sermons, knowing, as he put it, that his moments of inattention were caused by the body's tiredness and not by religious indifference.[22]

The King's piety impressed strangers who visited the camp in Courland. They noted the regularity with which he attended prayers and took part in the hymn-singing morning and night; they commented on the fact that the words 'With God's help' – the dedication used before the Narva and Dvina battles – were so often on his lips that they had become a phrase repeated by the soldiers. 'In battle', one diplomat reported, 'no soldier draws his sword without first saying "With God's help".'[23]

From the observation of the King's daily life in camp, deductions were made as to his character. His self-confidence, amounting to near arrogance, was stressed. His usual retort to those who conjured up difficulties, '*labri, labri, en françois, bagatelle, bagatelle*', was repeated with more aural than orthographical exactitude.[24] The dedication to the work in hand was commented on. The King, it was noted, no longer played cards and rarely hunted.[25] He had a stable full of fine horses, one of which was kept saddled day and night to permit him to leave for inspections and other trips at a moment's notice, accompanied only by the captain on duty and a page.[26] His long rides were becoming legend; he visited regiments and outposts so frequently that there was hardly an officer whose face, name and record was not familiar to him: no native Courlander, it was said, knew the roads of the Duchy as well as the King of Sweden.[27] Even the diversions he permitted himself – practising river-crossings on horseback, mock battles of attack and defence, the talk of campaigns and commanders[28] – could not be separated from the training of his calling. With royal ceremony when occasion demanded, such as the reception of foreign diplomats and emissaries, went an inscrutability about his next moves.[29] He was assumed to be ambitious. He was known to have been successful. He was summed up as a prince '*plein de feu et d'action*' whose valour was equal to that of his warrior ancestors. It was whispered that he believed he could not be beaten.[30] Such was the picture of the young Charles XII which was broadcast by word of mouth, by private letter and official dispatches all over Europe.

II

Much of it was true to life. But just as the simple personal habits and the informal manners in everyday life obscured for the foreign observers the gulf which existed between the Swedish King and his subjects, so the certainty of public behaviour overlay debates and uncertainties which had to be resolved

G

before action could be taken. Charles was *Herren*, the Master, even at time
when the Majesty, *Kungliga Majestät*, was laid aside.[31] Great freedom 〈
expression was permitted, and views on diplomatic and military issue
thought unpalatable to the King were frequently presented by word of mout
or by letters and memorials. At no time in Charles's career was Chancer
concern (from his own headquarters and from Stockholm) more acute tha
after 30 July 1701 when the King had put forward what could be interprete
as a dethronement demand in his letter to Radziejowski: Augustus (to who〉
Radziejowski communicated the letter) used it in Berlin to emphasize th
danger which Charles xii now presented to 'all crowned heads'.[32] It is true th〈
it was Chancery circles which had first put the idea of displacing Augustι
into Charles's head;* but they had intended that this should be effected b
secret diplomacy via the Sobieski and patriot groups, while Sweden official
kept aloof, and they had urged the King to reiterate assurances to the Polis
magnates that the Republic's neutrality would be respected as long as th
Elector's war effort was not supported.

Such assurances Charles xii had indeed sent to the Commonwealth as soo
as Augustus invaded Livonia in 1700; but the Chancery as a whole resente
the King's argument that it was incompatible with Sweden's honour to rene
them until an answer had been returned or an explanation offered for th
Republic's lack of protest at Augustus's having removed the Swedish repre
sentative from Warsaw.[33] Behind this resentment lay a collective Chancer
experience of the complexities of Polish politics, a memory of the difficultie
of the Polish campaigns of Charles x's reign, and a desire to make use of th
Spanish succession conjunctures. To the Chancery men, especially those i
Stockholm, this seemed a golden opportunity to achieve some of Sweden
desiderata. If Leopold was promised auxiliary troops by Charles xii, migl
not the town of Bremen or the principality of Hadeln or even a guarantee 〈
the Baltic provinces follow? If Charles joined the Grand Alliance, might n〈
minor military detachments to the Maritime Powers reap rich rewards? Eve
though Charles resisted the flattering letter in William's own hand, salutin
him as a future commander-in-chief of the forces opposed to Louis,[34] coul
he not explore possibilities which such a letter opened up? Why get deep int
the Polish mire if the roads to the west led to glittering prizes? No wond〈
that officials who reasoned in this way spoke of 'that cursed Polish dethron〈
ment',[35] which seemed to tie them to the east.

There existed an obvious dichotomy between the higher ranks of the civilia
bureaucracy and the military leadership. The Chancery officials tended to t
ignorant of, or not to give enough weight to, the military logistics of a give
situation. Most of them had achieved office and responsibility in the pacifi
years after 1679 and had been deeply imbued with the neutrality policy whic
Sweden had pursued in the Nine Years War. They were apt to assume th〈
negotiations alone could restore peace and make gains and they regrette

---

* See above, p. 168.

he growth of influence of the 'rash' military men which even a defensive war
rought in its train. On a lower, but very human, level they felt jealous of
he promotion prospects which the war put into the path of the officer class
nd bemoaned that the lure of the sword prevented the most intelligent and
est educated young men from entering their proper sphere, the civil
ureaucracy.[36]

The pull of the army, not only to defend Sweden against attack but also
ecause 'pen-pushers' seemed to have less of the King's respect, can be
educed from the letter in which Edvard Gyldenstolpe (the son of Charles's
ormer governor) announced to his father a break with family tradition: after
. grand tour of studies and travels, making useful connexions to fit him for a
iplomatic and Chancery career, he had decided the army was the only way
o rise 'these days'.[37] And the split among a civilian and an army group inside
eadquarters, centred round Piper and Rehnskiöld respectively, is amply
rought out in the correspondence of foreign observers who either stayed at
eadquarters for long periods or who made part of the campaign with the
'wedish army, even if we allow for some natural exaggeration. That split,
hough overlaid by concern for the prisoners-of-war, can still be noted during
he captivity in Russia.[38]

Charles relied more on his civilian advisers than either young officers or
ven wise grey-beards in Stockholm realized,* but he had the military require-
ents as his most pressing responsibility and these exerted a strong influence
n his political decisions. Sometimes they drove him to action considered
recipitate by the Chancery men. It happened on 30 July 1701 and it happened
n later occasions in the Polish years of the campaign. At such times one
xpression is apt to recur in confidential letters from civilians to colleagues at
ome: 'I fear the King is drawing the bow too tight.'[39] And in the equally
onfidential letters they received from Stockholm the sigh, 'I regret the King
oes not take the conjunctures sufficiently into account', is frequently heard.[40]
t is not surprising that such phrases are missing from the letters, diaries and
nemoirs of military men. They would be more inhibited by their sense of
ersonal loyalty to the King and less concerned about inquiries of the 'retro-
pect' kind than the civilians; but the main reason is, of course, that they
ccepted – as the King had to do – that military considerations exerted a
trong influence on political steps. Even where military criticism of Charles
xii can be deduced, as in the reports (written to defend their own reputations)
f Lewenhaupt and Creutz after the surrender of Perevolotjna,[41] this is
vithin the field of tactical errors and the chain of communication and not
vith decision-making either in politics or strategy.

In the autumn of 1700, Charles xii was not unmindful of developments in
he west. To him the non-commitment of Sweden was a given fact in view of
he military task ahead. The huge money offers by Louis xiv in compensation

* Charles's most immediate anxiety after Poltava was to get important Chancery officials
eleased and great though vain efforts were made for this purpose; cp. below, pp. 300, 323, 337–8.

for the military help France was bound to render as a guarantor of Oliva were
sidestepped since they were phrased in a manner which implied Swedish
moral support for Louis in Spain. They were, however, not directly refused
(Charles having learnt his lesson from the Chancery a year ago), and French
diplomats – though they had the fullest support from the Duke of Holstein
Gottorp – met with such evasive answers and such interminable delays that
they were provoked to the comment that the Swedish court was 'ruder and
more savage' than the Courland countryside of the raw autumn and early
winter.[42] Haersolte, representing William both as Dutch Stadholder and King
of England, was only slightly less despondent. Charles XII, he reported, always
spoke with gratitude of the friendship of William III,[43] but could not be
prevailed on to enter the Grand Alliance formed against France in September 1701 at The Hague. Sweden did, however, in that very month enter
into a convention of amity with the Maritime Powers in which Charles XII
pledged his word not to enter into alliances with rulers in enmity with
them.

The need to keep a close watch on conjunctures lay, from the Swedish
King's point of view, in the favourable opportunities these offered to some of
Sweden's enemies or to powers potentially hostile to Sweden. An alliance
between the Emperor and the Elector of Brandenburg had already been
signed in September 1700. By this Leopold had bought Frederick's military
support against France in return for the title 'King in Prussia': a title which –
though recognized by Augustus – was contested by the Polish Republic so as
not to render incontrovertible the loss of sovereignty over East Prussia.
Imperial and Saxon encouragement of the Prussian appetite for Swedish
Pomerania was suspected, and Swedish diplomacy began to counteract this
by cultivating good relations with Frederick of Brandenburg, holding out
hopes of recognition of his new title. Hanoverian* and Prussian adherence to
the Grand Alliance was not looked upon as any threat to Sweden, but the
King of Denmark's alliance with the Emperor in the spring of 1701, followed
by one with the Maritime Powers a little later in the year whereby Danish
troops were put at their disposal against France's if war should break out,
was alarming. Might not Frederick IV use his position to undermine the
Anglo-Dutch guarantee of Travendal and to weaken Imperial support for
Holstein-Gottorp? More sinister was the diplomacy of Augustus of Saxony.
In December 1700 he had signed an alliance with Louis XIV. He never ratified
it, but made good use of it to obtain better terms from the Emperor with
whom he negotiated throughout the autumn of 1701.† It seemed highly
probable that Leopold would have to buy Saxon support with treaty clauses
which were at least implicitly and possibly explicitly anti-Swedish.

There was therefore some need in the autumn of 1701 to make Brandenburg–Prussia and the Emperor aware that Charles XII might move west if his

---

* Georg Ludwig had opted for the Emperor against Louis already before the end of 1700.
† This alliance was signed in January 1702 and promptly ratified.

possessions in Germany were endangered; and the minor Swedish raids into Samogitia, a district which though part of the Polish-Lithuanian Common-wealth was nevertheless regarded by contemporaries as being 'German' and almost outside the Republic proper,* must be looked at in this light. Officially small detachments of the army crossed the Samogitian border (at the request of James Sobieski) to give protection for estates owned by the Sapieha family in that area – and as such they provoked counter-measures by Sapieha enemies on Swedish-occupied Courland – but they served also by their clear-ing of the Samogitian coast to remind the world that Sweden looked west as well as east in defence of her empire. This purpose could, however, have been achieved in other ways and the basic explanation for the prolonged stay of the King and the operational army in Courland lies in their long attendance on the cardinal's reply. When it finally arrived, it came in the name of the Polish Diet, to whom Radziejowski had communicated Charles's letter of 30 July. Its message, behind polite phrases was brief: would the Swedes please go away and not mix in the affairs of the Republic.⁴⁴

This was the most unhelpful answer possible from Charles's point of view since it gave no clarification of his relationship with the Republic. It con-tained no assurance that the Poles would deny Augustus a base for the 1702 campaign. Nor was there any phrase which would serve to discount the rumours of Polish designs, independent of Augustus, on Swedish Livonia. It is significant that it was after the receipt of this letter that preparations for a Russian campaign in 1701 were finally abandoned.

Charles himself must take the blame for the tone of Radziejowski's letter, since he himself had provided its ammunition by his dethronement sugges-tion. Many magnates who held that Augustus had trampled on Polish liber-ties and involved the Commonwealth in a Saxo-Russian war against Sweden when he had no right to do so, were simultaneously of the opinion that this was no business of Charles XII. Even the Polish patriots of the Jabłonowski and Leszczyński group, who favoured dethronement and war against Russia, were shocked when they heard the contents of the letter of 30 July. They wanted to achieve the goals they had in common with Charles XII by working on their compatriots by degrees, using Swedish money and discreet Swedish military pressure in the first place. They did not grasp the nature of Charles's military dilemma and underestimated his need to obtain clarification of the Polish situation within months rather than years.

Radziejowski's publication of Charles XII's letter was indeed intended to paralyse the patriot group while at the same time halting the Swedish army close enough to the Republic to be used by the neutralists in their struggle with Augustus. In the first objective the cardinal was successful for a longer period than in the second, since the totally negative answer he chose to send pushed Charles into measures which carried greater risks of Swedish violation of Polish territory.

* This was due to its ancient links with the lands of the Teutonic religious orders.

III

On 18 November the Sapieha brothers Benedikt and Kasimir suffered a defeat at the hands of the so-called 'United Families' of Lithuania (the Ogińskis, Wisńioweckis, Radziwills and Potockis) and fled to Polish Prussia. From there they wrote to Charles XII asking for support. James Sobieski had already from August 1701 entered into closer contact with Swedish head quarters by sending an emissary and by a correspondence, under the pseu donym of 'Creon', with Cederhielm. He wanted Charles to enter Poland to prevent Augustus suppressing Polish liberties and was liberal with advice as to the best means whereby Charles could unite the Commonwealth against the Elector-King.[45] No immediate commitment was made but in December Charles took part, with four hundred men, in a reconnaissance in depth of Samogitia during which – after minor skirmishes – the bridgeheads of Jurburg and Kowno on the Niemen were secured. The decision to move a major part of the army to Samogitia was then taken and after three weeks' absence the King returned to headquarters to arrange for the march south of fifteen thousand men in January 1702.

This move was a decisive one in several ways, not all of which were foreseen at the time. It clearly meant another postponement of the Russian campaign. For how long was uncertain – it would depend on the time needed to unravel what Cederhielm so aptly called 'the Gordian knot of our Polish dilemma'.[4] How Augustus was to be brought to sacrifice his alliance with the Tsar was immaterial to Charles XII. He was not bent, as negotiations later in the year were to show,* on dethronement at all costs, and would settle for alternative securities to deny the Elector of Saxony his Polish base. Samogitia, it was hoped, might serve as a halfway house from which the Poles – seeing the Swedes coming closer – might be pressed, as politely as possible, to clarify their attitude to Augustus's war on Sweden. It was also realized of course that the move might lead to longer and closer involvement with Polish affairs than was desired, but the length of time needed to unravel the knot was only dimly guessed at. Charles XII during 1701 commented to Cederhielm that 'we shall be fighting this side of the water for many a year to come',[4] but he was not sure whether the King was serious or not. If he was, how-ever, it is more likely that he had Tsar Peter in mind, or the formidable combination of the Tsar and Augustus, since events were to show that the King was slow in perceiving the subtleties and difficulties of the Polish situation.

Before departure Schlippenbach's army was reinforced and a militia organ-ized throughout the Baltic provinces in the hope of avoiding a repetition of the plunder which had taken place before the Russians had withdrawn for the winter across their own border. Four thousand men were left behind in

---

* See below, p. 190.

Courland, initially under Stuart's command, to protect Riga from the south, to deny Augustus a base and to keep the prospect of a Swedish-controlled Courland in being.

Charles's move south was preceded by manifestoes intended to maintain friendly relations with the Republic. He stressed the 'old and natural alliance' of Sweden and Poland against Russia and emphasized the desire of Sweden to preserve Polish liberties. Augustus himself – in Warsaw to exert pressure on the Diet – countered by hints that he would be prepared to sacrifice Courland or Polish Prussia to Charles XII in return for a Suedo-Saxon peace. Chastened by his experience over the 30 July letter Charles forbade any negotiation on these terms, arguing that the slightest nibbling of the bait would give Augustus an opportunity to publicize Swedish greed and turn the Poles as a body against them.

Neither of the two emissaries sent by the King-Elector to the Swedish head-quarters obtained audience with Charles XII. The first caller, already in January 1702, was Aurora von Königsmarck. Anecdotes and poems celebrating her visit to Bielowicze fostered the legend that this famous beauty, who had borne Augustus a son,* was sent to seduce Charles XII and so to entangle Mars with Cupid that the campaign against Augustus would falter. The fact that Aurora was more than twenty years older than Charles and that her beauty was thought by some rather faded does not in itself refute such speculations, but they seem to rest on slender foundations. She had plausible grounds for asking permission – which was granted – to visit headquarters: she was Swedish by birth and had relatives among the officers whom she wanted to meet. She was, however, given no opportunity to speak privately to the King. Political considerations apart, Charles had no wish to receive her. He had grown up at a court where royal mistresses were looked upon as 'a foreign custom'.† Moreover, his father had regarded adultery as a mortal sin and had passed on his strict moral code to his son. To receive Aurora in 1702 would appear, to Charles at least, as a condonement of adultery. When in Saxony in 1707 she was a guest at a Swedish wedding where he himself was present, he spoke to her politely but his basic attitude remained: consulted about what rank she should be accorded at the banquet, he left this to the hosts but queried whether a 'royal whore' ought to take precedence over any of the Swedish women guests.[48] Augustus's next emissary, the Saxon official Vitzthum, who approached headquarters in February, was not admitted to the camp and suffered a brief arrest on the grounds that he had no pass from the Elector to identify him and his business.

That Augustus had any serious intention of making peace at this stage is doubted by the scholar at present studying his policy from documents in the

---

* The famous soldier in French service, Maurice of Saxe, who in his *Reveries* commented on Charles XII's Polish campaign.

† It is not known whether Charles XII was ever told of his grandfather's illegitimate son who fell fighting on the Allied side in 1708, or of that grandson of Gustavus Adolphus's illegitimate son who fought with the Swedes in the Norwegian campaign of 1718.

Saxon archives.[49] He had an advantageous treaty with the Tsar* and hi
military preparations for the 1702 campaign were well advanced, with twenty
thousand Saxon troops ready to leave the Electorate to seek battle with
Charles on Polish soil. By special arrangement with Leopold the eigh
thousand Saxon troops destined for the Emperor's service were to be stationed
in Bohemia for the time being and could therefore be looked upon as a
reserve.

Military reaction to the Swedish crossing into Samogitia came with great
promptitude from the 'United Families' who saw Charles XII as an enemy
come to avenge the Olkienieki defeat of the Sapiehas. In reality there was at
this stage no Swedish commitment to Benedikt and Kasimir; but the guerrilla
warfare of Ogiński and Wiśniowiecki troops, added to military intelligence
about Augustus's preparations for the campaign, forced Charles's hand and
on 21 March a virtual alliance was made between the Sapiehas, invited to the
Swedish headquarters, and the King. The Sapiehas never became popular
with the Swedes. 'The slyest man I ever met', was the verdict of one official
looking back on a long life, of the elder brother.[50] Charles XII persisted in
regarding them as a family bent on selfish pursuits,[51] who would have to serve
as a stop-gap till he could make the patriot group and the one round Radziejowski cooperate with him. A formal alliance with the Sapiehas would justify
military action against the 'United Families', who had worried the Swedish
army by their guerrilla attacks. The merciless cutting down of four hundred
Swedes† by six thousand Wiśniowecki troops had especially shaken headquarters. Strategy would also be served by a Sapieha alliance since by virtue
of it Charles could proceed into the Commonwealth proper if need be.

The meeting with the Sapieha brothers on 21 March 1702 was therefore of
some importance. The conversation – as was usual between Swedes and Poles
at this time – was in Latin and German. Swedish protection and military help
was offered against Sapieha commitment to the dethronement programme.
One sentence by Charles has been particularly commented on because historians have read into it Charles's personal hatred of Augustus and his desire
for revenge. When the Sapiehas, not anxious to be pinned down, expressed
doubts whether anyone in the Republic really wanted to topple Augustus
from his elected position, Charles banged the table with his fist and said, with
emphasis: *Ego semel dice et face.*[52] The supposed hateful and revengeful
feelings are not substantiated. Apart from being contradicted by Prussian
diplomats at the time,[53] they would seem to be belied by the way Charles
wrote about his cousin in 1706 to his sisters. I bother to dispute them because
they seem an obstacle to a more historical, if still hypothetical, interpretation
of his use of the quotation. Like his fellow-monarchs, Charles was conscious
of the value of the given word and did not pledge it (and thus his honour)
lightly; and a more natural explanation would be that he in 1702 was in fact

* See above, pp. 158, 160.

† Hummerhielm, the officer commanding the detachment, was taken prisoner; news of the
catastrophe reached headquarters through some privates who got away.

assuring the Sapiehas of the firmness of his resolve not to leave them in the lurch if they took on their share of the bargain: to make the dethronement issue – so adroitly side-stepped by Radziejowski – a live one. If any more fanciful' notions need to be introduced, I would plump for youthful impatience with circumlocutory cleverness. This would at least be backed by Charles's persistent dislike of the different standards of morality accepted for relations between princes and those moral codes regarded as necessary and honourable in private life.[54] Experience made him slightly more adroit in – and more tolerant of – bending those codes in a complicated situation, but his upbringing and temperament made it impossible for him to be cynical about the pledged word.

After the meeting of 21 March, when the Sapiehas accepted the conditions laid down by Charles XII, events moved swiftly. The Swedes initially hoped to contain the Saxon troops in the Empire and orders were sent on 5 April for Nils Gyllenstierna to collect all available Swedish troops in the Empire – some eleven thousand in all – to intercept the Saxons on the Polish frontier of the Commonwealth. Some regiments were left behind in Samogitia and others, under Mörner, were temporarily stationed in Vilna, the Wiśniowecki stronghold. The main army marched along the Niemen as far as Merecz, where it crossed the river. It then divided into two columns and the army proceeded on the road towards Warsaw along different routes.* Recruits from Sweden were expected at Riga and these were put under Maidel's command as a reserve corps. The general idea was to stop Saxon troops coming into Poland or, if this did not succeed, to reach Warsaw before the capital was taken over by Augustus's German army.

Swedish movements were watched with mingled alarm and calculation in Warsaw. To avoid hostilities the Diet restored the Sapiehas to their dignities and offices in Lithuania and sent a delegation to Charles to offer the Republic's mediation in the Saxo-Swedish war. The terms proposed would severely curtail Augustus's power while averting the threat of Poland becoming the battlefield. The programme of the neutrality party had, however, little prospect of success since it appealed neither to Augustus, who wanted Polish commitment, nor to Charles who wanted the Poles to offer no help to the Saxon Elector even of an indirect kind. When Charles at last received the delegation on 23 April in Grodno (having found excuses not to do so early enough to interfere with the Swedish march), he greeted it in the friendliest manner but declared his inability to retrace his steps till the Republic gave proof of its neutrality: if the Poles thought it compatible with neutrality to let Augustus use their country as a base, they ought to concede him the right to seek his Saxon enemy on Polish soil. The dethronement concept was emphasized: the Swedish King would be glad to avail himself of their offices once

* One column, led by General von Liewen and the King, took the more direct route over Dlugowicze, crossing the Narew at Tykocin and the Bug at Wyszków, arriving at Warsaw on 14 May; the other, commanded by Colonel Spens, marched over Bielsk to the Bug to make certain of Brest-Litovsk and reached Warsaw at the end of May.

they had proved their neutrality by getting rid of an elected king who wa trampling their constitution underfoot.[55]

No hostilities accompanied the Swedish march since discipline was stric and there was no armed opposition from the Poles. Swedish propaganda wa much helped by the arrival of Olof Hermelin, a former professor of *eloquenti* in Dorpat, a fine Latin stylist who took up a senior position in the Chancery in-the-field. A memorandum on the Polish problem which Charles had aske for from Oxenstierna in Stockholm* was much studied at headquarters. Th chancellor expressed his conviction that the neutrality of the Republic wa more fiction than fact but urged Charles XII to respect the fiction in order t avoid an open break.[56] The King did his best to follow this advice.

Augustus had left Warsaw for the Cracow region as the Swedish arm advanced. He requested Radziejowski to join him, but the cardinal, true t his own political programme, played a waiting game and found some excus to move out of Warsaw to avoid being present when Charles and his me marched into the capital on 14 May. He was sent for by the Swedish King wh asked him to call an election Diet to permit the Poles to dethrone Augustu and proceed to the election and proclamation of a new king. Again th *primas* prevaricated: he held out hopes but delayed negotiations. Augustu was the first to gain two important concessions from the Senate: he was per mitted, in view of the Swedish presence on Polish soil, to bring Saxon troop into the Commonwealth and he was allowed to call on the Crown army of th Republic to protect its territory from violation. The order which he sen in early June to his Saxon troops to join him at Cracow was, therefore constitutionally correct and Charles XII could no longer argue that th King-Elector was trampling on Polish liberties.

At the same time, however, the neutralist Poles entered into negotiation with the Swedish King along anti-Augustan lines though they refused t proceed as speedily as Charles XII wished. The death of Jabłonowski, o 24 March, had been a blow to Swedish hopes. It offered Augustus the oppor tunity to nominate Lubomirski head of the Crown army – a commander who at least in the early stages of his career, would be dependent on the King Elector. The wise counsel of the late commander was much missed in th conference which took place on 5 June between Swedish headquarters and th Poles, the contents of which we know from a protocol in Hermelin's hand a well as from a memorandum sent by Piper to Charles XII and from comment by Cederhielm and Poniatowski who, as a member of the Sapieha mission now joined Charles XII and served him for as long as the Swedish King lived.[57] The Chancery wanted the King to desist from the dethronement programme but Charles XII – suspecting that the Polish motive was to delay his militar offensive – was still not ready to retract the demand. He would permit privat negotiations on alternative means of solving the Polish dilemma, but he wa

---

* Dated 5 March 1702, this memorandum is the last important one from his hand: he die aged seventy-seven in July 1702.

not prepared to make a public retraction of his demand as this would seem both inconsistent and dishonourable – 'indecent' is the adjective that stuck in Chancery memory.[58]

The urgent military need was to catch up with Saxon troops on Polish soil. Already on 24 May – as soon as it was known that Augustus had a perfect right to call his German troops into the Commonwealth – Charles ordered Gyllenstierna to seek a junction with the main Swedish army in the Cracow region. Mörner, who on 5 May had been ordered to leave Vilna, was on 7 June also detailed to direct his march towards Cracow. Both commanders were asked to keep in touch with the King who told them that he would go to seek Augustus. On 16 June Charles XII and some eight thousand men moved out of Warsaw and proceeded slowly in a south-easterly direction to permit the other two armies to catch up.[59]

IV

The battle of Kliszów on 9 July was the outcome of Augustus and Charles being equally anxious to fight before the other received reinforcements. There was an element of split-second timing in the calculations of both of them. By the middle of June Augustus had some fourteen thousand men and was keen to find Charles before he had been joined by Gyllenstierna. Charles could not fight till either Mörner – who had less of a distance to cover with his four thousand men – or Gyllenstierna with his considerable force (at least nine, possibly eleven thousand) had caught up with him. He was, however, desperately keen to achieve battle before the Polish Crown army – ordered to Cracow by Augustus – should arrive to take part in the battle: once the Swedes had spilt Polish blood it would be difficult to reach a solution of the Polish dilemma by negotiation. A captured Saxon prisoner on 21 June divulged Augustus's decision to attack in the near future.[60] On June 26 Charles learnt that Gyllenstierna would not be able to catch up with him in time;* and consequently moved in the direction from which Mörner was approaching.† The King took part in the preparations for battle, sat in on reconnaissance reports from cavalry detachments sent to spy out the Saxon position at Pinczów, and rode over to discuss the situation with Mörner as soon as he came within reach.

When Augustus came closer and settled nearer the Swedes at Kliszów, Charles favoured a surprise attack since the Saxons clearly imagined the initiative to lie with them, but he was prevailed on by his mentors in the art of war to wait for Mörner's army. In the evening of 8 July that officer, with troops tired from forced marching came into the Swedish camp as dark was falling. Battle was fixed for the following day, the troops to move off at

* The orders of 24 May had not reached Stettin till 14 June. Gyllenstierna left on 23 June, entered Commonwealth territory on 28 June and joined Charles in Cracow on August 19.

† Mörner's route was via Lublin and Kazimierz; Charles had gone past Opoczno and Radoszyce, and now moved east towards Kielce.

6 o'clock in the morning.* In the preparation for the battle we can mark yet another stage in Charles's development as a commander. His role is more independent and forceful – comparable to his growing command in the field of politics during 1701 and 1702 – and his typical style as a leader is more pronounced. The words chosen to announce a decision or brush aside an objection bear a stamp which from now one becomes associated with him and him alone. 'Hungry dogs bite best', was the retort to those who urged that Mörner's troops might need more time for rest. 'We'll soon conquer artillery for as much shooting as you want', countered the suggestion that it might be wiser to wait for Gyllenstierna's artillery.[61] In the battle itself Charles played a significant part so that the praise which has been bestowed on him for Kliszów, 'his most glorious victory',[62] is more deserved than the congratulations which came his way after Narva.

In effect the whole of the Swedish army showed at its best on 9 July. A silent march, without music or standards to attract attention, through wooded and difficult terrain ensured the desired surprise; a sudden, but planned, change from a frontal attack to a flank attack was the outcome of close study of the terrain; a sustained fight *aux armes blanches* forced the courageous Saxons to give ground.

Charles's own contribution was coolness in unexpected emergencies and quickness in reaching decisions on the left wing where he was in command. He did not hesitate when the Polish Crown army under Lubomirski† suddenly appeared on the scene of battle, however much he had dreaded (for political reasons) having to fight the Poles. He stuck to the battle plan when the Saxons crossed a morass (which the Swedes had reckoned impassable) to attack his wing in the rear; he cut off the retreat towards Pinczów – where Augustus hoped to regroup and offer battle anew – at the right moment. It was noted that he not only took part in the fight, but acted the role of the commander where necessary: riding about, watching the unfolding of the task of his wing in the overall pattern of the attack.

The Saxons had superior fire-power, but this was neutralized first by the speedier though far fewer Swedish field-pieces and by the capture, at an early stage, of forty-eight Saxon cannon which were now turned against their owners. The Saxon superiority in cavalry‡ had been countered by the Swedish attack at a gallop with not even a single salvo to precede it and by skilful manœuvres in tight corners. The Swedish infantry had walked – even run – to the attack in spite of *cheveaux-de-frise* and Saxon musket-fire. As Vellingk, who took over the section left without a commander when the Duke of

* The decision to fight on 9 July, the anniversary of the crossing of the Dvina, was thus an accidental one; but the anniversary was utilized for morale purposes and probably helped to forge a will to win.

† Augustus had been prevailed upon to postpone his attack on the Swedes till 10 July by Lubomirski who wanted the Crown army to cover itself with glory (and gain influence) by participation in the battle.

‡ Thirty-four Saxon squadrons counted 125 men each; twenty-one Swedish ones one hundred each.

Holstein-Gottorp was hit by a falconet ball, put it in his report: 'It was a battle which began with firm resolution, was continued with due caution and ended in the highest *gloire*.'[63]

The Swedish losses, from an army of some twelve thousand, were about three hundred dead and double that number wounded. Of the Saxon force of about sixteen thousand,* about two thousand were dead or seriously wounded and an equal number prisoners. The Swedish booty was rich. Trophies of standards, cannon and ammunition, uniforms and boots which came in handy for those Swedish regiments that were shabby, a field-chest full of money, and papers in the field-chancery which gave valuable insight into Augustus's diplomacy.

Charles xii's gratitude for victory was marred by the grief he felt for the death of Frederick of Holstein-Gottorp, mortally wounded in the battle. The King had never particularly liked his brother-in-law of the teasing tongue and the loose morals, but he loved Hedvig Sophia and suffered with her in her loss.[64] He did not take to himself any share of the victory either then or later. In so far as he singled out any one it was General Rehnskiöld: when the King in 1707 promoted him field-marshal and made him a count he cited Kliszów among his battle honours. For the rest Charles always praised the whole of the army. God had given victory because they had all given of their best.

---

* On paper the Saxon army counted 22,300 and the Swedish one 16,230; but neither was, according to the estimates of the military specialists, up to strength.

5

The Grand Design

Kliszów put the Polish part of Charles XII's 'grand design' into the realm of the possible. It no longer seemed visionary to think of the Republic, with its own Polish-born king, becoming Sweden's military ally against Tsar Peter for the benefit of both nations: the Commonwealth would, with Swedish help, regain land lost to Russia and, as a reward, Sweden would reap benefits along the Baltic coastline – Charles XII might, for example, be made Duke of Courland under nominal Polish suzerainty in the interests of the commercial aspect of the grand design. This stage one – so to speak – of the grand design was, however, not essential to the essence of it which remained, as always, the rectification of the frontier with Russia as *satisfactio* for the Tsar's attack; and Charles was very receptive in the post-Kliszów months to the alternative of peace with Augustus and benevolent neutrality from the Republic, so that he might move against Tsar Peter safe from attack on his flank. He felt confident that given such conditions the Swedes could tackle Russia without help. The Polish Crown army had not shown up well in the battle of Kliszów. Lubomirski's five thousand men had quickly been put to flight by numerically inferior Swedes led by Charles, and the King did not in the late summer of 1702 have exaggerated ideas of the military value of the Republic's alliance.

Yet the Kliszów victory was not of a kind which permitted Charles to dictate peace. The Swedish soldiers – and the horses* – had been too exhausted after eleven hours' marching and fighting on 9 July to cut off Augustus's withdrawal to Lemberg in Red-Russia. Here, where his support was strong, the King-Elector could collect his troops scattered in the battle and await his reserve army. He was still a military factor to be reckoned with, especially as he took immediate steps† to institute a closer collaboration in the field with Tsar Peter.[1]

Nevertheless, the impact of the Kliszów victory on the Polish Crown army and on Augustus's political ally, the Emperor, had been considerable. As soon as Charles's headquarters were settled at Cracow on 23 July negotiations

---
* A cavalry horse was reckoned capable of five hours' fighting in one stretch.
† These were effected through Patkul, who had been present at Saxon headquarters during the battle of Kliszów, but made his escape hidden in a peasant's cart.

or a Saxo-Swedish peace were begun under the mediation of Leopold's special envoy Sinzendorff.[2] The Emperor claimed to be speaking for Augustus in a general way and was undoubtedly himself very anxious for success: he wanted to free the Saxon army for his own war against Louis XIV. Charles XII was equally keen to see the Saxon army leave Poland and his Chancery officials, who longed for peace *per se*, excelled themselves in ingenuity. The negotiations broke down, however, on the inability of Sinzendorff to provide any proof of Augustus's desire for peace. All indications did, in effect, point to the King-Elector's determination to continue the war at all costs. Russian troops poured into Lithuania, the Tsar proclaiming himself the ally and protector of the Grand Duchy: others marched into Poland along the Lower Dnieper, ostensibly bringing Russian help for Polish landowners bothered by Cossack revolts. Augustus continued his negotiations to draw Prussia and Denmark into the war as active partners and his efforts in Copenhagen and Berlin were duly reported to the Swedes. Charles even began to doubt Leopold's impartiality: the Emperor's offer to James Sobieski of a governorship, with the title of viceroy, over part of the Austrian hereditary dominions looked suspiciously like a move to take Augustus's main rival for the Polish crown out of circulation.[3]

Nor did unofficial negotiations with various representatives of the Commonwealth lead to the kind of clear-cut result that Charles needed. Too many voices claimed to speak for Poland: the Sobieskis, the patriots, the Sapiehas, the cardinal, Lubomirski and, increasingly, the magnates of confederations forming or in being. The King's train of thought, and his feeling of being caught up in a tangled web, can be sensed from a letter he wrote to Piper on 29 August:

Since the Poles themselves made the first proposal for the dethronement, I desire that they themselves shall make it come to pass so that I need only support them till they have had their liberties confirmed. Either they must all say yes or all no; if they say no, then We must take Our measures accordingly; if they say yes, then I assume they will defend their new King. Believe that I would give Augustus peace immediately if I could trust his word; but as soon as peace is made and We are on Our march towards Muscovy, he would accept Russian money and attack Us in the back, and then Our task would be even more difficult than it is now.[4]

Time was the essence of the military problem, and in the absence of Polish unity and even of commitment by a majority of those who expressed themselves willing eventually to support Charles XII (wait and see, trust in our goodwill once peace is made, was what their messages boiled down to) the Republic itself – not only its symbol the crown – became the contested apple between the Saxon and the Swedish armies. Each army had to live, in large measure, from contributions levied. The Swedes did their best to distribute such burdens fairly. Magnus Stenbock, the 'Måns' of Charles's correspondence,* proved an efficient and fair director of the war commissariat.[5] The

* Sometimes 'Måns Lurifax', employing a childish nickname for the fox in Sweden.

Chancery was on continual watch against harsh measures by the military an
Polish complaints against Swedish officers and men were immediately investi
gated and brought to the King's notice.[6] Even so, it was unavoidable tha
regions affected by Swedish billeting and demands for food, fodder an
money should feel resentful, and that the rallying to the Swedish or the Saxo
side should be influenced by hopes of a lightening of the burden of contribu
tion, or by fears of the force at the disposal of either army. Such rallyin
tended in any case to be temporary: magnates frequently changed sides out o
concern for their estates, and caused growing disillusionment in the Swedisl
army. The King disliked being made a fool of by those who professed suppor
for his plans only to withdraw it as soon as it became expedient. Stenbocl
concluded that the only way to handle the Poles was to treat them as one di
a puppy: to stroke its head and smack its behind.[7]

The custom of the Poles seemed strange enough to Swedish eyes – the fac
that men kissed each other in salutation or when moved by joy or sorrow wa
much commented on[8] – but it was worse that the whole vast country with it
fourteen million people should offer no centre. Indeed, the country was geo
graphically too vast for either the Saxon or the Swedish army to control it b
military means. In the contest for Poland between Charles and Augustus
which lasted from 1702 to 1706, one can observe a Box-and-Cox patter
whereby armies ended a campaign in the position previously held by the
enemy: when Charles XII manoeuvred and fought his way to the north
Augustus moved south; when the Swedes had to move south-east, the Saxons
the Polish Crown army and the Russian auxiliaries filtered back to the north-
west. Victory in the struggle came to the Swedes because their superior
strategy enabled them to break this pattern; they split the enemy army into
a Polish–Russian part tied to the east and a Saxon part bottled up in the
west.

With the Swedes in Cracow in the late summer and autumn of 1702,
Augustus moved his army north to safety behind the Vistula and the Bug
river line. On the failure of Imperial mediation, there was no longer any need
for Charles XII to stay in the south and several factors exerted a pull towards
the north. It would not do to let the Tsar feel too safe from interruption. The
Russians had scored significant successes since Narva; the Swedish flotilla on
lake Ladoga had been routed by superior naval forces; Schlippenbach had
suffered a defeat at Hummelshof in July; the small garrison at Nöteborg at
the mouth of the Neva was besieged; areas which used to supply a super-
abundance of food were being laid waste and Swedish subjects were being
dragged into captivity by their thousands.* All the comfort Charles could
offer was a promise that the main army would reverse the situation as soon as
possible and that 'What Livonia in the meantime suffers, can, with God's
help be remedied by privileges and exemptions from taxes when God shall
give us peace.'[9] A move north would also serve the diplomatic negotiations

* One of these was Catherine, who eventually became the Tsar's wife.

with Brandenburg–Prussia and with England which were in train to restrain those whom Augustus courted most eagerly: it was necessary to obtain assurance of Brandenburg–Prussia's neutrality, and it was essential to check-mate Frederick IV of Denmark–Norway by obtaining from Queen Anne a renewal of William III's guarantee of Travendal.[10] Finally, secret appeals arrived from Radziejowski that 'something might be obtained' if Charles XII and his army came closer to Warsaw. The Cardinal could well be writing in his vein because he found Augustus and his troops too close for comfort; but his messages conjured up visions of negotiated safeguards and deserved investigation.[11]

The Swedish move north,[12] which finally began on 2 October, had been slightly delayed by an accident which Charles XII suffered on 19 September.[13] It was serious enough to spread rumours of his death across Europe; but there was in reality no danger to his life from the break – or serious crack – of the left thigh-bone which he sustained when his horse stumbled over a tent rope. The Swedes had been much impressed with the usefulness of Polish light cavalry for reconnaissance and patrol duties and had begun to recruit Valloche riders (known by the Swedes as *Valacker* or *Tovarich*) from Poles willing to serve Charles XII. The King was watching the new companies show their paces when the accident happened:* horse and rider fell, the horse landed on top of the rider, and the bone was damaged a little above the knee. It did not set perfectly – possibly because Charles moved about on crutches too soon – and one leg became shorter than the other, causing a slight limp. This seems to have become more pronounced as he got older and stiffer, and during the campaign in Norway in 1716 it struck those who saw him for the first time enough to mention it as a striking physical characteristic.[14] In 1702 the injury prevented him moving about the regiments in the way he normally did, and during the early stages of the move from Cracow he had to be content to be carried on a stretcher by relays of guards and to keep in contact with officers at a distance by letter. It was several months before he could ride again.

The route of the main army went along the Vistula, with heavy baggage and artillery being carried on river barges; while detachments fanned out in attempts to widen the area under Swedish contribution and control. In the Lublin region, the English diplomat John Robinson came to meet the army. His mission, to press for Sweden's entry into the Grand Alliance, was one which did not arouse much enthusiasm with the King (though that topic would obviously have to be touched upon in the Anglo-Swedish negotiations for a post-William convention); but he came straight from Stockholm, was well known at court and brought Charles welcome news of his family.[15] His young secretary, James Jefferyes, had Swedish army connexions, his father had served Charles XI for many years and his elder brother – after taking part

---

* Some eyewitnesses blame the accident on the King's galloping too fast; others claim that his horse was frightened by the shouts and cries inseparable from Valloche warfare.

in the Zealand descent – had fallen at Narva.[16] They were both given permis
sion to accompany the army as far as Warsaw, and diplomats from othe
countries also began to forgather in the Polish capital in expectation of th
arrival of the Swedish King.

II

Towards the end of March 1703 Charles XII arrived at Praga and settled hi
headquarters there, with the army in the neighbouring countryside. A stron
detachment under Rehnskiöld had separated from the main army in lat
December 1702 and continued along the Vistula in the direction of Thor
(Toruń), both to support the anti-Augustan forces in Great Poland and to re
connoitre the fortress in which Augustus – against the protests of the cardina
– had put a Saxon garrison. The main army had moved in easy stages, wantin
give Radziejowski time to secure a consensus of Polish opinion, and by th
time the cardinal began talks with Charles XII on 12 April he was empowere
to negotiate both on behalf of the Diet which he himself had called in Warsav
in March (and which on the whole was anti-Augustan) and by the rival Die
called by the King-Elector at Marienburg. In these negotiations Charles XII
pressed by his Chancery-in-the-field and increasingly anxious to cope with th
Russian threat,* made significant concessions: he agreed to avoid any refer
ence to Augustus's dethronement in written communications between himse
and the Poles and gave verbal promises not only to the cardinal but also t
Bishop Zaluski, and to a Marienburg delegation led by Morsztyn, to drop th
dethronement programme if the Poles would suggest alternative measures t
secure his flank. Such measures must be agreed to by a Diet representing th
whole Commonwealth, and till they were put forward he reserved his ow
freedom of action. Some historians have thought that this reservation spoile
the chances of success, others have assumed that Charles was not sincere,[1]
but his genuine interest in arriving at a compromise settlement is demon
strated by his lively concern with positive suggestions put forward in hi
own entourage. In particular, he thought well of a suggestion that Augustus'
son, the Electoral Prince, might be chosen King of Poland: if the princ
promised to keep Polish liberties and agreed to remain neutral in Tsar Peter'
war against Sweden that would be security enough – though it would be desir
able that the prince declare his loyalty to the Protestant Church so tha
religious tolerance might be promoted within the Republic.[18]

No suggestions at all came, however, from the Poles themselves. The
registered their pleasure in finding Charles XII 'sensible'; but they were to
split to agree on any political programme. Indeed, with Augustus in militar
control of the northern part of the Commonwealth, they were as much caugh
in the Polish dilemma as Charles and the Swedes.

Military necessity made it impossible for Charles to remain long at Praga

---

* The news of Nöteborg's fall in October 1702 had reached the Swedes during the march.

CHARLES XII's CAMPAIGNS
AND MOVEMENTS

0   300
Kilometres

NORWAY   SWEDEN

RUSSIA

Kristiania

Lastra Ed

Kristinehamn   Reval   Wesenberg

ederikshald   Stockholm   Narva
Fortress   Lais
Strömstad   Vadstena

Baltic Sea   Pernau

Hälsingborg   Riga
Landskrona   Karlskrona   Grubin   Bauske
Humlebæk   Lund   Würgen
Malmo   Ystad
Trelleborg   Bielowicze

Smolensk

Stralsund   Smorgonie   Tatarsk
Tribsees   Heilsberg   Radoscowicze   Koshukovichi
                  Boryzow   Holovzin   Malatitze
H   O   L   Y   Masurian Woods   Grodno   Mohilev   Mglin   Kostenichi
                  & Swamps   Starodub
        Thorn   Pultusk   P   O   L   A   N   D
Attranstädt   Punitz   Praga   Pinsk   Mezin
Leipzig   Blonie   Warsaw   Baturin
Kassel   Meissen   Rawicz   Lublin   Veprik   Kharkov
           Dresden   Kliszów   Krasnokutsk
O   M   A   N   Cracow   Sandomir   Poltava
Würzburg   Jaroslaw   Lemberg   Perevolotjna
Bamberg   AUSTRIA
Nürnberg

M   P   I   R   E
       Linz   Vienna   MOLDAVIA   Ochakov
          Budapest   Debreczen   Bender
    HABSBURG   DOMINIONS   Klausenburg

         HUNGARY   Rotenturm pass   Black
                     Pitesci   Sea
            WALLACHIA

Adriatic Sea

       T   U   R

          Timurtash
          Demotika   K   E   Y

Augustus was threatening to cut Swedish communications: anchored o Thorn in the west and relying on Wisńiowecki's hold on Lithuania, l stationed Field-Marshal Steinau on the Bug–Vistula line to hem the Swed‹ in all along the front. The danger had to be conquered by swift action. A soon as the Swedes began to test the Saxon lines to achieve a breakthroug‹ Augustus – anxious lest his centre army be encircled – ordered his infantı into Thorn while Steinau's cavalry was told to join Wisńiowecki that th‹ might fall on the Swedes in the rear when these, as expected, moved towar‹ Thorn in force.

On 18 April the Swedish army left Warsaw. The major part of it forced passage over the Bug close to the place where it joins the Vistula and move as expected along the river towards Thorn; but Charles XII, with a detachmeı of three thousand cavalry and dragoons moved east in forced rides to tack Steinau, if they could catch him, before he could carry out the King-Elector orders.

This expedition was the first one commanded by the King quite indepeı dently without any senior officer present, and though it was quite a minc affair it deserves some analysis for this very reason. On 21 April 1703 Charl‹ caught up with the Saxon commander outside Pułtusk, where Steinau and h 3,500 men had drawn up in battle-formation at the news that a Swedish forc was approaching. Steinau decided not to give battle, however, and both sid‹ raced for the bridge leading to the town on its island in the Narew rive: During the fight that developed on the bridge and in the narrow streets c Pułtusk, the Saxons lost two hundred men and eight hundred were take‹ prisoner by an accord suggested by Charles to avoid further loss of life. Th rest escaped and fled east as far as Osfidenka, leaving their baggage as booty for the Swedes. The victory was not on a grand scale and pursuit wa impossible with exhausted horses and men; but Swedish losses had been ligł – less than twenty – and the flank of the main army had been secured. Pułtus shows, military commentators agree, Charles's eye for terrain and his ligh‹ ning speed in action.[19] Important for the King personally was that things ha gone well, and though he minimized the action in his report to Rehnskiöł the relief of a pupil who feels he has not brought discredit on his teacher ca be read between the lines.[20]

One fact connected with Charles's correspondence with Rehnskiöld froı this expedition received some publicity: the King had left his cypher-ke behind and, when deciphering a letter from the general, had had to rely o‹ his memory, as also for those parts of his own reply which needed to be code‹ for security reasons. The cypher was of a relatively complicated kind and late investigations have shown that the King remembered it faultlessly – a fea which has been used to illustrate his remarkable memory and powers of con centration.[21] His memorizing the code is perhaps less surprising when on takes into account the amount of correspondence which passed betwee‹ Charles and Rehnskiöld at times when they were apart and the King was stił

nding his feet as a general in his own rights, but it remains proof of his keen-
ess on his job and of his delight in everything to do with mathematical
ymbols, even the figures in a cypher-code.

The victor of Pułtusk soon rejoined the main army, which proceeded to lay
ege to Thorn in order that the six thousand Saxon infantry now in the town
night not escape nor Augustus be given an opportunity to relieve the garri-
on: here was a chance to come to grips with a major part of the Saxon army.
y the middle of May the town was encircled, but the bombardment proper
ad to be delayed for nearly four months while heavy siege artillery was
rought by sea from Courland – the delay being mainly due to transit diffi-
lties in Danzig.* In the interval, attempts to relieve Thorn had to be beaten
ff. Such attempts were not made by the Saxon cavalry alone, for with the
wedes openly besieging a Polish town Augustus had in June 1703 obtained
ontrol over the Lithuanian as well as the Polish Crown army at a general
iet held at Lublin.[22] That the Commonwealth was not united behind Augus-
s was, however, demonstrated in July 1703 by the formation of a confedera-
on by the nobility of Great Poland. Its army was led by Stanislaus
eszczyński, who became the head of the patriot group when his father
.afał died in January 1703, much to the regret of the Swedes who had relied
n him carrying the Jabłonowski anti-Russian policy into effect in time.
tanislaus felt himself, and undoubtedly was, less fitted by political experience
an father or grandfather to take on the leadership; but for the Swedes the
onstancy of his anti-Augustan stand and the contacts with Turks and Tartars
d Ukrainians which he inherited from Rafał proved valuable assets.

In the fight to keep Saxon, Lithuanian and Polish cavalry from relieving
horn, the Swedes had the advantage of operating on interior lines. Detach-
ents from the main army kept the enemy on the far side of the Drewenz river
the north-east, while Rehnskiöld and his eight thousand men foiled efforts
cross the Warta in the south-east. The general, whose secondary objec-
ve was to secure supplies from the depot at Włocławek, outwitted enemy
valry, made himself master of the fortified town of Posen and gradually, with
tanislaus, won control of the whole of Great Poland for the confederation.[23]

The presence of the Swedish army at Thorn speeded up negotiations with
randenburg–Prussia and the Maritime Powers. In July a treaty was signed
cognizing Frederick's royal title, and the desired promise of neutrality was
ceived in return. In August Lillieroot, the Swedish ambassador at The
ague, obtained a convention whereby Queen Anne and the States General
peated their guarantees of the Travendal settlement. In return Charles had
sign a promise to enter into negotiations for Sweden's accession to the
rand Alliance, 'as soon as possible' – a vague enough phrasing but still one
hich went beyond earlier commitments which merely pledged that he would
rnish auxiliaries according to the 1700 treaty 'when he obtained peace'.[24]

---

* The town, a free city, was naturally anxious to remain neutral between Augustus and Charles
d made difficulties also about the transit of Swedish recruits.

This is proof not only of the Swedish need for constraint on Frederick IV o
Denmark–Norway but also of their concern at the Maritime Powers' critica
attitude to Sweden. The English and Dutch governments felt annoyed a
delays in supplies – such as tar – which they needed for their own war effort;
English and Dutch merchants feared Swedish designs not only on Courlan
but on West Prussia: Thorn was astride the Vistula which carried Polis
trade to the sea, and Danzig, subjected to Swedish pressure in various way
found ready support at The Hague and in London.[25]

Charles was genuinely surprised at the way the Maritime Powers – t
whom he felt tied by the bonds of alliance and to whom he had time an
again given his word that he would not aid Louis XIV – argued that the Swede
were helping France. Some of the Chancery officials took the point. Hermeli
explained to Charles that, whether willingly or not, he served the Frenc
cause in that Louis XIV 'took heart' from Sweden's non-commitment i
the War of the Spanish Succession. The King retorted that what he did, h
did out of concern for Sweden's interests;[26] but it may have been such argu
ments which brought him to the measure of moral commitment expressed i
the 1703 convention.

From Charles's point of view, he was making very real sacrifices for th
Maritime Powers. An invasion of Saxony would provide the ideal solution fo
his Polish dilemma. Indeed, many Poles asked him straight out,† Why don
you go and seek your Saxon enemy in Germany? Charles himself stressed t
Piper in August 1702 that if he now invaded Saxony, the dethronement of th
King-Elector in Poland would be an accomplished fact within six months.
Yet Charles respected the veto of the Maritime Powers until the summer o
1706. He did so, in the largest measure, because he could not afford to ris
losing the Anglo-Dutch guarantee of Travendal. This was a much more re
threat than the Imperial decree, issued as soon as the Empire declared war o
Louis XIV, that anyone attacking a member-state would become the enemy o
the whole of Germany. But there was also an element of real truth in Charles'
contention, though it was exaggerated for propaganda purposes, that he ha
felt in honour bound to respect the veto till the allied victories of Blenheir
and Ramillies made it clear that the Maritime Powers need no longer den
him a move which was, and had been all along, of inestimable value to h
own cause. Certainly in 1702 and 1703, after Louis XIV's victories at Fried
lingen and Höchstädt, any Swedish step which would play havoc with Angld
Dutch contracts for auxiliaries in the Empire was unthinkable for Charles:
would seem like a knife in the back of those who had helped him in 1700.

During the siege of Thorn, Charles was often in danger from balls an

---

* Swedish headquarters did what they could to speed supplies; it would seem as if a desire fo
higher profits in Stockholm was responsible for the delays.

† Contemporary Poles were presumably ignorant of the veto of the Maritime Powers on suc
an invasion, but Polish historians have echoed the question without investigating the reasons wh
Saxony was left in peace till 1706. There is, however, a general tendency among modern historiar
of the reign, e.g., Haintz, Rosén and Jonasson, to underestimate the importance of the veto.

bullets from the fortifications. Sometimes these were directly aimed at his own conspicuous figure; but he refused to avoid danger, arguing that if he did so, the morale of the soldiers, who had to take risks, might weaken. He himself had been entrusted with a young pupil for training in the art of war – Prince Maximilian of Württemberg, the youngest, at thirteen, of the many volunteers who flocked to the army[28] – and this may have had something to do with his concern to inculcate the belief that one was not hit till one's hour had come, or – as was already a common saying among soldiers – till the shot had your own name on it.

There was much speculation at times among the besiegers why one fighting man was killed and the next spared, sparked off perhaps by the fact that in one of the first days of the siege, on 18 May, a falconet ball ripped a leg off General von Liewen, while Charles, who stood at the general's side, resting his arm on the general's shoulder,* was unhurt. Even more remarkable, the ball continued its trajectory and passed just above the head of Prince Max who happened to have sat down to rest for a moment.[29] Von Liewen died the same night. The King grieved at the loss of an officer whose ability he greatly respected, one who had been his teacher in Poland in infantry tactics as Rehnskiöld had been for cavalry work. 'We shall find it difficult to replace him', he said as he helped to place the lid on the coffin.[30] Possibly some feeling that he had helped to expose Liewen to fire lies behind the risks the King took during the rest of the siege? He ordered bales of hay piled in front of his tent to be removed,† and made light of an incident in a trench on 9 September when the very brushwood on which his arm rested on top of the breastworks was shot away.

The siege of Thorn, once the heavy Swedish bombardment began on 14 September, was crowned with speedy success. The town had been well supplied with food and ammunition but the long months between May and September had taken their toll: there was sickness among the Saxon troops, food was getting short, and more and more houses were put in flames by Swedish fire-bombs. An assault, planned for 30 September, was cancelled‡ to avoid needless loss of lives once it became clear that the town and the garrison were equally willing to capitulate. This was done on 4 October. Five thousand Saxons were made prisoner and sent to Sweden: the town paid 100,000 *Thaler* into the Swedish war-chest and its artillery became Swedish booty. According to the custom of the age Charles entertained the Saxon generals to dinner and went out of his way to praise them for their stout defence. Swedish losses during the siege had been very light: forty killed and seventy wounded; though losses accepted to prevent relief of the garrison were estimated at several hundred.

---

* For this habit, see Motraye, *Travels, II*, pp. 6–7.

† The bales were put there to absorb shot after some had passed right through the tent, killing horses grazing behind it.

‡ The columns may have been lined up for assault to speed the capitulation; but the generally accepted story is that the King wanted to risk assault but was persuaded by senior officers to resist.

III

The repercussions of Thorn's fall were swift. Augustus had but four thousan
left of the Saxon army of thirteen thousand brought into play against th
Swedes in Poland; while Charles's army in the Commonwealth stood a
twenty-three thousand. The King had easy and safe communication wit
Sweden and good winter quarters in West Prussia. Outsiders looked upo
him as master of Poland's fate, and Frederick of Prussia suggested a partitio
of the Baltic coastline between himself and Sweden. His desire to lin
Brandenburg and East Prussia became obvious enough for Charles to rush
garrison into Elbing* lest the Poles should believe that he was willing t
sacrifice Polish territory for immediate diplomatic advantages which coul
not, in any case, fit into the grand design.

Prussian suggestions for a dynastic alliance through the engagement o
Frederick's son, aged fifteen, to Ulrika Eleonora, now also fifteen, were bette
received. The Prussian suit was pressed through Eosander,[31] a Swedish fort
fication officer and architect in Prussian service, who was sent to Stockholr
with a portrait of Frederick William. The princess liked the portrait an
enjoyed Eosander's talk about life in Prussia, so much nearer than Stockholr
to the cultural centres of Europe. Though Ulrika got on well with her siste
the younger girl could not help feeling the tension between the two parties t
the succession-struggle and was not above feeling flattered that her futur
status might be higher than that of Hedvig, a duke's widow, if she married th
son of a king.[32] She was therefore as well disposed towards the engagement a
her brother; but when negotiations started the dynastic alliance was foun(
from the Prussian side, to be but a variant of the political alliance whic
could only be had at the cost of Polish lands or part of Swedish Pomerani;
From 1704 onwards those ministers at Berlin who favoured a Hanoveria
marriage for the Prussian crown prince began an anti-Ulrika campaig
intended also to make her odious on personal grounds,† and won the day.

The certainty of Thorn's fall had persuaded Augustus, on 10 October, to sig
a new treaty with the Tsar. This mirrored his own weakened state as also th
successes scored by Peter in 1703.‡ At Birsen the Tsar had promised Livoni
to Augustus. The silence of the 1703 treaty on Livonia pointed to Peter
ambition to conquer and keep that Swedish province for himself. Moreove
the treaty specified that the fight against Sweden was to take place on Polis

* The Swedish detachment arrived on 1 December, two days before a Prussian force sent t
strengthen the hold Frederick already possessed, the Poles having permitted a small Brandenbu.
garrison as security for a loan.

† Ilgen told Frederick William that Ulrika suffered from bad breath and a weak bladder ar
was imperious and capricious into the bargain; a special emissary sent to Stockholm in 170
reported that the Princess was stupid, ugly, a veritable *Zwergin* (female dwarf).

‡ The Tsar had conquered Nyen, Koporaje and Jama and had begun to create strongholds of h
own, Petersburg and Jamburg; he had beaten a Swedish force of five thousand in June 1703 ;
Systerbäck; he had devastated eastern Estonia and parts of Livonia to facilitate future operatio
against Narva.

>il: Augustus, with Russian subsidies, was to create a new Saxon army and
> put this as well as the Crown armies of the Commonwealth into a joint
ampaign against Charles to be waged in Poland. Further, he had to commit
oth Saxon and Polish resources in full to the defence of Russia if the Swedes
1ould invade Tsar Peter's dominions, and he had finally to promise never to
nter into a separate peace with Sweden.

This treaty proved too much for the neutralist Poles. Legally, Augustus
'as within his rights since the Lublin Diet of June 1703 had given him per-
1ission to negotiate with foreign powers on behalf of the Republic; but they
:lt outraged that he put his own interests so much ahead of theirs. Only by
eposing Augustus, the majority of the group now argued, could they prevent
1eir country becoming the battleground for Tsar Peter's fight with Sweden,
fight of no possible benefit to them. In January 1704 Cardinal Radziejowski
alled a meeting in Warsaw intended to be a Confederation of the whole
Iommonwealth, though delegates from areas where Augustus's forces (i.e. in
outh Poland) or Russian troops (i.e. in Lithuania)* were stationed did not
ttend. Charles XII, who had established winter quarters at Heilsberg in
rmeland, sent two delegates to the meeting, the diplomat Wachschlager and
1e soldier Arvid Horn, known for his diplomatic and conciliatory ways. The
wedish army was distant enough, in Ermeland or in West Prussia, for no one
> hint that it might influence the delegates unduly.

Influence was, however, brought to bear in the political sense. Charles
'owned on the cardinal's suggestion that a formal deposition might be
voided by letting Augustus choose between his hereditary electorate –
'here he was at the moment residing – and his elective kingdom. Surely he
'ould opt for the former? The King wanted an unequivocal deposition, lest
ugustus should find a legal loophole through which he could creep back. To
btain it, he let his delegates exhibit those letters in Augustus's own hand by
'hich he had offered Charles part of the Republic's territory in return for a
axon peace with Sweden. This helped to sway some doubtful voters and on
'16 February 1704 Augustus was declared to have forfeited the Polish crown.

The first step in the Polish stage of Charles XII's grand design had thus been
chieved. But the second step was of equal importance, the calling of an Elec-
on Diet so that John Sobieski could be duly elected King of Poland. His name
'as freely mentioned at the Warsaw meeting and Horn had signified Swedish
ipport for his candidature. A certain amount of pressure was exerted by
harles in the hope that the cardinal, head of the Commonwealth during the
terregnum, should not be tempted to prolong it: such matters as payment for
1e Crown army and the easing of Swedish contributions, which the cardinal
ished to negotiate, Charles put off till the new king should be chosen.[34]

That Augustus, though deposed, was not powerless was shown when he
idnapped the candidate for the Polish crown and his brother on 18/28
ebruary and warned the remaining Sobieski, Alexander, that he accepted the

---

* With Russian support for Ogiński and Wiśniowecki the Sapiehas had fled to Courland.

crown at the risk of causing the deaths of John and Constantine in Saxo captivity. The set-back to Charles's plans was inestimable – probably th largest single cause for the failure of the grand design; but the aspect whic caused most comment at the time was that the kidnapping took place on th territory of the Emperor Leopold and that Augustus was not even repr manded. The Sobieski brothers lived in Silesia, at the castle of Ohlau – whic had indeed been put at their disposal by the Emperor – and at the news of Augustus's deposition they began their journey to Poland. A young Swedis officer, the Edvard Gyldenstolpe whom we have already had occasion t mention,* knew the brothers well from his European travels and happened t be in Breslau to recruit soldiers for the Swedish army at this time. He wa invited to travel in the Sobieski party. He was not free to leave at once, bu promised to catch them up and urged them to take an escort of armed men 'as times were uncertain'.[35] The Sobieskis held that this was unnecessary o Habsburg soil and did not take his advice. Their carriage had not gone fa when they were ambushed by thirty troopers whose officer arrested them i the name of Augustus. They were forcibly taken to Saxony and remaine imprisoned till Charles XII, in the treaty of Altranstädt of 1706, secured the freedom.

In their baggage was found correspondence, dating over three years, wit various Swedes, including Charles XII, and Augustus's justification for the imprisonment was that they were guilty of conspiracy with his enemy. Th was accepted by contemporaries, but the kidnapping which furnished th proofs was felt to transgress natural law and to be as inexcusable as th Emperor's silence was despicable.[36] One reason for Leopold's attitude, quit apart from his friendly relations and political ties with Augustus, may hav been his irritation at the way his Protestant Silesian subjects were takin courage from the proximity of the Swedish army: deputations from those place which were covered by Sweden's guarantee of the Treaty of Westphalia visite Charles's headquarters and appealed for his help to keep their churches open.

Augustus's coup put Charles XII in a terrible dilemma. He tried to persuad Alexander Sobieski to accept the crown, even if only as a caretaker for Jame but found him unwilling, because of Augustus's threat to his brothers' live It proved impossible to find a candidate on whom the patriots and the neutr lists could agree. Augustus made his way to southern and eastern Poland and was obviously still in the fight for the crown. The Swedes were driven t concessions, first to have the dethronement edict made public in May, then t have the date of the Diet to elect a new king fixed for 9 June (N.S.): mone was spent, larger sums promised and military support pledged for priva estates against Saxon revenge. With no agreement among the Poles Charle had to pick the candidate for the vacant crown. His choice fell on Stanislav†

* See above, p. 175.
† He went first to Cracow, where Rehnskiöld, stationed in the south throughout the winte caused him and his rival Diet to flee; then over Lemberg to Sandomir, where a new meeting of t Diet broke up at the news of Rehnskiöld's approach.

eszczyński; but Radziejowski and Lubomirski refused to work in his favour
nd the votes of a strongly pro-Sobieski group were only won at the cost of a
:cret undertaking by Stanislaus to be a caretaker king on behalf of James
obieski. It is possible that Charles XII knew nothing of the documents
'herein Stanislaus by his signature promised to relinquish the crown at
ames's bidding;[38] but in the absence of proof one way or the other, it is
]ually likely that he acquiesced since such an attitude would fit his concern
ot to break faith with the Sobieskis.

The most lively description of Stanislaus's election on 2 July (N.S.) 1704
)mes, not from the measured reports of Wachschlager and Horn, but from
1e autobiography (written in his old age) of the young Chancery official,
.euterholm, who at this time was Horn's secretary. Reuterholm's memory is
ot always reliable and he often repeats unfounded gossip,* but this eye-
·itness account carries conviction: the bishop of Posen, acting for Radzie-
·wski who had found an excuse not to preside, was the worse for wear after
rinking deeply at Horn's dinner-table. He had difficulty in making himself
eard on the open field where traditionally the ceremony took place above
1ose who protested either against the election or against Stanislaus. One
undred Swedish soldiers and their officers were posted 'at a good musket-
1ot's distance', officially to protect the electors, but – Reuterholm suspected –
lso to teach them 'to speak the right language'. All the Swedes present – 'I
id not spare my throat either', our witness confesses – shouted with the
oles when in the dusk of the summer evening the bishop finally achieved
1e response of a strong *Vivat Rex Stanislaus*, hats being thrown in the air as
n additional sign of consent.[39]

IV

'he shout of one of the Poles present, a certain Jerusalski according to
.euterholm, of *Nie poss wollem*,[40] later led Radziejowksi to doubt whether
1e election had been legal; but quite apart from the cardinal's prevarications
1e Swedes experienced grave difficulties in achieving the newly elected King's
)ronation. The full weight of Vatican influence – the Pope would have
cquiesced in a Sobieski – was brought to bear against the Polish protégé of
1e Protestant Swedish King.[41] The military threats of Augustus and Tsar
eter had to be conjured before Radziejowski could be persuaded to call a
)ronation-Diet, a task which occupied the campaign season of 1704.

Stanislaus himself was naturally anxious that as little fighting as possible
1ould take place on Polish soil, and urged an invasion of Saxony on Charles.
uch a project was, for reasons which we have already discussed, unaccept-
ble,† and an alternative was adopted – that of bottling up as many troops as

* It is from Reuterholm that we know of the rumour, cp. above, p. 91 that Charles XII before
700 had 'as close a knowledge as her husband' of Sarah, wife of Gustav von Düben.
† See above, pp. 142, 194; Swedish ties with the Maritime Powers had, into the bargain, been
einforced by a treaty of April 1704.

possible inside Saxony while fighting Augustus and his Russian auxiliaries
Poland. It is doubtful whether, as Swedish historians have argued, Charl
hoped to relieve pressure on the Baltic provinces during the 1704 campai
by drawing Russian forces into Poland: his aim was rather to beat August
before Tsar Peter sent more forces to help his ally by virtue of the 1703 treat
In this plan a measure of success* was achieved which laid the foundation f
the coronation-Diet of July 1705, the coronation itself on 24 September (N.S
and the Suedo-Polish treaty of 8/18 November along the lines of the gra
design.

But 1704 also brought set-backs. Charles and the main army had mov
away from Warsaw at the end of June, to join Rehnskiöld in the Sandom
region and press southern and eastern areas into acceptance of Stanislau
Their move naturally weakened Swedish defence of the west: a small garris
under Horn's command was left to succour Stanislaus in Warsaw, and Meije
felt had few Swedish troops for the protection of Great Poland since t
Poles were assumed to be able to hold the country for Stanislaus. Fiel
Marshal Steinau with a detachment from the Saxon army slipped through t
gap across the Silesian border; but Meijerfelt, on 9 August (N.S.), beat
larger number of Saxons who entered the Posen district under Gener
Schulenburg's command.[42] Shortly afterwards, however, while Charles ar
Rehnskiöld were scoring successes in the south-east, among them the co
quest of Lemberg,† the fortified capital of Red-Russian Poland, August
with some three thousand Saxons and nine thousand Russian auxiliari
conquered Warsaw, Stanislaus's Polish army withdrawing without a figl
Horn capitulated once the garrison roof was blazing over his soldiers' head
they were willing to fight but not to be burnt alive, their commander explain
when he justified his capitulation. This was laid squarely at Charles XII's ov
door, since he had left too few men in Warsaw to make a real defence po
sible.[43] The blame was accepted, and Horn and Reuterholm, who had becon
Patkul's prisoner and found him a fascinating conversationalist,[44] we
exchanged in March 1705.

In Lemberg Charles also received bad news from the Baltic province
Dorpat had capitulated to the Russians in July and Narva in August. T
Swedish garrisons and the army detachments which had attempted to relie
them had been short of food and clothes and were hopelessly outnumber
by large Russian armies skilfully deployed. The loss of Narva was partic
larly painful and could not be compensated for by the victory which Lewe
haupt and the Sapiehas had over Wiśniowecki and his Russian auxiliaries
Lithuanian soil at Jakobstadt on 18 July. One consequence of the summer

---

* I am unable to share Haintz's judgement, I, p. 101, note 1, that the campaign was a to
failure.

† The conquest on 25 August of this fortress never before captured – a virgin fortress, to use t
terminology of the age – created a great stir at the time. It was not rated highly as a military expl
by the conquerors, Charles XII and Stenbock, with a small force of dragoons: no skill had be
necessary, boldness was all and the small garrison had given in after a brief fight.

ents was that Lewenhaupt was given a general command of all Swedish
rces in the north-east to stop or delay large-scale Russian infiltration into
land.[45]

Such entry remained on the cards, however, presaged by that treaty which a
putation of Poles concluded with Tsar Peter on the Republic's behalf in
ly 1704. Superficially regarded, this treaty was complementary to that
ugustus had signed with the Tsar in 1703, but in it Augustus was to some
tent outmanœuvred, as it was the Republic which now received promises of
share of the Livonian conquest-to-be. Most of the clauses dealt with Russian
bsidies for Polish arms to be raised against Charles and with the Polish war
fort in case of a Swedish invasion of Russia. The way in which the Tsar tried
manipulate subsidies in negotiations with eastern Poles intent on extracting
e cash quickly mirrors the negotiations between Charles XII and the western
les in the previous year. The role played by Vatican diplomacy, anxious to
tain permission to proselytize inside Russia, in achieving the Russo-Polish
eaty was a significant one, and on the whole Tsar Peter was more successful
an Charles in making the Poles more dependent on himself.[46]

From mid-September onwards Charles XII and Rehnskiöld moved west to
ing the Saxons to accept battle as it had become clear that Tsar Peter –
tent on his own Baltic conquests – was not going to hurry to send fresh help
Augustus or to come to Poland in person to fight during 1704. A regular
ase began. Augustus and his three thousand Saxons left Warsaw at the
proach of the Swedes and crossed the Vistula with Charles in hot pursuit.
he two royal cousins caught a glimpse of each other on opposite sides of the
ver;[47] but Swedish attempts to get a bridge across in time failed and Charles
anged to a pursuit of Schulenburg and his four thousand Saxons with
eater expectations of success. The King and his cavalry regiments rode at
eakneck speed and caught up with Schulenburg at Punitz on the Polish
de of the frontier on 28 October 1704. Battle was begun, but darkness
scended before it had been properly joined, and before light the next
orning the Saxons managed to cross the Silesian border.

Charles and his men followed them a short distance on to Habsburg terri-
ry before turning back to deal with Russian and Cossack auxiliaries in the
reat Poland area. Uncharacteristic harshness was shown by troops under
harles's command, and at least in one case with the King's knowledge,
ainst detachments of these troops: they were cut down in revenge for the
aughter of Swedes earlier in the campaign.[48] The majority of the Cossacks
d Russians moved east as the winter approached, while Charles staked out
arters for his army along the whole of the Polish western border to prevent
hulenburg from re-entering the Commonwealth for the 1705 campaign till
should suit Charles. His own headquarters were settled at Rawicz near the
lesian border.

During the winter Patkul, fearing that Augustus might have to give way for
anislaus in Poland, tried on Peter's behalf to test Charles's willingness to

make peace with Russia. Offers and counter-offers persisted for a conside
able period, but when it became clear that the Tsar was intent on retainir
Swedish territory on the Baltic the negotiations petered out.[49] To Charles, a
to all Swedes in positions of responsibility at the time, it seemed traitorous t
give up any part of the Baltic provinces before coming to grips with the Rus
sian invader whom circumstances had favoured so greatly in 1703 and 170
Negotiations with Prussia were resumed on Swedish initiative; but Kir
Frederick put his claims higher than in 1703, trusting that the proximity c
Tsar Peter would make Charles more willing to satisfy Prussian desires for
corridor between Brandenburg and East Prussia. There was no willingness c
Frederick's part to go further than 'benevolent neutrality' in return, and as l
refused to commit himself to a recognition of Stanislaus these talks als
lapsed.[50]

Charles's main concern was his negotiations with the Poles to secur
Stanislaus's coronation. His strongest card was that he had stationed h
army in such a way that it would be impossible for the Saxon troops to com
back to the Commonwealth till the Swedes moved. From the Polish point c
view, Charles had secured a success in that he had chased the major part c
Augustus's Saxon army back into the Electorate in 1704: he was scorir
another by bottling up the Saxons throughout the spring and summer of 170
and thus spoiling the plans for a Russo-Saxon joint campaign for 1705. Th
number of those Poles who decided to take Stanislaus's side and obtain
treaty with Sweden which would offer some safety and hope for the futur
grew;[51] but it proved a time-consuming task to bring Cardinal Radziejowski t
the point of calling a coronation Diet, Swedish negotiators passing to and fro
Danzig, where the cardinal had taken refuge, and Charles's headquarters.

Even after the cardinal had agreed, at the end of May 1705, to call
coronation Diet for 1 July in Warsaw, the Pope's threat to excommunica
any son of the Church who participated in Stanislaus's coronation cause
further delay. So did Tsar Peter's massive movements of troops (he ha
between fifty and sixty thousand at his disposal at this time)[52] over Lithuan
towards Poland proper. But this year it seemed as if the Swedes could do n
wrong. A brilliant victory by Lewenhaupt over Sheremetev at Gemäuerthc
on 16 July stopped the Russians in their tracks and as Tsar Peter turne
towards Courland, the pressure of fear eased in Warsaw.[53] Augustus's direc
attempt to stop the coronation by sending General Paijkull – a Swedis
Livonian subject in Saxon service – to attack Warsaw with all the Saxons an
Poles he could muster in the Commonwealth was countered by the Swedis
Major-General Nieroth with far fewer troops and Paijkull was taken prison
on 21 July.*

On 14/24 September Stanislaus was crowned King of Poland. The place c
the coronation was Warsaw and not Cracow, the traditional shrine, and th
crown was a new one, paid for by the Swedes. The cardinal made a las

* For his later fate see below, pp. 217–8.

1inute offer to defy the Pope's ban, but Charles XII, suspecting his sincerity
nd fearing yet another delay, arranged for a Swedish escort to bring the
ishop of Lemberg to Warsaw. This prelate had some time ago declared him-
3lf willing to place the crown on Stanislaus's head, and was made *primas* by
1e new King on Radziejowski's death. Charles XII was present incognito at
1e ceremony, so as not to detract attention from the main figure of the day.
tanislaus made a handsome king and his personal style, especially his Polish
1oustache, was imitated by young men at headquarters. Max of Württem-
erg for one, from the evidence of his portraits, veered in adolescent imitation
etween Charles and Stanislaus.[54] Stanislaus was neither particularly intelli-
1ent nor ambitious, but the Swedes thought him more straightforward than
1ost Poles, which probably meant that they knew him better and were sure
1at he was on their side. He was a man of principle who strove hard to recon-
ile the interests of his own country and those of his Swedish ally. That these
1terests did not always coincide time was to reveal;* but he showed persis-
3nce in what he thought right for Poland and must be judged a puppet king
nly in the sense that his fortunes and his plans for the regeneration of his
ountry rested in the last instance on the military power of Sweden.[55]

V

Vith the coronation of Stanislaus, Charles had achieved the important second
tep of the first stage of the grand design. It now depended on him, rather than
·n the Poles, when the third and last step should be attempted: he had, at
1st, some freedom of action and a legally elected king of the patriot group
,ith whom to work. Negotiations proceeded, rapidly by Polish standards, for
treaty of peace and alliance between Sweden and the Republic, signed on
/18 November 1705. In it Charles guaranteed the territorial integrity of the
:ommonwealth and promised to help reconquer – against compensation –
he *avulsa imperii* lost to Russia.

Behind the compensation clause of the treaty lurked Swedish hopes of
bsorbing Courland, and possibly also Polish Livonia, thus rounding off the
3altic dominions with benefits both to commerce and to the budget of the
tate. Courland was not mentioned by name. The fact that Tsar Peter's troops
,ere occupying it at the moment the treaty was signed had little to do with
his. Lewenhaupt, with his relatively small forces, had not been able to follow
.p the victory of Gemäuerthof and had retreated to Livonia, leaving Cour-
and open to the Russians; but the Swedes expected to be able to chase them
·ut once the main army of Charles moved east. It was rather that Stanislaus
1ust not be handicapped in his task of uniting the Poles by a premature
lisclosure of the price to be paid for Swedish military help. It also
uited Charles's personal sense of honour to leave the transfer of the
luchy – on terms which did not conflict with his territorial guarantee of the

* See below, pp. 277 and 284.

Commonwealth* – to effective Swedish control till 'equivalents' could handed over to Poland. There was also a risk of whetting the Prussia appetite for Polish soil if future Swedish compensation was pinpointed.

But the treaty was specific in other respects: military cooperation betwee Stanislaus's Poland and Charles XII against Tsar Peter was arranged; the trac of the Republic, in the east as well as the west, was channelled into Swedis hands. The Warta river was to be deepened to facilitate trade with Stettin; th port of Polangen (which had become a strong competitor) in Courland wa to be destroyed. Various measures were stipulated which gave the merchan of Riga preferential treatment and virtual monopoly of all exports from th Dvina basin, though there was no intention of suppressing Polish domest and transit trade.⁵⁶ If the second stage of the grand design, the invasion (Russia, led to the kind of peace Sweden hoped for, further development (the commercial grand design would follow: with the *avulsa imperii* restored Poland, or at least in the Polish orbit of influence, the whole of the trade of th Dnieper basin might be linked to the Swedish Baltic ports. Memorand: official and unofficial, multiplied in Stockholm and elsewhere on futui opportunities.⁵⁷

Once the treaty was signed, Charles and Stanislaus attempted to come t grips with Tsar Peter in a winter campaign when hard frost would make th rivers and marshy bogs in the eastern parts of Poland passable. It was no intended to move the whole of the Swedish army east. It would be senseless t leave the west of Poland unguarded, since Schulenburg – in anticipation (the 1706 collaboration of Augustus and the Tsar – had between eighteen an twenty thousand men in readiness on the frontier. This army had a kernel (Saxon troops, with Swiss and German mercenaries and even a regimer recruited from French prisoners-of-war with the Allies. If the Swedes vacate the area round Warsaw, Schulenburg would march in with the speed of ligh ning. He had a great admiration for Swedish methods⁵⁸ and was keen t avenge the defeats of the 1704 campaign. Nor did Charles XII think it feasib at this time to launch the second stage of the grand design: but by splittir the army in two, leaving Rehnskiöld with ten thousand men in the west t handle Schulenburg while he himself with twenty thousand moved east, the: was some hope of achieving surprise and forcing Peter to accept battle at disadvantage. If luck were with the Swedes, the Russian army might be weak ened before the invasion took place. At the very least Charles expected t upset the plans which Augustus and the Tsar had laid for the 1706 campaig and to chase the Russians as far back as possible, at the same time alleviatir some of the pressure on Courland and re-establishing contact with Lewer haupt in Riga.

Charles's march was a speedy one. He left Błonie, just west of Warsaw o 29 December 1705 and on 15 January 1706 his army surprised the Russe

---

* It was visualized that Charles should become Duke of Courland on similar terms as the chil Duke, whose regent, by acting traitorously to the Republic, was deemed to have forfeited his lar

Charles XII in 1702,
from a painting by La Croix

Charles XII in 1706,
from a drawing by J. D. Swartz

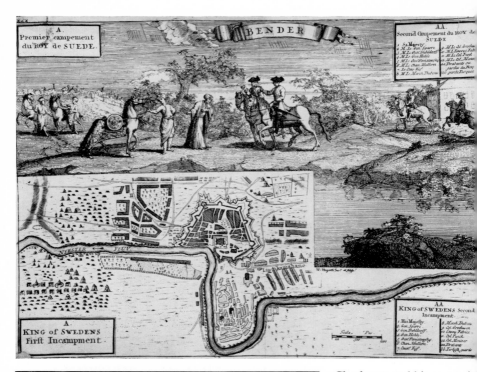

Charles XII and his camps in Bender, from an engraving

Charles XII in 1712, from a painting by Axel Sparre

axo-Polish forces, under the command of Augustus and the Tsar's General gilvie, near Grodno. The enemy did not want to accept battle. Ogilvie etired into the fortress of Grodno, while Augustus with his Saxons and Poles oved west to attack Rehnskiöld in the rear, Charles, with Stanislaus's olish–Lithuanian army taking part in his campaign, moved north towards ovno and sent messages to Lewenhaupt asking him to march (if at all pos-ble) into Courland and Lithuania so that the Russians might be forced into outh-eastern Poland and encouraged to make a stand. Lewenhaupt, with his avalry scattered and a sudden thaw making the roads impassable, was unable do this speedily,* but the Tsar was in any case unwilling to let Ogilvie risk a ght till the outcome of the Saxon attack on Rehnskiöld should be known. If ie Swedish general were defeated, then the time would be ripe to deal with harles, caught between the victorious Saxons and the large Russian armies. sar Peter, however, also prepared for a Saxon defeat. He was worried by evolts and uprisings at home, and began to plan scorched-earth tactics along ie whole of the Russian border with the Commonwealth,† in case Charles hould be tempted to make an invasion of Russia in 1705. He also withdrew is troops in Courland lest they should be surrounded and defeated.

Before Augustus and his eight thousand could get near Rehnskiöld, the wedish general marched to meet Schulenburg – already on the move towards im – and defeated at Fraustadt on 3 February 1706, in the most renowned attle of his career, an army double that of his own. The fight lasted only two ours. The clever feint which preceded it, the enveloping movement by the trong Swedish cavalry of both Saxon flanks while the numerically weak wedish infantry stood its ground bravely in the centre, the heavy losses iflicted on the enemy – all have combined to make Fraustadt the textbook xample of a decisive battle on a classical pattern.[59]

Charles XII was keenly aware of the importance of Fraustadt. 'The victory vhich God has given us this time is assuredly so glorious and perfect that ione could be greater', he wrote in congratulation;[60] and as soon as they net, Rehnskiöld was promoted to field-marshal and had the title of count onferred upon him.

Charles's own hopes of making the Russians stand in the east failed. He lrew his net as close as possible to prevent Ogilvie escaping; but this com-nander – ordered by the Tsar to move to the Ukraine at the news of Frau-tadt – got ahead of his pursuers when the Niemen, flooded with melting ice, lestroyed the Swedish bridge of boats at Orla. Charles attempted to take a hort cut through the Pripet marshes and catch Ogilvie to the south of them, iut progress was slow in the thaw and the pursuit had to be abandoned at ³iórsk, when, from the towers of the town, he saw the floods stretching as far is the eye could reach. The army was given a much needed rest from late April till the end of May.

---

* Later in the season he played a significant part in clearing Lithuania of Russian troops.
† See below, pp. 241–2, for the Zólkiew plan laid at this time.

H

The campaign in the east had important results even if the Russians ha
avoided battle: contact with Livonia had been re-established, the Tsar
troops had left Courland and Lithuania, Ogilvie and his men did not sto
till they reached Kiev, and the Swedes easily beat the Cossack forces se
against them. There was now room to manœuvre and to solve the Polis
dilemma if Charles acted quickly. Augustus was momentarily powerless i
the Cracow region, watched by Rehnskiöld, and his Russian ally was coope
up within his own borders. In May Charles moved to Volhynia, ensuring – a
in Lithuania in the spring – that the magnates, for however short a tim
rallied to Stanislaus. Secretly he began planning the march to Saxony.[61] O
4 August he informed Rehnskiöld of his decision to invade the Electorate an
showed him his detailed plans for the operation. His years as a pupil we
over in the military as in the political field.

On the Stage of Europe

Charles XII in Saxony, 1706-7

'he Charles who in August 1706 informed Rehnskiöld that he was moving 1e Swedish army to Saxony had come a long way from the youth who sailed 1to Pernau Bay on the yacht *Sophia* in October 1700. He was now twenty-four nd had matured in the hard school of the Polish war years. His optimistic ature had not been changed, but sad – and terrible – things had happened to im which left their mark. In many ways his personality was set between 700 and 1706, though his judgement, in my opinion, did not develop to its ullest extent till after 1709, during the years in Turkey.

The King had increasingly become cut off from home life, though emotion- lly he never severed the links which bound him to the family. During the vinters at Heilsberg in 1703 and those at Rawicz in 1704-5, Charles and the rmy felt 'near home'. The familiar German tongue was so much less strange han the Polish one;[1] communications with Sweden were easy and life took •n, at least at times, a semblance of peace. Wives visited husbands in high •ositions, brides of important officers and officials came out to wed,* there vere parties and balls. Music played, violas as well as the drums and hautboys •f military ceremonial occasions.[2] The King's sisters were anxious to visit .im. They pressed especially hard for permission to do so in 1704-5 when the vinter quarters were prolonged far into spring. Charles, however, feared for heir safety after Augustus's kidnapping of the Sobieski brothers and refused o run the risk of their being made the hostages of his enemies.[3]

Nor did he obey his grandmother's bidding to pay a visit home during the vinter and he brushed aside, politely, her reminders that it was time he got narried. Too much was at stake for him to leave Poland at a time of delicate .egotiations both in Warsaw and with powers abroad, and he pointed out hat he was already married, 'to the army', for the duration of the war.[4] It vould set a bad example, he argued, to think of his private affairs when the oldiers had no chance for home-leave and marriage; he did not want them to eel that he allotted himself privileges which the war denied them.[5] It is pos- ible that he was still thinking of his Danish cousin Sophia: it would be impos- ible to press his suit in Copenhagen as long as her brother's attitude was as

* Arvid Horn's marriage to Count Piper's sister-in-law in 1705 was a particularly splendid ccasion.

anti-Swedish as the Kliszów archives had proved. It is certain that he deliber
ately decided against marriage, and even experience of sex, till peace had bee
achieved.*

Links with home were sometimes forged anew, as when persons known t
him 'in the old days' came to serve him,[6] but they were more often broker
The four dogs he had brought with him from Stockholm died, the last on
during the siege of Thorn. We know their names – Caesar, Turk, Snushan
and Pompe – and know that it was Pompe of the well-known doggerel† tha
died last.[7] We never hear of the King replacing the lost dogs; this may b
because he stopped hunting, but it may also be part of a self-imposed sacri
fice. He was fond of his horses, but here we know that he schooled himself nc
to get too attached to any particular one: we are told that he picked whicheve
came handiest for his rides, for that very reason.[8]

He became used to the thought of death, and to taking the responsibilit
for causing death, though he could not carry the latter lightly. When it cam
to killing an enemy, he felt no pangs of conscience though he disliked mas
sacre and took the initiative for accords, as at Pułtusk, when he could;‡ but i
1704 he had the shattering experience of killing one of his own officers by
mishap that could have been avoided. On 5 May drills and exercises were i
progress, a regular enough occurrence. Axel Hård, who had recently returne
from service with the armies of Louis xiv, was training young officers – amon
them the King – in cavalry tactics. Putting his own sword at the back c
Charles xii, Hård asked: What would you do, Sire, if I were your enemy
The King wheeled round and fired his own pistol at Hård's chest, oblivious c
the fact that he had forgotten to remove the ramrod which, bursting int
three pieces, penetrated Hård's body. Some days later he died of wound fever
Charles's grief was intense.[9] It was later observed that the King throughou
his life observed four days of fasting and atonement every year. The signif
cance of two of them is not known, but one was the anniversary of Narv
and the other was 5 May.[10]

Charles never learnt to take losses in Swedish lives lightly, though foreig
observers often thought so because of the risk that seemed implied in th
gå-på tactics.[11] Unnecessary loss of life, brought about by guerrilla tactics o
what contemporaries thought of as the warfare of 'irregular' forces (such a
the Cossack regiments in the Russian army), was resented to such an exten
that he permitted retaliation. But even regular warfare, though necessary
seemed to him at times to demand too heavy a sacrifice from the nation. I
1704, when it looked as if the Polish situation might at last be solved, he sug
gested to Piper that perhaps it might be better if he challenged Tsar Peter t
single combat rather than go on wasting Swedish lives in a long struggle wit

---

* Cp. below, p. 377.
    † This runs on the theme that Pompe was permitted to sleep on the King's bed, a place many
young lady might envy him.
    ‡ He refused permission to kill Russian prisoners after Holovzin, when food was short fc
the Swedes.

.ussia. Surely it was better to risk one life, his own, than to let the war go on
nd on? The idea of such combats between individuals to settle issues between
:ates was still alive at this time (Louis XIV put it forward in his youth in a
>mewhat similar situation);[12] and Piper – who told Nordberg of his con-
ersation with Charles when they were both in Russian captivity – judged the
.ing both serious and sincere in his suggestion. He had some trouble in dis-
.ading him from publishing the challenge. His argument that the concept of
ngle combat was obsolescent enough to invite Russian ridicule did not make
uch impression; but his analytical deduction that Peter might accept the
hallenge, kill Charles and still not keep his side of the bargain but continue
1e war against Sweden did. The King desisted and laid such 'childish'
1oughts aside.[13]

The 'anti-war' aspect of the single-combat proposal may have been
rompted by a growing realization that the war would prove a long one. In
700 Cederhielm thought the King half-joking when he threw out a remark
1at 'we may be a long time on this side of the Baltic':* and Hermelin found it
ifficult to judge just how serious Charles was when at the end of 1702 he
ommented that 'We may be at war with the Poles for ten years and with the
.ussians for twenty.'[14] It is more than likely that Charles purposely exag-
erated to Chancery officials whom he found too optimistic as to the chances
f a quick peace; but he had from childhood on been given the campaigns of
Justavus Adolphus and other Swedish commanders in the Thirty Years War
> study, as well as those of his grandfather and father. Such reading had been
art of his military as well as his royal education; and he cannot but have
:arnt to reflect between 1700 and 1704 that the war in which he was involved
'as as intricate and difficult as theirs, and might evolve on a comparable
me-scale. That such remarks were not only for Chancery consumption is
lear from a comment he made in 1718 to Schwerin.†

Thoughts of his own death were forced upon him by seeing those related to
im by kinship or friendship die – Frederick of Holstein-Gottorp at Kliszów,
ieneral von Liewen at Thorn, his childhood page and 'old companion'
Jinckowström at Kalisz‡ in 1704 – and by pressure from others that he
ught not to take unnecessary risks. An answer of his, during the siege of
'horn when he was begged to take care 'for the sake of Sweden', has an
nigmatic ring: 'My death would be small loss to Sweden; I am not able to do
uch good for my country.'[15] Voltaire possibly had this remark in mind
'hen he suggested that Charles XII suffered from false modesty,[16] for it had
.een much quoted among army officers with whom he was in touch.[17] This
ccusation by Voltaire created great indignation among those who had known
'harles, it was a trait which they had never noticed in him.[18] A more likely
xplanation may be a regret, if a passing one, that he was stuck like a fly in
1e web of Polish politics and saw little likelihood of becoming the kind of

* See above, p. 178.　　† See below, p. 475.
‡ By a shot, possibly meant for the King, after the town had surrendered.

ruler he most admired: those who, like Henri IV of France, carried out reforr
and reconstruction at home as well as being successful abroad. And succes
in the war might in any case seem problematic in 1703, with neither stage on
nor stage two of the grand design within sight of completion. He certainl
believed that in the long life of the nation the life of an individual rule
mattered relatively little. 'Sweden will never lack for a king', was his commen
in 1715 when he was asked to settle the succession issue,[19] but this was in th
fully mature period of his life when his tongue had got sharper at times an
a tinge of disrespect for 'accepted opinion' had crept into the tone of hi
voice.

But though enigmatic or ambiguous remarks fell from the King's lips fror
time to time, those who shared the long Polish years with him remembere
other characteristics better: the way he worked and disciplined himself; hi
conscious attempts to share the hardships and privations of the campaigns
his secrecy about military moves and plans; his 'slyness' in finding excuses t
postpone political decisions till he judged the time ripe; his making light c
discomforts, and his laughter. He liked those who were basically serious bu
amusing in conversation and appreciated the verbal joke in particular. H
was still young enough to be acutely sensitive to the opinions of those h
respected and admired, and insecure enough to be ridiculously sensitive t
teasing,* but he was indifferent to what his enemies said about him and ofte
found cause for laughter in matters which the Chancery officials too
seriously. When these brought to his notice lampoons on him which the
wished to ban, he read them with genuine amusement, laughed aloud an
refused to let the Chancery take any action.[20]

II

In August 1706 those considerations which had hitherto deferred Charles x
from an invasion of Saxony no longer possessed the force which they had hel
between 1702 and 1706. The victories of Louis XIV in 1702 and 1703, whic
had threatened to permit French penetration into the heart of the Empire an
joint attacks on the Emperor Leopold's Habsburg lands by Louis, the Electo
of Bavaria and the Hungarian independence leader Rákóczi, were memorie
only: those of Marlborough and Prince Eugène had transformed the situatio
– Bavaria was lost, Louis XIV was on the defensive on his eastern frontier a
well as in Flanders. No longer could the Maritime Powers argue that ,
Swedish entry into the Empire in pursuit of Charles's attacker would tip
delicate balance against them in their own war with France.[21] There wer
indeed some at the King's headquarters who held that France was bein
weakened unduly: Charles ought to move closer to the western battlefields

---

* According to Bielke the King was hurt to the quick one cold evening in Poland when brother
officers noted that he wore gloves indoors: 'We'll soon have peace, Our Master has numb hands

eady to act as mediator,* or even to put his weight on the side of Louis XIV to prevent the Maritime Powers and the Emperor becoming too powerful.

With the new Emperor Joseph the Swedish King was not on particularly good terms. Like Leopold before 1705, he helped Augustus in various ways, specially by granting freedom of passage for Saxon armies to and from Poland via Silesia; moreover, he entered into closer negotiations with Tsar Peter than his father had done;† worse, he weakened the position of the Holstein-Gottorp family in relation to Denmark by giving support to Frederick IV in a contested succession to the bishopric of Lübeck-Eutin, traditionally held by the Holstein-Gottorpers and the Danish royal family in turn. Charles argued that he did not deserve such treatment. He had refused to listen to Hungarian appeals for help in 1704 – in spite of the Protestant religion of many of those who fought for their independence from Vienna – since he felt constrained not to aid those whom the Emperor regarded as rebels. Nor had he given public support to the Silesian Protestants, though in their case he had a treaty obligation which he meant to honour when opportunity offered.

Neither the wish to participate in a western settlement nor the desire to exert pressure on the Emperor moved Charles to decide on the invasion of Saxony: necessity drove him to it. Experience had shown that no decision could be reached with Augustus on Polish soil. The Saxon armies had been beaten, but with ever increasing numbers of Russian forces fighting on Augustus's side the Elector was not prepared to accept the military and political victories of Charles and Stanislaus of 1704 and 1706 as final. And if Tsar Peter had his way, to fight his war with Sweden on Polish soil, the grand design would be jeopardized by bringing suffering instead of support to Stanislaus and the Commonwealth. An invasion of Saxony seemed the only way to force Augustus to accept his defeat, an acceptance which was the prerequisite of the grand design proper. Swedish military gains of 1706 made the invasion possible; the European situation made it a justifiable risk. Some testing to ascertain whether the invasion could be avoided was done both by Augustus (who offered to give Lithuania to Stanislaus and Courland to Sweden) and Charles (who offered to desist from invasion if the Maritime Powers could persuade Augustus voluntarily to give up his claim to the Polish crown). Neither offer had any effect. On 7 July the Swedish main army broke up from Jarosław in Volhynia and directed its march towards Saxony, though its destination was kept secret; on 22 August it crossed the Silesian border at Rawicz; on 28 August it reached the Saxon frontiers.

There were few troops in Saxony – just the remnants of Schulenberg's army from the Fraustadt battle – and the general hurried these to safety in

---

* Louis had asked for Swedish mediation as early as 1704: the Maritime Powers had hinted, in the spring of 1706 but before the battle of Ramillies in May, that such mediation would not be unwelcome.

† An imperial diplomat signed a treaty with Patkul in December 1705 which promised Joseph Russian troops for the war with Louis against diplomatic help in favour of Tsar Peter, but this treaty was not ratified by Joseph.

Thuringia as the Swedes approached. The Saxon Council (the *Geheimrat*) wa determined not to sacrifice the Electorate for the sake of Augustus's Polis ambitions and sent two of its members (who had been empowered by th Elector as a last resort to relinquish the crown of Poland on his behalf) t Charles XII. Augustus was later to blame Imhoff and Pfingsten for havin gone beyond his wishes,* but in the circumstances the Saxons were frightene of the effect which too stiff a stand might have on their own country. O 4 September when the Saxon emissaries reached Charles's headquarters Bischofswerda, a Swedish garrison was already in Leipzig, another was on i way towards Dresden. In their negotiations with Charles, Piper and Hermeli as well as two plenipotentiaries from Stanislaus, the Saxons soon abandone their compromise plan – that Stanislaus might succeed Augustus as King Poland – and accepted Augustus's dethronement. Their real interest centre round the terms on which the Swedish army was to be given winter quarte in Saxony.

The Swedish King refused to delay his advance and on 14/24 Septembe when Charles had already reached the little castle of Altranstädt outsic Leipzig, terms were agreed: Augustus was to keep the courtesy title of Kin of Poland, but had to accept his dethronement and to agree that all decre promulgated by him since the day in February 1704 when the Warsaw Di dethroned him should be null and void. He had further to recognize Stani laus; to free all Poles imprisoned for political reasons, including the tw Sobieski princes; to end his alliance with Tsar Peter and hand over to th Swedes Russian troops stationed in Saxony. He also had to deliver up a deserters to Charles – and particular mention was made of Patkul who, sinc a quarrel with Augustus, had been a prisoner in Saxony since December 170 Finally, the Swedish army was to be permitted to stay in the Electorate ti the terms of the treaty had been carried out and guarantees of the peace b the Maritime Powers and the Emperor obtained. Contributions to enab Charles XII's army to be housed, clothed and fed during this waiting perio were arranged. A truce of ten weeks was publicly announced, but Charle agreed to keep the peace-treaty itself secret till Augustus – who commande the Saxo-Russian-Polish army in Lithuania while Tsar Peter was besiegin Viborg in Finland† – was safely out of Poland.[22]

Pfingsten, with a Swedish pass, was sent to find his Elector and obtain rat fication of the Altranstädt treaty. Once the signature had been penned he wa to inform the Swedish General Mardefelt that he and his four thousand men who had been left to help Stanislaus and his army of Poles and Lithuania under Potocki to safeguard Poland – should abstain from any act of enmit against Augustus. The Saxon councillor found his Elector earlier than h expected, for Augustus had not neglected the opportunity which Charles

---

* Pfingsten was arrested and imprisoned, but probably more to justify Augustus with Ts Peter than for any transgression of orders.

† The siege, begun in September 1706, proved unsuccessful; but in the post-1709 period t town was taken, see below, p. 334.

move towards Saxony offered: he had hurried west with Menshikov's cavalry hoping to make Stanislaus's position untenable. The news which Pfingsten brought him on 5/15 October was therefore extremely unwelcome, but after five days' deliberation he felt obliged to sign the ratification. On 23 October Pfingsten handed the document to Charles, much to the relief of the Swedes, since Augustus's consent had not been too confidently expected. But a few days later news arrived which raised the question of the Elector's sincerity: on 9 October – nine days after his signature – Augustus had taken part in an attack on Mardefelt at Kalisz. The Poles and Lithuanians fled and over half of the Swedish army (which included the 'Fraustadt battalions' of non-Swedish troops, particularly French, who had taken service with Charles XII after that battle) were cut down or taken prisoner.* Pfingsten had not informed Mardefelt of the peace signed and ratified; Swedish messages had not reached the general; and Augustus's secret advice to him to flee rather than stand his ground, he assumed to be a trap.[23] Kalisz had grave consequences for the Polish situation: Potocki's army lost heart; Stanislaus judged it wise to leave for Saxony; and a Russian occupation of the Commonwealth followed with Menshikov, dubbed Prince by the Tsar for his share in the victory, in command.

News of the defeat disturbed Charles since, quite apart from the loss of men, it augured ill for the Saxo-Swedish peace. To unmask Augustus with his ally and stop further double-dealing the Swedish King made the treaty of Altranstädt public on 5 November. By 12/23 of that month 'the sudden Peace in Poland' was known in the Dutch Republic and caused 'much Speculation'.[24] It was now only a matter of time before the news would reach Tsar Peter. Augustus left Warsaw secretly before the end of the month and reached Swedish headquarters on 7 December. He excused himself for what had happened and pleaded that he had acted under duress, fearing for his life if he gave Menshikov reason to suspect his loyalty to the common cause. He made much of his freeing the Swedes, including Mardefelt, who had been taken prisoner at Kalisz,† but did not mention that his last act before leaving had been to urge Menshikov to move more Russians into western Poland to strengthen the Russian hold on the country.

Charles professed to accept Augustus's explanation at face value. The two cousins got on well together on social occasions – Charles wrote to Stockholm that Augustus was 'jolly and amusing'[25] – but it soon became clear that the Elector was in no hurry to put the clauses of the peace treaty into effect.The elder cousin knew how important it was for the younger to take up the fight against Tsar Peter, and hoped to obtain some amelioration of the Altranstädt treaty if he delayed concurrence: as the campaigning season got closer, Charles might become meeker. And even if this hope should be disappointed,

---

* Seven hundred were killed, 1,800 taken prisoners; the rest got away.

† Charles also insisted on his freeing the 'Fraustadt battalions', which Augustus initially refused to do.

Augustus realized the desirability of keeping the road open for future cc
operation with Tsar Peter. It was important for him to delay as long a
humanly possible fulfilling those clauses against which the Tsar proteste
most strongly: the delivery of the Russian troops in Saxony to Charles XII an
the handing over of Patkul to Swedish justice.

For the Swedish army the period in Saxony was a period of comfort an
rest: in the campaigns to come officers and soldiers sometimes confessed tha
they had been spoilt for the hard life by those soft days in Germany wher
milk and honey flowed and where all Swedes felt buoyed up by the prestig
and respect and even friendship they met with as soon as the first panic ha
subsided in the Electorate. The Saxons, relieved at having escaped war, wer
impressed with Swedish army discipline* and fairness in assessing and extract
ing contributions. The bureaucratic machine examined all accounts with th
minutest attention to detail and Cederhielm stressed that he took care t
behave in Saxony 'as if I were the only Swede in the whole country'.[26] Th
native Swedish soldier was of peasant stock and a smallholder himself i
peacetime; he fitted in where billeted and helped tend the cattle and chop th
wood in his spare time.

The fact that many non-Swedes now came to enlist in Charles XII's arm
gave the Swedes added status as the kernel of the army. Fitted out in ne
uniforms – provided by Saxon contributions – they strutted a bit and caugh
the eyes of the girls. Legend has it that the illegitimate sons they left wer
numerous enough to form a regiment where Swedish paternity was a qualifica
tion for entry. Officers and officials of the time thought that 'many of th
army' would be glad to get out of Saxony before the fruit of the winter shoul
be known. There was a natural reluctance to tell tales about fellow-Swedes i
letters home and the Polish Valloche regiments were singled out as those mos
anxious to be on the move, but in civilian letters and in some war-diarie
there are comments which show that the Swedes also held some of their ow
nation responsible for children conceived in Saxony.[27] The Saxons themselves
while distinguishing between Poles and Germans in Swedish service and th
native born Swedes in respect of morals, soon learnt to take the official imag
of Charles XII's soldiers *cum grano salis*. 'It is true that they pray and sin
hymns more than others,' a Saxon clergyman noted in his almanac for 1706
'but they can swear as fluently as any other nation.'[28]

The leader of the Swedes was excepted from even such minor strictures i
matters of self-discipline. Throughout Charles XII's stay in Saxony he wa
scrutinized and watched as never before; he was confined to a comparatively
small stage and his every move, mood and habit was the object of notes anc
comment by hosts and visitors. The curiosity about him was boundless. In th
1706 *Dictionnaire Historique* thirty columns were devoted to him as agains
twenty-two for Louis XIV, stocks of engravings of him were quickly exhausted

* The strictness with which discipline was enforced – hanging for looting or acts of violenc
against civilians – was remarked on.

Swedes were importuned to obtain his portraits on rings or medallions for gifts and mementoes and 'a thousand questions' were asked of those who had met him.[29] Travellers managed to plan their routes so that the Swedish headquarters at Altranstädt could be included, and letters and diplomatic dispatches abound in pen-portraits of the Swedish King and stories about him in this period. The fact that he read a section of the Bible every day became known and was used to emphasize his devoutness, as was his strict punishment of blasphemy.[30] The circumstance that he had made an early pilgrimage to the battlefield of Lützen, where he demonstrated his familiarity with the history of Gustavus Adolphus and with the details of the battle,[31] was taken as an augury of his determination to protect Protestant rights in Germany.

The simplicity of his life seemed to observers to contrast with the power at his command. One of the more polished of the visitors, Lord Raby, Queen Anne's representative at the Prussian court, found the King's manners at times too rustic: his tale of Charles XII on a cold morning buttering his bread with his thumb* has been lifted from the Raby report to become immortalized in an English poem.[32] A young Swedish student, on his way home from Europe, found his King less elegant than Augustus. At first sight Charles struck him as not much different from the common run of shy Swedish peasant-lads, slightly gawky and awkward in the company of the great. But the mystique of the army and of tradition built round the King worked on him speedily. He listened to stories from relatives and friends in the Guards about Charles's courage and control of himself, of his fairness and dedication to the work in hand, and soon he could not look upon the King without experiencing 'something strange, impossible to put a name to, a kind of veneration not unmixed with awe'.[33]

To those who knew Charles best, those who had to deal with him in the course of his daily round, it was clear that the success implied in the Altranstädt treaty had increased his self-confidence. He was more willing to explain the reasons for his attitude on a given topic, in contrast to his earlier youth when a decision baldly announced made him seem both reserved and obstinate. He made it clear that he judged men by their worth, not by their birth. Noble and non-noble, if doing the same work, ought – in his opinion – to have equal pay. Old titles, he argued, did not have greater intrinsic worth than recent ones: it was the man that counted, whether the title was old or new, and if he had no title he might well live to deserve one.[34] In dictating orders and letters he strove to find good Swedish words (often coining them himself from regional dialects heard among the soldiers) for many of the foreign phrases in common use. 'It is marvellous to note,' wrote a secretary by temperament more inclined to criticism than to praise, 'what love the King has of our Swedish language.'[35] He disliked superstition: the argument used from Stockholm that Paijkull, who was said to possess the secret of making

---

* This may well be true: '*tumklining*' (i.e., thumb-buttered bread) survived till recent times in remoter Scandinavian country districts; for the King being willing to eat the thin Norwegian flat-bread spread in this manner in 1718; cp. below, p. 419, ‡.

gold, ought to be spared even if he had fought against the Swedes so tha
Sweden might benefit from his knowledge, was tainted, in his opinion, by a
belief in occult powers.[36] He disliked prophecy and showed little respect fo
those who tried to forecast the outcome of the Russian campaign by inter
pretation of obscure passages in the Book of Prophets.[37] He felt uneasy a
tittle-tattle meant to lower his opinion of any individual; the sign of his ange
when aroused at such and similar encounters was a heightening of colour an
a reiterated, 'What are you driving at?'

He liked realistic appraisals. He insisted that painters should paint what h
and they saw. A general, apologizing for the portrait sent home, explained t
his wife that the King had sat beside the painter and encouraged a true like
ness, not one thought polite or in the fashion.[38] Officials dispatching portrait
of Charles to Stockholm assured the royal family that it was the campaignin
in all kinds of weather which had made his skin so dark: the painter was no
to blame.[39] The portraits done from life of Charles XII at this time show no
only the wear and the march of time – his hair, receding, is already lookin
thinner – but also the greater security and command. In Poland, Charles ha
been struck by a painting which the French artist La Croix had made o
Stanislaus Leszczyński. It seemed to him true to life and he commissioned a
portrait of himself by the same hand.[40] The result is lively and striking
though somehow not convincing. A comparison of this portrait with th
series of studies and paintings which J.D.Swartz[41] executed in 1706 and 1707
demonstrates how much the earlier non-realistic treatment of the King'
clothes (La Croix painted him in conventional armour) and surroundings (o
flowing draperies) interfere with the character-study intended.

Swartz succeeds in bringing Charles before us; the uniform as he wor
it, the tent in which he lived, the features depicted with the realism which th
King insisted on (large nose and protruding lower lip clearly visible), and th
colouring true to life rather than to artistic convention. When these portrait
were sent home to Stockholm, numerous copies were made to satisfy th
demand for likenesses of Charles XII. Some of them were made by the fin
artist David von Krafft, who had frequently painted Charles before 1700, an
these have been much reproduced. As character-studies they are obviousl
less valuable than the originals by Swartz: they have become smoother an
more conventional – a representative portrait emerges which by its very natur
lacks breath of life and fresh observation.

III

The essence of the personality of the man who sat for the Swartz portrait
was not easy to capture. Few portraits, however 'like' the sitter, can revea
the person as he sees himself or as others see him. Certainly Alstrin, th
student-observer of Charles XII in Altranstädt, argued that no portrait he ha

---

* See frontispiece and illustration facing p. 204.

•ver seen of the King – and he must have seen at least some by Swartz – gave ιny idea of what he was 'really like'.* The impression of the King's character ιs strong in all the Swartz portraits, but a close study of them would seem to ιustify the conclusion that at times the painter saw signs, for all the solidity of ιhe posture and the gain in self-confidence, that Charles had not yet come to ιerms with himself though he had come to terms with his fate: there are ιortraits which show a face subtly at variance with the stance – with a ιuestioning look that seems to imply a youthful search for identity.

It has recently been argued that Charles XII never grew up, that, in the ιvords of Hans Villius, he remained an 'adolescent' all his life.[42] Such a ιweeping generalization must be, and has been, countered by reference to his ιnature handling of his task as a commander: as Gustaf Petri pointed out, no ιeneral could be as effective as Charles XII undoubtedly was if his personality ιad been wholly immature.[43] The discussion of the King's personality in ιerms of his emotional life is not a new one, but it used to be centred on whether he was sexually 'normal' or not. The fact that Charles XII was, as ιontemporaries put it, 'chaste' occasioned speculation in his lifetime: why, it was asked, did he play Mars without Love in attendance?[44] Rumours that he was a hermaphrodite circulated in the early twentieth century, but were stilled when, on the opening of his coffin in 1917, his corpse was observed to ιave a growth of beard. Homosexuality has not been specifically imputed to ιim though it has been hinted at by the epithet 'abnormal'.† Those who care to speculate on the comment in a letter by Reuterholm that Charles XII liked the Electoral Prince of Saxony 'who is very pretty',[45] might like to note that Reuterholm is the only contemporary to put on paper the story that Charles, before 1700, had known a certain lady at court 'as well as her husband did': Reuterholm himself did not, it would seem, want us to read too much into his choice of adjective for the Saxon prince. Those who find something odd about the friendship of Charles with the young Maximilian of Württemberg would gain a truer perspective of its teacher-pupil relationship from a reading of the life of Maximilian written by one who was in attendance on the prince from 1703 when he joined the Swedish army as a thirteen-year-old till his death in 1709. Charles then mourned the loss of 'his best friend', but it was Charles himself who had sent Maximilian from headquarters and put him in command of a company as soon as he was ready for promotion.[46] That Maximilian was heterosexual is shown by Fabrice's amusing and scandalous memoirs of their joint adventures in Saxony.[47]

The evidence we have of Charles XII's sexual make-up points to a normal interest in the opposite sex never consummated. The negotiations for a bride for him between 1697 and 1700, Hjärne's assurance that he was not impotent, and the post-1703 admonitions by his grandmother that he should marry 'for

* See above, p. 3.
† The French historian Nordmann (1962) has been the most explicit, calling for 'an investigation into the moral and psychological problems' posed by the sway of Görtz – whom he regards as a homosexual – over Charles XII.

the good of the country' would seem to preclude physical disabilities or peculiarities which would render marriage impossible.[48] Observers after 1700 noted that, though the King did not always speak much to the young ladies present at parties or on other occasions, he watched at least some of them closely and asked questions about them afterwards, identifying them by detailed descriptions of their looks and clothes; and, at least once, we know that he commented on the great beauty of one of them to fellow-officers.[49] He liked gallant stories,[50] and from his years in Turkey we know that he enjoyed the stories more spiced as he got older, 'though not too vulgar'. In talks with Löwen[51] he explained that he had remained chaste because he knew his own temperament well: it was ardent and he feared that if he gave in to temptation even once he would become a slave of his own appetites.* Where Löwen's memoirs can be tested by independent evidence – as they will be in this chapter on a matter of political importance – they give an absolutely trustworthy report of Charles XII's words, and I am therefore inclined to accept that the King did make the above judgement and that Löwen's memory of talk of gallant adventures and speculation on sexual prowess among the officers, in which the King took part and even encouraged others,† is substantially correct.

That Charles XII suffered from sexual frustration is demonstrated by the very appetite for talk about sex – discreet and possibly disguised even to himself before 1709, more open in the years 1709–14, when he also lacked the energy-absorbing military life of the years before and after his stay in Turkey. He seems early in the war to have evolved a theory which may have served as a rationalization for his own abstinence: officers, he held, were more proficient in their duties of war if they did not use up their strength in hunting animals or pursuing women.[52] His wish to have an élite corps of unmarried men expressed during the preparations for the Norwegian campaign of 1718,‡ may have been based on this theory. Similar ideas have been current in all periods among commanders in war. They do not permit us to draw valid conclusions as to Charles XII's own inclinations had fate not made him the commander-in-chief of an army forced into a long war.

Memories of revered parents and an adored elder sister may have a bearing on his sexual abstinence. He felt his separation from the family circle acutely. His sense of emotional isolation comes through in the letter he wrote to Hedvig Sophia early in 1705 begging her not to leave Sweden for Holstein-Gottorp: he realizes that she may 'also feel alone and lonely', but pleads with her to stay 'where we all belong' that 'I may have your dear company to look forward to if ever I get home again.'[53] 'We who are the only two left', is a recurring phrase in his letters to Ulrika Eleonora after Hedvig's death in 1708. He was moved to tears during the two reunions with Ulrika after 1715 (one in 1716, one in 1718) whenever he mentioned his mother's name. It could there-

* In this Charles may have been influenced by the talk at court of his having inherited his father's uxoriousness, see above, p. 105.
† See below, p. 376.   ‡ ibid., p. 466.

ore be assumed that he identified too closely with the women of his family
nd particularly with the elder sister, to develop normally. Certainly the news
f the death of Hedvig which was broken to him after the battle of Poltava
it him so hard that he refused to accept it for several months: he kept hoping
hat proof of it being 'false news' would soon reach him.* But it may equally
vell be assumed – and this seems a more likely explanation to the present
vriter – that the war which robbed him of the chance to marry the Danish
ousin (of the 'enemy' nation, as his mother had been between 1675-9) caused
he natural identification with the family to be prolonged beyond the age
vhen an independent emotional life finds its fulfilment outside the family.

The veneration of parents, the determination to keep promises made to
hem, exert a strong pull in such circumstances. Charles, succeeding to the
rown at fourteen, modelled even his signature on that of his father; that he
hould try to model his behaviour on his precepts is not surprising and may
ave contributed to that restraint which he explained to Löwen (and probably
lso to himself) as the outcome of fear of losing control. His father's abstin-
nce in similar circumstances, during the war of 1675-9 when he, a young
nmarried man, was fighting in Scania, was religiously motivated: he main-
ained in discussions with fellow-officers that no man 'given to an unlawful
ove of women could ever be truly courageous in time of danger, not only
pon the account that love did effeminate the spirits, but principally because
heir guilty conscience reproach'd them their unfitness to dye.'[54] It is not
nown whether Charles XI imparted these views in any detail to his son; but
t is unlikely that the personal letter which he left for his heir to read after his
leath should have remained silent on the issues of abstinence before marriage
nd on faithfulness after it. The obedience which Charles XII judged he owed
o his father is well exemplified by his unwillingness to pardon Patkul: quite
part from the bad example of letting traitors go scot-free, it would – he
rgued – be a blot on his father's memory to fail to execute a judgement made
y him.

IV

The year in Saxony proved a busy one. The work to get the army increased by
ome ten thousand men and drilled for the forthcoming campaign against
Russia went parallel with efforts to have King Stanislaus recognized and the
Treaty of Altranstädt guaranteed. The military tasks were straightforward
nd under Swedish control,† but the diplomatic ones proved difficult, and
uccess could be bought, if at all, only at a high cost. Frederick I of Prussia –
vho had been in negotiations with Charles XII since September 1706 for a
riple alliance of Protestant powers with Hanover as the third partner – gave
Stanislaus specific recognition in January 1707. In return Sweden had to
dmit Hohenzollern claims to Elbing‡ which Charles XII had resisted since

* See below, p. 313.   † ibid., pp. 232-5.
‡ The town was, however, to be occupied by the Swedes till Charles had achieved peace with
he Tsar.

1703.[55] The negotiations for the 'Evangelical Pact' strengthened Charles XII
hands in relation to the Habsburg Emperor, though the triple alliance in th
end did not materialize, pressure by the Maritime Powers on Hanover reduc
ing it to a dual confessional treaty signed by Sweden and Prussia in Augus
1707.[56] Joseph I was willing, in February 1707, to recognize Stanislaus
Charles XII in return would recognize the Archduke Charles as King Charle
III of Spain. Such commitment by Sweden in the War of the Spanish Succes
sion was, however, unthinkable. The Swedes held that the solemn assurance
they had given the Emperor (on 16 and 28 September 1706) that there was n
secret understanding between Charles XII and Louis XIV ought to satisf
Vienna in that matter.[57]

The very presence of the Swedish army in Saxony was, in the opinion of th
Emperor and the Maritime Powers, of benefit to France, and as tension grev
between Joseph and Charles fear rose in London and at The Hague that th
Swedes might be drawn into measures which would hearten Louis XIV: a
attack on the Emperor's Habsburg dominions by Charles XII to obtain redres
for grievances was thought possible and at times probable. In these circun
stances the Maritime Powers preferred to delay recognition of Stanislaus t
use it as a lever in a possible mediation between the Swedes and the Austrian

Swedish complaints against Vienna arose from the Emperor's receivin
into his service the 1,200 Russian auxiliaries in Saxony who according to th
Altranstädt Treaty should have been handed over to Charles XII. Josep
prevaricated, being anxious to preserve friendly relations with the Tsar, wh
might otherwise give support to Rákóczi and his Magyar and Transylvania
(Siebenbürgen) independence movement. Under Swedish pressure he brough
the troops back from their Rhine stations, but connived, in May 1707, at thei
escape from Austrian territory to Poland. Friction over this issue wa
increased by a diplomatic incident* in Vienna,[58] and by the killing of
Swedish corporal and the arrest of several officers in Breslau during recruit
ment for soldiers.[59] More significant was Joseph's delaying tactics in respec
of the Gottorp candidature for the vacant bishopric of Lübeck-Eutin. Th
King of Denmark agreed to abide by the rule of rotation as soon as Charle
XII arrived in Saxony, but the Emperor's refusal to endorse the Gottorp clain
raised suspicions that the position of Sweden's ally would be undermine
both from Copenhagen and Vienna once the Swedish army had moved out c
the Empire.

The projected evangelical triple alliance would have meant a desirabl
strengthening of Sweden's position in North Germany *vis-à-vis* the Austria
Habsburgs. The prospect of gaining Prussia, hitherto so resentful at Sweden'
hold on Western Pomerania, and Hanover, in the Vienna orbit since her 169.
promotion to an Electorate, as allies against the Habsburgs was most wel

---

* An imperial courtier, Count Zobor (Czobor), spoke slightingly of Charles XII and the Swede
at a party in the presence of the Swedish envoy, Baron von Stralenheim, who retaliated, accordin
to his own description, with *un couple de soufflers*.

ɔme. Frederick I, the instigator of the negotiations, had political reasons for ɪstrusting Joseph I at this time, but the confessional aspect loomed large with ɪl the prospective partners. The treatment of Protestants, whether Lutheran r Calvinist, by Leopold and Joseph, had shocked them: the fate of the Hun-arians sold as galley-slaves worried them more than did Louis XIV's treat-ɪent of the Huguenots, since Vienna's policy of suppression of Protestant ɪghts threatened to spread to areas covered by the Peace of Westphalia. The ereditary lands of the Habsburgs, including those of Bohemia, Moravia and ilesia incorporated by the Treaty of Prague of 1635, had not received a eneral guarantee of religious freedom in 1648 though Sweden had tried hard ɔ achieve this during the negotiations for the Peace of Westphalia. But certain reas of Silesia – the princedoms of Liegnitz, Brieg, Oels and Münsterberg as ʋell as the towns of Breslau, Schweidnitz, Jauer and Glogau – had received uch a guarantee.[60] It was against the closure of Protestant churches in ɪefiance of their 1648 rights that Silesians from the districts and towns in ɪuestion had appealed to Charles XII for help as early as 1704, and it was an ɪbjective of Swedish policy in 1706 and 1707 to act on their behalf both in lirect negotiations with Vienna and, more indirectly, in the negotiations for he evangelical triple alliance. By February 1707, Whitehall was plagued by ear of an imminent rupture between Sweden and the Emperor which would – rom the allied point of view – prove 'fatal to the liberty of Europe'.*

French diplomacy was, naturally enough, anxious to use Austro-Swedish ʳriction for Louis XIV's benefit. Officially the special envoys sent to Altran-tädt in February and March 1707 came to ask for Charles XII's mediation in he War of the Spanish Succession, but unofficially Count Erik Sparre (a ʒwede in French service) and Armand de Besenval (a French army colonel) ʋorked hard on Swedish officials and officers to make them dissatisfied with he prospect of a Russian campaign. The Empire in 1707 – so ran their argu-ɪent – was as rich a field for Franco-Swedish cooperation as during the ʲeventeenth century, and the Swedes would live to regret not taking the pick-ngs which offered: Louis XIV would mediate a Russo-Swedish peace and any ʲosses which that entailed would be more than compensated for in the gains ɔf an 'armed mediation' between France and the Grand Alliance.[61]

The Maritime Powers were not particularly worried by rumours of French ɔlandishment of individual Swedes. They were reasonably sure both of Charles XII's neutrality in the War of the Spanish Succession and of his firm ʳesolve to settle matters with Tsar Peter in a campaign that would move east ɪs soon as his military preparations were complete. But they became increas-ingly alarmed lest Austro-Swedish tension should explode into war: if Charles XII's troops crossed into Joseph I's hereditary dominions the Swedish King would, whether he wanted to or not, be in effect an ally of Louis XIV. The dissolution of the Austrian Habsburg dominions might well come to pass. In March 1707 the Estates of Transylvania recognized Rákóczi as their

* *British Diplomatic Instructions: Sweden*, ed. F. Chance, p. 33.

leader, and at the Diet of the Magyar Confederation which followed short
thereafter the House of Habsburg was declared to have forfeited all rights
the crown of St Stephen. Charles XII had in effect been non-committal enoug
to Rákóczi's diplomatic mission to Altranstädt to make him turn to Russ
for help,[62] but the very thought of a Protestant triple alliance in North Ge
many was anathema to the English and the Dutch since it implied a weakenir
of Joseph I, their Catholic ally in the struggle against France. Nor did the
relish the paralyzing influence which the presence of Charles XII in the Empi
had on the plans for the 1707 campaign against Louis XIV. Uncertainty an
long-drawn-out negotiations made it impossible to reckon with the ear
arrival of the German contingents in the Low Countries.

V

It is against this background that the visit of the Duke of Marlborough
Altranstädt between 27–29 April (O.S.) 1707 must be seen. Many legen
have become connected with it: the one that he bribed Count Piper with a
English pension to wean Charles XII from intervention in the western war an
hurry on the Russian campaign is perhaps the most long-lived. Count Pip
was not bribed, though his wife received a courtesy present of a pair
diamond ear-rings, with the consent of Charles XII; and even the secr
presents of £1,000 each with promises of annual pensions of the same amoun
to Hermelin and Cederhielm* had no effect on policy decisions. What wa
achieved was that young James Jefferyes† was permitted to go with th
Swedish army on the Russian campaign as a volunteer – in reality with th
twofold mission of reporting to Whitehall on the progress of the venture an
to be on the spot (if speedy success against Tsar Peter should free Charles x
for participation in the western war) to invite Charles XII's accession to th
Grand Alliance.

Here we come to the central objective of Marlborough's visit.[63] The Duk
given wide powers by the English government, wanted to satisfy Charles x
in some of his objectives in return for a promise of future moral if not militai
commitment to the Allied side. He was not willing to further the evangelic
triple alliance (indeed, his visit to Berlin after Altranstädt was intended t
prevent its formation as was the Allied pressure put on Hanover), but he wa
determined to obtain enough concessions from Joseph I in the Gottorp an
Silesian issues to prevent Austro-Swedish hostilities. He was also anxious t
give Charles XII sufficient expectation of support from the Maritime Powers i
respect of Stanislaus and the Treaty of Altranstädt so as not to delay Swedis
departure from the Empire.

In Turkey the Swedish King told Löwen that he had refrained from makin

* The story of this aspect of Marlborough's visit will be treated in its wider context in my fort
coming study, *Presents and Pensions: one aspect of Anglo-Swedish relations, 1688–1709.*

† For Jefferyes, see above, p. 189; cp. the introduction to his letters 1707–9, edited by th
present author, published in 1954 in *H.H.* 35: 1.

himself the arbiter of Europe when in Saxony, first of all because the struggle with the Tsar commanded all his military strength, and, secondly, because he had given his word to Marlborough to remain neutral in the War of the Spanish Succession against a promise that the Allies would keep his back free when he moved against Tsar Peter.[64] The truth of this report (which, incidentally, strengthens the trustworthiness of the memoirs as a whole) and the correctness of Charles XII's memory of the verbal promises exchanged, are demonstrated and deepened by letters between Marlborough and Godolphin in 1707 and by Swedish diplomatic correspondence between 1707 and 1709: what Marlborough had promised was support for Charles XII in respect of his troubles with Denmark and the Emperor as well as recognition of Stanislaus and guarantee of the treaty of Altranstädt; in return he had received a Swedish promise of cooperation with the Maritime Powers in respect of their peace with France. It was essential for Marlborough to make sure that Charles should not act independently, as an arbiter, in the War of the Spanish Succession and in his report to Godolphin he stressed that Charles XII 'had been pleased to give me particular assurances that he would adhere to no proposals that might be made him in relation to the mediatorship until he heard from me that the Queen thought it seasonable.'[65] From this base English statesmen built hopes that they had – at the very least – a mediator through whom 'we may yett have a good Peace' and – at best – a fighting ally.[66]

Marlborough was careful not to put his own promises on paper even to Godolphin. He knew full well the objections felt both at The Hague and in London against recognition of Stanislaus and guarantee of the 1706 peace between Charles and Augustus; but he and his colleagues in the Cabinet admitted the existence of the April 1707 promises when the Swedish envoy in London appealed for the fulfilment of them: and they were the object of much diplomatic activity after Marlborough's departure.[67]

Yet another fear was allayed during the Duke's visit to Altranstädt. There had been speculation among the diplomats there that if Charles XII had too speedy a success in Russia he would be able to impose a peace on the West to his own liking. Indeed, Robinson's pessimistic prophecies in this respect had helped to spur Marlborough on his journey:

That he will favour the Allys is very uncertain;* that he will force them to a disadvantageous peace is not improbable; that he will act against them is possible, and if he do so in all appearance he may do and we must suffer whatt he pleases. For supposeing the war in Poland and Muscovy at an end neither the Emperor, Denmark, Prussia nor any Prince or State of Germany will dare to appear against him. All will yield to his will and England and Holland must do so too or stand alone.[68]

But during Marlborough's visit such fears were allayed not only on the political plane, but also on the military one. The Duke himself talked of past and future campaigns with Charles XII and his generals and picked up enough gossip to conclude that the Swedes expected their campaign against Tsar

* Italicized words in cypher in original.

Peter to be no easy one and likely to span two years rather than one. Mar
borough's reported praise, on Queen Anne's and his own behalf, of the youn
King's generalship sounds fulsome to modern ears: the older man stressir
what happiness it would be for him to learn the art of war under Charles, con
veying the Queen's regret that her sex prevents her doing the same – th
veracity of such phrases have sometimes been doubted. But they ring true t
the phraseology of Marlborough and seem less strange if we recall Willian
III's flattering letter, penned in his own hand, to Charles in 1702. For his ow
part Marlborough was pleased with his success: 'I hope', he wrote to Brydge
'that it has entirely defeated the Expectations the French Court had from th
King of Sweden.'[69]

English pressure on Vienna not to drive matters to a breach with Charle
XII brought some results. Count Wratislaw was sent to Altranstädt in Jul
with the offer, as compensation for Swedish grievances in respect of th
Russian troops and the slight to Charles's honour, of free transit for th
Swedish army through Silesia when the offensive against Tsar Peter shoul
begin. With the help of the diplomats of the Maritime Powers, and in som
fear of the Swedish regiments who on 10 August began their march acros
Silesia, further concessions were wrested from the Emperor. On 22 Augus
1 September 1707, by the convention* of Altranstädt, Wratislaw gave up h
master's claim to Charles XII's military contingent (in his capacity of
German prince) for the war against Louis XIV, promised imperial approval o
the Gottorp candidate for the Lübeck bishopric and – what was far harder t
accept – the reinstatement of the Silesian Protestants to their religious right
of 1648.

The Emperor had been extremely reluctant to concede this, and eve
offered Charles one of the Swedish *desiderata*, Hadeln in Lauenburg, if h
would desist; a suggestion Charles felt it would be dishonourable to accep
He answered, politely, that he had territories enough and hoped with God'
help to retrieve what his enemies had robbed him of; but when the Imperia
representatives were out of earshot he was heard to mutter *Memini m
Alexandrum non mercatorem.*[70] He had to use threats to make Sweden's 164
guarantee a reality: he let it be known that he was prepared to interpret tha
guarantee to cover not only the Protestants in the enumerated places but in
all Silesia. Joseph speedily chose the lesser of two evils. By article 1 of th
convention the Emperor therefore promised to restore, in the enumerate
places, the churches and schools which had been closed or handed over t
Catholics since 1648, as well as all rights and income alienated since that date
and to maintain for the Protestants freedom of conscience and equal civi
rights with Catholics in the Silesian Estates.†

On the very day the convention[71] with Joseph I was signed, Charles lef

* I have chosen this term rather than treaty to avoid confusion with the treaty of Altranstäd
of 1706.

† A commission in Vienna, at which Baron von Stralenheim assisted, put the terms of the con
vention into effect in Silesia between 1707 and 1709.

Saxony to catch up with his army. The security he had gained to keep his back free during the execution of the grand design was not particularly strong. Augustus had not obtained an alternative kingdom which might make him forget the Poland he had lost. The Saxon Elector had declared himself a willing candidate for the crown of Naples and Sicily, and Charles XII had expressed his approval of the scheme,[72] but this was not a plan likely to appeal to the Emperor. Joseph had his eye on Spain's Italian possessions for himself rather than for his brother, whose claim to be Carlos III he only supported in respect of Spain, the Spanish Netherlands and the Spanish Indies. Frederick of Denmark had been impressed enough with Swedish power during 1706–7 to permit conferences to open at Hamburg, at which Robinson and Haersolte acted as mediators, to settle differences which had developed between Copenhagen and the Duke-Administrator of Holstein-Gottorp.[73] Frederick of Prussia had recognized Stanislaus and guaranteed the treaty of Altranstädt, but the recognition and guarantee promised by Marlborough had not yet materialized. The Swedes lived in hopes of at least English fulfilment of the promise since this would be a far more solid bulwark against Augustus's plans for revenge than the Prussian pact: a complement to the treaty of Travendal which had so far successfully contained Frederick of Denmark.

Military necessity made it impossible for Charles XII to delay his departure in the expectation of either recognition or guarantee from London and/or The Hague. The Emperor's ratification of the Altranstädt convention caught up with the army on 6 September (N.S.),[74] and it was hoped that Swedish reminders would elicit the documents desired from the Maritime Powers before the march was too far advanced.*

* In the event the recognition of Stanislaus by Queen Anne reached Charles XII in March 1708 see Hatton, *Jefferyes*, pp. 44 ff.); but England never guaranteed the treaty of Altranstädt of 1706. The States General gave neither recognition nor guarantee.

BOOK FOUR

The Campaign Against Russia

1

Plans and Preparations

everal considerations forced Charles XII to start his campaign against Tsar eter before the guarantees meant to restrain Augustus were complete.
The best moment for hitting at Sweden's eastern enemy might be lost if the wedes tarried too long in the west. Charles was well informed about domestic nrest in Russia, and the memoranda of Martin Neugebauer, former governor o the Tsarevich Aleksey, urged him to utilize both Moscow opposition against eter's policies and the Astrakhan Cossack revolt against Russian domination hich had broken out in 1705.[1] News of the unrest in Muscovy came also rom Polish sources, but it was Neugebauer who became 'the Russian expert' t Swedish headquarters since he had recent personal experience of its court nd was regarded as less prone to wishful thinking than the Poles.[2]

Furthermore, Augustus had fulfilled the terms of the Altranstädt treaty of 706. He had, though with bad grace, recognized King Stanislaus. He had, if alf-heartedly, reminded the Emperor and the Maritime Powers of his under-aking to obtain their recognition of Stanislaus and their guarantee of the reaty itself.[3] He had, in the night 27–28 March 1707, handed Patkul over to a Swedish guard.* His ally the Emperor had, in the convention of Altranstädt f 1707, given satisfaction for the clause in the treaty which Augustus had roken when he let his Russian auxiliaries go into Joseph's service. There was herefore no longer any legal basis for the Swedes remaining in Saxony.

It also had to be taken into account that the European situation might change in ways which would act in Charles's disfavour. If the Allies had a peedy victory over Louis XIV, anti-Swedish measures could be expected. The Emperor's resentment at Swedish interference on behalf of Silesian Protes-ants was well known: freedom of action might tempt him to revenge. The grumbles of Dutch and English merchants at high-handed Swedish treatment of Baltic trading-centres, such as Danzig, had accompanied all diplomatic exchanges between Charles XII and the Maritime Powers since 1703. The commercial classes of both nations feared that a victorious Sweden would exploit her monopoly in naval stores to force prices even higher and would also encourage Swedish shipping at the expense of that of other countries:[4]

* Patkul was executed in September 1707.

with the return of peace with France these critics might press their gover
ments to work for a partitioning of the Baltic into Swedish and Russi
spheres of influence.

That it was in Sweden's interest to settle scores with Tsar Peter before t
Allies achieved peace with Louis XIV was generally assumed, so much so th
the failure of the expedition against Toulon in 1707 was attributed to t
machinations of Charles XII rather than to Joseph I's preoccupations with h
Italian ambitions. It was believed at the time, and this belief has foun
credence among later historians, that the Swedish King (by a threat to inva
Silesia) had forced Joseph to drag his feet in the Toulon campaign and th
ensured that Louis XIV would be able to fight on. The Anglo-Dutch desire
find a scapegoat outside the Grand Alliance for the Toulon failure is natur
enough, but there is no evidence to support the conjecture of Charles
responsibility.[5] The accusation is, however, symptomatic both of the fear
Swedish power and of the understanding that peace in the west in 1707-8 w
not in Charles XII's interest. The sooner the Swedes could act against Ts
Peter, the less danger they ran that the second stage of the grand design wou
be imperilled by western or Imperial initiative.

Consideration of the Polish and Baltic situation weighed most heavil
Tsar Peter had intensified his pressure on Sweden's Baltic provinces duri
1706 and 1707 and Charles was most anxious 'to get them some air'; Russi
troops had flooded the Commonwealth and with Augustus's acceptance of h
dethronement the Tsar began negotiations with prospective candidates f
the Polish crown who could form a rallying point for anti-Stanislaus an
anti-Swedish forces. Peter's invitations to Prince Eugène and to the Sobies
brothers did not alarm Swedish headquarters since none of these were thoug
keen on the part; but the fear that Rákóczi – whose plea for military suppo
Charles had felt obliged to refuse[6] in spite of his expressed sympathy wit
the Hungarian Protestants – might accept the position as Stanislaus's riva
and thus imperil the chief gain from the invasion of Saxony was a strong spu
to action.

II

The military preparations for the Russian campaign had been well lai
Much time had been spent in Saxony in training foreign recruits to use th
Swedish drill and arms. Soldiers from the German Protestant states had bee
readily accepted with the exception of Saxons (some of whom, contemporari
tell us, managed to get into the army by giving false information about thei
domicile)[8] and had been formed into dragoon regiments for preferenc
Recruits from Sweden to bring native infantry and cavalry regiments up t
strength had throughout the war been transported across the Baltic, in con
voys protected by men-of-war, to the port nearest the army at any give
time.[9] There was no provision, however, in the Altranstädt treaty for th

ationing in Saxony of the large contingent of Swedish soldiers – some nine
ousand – which was needed to strengthen the army with native troops on
e eve of the Russian campaign, and Charles therefore directed that these
ould be landed in Swedish Pomerania in July 1707. There was some delay in
e embarkation of these forces and they did not join the main army till
ctober, when it was stationed at Słupca in Great Poland.

The army which after that date was ready to move against Tsar Peter used
 be given as forty to forty-three thousand strong: a figure based on numbers
vulged to foreigners in contact with the Swedish headquarters in 1707 and
 Swedish diplomats abroad. In recent years it has been challenged by Sture
aller who, from the muster-rolls of the War Office archive, arrived at a
ghting army of 33,000'* and consigned the contemporary estimate to the
alm of 'official propaganda'.[10] His own figure is now generally accepted and
chnically correct. But it should be noted that he counted only private
ldiers, and his figure may therefore be a little misleading to the non-
ecialist, to whom the army of Charles XII is unthinkable without its officers
d non-commissioned officers. Contemporaries would also have included
e men who served the army in non-combatant capacities, such as clergymen,
irgeons and apothecaries; nor would they have excluded the civil officials
ho at times took part in skirmishes and battles and shared the fate of the
my as prisoners-of-war after Poltava and Perevolotjna; or the servants of
fficers and officials. The most commonsense estimate would seem to be that
n the eve of the Russian campaign the army under Charles's command,
cluding all these categories, was not far from forty-four thousand.

In a rather special position were the foreign volunteers, at least one of
hom – James Jefferyes – was a secret diplomatic agent.† There were also a
w who made some stages of the campaign for political or ideological
easons. The Prussian von Siltmann,‡ sent on a mission by Frederick I, and
e delegation of Hungarian Protestants, led by the Slovak pastor Daniel
rmann,¶ are good examples of these categories.[11] Not part of the army
oper, though they swelled its numbers, were those wagoners who worked
or a relatively short period to transport supplies and ammunition, portable
ridges and mills: these were local civilians contracted to cover a particular
tretch of road. When their destination was reached, they returned home to
ake room for freshly hired men with knowledge of the road ahead.[12]

To the body of the main army Charles reckoned to join most of the Baltic
etachment (11,400 strong) under Lewenhaupt.[13] The army of fourteen
ousand men stationed in Finland under Lybeker might be brought into

---

* Composed of 7,100 cavalry, 9,600 dragoons, 14,200 infantry, 1,500 Valloches, and some other
nall units such as the King's drabants (150) and the artillery corps (150).

† Grofoy, a French agent serving Rákóczi's cause, was in a similar position in Saxony and
ithuania, but left in June 1708.

‡ He joined the army at the end of July 1708 and stayed till Perevolotjna.

¶ It stayed with the army from the end of July 1708 and went with Charles to Turkey after the
attle of Poltava.

play,[14] but in a separate operation against St Petersburg. The rest of Swede
forces, in number roughly equal to the main operational army, could take
part in the campaign: they would have to be left in the Baltic provinces, in t
German possessions and in Sweden* for defence.

Both the main army and the subsidiary ones had by this time been fitt
out and armed in ways which suited the fighting tactics developed during t
war. They all had the so-called 'Charles XII's sword': a lighter and mo
pointed model ordered in Sweden or in the German provinces from 17
onwards to replace that of the previous reign.[15] Most of the soldiers who h
gone with Charles to the Baltic provinces in the autumn of 1700 had carri
the flint-lock musket introduced by Charles XI; by now the cavalry had al
been issued with flint-lock pistols.[16] Quantities of gunpowder had be
bought, though the Swedish army used relatively little ammunition becau
of its emphasis on attack with *armes blanches*. The artillery taken along w
small in number compared with the heavy booty sent home after Kliszów
blown up after Lemberg. The uniforms were new for the most part. T
Swedish veterans who had been likened to gipsies when, weather-beat
and ragged, they marched into Saxony[17] walked out well shod and dresse
The Swedes wore the familiar blue and yellow with cloaks of darker blue
grey, but in some regiments at least the elkskin breeches had been replaced
cloth ones and in some a kind of greatcoat, a cloak with sleeves call
paijrock, was issued.[18] The non-Swedish regiments wore clothes which vari
from this pattern, but on the whole it was a uniformly dressed army whic
embarked on the Russian campaign. Bibles and hymn-books and medic
supplies had also arrived from Sweden, or had been bought locally,
considerable quantities.

Food for at least the first six weeks of the campaign had been stockpile
and divided between the regiments, after that ready money and cred
arrangements would replenish the stores. The Swedish soldier's diet was, c
paper anyhow, a liberal one, rich – as historians interested in nutrition ha
pointed out – in calories.[19] Its staple items were bread, dried lentils and bee
but the quantities of meat, bacon and fish were generous. Tobacco was issue
weekly and brandy or other spirits was part of the rations for difficult tas
or in inclement weather. There was a prohibition against eating raw fru
and against the brewing of mead from fruit and honey during the marches fc
fear of stomach infections. The basically sound and sufficient food, couple
with the strong constitutions of hand-picked recruits, made for toughness an
hardihood even at times when the diet fell far below that scheduled on pape
both in the Polish marches and in those on Russian soil, the Swedish arm
of 1707–8 was to suffer great hardships when plans to obtain fresh suppli
broke down.†

* There were at this time some eleven thousand troops in each of the two main subdivisions
the empire and seventeen thousand in Sweden.

† See below, pp. 257–8, 266–8, 270–3.

The road ahead had been the object of much study during the year in ₄xony. Gyllenkrook, the quartermaster-general who was Charles's acknow-dged 'expert on roads', worked from Polish and Russian maps procured ₊r him from many sources, one of them a fine map of Russia which Augustus ₁d given to Charles as a present. The King took a close interest in the pro-₋ess of Gyllenkrook's work, but with the object of maximum surprise the ₋eatest secrecy was observed about the actual route to be chosen. Gyllen-rook recounts in his memoirs that many approached him to find out the ₖely direction of the march, but that he himself was unable to make a guess ₎ it because of the multiplicity of alternatives implied in the local maps of vers and roads demanded from him. Charles was apt to tease Gyllenkrook a ₜtle when he became too insistent with advice or too keen to be in the know, ₙd it was with some relief that the quartermaster-general was assured by ₎ehnskiöld that the King did have a plan for the campaign: he had begun ₎ believe that there was no plan at all.[20]

Steps were also taken before the departure of the army from Saxony to ₋rengthen the Royal Council at home. This body had lost several of its most ₐluable members: Count Oxenstierna had died in 1702, Count Wrede, head ₊ the College of Commerce, was temporarily incapacitated by a stroke,[21] and ₋illieroot had not long survived his recall from The Hague. Some of the ₋usted and experienced officials, such as Åkerhielm of the Chancery, had also ₋ied and it was not till 1713 that his son (educated at Oxford at Queen Anne's ₓpense in an attempt by Robinson to establish a useful connexion) joined the ₋ing at Bender and became a trusted member of the Chancery-in-the-field.[22] ₋here were in 1706 some rising men in the Chancery, among them Samuel ₋arck, who succeeded Åkerhielm and corresponded regularly with Olof ₋ermelin at headquarters; but the King felt that Sweden needed to be stiffened ₋r the tough struggle ahead by an influx of men who had worked with him ₊etween 1700 and 1707, who would know the needs of the army and be able ₎ act independently in the interests of the grand design if communications ₊etween himself and Sweden – which had hitherto been regular and relatively ₐsy – became slower and possibly perilous. Two trusted officers were now ₙade councillors; Stenbock, who had proved his value as an organizer and ₋orn, who had equally proved his as a diplomat. Both left the King before ₋he army broke up to begin their tasks in Sweden.* Others in less high ₋ositions also went to posts at home, among them Reuterholm,† who had been ₋harles's secretary for some time, and through whose pen we catch candid-₋amera pictures of the King in Poland and Saxony; the impatient King not ₋othering to pull off his gloves before signing a letter and making a botch of ₋t; the 'sly' King slipping out of what the secretary regards as already settled; ₋he King at work, going through an important draft dispatch line for line, ₋eighing every word and making numerous changes in his own hand.[23]

* Stenbock also had work to do in Scania as he was appointed governor-general of this district ₋n succession to Rehnskiöld, for whom a deputy had acted between 1700 and 1707.
† At the end of 1707 due to failing health.

III

It was with regret that the field Chancery officials and many officers as we bade farewell to Germany, even though they realized that the Russian cam paign was necessary. They spoke to each other, and wrote home, of the way in which the interests of Sweden and the dynasty might benefit from a long stay or a speedy return: Charles could retake the principality of Velden which rightfully belonged to his family and make good his claim to Jülic Cleve and Berg; here, at last, was the perfect opportunity to incorporate the town of Bremen which Habsburg trickery and power had denied Swede ever since 1648. They spoke, with equal sincerity, of Charles's mission Germany: God had called him to protect the Protestants in the Empire and the Habsburg dominions. Only a beginning had been made in 1706 and 1707 it must be hoped that the King would be permitted to resume with vigour the fight both for Hungarian and German Protestantism.[24]

Presumably they talked of, or at least hinted at, such objectives to Charl XII; but none of these reached the list of high priorities with the King. In h review of past policies with Löwen in 1713 they are not mentioned beyond regret that he was not able to do all he might have wished for religio toleration.[25] The King's whole attention in 1707 was focused on the strugg with the Tsar and his time was taken up with the manifold preparations ar contingency planning which the coming campaign demanded. Charles ar his closest collaborators realized that the struggle with Russia would be hard one. The King did not share the optimism of those officials and office who – because they felt emotionally committed to the Protestant crusade preferred the western theatre of war to the eastern one – convinced themselv that it would be easy for Sweden to frighten the Tsar into making peace. Russia robbed of allies, so ran their argument, would soon be brought to s sense, and the coming campaign might be one of manœuvres rather than har fighting that would risk the army. From scattered bits of information (tru enough as far as facts were concerned) a prognosis of such an ideal campaig was formed: the Swedes might have to leave a sizeable army in Poland sustain the cause of King Stanislaus – even a figure of sixteen thousand wa mentioned – but if the main operational army and the forces in the Balt under Lewenhaupt joined, some forty thousand could still march along northern invasion route to threaten Moscow; the Tsar would simultaneous be threatened by Tartars and Turks from the south* and would be gla enough to buy peace at the cost of restoring what he had taken from Swede and to offer some *satisfactio*, either in the Pskov area which would benefit the frontier of Finland, or in money which could finance further ventures i Germany.[26]

Such and similar speculations – committed to paper either by their autho

* See above, p. 193.

letters home or by those in whom they confided – contrast sharply with the
lence of the King and of the two men whose judgement he most respected.
he tension between Rehnskiöld and Piper has already been mentioned.*
ach had his own partisans. Those who found the field-marshal easy and
pproachable liked to contrast him with a touchy and irritable Piper, much
ncerned with status; while those who praised the wisdom and caution of
per thought Rehnskiöld arrogant and dominating under a cloak of bon-
omie. Foreign observers were apt to attribute the two camps at headquarters
evidence of a struggle between Piper and Rehnskiöld for ascendancy over
e King; and though Charles had equal regard for them and felt equal need
'them, so that there was no question of a straightforward competition, there
an element of truth in it: Piper was against taking risks and felt that
ehnskiöld encouraged rather than restrained the King.[27]
In the later stages of the Russian campaign and in the post-Poltava years,
per let his confidants know that he had 'all along been of a different view'
out the whole venture, hinting that he had been overruled both as to the
rection of the Swedish thrust and in the continued advance once difficulties
ppeared.[28] But he must have known that Rehnskiöld could be as little to
ame as himself: since 1706 the King made his own military decisions as well
the political ones, however much he valued the collaboration of his chief
lvisers. Whatever qualms Piper felt in 1707 and 1708 he kept to himself,
was too loyal and too conscious of security needs to voice objections
tside the King's chamber of a kind which might reveal details of the plan
'campaign to come. And Rehnskiöld was as tight as a clam on all contin-
ncy planning. Indeed it was he who had impressed on Charles XII the
osolute necessity for secrecy in operational moves. There is a tell-tale letter
om the King to Rehnskiöld in the early years in Poland: Charles, referring
a failure due to a leakage of information, goes out of his way to stress that
is not the guilty party.[29]
Scarcity of detailed information from those in the know of the planning
ages of any campaign in the war is therefore the rule; but the Russian
mpaign presents a particular problem which has made historians scan all
ailable material for the merest hint of Charles's plan of operations. A
construction of the plans of campaign with evidence of changes made
cording to shifting conjunctures is possible for the whole of the war – with
e exception of the years 1707–9 – from an abundance of 'official' sources in
e form of reports, memoranda, relations of various kinds and especially
om the march-'tickets' of the day which give indications of forward planning
en where the actual route has to be changed.† 'Unofficial' sources in the
rm of diaries, letters and memoirs can be checked against the 'official'
aterial. For the Russian campaign, however, the 'official' documents are
the main lacking; though the material behind some of the 'relations' – prin-
pally those intended for propaganda purposes – has been reconstructed by

* See above, p. 175. † ibid., p. 161.

I

the clever detective work of Hans Villius and others.[30] At the time t
Swedish army broke up from Saxony, all papers not needed in the Chancei
in-the-field were sent to Stockholm. Adlerfelt, the historiographer royal, se
home his manuscript history of the campaign at the same time: hence o
abundance of official material for the years up to 1707. Three regiments se
back their papers, including muster-rolls for 1702–7, in March 1708 and f
these particular regiments we possess some information that covers the eai
stages of the campaign and helps to illuminate it.[31]

It used to be believed that part of the papers of the field-Chancery and
the army for 1707 to 1709 had fallen into Russian hands at the defeat
Poltava or at the surrender of Perevolotjna; but Swedish searches for them
Russian archives have been fruitless,[32] and it is now generally held that t
order which Charles XII gave that all archives should be burnt or sunk in t
Dnieper in the very night when he separated from the main army was carri
out. A recent Russian study of the Great Northern War seems to me to gi
indirect but conclusive proof that this is so: in the posthumously publish
monograph by Tarle there is no trace of papers which could have emanat
from the supposedly captured cache, though he meticulously examin
intercepted Swedish letters and information obtained from Swedi
deserters.[33] If the field-Chancery or other important papers from hea
quarters had fallen into Russian hands, it seems unlikely that Tarle wou
have neglected to utilize them; that they should have been captured, but n
preserved seems even more unlikely, since less significant material h
obviously been carefully kept.

The loss of the headquarters archives defies the historian's search f
certainty about Charles XII's plan of campaign against Tsar Peter. Much ca
be deduced, and has been deduced, by scholars in recent years; but there is i
concensus of opinion about the campaign as a whole. Discussion has be
lively and continuous, but it has been dominated either by preconceived ide
about the King or by too rigid an interpretation of the sources which a
available. Some historians have argued that what actually happened at vario
stages of the campaign had in effect been planned and that changes whic
superficially seen, may be interpreted as forced upon Charles by circumstanc
are in reality feints which form part and parcel of a 'master-plan' from whi
the King never deviated. In the thesis held by historians of this school, Charl
never aimed at Moscow, but feinted such a move before turning south
base his invasion more broadly with the cooperation of Poles, Cossacl
Turks and Tartars.[34] Others have maintained – taking Gyllenkrook's wor
literally – that Charles had no plan beyond a concern to push ahead and ma
use of circumstances and opportunities as they offered: indeed he was
contemptuous of the Russians, according to the tenets of this school, that
assumed very little effort would be needed to defeat the Tsar's army ai
topple the Tsar from his throne.[35]

There was undoubtedly among the Swedes, as in Europe generally, ₁

nderestimation of the new army which Peter had forged after the defeat of
arva. This underestimation was typical even of foreigners who lived in
ussia. Whitworth, the English resident in Moscow, wrote in 1707 that of all
ussian native officers there were only two sufficiently qualified to be worth
aptain's rank in the west.[36] Swedish feelings of superiority can be deduced
om the surprise with which Jefferyes heard them admit, once the campaign
ot going, that the Russians were better fighters than in earlier years: they
sed to bury themselves up to their ears behind fortifications out of sheer
ight, now they came out and fought with bravery and tenacity.[37]

But Swedish contempt for Tsar Peter must not be exaggerated nor be
tributed to the higher ranks of officers at the time of the planning of the
ampaign. It is true that many officers when prisoners-of-war in Siberia,
here pietism became their main spiritual comfort, interpreted the Swedish
ilure as God's punishment on them for having been too proud of their own
my and too contemptuous of that of the Tsar; and it is worth noting that a
haplain at Charles's headquarters in Turkey referred in a sermon to the
efeat of Poltava as Heaven's retribution for Swedish presumption and
ovetousness: they had tried to do 'too much' for the Poles and the Cossacks
nd they had coveted extension of their own frontiers.[38] There is, however,
nd element of rationalization in such attitudes; and the assumption of too
reat a contempt is put into better perspective when seen against the careful
reparations which were made for what headquarters reckoned a difficult
sk. Professional commanders, whether Swedish or European, did not
nderestimate the tenacity or the power of the Tsar. A comparison between
wo comments sent to Whitehall about the prospect of Charles's grand design
1707 is illuminating. Robinson, the diplomat, wrote (the words here
alicized in cypher): 'things will go *in Muscovy to the King of Sueden's mind.*'[39]
Iarlborough coolly advised that there was no hurry to pay the pensions
romised to Hermelin and Cederhielm till the outcome of the struggle
etween the King and the Tsar could be seen.[40]

IV

ecent comparisons between Polish, Ukrainian, Turkish and Swedish
aterial have swept away the single master-plan thesis, with everything cut
nd dried for the whole campaign, for ever. Charles – as Dr Kentrschynskyj
his biography of Mazepa has convincingly demonstrated[41] – did not enter
to specific agreements with the hetman of the Ukraine before starting his
perations against the Tsar, nor did he utilize the mission by Mehemet
ga, the emissary of the Crimean Khan and the Sultan, to Swedish head-
uarters early in 1708[42] for the purposes of political negotiations. On the
ontrary, he side-stepped Stanislaus's efforts to obtain assurances that the
hole of the Ukraine should be reunited with Poland and even forbade his
olish ally to press Mazepa into a premature revolt against Tsar Peter. But

this absence of firm commitments by Charles XII must not be taken as pro
of the opposite thesis – that of no planning at all. In my view, the King
encouragement of Polish diplomacy in the east,[43] an interest close enough
amount to a virtual supervision of it, points to a measure of planning a
control which Mazepa's biographer is loath to admit. Whether Charles
insistence that the final decision must be his proceeded from Swedish kno
ledge at this early stage of the inherent conflict between Mazepa's aim
complete independence of the Ukraine, both from Russia and Polan
and Stanislaus's hopes of complete incorporation of the Ukraine wi
Poland – a conflict which has been so brilliantly analysed by Dr Kentr
chynskyj – is difficult to say. I am inclined to think that this conflict was n
fully grasped by Charles till he himself arrived in the Ukraine.

But there is much we can know with certainty. The King realized t
possibilities implied in the revolt of the Astrakhan Cossacks, 1705–8, in tl
rising of the Don Cossacks under Bulavin in 1707, in Bulavin's attemp
to exploit the unrest of the Zaporozhian Cossacks, and in the ambitions
Mazepa to free the Ukraine from a Russian overlordship. Stanislaus throug
his agents kept in close touch with all these areas of unrest, reported
Swedish headquarters and received what amounted to orders about the ne
move. Swedish high officials reckoned with Mazepa as a possible ally fro
1706 onwards.[44] Similarly, the Polish contacts with the Tartar Khan of tl
Crimea and with influential Turks at Bender and in Constantinople we
encouraged by Charles XII from 1701 onwards, and Swedish headquarte
assumed that the Khan and/or the Sultan might become partners wi
Sweden in a loose anti-Russian confederation due to their desire to rega
Azov.[45] In the negotiations which Mehemet Aga had with the Swedes durir
his 1708 mission commercial questions were the ones discussed; but the
would not preclude political cooperation at a later stage – indeed, on tl
pattern of 'normal' Turco-European relations with powers that were n
near-neighbours, commercial treaties were the channels through whic
political cooperation took place.

The lack of specific commitment in the east is most easily explained by tl
freedom of action Charles XII hoped to preserve: 'We must wait till we con
closer' was his motto for this campaign as for others. The contacts establishe
were valuable and might be further utilized; but they were there as bulwar
and buttresses to facilitate moves that might, or might not, become necessar
Open Swedish contact with those in rebellion against the Tsar might – an
here I move to the realm of semi-conjecture – at the opening of the campaig
have seemed to smack too much of the way Augustus and Peter had mac
use of Patkul. Any three-cornered agreement between Charles, Stanislaus an
Mazepa, or between Charles, Stanislaus and the Tartar Khan, or Charle
Stanislaus and the Porte – given that any of these could be obtained – wou
involve responsibilities which might interfere with the main objectives of th
campaign: the freeing of the Baltic provinces from the Russians where thes

ere in occupation and the achievement of a peace along the lines of the
rand design.

The plan of campaign to achieve such aims can, in my submission, be
stablished with near certainty, though some aspects of the plan were
eliberately and for good reasons left fairly vague. Charles was determined to
revent the Baltic provinces, which had suffered so much by the absence of
ae main army between 1700 and 1707, becoming the battlefield for his
ruggle with Tsar Peter. He was hardly less determined that Stanislaus – with-
ut, as yet, sufficient great-power guarantees for his throne – should not
opardize his position by Charles fighting the Russians on Polish soil. The
ussian forces must therefore be manœuvred out of Poland and pushed as
ose to their own frontiers as possible. His 'secret weapon' – jealously
uarded – was a march through the Masurian woods and swamps,* never
efore traversed by an army, to force the Russians out of those well-fortified
nes in Poland which they had created during the year the Swedes spent in
axony without a battle. Some fighting in Lithuania was unavoidable, but
was hoped to push into Russia proper as soon as feasible.

From the Polish-Lithuanian Commonwealth many at headquarters
xpected – on the analogy of the plan abandoned in 1701† – that Charles
ould proceed to the Baltic Provinces to rid them of Russians and push Tsar
eter back from the Gulf of Finland. Some historians have argued that if the
ing had done so his campaign would have stood better chances of success;[46]
thers have countered that these provinces were too exhausted to serve as a
ase for the attack on Russia and have pointed to the political complications
at might ensue with the local population if their land became the battle-
eld even for the first stage of the Suedo-Russian fight.[47] In any case it seems
nlikely that a mere holding operation on the fringes of the Tsar's dominions
e.g. an occupation of the triangle Pskov–Novgorod–St Petersburg – could
ave brought about a decision of the kind envisaged in the grand design.
harles and his military advisers were convinced that without an invasion
eeper into Russia they would not get a 'lasting peace'. Such an invasion
ould, of course, be mounted from Pskov along the road to Moscow, but the
istance from Pskov to the capital was long and the route went through
latively barren country.

The barrenness of the land might not matter much in the last analysis,
nce supply trains could be organized for any route of attack chosen; and I
ould therefore place the desire to spare the Baltic provinces and the need to
ake the shortest possible route to Moscow above this consideration in a
econstruction of Charles's reasoning. It must have been known at the
wedish headquarters – or it became known during the early stages of the
ampaign – that the Tsar had decided to burn to the ground those parts of
ie Commonwealth which he was forced to evacuate in order to offer the
wedes no sustenance and delay or make impossible their advance; also that

---

* See sketch map facing p. 159.   † See above, p. 161.

he intended to continue this policy inside Russia proper if Charles succeed
in chasing him out of Poland–Lithuania. The forthright comment attribut
to the Countess Sieniawska[48] when she heard of his intention to create
barrier of ravaged land between the Swedes and Moscow* may well
apochryphal; but if Charles had not become convinced of the probability
Tsar Peter putting the Zólkiew plan into effect also for Russia, how can o
explain his orders to Lewenhaupt in the spring of 1708 to collect a vast supp
train of ammunition, stores and food which were to join the main army at
rendezvous to be fixed at a later date?

V

There were four possible road-networks by which Moscow could be reache
or threatened from the west. The most northerly one went over Pskov; t
next one over Smolensk; then came the one through the Severia district ov
Briansk and Kaluga; finally the one furthest south from the Ukraine a
Tartary which centred on Poltava and moved over Kharkov and Tu
towards the Russian capital. The first route we have already ruled out; and
early choice of the two southernmost routes is rendered less likely by t
undoubted annoyed surprise of Mazepa when he learnt that Charles w
moving towards the Ukraine,[49] and by the very convincing arguments whi
Einar Carlsson brought some years back against the theory that the wint
campaign round Poltava early in 1709 was a push along the southern roa
network which was foiled by an unexpected thaw. His contention, that it w
a limited operation to ensure safe winter quarters to permit negotiations f
prospective allies in the Crimea and Constantinople, has now been accepted.
Military historians of a calibre to command respect still emphasize, howeve
that the move to Severia to use the Kaluga road, or to Ukraine to reach t
same road over Novgorod Seversk, was, in all probability, a calculated mo
to the south to steal a march on Tsar Peter after a feint directed towar
Moscow.[51]

Absolute certainty on this point cannot be reached, but some material h
recently become available which has convinced the present writer that t
shortest route to Moscow – the one over Smolensk – was the one Charles
planned to use, if at all possible, and that the turn to the south was forc
upon him. Mazepa's discomfiture does not by itself provide a proof of th
since the King could have made up his mind without informing the hetm
that Severia was to be his route; nor does the hasty improvisation of Swedi
propaganda in the Ukraine, clearly demonstrated some time ago by Kentr
chynskyj.[52] But the revelation by Tarle that Swedish propaganda in Russia
prepared well in advance, was distributed ahead of Charles's army beyor
Smolensk, on the route to Moscow, becomes of the greatest significance wh

---

* To the effect that to do so would be comparable to a husband cutting off his balls to sp
his wife.

.ken in conjunction with the obvious lack of planning of propaganda ₁aterial prepared for the southern routes. Tarle himself was not interested ₁ the problem of the direction of the Swedish thrust; but in order to illustrate ₁e loyalty of Russians in the path of the Swedish advance he tells us of a local ₂adman of a village north-east of Smolensk who sent to Moscow a manifesto .stributed by the Swedes in his area. It was printed in Russian, bore the ₁print of Danzig, and assured those that read it that they would be well ₂eated as long as they remained in their homes and left the Swedish soldier ₁molested.[53]

The fact that such manifestoes – much along the lines of those distributed y the Swedes in Zealand, Poland and Saxony – had been printed well in ₁dvance does not in itself tell us anything about which of the four routes to ₁oscow Charles planned to take. But the circumstance that it was distributed ₁ the Smolensk region, ahead of the town which the Swedish army never ₂ached – it turned south within miles of the town on 20 August 1708 – does ve us, in my submission, a substitute for those march-'tickets' and entries f quarters and territories for grazing horses which have been lost. I would ₁erefore argue that this indirect evidence permits the conclusion that Charles ₁d aim at Smolensk and that he was forced – by circumstances which will be ₁alysed below* – to abandon this route for one or other of the two southern ₁es.

Contemporaries, especially non-Swedish contemporaries, believed that ₁harles intended to go to Moscow (the route did not interest the non-₁ofessional) for the purpose of dethroning the Tsar as he had dethroned ₁ugustus.[54] It is true that some, such as the Russian expert Neugebauer, ₂commended Peter's deposition and the enthronement of Aleksey.[55] But ₁harles himself, when he was prompted on this topic by Löwen in 1713, made ₁ distinction between elective monarchs and hereditary monarchs. Augustus, ₁e argued, had been an elected king and it was therefore morally justifiable ₁ contribute to his deposition at the request of the Poles: Charles made a ₁mparison with the ease with which the Allies felt free to change sides over ₁e Spanish succession – switching between Philip v and Carlos iii and back ₁ Philip again – just because Carlos ii had no heir of his own body.[56] If the ₁ussians had chosen to depose Tsar Peter, Charles continued, he would not ₁ave been surprised: from what he had seen and heard of the despotic aspects f the Tsar's rule he concluded that he would rather be the poorest peasant in ₁weden than the mightiest subject in Russia, for even the lowest in his own ₁nd were safe from arbitrary government.[57] It is therefore likely that Charles, ₁ke Louis before him in respect of the Jacobites in the reigns of William and ₁nne, would have been content to benefit from the deposition of the Tsar ' he had been deposed by his own subjects. Swedish wishful thinking toyed ₁ 1707–8 as in 1717–18,† with the idea of how much easier Sweden's task ₁ould be if the head of the Russian state was the weak Aleksey rather than

* See pp. 264 ff.   † See below, p. 456.

the vigorous, capable and unrelenting Peter; but there are no grounds (
which we can substantiate a disbelief in Charles's word that the dethron
ment of Tsar Peter was not part of his grand design. If he succeeded :
making the Tsar agree to the main terms of that design, at whatever sta;
on the road to Moscow this proved feasible, he would be willing to stop h
advance.

The grand design was, the King hoped in 1707 and the early part of 170
to be supported by subsidiary operations where these proved possible. B
there was an element of uncertainty in two of these. First of all, the situatic
in Poland would remain unsettled until the promised recognition of Ki
Stanislaus and guarantee of the treaty of Altranstädt arrived from Londo
The Swedes at this time had little faith in Dutch willingness to take risks f
the sake of Charles XII – 'they have conceived a conviction that the Stat
General feel some enmity towards them', Robinson reported on the eve (
the departure of Charles's army;[58] but the putting into effect of the promis
made by Marlborough was reckoned the best possible insurance again
Augustus meddling in Polish affairs once the Swedish back was turned. Muc
would of course also depend on the success or otherwise of Charles's ow
army; but if fortune was only half-smiling and the British guarantee of Altra
städt arrived then Stanislaus would be able to cooperate with the main arn
by a diversion in the south to justify this share in a reconquest of the *avul*
imperii. At the very least he and any Swedish troops left in Poland would for
a strategic reserve. Another diversion contemplated, but again one th;
depended for its effect on the conjunctures, was a plan that Lybeker, i
command of the Finnish army, should attempt to retake Ingria and especial
St Petersburg, once the Russian forces there had become weakened by witl
drawals to the home front. Orders were sent to Stockholm for supplies to t
sent to him so that he might take the offensive should circumstances permi
A naval blockade of St Petersburg was also recommended, as was tl
building of galleys and other ships to restore the lost command of the lak(
in the frontier region.[59] As the main army moved into Russia proper an
forced evacuation of the Tsar's occupation troops in the Baltic province
so – it was hoped – would Lybeker's forces be able to restore Swedish contr(
and possibly move forward into areas ear-marked by the grand design f(
satisfactio.

The one move planned in detail for a subsidiary army, that of Lewenhaup
was in the nature of a junction with Charles's own army once the Russia
pressure on the Baltic provinces should have eased: its purpose was to brin
food and supplies to the main army to nullify the effects of the Tsar's scorche
earth policy. In the event, it was the failure of Lewenhaupt to join the mai
army with the essential supply train at the time envisaged which endangere
the whole campaign and set the stage for the unrolling of that Greek traged
into which the grand design of Charles XII developed. It used to be fashionabl
to lay the whole blame for the failure of the junction, and thus of the gran

esign, on Lewenhaupt alone.* This will not do.[60] As in every tragedy the ero helps to ruin himself when once he is caught in the web of fate. The lowing down of the timetable for the main army by a fruitless wait for that einsurance from London which would secure Stanislaus's position by estraint on Augustus; Lewenhaupt's difficulty of finding horses for the supply rain; the exceptionally rainy summer which made the roads into seas of mud lifficult to navigate for the heavy wagons; the total destruction of the Russian ountryside – these are some of the complex reasons for the supply train not eaching the King as planned. But among them must also be counted Charles II's own optimistic belief that the junction – whatever the difficulties – would e effected in time.

* See, e.g. F. S. Bengtsson, *The Life of Charles XII*, pp. 292–3: he builds on Hallendorff and tille who, unrealistically, assumed that the supply train ought to have kept up the same speed s the King's army.

2

Across the Rivers

The heart of Russia – which had to be threatened if not conquered during stage two of the grand design – lay well protected behind rivers: the Berezina the Drut', the Vabich', the Dnieper and the Sozh would have to be crossed on the Smolensk–Moscow route; and Besed', the Iput', the Desna and the Oka covered the Kaluga–Moscow approach and the many tributaries of the Dnieper (the Psiol and the Vorskla among them) as well as those of the Volga would provide defence for the capital along the Kharkov–Tula route even before the invader reached the Moskva river.

Before even the Berezina could be reached the Swedish army would have to cross vast distances of the Polish–Lithuanian Commonwealth where the Russian troops had taken positions along the Vistula. Tsar Peter was determined to confine the battle to non-Russian soil for as long as possible, and had let Menshikov ravage the country between the Polish border and the Vistula to delay and weaken Charles XII's army: Rawicz, the King's headquarters of 1704 and 1705 had been razed to the ground and the Swedish soldiers were shocked at wells and rivers poisoned by the floating corpses of Poles who had tried to resist the burning of their homesteads. 'Kalmuks and Tartarians – who have no regard either for friend or foe', wrote Jefferyes, were still strafing the countryside when the Swedes crossed the Oder at Steinau and entered Polish territory on 7 September.

II

Before leaving Saxony Charles XII paid a surprise visit to Dresden with a small suite of seven persons and spent the afternoon with the Elector. On his return to headquarters high officers and officials blamed him for having taken such an unnecessary risk: Augustus might have used the opportunity to make an attempt on his liberty or his life. The incident was put down to a royal whim, though the charitable assumed he had wanted to bid his cousin and host a courteous farewell. A desire to see the Saxon capital may have been equally responsible. His excuse to the companions whom he had brought out for a ride along the Elbe without any destination being mentioned would eem to point to this: 'We might as well ride into the town now we have got so close.'[2] He always enjoyed seeing new places and most of his time in Dresden was spent in making the rounds of buildings and collections with Augustus. He also called on the Dowager Electress, his mother's sister, and it is possible that a wish to see someone of the family to remind him of home (and even of Sophia whom he only knew from her portraits) also played its part: the women of the Danish royal house bore a strong resemblance to each other.

He was in any case conscious that the impending campaign would cut him off from Stockholm more than those of previous years. Hitherto letters from his grandmother and his sisters and their presents, such as the orange marmalade he particularly liked, had reached him with fair regularity. So had the letters from court officials whom he specially valued, such as those from Tessin which gave news of the rebuilding of the royal palace. Postal communication would of course be kept up even after the campaign against Tsar Peter had started, but his knowledge of the route which he and Rehnskiöld had decided on and the full implications of the grand design which were now worked out made him face the fact that contact with home would be slow, spasmodic and even hazardous.

There was greater risk, more personal responsibility but also greater opportunities in the coming campaign than in those between 1700 and 1707. Against the King of Denmark the Maritime Powers, by covering the Zealand descent, had acquired a voice, and a deciding one at that, in the settlement of Travendal and could lay down vetoes for the field of future operations; against King Augustus the Polish anti-Saxon groupings of various kinds had similarly offered a point of support while yet circumscribing his freedom of action in various ways. This time greater liberty to manœuvre had been obtained: the commitments to King Stanislaus and the Republic had been kept so deliberately general that Swedish ascendancy in the councils of war and peace existed. But the element of risk, implicit in an appeal to the dice of war, was correspondingly greater. Frederick of Denmark had bowed to superior pressure from many powers so speedily that Charles XII's advisers had relatively little difficulty in persuading him it was his duty as a Christian ruler to accept the peace of Travendal even though Swedish objectives had not been fulfilled. King Augustus's peace offers had been so frequently proved insincere that no well-informed statesman or diplomat, whether Swedish or European, took them seriously. The decision by the sword was therefore felt to be just and had created no moral problem for Charles XII, even when there had been temporary differences in the field-Chancery about how to conduct the political aspects of the Polish campaign. Tsar Peter, however, was manifestly sincere in his peace offers: through many channels, particularly that of English diplomacy,* he made it known that he would be willing to stop the war if Charles XII would cede him outright that part of Ingria where St Petersburg had been

---

* He used Charles Whitworth who was accredited to him from Queen Anne and sent an experienced diplomat of his own, Matveev, to London between 1707 and 1708.

founded, and also the town of Narva for a given number of years, Dorpa
and other places he had occupied would be returned.[3]

With the wisdom of hindsight some historians have argued that acceptanc
of these terms in 1707 would have saved Livonia for Sweden, if not Ingri
and part of Estonia, and would have prevented the great losses which Swede
sustained at the peace settlements of 1719–21.[4] At the time, however, Charles'
decision to refuse any terms but the restitution of the *status quo* was based o
sound reasoning: Russia, whose potential power was being so energeticall
channelled by Tsar Peter, would prove a permanent threat to Sweden'
great-power position if access to the Baltic was conceded.[5] Would Russia res
content with a small part of Ingria and would Narva be given up after th
terms of years stipulated had expired? Was it not more likely that Russi
would aim at an ever greater share of the export and import trade, with it
dues and tolls paid in that ready money so necessary for the running of th
Swedish administration? She could use the Narva connexion with Englis
merchants and shipowners and would she not be welcomed by the Maritim
Powers as a counterweight to Sweden? Could Sweden, armed and trained t
the pitch of 1707, be expected to cede such vital areas of her state – the ver
lynch-pin between Finland and the Baltic provinces – without a fight? Was i
even morally right? Against Tsar Peter's argument that whatever treaties hac
been signed in the past by himself or his predecessors Russia had achieved
right to parts of Ingria and Estonia by virtue of the twenty-year occupatio
in the early sixteenth century, Charles took his stand on the peace treaties o
Stolbova of 1617, of Kardis of 1660 and of later renewals of these Suedo-
Russian treaties regulating the frontiers between the two states. As soon a
Tsar Peter offered to restore the *status quo* which had existed before th
Russian attack of 1700, it would be his Christian duty to accept peace: til
then the sword must decide. That most Swedes in positions of influence anc
with economic power shared this view is shown by the extreme tenacity
whereby Sweden – even after the death of Charles XII – continued the wa
against Russia.* Some of them held land in the Baltic provinces; many more
were concerned with the trade and the income which the state derived from
these territories and with the vital imports of grain which helped to feed the
population of Sweden and Finland; and among all sections of the people there
was fear of the domination which Russian naval and military power might bring

Yet Charles XII's personal responsibility in 1707 was a real one. If he hac
decided to accept Tsar Peter's terms, it is conceivable that the ensuing peace
could have been made palatable to the Swedish nation by reference to the
temporary nature of the cession of Narva and by stress on the fact tha
Sweden might reconquer the lost part of Ingria at a future date when Russia
should find herself without the kind of leadership provided by Tsar Peter.
That we should find it inconceivable for Charles to adopt such a view is
attributable not only to his sense of duty as defender of the state which hac

---

* See below, pp. 511–13.

been handed down to him by his father, but also to the heart of the Swedish dilemma ever since she had been drawn into trans-Baltic ventures: once the army of a country basically poor in manpower had been mobilized and trained in action, the disbanding of it was virtually impossible before a radical solution to the problem which had called it into being had been attempted. While Charles XII and Tsar Peter thus stand poised against each other in 1707, the shadows of Gustavus Adolphus and of Charles X imprint themselves on the mind's eye.

III

The morning after his visit to Dresden, Charles hurried to catch up with the main body of the army which had crossed the Polish border at Steinau on 7 September. On the 11th the King and his party, whose ride through Silesia had provoked scenes of Protestant enthusiasm which worried the Habsburg authorities and embarrassed the Swedes, stood on the soil of the Commonwealth once more. Divided into six columns the army now marched through the ravaged countryside till between the 17th and 19th it was distributed in Posen, east of the Warta river with headquarters at Słupca. During this stay, which lasted till 2 November, the nine thousand recruits from Sweden arrived and the whole army was inspected by the King and trained in new drills issued at Słupca. The wasted land west of the Vistula offered little food and shelter, and Charles was anxious to cross the river as soon as possible in the hope of finding better supplies.

On this river, and in the neighbourhood of Warsaw in particular, the Russians had strong defensive positions: Menshikov – in command of the Russian forces after Tsar Peter had left for a visit to Moscow – expected the Swedes to aim at the capture of the Warsaw to Grodno road. Menshikov did not intend to cross the Vistula to attack Charles before his crossing (a risky operation in the wasted countryside), but planned to fight him at Pułtusk for the important Narew river passage. The Valloche companies proved good reconnaissance troops and Charles XII was reasonably well informed of the dispositions of the Russian army in Poland. Places for crossing the Vistula were therefore chosen well to the north, on a stretch of the river between Thorn and Płock, and the only difficulties the Swedes had to contend with were the vagaries of wind and weather. The snow was deep and soldiers suffered from frostbite and illnesses aggravated by the cold; several attempts to throw bridges across the river failed. After Christmas the cold became severe enough to put three inches of ice on at least parts of the stretch selected and – between 28 and 30 December – the army could cross the river. Straw and boards, sprayed with water that soon froze solid, reinforced the ice so that wagons and artillery could be moved to the other side. 'They have executed their design', wrote Jefferyes* from Drobin (where

---

* For his presence with the army, see above, p. 224. His letters, hereafter cited as Hatton, *Jefferyes*, form a valuable, relatively unbiased source of the campaign.

headquarters was established for a few days), 'without any other loss than that of 2 or 3 wagons which went to the bottom of the river.'[6] The crossing had, however, had its hazards, recounted in diaries of the campaign, and unknown to Jefferyes there were both men and horses which drowned in the Vistula.[7]

The days in Drobin were busy ones. The army had expected some weeks of rest in good quarters,[8] but Charles wanted to make sure of the outflanking movement he had prepared in general terms and which now was worked out in final details: by marching through the Masurian woods and marshes – never before used by an army – he planned to force Menshikov out of the whole Narew–Niemen line without wasting lives in a battle. Speed seemed doubly necessary in view of disquieting rumours in letters from Saxony 'that there lately has been money coin'd by King Augustus' ordres with the Polish arms and 12 pieces of cannon founded with the same arms'. This, Jefferyes reported, 'has occasion'd some speculation at this Court.'[9] And well it might, in view of the continued absence of Anglo-Dutch guarantees of the treaty of Altranstädt or even of simple recognition of King Stanislaus. Recognition of Stanislaus by the Porte had, however, arrived with the Turkish Mehemet Aga from the Sultan in an indirect way: the governor of Silistria, Yusuf Pasha, had sent the envoy – who caught up with the Swedish headquarters before the crossing of the Vistula – with letters to Charles XII and Stanislaus written, as he said, at 'the Sultan's request'. Ahmed III congratulated Stanislaus on his accession to the throne of Poland, felicitated Charles XII on his past successes and thanked him in particular for having freed the Turkish prisoners-of-war at Lemberg in 1704.[10] Rumours had it that the Aga had 'ordres to make an offensive and defensive league with the K. of Sveden against the Muscovites',[11] but in reality the talk was in rather general terms on both sides and trade rather than politics was touched upon by the Swedish Chancery officials.[12] The King received the Aga in a friendly manner, gave him presents and joked at his surprise at not finding Charles surrounded by his whole army.* There was, however, a considerable gain for Stanislaus's position in Poland from the Turkish mission; while contact between the Porte and the Swedes had been put on a direct and official footing for the first time, so that it could be picked up again without Polish emissaries if need be.[13]

The success of the Masurian route was destined further to enhance Stanislaus's position in Poland through the prestige and power which Charles achieved. Three roads existed through the woods and swamps to the town of Kolno, twelve miles south-west of Grodno; the most difficult part would be between Kolno and Grodno since there was only a single spot, Goniadz, where the river Bobr could be crossed, irrespective of whether the Russians had destroyed the bridge or not – here the marshes were deep and endless. To get any army safely across, let alone one of the size of the Swedish one in 1708, would need superb organization, though if the cold lasted the task

---

* He could now, the King told him, return home and say that he had been in the midst of the Swedish army and not seen a single regiment: a stranger tale than if he had seen them all.

would be eased. The march plan, dividing the army into three columns, was set up by Gyllenkrook and Charles XII who led the middle one himself.* The route was covered with speed (given the character of the terrain) as far as Kolno; from there the King and a smaller party hurried to Goniadz and since they found no bridge began to construct a pontoon bridge, three thousand metres long, for the crossing.

The weather had, however, turned mild and the army suffered both from the soft roads and the lack of provisions. Fodder for the horses was particularly difficult to come by.[14] The peasants who lived in the district had sometimes to be threatened in the crudest form to divulge the whereabouts of supplies which they had hidden to soldiers whose food wagons had got stuck in the mud or needed repair. Edvard Gyldenstolpe wrote home of the regret which he and fellow-officers felt at having to capture a child and pretend to be prepared to hang him in order to make the mother give the information needed. Some regiments he hinted had even to make a reality of the threat before the peasants became cooperative.[15] Sometimes the inhabitants took their revenge in a form of guerrilla warfare. 'We have', wrote Jefferyes on 20 January, 'hitherto mett no ennemy's but the boors, which keep themselves upp in the woods, and very often when the regiments pass, show themselves to the number of 4 and 5,000; these incommode the army very much, being covered by the wood, whither they have their refuge when they have done any mischiefe'.[16] At least once a group of them armed with rifles built a barricade across the road to stop the King's detachment and one of them, who advanced with a white shirt over his clothes to investigate what terms the strangers wanted to offer in return for their passage, was shot by a Swede.[17] That this was done on Charles XII's express orders has sometimes been maintained in historical literature; but eyewitness accounts note the King's anger and regret that the life of one who trusted to the rules of civilized warfare should have been taken.[18] Charles was, however, ruthless in repressing the guerrilla warfare met. If his soldiers were bodily harmed or killed (as for instance when some of them were burnt to death in their quarters at night) reprisals were ordered by the King. Men of the village, if caught, were to be hanged to make others desist from acts of violence and the village itself was to be burnt once the last regiment had passed through.[19]

In spite of difficulties the cohesion of the march was maintained. Engineers improvised means for crossing marshy land, wagons were repaired, and the 'dayly fatigues'[20] endured so that the relative progress or each unit worked according to plan.† After the crossing of the Bobr Charles, Rehnskiöld,

* This column marched through Ciechanów, Przasnysz, Bodowelanki to Kolno; the column nearest the East Prussian border (which also counted Stanislaus and his Polish–Lithuanian forces) went past Mlawa and Chorzele, while that closest to the Narew, consisting of dragoon regiments and Valloches to protect the army against surprise, rode through Novemiasto, Maków and Wizna.

† The preparatory work which established the proper distances between units and allocated quarters has been investigated by Gustaf Petri in volume III of his regimental history of the life-grenadiers (Stockholm, 1958), pp. 221 ff.

Creutz and Prince Maximilian hurried ahead with cavalry troops. On 2 January the King and six hundred men rode over the frozen river Niemen having fought a battle in the evening of the 27th with Russians posted at th bridge – and occupied the town of Grodno which Tsar Peter and his me had evacuated a few hours earlier when news of the Swedish approach reache them. The whole of the Narew–Niemen line had now fallen to the Swede without a battle. As far as Kolno the march had remained a complete secret after that rumours of it had reached Menshikov who put his army in safet beyond the Niemen, withdrawing the infantry close to the Russian borde between the rivers Dvina and Dnieper. Poland had been saved from being th battlefield for the Russo-Swedish confrontation and stage two of the gran design had opened well by forcing the Russians back towards their ow country,[21] though there were still a great many of them on Lithuanian soil.

Tsar Peter, realizing that the Swedes were not yet in Grodno in force decided on a counter-attack and in the night of 29 January sent one of hi German officers, Brigadier-General Mühlenfels, with three thousand men t attack Charles's six hundred Swedes, most of whom were thankfully aslee in bed having spent the previous night in the open at the Niemen bridge. Th sentries heard the approach of the Russians, the alarm was raised,* and afte some fighting in the pitch dark, when the Swedes recognized each other mainl by the sound of their voices, Mühlenfels withdrew.† Charles in his tur attempted a pursuit of Tsar Peter as soon as more troops had arrived and h had given Gyllenkrook orders to prepare for the move of the whole army (th last sections of which were now within ten miles of Grodno) to Minsk. Thi was not the direction which Tsar Peter expected Charles to take: he assume that from Vilna on the Swedes would push northwards over Dünaburg t free the Baltic provinces. For that reason he had already at the end o January ordered that all inhabitants of Dorpat should be moved to Russi and the town prepared for a strong defence with mines for its destructio placed in position: officials in Ingria were told to destroy the countrysid completely and concentrate supplies and ammunition in the towns to offe resistance there to the Swedish troops whether they approached ove Lithuania–Livonia or from Finland. Peter and his generals realized, however that more was at stake than the Baltic provinces and elaborated on th Zólkiew plan to prevent the Swedes from penetrating into Russia. A broad belt of inhospitability – two hundred kilometres in depth – was planned alon the western border from Pskov over Smolensk down to Cherkassk. Within i the peasants were ordered on pain of death not to keep hay or grain in barn or houses but to dig it into the ground or hide it in the woods and to prepar

---

* This is the occasion – made much of in picturesque historical treatments – when Charles xii got on horseback so speedily that he forgot to put his boots on.

† Mühlenfels was put under arrest by the Tsar (officially for his failure to destroy the Niemen bridge before 27 January); he escaped but fell into Swedish hands en route for Germany. He took service with Charles and proved useful for his military knowledge of Russia. He was captured by the Russians at Poltava and executed.

hiding-places for themselves and their cattle far from the main roads, to which they would repair when the Swedes approached. In Moscow Aleksey – seventeen years old – was put in charge of the work to prepare the town against a siege.[22]

IV

In February 1708 Peter moved faster* than Charles, whose pursuit with few and tired troops was soon abandoned. From Vilna Charles went to Smorgonie, between Vilna and Minsk, which was reached on 12 February. The rest of the army caught up and quarters were allocated in the triangle Vilna–Smorgonie–Bielica. The King's rapid chase of Peter's army had prevented wholesale destruction of the area as laid down at Zólkiew but some parts of Lithuania had suffered more than others. 'The Muscovites', wrote Jefferyes from Bielica on 15/26 February, 'still continue their old method of running away, as the Svedes doe of pursuing them, but they have one advantage of us, that they have provision in abundance, which we suffer for want of, for commonly they take care to leave nothing behind them, and what they cannot consume they burn.'[23] Those who had taken part in the 1706 campaign to the districts east of Grodno remembered the Lithuanian peasant's habit of digging his stores into the ground in troubled times and knew the tell-tale signs (such as the early melting of snow in relation to the surrounding field) which indicated where profitable digging could commence.[24]

Shortages helped to undermine the health particularly of the recruits freshly arrived from Sweden who caught dysentery and 'hottfeaver'[25] so badly that many of them died. The King himself was confined to his room for a few days with a bout of dysentery. 'The Physitians', Jefferyes explained, ascribed this 'to His Majesty's drinking no other liquor but water; this custom His Majesty has since thought fitt in some sort to reform and begins now to drink small beer, but that of so mean a sort, that were it not for the name, he might as well make use of the pure element.'[26] But with the opportunity for treatment during rest and with more regular food – Jews and other merchants from Königsberg soon began to call with full loads on the army[27] – the condition of the soldiers rapidly improved. Soon the usual exercises in drill and fighting-tactics recommenced with some modifications, signed by the King early in March, of those issued in the previous October at Słupca.[28] On 3 March, mainly to ease the supply position, the army moved closer to Minsk and headquarters was settled near Radoszkowicze till early June.[29]

The Swedish success in outmanœuvring the Russians had favourable repercussions for King Stanislaus and his position in the Commonwealth. Vilna gave its allegiance to him (and under pressure from the Swedes contributed thirty-five thousand crowns to the good cause) and the Sapieha and

* The Tsar and his troops stayed at Vilna between 28 January and 3 February and then moved to Czaszniki and Besenkovici on the Dvina.

Wiśniowecki families were reconciled to his kingship, though that of Ogińsk
always opposed to the Sapiehas, was not. Negotiations to wean Sieniawsk
the commander of the Polish Crown army, from his alliance with Tsar Pet(
were – for the present at least – in vain, and it was clear that Stanislaus woul
need a stiffening for his Polish and Lithuanian troops to enable him to kee
control of the Commonwealth when Charles XII continued his march toward
Russia proper. For this purpose eight thousand troops in Swedish service – a
German hired regiments stationed in Pomerania, Elbing, Posen and th
Danzig area – under the command of General Krassow were detailed to wor
under Stanislaus's orders in Poland.[30] The fear that 'the nobility of Grea
Poland would desert K. Stanislaus as soon as the Svedish army should remov
from these parts', made Charles XII 'very impatient' to receive the promise(
recognition and guarantee and Queen Anne was pressed, via Jefferyes an
Robinson, to present both, or at the very least the recognition.[31] The succes
of the winter campaign had some effect even in London. Robinson (who wa
in Hamburg at this time)* argued that the 'agnition' would offend the Tsa
less than the guarantee and recommended it since it looked as if the Polis
Crown army was rallying to Stanislaus. This advice was acted upon and o
April 18 (O.S.) recognition was granted, though news of it did not catch u
with the Swedish army till mid-June.[32]

At headquarters in Radoszkowicze the signs of impending move multiplie(
from early May. Gyllenkrook worked on the maps with the assistance of th(
King whose answers to queries seemed as irritatingly frivolous as ever. Th(
march route was made up as far as Mohilev, a fact which pointed toward
Moscow and not, as Gyllenkrook thought most sensible, to the Balti(
provinces. General Lewenhaupt arrived to receive his orders for the comin,
campaign and returned to Courland and Riga to gather the supplies – foo(
and ammunition for three months for both the main army and the 12,500 o
so men he was to take along with him – a task that would need thousands o
wagons and horses.[33] All correspondence with Moscow was prohibited and a
censorship was established for letters sent from the army by foreigners a
well as Swedes lest information helpful to the enemy should wittingly o(
unwittingly escape. Information about enemy concentrations was obtaine(
by Valloche reconnaissance and studied. The King inspected regiments an(
watched how well they performed their charges, evolutions, wedges an(
squares. Food was collected for six weeks for the men and the rate of growtl
of the new season's grass was keenly watched since that would provide fodde
for the horses.[34] Jefferyes felt that the Swedes had probably outstayed thei
welcome. As early as mid-April he wrote from Vilna:

the poor inhabitants are long ago tyred of the Svedes company; nor can it b(
otherwise when they exact such great contributions from them, who expected favou(
and protection, this is the reason that some have dyed here of near grief to se(
their familyes ruin'd, and others with bagg and baggage steal from their habitation:

* For Robinson's stay in Hamburg during the campaign see above, p. 227.

the night and betake themselves to the King of Prussia's dominions; so that a little time the Svedes will make themselves as odious to their friends here, as they are terrible to their ennemyes, for they destroy the one with weapons, and the other with contributions.[35]

An expression of regret by the Swedish King for such burdens laid on allies has been preserved by an eyewitness from this period. The little girl of eleven whom we have already quoted on Charles XII's appearance in 1708* told – but so many years later so that she probably recounted family tradition rather than her own memory of the words spoken – that the King, when he took leave of her father and thanked him for the hospitality he had enjoyed (and insisted on paying for) in his home, assured him that he would in the future 'find means to make good what Poland has had to suffer'.[36]

V

The mood at headquarters in April and May 1708 was on the whole one of cautious optimism; all were 'overjoyed' at the news of the Bulavin revolt: sixty thousand Cossacks had poured into the dominions of the Tsar and 'burn and destroy at the same rate the Muscovites have done in Liefland'.[37] That Tsar Peter seemed aware of a weakening in his position was deduced from the fact that he sent the Swedish resident, Thomas Knipercrona, who had been under arrest in Moscow since the outbreak of the war, to Radoszkowicze to suggest a cartel for the exchange of prisoners or at least the setting at liberty of the Tsar's representative in Sweden in return for Knipercrona's freedom.[38] Was this the harbinger of a willingness to restore the *status quo*, some speculated? Others spoke of information that the Tartars would begin to move as soon as the Swedes were in march towards Moscow. Jefferyes heard 'by a sure hand' that 'the warr is to be declar'd in their own name but the Svedes keep underhand a certain person who is to instigate them, and if need be, lead them on'.[39] Officers joked or flattered the King. Axel Sparre, from whose hand we have several drawings and paintings of Charles XII,† reminded him of an old prophecy in the Sparre family that one of that name should become governor of Moscow; Anders Lagercrona made a prophecy of his own: the Muscovites would not dare to oppose the march to Moscow.[40]

But there were other and darker prophecies. Some who studied the Bible diligently found chapter and verse that spoke of a catastrophe to come which seemed to fit the present venture only too well: they whispered of God's punishment to come in a terrible defeat.[41] Others were oppressed by a feeling of the risk involved in moving so far from the home base. Comparisons were drawn – and pointed out to the King – with Louis XIV's rash push into the Empire which led to a French defeat at Höchstädt in 1704.[42] The 'melancholy aspects' of Piper, Lewenhaupt and Gyllenkrook were observed.[43] They

---

* See above, pp. 16–17.   † See illustration facing p. 205.

sighed, more or less publicly, over the hardness of the task ahead, the inscru
ability of the details of the King's plans and the element of dare-devilry in h
reiterated 'We must take risks while luck is with us'. Rehnskiöld was staunch
reassuring: the King did not take his responsibility lightly and he knew for
fact that the King was often awake at night working and worrying while the
were fast asleep. His belief in *Lyckan* held no flippancy but arose from h
deep trust – which the field-marshal shared – that God was with him an
would bring about the glorious accomplishment of his design.[44]

Tension of this kind among the high officers and officials in a period
enforced waiting for operations to start again was natural enough given th
clashes of temperaments between them and the feeling of responsibility f(
the outcome which they all shared. There is evidence that Charles XII wa
aware of it and was anxious that it should not spread to the officers at larg
and affect the morale of the army. An apothecary at headquarters noted in h
diary that he sometimes saw the King in the evening walking about by him
self: if he heard jolly laughter coming from a place where officers were gathere
together, he passed that billet by; if he found one where the atmosphe
seemed to be too quiet, he joined the company and cracked a joke or two.'

Between 6 and 8 June the army broke up and operations commenced. Th
Russian forces had – in view of the uncertainty of the direction of Charles
thrust – been split into strong separate armies. The main one (some sixty
seven thousand strong), under Menshikov and Sheremetev, was given th
task of covering both Pskov and Moscow, though a detachment of 16,50
men under Bauer was left in Dorpat ready to reinforce either Sheremetev c
the army (of twenty-four thousand or so) under Apraksin in Ingria if S
Petersburg should be threatened. The Tsar still believed that the main attac
would hit the Baltic provinces and paid a rapid visit to St Petersburg to chec
its defences;* Menshikov was beginning to think (from news received vi
Constantinople) that Kiev and Little Russia in general was Charles's objec
tive.[46] From reconnaissance made, Charles knew that the main Russia
army stood close to the Russian border between the Dnieper and the Dvina
though with considerable detachments of cavalry between the Berezina an
the Dnieper, to take the first force of the Swedish advance. The stronger c
these, under Field-Marshal von Goltz, straddled the main road betwee
Minsk and Smolensk at Boryzów on the Berezina; a much smaller one wa
stationed further south on the same river at a place called Berezina-Sapiehska
to guard the road to Mohilev. By sending cavalry under Sparre to make
feint at the Boryzów position and marching the whole of the army for som
distance in that direction before regaining – along minor roads – the route t
Berezina-Sapiehska, Charles achieved a crossing of the Berezina river a
small cost. Between 16 and 19 June, bridges were built, Sparre's force
incorporated with the rest of the army, cannon brought up to silence th

---

* It was during this visit (from mid-March onwards) that he fell seriously ill with fever and ha
to stay much longer than expected.

musket-fire from the Russians who guarded the pass on the far side and the passage successfully forced.[47] Prince Maximilian was wounded by musket-fire (two bullets went through his left side but luckily without damaging his guts) and was much praised for his bravery in having attempted, with other officers, to shield the King.[48]

The Swedes admired the skill of the manœuvre thought out and executed by Charles XII,[49] and the Russians admitted that they had been fooled.[50] Tsar Peter begged his field-marshals, if at all possible, to postpone a main battle till he should arrive on the scene. The decision which had been taken in the council of war early in March (before the Tsar left for Ingria) to create an even more completely devastated zone than the one planned at Zólkiew was now put into effect so that the Swedes might be denied all sustenance whether they aimed at Pskov, Smolensk, or Kiev: along all roads – main and side ones – every building, every scrap of food and fodder would be burnt as soon as Charles's approach seemed at all likely. The enemy must march into a desert of desolation and every attempt must be made to harry him from the rear and from the flanks as he ventured forward.[51] It was an awareness that the Russians would continue the scorched-earth tactics which they had already employed in Poland and Lithuania with considerable success which had decided Charles to bring the supply-train ordered from Lewenhaupt into being: food of one's own was essential in a country where the Tsar was more powerful than he had been in Poland. Rumours of his determination to devastate his own country were current at the Swedish headquarters through the Poles who represented Stanislaus with Charles, Count Poniatowski as a diplomat and Count Urbanowics as leader of a Polish and Lithuanian token force: the story of the Countess Sieniawska's retort to the Tsar* was clearly relished and repeated in letters to Stockholm.[52]

VI

Temporary food-shortages when soft roads made it difficult for supply wagons to catch up with the soldiers were always a hazard on campaign; and as persistent rain started shortly after the Swedes left Minsk the march to the Berezina and through the marshy land beyond that river was handicapped by a slowing down of the supplies. Charles had hoped, immediately after the crossing, to catch Goltz and his Boryzów detachment in the rear;[53] but Valloche reports that at least twelve thousand Russians were gathered behind the Drut' river (and its tributary Oslik) in the neighbourhood of Bialenicze made him change direction and make what speed he could along the muddy roads – where supports of wooden boards and fascines had to be laid for miles at a time – in the hope of battle with this larger force. By the time he arrived, on 26 June, the enemy had, however, withdrawn, and the tired Swedes went into camp near Bialenicze for a few days. Jefferyes found a

---

* See above, p. 242.

moment to write to Whitehall to report the reason for the slow progres
thirty (continental) miles in three weeks: the 'continuall rains' and the effor
of the enemy 'who had cutt down the wood, through which we have pass'
for severall miles together, to hinder our passage'. He marvelled at the wa
the soldiers had behaved:

> I cannot on this occasion pass by the praises due to the Svedish troops, fc
> whether I consider the great hardship they have been obliged to undergo, by forcin
> their way through places allmost impassable, and by wading through morasses u
> to their middle, or I consider their patience in suffering hunger and thirst, they bein
> for the most part reduc'd to coarse bread and water, I must conclude they are a
> good subjects as any Prince in Europe can boast of.[54]

The stop at Bialenicze was not of long duration. Reconnaissance showe
that the Russian troops which had been stationed on the Drut' had joine
what seemed the main army a few miles further east by the river Vabich' near
place called Holovzin. Deserters told that at least thirty thousand men wer
there and more expected; battle was – so they said – to be risked. Sheremete
was in command and Menshikov represented the Tsar. Here was the chance o
battle at last, and on 30 June the King and part of his army, the infantr
at its head, set out to seek the enemy. With dramatic suddenness – so th
colonel of the regiment of Foot Guards (*Livgardet till fot*), Posse, described it i
his diary – they came out of a wood to see the church tower of Holovzin an
Russian troops ready to attack.[55] On the Swedes forming a line, however, th
enemy withdrew to the other side of the water to the defensive position
where the Russian field-marshals were collecting their forces. For sever
days Charles waited, both for more troops to catch up with him and to wor
out a suitable plan of battle by good reconnoitring of the terrain. Jefferye
who was no military man in spite of his captain's title,* wondered at th
delay ('there being but a little river between us and the ennemy, fordable i
several places') and found it strange that the King suffered 'His ennemy t
batter his camp, and to fall in among his troops'.[56]

The site was not an ideal one for battle from the Swedish point of view.
The major body of the Russian troops (we now know that some thirty-eigh
thousand in all took part in the Holovzin battle) had protected themselve
with earthworks and *chevaux de frise* and occupied two different position
(one under Sheremetev, one under Repnin) separated by a marsh and als
by a wooded stretch through which a tributary of the river ran. To the nort
of Sheremetev, beyond a deeper and more extensive swamp, Russian infantr
under Hallart was stationed and to the south of Repnin was Goltz with Rus
sian cavalry regiments and Cossack and Kalmuck troops. It was possible wit
feints and the spreading of false rumours through ostensible deserters to kee
the Russians from concentrating their forces further: Hallart was in this wa
kept to the north and out of the battle. But the frontal attack which th
situation demanded had the disadvantage that there was nothing to pin th

* For this title see Hatton, *Jefferyes*, pp. 13–14.

enemy against: with fairly open woodlands and fields to the rear of the Russian fortifications it would be easy for them to make their escape if the fight went against them. Charles reckoned to have nearly twenty thousand of his troops at Holovzin by 3 July and at midnight on that date the Swedes were ordered to get ready for battle as silently as possible.

The King had decided to cross the river so that from the wooded terrain, regarded by the Russians as impenetrable, he could attack Repnin without Sheremetev coming to his help. At 2 o'clock in the morning the artillery had been moved to prepared positions and the grouping of the soldiers was complete. At first dawn when the Swedes began to place their pontoon bridges across the river, the Russians became aware of the coming attack and so as not to lose time some of the Swedes, with Charles at their head, waded across the river. The weather was unkind, with rain pelting down during the preparatory stages of the battle. The going was hard through marsh and wood and the fighting was even harder. The King led the infantry, which coped with Repnin's forces, Rehnskiöld the cavalry which grappled with those under Goltz. The Russian infantry were not willing to expose themselves to the Swedish attack with *armes blanches* and an exchange of musket-fire – untypical in the battles of Charles XII – became the prevailing pattern. 'About 5', wrote Jefferyes in his report of the day, 'the battle grew hott, so that in a whole hours time nothing was heard but a continuall firing from the musquetry on both sides ... the ennemy discharged commonly their guns at 30 or 40 paces distance, then runn, chargd again, rallied and so discharg'd, which hunting fight lasted till 7 o'clock.'[58] By that time the enemy had retired from the field and could not be pursued effectively. The Swedish cavalry, numerically inferior, had to make brave stands before they broke enemy morale; but even when they went over to the offensive they found it hard to catch up with those enemy squadrons who left the field and disappeared in the marshy and wooded terrain. Sheremetev's forces also withdrew from the field and an attempt he made to cross into the Swedish camp was foiled by fresh forces arriving in the town. So was Charles XII's plan to lead an attack on Sheremetev with these same troops, by a message – later proved to be a false alarm – that his cavalry was in difficulties and needed his presence.

The flight of the Russian army from the position covering the Dnieper was a blow to Tsar Peter.* Repnin was court-martialled and lost his command; but the Swedes thought he had given them a hard fight. They had lost 267 men, among them the commander of the drabants, General Wrangel, and thirteen of that small élite corps. More than a thousand men were wounded. When they discussed the battle they were, in Jefferyes's words, 'forc'd to own the Muscovites have learnt their lesson much better, and have made great improvements in military affairs since the battle of Narva and if their soldiers had shew'd but half that courage their officers did (which for the most part

---

* The losses, in view of Russian resources in manpower, were of less importance: they amounted to 977 dead and 675 wounded.

are foreigners) they had probably been too hard for us in the late action.'
Certainly the battle had not been a decisive one; but it had (and for tha
reason, as well as for the tactical difficulties which had been overcom
Charles XII reckoned it his most important victory)[60] opened the road to th
Dnieper.

When the dead had been buried, the wounded dressed and arrangemen
made to send back to Sweden those unlikely to recover speedily, the arm
continued to that broad river which they reached on 9 July. They found n
opposition in the way of their crossing it, for the Russians guarding it ha
already fled east at the news of Holovzin. The King halted the army on th
western side of the Dnieper, by the town of Mohilev; but it was not thoug
likely that he would stay long: the big river barriers had been conquered an
the road to Moscow seemed open.

3

The Blows of Fate

Mohilev, Jefferyes wrote, 'is one of the Kings of Poland œconomyes, pretty large and surrounded with an old wall; the Jews here have engross'd most of the trade from the Christians which in peaceable times used to be pretty considerable from Mosco and other places.'[1] Here Charles XII stayed after July for much longer than the army had anticipated. Speculations and explanations were rife. The endless rain continued, the number of sick in the army increased: the King was concerned, Cederhielm wrote his brother, that those who were ill should be nursed in proper houses and that the army should rest and collect food for another six weeks' period.[2] But the real reason was to permit Lewenhaupt to join the main army or at least to let him move close enough for safe contact.

Lewenhaupt had returned from his visit to headquarters at Radoszkowicze to Riga early in May but had not found it easy to collect the masses of supplies and the large number of wagons and horses needed. The last days of June had come before he was able to send the supply train and his army of 12,500* along the route which the King's orders, received on 3 June, laid down for him as far as the Berezina and where he, at Berezina-Pazowska, was to collect fresh instructions for the next stage of the march. He himself remained at Riga till mid-July but caught up with his men on 29 July.

Historians anxious, whether consciously or not, to shield Charles XII from criticism have blamed Lewenhaupt for excessive slowness: if only he had been quicker in collecting supplies, speedier in setting out himself, more active in hurrying the supply train on – so goes the argument† – then he would have joined Charles XII at the right time and the invasion of Russia would have had, at the very least, a much greater chance of success. But Lewenhaupt was the victim of the same rainy summer which had made the march of the King's army difficult and slow; and the average speed of his supply train is respectable when the weather and the conditions of the roads are taken into account.

---

* Five thousand cavalry and 7,500 infantry.

† The condemnation of Lewenhaupt by some historians, especially Hallendorff and Stille, for the slowness of his march is no longer accepted: it is unrealistic to argue that the supply-train ought to have kept the speed of an unencumbered army on the march. Bengtsson is particularly hostile to Lewenhaupt.

Everything was harder in the rain even for the operational army: fascines c
twigs and wooden boards had to be laboriously constructed to help artiller
and heavy supplies along soft roads; the leather sections of a portable bridg
became so sodden with rain that thirty-two stout guards, detailed to carr
each section, had to rest after every twenty paces. There were temporary, bu
acutely felt, shortages of food when wagons stuck fast in the mud. And thoug
the grass grew in the rain it looked as if the corn would never ripen in the we
and watery borderlands between Lithuania and Russia.

The period which Lewenhaupt used to collect his supplies, was, howevei
some three weeks in excess of what the King had estimated – three very vita
weeks as things turned out – but the question whether Charles brushed asid
objections from Lewenhaupt or whether Lewenhaupt himself was taken b
surprise by the problems he had to overcome to get the supply train movin
cannot be answered.[3] News of Lewenhaupt's having left Courland reached th
main army; but with the secrecy surrounding the objectives of the campaig
nothing was known (except to those closest to the King) of the purpose of hi
movements: 'Whether he is to joyn us, or act separately', wrote Jefferyes, 'i
talk'd of with uncertainty.'[4]

To Tsar Peter Lewenhaupt's leaving Livonia and Courland was significan
in itself since it disproved his theory of a big offensive in the Baltic provinces
he now assumed that the Swedish subsidiary army was bound for the Ukraine
His fear for St Petersburg was at least eased. Dorpat had been burnt dow
and its walls shot to pieces already in early July when Peter wanted Bauer t
cover Pskov; but with Lewenhaupt out of the way Apraksin had enough me
to deal with whatever Lybeker from Finland and Stromberg with the remnant
of the Swedish forces in Livonia might attempt against Ingria. In this calcu
lation the Tsar was proved right[5] and the Swedish combined naval an
military plan to regain St Petersburg miscarried absolutely.*

Charles's prolonged stay – a whole month – at Mohilev created much specu
lation since the real reason for it was not known. In Hamburg his stop o
what western Europeans still called the 'Boristhenes' gave occasion to th
report of a 'cessation of arms' between Sweden and Russia.[6] Jefferyes, wh
passed his time in Mohilev seeing what sights the place offered, felt he ha
already come into Russia. In the churches of the 'Greek-Schismatick' religio
the priests spoke only Russian and he was told that the wax candles on th
altar tables, 'small and great promiscuously mix'd together, and above then
all a very large one', signified 'the Greekish congregation, and the Czar a
the head thereof'. He accepted the official reason given why the bridges lon
since laid across the Dnieper remained unused: the army needed to collec

---

* Stromberg was beaten by Apraksin at Wesenberg in Estonia before Lybeker with his te
thousand men forced the Neva crossing on 29 August. The wet summer caused supply difficultie
also for Lybeker. False information, deliberately planted by Apraksin, about the strength of th
Russian forces made him abandon the plan to attack St Petersburg and ship his army home o
the Swedish fleet of twenty-two men-of-war which cruised off Ingria waiting to play its part in th
combined operations to chase the Russians away.

ιore food.[7] It was known through deserters that the Russians had retrenched
ιemselves at Gorki, between Mohilev and Smolensk, in some strength
:hirty to forty thousand was mentioned) 'and are resolv'd, as they give out,
) wait our coming.' There was some impatience to be on the move. 'We
ιink, from out late experience', Jefferyes continued – having recovered his
erve with his Swedish comrades – 'their resistance will not be of very
angerous consequence, especially if they have made choice of an open field
/here our troops can have room to exert themselves.'[8]

The Swedes were not entirely undisturbed in Mohilev and surrounding
istricts. Small Russian detachments were stationed on the other side of the
ιver and some of their men 'like water-doggs swimm over, and steal away our
orses'.[9] Occasional raids were made and prisoners taken. Propaganda in
ᵢerman was also spread in the Swedish camp, shot over in hollow cannon
·alls, to counter Neugebauer's famous *Pasquillade*.[10] His name was not
ιentioned. The Swedes were made the authors of the charges he had publicly
·velled against the Tsar: 'that foraigners were used in the Muscovite army
.ot only with disdain and contempt, but frequently forc'd to quitt their
ervices without pay'. As a counterblast the leaflets – in Jefferyes's translation
· were to assure all who received them:

hat the aforesaid report was false and malicious, and for encouragement of any,
specially of the German nation, who would quitt the Svedish service and engage
.imself under them, that all such should have their sallarys duely paid them, and
.ismission when they pleas'd to give over their services, besides which they should
·e fournish'd with passports and letters of recommendation to what prince or state
ᵖever they had in mind to engage themselves.[11]

It so happened that the manifestoes did not fall where the German regiments were stationed,[12] but it was not thought that the Russian promises
vould affect them when the news spread.[13] There had been some desertion
ᵣom these regiments during the difficult march through Masuria when East
·russian territory was temptingly close.[14] To exchange the service of the
ₛwedes for that of the Russians – at a time when the Swedes had achieved so
ιany difficult crossings at small cost and forced the Russians on the defen-
ive – was another matter: Charles XII found so many local men of standing
vanted to join his army for the invasion of Russia proper* that there was talk
·f setting up a special regiment for them.[15]

The long wait in Mohilev produced rumours of peace also inside the
ₛwedish camp. The commander of the Valloche corps, the Livonian-born
ₓanefehr, had been captured in a raid by enemy Kalmucks. He was taken to
ᶜsar Peter, now present at the Gorki fortified position, was well treated and
·ermitted to write a letter to King Charles which was sent by trumpeter to
he Swedish army. Since its contents were kept secret, speculation was rife

---

* Their purpose, according to Jefferyes, was 'to follow the Svedish army into Muscovy, where
hey think to revenge the injuryes the Muscovites have done them here': Hatton, *Jefferyes*, p. 57.

that it contained terms for an accommodation, but though many expresse
their wish for peace few thought that the Tsar with his large army would giv
that 'very sufficient satisfaction' which Charles was known to demand.[16]

II

Between 5 and 9 August the Swedes crossed the Dnieper. On the 10th th
march in four columns began in a south-easterly direction. It was a brie
march, three miles only, to Stalka on the small river Resta, followed by
whole week's stop; but the direction of it had the significant and desire
result of moving the Russians out of the Gorki positions they had built o
the road to Moscow in haste to protect Severia. Menshikov, with his insistenc
on the greatest danger for the southern as opposed to the northern parts o
the Tsar's territories, seemed to be justified. The Bulavin revolt was on th
point of being beaten, but if Charles and Stanislaus with their armies brok
into the south, what new revolts might not follow, trusting to the help o
Swedes and Poles? The Russian forces were therefore regrouped to preven
the Swedes moving into Severia and strong cavalry forces were sent fror
Gorki to Proposh and Cherikov on the Sozh river. That the Swedish move wa
a feint which succeeded is clear from evidence in Cederhielm's letters.[1]
Jefferyes (who had good contacts in the Chancery) reflects the pride felt in
ruse that worked: 'His Majesty having left Horke,* where they [the Russians
had retrenchd themselves, to the left, we are assur'd their cavalry has allread
quitted that place, and we think their infantry will do too, after infinit
labour spent to no purpose in making lines and other works for thei
defence.'[18]

Charles XII was, however, becoming seriously hampered in his freedom o
action by concern for Lewenhaupt. The supplies as such were not urgentl
needed as yet, but Lewenhaupt and his men must not be left so far behin
that the Russians might discover and attack an isolated supply train. Th
King's plan had been for a junction of Lewenhaupt and the main army befor
the crossing of the Dnieper and the invasion of Russia proper. It was clea
from Lewenhaupt's letters to headquarters that the delay in starting and th
terrible roads of the wet summer had slowed his progress far below tha
estimated as possible, but even so it was assumed that by 15 August at th
latest he could have caught up with Charles.[19] But 15 August – with Charle
and his army waiting in their 'Camp 3 miles from Mohilev'† – came and went
Operations must be resumed, but they would have to be kept close to th
Dnieper lest Lewenhaupt be endangered or the main army penetrate too fa
into Russia without the security of future supplies. If the enemy could b
made to stand and deliver battle before the junction, that would be the idea

---

* I.e., Gorki.
† Jefferyes – to whom the name of Stalka was probably not known – dated his letter of Augus
16 in this manner: Hatton, *Jefferyes*, p. 56.

olution: Charles had men enough. The main purpose of the King's strategical
manœuvring[20] after he broke up from Stalka on 17 August was therefore to
seek battle in circumstances as favourable as possible to Swedish tactics; but
f necessity he had to plan his moves so that the Russian army should not
e able – if their scouts discovered Lewenhaupt's approach – to intercept the
junction. Charles sent out several parties to obtain firm news of the supply
rain,[21] and the expectation of the return of such scouting-parties was the
main reason why the army, having broken up from Stalka on 17 August,
marched only short distances each day.

The river Pronya was crossed, but not many Russians were seen till Cherikov
n the Sozh was reached on August 21. Here the Swedes remained for several
ays on one side of the river within sight of a considerable body of Russians
n the other bank. In Cherikov Charles ordered Gyllenkrook to prepare the
marching-orders for individual regiments to move away from the southern
reas which he had let the Russians assume they intended to invade and turn
harply north-east, in the direction of Smolensk, with the next camp planned
or the area round Mścisław. On 23 August the Swedes moved. Tsar Peter,
who with his main army had gone as far south as Krichev, now became aware
hat the Swedish march towards Severia had been a feint and all Russian
orces – bar a few cavalry regiments left opposite Cherikov – were ordered to
urn north once more to cover the approaches to Smolensk. On 27 August
Charles learnt that the Russians were on his own side of the Sozh river,
etween him and Smolensk, and concluded that battle could be expected
within the next few days.[22]

Battle of a sort did ensue, but not of the kind which Charles had hoped for.
'sar Peter grouped his forces along the river Belaya Natopa north of Mala-
tze* in marshy country astride the Swedish route. When the Swedes arrived
hey found, to quote Jefferyes's report, 'the ennemy had sett out severall
osts on horseback by the side of a morass, and perceiv'd soon after their
whole army encamp'd by a wood, having the said morass before them, which
over'd their front and both wings.'[23] King Charles collected his army and
et it encamp along another river, the Chernaya Natopa, which bordered the
marsh. In the night of 31 August a body of Russians thought to consist of
ine thousand infantry and four thousand dragoons crossed the marsh, and
t 7 o'clock in the morning, helped by a thick mist, attacked two of the
Swedish regiments which were isolated beyond the right wing of the camp.
These suffered a fair number of casualties before they received help which
orced the Russians to retire. This skirmish was assumed by the Swedes to be
he opening stages of a regular battle, and the next day Charles XII made his
dispositions. In the night of 2 September the army divided into two groups,
ne under the King and one under Meijerfelt, and crossed the Chernaya Natopa
n bridges constructed the previous day. At Walowniki battle formation
was set up in the hope that the Russians would accept a fight. The marshy

* I have used the spelling of Swedish historiography for this battle

terrain made an immediate frontal attack by the Swedes impossible, an
when on the morning of 3 September Rehnskiöld and other officers recor
noitred close to the Russian lines they found these had already bee
evacuated: they were in time to see the rearguard of cavalry leaving.[24]

The attack by the Russians on the morning of 31 August made a stron
impression on the Swedes. Deserters told them that the Tsar's intention ha
been to draw a large part of the Swedish army to the point of the skirmish s
that he 'might without great resistance pass the morass somewhere else t
attack the rest of our army, but finding his forces repuls'd ... he desisted fron
that design.'[25]

The Swedes lost nearly three hundred men and had about five hundre
wounded at Malatitze. The enemy lost more – seven hundred killed and som
two thousand wounded – but the hard fighting was proof of improvement i
Russian morale.[26] Jefferyes wrote:

> The Svedes must now own the Muscovites have learnt their lesson much bette
> than they had either at the battles of Narva or Fraustadt, and that they equall
> not exceed the Saxons both in discipline and valour; 'tis true their cavalry is nc
> able to cope with ours, but their infantry stand their ground obstinately, and 'ti
> a difficult matter to separate them or bring them into confusion if they be nc
> attacked sword in hand; nevertheless 'tis most probable they will not hazard a battl
> with us, but endeavour by surprises and by cutting of our provisions to moulde
> away our army, which is very practicable in this country, where the inhabitant
> having burried their provisions quitt their houses and the ennemy burn whateve
> they come over. As yet we are in a tollerable condition as to necessaryes, but i
> the ennemy pursues the same methods in his own country which he has begun i
> this, I verily believe he needs make use of no weapon against us, but that hunger an
> want will drive us out.[27]

III

Such surmises were borne out during the march of the Swedish army afte
4 September when Charles left Walowniki.* Deserters told them that the Tsa
with all his infantry and some of his cavalry had crossed the Sozh and mad
for the Russian border. Big cavalry detachments had been left behind, how
ever, to harry the Swedes in their route which still aimed for Smolensk
among them the twenty thousand which had recently arrived under Baue
from the Baltic provinces. On 8 September an attack was made during th
Swedish march by four thousand Russian dragoons. Hidden in a thicket the
suddenly came out 'in a full body' and put the companies they surrounded i
some disorder. They were easily repulsed and left both dead and prisoner
when the rest of the regiments counter-attacked;[28] but on 10 Septembe
a tougher fight ensued at Rajowka. This was specifically aimed at the King i
person; Charles was riding before a troop of horses and was 'attacked an

* From Walowniki, two days' march brought the army to Iwany where it stayed from 6 to
September; on the 10th Rajowka was reached; on the 11th Tatarsk and Starysze on the Russia
border. Here the army remained till 15 September.

urrounded before any sufficient assistance could come up, by upwards of 20
quadrons, who cutt down of the Kings troops alone near 30 men.'[29] The
King's horse was shot from under him, he mounted that of his adjutant-
eneral who had been killed; Prince Maximilian with great presence of mind
retended to be a Russian officer and gave the words of command when he
y chance found himself in front of an enemy squadron.* The Russians were
ut to flight but suffered few losses before they rejoined the large body of
avalry which Menshikov had posted safely behind swampy ground. Again
Charles hoped that battle would be joined. He stopped at Rajowka that
ight 'with the intention [Jefferyes explained] to attack the ennemy early
ext morning, if he had stood firm, but towards the night he sett fire on
ll the villages on the other side of the morass and so decamped about mid-
ight.'[30] The situation was beginning to look grim. The food supplies
ollected in Mohilev were running low. 'I cannot enough describe to
'our Honour', wrote Jefferyes on 12 September to the Secretary of State in
Whitehall:

ie great vigilance of our ennemys, who use all the methods of the most experienc'd
oldiers to allarm us, and keep us for the most part both day and night with one foot
a the stirup, these continuall fatigues and the want of provision which begins more
nd more to press us has allready occasion'd murmuring in the army, and will be
f worse consequence if shortly there be not some alteration for the better: we are
ow forc'd to live of what we find burryed under ground and this is the way we
ropose to maintain in for a while, but should a suddain frost come and deprive us
f that expedient, instead of a formidable army, I fear his Majesty would bring into
tussia a parcell of starv'd beggars.[31]

Conflicting news arrived about Lewenhaupt's progress. Some Valloche
scouts returned about this time with the news that the general had passed
ie Dnieper in the first days of September† and had now got as far as Chausy
n the river Pronya; others reported that he was still as far back as Mohilev
nd had not actually crossed the Dnieper.[32] None of the reports was based
n actual contact with the general. Historians have assumed that Charles XII
nd his advisers accepted these reports and believed that Lewenhaupt was at
east as far advanced as the Dnieper.[33] It is true that in the army the report
f Lewenhaupt's having 'past the Nieper 10 dayes ago, with 12:m men' was
urrent on 12 September;[34] but I am inclined to conclude that this was per-
iitted to leak out to quiet the 'murmurings' Jefferyes reported: if food was
hort, it was important to sustain morale not only by Charles XII refusing to
ccept any more – or better – food than his men,[35] but also by giving hopes of
upplies being close at hand. There are several factors which support such a
onclusion. No hope of an immediate junction was encouraged. Coupled

---

* When he returned to the Swedes 'he had like to run as great a hazard of loosing his life, for
iese taking him to be an ennemy, made severall shott at him, which to his good fortune missed
im': Hatton, *Jefferyes*, p. 61.
† The Dnieper was in effect reached on 21 September.

with the news of the general having crossed the Dnieper was the cautiou
'but 'tis thought he will not joyn our army till we come nearer Smolensko.'
And headquarters possessed sure news that on 29 August Lewenhaupt ha
reached no further than Dolginow, halfway between Vilna and the Dnieper
on that day at that place a messenger from Charles XII reached the genera
and returned with firm news of the supply train.[37] In the terrible state of th
roads, which Charles knew only too well from personal experience, it is nc
likely that he should have become convinced that Lewenhaupt had covere
distances which – even as the crow flies – meant 230 kilometres (to Mohilev
or 270 kilometres (to Chausy) in ten to twelve days. The average dail
speed of the supply train was known: between eight and nine kilometres b
present reckoning. Finally, if Lewenhaupt was known to be as close as wa
indicated by the reports received – and spread – would the decisio
which Charles reached at Tatarsk between 11 and 14 September have bee
necessary?

V

At Tatarsk, on the very border of Russia, came an agonizing moment c
decision. We know it was agonizing because commentators and diaris
noted the prolonged talks that took place between the King and his adviser
We know the outcome of the talks – a move away from the direct Smolens
route to Moscow – and we know that Charles consulted Rehnskiöld an
Piper in particular. Meijerfelt was present,[38] as well as the two chief adviser
when Gyllenkrook was given the decision to move south, and it is possibl
that he also had been consulted.* A hint in a letter he wrote to Charles man
years later, in the autumn of 1718, would seem to support this, for he preface
the advice he there gives on an issue that to him seems important† with th
words that he has 'once before' taken the liberty to speak very frankly whe
vital decisions had to be taken. We have no reports of what was actuall
debated and discussed – apart from the advantages of a more souther
invasion route which can be deduced from what Gyllenkrook was told at hi
interview with the King – but four facts were inescapable and must have bee
taken into account. The army was short of food; Tsar Peter was putting th
country between Tatarsk and Smolensk on fire using his Kalmucks an
Cossacks to lay it waste; there were murmurings among the soldiers; an
Lewenhaupt was not likely to join the main army with his supply train fo
several weeks.

Scouting parties sent into Russia brought back news of the Tsar's scorched
earth tactics; from the Swedish camp the horizon was obscured by flame

* I am inclined to believe – though I cannot prove this conclusively – that Meijerfelt may hav
been consulted on the morale of the non-Swedish troops; but he may also, vide Bennedicl
K.F.Å., 1911, p. 105, have been the major-general in attendance on the King at the time.
† See below, p. 472.

nd smoke – it hid the sun for days, wrote one diarist.[39] 'The country we
:ayed in was desolate', wrote Jefferyes, 'we found nothing but what was
urnt and destroyed, and of large villages little left but the bare names, we
ad also news of the like destruction as far as Smolensko.'[40] Smolensk was
nly seven Swedish miles away, Moscow forty. The Russians lay behind the
ver Gorodnya, close to Tatarsk. Their position might be strong, but Charles
ad repeatedly succeeded in manœuvring them out of well-chosen strongly
arricaded river positions and the main army was not short of men, but of
)od. To be so near the goal, to have manœuvred and marched and covered
ıch vast distances and fought successfully for over a year, and yet so far,
·as bitter indeed. But it would be impossible to push on without Lewen-
aupt's supplies; equally impossible to wait for him at Tatarsk and risk
ıutiny or large-scale desertion.*

If a change of route had to be made, it would have to be made speedily if
ıe campaign as a whole was not to be endangered. There had always been
n element of flexibility in Charles's plans: 'We must wait till we get closer'
pitomized the fundamental willingness to make changes according to circum-
ances. The supply-train idea – essential to the direct Smolensk–Moscow
)ute once it seemed on the cards that Tsar Peter would devastate his own
)untry – had miscarried. The main army had wasted the most valuable
ımpaign months of the year – ever since 4 July when they had gained access
) the Dnieper – in what was essentially manœuvring to permit Lewenhaupt
) make the junction planned for 15 August at the latest.

But supplies could be got to the south. No devastation had taken place in
everia. And from Severia roads also led to Moscow. The route would be
)nger, but not so long that a decisive battle could not be sought after a
:latively short delay. In the evening of 14 September orders were given for
ıe change of direction of the thrust. An advance force of three thousand
ıen† under the command of Lagercrona was sent in the night of 14–15
eptember with orders to speed to Krichev on the Sozh and from there, leaving
art of his force to start bridging that river for the main army, to cross into
everia and make sure of Drokov on the Iput' – a small town which com-
ıanded the road-network leading to the fortified places of Mglin and Pochep.
.t Drokov he was to await further orders, but it was made clear that the main
bjective of the operation was to secure Starodub, the capital of Severia. In
ıe evening of the 14th three couriers were also sent to Lewenhaupt, along
ifferent routes to secure arrival of at least one of the messages, to order him
) point his own march towards Starodub. In the early morning of the 15th –
ıe hour before daybreak – the regimental quartermasters were called to the
:ing to receive the orders for the march. The army was divided into three
)lumns and started its move south a few hours later.[41]

---

* For the beginning of desertion, see Grund's and Whitworth's dispatches from Moscow
ıoted by E. Carlson, *Sveriges Historia*, III, 373.
† A thousand cavalry, two thousand infantry composed of guards and detachments from other
.ack regiments.

K

The prospects for a successful grip on Severia seemed good. Th
Russians were further to the north-east than the Swedes, Charles had
shorter and more direct route to Starodub than Peter.* But luck wa
no longer with Charles. Fate reined blow upon blow upon him in the summe
of 1708.

The initial stages of the move south went well. Marching at full speed th
main army reached Krichev on the Sozh on 19 September and crossed th
river on bridges constructed by Lagercrona's men. The terrain between th
Sozh and the next river, the Iput', was, however, difficult to traverse – te
kilometres only, but thickly wooded in parts, marshy and waterlogged :
others. The Swedes, short of food and worn by the hazards of the summe
found this stage a tough task. Distemper began to spread. Men died. Whe
Charles XII at the head of the army on the 21st reached Koshukovichi (abo
halfway between Krichev and Drokov where he expected to meet Lagercrona
he learnt that Lagercrona had taken a wrong road† and was heading too fa
south, away from Drokov and the route to the Mglin and Pochep. These tw
fortified towns – the very entrances to Severia – were vital. The Swede
needed to occupy them before the Russian army arrived so that they migh
close the gates of the province in the Tsar's face. The King hastily picke
another advance guard which he decided to lead himself, suppressing anxie
about further unwelcome news which reached him at Koshukovichi: a lette
from Lewenhaupt revealing how far he was removed from the main army – h
did not estimate to reach the Dnieper till 22 September.

With his small force picked from those who first came out of the Krissowe
woods Charles XII now hurried on. Drokov was reached on 24 September,
bridge was laid over the Iput' and on the 27th they occupied Kostenichi, th
Cossack fort of Mglin, without fighting since its garrison had already fle
On arrival, however, the King learnt that his calculations had rested on a
least partly false premises. Tsar Peter, when he moved the Russian arm
north after Charles's successful feint in late August, had left a detachmen
under General Ifland to guard Severia, and men from this force were alread
in possession of Pochep. Russian dispositions had been better than expecte
and Swedish reconnaissance had been less thorough than could have bee
desired.

There was still a chance, however, that Severia might be gained as a Swedis
base. The main Russian army had not yet reached Severia and Lagercrona
mistaken route might turn to good purpose if he showed initiative enough t
occupy Starodub. Messengers were sent to him, but they arrived too lat

---

* This circumstance in particular supports the thesis that the thrust towards Smolensk was
feint and that the breakthrough to Severia was an integral part of Charles's original plan, but s
above, pp. 242–3.

† Lagercrona, who was not popular in the army, has been blamed both by contemporaries an
by most historians for having – on local advice – taken a short cut which led him astray: but
Ifland had been in Pochep since August this mistake cannot have had the dire consequenc
attributed to it.

agercrona had realized that his short cut took him far south of the route aked out for him, indeed to the very vicinity of the Severian capital. The nior officers with his expedition took the common-sense view that since ey had strayed so near Starodub they might as well secure this obviously nportant point. Lagercrona overruled them – though he knew that Starodub as one of the objectives of the King's move to Severia – because he regarded as his duty to follow orders implicitly and make sure first of the place Charles ad asked him to take: Mglin. In retrospect Lagercrona's decision outside the everian capital had far more serious consequences than his original mistake, r on the day after he turned his force north Russian troops sent by Ifland ccupied Starodub.

Nordberg knew 'ambitious' officers of Lagercrona's hand-picked corps ho grieved to the end of their days at his fatal neglect of their advice; agercrona for his part regretted the loss at Perevolotjna of the written orders e had received from the King which proved that the responsibility for the alamity was not his. Charles XII was disappointed enough to burst out, Lagercrona must be mad', when he was told of the opportunity missed; but e never blamed Lagercrona in public and received him well on his return.[42] On flection he must have realized that Lagercrona had done what he thought est and that he was, at the moment of decision, as unaware of the presence f Ifland's corps inside Severia as the King himself had been when he raced r Mglin. The improvised nature of the move to Severia, with its insufficient telligence preparation, was punishing them both.

Charles XII had cause to worry. By 1 October he knew that Starodub was in ussian hands. His own army, coming out of the dreadful march through the oods, was in no state to seek immediate battle. Intelligence reports indicated at Tsar Peter had cut off Lewenhaupt and was preparing to attack him. umours even had it that a battle had been fought and that Lewenhaupt had een defeated. The worry about Lewenhaupt's safety, the fear of endangering im and his men by increasing the distance between the main army and the pply train, had been one which Charles had lived with ever since he crossed e Dnieper. 'Now the Russians have fled back to their own country', ederhielm commented after the Malatitze battle, 'Lewenhaupt will be safe.'[43] the nerve-racking period when the race for Severia was known to be lost d the fate of Lewenhaupt's army was in the balance this anxiety became ute: Charles found it difficult to sleep at night. Work had often kept him sy at night-time, but with work done he slept like a child. Now he wandered the quarters which Colonel Hård shared with Gyllenkrook. He never said hat worried him, but they guessed and tried to distract him as best they uld with stories of this and that and indifferent discourses on safe sub-cts. As the night wore on the two would sometimes accompany the King ck to his own tent and sit about just to keep him from brooding alone hile he stretched out, fully dressed, on his bed for at least some bodily st.[44]

VI

The morale of the Swedish army had been strengthened by the move to th
south which was interpreted as a happy omen.* It was generally suppose
that Charles would now move to the Ukraine, 'a country belonging to th
Muscovites, very plentifull of all necessaryes and where no army as yet hi
been.' It was further surmised that an invasion of the Ukraine 'will not onl
fournish His Majesty provision for his army, but give him occasion of brin;
ing General Mazeppa, who commands the ennemyes Cossacks, and who hi
his estate in this country, to some reason.'[45]

Among the initiated who knew of the Polish–Swedish contacts wit
Mazepa, there was naturally no emphasis on bringing Mazepa the enem
to reason, and much talk of cooperation with a prospective ally. Whe
Gyllenkrook was called to Charles's quarters in Tatarsk to be told of th
decision to turn south, he found Meijerfelt there, as well as Rehnskiöld an
Piper, and as both Meijerfelt and Gyllenkrook have left independent bi
collaborative records of what was said on that occasion we have here th
'official' version for the turning away from the Smolensk–Moscow roa
to the south. Messages had arrived from Mazepa, Gyllenkrook was tol
by the King, begging Swedish help and protection since there was no sig
of Stanislaus who was supposed, according to Polish–Ukrainian verb;
agreements, to be close enough to protect Mazepa when Charles moved o
Moscow.

Such messages had indeed arrived. The Ukrainian hetman was in a grei
dilemma in the summer of 1708. He wanted to reinsure against all risks an
ran into great difficulties as the Swedish army neared the Russian borde
Proofs of his contacts with Stanislaus had been laid before the Tsar and b
was commanded to the august presence to explain himself. He had no doul
that he could do so satisfactorily, but he wanted to delay his visit till the ou
come of the Russo-Swedish war could be seen more clearly. His excuse
became difficult to sustain: from serious illness he moved to death-bed an
had to be given the last sacrament to allay the suspicions of the Tsar's emi;
saries sent to fetch him; but letters written from him, or on his behalf, wer
most patriotic in sentiment and begged help against the Swedish invade
At the same time he appealed for help to Charles XII whenever it looked as
the war might move closer (as during the August feint towards Krichev whicl
Mazepa reckoned, might be the opening of a joint Polish–Swedish campaig
in the south) or when it seemed (as during Charles's renewed march in th
Smolensk direction) as if Moscow was threatened. That his appeals wer
'diplomatic' rather than genuine is clear from his consternation and ang(
when he realized that Charles was on the road to Ukraine. From a variet

* Cp. Jefferyes's comment that the news of the Russian destruction as far as Smolensk had th
'happy effect' of Charles turning his march to the right, supposedly to the Ukraine: Hatto
Jefferyes, p. 62.

r motives, of which we know nothing for certain though pride and concern
>r officer morale must have played important parts, the Swedish King chose
> interpret Mazepa's appeals as urgent and specific cries for help. Gyllen-
rook was told that Charles, since Stanislaus was not able to sustain Mazepa,
·lt in honour bound to march to the hetman's protection against the Rus-
·ans: he would give up his own '*dessein*' – which had been to march on
·molensk and Pskov – and turn instead to the Ukraine.*

The specific mention of 'Smolensk and Pskov' is intriguing and may have
·een used to please Piper and Gyllenkrook who had never been keen on
·xtending the operations close to Moscow; but the King may have had his
·wn reasons for not mentioning the Russian capital. The painfulness of having
·ad to give up the Smolensk road and/or the concealed hope of reaching the
·ıme goal via the Severia route are possible explanations, but there is no
·ay of delving into Charles's mind at this time.

In the event the failure of the Severia venture has, in the memoir-literature
·om the period, made the Ukraine stand out as the goal – Severia becoming
·ıt a brief stopping-place on the road to Mazepa. The propaganda value of
·Iazepa with the Swedish army contributed to this but even Gyllenkrook –
·ho had himself set up the march-route for the Lagercrona corps – forgot, in
·ɛtrospect, the role Severia might have played in the campaign if Mglin,
·ochep and Starodub had been secured. The relative importance of Severia
·ıd the Ukraine and the true relations between Charles and Mazepa have,
·owever, been clarified by specialists like Petri and Kentrschynskyj and there
·   no doubt that Charles hoped much from the race for Severia and was
·isappointed at the lack of success.[46]

One reason for this lack of success was the exhaustion of the Swedish army
·hen it emerged from the Krissower woods. The march between Krichev and
·Iglin had been costly. The losses in men from illness and hardships and
·ıemy raids are not known; but Jefferyes reported that all characterized
·ıem as 'heavy'. He wrote on 7 October:

The late march His Majesty made since we left Cruickzow [i.e. Krichev] the 20th
·ıst has been through vast woods and wildernesses, and must have cost His Majesty
·ɛar, since for 25 miles together very little subsistence has been found for the army
·ıd nothing at all for our horses; add to this the continual fatigues of marching
·ery day, the vigilance of our ennemys who kept us day and night on our watch,
·ıd distemper which for a time swept abundance away, 'tis thought we have lost
·ore in this ramble than if we had given the enemy a battle.[47]

·here had obviously been some wasting of Charles's army throughout the
·ımpaign; but the casualties of this atumn march probably outweighed those
·˙ Holovzin, Malatitze and Rajowka put together: when the winter cold of
·ecember 1708 to January 1709 had taken its toll the army of thirty thousand

* The bias in Gyllenkrook's memoirs demonstrated by Villius and Westin does not necessarily
·ect the facts of the Tatarsk conversation, though his picture of the King who knew not where to
·rn may not be a true one.

strong which had separated from Stanislaus in July 1708 had dwindled t twenty-five thousand.

Losses apart, the army which came out of the woods (the last ones arrive only on 2 October to encamp and rest in the neighbourhood of Mglin) wa in no fit state to proceed immediately to an attack on Ifland either in Poche or Starodub. Diarists noted how sparse their diet had been; roots and berrie they came across were the only items they had to supplement the bread ratio Such uncooked food was not much use to invalids. Ensign Piper, who wea from dysentery and fever travelled in his colonel's coach, survived on h coarse rye rusks and his two bottles of brandy,[48] but he and the others wh got through needed time to recuperate. Even those free from distemper ha suffered from the weather: thunderstorms and rain had been their lot throug out the march. The peasants who lived in the Mglin neighbourhood had fle at the approach of the Swedes, but without destroying homes and stores so t army was able to find good quarters and sufficient corn to bake good brea

News which reached King Charles during the time the army rested (t 11 October) was disheartening. On 1 October he learnt that Starodub ha been taken by the Russians. A few days later the uncertainty which he an others had increasingly felt about Lewenhaupt's safety was resolved, b with news of the general's defeat at Russian hands, Jefferyes wrote c 7 October:

> Yesterday, we heard great firing of gunns from a town half a mile from this plac in which lyes a Muscovite garrison; we are sinse informed it was for a victory t Muscovites have had over Count Leyonhaupt by the river Doza, of which here yet no certain account come in; but I presume that action has not gone according wish, sinse most here endeavour to conceal it, and those that discourse freel speack of nothing but the praises of that count for his good conduct during t action, and in his retreat after.[49]

With the turn to the south, the supply-train aspect of Lewenhaupt's ventu had lost most of its importance, while the prospect of reinforcement in me had gained in view of recent losses: the addition of eleven or twelve thousar men when the junction was effected was emphasized in morale buildir propaganda.[50]

The historical discussion whether Charles XII needlessly exposed Lewe haupt to defeat[51] seems to the present writer as pointless as the debate c Lewenhaupt's responsibility for the failure of the Russian campaign plan Charles XII. The contention of those who hold that the Swedish King wa convinced, before he took the decision at Tatarsk on 14 September th Lewenhaupt was safely beyond the Dnieper[52] seems, from what has bee argued above, untenable; but that the King had any other choice but t attempt to secure Severia irrespective of how far Lewenhaupt had reach on his road to the junction seems equally unconvincing, unless retreat ar abandonment of the invasion of Russia altogether is considered a valid choi from Charles's point of view. There was no sure knowledge of Lewenhaupt *hereabouts in the vital days of 11–14 September; it was permissible to hope *at his march once one of the King's couriers had reached him could be nked into the Severia venture and that he might even play an important role a it by securing Starodub.[53]

The King's move south had, however, by its very nature opened a gap etween the main army and Lewenhaupt: the Russian *corps volant* of 11,500 men under Tsar Peter's own command came too late to hinder Lewenhaupt's crossing the Dnieper but soon enough, with the help of General Bauer's oops, to win a victory at Lesnaja on 29 September.* The battle was a hard-jught one. The issue, Tsar Peter wrote, was in doubt throughout the day; but though Lewenhaupt stuck to the battlefield after fighting had been broken ff, by nightfall he was forced to leave behind the supply train (largely lundered already by Cossacks) when he and the army marched off the jllowing morning.[54] King Charles never blamed Lewenhaupt either for the ow march or for the defeat at Lesnaja; he argued that the general had done is best and deserved praise for his stand. But Tsar Peter called Lesnaja – the rst Russian victory over the Swedes in a regular battle – 'the mother of oltava'. There is evidence of a slackening of morale on the Swedish side some soldiers after the defeat broke into the wagons and drank themselves enseless; some deserted)[55] and of increase in self-confidence and belief in nal victory on the Russian.

News of the battle of Lesnaja sealed a decision which Charles seems to ave contemplated at the first rumours of the defeat, when he already knew that the pass at Pochep was in Russian hands and that the race for Starodub as lost. We learn from Jefferyes that on 7 October an express was sent from *e King to Mazepa at his capital in Baturin to desire winter quarters in the Jkraine.[56] This information he no doubt got from his friend Cederhielm in *e Chancery-in-the-field and this, rather than the 'official version' referred) above, presents the real situation and pinpoints the time when it was ecided that Severia and the Kaluga–Moscow road was as unobtainable as *at of Smolensk–Moscow and that Mazepa would now have to be brought *to play. Safe winter quarters could not be had in Severia in the given rcumstances: Sheremetev with twenty to thirty thousand men had entered *rough the Pochep gate and was already troubling outlying regiments and *aller forces sent out foraging.[57]

That Mazepa would reply in a positive way to the King's request was taken)r granted, since hints at the previous contacts with the Ukrainian hetman ow went from mouth to mouth. Spirits rose at the prospect of ease and lies: 'We find ourselves at present', wrote Jefferyes, 'with the hopes of)ming into a country flowing with milk and honey; that Count Lewenhaupt ill soon reinforce our army with the addition of 11 or 12:m men and that eneral Mazeppa will declare for us.'[58]

---

* 28 September according to Russian style; I have used the Russian name for the place of the .ttle (Polish, Lesna).

4

The Fight for the Ukraine

Once the decision had been taken to move to the Ukraine, to utilize th
southernmost base and the southernmost route for an attack on Moscow i
the spring of 1709, speed was vital. More Russian forces were streamin
south: the race for the Ukraine was already on. Some Swedish regiment
were sent off before 11 October, the date on which Charles XII left Kostenicl
and moved south. Preparations were feverish also in the non-military fiel
The first manifestoes in Ukrainian, asking the population to regard the Swede
as their friends and Charles XII as their protector were now set up an
distributed ahead of the army.[1] During the march, which avoided Starodu
with its Russian garrison, Iffland with Russian cavalry unsuccessfully trie
to oppose the Swedes at the crossing of the river Vablya. Here Lewenhaup
joined the army with seven thousand fit men out of his original 12,500. Hi
infantry had suffered most in the battle of Lesnaja and the remnants of
were used to fill vacancies in the main army; his cavalry maintained i
separate squadrons but was incorporated into the main army. In Panurivk
where the army rested for a few days, an emissary from Mazepa arrived wit
a positive answer to the letter sent by express to the hetman: quarters wer
offered and cooperation promised. At the same time Mazepa strongly presse
Charles XII to direct his march to the fortified town of Novgorod-Seversk o
the river Desna, on the plea that if that fortified town fell into Russian hand
the Ukraine would be endangered.* An advance guard under Creutz set o
on 20 October; the main army followed as rapidly as possible in snow
weather which made it difficult to distinguish friend from foe when skirmishe
developed. It was only at a distance of three hundred paces that snow-covere
mantles, thrown back for action, revealed enough red and green to warn on
Swedish battalion of the need to take the covers off their muskets to aim a
Iffland's troops.[2]

Though Creutz marched night and day, the Russians were in Novgoro
Seversk before him.† Superior numbers, excellent reconnaissance, above a

---

* Charles XII had intended to take a more direct route to Baturin; and Kentrschynskyj in h
Mazepa biography agrees that it is 'possible' that the Swedes lost time by the move to Novgoro
Seversk to which Mazepa, still reluctant to commit himself openly, pressed Charles.

† Creutz reached Sheptaki, close to Novgorod-Seversk, on 22 October.

he exhilaration of knowing that the invincible Charles had been forced ɔ dance to the Tsar's pipe and was being manœuvred further away from Moscow every day acted as a tonic on Russian officers and men. The broad Desna, which formed the border between Severia and Ukraine proper, would ave to be crossed without control of this key town. Charles stayed at ,arinowka from 27 October while reconnaissance and preparations for he river crossing were made.

During the stay here Mazepa with a suite of two thousand Cossacks[3] joined he Swedes, driven to this step by information that Menshikov was on his way ɔ Baturin. The hetman, educated and amusing, though judged shrewd and alculating by the Swedes, conversed with Charles and his advisers in Latin. lis proud head with its white tufts of hair made an impression; the length of is moustaches and the smallness of his hands were commented on. The ,wedish King promised to avoid, if at all possible, Ukraine's becoming a ℜusso-Swedish battlefield or at least to keep his fight with Tsar Peter to the 'utskirts of the country. No secret alliance guaranteeing Ukrainian indepen- .ence was made,* since Charles wanted to keep a middle – and dominating – 'osition between Stanislaus and Mazepa. Promises were made that Russian 'ower in the Ukraine should come to an end but these did not conflict with ℂharles's commitment to the Republic. It seems as if Charles had in mind a economiliation between Mazepa and the Commonwealth whereby Polish laims on western Ukraine† were to some extent satisfied, while the rest of Jkraine became independent under Mazepa. In either case Sweden's com- nercial interests in the hemp of Severia and Ukraine would be recognized nd the trade-routes with Turkey and the Near and Far East be channelled to he Swedish Baltic ports.[4]

On 2 November, in Mazepa's presence, the Swedes successfully forced the Desna passage at Mezin against determined opposition from a considerable ℜussian army. The tactical operations which achieved this at little cost have 'een much praised, but the success – compared by admirers to Alexander's rossing of the Ganges[5] – was to a large extent nullified by Menshikov's and he Tsar's rapid responses to Mazepa's putting himself under the protection 'f Charles XII. Menshikov, denied access to Baturin on 26 October, informed 'sar Peter on the 27th of Mazepa's betrayal of the Russian cause. The Tsar, 'elieving the hetman's lies about being on his death-bed, had indeed sent Menshikov to Baturin to secure a loyal successor. Now the game was up.)rders reached Menshikov in the night of 2–3 November to besiege Baturin. ℬy this time the Tsar knew of the successful Swedish crossing of the Desna nd with only four miles between Charles XII and Baturin, Menshikov was told hat it was now or never. He skilfully used both promises and threats to xploit the dilemma of the Cossacks left in Baturin and after a two-hour

---

* This was asserted by some of the memoir-writers, but has been disproved by Kentrschyn- <yj, *Mazepa*, pp. 333 ff.
† The treaty of Warsaw of 1705 had guaranteed the borders and rights of the Commonwealth s laid down in the treaty of Oliva.

storming on 3 November the fortress gave in. To prevent recapture by th Swedes, who had more troops than Menshikov, the whole town was destroye by fire. The destruction would, Tsar Peter emphasized, serve as an exampl to other would-be traitors.

The blow was serious for the Swedes. Magazines of arms and ammunitio were destroyed* from which they had hoped to compensate for the loss (Lewenhaupt's supplies, and the effect on the Cossack population was alarn ing. Instead of Mazepa leading the whole of the Ukrainian people into th Swedish camp, diplomatically if not militarily, a split developed betwee those who took the side of Mazepa and those who swore allegiance to th new hetman proclaimed by the Tsar. A civil war inside the Ukraine, remini cent of that fought in Poland between 1702 and 1706, was the result. Mazepa dream not to hazard, but to obtain Ukrainian independence by negotiatio from a Tsar hard-pressed by Swedes close to Moscow was at an end.[6] Fro this time he remained committed to Charles XII, the sole hope for his pla for Ukraine's independence. He proved a loyal ally to the end of his da and made great sacrifices of money and effort to further the Swedish caus

II

On 11 November Charles and the first regiments of the army passed throug the still smoking ruins of Baturin and made a temporary halt there till th last troops had caught up on 14 November. The countryside charmed th Swedes: the land did seem to flow with milk and honey as promised† – there wa corn, fruit, tobacco and cattle in abundance. All aspects pleased after a yea spent in areas largely abandoned and devastated.[7] The inhabitants seeme to some, less attractive. Strange language, dress and customs often produc fear which is given vent in contemptuous remarks. A German soldie making the campaign has left on record his revulsion against the Lithuanian whom he first met after the passage through the Masurian woods: dirty lik pigs and untrustworthy.[8] Swedish veterans of 1702–6 had learnt not to judg the Lithuanians en masse in so sweeping a manner, but in 1708 we find entrie in some diaries that the Ukrainians are 'a sour and swinish lot'.[9]

It was natural enough that the Ukrainians in the villages and towns whic Mazepa allocated south-east of Baturin as winter quarters for the Swede should feel bewildered and resentful. The foreigners had a strange and heret religion (a theme that the Russian propaganda harped on with some success and brought vast numbers of the Tsar's troops to a country whose inhabitan had served as auxiliaries in the Russian army but which had not for sever generations suffered the fate of being a battlefield. Tsar Peter tried hard t race Charles for the fortified towns of Romny on the Sula river and Hadyac on the Psiol, but that race was won by the Swedes, helped by Mazepa'

* The cannon of Baturin were saved for the Tsar, see *Wittram*, I, pp. 301–2.
† In war diaries and letters the wild crocus, hyacinths and tulips of the following spring a noted with delight.

nowledge of the country. The settling down in the quarters inside the Prilyk–
omny–Hadyach–Lokhvitsa square was, however, not achieved without
>me skirmishing with the Russian forces; and Tsar Peter was determined not
> let the Swedes enjoy peace in their new-found homes.

The winter, which had started early and became colder than any in Euro-
ean memory, favoured Russian attacks since the rivers froze and no longer
ut obstacles in the way of free movement. The tactics were reminiscent of
lose employed earlier: the Russians would gather troops at a particular
oint to tempt Charles to collect his own forces; but once he marched towards
lem in the hope of achieving a regular battle, they would withdraw. This
appened at Smeloye towards the end of November: when the Russians had
ithdrawn (on 24 November) Charles gave permission for his troops to loot
le town – a rare occurrence indeed with the Swedish army of this time – to
tilize Russian magazines stored there. Each regiment was allotted a section
f the town and, plunder over, Smeloye was burnt to the ground.[10] The war
ncreasingly took on a ruthless character. Though the Swedes were far from
loscow, they were now in territory which Tsar Peter regarded as Russian –
hatever Mazepa and many Ukrainians felt – and it was important for the
sar to weaken Charles's forces as much as possible during the winter lest
e should form a focus for Cossack revolts against Russian overlordship in
le spring. It was even more essential for Charles XII to maintain his army with
le minimum of losses till spring should make possible a new thrust. He could
ot afford to see his numbers whittled away in winter skirmishes.

Historians, handicapped by the loss of the field-Chancery papers, used to
elieve that Charles's operations in the winter of 1708–9 were part of an
ttempt to push towards Moscow making use of the hard winter when marshes
nd rivers would carry men and guns and baggage-wagons: this campaign
as, it was held, at first successful but was then stopped by an unseasonable
law in February.[11] A careful study of available material led Einar Carlsson
1947 to maintain that Charles XII's purpose from the end of December 1708
> mid-March 1709 was to chase the Russians from the whole area west of the
orskla river so that the Swedes might enjoy safe winter quarters.[12] Carlsson's
nclusions have in their turn been attacked,[13] but it seems more likely than
ot that Charles XII intended a temporary stop in the operations and that safe
uarters were his prime consideration. This fits the political situation of the
me. The Swedish army was still quite strong and its reputation high. Indeed,
le weakening in Charles's position which is easily discernible to us was largely
idden to contemporary observers of the campaign. Russian losses in men
ad been heavier than those of the Swedes;* Peter had not risked a battle with
harles after the Holovzin defeat and this was attributed to fear of the Swedes'
vincibility rather than to the Tsar's calculated plan of tiring the enemy.

But Charles himself and his advisers were well aware that a winter cam-
aign against Moscow was out of the question in the circumstances. Their

* See below, p. 287 for a comparison of the losses for the whole campaign up to Poltava.

need was a peaceful winter which would permit planning and negotiation
for a resumption of the campaign in 1709. Reinforcements must and coul
be got, it was assumed, from Krassow and Stanislaus; the Cossack, Tarta
and Turk situation would have to be examined since a thrust from the dee
south – the very longest route to Moscow – could do with the boost of allie
effort; supplies of all kinds would have to be arranged and contacts mad
with merchants who – as at Vilna – would be only too eager to dispatch wha
was ordered in return for cash and credit-notes. The Tsar, worried as to th
possibility of a winter push by Charles, attempted to close access to th
Kharkov–Bjelgorod–Kursk–Tula–Moscow route. He put garrisons into th
fortified places on the road to Kharkov: Poltava was one town which no
received a Russian garrison, Veprik another. In mid-December, when th
Swedes had settled down in their quarters and the cold was intense, h
launched a surprise attack against Hadyach.* He occupied the outskirts c
the town – which at this time had few Swedish troops – on 19 December
Intelligence reports warned the Swedes what was on foot and Charles ordere
the whole of his army to move towards the town both to prevent a Russia
occupation of it and in the hope that the Tsar might accept battle. The Kin
reached Hadyach with some of his regiments on the same day, a few hour
after the Russian advance troops had marched into its suburbs; but Tsa
Peter who stood with his main army half a mile distant, immediately withdre
to Lebedin which had been his headquarters ever since Charles and Mazep
crossed the Desna.

The weather proved a more determined enemy than the Russians. Th
Swedish regiments had a tough march in deep snow to reach Hadyach. Th
nights then turned bitterly cold and caused suffering to those who had t
camp outside the town at night. Fever incapacitated many and some froze t
death. Long queues of coaches and wagons slowly filtered through the narro
gates of Hadyach between 22 and 24 December when the King and the arm
continued operations with the lightest of encumbrances – one wagon wit
bread, one with ammunition for each company and one packhorse for eac
officer – and all sick persons as well as baggage, supplies and part of th
artillery were for safety's sake to be brought into Hadyach. From one man o
the sick list, the ensign Piper whom we have mentioned earlier, we have
graphic description of what the slow crawl into Hadyach meant in a night c
biting wind. The driver of his coach froze to death; a young volunteer wh
sheltered with him for a while forgot to draw the leather curtain of th
window on the windy side when he left. Piper was too weak to do so himself
his feet became frostbitten in spite of his three pairs of socks and his quilte
cover. In the end his servant found him and carried him on his back, crawlin
between carriage wheels and horses' hooves, into the town.[14] It was Christma
Eve: the most festive day in the Swedish Church calendar.

---

* In the older historical literature, and also in *Haintz*, I, pp. 151 ff., the ensuing campaign i
seen as arising from Charles's initiative, part of the push towards Kharkov and Moscow.

III

'he intense cold hit Charles and the main army as well. On 23 December ১ey set out with the objective of retaking the Cossack fort of Veprik, roughly mile to the east of Hadyach, and to chase the Tsar from Lebedin so that they ⅱight be safe from fresh interruptions.[15] The Russian troops stationed near 'eprik withdrew at the approach of Charles and the Tsar left Lebedin for ɔsitions further east at Sumy. The weather paralysed operations. On ;hristmas Eve, we learn from one diarist, 'His Majesty stood still because ↱ the terrible cold.'[16] No service could be held during the Holy Days – ossibly the most telling testimony to the fury of the winter.[17] Some regiments ʌere quartered in the suburbs of Veprik (which the Russians had not had me to burn) in the evening of 23 December; but most of the rest, en route ɔr Lebedin, found no roof for their heads* till Senkov was reached after ;hristmas.

As soon as the worst of the cold was over, the attempt to secure Veprik was ɛstarted. The fort was at the top of a hill and defended by earth ramparts ⱱhich the garrison turned into walls of ice by pouring water on to them. The arrison was small, some 1,500 Russians and a few hundred Cossacks with ɨfles, fine marksmen who made good use of that weapon's superiority over he muskets of the westerners. On 7 January, after the Russian commander ad refused to surrender, the storming of the fort commenced, three thousand ʌwedes – six infantry regiments and two dragoon regiments – being detailed ɔr the task. It was intended that Swedish artillery should immobilize the efenders while three columns mounted the attack. This miscarried, partly ৷ecause of mistiming in the cooperation between the columns, but mainly ৷ecause of the accurate and murderous fire from the fort. The Swedes were ৷icked off as they raised the storm-ladders into position; officers leading heir men in waves of assault were easy targets for the marksmen. Darkness nade the Swedes abandon the attack.

In two hours of a short afternoon the Swedes had lost four hundred men ₋nd had about six hundred wounded. Among the wounded was General ⱡehnskiöld. Splinters from a grenade had hit him, but the contusion in his hest was more serious; he never recovered his health completely. The losses n officers who had been killed outright or who died from their wounds were ɾightful for the regiments that took part: Edvard Gyldenstolpe† was killed, ⱡis brother Karl died, 'not from his wounds', wrote Meijerfelt, 'but from grief ₋t having lost his brother'.[18] The army mourned these and many others, ₑeling that the flower of the officer-corps had been taken from them.[19] It was ≀ttle comfort that the Veprik garrison gave in in the night of 7–8 January

* The village of Plechivets, north-west of Veprik, accommodated part of the army over ;hristmas.

† Edvard, for whom see above, p. 175, in Meijerfelt's regiment of dragoons was killed before the torming proper commenced.

and that its men marched out to deliver up their arms and become prisoners of-war.

Charles XII had been persuaded by his senior officers not to risk his lif by taking part in the storming. Piper found him 'grieving much in his min over the unhappy action at Veprik'.[20] It had been essential to eradicate th threat from a Veprik in Russian hands, but it is an open question whether th King might not have prevented the losses by offering the garrison a capitula lation on terms in the morning of 7 January. It seems certain that officers having prevailed on Charles not to risk his life, felt in honour bound to b reckless of their own till the storm was called off.

The attitude of the Swedish officer of the Caroline army to death in battl was – where we can check it – that of the ethos of the period, the one in whicl Charles XII himself had been brought up. Gay and extrovert characters sucl as Edvard Gyldenstolpe and Maximilian seem to be paying lip-service t convention when they write of death ending the troubles and tribulations o this earthly life which has to be suffered before the joys of paradise can b tasted. But they ring true when they write of their belief that God has decide the time to gather each one of us home and that death for one's country o cause is a good way to go.[21] Here they remind us of Charles – on a late occasion – stressing his soldier's preference, once God's hour has come, to di to the music of the military cannonade rather than on a sick-bed at th ministrations of the medical men and to the lugubrious tolling of bells.[2] The King was at this time, for it was during the siege of Stralsund in 1715 in duty bound to make light of danger to stiffen morale, but apart from th slightly jocular overtones this remark fits the expressions he uses in letter when he mentions individual casualties: God* would not suffer him to liv any longer.[23]

IV

To the experience of Veprik Charles XII and his foremost civil adviser, eacl equally saddened, reacted differently. The postal communication with Polan and Sweden had been uncertain ever since the crossing of the Desna; eve before this (since 15 September) letters from Swedish officers and official had been penned with one eye on the possibility that the enemy might intercep what they had written.[24] Little or no news filtered to the Swedes from out side,[25] but it was known that Tsar Peter had dispatched an army towards th borders of Poland. In these circumstances there was some anxiety both i respect of the situation in Poland and about the safety of Stanislaus an Krassow if they were ordered to join Charles in the spring. Piper – feeling hi responsibilities the more strongly since Rehnskiöld was ill – advised a tem porary withdrawal to the Dnieper to re-establish contact with Poland and t

---

* The replacement of 'God' with 'Fate' in such letters after 1715 will be discussed below pp. 311–12.

make sure of reinforcements.[26] This was unacceptable to the King who decided to continue his plan for clearing Ukraine of Russians to preserve his own troops and prepare for a 1709 resumption of the campaign.

A limited Swedish offensive started in mid-January when the Tsar began a regrouping of his forces which argued fresh attacks on the Swedish winter quarters. Charles, with a minor detachment of cavalry and infantry, raided the Russian positions, drove Rönne's forces from Krasnokutsk and Gorodno, and withdrew to the south when a large body of enemy troops came towards him: on 23 February his force was at Oposhnya on the Vorskla river. Throughout this month-long raid the Swedes, at Charles's express orders, burnt every village and town they came across. The Swedish King was applying the tactics Tsar Peter had taught him: to lay down such a belt of desolation and waste that enemy penetration would be impossible. The destruction went against the grain with the majority of the Swedish soldiers. Diaries of those that took part speak of the pity they (and the King) felt for those made homeless and of their attempts to help refugees.[27]

The weather helped Charles.* In mid-February a thaw set in unexpectedly. It rained as if the heavens had opened and the hard frozen earth was changed to flooded marsh and swamp it seemed within minutes. But though this incommoded the Swedes, it gave added protection against Russian operations and eased the task of Rehnskiöld, left in command of the main army, who had been bothered by Sheremetev's Kalmucks and Cossacks. During the month of March the whole Swedish army with all its baggage could move, without being disturbed by the enemy, to the new positions marked out for it by Charles between the Psiol and the Vorskla rivers, closer to the route to Moscow which the King hoped to make use of before too long. The policy of destruction was continued, again for reasons of security, in respect of towns evacuated: Rashoka, south of Hadyach, to which a small Russian force had penetrated, was plundered and burnt on 11 March; Hadyach itself was destroyed by fire on 15 March after the Swedes had been permitted plunder once more.

Charles XII's grouping of his forces in their new quarters during March and April tells of his future plans. His main strength was placed along the Vorksla river in a line from Oposhnya in the north to Stari Senchary, two miles south of Poltava. In Poltava, the key fortress commanding the road to Moscow that went over Kiev–Poltava–Kolomak–Kharkov–Bjelgorod–Kursk–Tula, the Russians had significantly strengthed the garrison before posting their main army in the area of Kharkov. Advance Russian detachments under Goltz had been sent west of Kiev, to intercept Stanislaus and Krassow; pro-Russian Cossacks, under the rival hetman Skoropadsky, had been stationed on the lower Psiol to seal off the Zaporozhian Cossacks from the Swedes. To guard against surprise attacks from either of these corps Charles posted strong

---

* According to an older deduction, still maintained by Haintz, I, 2nd ed., p. 255 (after consideration of Carlsson's evidence), it stopped his advance. In view of the few troops which Charles had with him on the expedition, this does not seem tenable to the present writer.

cavalry detachments at Reshetilovka and Shishaki on the Psiol river. Th
Swedish position obtained by the spring of 1709 was quite a favourable one
The army was settled in a square fifty to sixty kilometres each way, betwee
two rivers, with the advantage of fair concentration of forces with fai
accessibility to supplies, particularly (as Tengberg has pointed out) durin,
those periods – four in the year – when the Cossacks fasted.[28]

The Swedish move further east and south had one other purpose: t
facilitate contacts with the Zaporozhian Cossacks with whom Mazepa ha
been negotiating on Charles's behalf. The hetman of these Cossacks of th
Dnieper, Konstantin Hordienko, made common cause with the Swedes on 2
March and took on the guard on the Vorskla between Stari Senchary an
Perevolotjna, the place where the Vorskla flows into the Dnieper. Here th
Zaporozhian Cossacks kept their fleet capable of moving three thousand me
across and along that broad river, too wide for any bridge-building know
to that age. It was for the boats rather than the 1,500 Cossack cavalry tha
the Swedes desired cooperation with Hordienko: his fleet might be neede
to bring the army of Stanislaus and Krassow and Swedish recruits over th
Dnieper at a place not expected by the Russians. But while the hetman an
a thousand of his men were at Charles's headquarters negotiating terms
Russian Cossack and other troops moved speedily from east and west t
raze the Zaporozhian strongholds at Koleberda and Perevolotjna and bur
the fleet.* With the coming of the Zaporozhians Charles entered into a forma
alliance with Mazepa and Hordienko:† by a written resolution of 30 Marc
the Swedish King bound himself not to make peace with the Tsar till the ful
independence of the Ukrainians and Zaporozhians from Russia had bee
obtained, agreed to regulations which sought to minimize friction betwee
the Swedish army and the native population, and promised to move out of th
Ukraine as soon as the military position would permit.

Mazepa's position was greatly strengthened by these written assurance
which amounted to a treaty. Charles XII had taken care not to choose a for
of words which prejudiced the Polish cause but the whole basis of his relation
ship with Mazepa changed from one of vassalage to one of equality amon
allies. The hetman showed his appreciation by becoming Charles's banker
sixty thousand *Thaler* needed to pay the Valloche regiment and for othe
expenses was handed over against a Swedish bill.[29]

V

The lightning raids by which the Russians destroyed Zaporozhian fleet an
strongholds were a blow both to Hordienko and to Charles XII; but the new
allies were all the same useful. Through their lands and with their help posta

* In May followed the destruction of their capital, Sich; for the consequences of this see below
p. 287.
† For the preceeding agreement between these two on the return of democratic government i
the Ukraine see Kentrschynskyj, *Mazepa*, pp. 355 ff.

communication with Poland and Sweden became secure once more;[30] luxuries or near-luxuries which had been lacking, such as wine and spices, were imported by them from Turkey for the Swedish army;[31] contact with the Crimean Tartar Khan and even with the Porte became easier. From March 1709 Mazepa and Piper began a joint diplomatic offensive against Tsar Peter with the Turks. Colonel Koltza of the Valloches was dispatched with messages to Bender and letters which invited the Sultan – via Yusuf Pasha, the Seraskier of Bender – to cooperate with Sweden and Ukraine in fighting the Russians.[32] Letters to the Council in Stockholm reiterated the orders of November 1708 to send recruits to Pomerania;[33] those to Krassow instructed him to reinforce his army with men which could be spared from the Swedish provinces in the Empire in preparation for his and Stanislaus's junction with the main army;[34] those to Stanislaus informed him of the support which was expected from Devlet-Gerei as a result of negotiations now in progress between the Tartar Khan on the one hand and Hordienko and Mazepa on the other.[35]

Some time would naturally elapse before certain news could arrive of the outcome of the approaches and the practicability of carrying out orders. That King Charles was in an optimistic frame of mind is clear from the fact that he did not respond positively to Russian suggestions for peace which reached him on 1 April. On that date a Swedish officer* taken prisoner at Lesnaja was sent to the King's headquarters, ostensibly to negotiate an exchange of prisoners. He was also empowered to say that the Tsar 'was inclind to make peace, but would not be persuaded to quitt Peterbourg.'[36] The letters which were sent back on 1 May ignored the peace feelers and were judged to have displeased the Tsar since the officer in question 'was presently sett under a stronger guard than formerly, and has not sinse been permitted to come hither'.[37]

The sufferings of his army in the winter of 1708–9 had saddened Charles XII. His reactions can be better studied in the war diaries which have survived than in the King's own letters and instructions. Young Piper had resisted the surgeon's suggestions that both his legs be amputated to cure his frostbite, but some toes on each foot and part of both heels had had to be cut away. When Charles visited him, he made light of the injury in Piper's presence. The ensign notes that the King used his '*Hå, lappri, lappri*',† put his own leg on to the saddle of a horse, indicated with his hand on his boot the loss of half the foot and said he had known men who had lost that much of their foot and who, when their boots were stuffed to supply the missing part, had walked just as well as before. But to the colonel of the regiment, when they rode away together the King said: 'It is hard on that one, he is so young.'[38] This blend of compassion and determination to stiffen morale meets us also in other entries which tell of odd meetings with the King and notes the words

---

* He was Erik Johan Ehrenroos, ennobled von Klinthen, chief accountant of the army of Lewenhaupt.

† 'Ho, small matter, small matter'.

he used to soldiers or officers on sentry-duty or at work in the trenches befor Poltava.[39]

This siege was prepared during April, but the first trenches were not opene till the night of 1 to 2 May. Even after this the operation went on so slowl that it exasperated the siege experts – Gyllenkrook among them[40] – and mad the army ponder what the King's real intention was. The shortage of 'powde and ball' was not sufficient explanation though stocks were running low Nor did it seem enough to say that 'Generall Mazeppa has had a hand i perswading His Majesty to it'. The majority of the uninitiated believed – an their testimony misled historians for generations – that Charles XII used th siege of Poltava as a bait to tempt Tsar Peter and his army to cross the Vorskl and risk a battle. Again and again one meets this guess in diaries and letter Jefferyes reported to Whitehall that:

the general opinion is, that His Majesty has undertaken [the siege] to bring th Muscovites to a battle in case they have a mind to succour [Poltava]; we have severa times been in hopes this bate would take, the Muscovites have passed the rive Worsklo and have advanced towards us, and we have 3 severall times been rang'd i order of battle to receive them, but when we have advancd, they have either give way, or else we have found them so deeply burryed in the earth, that we have no been able to attack them, without hazarding the loss of our infantry.[41]

It is only recent patient research,[42] utilizing also the Russian records, whic has uncovered the real reason for the delaying tactics of Charles XII betweer March and June 1709: his need to wait for news from Stanislaus and Krassow from Devlet-Gerei and from Yusuf Pasha. It is true that in the meantim Charles would have welcomed a battle if one had offered in condition favourable to the Swedes; but Tsar Peter was engaged on a diplomati offensive to counteract that of Charles, and the Russian army had orders t harass the Swedes without taking undue risks. From the far side of th Vorskla attempts were made to carry out these instructions. Some failed Towards the end of April, before Charles moved from Budyshchi* to Poltava a surprise raid on his headquarters was discovered and foiled; early in May plan to free the 1,500 Russian prisoners taken at Veprik miscarried; efforts t relieve the garrison of Poltava by the Russians were stopped,† as were effort by the garrison to break out.[43] Others succeeded. Twice regiments were singl attacked and sustained heavy losses;[44] on 15 June the Veprik prisoners were freed and Swedish baggage was plundered. The absence of spectacular Swedish successes was dispiriting to the army in general. 'The beginning of this year', wrote Jefferyes on 27 June, 'has not been so successful to us as we thought it would, the losses we have had at severall times, though not very considerable, yet are greater than we well can beare in the circumstances we now are.'[45]

* Headquarters had been at Budyshchi (Budiezin in contemporary spelling) since the King's return from the winter offensive.

† Though in the night of 16 May 1,200 Russians, commanded by a Dutch officer managed to trick their way into the garrison: see Hatton, *Jefferyes*, p. 73, for the method used.

The Swedes were indeed being slowly confined by Russian action to an ever narrowing space from which they would eventually have to break out: by the end of May Charles had concentrated all his troops in the near neighbourhood of Poltava. His infantry was divided into two groups, the larger one at Poltava itself, the other at Shuky; his cavalry was strung out west of the town in a line from Shuky in the north to Stari Senchary in the south. The Russian army, under Menshikov's command in the Tsar's absence* was similarly concentrated on the other side of the Vorskla river, encamped at Krutoy-Bereg opposite the town of Poltava; but strong Russian Cossack troops were stationed in the rear of Charles's army on the Psiol river. The regular Russian forces had during the campaign suffered heavier losses than had the Swedes: it has been estimated that Charles's army by the spring of 1709 had been reduced by less than one-fifth (from some thirty thousand to some twenty-five thousand) while Peter's army had been reduced perhaps by one-third.[46] But the Tsar could fill the gaps in his ranks with greater ease than Charles who had to await reinforcements from afar. At the beginning of June when Peter arrived in the Russian camp it soon became known to the Swedes that he had brought eight thousand recruits to add to the six thousand with which Sheremetev had already increased the main army.

The Swedes lived for some considerable time in hopes of a junction with the army of the Tartar Khan. In mid-May two Tartar colonels arrived in response to Count Piper's letter of 30 March to open negotiations on the terms of collaboration between Devlet-Gerei and Charles XII. The Khan's main demand, that Charles should sign a treaty binding himself not to make peace with the Tsar till Crimean objectives had been achieved, was agreed to in principle; and an escort was sent to meet the Tartar delegation said to be on its way to Swedish headquarters for the formal negotiations of the alliance.[47] In the army news spread that 'the Tartars made themselves ready to come and joyn us'.[48] The number of thirty thousand was freely mentioned – based on letters from Sandul Koltza to Mazepa and Poniatowski[49] – and it was assumed that the Sultan was willing to support the Swedes either directly or indirectly by giving the Khan his blessing.[50]

Tsar Peter's diplomatic counter-offensive, as well as the Russian destruction of the Zaporozhian capital at Sich on 14 May, brought a halt in the negotiations. Communications with the Crimea were, at least temporarily, interrupted; the Swedish escort to meet the Tartar delegation had to turn back to headquarters; and the delegation itself returned to the Khan. The fact that Charles XII had not been able to protect his Zaporozhian ally offered food for thought; so did the rumours spread by Tsar Peter that the Swedes were in the process of making peace with the Russians, a peace that was to be cemented by a marriage between Charles XII and the Tsar's sister.[51] More significant was the effect of Peter's threats and promises in Constantinople. Russian naval preparations at Azov, and fear that the Habsburgs would use

* The Tsar was ill in Azov from the end of April till the beginning of June.

the opportunity of a Turco-Russian conflict to attack the Porte, gave th
upper hand to those who wanted to avoid commitment in Charles XII'
struggle with the Tsar, or at least to postpone it till Swedish success seemec
more certain. In mid-May the Sultan sent orders to the Khan, whose armie:
had indeed moved to the Ukrainian borders, forbidding his junction with th
Swedes. Copies of these instructions were shown to the Russian diplomat i
Constantinople.[52]

VI

The results of Russian successes in Poland as well as at Constantinopl
became known in the Swedish headquarters on 22 June when severa
messengers arrived together: Colonel Koltza from his mission in Bender,
new delegation from Devlet-Gerei and the Swedish diplomat Klinckowströn
from King Stanislaus and Krassow.

The news they brought was, taken together, of the utmost consequence
Headquarters now learnt of the dismal situation in Poland: of the weakenin
of Stanislaus's position after April 1709 through military successes gained b
Sieniawski supported by Russian forces under Goltz; of Krassow's mov
towards Pomerania to protect the recruits expected from Sweden in cas
Augustus should attack them in their march. It was clear that no reinforce
ments could be expected for Charles either from Poland[53] or from Pomerani
– Russian troops barred the way and neither Stanislaus nor Krassow wer
strong enough even to attempt a breakthrough.* From Devlet-Gerei cam
at this stage no hint of the Sultan's veto of his military plan. Indeed, h
stressed his eternal friendship and his determination to 'risk all' in cooperatio
with Charles XII and explained the delay in setting his troops in motion a
caused by the false rumours the Tsar had spread about a Russo-Swedisl
peace.[54] The Khan's goodwill was believed. It was not only for the sake o
morale that headquarters let it be known 'that the Tartars are in earnest
their ministers who arriv'd here some dayes ago, have inform'd us that 40:n
stand ready expecting His Majesty's ordres, whether they shall joyn us, o
make an incursion into Muscovy by any other way'.[55] But taken in conjunc
tion with the non-committal answer which Koltza brought from Bender† i
was clear to headquarters that the Porte was not willing to act speedily an
might be restraining the Khan.[56]

There was a difference, which was disturbing, between the objective o
Devlet-Gerei's first mission – the one that turned back after the Tsar'
destruction of Sich – to negotiate a specific treaty of alliance preparatory t
military cooperation and the vague, if grandiose, talk of the second mission
And while the Pasha of Bender returned a most polite and pleasant missive i

* Polish historians investigating the year 1709 speak of 'The dissolution of the pro-Stanislau
camp'.
† Yusuf Pasha's letter is printed in Nordberg, I, pp. 931 ff.

answer to Count Piper's letter of 30 March, he stressed that a formal embassy from Charles XII to the Sultan at Constantinople would be a prerequisite for collaboration between the Porte and Sweden. That such insistence, by necessity, removed collaboration from the immediate present to the more or less distant future was obvious. By 22 June one might therefore be justified in deducing that Charles XII and his senior advisers realized that the long wait at Poltava had not justified expectations: speedy reinforcements, in men and supplies, which would form a secure base for a new thrust towards Moscow could no longer be expected with any confidence.

The setback for Swedish hopes was not divulged to the army at large. The Tartar promises were made much of and all that was said about Stanislaus was that when Klinckowström had left him, he 'had gott together a considerable army of Svedish and Polish troops'.[57] It was the more necessary not to alarm the soldiers and officials since a shattering blow to the morale of the whole body of Swedes had fallen on 17 June. In the morning of that day, on the King's twenty-seventh birthday as many noted, Charles XII had been hit in the foot by a rifle bullet: 'tis remarcable', wrote Jefferyes, 'that His Majesty was never wounded before this time, and that the first time was upon his birthday.'[58]

5

Poltava and Perevolotjna[*]

The beginnings of the battle of Poltava can be traced back to the night of 1.
to 15 June when the Russians made an unsuccessful attempt to cross the rive
Vorskla. The Swedes had defied all frontal attacks on their Poltava positions
and Tsar Peter and his military advisers had reached the conclusion that thei
only hope of relieving the Poltava garrison would be to cross the river fa
enough away from the Swedish army to ensure a relatively safe passage. Onc
on the same side of the river as Charles XII, they hoped to be in a bette
position to prevent the important fort, commanding the southern route t
Moscow, from falling into Swedish hands.

The belief, evident in older historical literature, that the Tsar only decidec
to cross the Vorskla after he learnt of the Swedish King's injury on 17 June
has given way before knowledge, from Russian sources, of the first faile
attempt.[1] On the night of 16 to 17 June the Russians planned a repeat wit
larger forces at Petrovka, while mounting diversionary attacks along th
whole front of the Swedish position to give the Petrovka force time to dig in
They were conscious of the need to hurry if they were to save Poltava. It
commander had sent word that he could not hold out much longer, and the
Tsar worried that Tartar support might arrive for Charles XII in spite of th
Sultan's veto: with Poltava in Swedish hands and reinforcements in men th
road to Kharkov – and Moscow – might be at stake. Such a developmen
could be prevented, it was argued, if the Russians managed to cross the
Vorskla with the major part of the army. They could then dig themselves in so
securely that if Charles XII decided to attack, he would do so under disadvantageous conditions facing heavy artillery fire. If he decided not to attack, the
Russians could from their fortified camp carry out flanking raids to weaken
the already diminished Swedish army.

Swedish intelligence, through information from deserters and from
reconnaissance reports, was well aware of what was on foot. The whole army
was at action stations throughout the night of 16–17 June. It had been agreed
to let the Russians come over in some force, so that the Swedes might have a
chance to do battle with a large section, yet not so large as to constitute the

[*] In Ukrainian, Perevolochna, but I have preferred to use the transliteration of Swedish
historiography.

vhole of the Tsar's army. Rehnskiöld with ten cavalry and eight infantry egiments was sent to Petrovka to prepare for this battle and reckoned that ae would have to face twelve dragoon and three infantry enemy regiments: a avourable proportion from the Swedish point of view. Charles XII was in :ommand at Poltava and it had been agreed that as soon as the situation here was under control he would join Rehnskiöld and take part in the battle.

Before he could do so, however, he was wounded. At about 8 o'clock in the norning he inspected the defences at Nizhnyi-Mlini just south of Poltava vhere Russians under the command of Hallart had already been driven back. \s he rode up the bank from the river a rifle bullet shot from an island in the /orskla hit his left boot from behind and passed into the foot.* Poniatowski, vho was with him, noticed that he was hurt but was told to keep quiet about he injury. The King informed Lewenhaupt, whom he left in charge, that he vould have the bullet removed; but he continued his rounds of inspection for everal hours and it was 11 o'clock before he came to his own quarters. His)aleness and blood dripping from his boot to the ground wherever he stopped 'or any length of time had been noticed: when he fainted on dismounting he word that the King was wounded spread like wildfire. The bullet did not aave to be cut out; it was found to have passed out by the big toe and he surgeons got busy picking bone splinters out of the wound. The King aeld his own foot while this was being done and assured those who condoled vith him that he would soon be on horseback once more.[2]

But the weather of that summer was, to the Swedes anyhow, 'unbearably 1ot'. Wounds went septic and putrefied easily. Charles XII became feverish n the afternoon, blood-poisoning set in, and between 19 and 21 June the <ing's life was in the balance: on the latter date the medical men gave him)ut two hours to live. When he was weak and feverish, he found comfort in 1aving Hultman, his servant, tell him old sagas and *contes*. It is significant hat the ones he liked to hear over and over again were those which can be :onstrued as having a bearing on his own life and hope: Rolf Götrikson .uccessfully fights the enemy and claims his bride with the peace, Prince 3ideon wins the Princess of Aragonia, the jewel in her father's crown.[3]

On the 17th, while the King was still able to give orders, he left the decision vhether to fight at Petrovka or not to Rehnskiöld. The field-marshal con-.ulted his fellow-officers of high rank. They all agreed not to risk battle,)artly because of Charles's injury but also because the Russians were found deeply entrenched'[4] when the Swedes arrived at Petrovka. Some historians 1ave argued that Rehnskiöld's decision not to attack on the 17th was respon-.ible for the catastrophe that followed on 28 June: if he had thrown the Rus-.ians back across the Vorskla, so runs the argument, Tsar Peter would have eceived a serious check and might have desisted in his attempts to move the vhole of his army to the Swedish side of the river.[5] Such judgement seems to ·est on supposition rather than evidence: the Tsar would not have been easily

---

* The bullet had a slow speed; it may have ricocheted from the island eighty metres away.

discouraged since he regarded the situation as urgent. On a day when th common soldier at Petrovka wondered what had happened to delay the Kin and speculated on his fate,[6] it is not strange that the officers in the know shoul decline to hazard battle till the extent of the injury had been assessed.

Charles's wound was known to Tsar Peter in the evening of the 17th,[7] an it obviously encouraged the Russians. At about 11 that night an assault wa launched to relieve the fortress by a frontal attack, but after half an hour' fighting the enemy retired on finding the defence firm. Then between 19 an 21 June, the days when Charles's fever was at its height, the whole of th Russian army remaining on the eastern side of the Vorskla crossed the rive near Petrovka and moved into a fortified camp at Semyonovka. The Swede expected a Russian attack or at least a willingness to accept battle on th 22nd. Early in the morning on that day Rehnskiöld was ordered to put th whole of the army into battle position on the field north-west of Poltava The command was to be his, but the King – weak though free of fever – le himself be carried on a stretcher slung between horses in front of his army t heighten morale. The Russians refused to fight, however, and at midda Charles ordered his men to disperse to quarters allotted in such a way that would be easy to recall and regroup them at need. It was while Charles wa lying in his stretcher before the army that the messengers of 22 Jun approached him.

II

The news which they brought* differed in its effect on those of influence a headquarters. Count Piper was for giving up the siege of Poltava and returr ing to Poland to save the situation there. The risk of carrying on withou speedy reinforcements seemed to him too great. He was also in favour c pursuing negotiations with the Tsar more energetically. Menshikov ha written to him recently and proposed 'to come hither in person to enter upo a treaty, if His Majesty will grant him safe conduct'.[8] The time seemed t Piper to have come when sacrifices would have to be made to put an end t the Russian campaign. Such sacrifices could be regarded as temporary; ther would always be an opportunity to renew the war at a more favourabl opportunity. The Chancery as a whole shared these views.[9]

It was not only the officials who longed for peace.[10] The army was gettin tired. 'Though we speack but little of peace at present', Jefferyes reported 'yet here are but few among us who do not heartily wish for it, for the officer as well as the common soldiers begin to be tir'd of their continual fatigues The conviction that the Russians would not come out and fight a regula battle had a depressing effect in the hot summer which encouraged illness an caused lassitude. On 26 June the Russians moved their camp closer to Poltava to 'within cannon-shott' of Charles's army, and entrenched themselves s deeply that the Swedes concluded that 'they do not design to give u

* See above, pp. 288-ᴖ

attle, unless we attack them in their trenches'.[11] On such an attack
Charles XII nevertheless decided. There was no point in waiting now;
einforcements from Poland and Sweden could not be expected for the 1709
ampaign. A successful battle would be the only means of drawing Tartar
nd Turkish support to sustain the continuation of the campaign. A battle,
ven if not outstandingly successful, would moderate the Russian demands if
eace negotiations matured, and – as officers commented – permit a return
vith honour' to the Polish base.[12] Those who guessed that the King would
ot grasp Menshikov's peace overtures over-eagerly were proved right.[13] To
Charles a cession of Swedish land would be binding for his lifetime: he was
ot, he later explained, one of those rulers who could sign a treaty and then
nd an excuse to break it.[14]

A retreat to Poland would not raise such moral problems as a 'bad peace';
ut Piper's suggestion struck at his honour and pride as a soldier. Was it not
owardly and senseless to go back across the Dnieper without risking a battle?
'sar Peter had more troops, but the disproportion between the two armies
vas not alarming. He reckoned that with troops detailed to cover the fort
f Poltava to prevent the garrison breaking out, and with a detachment to
rotect the baggage and field-cannon, he could muster twenty thousand for the
attle. The Russian entrenchment contained forty thousand, but if clever tactics
vere employed they might not be able to exploit their superiority in numbers.[15]

The fact that he himself was injured and would not be able to take an active
art in the battle was regrettable, but the situation did not permit delay.
Jniforms and boots were worn, ammunition was running low. The Rus-
ian camp and fortifications on the far side of the Vorskla had been destroyed
y the Swedes after 22 June and 'some of the ennemys baggage' appropri-
ted;[16] but food was already becoming short through Russian raids on
wedish sources of supply in the Ukraine and would become shorter still
vhen the Cossack fast ended on 30 June. There was yet another factor which
ounselled an early attack: Swedish reconnaissance troops reported that the
econd Russian encampment was so situated that the attacker might have a
etter chance than the defender. Here the position seemed not impregnable
s at Malatitze; here there was no easy route of escape as at Holovzin.

The rear of the Russian camp was against the Vorskla at a point where the
ank was steep and the river bed so broad and marshy that it would be
ifficult to recross it. The only retreat possible was the way they had come:
ack to the ford at Petrovka. The site for the entrenched camp was well
hosen, with thick woods on one side of it and marshy and wooded land on
he other. The only open approach from Poltava had been closed by a row of
ix redoubts set at intervals of about two hundred metres.* The camp itself
vas protected by walls studded with seventy cannon. Inside these walls the
Tsar's thirty thousand infantry sheltered. His cavalry, ten thousand strong,
vas stationed between the retrenchment proper and the redoubts.

* See plan, p. 295.

The Swedish plan of attack worked out by Charles XII and Rehnskiöld wa to speed through the approach, ignoring the fire which would no doubt k directed at them from the redoubts as they neared the camp. When reachir the far corner of the camp, they would then turn sharp right to cut off tk escape to Petrovka. It was hoped they could pin the enemy into a corn before the Russians had time to range themselves properly for battl The direction of the Swedish attack would prevent Russian relief of tk Poltava garrison as well as raids on the Swedish baggage and artillery a Pushkarivka.

On Sunday 27 June after the evening service the generals and colone of the Swedish army were called to Charles's quarters and handed the orders and plans for the first stage of the battle to be waged the next day. Rehnskiöld was to have the command, but Charles was to be with the army carried by guards on a stretcher. It was on this stretcher that he inspecte the infantry in the late evening. On it he was carried at the head of the troop when they marched to the rallying-point at midnight. Here a division int four columns was effected and they settled down to rest and wait for first ligh and the junction with the cavalry which was gathering in six columns. Und Rehnskiöld Lewenhaupt was in charge of the infantry, nine thousand in al and Creutz of the cavalry, some thirteen thousand. The artillery, thirty canno in all, was left with the baggage as it had no role to play in the attac planned.

It might be thought that the presence of a king, who had wielded so command since the start of the campaign but who was now an invalid – unabl to ride his horse – would prove a liability to the officers charged with the hand ling of the battle. Certainly there is evidence that nerves were taut amon several of the high officers in the early stages of the operation.[17] But Charle XII's presence was taken for granted and would be helpful for morale when th time came to attack with the naked sword. Probably he himself would hav found it unbearable to wait remote from the battlefield even if anyone ha suggested he should stay away. He had been under some strain throughou the long wait at Poltava, strain which he tried to resolve by praying for God' guidance. We know little, if anything, of Charles's private devotions an personal attitude to prayer. But from this very period an odd scrap o information has come down to us. A young officer, on patrol in the night o 6 June, happened to pass by an orchard near Charles's quarters and wa astonished to see his King kneeling under a cherry tree in an attitude o prayer. The officer withdrew without being seen, but made a note of th incident in his diary.[18] That Charles XII, a reserved person, thought himsel totally unobserved and alone is obvious; that he should have wandered abou in the hot summer night is not surprising; that his thoughts should have bee such that he felt impelled to pray on his knees there and then is illuminating

* In the afternoon Rehnskiöld, Piper and Colonel Siegroth had been called to the King's roon to discuss the battle and Gyllenkrook had, with the field-marshal, worked out the necessar orders and march-'tickets'.

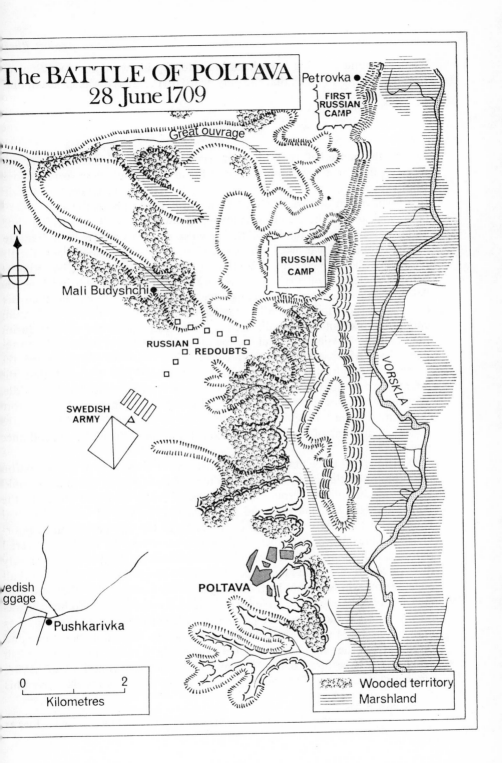

The BATTLE OF POLTAVA
28 June 1709

Petrovka

FIRST
RUSSIAN
CAMP

Great ouvrage

N

Mali Budyshchi

RUSSIAN CAMP

RUSSIAN REDOUBTS

SWEDISH
ARMY

VORSKLA

POLTAVA

Swedish
Baggage

Pushkarivka

0   2
Kilometres

Wooded territory
Marshland

That he found comfort is perhaps indicated by his words to Axel Sparre
few days before 17 June, that the only peace that mattered was 'peace in one
own mind'.[19]

III

During the pause before battle commenced, some heard the sounds of me
working not far away. Sounds carried far at night, but these seemed close
than expected, given the distance of the Russian camp. Gyllenkrook, wit
two fortification officers, went off to investigate. At about the same time
became clear that the enemy was aware of Swedish activity: warning shot
and drums beaten for alarm told their own story. It was not yet light, but afte
a brief council of war at Charles's stretcher, Rehnskiöld gave orders for th
infantry to be formed into two lines so that the attack might be mounte
before the element of surprise was totally lost. While this was being done, th
field-marshal did some reconnaissance on his own.[20] What he then dis
covered, as did – independently – Gyllenkrook and his officers, was alarmin
enough to necessitate immediate changes in the plan for the attack: durin
the night the Russians had built a line of four redoubts at right angles to th
line of six which protected their camp. These new redoubts divided th
plateau, through which Charles and Rehnskiöld had planned that th
infantry would march in their lines of battle formation, down the middle
The last of the redoubts were not as yet completed;* it was the noise from
the men working on them, quite close to the Swedes, which had been hear
once the marching of Charles's army had stopped and the night was still onc
more.

Decisions had to be made quickly. Orders were given to stop the formatio
into lines of battle and to regroup into five columns so that the plateau coul
be crossed in column-formation and lines of battle reformed closer to th
Russian camp. Gyllenkrook and Siegroth, the 'colonel of the day',† spe
round with the new orders. The commander of the middle column, Major
General Stackelberg, was specifically asked to attack the newly discovere
redoubts in his march. Since it was in the attack on the third of the four newl
discovered redoubts that an unexpected snag developed, which had a snowba
effect on the whole action, high officers naturally enough later discussed hov
mistake number one could have been avoided. Lewenhaupt, who himself wa
on the far right flank and not present when the change in dispositions wa
made, considered that if the columns had marched close together, three and
three, leaving the redoubts as isolated as possible in the middle, the Swedish
army might have fared better.[21] That Rehnskiöld was conscious of havin
made a mistake himself at one stage of the battle of Poltava is clear from hi

---

* See plan, p. 295.
† This Swedish term indicates the colonel who, according to a fixed rota, served the King a
chief staff officer.

gh as a prisoner in Russia: 'One mistake can darken all previous *gloire*'[22] – nd it is possible that it was his own immediate reaction to the problem posed y the new redoubts that weighed on his mind. Charles XII, who had nothing ut praise for the conduct of both these generals in the battle, is known to have ttered one criticism: 'Here the reconnaissance was not well done', but this eems to have been expressed during a later stage of the battle when the ussians marched out of their camp.[23]

Whether different dispositions once the discovery of the new redoubts had een made would have significantly altered the outcome must remain specu- tive. What is certain is that Rehnskiöld and Charles XII had very little time which to adapt their plan to the new situation. The Russian artillery began play on the Swedish army even before the reforming into columns was mplete. It was essential to move as soon as possible since a stationary rget brought casualties with consequent loss of morale.* As the sun rose – at o'clock – battle commenced.

The first and second redoubts fell to the Swedes speedily, but the third was bravely defended that six battalions under Major-General Roos were ught up in the attack and so severely mauled that they eventually lost ntact with the rest of the infantry and wandered, much depleted in numbers, to the woods east of the line of the six redoubts.† Two further battalions, nder Major-General Sparre, were also held up but succeeded in rejoining e main army. It was not easy to find one's way if once separated from the her columns. Russian cavalry had left the line of the six redoubts to attack the dvancing Swedish infantry, Swedish cavalry hurried to meet the enemy. ust thrown up by galloping horses added to the cloud of smoke from the cessant enemy artillery fire. The lack of visibility was such that the Russians uld unnoticed send a detachment under Menshikov from their camp to ttack the isolated Roos (whose plight had been reported by their scouting oops) and to liberate, if possible, the garrison of Poltava.

The strength of the Russian fire was such that it may have contributed to e Swedish main army, once it had successfully forced the line of the six doubts, collecting in the wooded terrain of Mali Budyshchi, since this lay in dip which offered protection from the Russian cannon and mortar balls. ussian historians certainly interpret the Swedish move to the west as one of ight from their murderous fire.[24] But it seems more likely that this was a lanned move. One lieutenant mentions Mali Budyshdh as '*unsern rendez- ous*';[25] and high officers and officials gathering there congratulated the King on successfully achieved first stage of the battle.[26] This is not to underestimate e force or importance of the Russian artillery park, which prevented the wedish cavalry from pursuing effectively the Russian cavalry after this had

---

* Several war diaries note heavy casualties from the first cannon balls: Weihe tells of the ecapitation of two grenadiers from the first shot and of a captain and four musketeers from the cond.

† Roos was handicapped by the circumstances that Colonel Siegroth was mortally wounded in e early stages of the fight for the redoubt, before he could persuade Roos to extricate himself.

been forced to give up the territory between the six redoubts and the cam The damage wrought to the King's stretcher by a Russian cannon-ball an the loss of life among those who guarded him was alarming to the high office who felt responsible for the King's safety. In retrospect some critics on th Swedish side, Lewenhaupt among them, thought Charles XII's decision t leave the larger part of his artillery behind at Poltava a grave mistake (on four field-guns were taken along);[27] though it should be remembered th these critics did not know the battle-plan in its entirety and the way in whic it depended on speed for successful execution.

The most serious consequence which followed Roos's separation from th main army lay in its detrimental effect on the speed of stage two of the battl The absence of his troops was discovered at about 6 o'clock, when the arm was collecting after the breakthrough of the line of the six redoubts, an adjutants as well as a dragoon regiment were sent off to get into touch wit him. A little later, when news arrived that he was in serious difficultie two cavalry regiments and two infantry battalions were dispatched to hel extricate him. Precious half-hours came and went.

At 8 o'clock it became clear that Rehnskiöld could not afford to wait muc longer. The Russians, with plenty of time at their disposal, put their cavalr commanded by Bauer, in a position which might threaten the Swedish flank. Some infantry regiments were ranged in lines outside the camp in case th Swedes made a frontal attack.[28] In view of the reduced number of their ow infantry – Lewenhaupt had at this time only ten battalions with him – th Swedes decided not to risk a frontal assault and between 8 and 8.30 in th morning the army prepared to attack the Russian cavalry and the right flan of the camp. While this was being done, the two infantry battalions sent t help Roos returned to report that it was impossible to break through th enemy forces which had isolated him, and it became clear that the Swedis infantry available for the second stage of the battle was reduced by hal Adjutants sent to ask Mazepa to bring the artillery and the regiments left Pushkarivka to the main army also failed to get through:[29] neither reinforc ment nor protection against the Russian big guns could be obtained.

A little before 9 o'clock came the most alarming news of all, somethin totally unexpected. While Creutz and Rehnskiöld were, separately,[30] obserˇ ing the enemy's movements from small hills in the terrain, they noticed th the whole Russian army was in movement. Dragoon regiments were bein sent off and it could easily be guessed that they were meant to link up wit Skoropadsky's Cossacks stationed in the Shuky region. Infantry regiment in great strength were leaving the entrenchments to form a strong left flan outside the camp. The Russian cavalry – which the Swedes had aimed t attack – was in the process of withdrawing to be incorporated into a Russia army marching for the first time in the war to a regular attack on Charles X

---

* They collected in the shelter provided by a deep Ukrainian river-valley, called the great *ouvra* by the Swedes, the *Schlucht* by the Germans: see plan, p. 295.

IV

ehnskiöld consulted briefly with Lewenhaupt how best to meet this attack. hen he told the King. Gyllenkrook noted Charles's suggestion, 'Would it ot be best if we attacked the cavalry first and got rid of them?', and also his greement, 'Well, well. You must do as you will,' when the field-marshal old him this was impossible.* 'No, Your Majesty,' Gyllenkrook heard ehnskiöld say, 'we must march against them.'[31]

At 9 o'clock therefore the Swedish army turned and moved south to get to a position parallel to that of the Russians. The Swedish cavalry was rdered to range itself behind the infantry. Lewenhaupt reckoned that his velve battalions counted at most four thousand men, and formed them into ne line. His left flank was protected by a marsh. Opposite him he had two acked Russian lines of infantry, longer than his single one, supported by venty field-guns. Lewenhaupt in his report of the battle estimated the guns : 'nearly 100', and the Russian infantry at twenty-two thousand, but this too high: the Russian first line of twenty-four battalions was ten thousand rong, the second (of eighteen battalions) eight thousand.[32] Even so, the nemy superiority in numbers was terrifying. So was their superiority in re-power. The command of the infantry was held by Sheremetev; Bauer nd Menshikov – who had returned after a vain hunt for Roos† – were in narge of the cavalry wings; the Tsar acted as head of an infantry division.

The Swedes attacked first to gain a moral advantage. Lewenhaupt led a narge with *armes blanches* by the Swedish right wing which made the ussians fall back and gave the Swedes some field-guns to turn against their nemy. But a gap appeared between the élite regiments of the right and those f the left which could not keep up the same pace. Russian troops poured to the gap and widened it. Panic gripped men whose colonel was wounded nd the Swedish line began to give way. Even Lewenhaupt when he came on ne scene could not make the men stand. 'I rode up and down in front of nem,' he later reported, 'I begged, threatened, cursed and hit out. All was vain, it was as if they neither saw nor heard me.'[33] Swedish cavalry of the ft wing formation came to the sporadic support of the hard-pressed infantry, ut could not in the long run maintain itself. Rehnskiöld, who had come their help, was among those taken prisoner here. The right wing was nable to develop its own attack on the Russians properly, partly because of nfavourable terrain but also because of the way the infantry attack had had start before the cavalry had completed its regrouping. Menshikov's forces ained on the Swedish cavalry right, and Creutz was not able to make it stand ll it reached Mali Budyshchi in its retreat.

* Speculation by some historians how the battle would have ended if Charles xii's suggestion d been attempted seems vitiated by the fact that (unknown to the King it would seem when he oke) the Russian cavalry had already begun to withdraw.

† Roos had, about 9 o'clock, effected a retreat to Poltava.

Within half an hour the battle was over. The Swedes were either casualti of the battle (killed or prisoner-of-war) or had retired to Mali Budyshchi even fled to the safety of the baggage and reserve regiments at Pushkarivka.

Charles XII on his stretcher had been at the head of the right infantry win When the panic spread to that sector of the thin line, his cry of 'Swede Swedes'* went unheeded. His stretcher was hit by musket bullets and de troyed. It looked as if the King would become a prisoner of the Russia approaching ever closer. Lewenhaupt's call that the King was in dang brought, however, a front of soldiers willing to delay the enemy by layi down their own lives for his. Charles forced himself on to a horse, the ba dages on his foot came undone, blood dripped from the wound that open with the unwonted activity. The horse was shot under him and was replac by that of Johann Gierttaⴕ of the drabants. When the King reached Ma Budyshchi he channelled the flight of the survivors into an orderly retre with Creutz's and Lewenhaupt's help.

The Russians did not pursue the Swedes. The fight had been one betwe infantry in the main, and the foot soldiers of Tsar Peter were nearly as shak as those of Charles. Cavalry regiments from Pushkarivka and field-guns fro the artillery park coming to the help of the main Swedish army were enou to stop the Russians in their tracks.

At Pushkarivka Mazepa and Hordienko had put their Cossacks in posture of defence, and it was here that the remnants of the Swedish regimen collected. Roos had capitulated when Russian troops reached Poltava at o'clock and told him that the battle was lost;[34] but the two regiments le to guard Poltava managed to fight their way to Pushkarivka. By midday mo of the beaten army had reached the safety of the baggage and could rest a refresh themselves. Charles was among the last to reach Pushkarivka. Hultma rebandaged his foot and got him something to eat. He asked for Rehnskiö and Piper and wanted to know the fate of Prince Maximilian who as colon of the Scanian dragoons had fought on the left wing.[35] When it was cle that all three were missing, he sent Meijerfelt to the Tsar in the hope arranging their exchanges if they were still alive.[36] The Swedes had left son ten thousand on the battlefield, 6,901 deadⴙ and 2,760 prisoners of t Tsar.[37]

The three whose absence worried Charles most were prisoners: Prince Ma had in vain tried to cut his way to the King;[38] the Field-Marshal – when was lost – was seen to ride away to surrender his sword; Piper and Cederhiel gave themselves up;[39] Hermelin died, possibly killed by enemy Cossacks

---

* His call of 'Svenskar, Svenskar' is noted by diarists.

ⴕ Giertta dismounted to save the King, but survived the battle.

ⴙ Among the dead were 301 officers; among the prisoners-of-war 260. Russian losses we relatively light: 1,345 killed and 3,290 wounded.

¶ The rumour that the Tsar had killed Hermelin, whose propaganda had annoyed him, anger, has never been proved. For an examination of the problem see Olsson, *Hermelin*, pp. 594 and Waller, *K.F.Å.*, 1955.

Adlerfelt had been killed at the King's side during the battle. The manuscript of his history of Charles's wars was safe in the baggage of Prince Maximilian* who brought it out of Russia when he was freed. Though the Prince died before he reached home, his tutor and secretary, Bardili, took care that Adlerfelt's book, with its many anecdotes from the campaign that the 'Little Prince' had shared with Charles XII, was not lost.[40]

V

With the troops that remained – some sixteen thousand – Charles XII intended to make his way to Poland. In theory several routes were possible to effect a junction with Stanislaus and Krassow. In practice the presence of Russian and Skoropadsky troops in the Kiev region and the destruction of the Zaporozhian fleet made any move in a western direction hazardous. The Swedes would have to return to Poland therefore over Zaporozhian and Tartar lands. The most feasible way, in view of the scarcity of boats or other material for a crossing of the Dnieper, might be a crossing of the Vorskla at the several fording-places known to Hordienko's Cossacks and to reach the road which ran south from Kharkov to the lands of Devlet-Gerei. From the Khan's territories, as also from the Moldavian parts of the Sultan's dominions, Podolia and Volhynia could be reached with relative ease. If enough boats or rafts could be got together, it might be possible to cross the Dnieper at Perevolotjna and make a speedier march into Poland through Zaporozhian territories without touching those of the Khan or the Porte.

In either case a march directed towards Perevolotjna was the first step. The traditional picture of Charles as ill with fever once more, incapable of taking decisions,† on the retreat from Poltava, has faded before that of modern research which shows us the King, unable to ride a horse and transported in a coach, but in full control of the march. To depict this march as a headlong and disordered flight – as has sometimes been done[41] – would be misleading. Even if the rationalization of the battle of Poltava as a failed attack on a fortified camp‡ came later, when nerves had settled down and officers were writing up the action,[42] the feeling of being an army with a 'victorious' reputation[43] had a steadying influence. The baggage was sent ahead in the afternoon of 28 June, infantry and cavalry followed under Creutz's command. The Russians might be expected to start a pursuit, so the march continued throughout the heat of the day and well into the night. While the troops rested for some hours, Creutz arranged for horses to be made available for the remaining infantry so that greater speed would be possible on the 29th.

* Adlerfelt was the 'cavalier' in attendance on the Prince.

† This picture was, probably subconsciously, motivated by a desire to free Charles from responsibility for this stage of the campaign.

‡ Gustavus Adolphus's failed attack on Wallenstein's camp at Nürnberg was used as a comparison.

L

The artillery and the precious wagons which carried the cash belonging t
respective regiments reached Perevolotjna in the evening of 29 June. Betwee
29 and 30 June the whole army and most of the baggage arrived. Creutz, wit
the rearguard, caught up at 4 o'clock. To his conference with Charles h
brought news that the Russian pursuit had now started: regular Russia
troops, not only Cossack detachments, were on the march, though thei
number was not known. Furthermore, no suitable places for the crossing o
the Vorskla had been discovered though he had been on the look-out fo
them.[44] The King's news was not encouraging either: Gyllenkrook had jus
reported to him that it would not be possible to get the whole army acros
the Dnieper before Russians in pursuit could be expected to catch up with th
Swedes at Perevolotjna.[45] Meijerfelt could be relied on to do his best to post
pone such pursuit;* but that it would be mounted was regarded as certain

The decision was now reached, not without some pressure by the generals
and Gyllenkrook on Charles XII in respect of his own role, that the arm
should cross the Vorskla in the morning of 1 July and aim at the territorie
of Devlet-Gerei under the command of Lewenhaupt supported by Creutz
The money in the regimental chests would be divided among officers and men
So would ammunition and food to the amount of what each individual coul
carry on his own horse. In this way supply wagons and baggage would no
impede their march. There was a faint hope of getting artillery and baggag
over the Dnieper if the pontoon bridge started on 29 June could be completed
In any case Mazepa and Hordienko and their more important followers mus
be got to safety across the Dnieper as a matter of priority: for if the Swede
should be defeated in a battle with the Russians, the Cossacks would b
treated by the Tsar as rebels. Torture and execution would be their lot. I
would be a blot on Swedish honour to deliver their allies to such a fate. Th
King, with as many wounded Swedes as possible, a small staff and a stron
escort would also cross the Dnieper and with Mazepa and Hordienko a
guides take a short cut across the Zaporozhian desert to reach the Sultan'
dominions and make preparations for a reunion with his army and the marc
back to Poland. The rendezvous was put at Ochakov on the Black Sea
equidistant from Bender and Perikop, the Khan's capital. It was reckone
that Devlet-Gerei and the Seraskier of Bender would help speed the army'
return to a secure base, if only from fear that Tsar Peter was becoming to
powerful. Money for Charles's immediate needs was also to be ferried across
as were Mazepa's two barrels of gold and several chests of valuables.[46] Wor
was put in hand to effect these plans during the night of 30 June–1 July.

It was realized that, since the whole of the army could not be put to safet
across the Dnieper, it would be preferable to move it away from Perevolotjn
and let it retrace its steps for some distance along the Vorskla river in pre

---

* He did, by the initial impact of his report of Charles's willingness to negotiate peace, obtai
half a day's postponement.

† Charles had only five left of his ten major-generals and generals, and one of them, Axe
Sparre, was wounded.

parations for the morrow's crossing to its far side. But discipline had already begun to slacken. Charles XII's order forbidding individual soldiers or companies to make their escape over the Dnieper shows that such attempts had started. Even more significant is the fact that this order was not universally obeyed. The feeling that safety lay beyond the broad river while a trap might be sprung on its tributary lit the first flicker of panic. It was partly from a hope that daylight might extinguish it that the move from Perevolotjna was postponed till 1 July. Dusk was already falling and it would not be easy in the prevailing circumstances to collect the troops for the march.

Lewenhaupt was on the list of officers whom Charles wanted to take with him to Turkey, as his linguistic abilities would be helpful to a field-Chancery robbed of most senior staff. But when he specifically asked to share the fate of the army he was, as the senior officer, put in command. He promised the King that if the Russians caught up with him, he would fight the enemy. This promise Charles assumed to be an unconditional one. But Lewenhaupt, by the form of words he chose, regarded himself as bound to fight only if the Russian challenge came after he had got the army away from Perevolotjna.[47]

VI

During the night Charles was ferried across the Dnieper on a stretcher.[48] His coach was brought over after him, the weight of its wheels distributed over two boats. The Cossack leaders were already on the far side since the evening of 30 June, so was the Hungarian Krmann* and his companions. Fishing boats plied to and fro with the wounded; the Swedes of the escort and the Cossacks swam across led by Zaporozhians who had a special knowledge of the river and its currents.† In the early morning of 1 July a train of carriages and coaches, with an escort of nine hundred Swedes and some two thousand Cossacks, began the trek through the desert, leaving the rest of Mazepa's and Iordienko's men (estimated as between five and six thousand) to march to the Crimea with the Swedes. One of the diarists who had crossed the river noted the uneasiness he and his companions felt at seeing no sign of movement away from Perevolotjna by the time they themselves turned south.[49] Another remembered that clouds on the far horizon were thought by some to be the dust from Tsar Peter's cavalry approaching.[50]

These two entries have since been used in an attempt to prove that Charles XII consciously left his army in the lurch and saved his own life at the cost of certain captivity for his men. He did so, it is argued, out of fear of becoming the laughing-stock of Europe if the Tsar should drag him through the streets of Moscow like a captive bear.[51] It is true that Gyllenkrook had used such arguments when he joined his voice to that of the generals who begged Charles

---

* Krmann's notes and memoirs of the trip are one of the more important sources.

† The method used was for one Cossack rider to lead a party across sitting on the back of a horse accustomed to swimming the river; the other horses followed this leader, each dismounted rider holding on to the tail of his own horse.

not to risk capture.[52] It is also true that preparations for the reception of th
Swedish army at Ochakov could have been made by others and did nc
demand Charles's own presence. But given the injury which prevented th
King from being of any use in further battle, and which would indeed mak
him a liability to an army that needed to move fast in the hope of avoidin
battle, the decision seemed one of common sense. Certainly it was of som
importance that news of Poltava should reach Sweden and Poland – an
Europe at large – not only from the Russian side. There was no time to pe
such dispatches at Perevolotjna, and Charles XII – writing to Stockholi
from Ochakov – gave as his main reason for speeding to that place the need t
tell also the Swedish side of the story lest people at home and Sweden's frienc
abroad should fall victim to Russian propaganda.

Charles XII initially put up a spirited fight on 30 June against those wh
argued that his place was no longer with the army. When Gyllenkrook hinte
that the men might refuse to fight, the King returned the oft-quoted, 'The
shall fight when I order them'; but reflection forced the conclusion tha
command was not compatible with lying on a stretcher or sitting in
carriage.

The King's tent had been left at Perevolotjna. In it Lewenhaupt and Creut
snatched a few hours sleep. Neither of them gave a clear lead as 1 Jul
dawned. They were both exhausted from the mental and physical strain c
the last few days. The weather was still unbearably hot. Lewenhaupt wa
weakened by diarrhoea. It was natural that – in retrospect – both he an
Creutz should emphasize the lack of will to fight in the army; but the cor
temporary evidence shows that there was less panic on 1 July than on th
previous afternoon and evening and that where men were ordered to saddl
up and parade they did so.[53] The failure of nerve was in reality among th
higher officers, who dreaded a trek into the unknown – to infidels, Turks an
Tartars – more than they dreaded captivity with the Russian 'European' army
officered by men who spoke German and French and shared a professiona
code of conduct. Had no Russian force appeared at Perevolotjna in th
morning of 1 July, Lewenhaupt and Creutz would no doubt have got th
Swedish army away. But at 8 o'clock Menshikov with six thousand men an
perhaps two thousand Cossacks – a force therefore considerably smalle
than that of the Swedes – appeared on a height above the river and sent
trumpeter to the Swedish camp. Lewenhaupt dispatched Creutz to parle
with the Russian prince to gain time; but once talks had started the temptatio
to enter into a capitulation was irresistible. The Prussian von Siltmann, wh
joined Menshikov as soon as the Russians arrived, played an important i
obscure role in these talks.[54]

When terms had been offered, Lewenhaupt consulted all officers of colonel'
rank and above* whether these should be accepted or a fight risked ii
unfavourable circumstances. On being asked in this council of war wha

* Only two major-generals remained as Sparre and Lagercrona were with Charles,

Charles XII's orders had been, he suppressed all details of the Vorskla crossing and the Ochakov rendezvous and confined himself to saying that his only order was that the army should defend itself 'as long as we could'. His sending the colonels to ask the soldiers if they were willing to fight has been criticized by historians as a breach of Caroline army practice.* His dissatisfaction with the answer brought back by every one of them, 'We will fight if the others do', and his second dispatch of the colonels to the men to impress upon them the seriousness of the situation and the might of the enemy has counted even more against his reputation. Charles XII, who respected him as a fine and brave soldier, thought that Lewenhaupt 'must have taken leave of his senses' when he learnt of the surrender at Perevolotjna.

In Lewenhaupt's defence it must be stressed that he regarded the situation as hopeless and saw it as his Christian duty to save the army from what he could only think of as a needless and purposeless bloodshed. He knew that at least six thousand soldiers ranged in disciplined order had expressed their willingness to do their duty; he had been told that Russian attempts on the Swedish flank had been beaten off with ease. But his conception of his duty blinded him to these facts and made him see only those that pointed to a catastrophe: the unsuitability of the Perevolotjna terrain for a battle, his vain search for the Tartar officers who were to serve as guides for the trek to the Crimea. Above all he remembered that some soldiers had refused to continue the fight at Poltava: might not the same happen again?[55]

Charles XII took a good share of the responsibility on himself. 'I was guilty of an oversight,' he wrote to Stockholm at a later date, 'in that I forgot to give the other generals and colonels who were there the orders of which only Lewenhaupt and Creutz had knowledge. But for this, nothing would have happened as it did; for all the colonels were at a loss, not knowing what orders had been given, nor which way they were to take with their regiments, nor where I myself had gone.'[56]

It has been suggested that the Swedish officers at Perevolotjna were concerned not to lose their baggage.[57] The King's orders to sink the Chancery-in-the-field papers and the regimental records into the Dnieper had been obeyed,† but the orders to burn the baggage and destroy everything that had to be left behind had not. But surely the after-effect of Poltava, the fear of an uncertain future, the welcome prospect of an end to the fighting after long years, and the hope of speedy repatriation[58] through exchanges with Russian prisoners held in Sweden operated more strongly on the officers who gave Lewenhaupt the answer he wanted the second time round. Defeatism was in the air. At 11 in the morning the Swedes capitulated: 1,161 officers and 13,138 non-commissioned officers and men filed into Menshikov's camp and laid

* That the soldiers themselves, even those of the non-Swedish regiments, thought so is clear from the answer overheard by ensign Piper: 'Why do they ask us? They never did so before. The command then was *Gå på*. We cannot guarantee that we shall beat them, but we will do all in our power to do so.'

† See above, p. 238.

down their arms. The capitulation said nothing of the Cossacks and Zaporo
zhians. Many escaped, but many were caught and Swedes who saw thei
mutilated bodies dangling from Russian gallows felt that they had acted witl
little honour towards their comrades-in-arms.[59] Their own surrender some –
perhaps most of them – felt a disgrace.[60]

Perevolotjna had completed that destruction of Charles XII's army whicl
Poltava had begun. The campaign against Russia was lost.

The Years in Turkey

BOOK FIVE

The Years in Turkey

1

Grief and Grief Overcome

From the far side of the Dnieper the Swedes, guided by the Zaporozhians and Mazepa, began to move through the no-man's-land which separated the territories over which the Tsar claimed sovereignty from the Sultan's dominions. This 'desert' – the dry steppe of tall grass – had been created that it might serve as a buffer in peacetime; but Mazepa and some of the Cossacks knew the paths that led through it from participation in wars against the Turks. There was little food to be found, but the Zaporozhians taught the Swedes how to catch hares and birds with their bare hands and how to light a fire from a mixture of dried horsedung and grass. The Cossack way of curing horse flesh under the saddle was also imitated. Water was more of a problem. Wild cherries slaked the thirst off and on, and Charles XII's servant, who had the knack of locating streams, usually managed to bring his master something to drink even if he had found it necessary to filter the river-water through a hat.[1] The heat was nearly unendurable in the middle of the day and the habit of taking what rest one needed then instead of at night was soon adopted.

The worst fear was that of pursuit by the Russians. Mazepa had sent Charles XII's coach and six hundred Swedes, with a party of Cossacks, away to the south before dawn. He himself, confined to his coach by ill-health, waited till the rest of the Swedish–Ukrainian group destined for Turkey had come across and arranged for smaller detachments to take different routes lest Russian troops should find it too easy to discover the track followed. By evening he caught up with Charles and they made what speed they could, hampered to some extent by the heavy wagons which carried the Ukrainian treasure. Without this, however, the expedition itself would have been impossible,* and a strong Swedish escort protected the precious cargo. On the fourth day the border between Zaporozhian and Ottoman territories was reached at the river Inhul, a tributary of the Bug. Nominally the Swedes and the Cossacks now stood on soil that belonged to the Tartar Khan of Crimea, but they were still in country that was both unpopulated and uncultivated and

---

* Kentrschysnkyj, *Mazepa*, pp. 443 ff. has analysed the importance of this treasure for the participation of *Mazepa's* Cossacks and those of Hordienko in the expedition.

could not feel secure from the Russians till they had entered Ochakov on the far side of the Bug. There had been some losses among the exhausted and wounded, and (unknown to the main party) one detachment had been captured by Russians already on 2 July. On 7 July they reached the shores of the Bug and believed themselves within sight of safety: the Russians would not dare to pursue them on well-defended Turkish territory. Poniatowski had gone ahead to make arrangements with the local Pasha, Abdurrahman, for transport. Formalities and bargaining took much more time than expected, two whole days, and while the ferrying was still incomplete, six thousand Russians under the command of Volkonsky reached the place of crossing.

Volkonsky and his men had started from Perevolotjna as soon as the capitulation had been signed on 1 July; but the Zaporozhian feints, and even more the hunt – which proved successful – of a small Swedish force under Melander which had strayed from the route of the main party lost the Russians valuable time. When they did get on to the track of Charles and Mazepa and raced to the Bug, they found that the two men they had hoped to capture had escaped. But six hundred Swedes and Cossacks were still on their side of the river and were immediately attacked. It was agonizing for those who had reached haven on the other bank to watch this hopeless struggle. The Swedish half of the combatants were offered and accepted a pardon; the Zaporozhians – who knew that no quarter would be given – either perished in an improvised entrenchment or were cut down.[2] Charles had to witness the difference in treatment meted out to his men and those of his allies. Though he had not handed the Cossacks over to the mercy of the Russians by a conscious decision, it was still grievous to accept his impotence to save men who had trusted to his military power and protection.

II

At Ochakov Charles's first task was to send letters to Sweden and Poland. The very night of his arrival expresses went to the Council in Stockholm and to Stanislaus and Krassow. The draft of the letters they carried had been largely written by the King himself. No mention was made of the wound which still incapacitated him. The 'reverse of fortune' at Poltava was admitted, but calmness and fortitude was counselled: Sweden was bidden to replenish the regiments which had suffered most in the battle without delay; Stanislaus and Krassow were asked to cooperate and hold themselves in readiness for a junction with Charles XII and his army approaching across the southern frontiers of Poland.[3] To the Khan of Crimea both Charles and Mazepa sent emissaries. From the King the secretary Klinckowström went to ask in his master's name that the Swedish army – approaching (as it was assumed) from Perevolotjna – should be well received. Mazepa's legate promised a generous money reward for similar help for his Cossacks. Martin Neugebauer was dispatched to Constantinople to ascertain Sultan Ahmed's attitude to the post-Poltava state of affairs.

There were already signs that this attitude was ambiguous. On 11 July the Seraskier of Bender, Yusuf Pasha, arrived at Ochakov with greetings from the Sultan but he also carried an invitation (which sounded like an order) for the visitors to leave Ochakov for Bender. This move was not popular with either the Ukrainian hetman or the Swedish King; they found the Sultan's slow methods worrying and realized that they would be more at his mercy if they moved as far from the rendezvous with the army as Bender. But they had no choice and took comfort from the fact that Bender was on one of the routes to Poland. To the Cossacks this invitation seemed alarming. Bender was in Bessarabia, far removed from home; in the opposite direction from the one in which they had expected to travel. The Tartar Khan was a prince with whom they had long been in negotiation; Yusuf Pasha and the Sultan were unknown quantities. In the night of 11–12 July there was a near-revolt among the Zaporozhians, and Mazepa and Charles had to play on many strings to keep them to the Swedish alliance and persuade them to participate in the move to Bender.[4]

The fact that Charles XII and Mazepa had sought asylum in his territories imposed on Ahmed III and his advisers a duty according to the Islam religion not to deny them such asylum, but offered also the opportunity to use the presence of the visitors as a pawn in the diplomatic tug-of-war in progress between the Porte and the Tsar for and against confirmation of the armistice of 1700.

News of the Perevolotjna surrender, and of the quick move of masses of Russian troops into Poland which followed it,[5] made Charles XII aware that he was reduced for some considerable time to be a pawn in other men's games. Odd rumours of the capitulation reached the Swedes towards the end of July, but certainty did not have to be accepted till Meijerfelt arrived in Bender on 2 August. It was a blow from which Charles XII never recovered, though those who were present tell us his face remained stoically calm when he heard the news.[6] But the deep impression it made on him can be seen from a comparison of the letters which he wrote which touched upon Poltava and Perevolotjna. In his report on Poltava, he praised the behaviour of his men and explained the 'setback'* which had brought such heavy losses by the advantageous position and the firmness in attack of the enemy. In its several pages there is no reference to God or to heavenly punishment that might be intended by the 'setback', but the expression 'a fated and unlucky happening'† hits the eye. This is the first time that the word 'fated' is mentioned in the letters which have survived from his pen; later still the adjective gave way to the noun when he had, in private letters, to impart news of the death in battle of individuals known to him. *Ödet* – Fate with a capital – meets us again and again in the letters of his later years. But whether this sprang from an aversion

---

* Swedish: '*avbräck*'.   † '*Ett öde och olyckligt tilfälle*'.

to link God with sorrows inflicted or from an unwillingness to accept chastise
ment at God's hands or even from some modification of his religious belief
we cannot tell. In conversation about Poltava, as contrasted with his letter
about that battle, he once apportioned blame, in an indirect manner. During
the march to Perevolotjna criticism of Rehnskiöld was heard. He had been
difficult and on edge and not really in command of the situation, officer
commented. Charles jumped to his defence: if all had done their duty as well
as the field-marshal, the battle would not have ended as it did.[7] The King's
loyalty to an old teacher and comrade-in-arms is not surprising,* but if he
had any 'guilty men' in mind he did not then name them.†

For Perevolotjna he roundly blamed Lewenhaupt and himself. He found
extenuating circumstances for both culprits when an appeal by Lewenhaupt's
family to have him exchanged, supported by Ulrika Eleonora, in 1712 forced
him to speak of the capitulation. His own omission to inform all generals and
colonels of the orders he had given to Lewenhaupt and Creutz could 'to some
extent' be excused by his injury and by the fact that those who were fit did not
think of reminding him of the need to do so. As for Lewenhaupt, he did not
believe that the general had acted from ill-will or fear for his own skin, but
he must have been 'too confused and defeatist to tackle the task in the way a
general ought to when things are difficult'. It was indefensible, Charles concluded, to show such timidity as Lewenhaupt had done. The report of the
surrender which the general had sent to his wife, and which through her had
reached the King at Bender, tried to show that the guilt lay with the troops,
who refused to fight. Charles argued that it proved the general's guilt. It was
Lewenhaupt who had acted against a specific order and against the soldier's
code of conduct. 'In the most shameful manner' he had caused 'irreparable
damage, which never could have been greater if he had risked the life of every
man.'[8] It was the smear on Sweden's military reputation which grieved Charles
most. He refused to have Lewenhaupt exchanged[9] just because he was
the one who had dimmed Sweden's honour at Perevolotjna; he sought at
Stralsund and in the new armies of the Norwegian campaign to create a spirit
among the officers which would make unthinkable a repetition of conduct he
regarded as unforgivable. That Charles lacked psychological insight into the
state of mind of Lewenhaupt and Creutz after Poltava is clear. Bodily removed
from the scene of Perevolotjna, he could not in imagination visualize the
situation as it seemed to those he had left in charge.

To the grief over Sweden's loss of *gloire* was added a grief which hit him
even harder: the death of his elder sister Hedvig Sophia. An army could be
recruited afresh, *gloire* could be regained – her loss was final enough to throw
him into the depth of lonely despair. She had died in an epidemic of measles
on 11 December 1708,[10] but the news of her death had only reached the

* Rehnskiöld for his part would not tolerate criticism of Charles XII among officials and officers
who were, as he, prisoners-of-war in Russia: see Westin's essay on the captives in the *Festschrift*
to Folke Lindberg.

† See below, p. 378, for his 1712 criticism of Roos in a private conversation with Löwen.

Swedish camp at Poltava on 22 June 1709 with Klinckowström. Because of Charles's own illness it was decided to keep it from him for a while. No one had wanted to add to his worries after the battle and during the journey to Ochakov. His injured foot gave him considerable trouble; and after Bender had been reached* Neumann carried out, on 26 July, an operation to cut away the top joint of the middle toe and take out a 'dead' bone† from the foot.[11] Only when it was clear that this operation would not lead to complications, was the decision taken to break the bad news to him.‡ The impact of it was shocking to those who had been used to a King in control of his emotions. He could not stop crying and covered his head with his cloak to hide his grief-stricken face. He shut himself for days on end in his tent and refused to see even the closest of old comrades who shared the Bender quarters. This need to be alone to master sorrow is not uncommon. With persons of royal rank, always surrounded by aides or courtiers, it may be particularly strongly felt. Certainly it was the typical reaction of Charles's relatives to loss of those dear to them. Charles XI refused to see anyone after losing Ulrika Eleonora;[12] Hedvig Sophia, when the news of her husband's death at Kliszów reached Stockholm, shut herself up and would not let anyone near her for days; Ulrika Eleonora the younger reacted in this way when she felt mortally wounded at losing not her husband but her husband's love.[13] Hedvig's son, Charles Frederick, could not bear the company of others after Charles XII was killed in 1718.[14]

That the wifeless Charles, with his strong attachment to parents and sisters, should follow the family pattern of behaviour in deep grief is not surprising and probably more 'normal' in the circumstances than not. But the fact that he could only master his grief by taking refuge in a belief that the news was false – even though transmitted to him in a letter of condolence signed by members of the Swedish Council – shows how near the edge of a breakdown he was. For nearly a year he hoped that the 'too terrible, quite unexpected, *rumour*¶ which totally numbed me' would be contradicted. It was nearly a year before he admitted in a letter to his younger sister that he had accepted the truth of Hedvig's death. Even so, he – who was usually so direct – could not bring himself to put down the words 'dead' or 'death'; nor could he more than hint at the comforting belief in a reunion after death. 'All hope', he wrote on 12 June 1710, 'has now disappeared in that matter which I had convinced myself I should never have the bad luck to survive … my grief will never quite cease till that which has been separated comes together once more.'[15]

---

* The departure from Ochakov was on 14 July, the entry into Bender was on 22 July.

† This bone was put in a blue velvet bag which Neumann placed in the King's coffin in 1718.

‡ Some memoir writers, e.g. Bielke and Poniatowski, recall this news as having been broken to Charles at or near Ochakov; but I have preferred Hultman's version deducing (possibly wrongly) that his close attendance on the King at the time of the operation may have etched the vital period on his memory.

¶ Italicized here, not by the writer of the letter.

III

Grief brought him closer to Ulrika Eleonora. The child he had said good-bye to in 1700, and written to in the intervening years in terms of elder brother to a very much younger sister who must not be burdened with affairs of state, now becomes his confidante in matters of policy. Indeed, Charles XII's letters to Ulrika Eleonora are our most significant source for his innermost thoughts on war and peace for the period between Poltava and his return to Stralsund in 1714. And in the emotional sense he seems to have concentrated on her the love he had borne the lost parents and the elder sister. He was always conscious of the two of them as the only survivors of the family and his appeal to her, when there were differences of opinion between himself and the Council in these difficult years was, again and again, that 'we two who are the only ones left, must stick together and be agreed.'[16] Hedvig Sophia's son – whom he had never seen – meant little to him in these years. Charles Frederick was someone unfamiliar and even resented. When portraits of the boy-Duke arrived, or letters from him, Charles found old wounds open again. He cried at something in the boy's features which reminded him of Hedvig Sophia; he thanked him indirectly – via Ulrika Eleonora – for his notes, rationalizing his own dislike of starting a direct correspondence by a belief that his bad handwriting would either not be decyphered by the boy or would serve him as a bad example.[17]

As Charles XII's stay in Turkey became so much longer than anticipated, he found himself with time on his hands for the first time in years. Correspondence with Stockholm, work on a reform programme in Sweden which was meant both to promote the war effort and to make government more efficient and just,* diplomatic negotiations and the running of the Swedish community at Bender, were absorbing enough but not as demanding as the years on campaign and Charles later referred to 'our lazy-dog-days in Turkey'. There was therefore an opportunity to take up interests that had been neglected and to develop new ones under the impetus of a new environment. That these hobbies formed part of the process by which Charles XII tried to overcome his grief at Hedvig Sophia's death seems clear by the very intensity with which he pursued them and the speed with which he adopted them as soon as headquarters had been established at Bender. It is also worth noting that those he first embarked on had a connexion with the family and particularly with the memory of his father.

Among the officers and Chancery officials Charles had brought to Bender were several good draughtsmen. The training of the fortification-officer provided, as a Swedish expert† has pointed out, the best education for draughtsmen, engravers and architects till the foundation of the Academy of Drawing (*Ritareakademien*) of 1735; and one of these officers, the drabant

---

* See below, pp. 337 ff.   † Ewert Wrangel, *K.F.Å.*, 1931, pp. 121–2.

Cornelius Loos, was charged, with two assistants, to draw the figures to illustrate the drills for infantry and cavalry which Charles XII had worked out between 1700 and 1708. The work began immediately after the Swedes had reached Bender and continued for five months, 'in the King's own room' under his supervision and with his cooperation.[18] It was meant as a tribute not only to the army that had fought for nine long years but also as a memorial to Charles XI who had laid the foundation of that army. The result, a thick folio volume bound in leather, now in the Swedish War Office archive, is a superb example of Caroline craftsmanship as well as our most important material for an assessment of Charles XII as a tactician.

A connexion with the memory of his parents can also be traced for the three expeditions which Charles XII sent from Bender to what contemporary Swedish usage labelled 'the Orient': Asia Minor, the Levant and Egypt. Charles XI had given financial support for the travels and purchases of manuscripts by scholars such as J. G. Sparwenfeldt, G. Peringer-Lillieblad and Olof Celsius for religious reasons, and had been fascinated by the less scholarly but grandiose speculations of the Rudbecks, father and son, on the historical and linguistic links between Sweden and the Holy Land. Ulrika Eleonora had shared her husband's interest both because of her piety and because of her love of learning for its own sake. Erik Benzelius, to whom Charles XII's education in Church history had been entrusted was – as were his famous sons in their turn* – drawn to Oriental studies.

It is not surprising therefore that Charles should turn his thoughts to 'the Orient' when fate had taken him as close as Bender to the lands of the Near East. It was out of the question that he himself should make a journey: his duty was the war which he expected from month to month would absorb all his energies once more. But there were others, equally interested and more competent from the scholarly point of view, who could be given the means to undertake expeditions and bring back drawings and reports which would let him take a vicarious share in the journey. One of these was Mikael Eneman, who in 1703 had defended a thesis on *De sepulchro Christi* and who from 1707 had been one of the King's chaplains. To give him an opportunity to continue his studies Charles sent him to Neugebauer in Constantinople as soon as it became clear that the stay of the Swedes in Turkey would last some time. Eneman was to act as chaplain to the embassy, and one of the regimental chaplains, Sven Agrell, was sent as his assistant.

There were quite a number of Swedish subjects in Constantinople in 1709 quite apart from those sent by Charles from Bender to the embassy.† Men, women and children who had been taken by the Russians from the Baltic provinces and sold as slaves to the Turks were freed by the Sultan out of courtesy to Charles XII and out of gratitude for his having set Turkish

* Benzelius and his three sons all became in their turn archbishops of Uppsala.
† Among the embassy staff one may note the secretary Gustaf Celsing since two of his sons became envoys at Constantinople and 'Oriental' scholars.

prisoners at liberty in Lemberg in 1704. Most of these seem to have joined the Swedish community at Bender (for we find entries in the consistory protocols of the clergy concerning women who were Swedish subjects)[19] and Eneman was not burdened with pastoral duties. The King included him in the first expedition which he dispatched, consisting of the three draughtsmen of the Swedish drill-volume: Cornelius Loos, Conrad Sparre and Hans Gyllenskepp.* These officers set out from Bender on 11 January 1710, that, in the words of the Chancery diary, they might go 'to Jerusalem and Egypt to examine the rarities and monuments there and make drawings of them'. In Constantinople they were to pick up Eneman, but he – presumably because he needed more time for his preparatory studies – asked and was granted permission to defer his trip.

Loos's detailed journal of the first expedition was lost in the *Kalabalik*,† but a brief itinerary of the distances covered from 11 January 1710 till 28 June 1711 saw them safely back in Bender is entered in a beautifully clear script in the margins of the big map of 'Turkey and the Near Orient' which Loos drew to serve as a background for his report and which, in itself, is a contribution to the cartography of the area. A specification of the most important ruins and antiquities visited has also survived, as have many of the drawings made.[20] Charles XII enjoyed studying the collection brought back by the expedition so much that the drawings were kept in a chest in his own room. It was stolen during the *Kalabalik*, but a fair portion of them were bought back into the King's possession through the offices of F. E. von Fabrice, the Holstein representative at Bender. What disappeared is only too clear from the list which Loos set up in 1736 of the items he had handed over to Charles on his return: apart from the Journal itself there had been a collection of between five and six hundred antique medals, engraved stones, small 'heathen figures' of bronze, coral, stone or wood and other curiosities; drawings and plans of Constantinople, charts of the Dardanelles, drawings of the islands, especially of Rhodes, with castles, fortifications and antiquities; views of the towns of Egypt, Judaea, Samaria, Galilaea, Syria, Phrygia and Anatolia, with drawings of everything remarkable: aqueducts, colonnades, cloisters, mosques and pyramids (and particularly the great pyramid of Cheops),‡ mummies, the 'Superb and Magnificent temple of Baal', remnants considered to have been Troy, the ruins of Palmyra. Innumerable inscriptions had been copied. The biblical references had been carefully followed up to provide a pictorial companion to the Bible, but of these (listed by Loos) only a single one has survived. Of the many drawings of the Sophia mosque only one was missing in 1736, but since then several have disappeared.

* Captain Sparre, a nephew of Axel Sparre, had served in the French army after completing his studies at Uppsala; Gyllenskepp, a lieutenant in the Lifeguards, had also studied at Uppsala.

† For the *Kalabalik* see below, pp. 357 ff. The expedition travelled on a Turkish man-of-war from Constantinople on 31 March 1710 and reached Alexandria on 18 May; the journey back was overland.

‡ Sparre has left a detailed description of this pyramid which was printed in 1762 (*Nya Svenska Biblioteket*, I, pp. 311 ff.).

What was saved from the *Kalabalik* gives some indication of Charles XII's interests at that particular time: he was obviously studying the Constantinople views and the series of drawings dealing with the Sophia mosque and some influence from these sources has been inferred in his replanning for parts of Stockholm.[21] Three other chests containing the results of the Loos expedition are known to have been burnt since they were stored in the loft of the King's house and this was set alight by the Turks during the struggle. In these were stored 250 drawings, the collections of antiquities and of botanical specimens.* Some individual items were preserved because they had been presented by Charles to members of his court and were brought back to Sweden by them, such as the series of paintings and tableaux of Turkish costumes, male and female, and the 'especially beautiful and costly model of the Temple of St Helena in Jerusalem, which contains the grave of Christ and the mountain of Calvary.'† Others, which were the private property of the three members of the expedition, have also survived, and from the letters and papers of these three the scope of the whole collection has been reconstructed.

IV

It had been Charles XII's intention to have a selection of the drawings which the expedition brought back engraved on copper by Tessin and published as a companion work to the famous *Suecia Antiqua et Hodierna* of Erik Dahlberg. These magnificent drawings, celebrating Swedish towns and the palaces and gardens of the royal family and nobility, had been done in the reign of Charles XI, but it was due to the combined efforts of Charles XII and Tessin that they were now being prepared for publication.‡ With the projected companion-volume from 'the Orient', the King wanted to pay a pious tribute to his father's interest in the Holy Land, while at the same time demonstrating that the Swedes were not narrowly chauvinistic in their admiration of views and buildings. Even after the drawings of biblical places had been destroyed, the King persisted in the scheme. It was hoped that Loos, from his sketchbook, would be able to provide new drawings of at least some of the missing ones: these, with what had been saved, he expressed a determination as late as 1718 to publish 'as soon as possible'.[22]

Since he had publication in mind, Charles examined the drawings and tested their authenticity where possible. He had congratulated the members of the expedition on their return and promoted them in rank; but he was not unaware that as far as the collection of antiquities and curiosities brought back was concerned the more learned of his entourage accused the officers of occasional gullibility. Monks and Jews, Agrell noted in his diary, had spun the simple soldiers many a tale.[23] In at least one case the King's suspicions were aroused as to whether a drawing was based on personal observation.

* The fate of the collection of 'curious animals' brought back is not known.
† These were given to Baron von Düben, marshal of the court, who handed them over to Tessin.
‡ The first plates for the work were printed in 1717.

The Huguenot traveller A. de la Motraye, who was introduced to Charles i
1711 by Fabrice, hinted broadly that the ruins of Troy had been copied b
Loos when in Constantinople from drawings done by himself. The King, wh
knew from conversations with Sparre and Gyllenskepp, that his own exped
tion had only observed these ruins from a distance while on board shij
thought of a way to show Loos that he would have preferred to be informe
which drawings were originals and which were copies. He borrowed Motraye
manuscript with its illustrations and called Loos to him: 'Come, let me sho
you the same Trojan ruins that you yourself saw.' But he comforted the en
barrassed officer by stressing to him, as to Motraye, that the traveller po:
sessed, in some measure, the same privilege as the poet – to weave a web c
magic.[24] It is possible that when Loos completed his drawings in Bender h
used both his own sketches and those of other artists that he had been able t
copy while on his journeys; in the case of his large view of Palmyra it is know
that some Frenchmen had executed drawings to which he might have ha
access in Damascus before they were sent to be engraved in Paris. B
the range and quality of drawings from Loos's hand which still survive a
such that modern experts confess that publication of them in the eighteent
century would have given him an honoured place in the ranks of Europe
antiquarians.[25]

Two later expeditions financed by Charles took place in 1711 and 171
respectively.[26] Both had for their main purpose the promotion of Ne
Eastern studies in Swedish universities by giving promising scholars th
chance to travel and to purchase manuscripts. With Eneman who set out i
August 1711 went also a young notarius in the College of Commerce, Joha
Silfvercrantz, that he might estimate prospects for Swedish commerce in th
countries through which they travelled. It was only during the Nine Yea
War that Swedish and Danish ships began to penetrate into the Medite
ranean and caused some anxiety to Dutch shipping circles;[27] and Charles an
his advisers were keen to have first-hand reports on conditions in the Ne
East. The representative of the Dutch Republic at Constantinople, Jaco
Colyer, gave all possible help and introductions to Dutch consuls en route t
Eneman's as to Loos's expedition, probably unaware of the interest in com
mercial matters of Eneman's companion. Eneman and Silfvercrantz suffere
more from climatic conditions and the hardships of travel than had th
toughened officers of the first expedition. After the voyage to Alexandria
through Smyrna and the islands of the Ionian archipelago – the journey cor
tinued to Palestine and Syria, and here Silfvercrantz had to be left behin
mortally ill. He died in St Jean d'Acre in July 1712.

Eneman's return to Constantinople (which he reached in June 1713) wa
delayed by illness as well as by his scholarly studies. Even before his retur
Charles XII had made him professor at Uppsala, but he kept him at Bender fc
two months so that Eneman might spend an hour each day giving him infor
mation about what he had seen and what manuscripts he had obtaine

neman – who was the first Swede to visit Mount Sinai – had kept a detailed
diary during his nearly two years of travels,* and had also written a report on
the antiquities of Constantinople.† His career at Uppsala ended, however,
before it had properly begun: he died from 'pleuritis', contracted during the
expedition, a few days after his installation in October 1714. His letters to
Olof Rudbeck the younger, to whose daughter he was engaged, give much
information about his researches and about the interest which Charles XII
took in them.[28]

The third and last expedition was a solo one, undertaken by Henrik
Benzelius, a son of Charles's old teacher. This young man had chosen
'Alexandria' as the topic of his Uppsala thesis in 1709 and made his way to
Bender in 1713 to get closer to 'the Orient' in which he was so passionately
interested. He arrived at the royal headquarters shortly before the *Kalabalik*,
when the King's fortunes were at a low ebb; but in January 1714 he was given
a royal bursary to study in Constantinople and to travel in the Near East.
He journeyed, often on foot, in Egypt and Palestine and his command of
Arabic and Hebrew was so impressive that his name was long remembered
as one who had no compare among foreign scholars. In the summer of
1716 he returned to Europe and continued his studies at various universities, again with financial support from Charles XII. In November 1718 news
of the King's death reached him on his way from Gothenburg to the
headquarters at Frederikshald where he was meant to give a report of
his work. As professor at Lund he began to work through the material of
all three expeditions in the hope that some of it might be published, but all
that was done in his lifetime was the printing of part of Eneman's diary in
1740.[29]

V

Apart from talk with the draughtsmen and scholars who returned from the
first two expeditions, Charles XII during his years in Turkey enjoyed conversations with those who came as travellers or on diplomatic business to his
headquarters. One of these was Friedrich Ernst von Fabrice, the Hanoverian
in Holstein service, who arrived in Bender as early as the end of June 1710.
He had fresh news from Stockholm – a town he noted in his memoirs to be
one of the most beautiful in the world' because of its position, 'not inferior to
that of Constantinople', and its many palaces[30] – where he had been sent by
Stanislaus and Krassow in 1709 to report on the situation in Poland. Charles
remembered him from the Altranstädt period and enjoyed in Turkey as in
Saxony the fund of stories of the much-travelled diplomat, often of a gallant
kind or involving the methods used in diplomacy by people known to both of

* This diary, in two volumes, was published in full in 1889 on the occasion of a Stockholm
scholarly congress.
† This was printed in 1768.

them.* He was also one of the partners with whom the King played chess fo relaxation. Charles never reverted to the card playing and gambling he had foresworn as a very young man but he enjoyed a game of chess which h played only for a short while and left to be continued till the next half-hour h could spare. The passion with which Fabrice and Grothusen played chess both hating to be the loser and refusing to speak to each other for days after a match, astounded him: it was only a game.†

From Fabrice's memoirs and the diaries of Swedes at Bender it is clear that the King often had to smooth out quarrels between men who were quick to take offence, cooped up far from home with too little to do. Fabrice, as a strong partisan of the Holstein interest, was particularly prone to be involved in bitter disputes which sometimes degenerated into fights. He tells how Charles once separated himself and Major-General Daldorff and demanded an explanation for the fight. The officer was forced to apologize to the diplo mat, but the King told Fabrice that he must not be too hard on the brave ma who had not yet recovered from a terrible war wound: a Cossack had spli open his stomach so that his entrails ran out.[32] Charles's attempts to explai the reason for the behaviour of those who were with him in Turkey – an Fabrice's story is only one of many which bear in the same direction – show greater understanding of human motives than in the busier campaignin years. He had more time to ponder over men and life in general. The study o literature[33] also helped to raise questions of behaviour. He enjoyed readin (or being read) French plays and especially those of Molière, Racine an Corneille. He disliked Boileau's treatment of Alexander but enjoyed discuss ing the motives and actions of the characters in the plays read.‡

His interest in cameralism and in writings on economic matters in genera was stimulated, even beyond the task in hand, by his conversations wit Casten Feif, one of the Chancery officials who had escaped capture at Poltav and who was now put in charge of what might be termed domestic Swedis affairs (as opposed to those of diplomatic relations which were handled b von Müllern). Through Feif's correspondence with Horn and Tessin i Stockholm we get a good insight into Charles's development in respect c 'politics' and can discern that his interest in 'reform' was intellectually base as well as practically motivated. In foreign affairs the element of secrec involved prevented a completely open discussion, except with Ulrika Eleonor when he could send a letter by absolutely 'secure hand'. He learnt a good dea

* A typical example, involving both themes, is one recounted by Fabrice in his memoirs: whe he told Charles of the way in which Lord Raby was able to procure important news for Quee Anne through his affair with the Prussian King's mistress, the Countess of Wartenberg, Charl retorted that he now realized why Fabrice was paying court to the Finnish housekeeper of h Chancellor, Baron Grothusen.[31]

† Both Ture Bielke and Fabrice in their memoirs comment on Charles's habit of attackin with the king when playing chess.

‡ Such interest was not confined to literature and history; one of his first questions to Jeffery in 1711 was to have the differences between the Whig and Tory parties explained: see Jefferyes letter of 18 May 1711 in *H.H.* 16: 2.

rom the diplomatic work of Poniatowski at the Porte which he himself had
o supervise without the benefit of memoranda from Hermelin and Ceder-
ielm; and became absorbed and fascinated by the larger views as well as by
he day-to-day handling of problems. The political situation – which entailed
moving closer to France and away from the Maritime Powers – was one which
he accepted only with reluctance and he therefore tended to avoid personal
ncounters with the representatives of these powers in Turkey. One exception
was Jefferyes – taken prisoner at Poltava but eventually released by the
Russians – since Queen Anne sent him to Bender on a special mission to
Charles XII.[34] The Swedish King could therefore not avoid him, but a
barrier was erected between them because of the diametrically opposed views
f Charles and the British statesmen in power as to the desirability of
neutralizing the Empire for as long as the Northern War lasted.*

A somewhat limited contact can in any case be observed between Charles
nd most of his officers and officials, due to the fact that each class tended to
ave a specific range of interests and duties only in common with the King.
He swopped stories mainly with the officers, relatively unemployed as many
f them were, during and after rides taken for exercise; he discussed admini-
trative work and reform with the officials. He tended to leave both categories
lone in their off-duty hours if they arranged entertainments for themselves:
e gather from memoirs and diaries that he had a habit of looking in from
he outside when some of his suite went for a second and richer supper, after
hey had shared his, concocted by Fabrice's famous cook or Grothusen's
adequate one.[35] He was not a frequent guest at the parties arranged and did
ot, for example, participate in the big feast, somewhat mockingly but
splendidly arranged by Fabrice, for Axel Sparre's sixtieth birthday.[36] Jests
ften served to hide his innermost thoughts.

But at least once, late in his Turkey period, he found a visitor to whom he
ould speak freely. This was Axel von Löwen, who stayed at Bender for at
ast a month in May–June 1712, having arrived to discuss the situation of the
wedish army in North Germany. Löwen was an officer whom Charles had
ermitted to take service[37] with the armies of the Allies in the War of the
panish Succession and who had fought at Oudenaarde and Malplaquet: they
ad therefore a joint interest in the art of war, in the genius of commanders
nd in the fate of nations at war. The fact that Löwen was visiting Bender on a
latively short mission also made it easier to talk openly to him than to those
ho were with the King every day. In any case, possibly responding on a
ersonal level to something he respected in the other man,† in their conversa-
ons Charles reviewed his own past actions and policies in a markedly objec-
ve manner against the background of the whole stage of European politics of
s age. But before Löwen reached Turkey much had happened to encourage
harles to analyse himself and his position.

* See below, pp. 328 ff.
† It may be worth mentioning that Löwen and Rehnskiöld, like Charles, had been orphaned
an early age.

2

War in Dependence on the Porte

The Swedes found the countryside surrounding the fortified town of Bend᷉
very pleasant. Already during the march from Ochakov they had commente
on the fruitfulness of the Sultan's dominions. The contrast with the desert ⟨
the steppe made it seem near miraculous: the plenitude of fruit-trees, tl
ubiquity of exotic products, the lushness of it all, are recurring themes
diaries, letters and in memoirs.[1] They were charmed by ceremonies in the
honour: the magnificent escort of Yusuf Pasha, the reception once they we
across the Dniester and were 'saluted by above 100 canon from the City, and tl
great Turkish field music', welcomed 'by all the Turkish Quality of the Por
then at Bender, and provided with an 'abundance of fine Tents'.[2] The town itsel
on its imposing 'Eminence', they found 'very nasty' with streets 'narrow ar
irregular', though it was to improve greatly during their stay in Turkey. Wi
important visitors, with diplomats and merchants and travellers coming ar
going, 'fine houses and buildings were erected and the fortifications mended ⟨
round the City' – even pavements were constructed from 'square boards fastne
together by wooden pins'. At least ten new mosques were built, 'one of whi⟨
is extraordinarily beautiful and large, and stands in the middle of the City'

The population was a mixed one; there were Greeks and Armenians
some suburbs who had churches in common; there were Jews with their syn
gogue; there were Lipkani Tartars and Multuans who shared the northe᷉
suburbs though the former were followers of Islam and the latter 'pretend᷉
to be Christians'. The cleanliness of the Turks impressed them[3] as did the fa᷉
that they were 'obliged to go every day to their devotions'[4] – a contrast wi᷉
the Swedish custom of Saturday bath and Sunday church. The climate w᷉
acceptable, even if sometimes too hot in the summer; and in the winter snc
fell and reminded them of home.*

The heat of August 1709 was used by Charles XII as an excuse to move o᷉
of Bender as soon as he heard from Meijerfelt of the surrender at Perevolotjr
He pitched his camp opposite the town, across the Dniester, 'on that side
the River which is towards Germany'. The choice of site was not fortuitous.
was believed to be influenced by easy access for provisions – the Turks w᷉

* Fabrice tells us of sledges being constructed by the Swedes for use in winter, *Memoir*
p. 48.

pplied the Swedes no longer needed to ferry their wares over the Dniester –
d by the 'very pleasant prospect of Mulberry and other trees, which grew
und about it'.[5] But greater freedom of action for Charles and his troops was
stronger attraction. Reunion in Poland with the Swedish army which had
rvived Poltava was now out of the question and contact with Krassow and
anislaus was imperative.

With the move out of Bender, Charles XII parted physical company with
azepa. The hetman was ill and bedridden and was quartered in a house in
e town so that he might be nursed properly. But cooperation and trust
mained. Charles XII indignantly refused the Tsar's offer – conveyed through
eijerfelt – to free Piper in return for Mazepa being delivered to 'his justice';[6]
d Mazepa put his Cossacks (who made their own camp at Varnitza, about a
arter of an hour's march from that of the Swedes) at Charles's command
r the exploratory military ventures in Poland which he knew the King had
mind. Collaboration between the Swedes and the Cossacks continued even
ter Mazepa's death on 22 September, under the new hetman Orlyk, though
lations were to some extent strained by Charles XII supporting Mazepa's
ir, his nephew Voynarovsky, in his race with the Cossack leaders for the
asures left by his uncle.

On his death-bed Mazepa had tried to satisfy his nephew – who himself had
wish to be hetman – by allocating as his share of the inheritance the money
e Swedes owed Mazepa, and leaving the riches he carried with him (bar
me valuables handed to the nephew) to the hetman who would be elected
s successor. The distinction between private and public hetman Cossack
operty was a difficult one to draw and customarily both had passed to the
w hetman. But Voynarovsky regarded all the gold and precious stones
rried to Turkey by his uncle as his own rightful inheritance and Charles XII
rmitted him to lay hands on the whole fortune before a new hetman had
en elected.[7] The hope that Voynarovsky should prove a liberal lender may
ve influenced this decision; but it may equally well have been caused by the
eak which had taken place between Mazepa and the other Cossack leaders
ortly after the arrival in Bender. These, the members of the *generalstarsjyn*,
d moved to Jassy, separating themselves from Mazepa and Hordienko and
e rank and file of Cossacks and Zaporozhians. It is possible that news of the
edish surrender at Perevolotjna occasioned this move: the power of the
ar now seemed so great that it would be politic not to remain closely identi-
d with Charles XII. It is certain that they disagreed with Mazepa's policy
the last months of the hetman's life: he accused them, in Hordienko's
esence, of defeatism and of plans to make their peace with the Tsar through
e offices of the Hospodar of Moldavia.[8] In these circumstances it is under-
ndable that the Swedish King – whether he fully grasped the distinction
ween the private and public share of Mazepa's fortune or not* – should

Kentrschynskyj, *Mazepa*, pp. 249 and pp. 466–7, regards Charles as guilty of breaking the
st Mazepa had placed in him. This may be so, but the source-material quoted does not support
n a verdict.

be reluctant to entrust the riches stored in the hetman's bedroom for sa
keeping to men of whose intentions Mazepa had been strongly suspicious.

At the time of Mazepa's funeral on 25 September – undertaken with
much pomp and circumstance as conditions permitted[9] – Charles had begr
to hobble along on crutches, and to ride with a support for his leg.[10] Lor
before that time he had sent out an expedition of some hundred Swedes and
large Cossack force under the command of Gyllenkrook to test whether
would be possible to cross from Moldavia into Poland and to make conta
with Krassow and Stanislaus: indeed, as Nilsson has shown, an advance-par
for himself and his entourage as soon as he was fit enough to travel lor
distances.[11] The peace-terms which Meijerfelt brought from the Tsar we
totally unacceptable and it was necessary to think of means to resto
Sweden's fortunes enough to make Peter change his tune. For, flushed wi
the victory of Poltava and the capture of experienced soldiers and office
at Perevolotjna, Peter demanded the fulfilment not only of his own objectiv
but also those of his former allies. Travendal and Altranstädt were to
rescinded: if Charles wanted peace he must hand Scania, Halland and Blekin
to the King of Denmark and must recognize the Elector of Saxony as King
Poland once more though he need not hand over Swedish territory to Augu
tus. The booty Augustus had planned to obtain for his own part in the an
Swedish coalition was, in the terms which Tsar Peter handed Count Piper –
be sent with Meijerfelt to the King – transferred to Russia's share; the whe
of Swedish Livonia was to be signed away to the Tsar as well as Eston
Ingria and Karelia. A further and final demand was that the Kexholm *I*
(district) of Finland must also be sacrificed: Peter's 'window on the west' mu
be safeguarded against being shattered by the Swedes in future.[12]

Poltava had made a profound impression on Europe. The Tsar's 'comple
victory', the 'entire defeat' of Charles,[13] was well publicized in official a
private letters sent to the capitals of the whole continent.[14] Descriptions
how the Muscovites had celebrated their victory '3 dayes after another' wh
still at Poltava[15] and of the magnificent December procession in Moscow
which the Tsar had signalized the changed state of affairs circulated: Swed
officers and officials in ascending rank, Rehnskiöld and Piper at the er
being marched through the streets of the Russian capital made explicit t
turn of the wheel of fortune.[16] Discussion of faults of omission or commissi
was rife, both among the captured Swedes of any influence,* and amo
observers, more or less well informed. Presumption and consequent puni
ment was a main theme in these discussions,[17] and even in sermons preach
at Bender,† while Europe outside Bender and Russia speculated whetl
Charles was dead or alive.[18]

But Tsar Peter did more than celebrate and publicize. A council of war v

---

* Jefferyes is a good source for this, see Hatton, *Jefferyes*, pp. 82–3; so is Whitworth, the Eng
diplomat in Moscow, see S.P. 91, vol. 6, letter to Boyle of 8/19 September 1709.
† E.g. in Eneman's sermon of 6 August 1709.

:ld between 14 and 16 July near Poltava. As a result large detachments of
e army were sent to put the Swedish Baltic provinces – and especially
ivonia – into the Russian fold, while others marched into Poland. Negotia-
ons, conducted mainly by the Tsar himself, in Lublin and Thorn, with
axons and Danes, utilized the strong Russian position to achieve a resurrec-
on of the anti-Swedish coalition of 1700 on terms more acceptable to the
sar. The promise, in a secret article only, of the treaty with Augustus of
'20 October that Livonia should be ceded to the Elector once Russia had
onquered it, was hedged about with conditions;[19] and the treaty with
rederick IV of 11/22 October put no limitation on Russian prospective gains
nce it stipulated that each partner should keep what he conquered.[20] Only in
egotiations with the King of Prussia at Marienwerder did the Tsar draw a
ank: Frederick I was not ready to enter the coalition on terms as bleak as
lose offered.[21]

In Turkey Tsar Peter worked at first to obtain the delivery of Mazepa, and
le containment of Charles* so that he should not escape to Poland before the
ordon of Russo-Saxon troops was drawn tight enough to catch him. The
lreat that the armistice of 1700 might be denounced by Russia was freely
sed, since that truce stipulated that neither should harbour rebels against
le other.[22] The Turks made use of arguments, fed them by Neugebauer,
oniatowski and the French diplomat Ferriol, that Mazepa was no longer a
ussian subject but a Swedish one;[23] and in January 1710 Tsar Peter relin-
lished the pressure and agreed to renew the armistice of 1700. By this time
Iazepa was long since dead and Charles had been taught a lesson when the
orps he sent towards Poland under Gyllenkrook had, on 24 September, been
iptured on Moldavian soil (at Czernowitz), having been betrayed by the
ospodar who permitted Russian troops to enter Turkish territory.† Any
tempt of Charles and the rest of Cossack–Swedish forces to make a direct
ıd immediate breakthrough into Poland became hopeless as Saxon and
ussian troops secured control of the major part of the Commonwealth. In
ırly October Krassow – who had hoped to make his way to the King in
ender – marched through Brandenburg territory to Swedish Pomerania to
roid capture[24] and King Stanislaus followed as a refugee from Poland.[25]
nly a part of the Polish Crown army under Potocki eventually reached
ender after having escaped through Hungary.[26]

The problem that faced Charles XII was therefore: which way could he take,
ith reasonable safety, to reach his Swedish territories? Poland was out of the
lestion. The route over Moldavia and Hungary had risks of its own: prob-
ole treachery of the Hospodar, and possible commitment to Rákóczi if they
ot safely through Moldavia.‡ And even if he and his men could pass freely

---

* His delivery, though asked for, could hardly be expected in view of Islamic laws of asylum.
† The Hospodar was later deposed and imprisoned for having permitted the Russian violation
the border.
‡ That this was not a groundless fear is shown by the fact that Potocki's forces were forced to
ght Habsburg troops on Rákóczi's behalf before they could continue their journey.

through Hungary in the political sense, the plague which started in easte
Europe in 1709 (and spread also to the Baltic provinces and from there,
1710, to Sweden itself) closed the frontier between Hungary on the one ha
and Austria and the Empire on the other between the autumn of 1709 a
the summer of 1714.[27] A ship to take him and those officers and officials
particularly wanted to accompany him was offered repeatedly by the King
France and by each of the Maritime Powers.[28] Security could not be guara
teed as the War of the Spanish Succession was still raging and the privatee
of one belligerent might capture the ship put at his disposal, whichever side
entrusted himself to, before it reached a Swedish port. The choice between t
belligerents implied in these offers was naturally repugnant to him: he wou
lose what freedom of action on the European scale remained, and Sweder
balancing policy would be at an end. In any case his departure by sea wou
mean leaving most of his men and his allies in the lurch. Even the suggestio
of a Swedish ship which was to come to Constantinople to fetch him, p
forward by Stockholm councillors in 1711, was not acceptable. The King
answer, 'I have decided not to trust myself to the sea',[29] has put some h
torians in mind of his seasickness when he crossed the Baltic in the autun
of 1700. The fact that Denmark–Norway was at war with Sweden probab
had more to do with the refusal: his ship would run the gauntlet of enen
privateers and warships, particularly in the Skagerak.

His efforts to get home therefore came to centre on two possibilities: on t
hope of a strong Turkish and/or Tartar escort before Tsar Peter and August
had established complete control of Poland and – once too much time h
elapsed to make this more than a forlorn hope – on the plan for a stro
Swedish force to battle its way through Poland towards Bender so that
should be put in a position of independence once more. Both hopes we
affected by the prospect of bringing the Tartar Khan and the Sultan as alli
into a war against Tsar Peter; and Swedish diplomacy directed from Char
XII's headquarters was, between 1709 and 1713, actively engaged in supporti
those at the Porte who favoured war with Russia so that Turkey might rega
Azov.[30] Its greatest success came in November 1710 when Ahmed III declar
war on Tsar Peter. From this war, and from Russian non-fulfilment of t
terms of the Peace of Prut of July 1711, followed renewed hostilities and thr
further declarations of war: in December 1711,* in October 1712, in Ap
1713.† But the success proved a very limited one. Turkey never entered into
formal alliance with Sweden and Charles could not influence either the ca
paigns or the peace-makings. The main reason for this is to be found in t
vicissitudes of the Swedish expeditionary force he expected, and in the sp
which developed between himself and his Council in Stockholm as to t
policy which would most benefit Sweden. Their differing attitudes led, for

* This war was ended by the Peace of Constantinople of April 1712.
† There was no formal peace-making between the last two declarations of war; hostilities w
concluded by the Peace of Adrianople of June 1713.

:riod, to two separate Swedish foreign policies and weakened the King's
ɔsition at least as much as the slowness in fitting out the expeditionary force,
s naval escort and supply ships.

III

was not easy for Charles XII to look at Sweden's situation with the eyes of
ιe men left in charge in Stockholm.[31] King Frederick of Denmark and
ugustus of Saxony had renewed their alliance and decided to attack Sweden
ιce more even before their formal treaties with the Tsar. Indeed, they hoped
/ quick action to render themselves more independent of Tsar Peter whose
owing power was creating fear as well as respect. They realized that, while
ιe War of the Spanish Succession lasted, they would have to leave Sweden's
·erman possessions undisturbed; but promises were made to Frederick I of
russia of future compensation in Swedish Pomerania which secured his
ɔmmitment to refuse Swedish troops any march through his territories as
·ng as Denmark and Saxony were at war with Charles XII.[32] And Frederick I,
ith an eye to these prospective gains, was active in promoting the negotia-
ɔns with the Maritime Powers which led to the Hague conventions of 1710*
·r the Neutrality of the Empire.[33] Such a neutrality was highly desirable for
ιe Allies who fought Louis XIV in the field and at the conference table
:tween 1709 and 1713: how could the French be brought to reason if there
as hope of the Empire being set ablaze? how could the German princes be
;pected to keep their troops in the pay of the Allies if a free-for-all developed
·r the partitioning of Sweden's provinces in Germany?
It was with the 'protection of Charles XII's German possessions' that the
nglish and the Dutch salved their public consciences. They pressed this point
. Stockholm, and they sent Jefferyes to Bender to obtain the King's signature
· the Act of Neutrality. Less was said of the fact that the neutrality com-
·ised also Poland, Sleswig, Holstein and the whole of Jutland. That the
[aritime Powers were not taken in by their own propaganda is amply clear
ɔm contemporary official correspondence: the policy was forced upon them
/ their own need and made easier, for some of the statesmen involved at
ast, by a growing resentment at an ally who would not realize that he was
:aten. Bolingbroke, with Poltava in mind, preached untiringly that after
ιch a defeat Charles XII must begin to think of sacrifices of territory rather
.an of keeping on with the war.[34]
But, realizing that the Act of Neutrality had for its purpose the denial to
harles XII of his German base – the only territory where the Swedish
.peditionary force could land before undertaking its march to Poland – his
fusal to sign came as no surprise to London and The Hague. Indeed, the

* The first convention, signed at The Hague on 31 March (N.S.) 1710 by the Emperor, the
aritime Powers, Hanover, Denmark, Saxony, Prussia and Russia, was arranged during the
et of Regensburg in January 1710; the second convention, stipulating a corps of twenty-one
ɔusand men, was signed in December 1710.

statesmen of the Maritime Powers showed a marked reluctance to furnis
their share of the corps stipulated if the Empire's neutrality were violated, nc
only because they found it hard to spare the troops but also because the
realized the use which Frederick of Denmark and Augustus of Saxony wante
to make of it: the corps was intended to guard Denmark from a rear attack b
Swedish troops and leave that country free to concentrate on a reconquest c
all the peninsular territories the Twin-Kingdoms had lost to Sweden in th
seventeenth century: Scania, Halland, Blekinge, Bohuslän, Jämtland an
Härjedal.

This attack, mounted in November 1709 simultaneously from Denmar
and Norway, had at first a fair amount of success, but the loyalty of th
Scanians to Sweden* and the great victory of Magnus Stenbock at Hälsin;
borg on 28 February 1710 forced the Danish King to withdraw (saving abo\
half the army employed in the campaign) to his own side of the Sound. .
renewed descent was much urged by Augustus in 1710, he himself bein
willing to add Saxon troops to those put at Frederick's disposal by the Tsa;
and it was for this reason that Dano-Saxon clamour for the neutrality cor
increased throughout the summer of that year.[35] The discomfiture c
Frederick IV was not entirely unwelcome to the Maritime Powers. He ha
broken the Peace of Travendal, of which they were guarantors, and they ha
not lifted a finger to stop him. Active help by a 'neutrality corps' to restor
Frederick IV to complete control over the Sound was, however, not in th
interest of either of the Maritime Powers. It was hoped that his having bee
thrown out of Scania in 1709 might make a general restoration of the peace i
the North easier, and there was no grief in Whitehall when the plan for
combined Dano-Saxon–Russian descent on Scania had to be given up i
October 1710.

Tension was developing at this time between the two Maritime Powers. Th
new ministry in Whitehall was determined to gain the upper hand in th
arrangement of peace terms with Louis XIV, and the great energy and ruthle;
independence typical of English statesmen between 1710 and 1713 in the
relationship to the Dutch[36] is noticeable also in the intensive peace campaig
which they mounted in Stockholm in 1710. They were to some extent su;
ported by the diplomats of the States General, but the initiative came fro;
London and English statesmen were fully aware that they, with the objecti\
of restoring peace in the north as well as the south, were driving a wed;
between Charles XII and his Council. It was the Swedish Council, howeve
that had unwittingly placed the instrument which they could use into th
hands of the English when in June 1710 it sent Robert Jackson, the residei
diplomat of Queen Anne, to London to ask for help from the Maritin
Powers according to the guarantee of Travendal: they painted the plight c

* This was in contrast to the happenings of the Scanian War (1675–8) of Charles XI's reign, a;
indicates the degree of real incorporation with Sweden which had taken place. Fear of revo
however, occasioned Swedish preferential treatment in regard to taxation, etc., in 1709 and 17
in the threatened areas.

1eir country in such sombre colours that their arguments were turned gainst themselves.* If Sweden, Whitehall argued, would be ruined if England id not come to their help, the time had come not to throw good money after ad: peace must be made with or without Charles xII's consent.[37]

The difficulties of the Council were considerable, and when added together roduced a defeatism in some of its members which paralysed its work as a ody. They started out well, recreating with energy and initiative the regiments rdered by the King from Ochakov to replace those lost at Poltava.† But these ·oops – together with the seventeen thousand soldiers stationed in Sweden 1roughout the war for its own defence – had to be used against the Danish >rces in Scania. And though Frederick IV's army was thrown back across the ound, a large part of it remained in being‡ and new attacks would probably ave to be met, both from Denmark and from the Norwegian frontier. Such rospects inhibited the Council from sending the army to Germany as Charles II demanded.

The concern for defence in the east was also beginning to stir the hearts of 1ose who carried the responsibility in Stockholm. Tsar Peter had occupied 'ourland in October 1709 and prepared a siege of Riga for the spring of 1710. ' Riga and the remaining fortified places (Dünamünde, Pernau and Reval) 1ould fall to the Russians, could not the Council expect that the Tsar – lready in command of Ingria – would bring his attack closer to the heart of weden–Finland? That he aimed at the incorporation of all the Baltic rovinces was not openly said in the manifestoes which he spread among the ierman-speaking burghers of Riga and Reval, though they were promised 1e restoration of privileges lost when Swedish absolutism had been intro-uced.[38] Their future as the treasured link between the Tsar's older posses-·ons and the west could not yet be expressed in view of the delicate state of .usso-Saxon–Polish relations, but there was no doubt that the Tsar wanted to ·ess Sweden hard and Finland would, it was surmised, soon feel the force of is offensive.

Hot on the heels of these fears for the safety of the homeland itself came orries about shortages of money and supplies. The harvests of 1708 and 1709 1d been bad ones. Bureaucratic demarcation lines and personal rivalries ·eated obstacles in channelling what was available to the spot where the

* An earlier instance of the Council's appeals being turned against it can be made out for the eutrality conventions, since the Council – immediately after they had heard of Poltava – asked e Elector of Hanover and the Maritime Powers to work with the Emperor and the Empire for a 1arantee of 'security' for Pomerania, Wismar, Bremen and Verden.

† This was achieved by the doubling-up procedure laid down in the regulations of Charles XI's ign, see above, p. 114.

‡ It has been surmised (e.g. Haintz, II, p. 84) that Charles XII refused Stenbock the field-arshal title which the Council proposed as a reward for the victory at Hälsinborg because he ·nsidered that a more skilful use of the opportunities would have produced greater Danish losses; it seems more likely that Charles, well aware of the impossibility of laying down rules for 1at ought to be achieved by a battle, did so because of his general dislike of being dictated to by e Council in matters of army promotion; cp. below, p. 338.

King wanted its concentration: the naval escorts, the transports and supp
ships for the expeditionary force.[39] Finally, the plague which reached Stoc
holm in June 1710 and spread from there to central and southern Swede
carried by rats in a ship which came from the Baltic provinces, caused disloc
tion in the government machinery and had a lowering effect on morale by t
misery and grief it brought.[40]

Charles realized that Poltava and Perevolotjna combined would tempt h
Danish cousin to reopen the war and gave the Council permission (before h
knew that hostilities had commenced) to negotiate with Frederick IV in t
hope of avoiding a break. After the victory of Hälsingborg he twice en
powered it to make a separate peace with Denmark.* He also encourage
negotiations between Mauritz Vellingk, the governor of Wismar (till Octob
1710 and then of Bremen and Verden), and the Danes for the same purpos
these persisted till 1712 and were assisted by the Duke-Administrator
Holstein-Gottorp and his shrewd and diplomatically gifted minister Geo
Heinrich von Görtz.[41] It is not likely that Charles expected any of the
negotiations to succeed since he insisted that the foundation for the separa
peace must be the Peace of Travendal: King Frederick could hardly be su
posed to relinquish the chance of improving upon that peace without a pr
longed fight.† The King's main purpose must have been to weaken t
anti-Swedish coalition in the west while time was gained to get the expeditio
ary corps to Swedish Pomerania. His purpose is clearly seen in March 171
when he let the Danes know of peace overtures he had received fro
Augustus through a French diplomat in Constantinople.[42]

The fact that the Council accepted the neutrality convention‡ and open
negotiations on the transfer of the Swedish army in Pomerania to the Mar
time Powers opened a split between King and Council which could not eas
be healed. Charles did not believe that his councillors acted from ill intentior
but the public display of a divided approach to Sweden's problems was in h
opinion harmful to the country's prestige,[43] a counterpart on the civil side
government, one may surmise, to Perevolotjna. On 4 December 1710 h
forbade the Council to proceed any further in respect of the neutrality co
vention.[44] Through Swedish diplomats in the capitals of the Allies he let it b
known that he had no intention of disturbing the peace of the Empire: h
would give his word not to attack Saxony or any other German territory, b
he would not and could not sign a convention which by interning his Pom
ranian army and robbing him of the use of his bridgehead to the Contine
made nonsense of his own policy.

---

* These powers of 26 April 1710 and 10 January 1711, are printed in *Historiska Handlingar*,
pp. 41 ff, and VII, pp. 32 ff.

† Indeed, by March 1711, the Maritime Powers were told that Frederick insisted on all t
territories mentioned in his treaty with Augustus as well as on the island of Gotland.

‡ The acceptance was, however, subject to the King's final approval and conditions were la
down – e.g. the immobilization of the Danish army, to make Sweden more secure. The reservatio
were not publicized by the signatories of the convention, while the acceptance was – hence t
damage to Charles's prestige.

IV

᾿ this time Charles's hand was freer in relation to his Council, the Allies
d the anti-Swedish coalition because of a Turkish declaration of war on
ar Peter of 21 November 1710. Allied diplomacy had done what it could to
event the break, Austria had even threatened to become Russia's ally.[45]
ench diplomacy at Constantinople – gaining on that of the Maritime
▸wers – had fanned the embers which Poniatowski and the Tartar Khan had
,* Now was the time for Ahmed III, while Austria was still engaged in war
th Louis XIV, to retake Azov; once the Emperor had peace in the west,
ɔ chance might be lost forever, and worse, Turkey might then risk a two-
ɔnt war, Austria taking up the attack which had been but temporarily
andoned in 1699 to permit Leopold to claim the Spanish succession for his
ɔuse, Russia denouncing the armistice of 1700 (which had been renewed,
t not converted into a peace) and continuing her expansion from the base
Azov.[46]
The news of the victory at Hälsingborg increased respect for Sweden's
litary power in Constantinople. If the expeditionary corps arrived in time,
ʌarles had high hopes that at least part of the Turkish war effort in the
ɔming campaign would be directed against Russian troops in Poland and
ʌs facilitate his own junction with his Pomeranian army and the new corps.
: had in December 1709 replaced Krassow with Nils Gyllenstierna in
ʌom he had greater faith;† and on 2 July 1710 he reminded the Council of
: urgent need to dispatch the expeditionary corps. The combined armies
re to be under the command of Gyllenstierna and King Stanislaus till they
ned him.
The Turkish and Tartar campaign in which Charles now had some prospect
taking part was discussed in Bender when Devlet-Gerei visited the Swedish
ng in December 1710. The Tartar army was to open the campaign in
1uary 1711 in preparation for the main Turkish attack of the summer of
ɪ 1 : the Khan's thrust would be against southern Russia and attempts would
made to bring Polish Ukraine into the fight. Several Swedish officers were
ached to the Tartar army, among them Lieutenant-Colonel Lagerberg
ose main task, according to the written instructions which Charles XII gave
n on 20 December, was to work for an alliance between Sweden and the
ʌanate. Potocki's Poles and Orlyk's Cossacks cooperated in the Tartar raids
ich began according to plan. We have details of them from Lagerberg's
.ry which has survived.[47] The whole area between the middle Dnieper and

In the forlorn hope that the war might reactivate Hungarian struggles against Joseph 1: on
▌ay (N.S.) 1711, peace was made between the Habsburgs and the Hungarian Estates and
.óczi, in exile, was informed of the fact.
Gyllenstierna, governor of Bremen and Verden, was in October 1710 made president of the
▌ege of War in Stockholm; Dücker was then put in charge of the Pomeranian army; cp. below,
39.

the upper Don and Donez was laid waste, making it impossible for the Tsar
use these districts in the struggle to come. But though Poland was seethi
under Russian pressure and it was confidently predicted that many wou
join the Swedes if they marched in from Pomerania, few risked cooperati
with Potocki (backed as he was by the plundering and burning Tartars a
Zaporozhians)* and no general revolt against Augustus and the Tsar bro
out.

The opening stages of the winter campaign of 1710–11 brought, howev
some relief of the pressure on Sweden in the North. Russian troops we
drawn to the south to meet the new challenge with the help of the Moldavi
hospodar Demetrius Cantemir who was in secret understanding with the Tsa
Peter's diplomatic preparations, apart from those which envisaged a gene
Christian revolt against Islam fanning out from Moldavia,† included
mission to Venice to gain that republic's participation in the war. The Ve
tian state, which had gained the Morea in the War of the Holy League, w
not anxious to risk losing this important area and remained neutral.

Towards the end of March 1711 the various contingents of the Sulta
army began their march to the Danube to meet the Russians. The major p
of the Khan's forces were also dispatched to the Danube rendezvous, bu
detachment of Tartar troops, supported by the Turkish fleet, was to strike
Azov and Taganrog.[48]

Charles XII had two representatives with the main army. Lagerberg was s
in attendance on the Khan and Poniatowski was accredited to the Gra
Vizier, Baltadji Mehemet, who had supreme command of Ahmed's forc
Historians of the Prut campaign are of the opinion that the plan for it v
largely made up by Charles XII.[49] They base this on a letter which the Ki
sent to Funck, his representative in Constantinople, on 27 July 1710, o
lining what was going to happen in 1711.[50] I am inclined to believe that t
letter represents less a cut-and-dried plan presented to the Khan and t
Sultan than a blue-print for the way the King hoped the campaign wo
develop. The Moldavian venture – which it is quite likely that Char
strongly recommended but which must also have been on the Turkish agen
to make sure of the loyalty of a difficult border region – would draw Russi
troops away from Poland and thus facilitate the entry of the Swedish expe
tionary corps; the forces that moved towards Azov and Taganrog could, o
these fortresses had been taken, push towards the Donez and the Don and
far into southern Russia as possible, tying down troops so that the advance
Stanislaus to join with Charles would be made easier. Possibly revolt agai
the Tsar would follow in Russia.

Such hopes were, however, all built on the timely arrival of the Swed
army; and Charles must have been aware of his lack of influence on Turk

* Lagerberg recounts that sixty thousand Tartars and two thousand Zaporozhians took par
the raids, but no check on these figures is available.

† A Russian diplomat was sent to Rome to ask the Pope's blessing for this crusade: see Ha
II, p. 103, based on Venetian and Vatican archive-material.

•lanning till he commanded an army once more. From the concentration of ˈurkish forces in the west it was clear that the Sultan was concerned to pre-ᵉnt Moldavia and Wallachia from making common cause with the Tsar and ᴏ dissuade the Austrians from military action. Forces allocated for the Azov ᵉnture were small. No army had been detailed for a push towards Kiev, and ᴛere was no guarantee that the Turks would ever move into Poland to drive a ᵥedge between that country and Russia. No treaty had been achieved for ᴄharles either with the Khan or the Sultan, though he had tried to obtain ᵣm agreements with both.

This does not dim the brilliance of the opportunity which existed for ᴄharles XII in 1711 if his own forces arrived soon enough to take advantage of ᴛe situation: then his whole plan – a variant of the grand design with Turkish ᴺnd Tartar support – might be set in motion once more. His plans, discussed ᵥith the Khan and his own officers and officials, were therefore more than ᴀaydreams. That they lacked a solid foundation was due to faulty communica-ᴛons between him and the Council. This was not primarily a matter of •hysical distance between Stockholm and Bender. Letters to and from his ᴀapital arrived with fair regularity through the Swedish embassy in Vienna, ᴛhough there were occasional long delays.* It was rather a lack of communica-ᴛon on the level of grasp and understanding of the problems which seemed ᴺost pressing to each side. To the King everything depended on his being put ᴺ a position to use the opportunity which his diplomacy had helped to achieve ᴛ the Porte; to the Council the first priority was to ward off the dangers ᴛhat threatened the homeland.

It would be wrong – as has sometimes been done – to blame the Council for ᴛe King's losing his chance in 1711:† the most that can be laid at their door ᵥ a failure to state clearly that the expeditionary corps was out of the question ᴺ the circumstances in which they found themselves. This they did not do. It ᵥould seem that those among them who regarded the expeditionary corps as ᴀ crazy and impossible venture and worked actively against it between 1709 ᴺnd 1712 were restrained by the respect they felt was due to the monarch: ᴛhey believed that the King would deduce that dangers close at hand made it ᴺmpossible for them to obey his orders. Charles, looking at Sweden's con-ᴅition from afar, assumed – since he was not told to the contrary – that the ᵪpeditionary corps would reach him in time. He built on what information ᵥas available to him and drew conclusions which were logically defensible, ᴇet untenable because his premises were incomplete. He knew, for instance, ᴛat the Dano-Saxon–Russian descent on Scania had been given up by ᴐctober 1710 and that the Swedish navy had destroyed a large part of a con-ᵥoyed Danish transport fleet returning empty from Danzig (where it had ᴀailed to pick up the Russian contingent) in the battle of Kjøge Bay near

* E.g., Charles's order of 9 March 1711 to remind the Council of his need for the expeditionary ᴐrps took five months to reach Stockholm.

† This view, strongly held by Bennedich in *Karl XII på slagfältet*, IV, pp. 889 ff., has permeated ᴀuch writing on the period.

M

Copenhagen. From this he concluded that the Council could now procee with the Swedish transport to Pomerania: the danger of an invasion c Sweden itself was past and the Danish navy ought not to present a seriou obstacle to the Swedish naval escort.[51] What he did not know was that th Swedish navy was not up to strength and that the Council had not mad arrangements for transport ships.

Each side lacked imaginative understanding of the other's predicament. Th King did not realize the moral effect in Stockholm of Viborg's capitulatio in June 1710 and Riga's in July 1710:[52] how these made his Council clutc at the hope of deliverance by the Maritime Powers rather than by their fa away King. Nor did he guess that to the Council he himself seemed to b cutting down their hopes by gratuitous insults to London and The Hague: hi non-acceptance of the Neutrality convention,* his insistence that the Swedis blockade of Russian-occupied Baltic ports should be strictly maintained, s that neutral trade to these parts was effectively and not only theoreticall prohibited.† The Council for its part gave no thought to the realities behin the King's plan for defeating the Russians and freeing the Baltic provinces i cooperation with Turks and Tartars in a southern offensive. In their pre occupation with matters close at hand, they did not even give serious attentio to the problem of how Charles might safely reach Sweden without losing hi freedom of action in the process.

V

It has been contended‡ that Charles XII's gravest mistake in the whole of hi career was not to have taken a personal part in the Turkish campaign i Moldavia even though no army of his own arrived in time. The hypothesis o which this rests is that his moral influence would have been enough to prevent the Peace of Prut or at least to obtain terms favourable to Sweden in tha peace treaty. Such a supposition is not well founded. We know, and this i probably why the contention has been widely accepted, that Tsar Peter when cornered at Prut – was willing to give up most of his Baltic provinces; we know that Poniatowski¶ believed that things would have worked out bette if only the King had been present.[54] But there is no evidence which permi the conclusion that Charles would have been able to influence Turkish polic in the field or at the conference table till he had regained an independen command. Indeed, the evidence we do possess points the other way: neithe

---

* He had announced this already on 31 November 1710, but formal refusal followed on 1 March 1711 after Jefferyes invited his accession on behalf of the Maritime Powers and th Emperor.

† By a declaration to Jefferyes dated 2 May 1711, when it had become clear that the Counc was not enforcing the prohibition.

‡ See, e.g., Stille, Kurat, Haintz.

¶ In his memoirs he blames Müllern and Feif for dissuading Charles XII from accepting a invitation by the Grand Vizier to visit him at his headquarters.

he Sultan nor the Khan had accepted his offer of alliance and they had there-
ore not tied themselves in the slightest beyond Ahmed III's offer – conveyed
n the autumn of 1709 – that he would put at Charles's disposal an escort to
ee him safely home to his own dominions.[55] And this escort had not been
orthcoming while the situation in Poland had been fluid enough to render it
ikely that such a plan would succeed: instead Charles had been kept at
3ender and used as a pawn in Turkish diplomacy to obtain the January 1710
eaffirmation from the Tsar of the armistice of 1700. Even after its declara-
ion of war against Russia, the Porte played a waiting game as far as Sweden
vas concerned. The assurance which Funck received in May 1711[56] that
\hmed would not make peace with the Tsar without taking care that Charles
vas included could be interpreted, and was so interpreted at the Peace of
'rut, as referring to the Sultan's promise of a safe escort for the Swedish King
hrough Poland.

When Tsar Peter's army of more than fifty thousand men reached the Prut
iver in July 1711 it found itself, to its surprise and horror, in a position where
etreat was impossible and where it would have to fight against overwhelming
>dds.[57] Provisions were hard to come by; the need for water in the hot sum-
ner restricted its movements to the river since the enemy had made the wells
inusable; its connexions with bases in Poland and Russia were broken
hrough massed Turkish, Tartar and Cossack horsemen in the rear of the
['sar's army. The Turkish forces, with Tartars, Cossacks, Poles and Swedes
.mounted to more than one hundred thousand men.* Peter felt sure that a
ough peace would be imposed on him, but neither he nor his negotiator
>hafirov lost their heads and were rewarded with terms that in the circum-
tances seemed ridiculously light. The Grand Vizier, influenced more by fear
hat Austria was on the point of mobilizing against the Porte than by the
>resents which were heaped upon him,[58] agreed on 11 July to peace on the
ollowing conditions: the return of Azov to Turkey, the destruction of Russian
>order fortresses constructed since 1700 in the Azov area; the evacuation of
²oland by Russian troops; and an undertaking that the Tsar put no obstacles
n the way of Charles XII's return to his Swedish territories.[59]

As soon as negotiations began, Poniatowski and Lagerberg sent messages
o Bender to urge the King to join them in an attempt to persuade the Grand
/izier not to waste his glittering opportunities: they realized the Tsar would
>uy peace dearly. Charles reached the Turkish camp in the afternoon of 12
uly. By that time Baltadji Mehemet had already signed the peace and the
Russians were preparing to leave for the frontier escorted by Turks and
'artars. Poniatowski and Charles's interpreter, Savary,† were present at the
nterview between the King and the Grand Vizier. Charles received short
hrift: nothing had been heard of the Swedish army supposed to break into

---

* See Kurat, *K.F.Å.*, 1939, pp. 132 ff., for this estimate, more reliable than the two hundred
1ousand often given.
† His notes on the interview are printed in *K.F.Å.*, 1913, pp. 223 ff.

Poland;* peace was now made and Charles would be able to go home i
safety, the Tsar having left Shafirov as hostage for his faithful execution of th
terms signed.

It was not to be expected that Charles should regard this as sufficier
security. Tsar Peter was, in his opinion, capable of sacrificing his negotiator
he was minded to break the treaty. And even if Russian troops did withdra
from Poland, this still left Augustus of Saxony. Augustus had broken th
Treaty of Altranstädt, and Charles himself had been forced to declare wa
on the Elector after the Turkish break with the Tsar in November 1710 le
the Swedish army expected from Pomerania might be treated as irregula
forces once they reached Polish soil. Since the Turks were not at war wit
Augustus it was understandable that nothing had been stipulated about Saxo
troops in Poland in the Grand Vizier's treaty with the Tsar; but the lack o
any reference to Augustus put Charles in an unenviable position. That he fe
the indignity as well as the impotence of it seems clear from his parting wore
to Baltadji Mehemet. He raised his fist and said: 'This treaty I'll make yo
rue, that is as true as that my name is Charles.'†

That he lacked power to make his threat a reality till the Swedish exped
tionary corps should arrive, was made even more obvious to him in the day
that followed. His letters and memorials[60] protesting against the treaty o
Prut and suggesting ways and means for reopening the war had no effect i
Constantinople, Ahmed III ratified the Peace of Prut and voices were raise
which argued that now Azov had been reconquered, it was time to forge
eastern troubles and move to the west: to the reconquest of the Morea fro
the Venetians.

* For Turkish inquiries throughout the campaign to know whether this army had arrived s
Lagerberg's diary, p. 177.
† The gesture and the accompanying words were thought crude enough for the Swedi
authorities in 1740 to have them taken out of Nordberg's history of Charles XII before publicatio
They were later printed in the *Anmärckningar*, pp. 42–3, in which Nordberg in Copenhagen (175
published additions to his history.

3

The Beginnings of Reform

The way in which the great opportunity of 1711 had been lost turned Charles XII's thoughts to ways and means to stimulate the Swedish war effort in spite of the distance between himself and Stockholm. It was no easy matter. He had lost his most experienced and forceful Chancery officials. Feif, who handled his correspondence on domestic affairs, had been a member of the *kansli* since 1682 and was both capable and energetic, with useful contacts in the world of commerce and technology.[1] But he had to be tactful and cautious in his role as a mediator between the King and the Council, and was conscious of the difference in rank and office between himself and those he corresponded with on the King's behalf more privately, as, e.g. Horn and Tessin.

It was not easy to get the kind of information which Charles desired. When direct questions were asked, Feif was told in private letters that the Council and the Colleges suspected the King of 'wanting to change everything'. This was not so, wrote Feif in June 1710:[2] the desire for news of all kinds sprang from Charles's concern to overcome a feeling of being out of touch, and he advised Horn to write freely and directly to the King to improve the latter's contact with Stockholm. But the information sent from the Council or from individual councillors remained sparse. Weighed down by the feeling of responsibility in a difficult situation, and conscious of differences of opinion, the Council sent its secretary out of the chamber when important matters were to be debated. Hence no minutes were kept of the discussions which led to decisions in 1710 on such important issues as the Neutrality convention, the suggested hire of Swedish troops to the Maritime Powers, or the blockade of the Baltic ports now in the Tsar's control.[3] It is not strange that Charles XII had a feeling of being kept out of deliberations, and indeed of being ignorant of what his councillors decided amongst themselves. He experienced a similar feeling of frustration when it came to contact with those few Swedes who were permitted to go on parole from their Russian captivity to Stockholm. One of these was Cederhielm, sent to test the Council's opinion of peace-terms with the Tsar; and Charles's anxiety to discuss matters affecting exchange of prisoners and officials is evident from Feif's postscript to the letter of 27 June 1710 already quoted: 'Cederhielm shall join us when WE come closer' – stressing the King's hope to talk himself to Cederhielm when either with the help of a Turkish escort or that of the Swedish expeditionar corps, he had moved into Poland once more.[4] He felt slighted when appoint ments were announced without prior consultation with him. The King wil agree to what is *proposed* to him, Feif commented, but he would like to b informed before appointments and promotions were made public.[5]

Initially Charles had hoped much from Arvid Horn. He, who had been a officer, was assumed to be alive to the military needs of the King at Bender Through Feif he expressed his satisfaction that Horn was now head of th Chancery and, as a pleasantry, commented that it would serve to convince th world that a soldier was capable of turning his hand to all things; he con gratulated him on his third marriage and complimented him on having chose to ally himself with the Nils Gyllenstierna family.[6] Disillusionment set i slowly. First with the Council as a whole, later also with Horn, when h found them lacking in energy in pursuing orders he sent from Bender.

The King needed money; to pay his drabants, to keep the Swedish an Polish troops, to help the Cossacks, to succour the Swedish prisoners-of-wa in Russia,* to send presents of politeness to the Khan and his officers, and t enable Poniatowski in Constantinople to compete with the Russians i distributing bribes. He therefore asked that sums allocated for his expense for 1709 and 1710 should be sent to Vienna that he might pay the mor pressing of his bills.[7] It was galling to be dependent on Turkish charity even Islamic law prescribed that the Sultan should furnish those he gave asylum with food and other necessities. It was humiliating not to be able to repa Voynarovsky and worse still – when money from Stockholm was slow i coming and anyhow insufficient – to have to beg new loans from the hetman' nephew and to let Swedish diplomats scour Constantinople for banker willing to furnish cash.[8]

In such circumstances it was difficult to bear with equanimity the constan harping by the Council on how bad things were without any compensatin suggestions as to how the situation might be remedied. The Council's letter were so full of reiterated general complaints – the heavy burden of the war the ravages of the enemy, the stop to commerce and shipping, the bad harvest and the resulting poverty of the nation – that by 3 February 1711 the Kin proposed that in future a single sentence might suffice on this topic: whethe things were the same, or worse.[9]

Charles's decision to infuse new blood into the Council constituted his firs and relatively unsuccessful attempt at improving relations between himsel and Stockholm. In 1710, as evidence mounted that the Council as a whole wa working against the expeditionary corps, he made two men councillors wh might be expected to understand his own policy and support it. Nils Gyllen stierna was one of them, the former governor of Bremen and Verden to whom

* Almquist, *K.F.Å.*, 1947, pp. 14 ff., has stressed the Council's slackness in this respect an pointed out that no real improvement in the prisoners' lot came till Charles XII's return to Sweden

ie had given command of the expeditionary corps-to-be after Krassow's dismissal: he was now made president of the College of War. Gyllenstierna, however, regarded his promotion as a vote of non-confidence in him as a commander and blamed King Stanislaus for having made him suspect with he King.[10] In any case, he made common cause with those influential councillors – prominent among them Wrede, head of the College of Commerce and Horn of the Chancery – who regarded the 'war in Poland', as they termed the expeditionary corps plan, a luxury Sweden could no longer afford. The other new man, Magnus Stenbock, proved as vigorous an exponent of Charles's policy as could be desired, but he found himself for that very reason isolated in the Council. He was listened to with greater respect than the lone councillor* who advocated a devaluation of the currency as the solution for Sweden's temporary difficulties – he was after all the victor of Hälsingborg – but he made little headway. Quite apart from his being the King's man and therefore swimming against the stream, his fellow-councillors found him touchy, suspicious and impatient and therefore not easy to work with.

Charles, hardly less impatient, but hiding his suspicions as best he and Feif could manage, tried to alter the balance within the Council by removing, in he politest possible way, the man he assumed was leading Horn astray, Count Wrede: his age, the King decreed, earned him a well-deserved rest from public office.[11] At the same time King Stanislaus, who arrived in Sweden in September 1711, rose in influence and began to serve as an unofficial 'mediator' between Charles and his Council through his collaboration with Stenbock.[12] This was due more to their common concern at the danger to Sweden's German provinces in 1711 than to deliberate policy; but the King learnt a lesson from the effective cooperation between these two (and Wachtmeister of he Admiralty) which – at the very end of 1711 – forced the anti-Swedish coalition to abandon its blockade of Wismar, Stettin and Stralsund and its attack on Pomerania. Dücker, escaped from Russian captivity in time to take part in the defence of Scania, was now in command of the Pomeranian forces.[13] He acted with promptitude and energy but without the five thousand troops which were transported and convoyed from Sweden to Pomerania and Wismar he could not have met the danger. In spite of the Council's dislike of Stenbock and Stanislaus† (who – with considerable justification – was held responsible for informing Charles XII of the way its policies in 1710 and 1711 ran counter to that of the King) all councillors willingly cooperated in the defence of the German provinces. It was this defence which Horn and Wrede had hoped to achieve at what they considered a low cost by cooperation with the Maritime Powers and the signature of the Neutrality convention; Horn had even tried to keep Charles's refusal of that convention a secret in order to postpone attack by the anti-Swedish coalition in the Empire.[14] But once the

---

* Jakob Reenstierna.

† The expenses for him and his family, amounting to one thousand *riksdaler* a week in cash, plus supplies in kind for their kitchen, were also resented; for the amounts paid see D.Lundström, *Magnus Stenbock i Stockholm 1712*, pp. 21–2.

attack began, the need for military counter-measures was appreciated an‹ support given to Stenbock, though opposition to the King's wider plans fo‹ the expeditionary corps persisted.

The information which reached Charles from Stenbock and Stanislaus, a well as from other sources in 1710 and 1711, made him contemplate th‹ desirability of bypassing Council and Colleges in times of urgent necessity individuals had proved the more effective helpers.

II

A direct connexion can thus be traced between Charles's experience with th‹ Council and the Colleges in 1710 and 1711 and his increasing reliance o› individual collaborators who possessed the energy to force or the wiles to eas‹ his policies through committees which sabotaged them or through bodie which by their very organization were resistant to change and abhorrent o improvisation. The beginning of this policy was haphazard, forced on th‹ King by necessity. The first step came on 23 February 1712 when he remove‹ the business of the expeditionary corps, 'the transport' as it was known i› contemporary correspondence, from the Council and transferred respon sibility for it and control of it to Stenbock.[15] This seemed the only hope onc‹ it had transpired that the forces which had been moved to Germany were, b‹ calculated intent on the Council's part, not large enough to be useful to him i› the second Turko-Russian war which had broken out in December 1711.* His own diplomacy at the Porte – as well as the news of the landing in Pome rania of troops from Sweden, which were presumed to be the expeditionar‹ corps at last on its way to Poland – had contributed to this rupture betwee› the Sultan and the Tsar; if Charles wanted to avoid a repetition of his fate i› the Prut campaign he would have to resort to drastic measures.

He hoped to avoid an open break with the Council. Through Feif he trie‹ to rally that body behind Stenbock and Stanislaus: Horn was told that Stanis laus praised him in his letters to the King; plans put forward by Gyllenstiern‹ were approved in flattering terms.[16] Feif appealed to the chancellor in term‹ which can only be termed imploring. 'I beg for the sake of God', he wrote o› 12 March 1712, 'that Your Excellency will promote the newly ordered trans port, otherwise all our work here will fall to the ground.'[17] The reason for thi‹ tone lies partly in the emotional response he hoped to awake in Horn, bu partly also in the growing realization that it was more likely than not that th‹ expeditionary corps would arrive too late to permit Charles XII to reactivat‹ the grand design.

The Khan was a visitor at Bender at this time† and optimistic plans fo‹ Swedish–Tartar cooperation were in the air, though the experience of the Pru

---

* See below, p. 350.

† It was during this stay that Axel Sparre painted companion portraits of the Khan and th‹ King. Both – according to Feif's letter to Horn of 26 March 1712 – were thought fine likenesses

ampaign urged caution and scepticism on both sides. The question of his afe return home began to be uppermost in Charles's mind. It would be unwise o reckon on more than a Turkish escort through a Poland freed from Russian roops unless there was certain news of the landing of the expeditionary corps n Germany, but – it was emphasized in letters to Horn – the Swedish army vould still have to march 'a good bit into Poland' to meet Charles and his ender flock.[18] Behind this demand the determination to help Stanislaus .gainst Augustus can still be espied, but a real concern that the King, without uch an army rendezvous, would be exposed to the danger of capture either n Poland or in Germany is more noticeable than in 1710–11.

When history had repeated itself and the non-arrival of the expeditionary orps within what the Turks regarded as a reasonable time had produced the 'eace of Constantinople between the Sultan and Tsar Peter in April 1712, with- ut Charles being able to influence that peace in any way, the King openly oiced his dilemma. News from the Empire that the Russians – freed from the outhern theatre of war once more – had joined the Saxons in sieges of Stettin .nd Stralsund[19] made his dilemma worse. 'If the transport does not come oon', Feif wrote in July, 'His Majesty must conclude that he is not wanted at Iome; for where can His Majesty otherwise direct His march? His Majesty annot let himself be imprisoned either in Stade or in any other place in 'omerania; nor can he wander round Poland with the Turks from one place o another while his enemies are in Pomerania.'[20]

It was with an appeal to save 'our Swedish Isaac' from his stay with 'Turks .nd Heathens' that Stenbock turned to the burghers of Stockholm to get the ash he needed for the expeditionary corps.[21] But the eyes of merchants and nanufacturers alike were directed to the west rather than the east: Stenbock's int that the corps would bring the Sultan to declare war on the Tsar once nore fell on deaf ears, while the burghers made him promise to make sure of ree trade through the Sound, 'if not for this year, at least for the next.'[22] It vas not strange that the burghers, and the Council as a whole, should have heir attention riveted on the danger still presented by Denmark. Plans for the lescent on Scania were, at least temporarily, laid aside; but in the summer of 712 Frederick IV had begun an attack on Bremen and Verden, and, as)anish naval power was considerable, an attempt at a total blockade of weden from the west might be made: Gothenburg's link with the North Sea night be cut as well as the Swedish passage through the Sound.

Whether this promise affected, as has been argued, Stenbock's operations nce the expeditionary corps of sixteen thousand men had been landed on the sland of Rügen in September 1712, is a moot point and will be discussed in nother connexion.* For our present purpose it is important to note that tenbock's and Stanislaus's success in getting the corps ready, in fitting out he men-of-war needed to obtain control of the Baltic for the crossing, in ecuring transport ships and the masses of supplies of ammunition and food

* ibid., pp. 361–2.

needed for the proposed campaign, confirmed Charles XII in his belief that action by individuals was more suitable for the war he had to fight than th old-fashioned methods of Council and College responsibility. From now on he begins to rely on men who served him more as cabinet ministers than a heads of bureaucratic departments which had not kept pace with the times The foreigners among these men have impressed themselves on contempor aries and posterity alike: Stanislaus, Poniatowski, Frederick of Hesse, Georg Heinrich von Görtz and a host of other Holsteiners. Charles had man Swedish 'ministers' in the post 1712 period; but the majority of those wh were part of the old bureaucratic system resented his employment of non Swedes. These were accused of circumventing the channels hitherto used, thu lessening the rightful prestige and power of those in regular office.

Charles XII was insensitive to this dislike of his foreign helpers once h came home to Sweden; he wanted Swede and non-Swede to cooperate together to sustain the war effort. That his dissatisfaction with the organiza tion he had inherited went deeper than an *ad hoc* attempt at coping with th problems of the war-period is, however, clear. It is evidenced by his work fo the rationalization of the administrative machine and especially the Chancery which culminated in his reform programme of 1713. From the 1670s onward there had, in Sweden, been a tendency for specialized sections or 'expeditions to develop within the *kansli*, but – comparable to what was the case in th Secretary of State's offices in Whitehall before the reform of 1782 – individua officials were usually responsible both for domestic and for foreign business In 1705 Charles XII had decreed two distinct divisions: one for domestic an one for foreign affairs. This distinction was largely obscured in the Chancery in-the-field before Piper's captivity, but it was reaffirmed when Charles in Turkey allocated to Feif and his officials domestic matters and to von Müller and his staff the handling of foreign affairs. Both were to leave responsibility for policy decisions to him.

On 26 October 1713 the King published, from Timurtash,* a full-scal reorganization of the whole administration, covering not only the *kansli* bu also the other Colleges. The *kansli* remained in being, but its role was confine to deliberations on foreign policy and conservation of royal archives, librarie and postal communications. Six 'state expeditions' covered the rest of th administration. Two dealt with the day-to-day handling of foreign affairs divided according to areas: the 'German expedition' covered the Empire Denmark, Switzerland and Italy, leaving relations with the rest of Europe to its sister 'expedition'. Three handled domestic matters: a 'military expedition was to deal with naval and army affairs; an 'exchequer expedition' had as it sphere the economy of the state in general; a 'trade expedition' had respon sibility for commerce and manufactures, the mining industry and the coinage banking and the customs. The towns also came under this expedition as di Church and education.

* For Charles's move to this place, see below, p. 365.

Each of the five expeditions mentioned above had an *ombudsråd* at its head, word suggested by the King in preference to the '*Geheim Kabinett*' counillor (*råd*) put forward – implying one who mediated between the King and the administration. The task of each *ombudsråd* was to discuss the activities of his own department with the King and to execute decisions reached with the help of the secretary, under-secretary and other personnel of the expedition. It was part of his express duty – and here we find echoes of Charles's experience with Council and Colleges between 1709 and 1713 – to take the initiative and to lay before the King plans which would be for the 'service of His Majesty and the benefit of the State'.[23] Cooperation between departments was arranged: when matters of domestic policy were discussed the three *ombudsråd* or the 'home' departments should meet the King in a body; those of both 'foreign' departments were to be present in the *kansli* when the foreign dispatches were read while the president of the *kansli* and his two next in command (the *kansliråd*) were to have access to the meetings where the 'foreign' *ombudsråd* discussed the affairs of their departments with the King. When issues of great importance were to be decided, such as the budget for the coming year, all the *ombudsråd* were to meet the King in a *konselj*, i.e. a cabinet council.

The sixth expedition was one which had already become a separate institution, the 'revisions-expedition'. The head of this department was now given the title of *högste ombudsman*. His general brief was to see that the law of the land was obeyed and to keep an eye on the proper, efficient and fair functioning of the administration. It was his duty to see that executive instructions were carried out and to suggest modifications of existing instructions and regulations if changing circumstances or conditions begged reform.

From Timurtash Charles XII nominated *ombudsråd* for the five departments as well as a *högste ombudsman*. The latter began his work more or less immediately since he already had a base in the revisions-expedition; but though the regulations for the whole reorganization were sent to the Council in Stockholm in January 1714 they were not (for reasons which have not been clarified) discussed in that body till October 1714 and they were not carried into effect till the King's return to Sweden in 1715.*

III

It was also in Turkey that Charles XII began work on an overhaul of the tax system, and here he had a more immediate, if limited success. The impetus for changes decreed was on the one hand the need to raise money and on the other a dissatisfaction – stimulated by discussions at Bender with Feif and Silfvercrantz – with the existing Swedish system that seemed neither fair nor efficient.[24] Sweden's taxes pressed hardest on the poorer classes. When it became clear that further taxation was necessary after 1709, the meeting of

* See below, pp. 439 ff.

representatives of the Estates which the Council called in 1710 proved un
willing to listen to ideas which would alter the incidence of taxation as hithert
levied, though they did not object to the doubling of the taxes in existenc
since 1700 to finance extraordinary expenses of war. These were: a contribu
tion of ten per cent of all salaries, five silver *daler* for each unit of noble lan
and two silver *daler* for each unit of Crown land and land of the tax-payin
farmer. Every taxable unit of land (the *hemman*) also paid 1½ silver *dale*
towards the expenses of moving the troops, the so-called *durchtågsgärd*.*

The publications of the cameralists in Austrian service – von Hörnigk
Becher and Wilhelm von Schröder – were studied and debated at Bender an
in particular the 'Dutch tax' described by Schröder in his *Fürstliche Schatz
und-Rent Cammer*:† a percentage tax on the total fortune of the inhabitant
which enabled the Crown to share in the increase of wealth which came wit
good conjunctures. By 4 June 1712 instructions were sent to Stockholm t
levy such a tax to replace all the older contributions from 1713 onwards. A
subjects were to disclose their assets in money and property. Shares in com
panies at home and abroad and valuables were included, but salaries an
pensions were to be exempt. It would be in the interests of all to make the
declaration as high as possible, it was argued, since the percentage was not t
be fixed till the 'self-assessments' had been collected: if undervaluing too
place, the percentage had to be high.

The work involved was entrusted to that committee of the Estates whic
managed the affairs of the Swedish Bank, though – as the name for the ne
organization, the *kontributionsränteri*, indicated – its affairs were to be kep
separate from the Bank as such and a royal councillor, Reenstierna, wa
put at its head to form the link with King and Council. That Feif expected th
new measure to be unpopular is clear from his stressing that the reform wa
'the King's own work'; he tried to turn away wrath by stressing that all a
Bender had already begun to assess themselves according to the new taxatio
system.[25] Reenstierna, keen on financial and taxation reform, had the ne
office working by October 1712 and tax was levied according to the ne
principle for 1713. The tax was, however, fixed at only one per cent, though
was realized that this, even with a further one per cent claimed later in th
year, would fall short of the Crown's needs. Undervaluing had been prevalen
but the eight per cent which modern historians have estimated as the figur
which would have produced the money needed was one of which the men i
charge of the *kontributionsränteri* fought shy. They adopted a collegial for
of responsibility for decisions and refused to give it up even after Charles x
had explained that he had not intended them to work in that way: he ha
hoped to promote in the new office more vigorous action and more individua
responsibility than in the traditional civil service.[26]

Charles's reform in the system of taxation was unpopular with the prope
tied sections of society and the Diet called by the Council in 1713 decided t

* Cp. above, p. 130.   † Published in 1686 and requently reissued.

eturn to the old system for 1714. The King overruled this decision on 23 April 1714, though he suggested – since there had been complaints that the work was too much for the board of the Bank – that a new committee, nominated by that board, should be put in charge of the tax for 1714. The percentage was put at two per cent for that year and though the income fell far short of estimated expenses, Charles and his advisers stuck to the priniple of the new system. After the King's return to Sweden the lack of drive in he *kontributionsränteri* was compensated for in that a new office, the *upphand-ingsdeputation*,* took over much of the direction of the work, including that of obtaining and handling loans. Charles had stipulated this as one of the original functions of the *kontributionsränteri*, but had received little response from the board of the Bank.

The link between the 1712 reforms and the Bank is an interesting one and shows an awareness in Bender of Dutch and English ideas on finance as well as on taxation. An attempt to lend the new tax respectability by its connexion with the Bank and a hope that the Bank, handling the money that came in, would become the collaborator of the Crown once more can also be discerned. Until 1709 the Bank had shown no scruples in lending the Crown money; but since Poltava it had closed its doors decisively. This was the more alarming since it was after 1709 that Charles XII really needed to raise money.

The scale on which he needed it is seen from the desiderata with which he sent Ehrenskiöld – a Chancery official good at raising money – from Bender to Stockholm in 1710: large sums were needed for Swedish prisoners-of-war in Russia; for the payment of soldiers with the King in Bender and in the German provinces; and, above all, for the fitting out of the navy on which all the King's future plans depended.[27] Ehrenskiöld tried to raise these sums, or part of them, with those known to have cash and international financial connexions – the burghers of Stockholm. He found them not unwilling if in return the King would grant them advantages such as 'free trade': no payment of tolls and dues in the future. The Council recommended such concessions to Charles XII, but he – from a desire to protect and encourage Swedish manufactures – preferred to attempt other solutions to his financial difficulties.

Before 1709 Sweden had not had to raise loans abroad: the largest one, in 1701 from the Dutch Republic of 750,000 florins, was secured on the toll of Riga and paid off by 1710.[28] Between 1710 and 1713 Ehrenskiöld travelled on the King's behalf, visiting his contacts in Hamburg and Vienna, or was busy at Bender with projects for the floating of loans. These projects served as models for the financing of the war effort between 1715 and 1718; but they were difficult to launch from Bender, or even during Ehrenskiöld's stays in Germany, because of the problem of raising the necessary securities in Sweden. Individual councillors and rich subjects were generous in lending the Crown money if convinced of the urgency – as, e.g. when the forces of 1711–12

* See below, p. 436.

had to be fitted out[29] – but there was not enough confidence or even insight to make long-term planning feasible. With the Russian control of the Baltic provinces the mainstay for the financing of loans had gone; and panic (which was not well founded, but none the less operative) weakened Swedish securities, such as the dues on imports and exports, when Denmark–Norway had become an enemy once more and the trade through the Skagerak and the Sound were no longer deemed safe. The logical step, which was not fully exploited till Charles's return when he had secured Görtz to help implement the Bender schemes, was to utilize Sweden's resources in copper and iron a exportable raw material, as backing for coinage and as securities for loans But that the work of the reform period proper began in Bender is indisputable even the issue of obligations and paper money were debated and planned between 1711 and 1713.[30]

As a stop-gap, to cover expenses which had to be paid from Bender, loans were taken where they could be got on what securities could be arranged.* Some loans were arranged with no other backing than the King's word. This was the case with the two large sums which the Sultan lent Charles XII in 1710 and 1712: 400,000 and 500,000 riksdaler respectively; and also with the smaller sums which individual Turkish subjects (Greeks and Jews among them) risked advancing to the Swedes in the difficult year 1713–14. When the foreigners at last left for their home far in the north, a motley band of creditors and representatives of creditors came with them to collect the debts due.[31]

IV

Parallel to reforms which were effected or planned in administration and taxation ran a growing concern on how to make the fullest use of Sweden's resources. The King's concern that the land under cultivation should not diminish is evidenced by his order of 21 May 1711: the Council was told to make sure that farms left derelict due to the ravages of the plague should be speedily resettled by soldiers who had left the army through age or war injuries. This was effected and the number of derelict farms (a problem since the great famine of the 1690s) decreased between 1713 and 1715. As the harvests of these years were good ones, the prosperity of the countryside increased after the bad years of 1708–11.

In a community where the majority of the inhabitants tilled the soil the King and his advisers hoped to encourage the peasants by converting their rents and dues from kinds to cash. The peasants themselves had increasingly come to favour payment in ready money; and preparatory work for the assessment of a fair ground-rent had begun after the resumption of Crown land was complete. The war of 1700 had interrupted the detailed investigations which were needed for the new jordebok (land register) but at Bender

---

* E.g., the loans with foreign bankers in Constantinople and the loan which Ehrenskiöld arranged in Vienna to finance the return in 1714.

discussions on the simplification of taxation which rested on land were resumed. Administrative convenience was one of the attractions of reform – more money flowing more easily into the coffers of the Crown was expected* – but the improvement in the lot of the peasants which standardization and fairness of taxes and dues would bring was also prominent in the discussions. In June 1713 Charles ordered that Sweden's district governors should restart the work on collection and collating information for the register so that a single land-tax could be introduced.[32] The change envisaged was not one that was relished by landowners whether large or small. With an up-to-date registering of land they expected to have to pay more tax than previously; and as payment in cash from their tenant-farmers was sure to displace payment in kind as soon as the tax-paying peasant was ordered to pay the Crown in ready money, they were also faced with the prospect of losing what benefit they had enjoyed in a period of rising prices from their rents. The work proceeded but slowly before the King's return; and even after 1715 so much preparatory work had to be done on the register that the reformed land-tax was not brought into use till January 1718.†

It was impossible from Bender to do more than send reminders about the necessity to work on the new land register, but plans which it was hoped would benefit Swedish mining and metallurgy and the manufactures in general could be more actively tackled by correspondence with individual experts. One of the most important of these was Christoffer Polhem, a mining engineer and inventor who had travelled widely abroad and who kept abreast with technological progress in Europe. He was – like Ehrenpreus, the director of customs – interested in broad economic and financial trends and wrote at least sixty memoranda on such matters. In them he quoted German camera-lists (such as Becher's *Politische Discours von den eigentlichen Ursachen des Auf-und-Abnehmen der Städte, Länder und Republiken*) as well as from English and Dutch practices which he had observed.[33] A lively exchange of ideas followed between Bender and such would-be reformers in Sweden; Feif and Silfvercrantz being used to wield the pen till Charles XII could meet his correspondents in person.‡

A fairly strict mercantilism was aimed at. Sweden was to make better use of her resources such as copper, tar and iron, and obtain higher prices for the export of them as raw materials. The mining industry was to make use of the latest inventions, most of them from Polhem's drawing board and work bench; and manufactures were to be encouraged as well as trade. That both should flourish untrammelled was the motive for that complete separation, in 1711, of the College of Commerce from that of the *kammar* (Exchequer) on which

---

* Those who argued in favour of the change in Sweden, such as Fröhlich who had been connected with the register in the 1690s, stressed that the work would be halved and opportunities for cheating would be eliminated.

† See below, p. 470, for the new system being abolished after Charles's death and not reintroduced till 1869.

‡ For such meetings, see below, pp. 399, 430.

it had been in some dependence since 1679. The division of the College into three sections, intended to rationalize the work, which Charles XII decreed at the same time was not carried into effect; but the energy and efficiency of *kommerskollegiet* after 1711 is very noticeable.[34]

One interest which the King and Polhem shared was in improved communications: plans for new docks at Karlskrona and for canals between lake Vänern and the Baltic and lake Vättern and the Kategatt, with locks on the Göta river, were made already in the correspondence of the Bender period. Contracts, such as the one for the Göta canal, were signed on the King's return. Charles XII, wrote Feif to Polhem, has 'a particular bent for Mechanics, and reads everything you have to say on such matters with so much pleasure that he wishes you to write in more detail; he also wants you to make small models of cranes and pontoons and threshing machines to be used on campaign so that you can take them with you when you will be ordered to meet him, as soon as he gets close to our own borders'. The King asked for samples of the watch industry which Polhem had started in 1710, sent drawings of the mills which had been improvised during the war and of anything he had noted which seemed useful, such as Turkish baking ovens economical in fuel consumption. He was full of suggestions. Could they not manufacture sewing-needles and pins in Sweden? Was it not a shame that these had to be imported when the raw materials needed were found at home? Might not copper and brass be exported to the Mediterranean countries where there was such a demand? 'If God gets me home', Feif quoted Charles as saying, 'I'll see that all kinds of manufactures are encouraged.'[35]

Feif's own experience in manufacture illuminate that part of the correspondence which deals with problems of training skilled workmen; and the general mercantilist ideas which permeated the discussions at Bender can be deduced from the information that Charles intended, as soon as possible, to free all manufactures from export dues. It was hoped that since Sweden possessed important raw materials goods manufactured from them would be able to compete successfully with those of other countries once the export duty was taken off.

Charles secured money for the *Labora Mechanicum* (established in 1697) so that Polhem's genius for invention should be encouraged, and expressed his sadness that there was not enough love of the arts and sciences in Sweden, nor money at the moment to support them as he would wish. In the future he would certainly arrange travelling scholarships for those who wanted to study sciences abroad.[36]

From the masses of information available to us of Charles XII's interest in and orders for specific reforms and innovations during the years he spent in Turkey, we can conclude that the so-called 'reform-period' between 1715-18 owes more to the Bender discussions than to the initiative of von Görtz, with whom they are generally associated. Görtz was a helper of tremendous energy and experience, who sacrificed his own fortune (and in the end paid with his life) to improve that of Sweden. Even so, those who with the King as a driving force planned (and to some extent began) the modernization of Sweden from Turkey should not be forgotten, nor those who contributed to the work by their correspondence with the King at Bender.

Two reforms are symptomatic of them all. Sweden found herself saddled with a calendar which differed both from the old unreformed Julian calendar and from the Gregorian New Style in general use on the Continent. England used the Old Style (and did so till 1752), but the Swedish Style, the modified Julian calendar, had – by cutting a day off the Old Style in the year 1700 – moved one day ahead of the Old Style while still remaining ten days behind the New Style. In the campaigns of 1700–9 the Swedes, as far as dating was concerned, had the worst of both worlds since the plan for dropping another day in 1704 (the next leap year) had been forgotten. The amount of correspondence with Europe in the Bender period convinced the King that there was little point in waiting for decades to lose the difference of ten days: better to retreat to the Old Style which was – mainly because of England's increasing commitments on the Continent after 1688 – acceptable to the west and understandable in the east since Russia also kept to the Julian calendar. Charles therefore decreed that the month of February 1712, a leap year, should contain thirty days instead of twenty-nine.[37] On that day Sweden obtained conformity with England and Russia in that the Swedish Style from 1 March 1712 was identical with the Old Style. It was no use working in isolation or going it alone and the jump to the New Style could not be accomplished in one bold leap.

While willing to go back, Charles was also keen to go forward. He became interested in the vaccination method with which the Turks prevented smallpox epidemics and in 1713 paid one hundred ducats to the Greek Emanuel Timoni, the Sultan's foremost medical adviser, for a copy of the manuscript which described this novel method for controlling one scourge of mankind.[38]

4

The *Kalabalik*

Charles XII's attempts to undo the Peace of Prut were, in the long run, success-ful though this was due more to Russian non-fulfilment of the terms of tha peace than to the power wielded by the Swedish King in exile. But Charles's diplomacy knew how to exploit the fact that Tsar Peter, once he had escaped from his dilemma at Prut, showed little inclination either to give back Azov or to move his troops out of Poland.[1] His pressure was reinforced by the Tartar Khan and by Turkish officials opposed to Baltadji Mehemet Pasha. On 20 November (N.S.) 1711 the Grand Vizier was dismissed from office and though the appointment of Yusuf Pasha,* a former Janissary commander, did not – from the Swedish point of view – promise well,[2] war was declared on Peter on 10 December (N.S.). News that Swedish troops had landed in Pomerania † did to some extent influence this step as it was assumed that these were the expeditionary corps so long expected; but the knowledge, which eventually percolated, that Stockholm intended a strengthening of the German provinces only and that the force landed was not of the magnitude demanded for a breakthrough into Poland weakened Charles's position once more.

The diplomats of the Maritime Powers worked hard to make the Turkish declaration of war a token one only.[3] The Tsar for his part had no desire for a repetition of the Prut campaign, and in February 1712 he was persuaded to hand over the Azov fortress and to raze the fortified places stipulated in the Peace of Prut. On 16 April (N.S.) 1712 his representatives in Constantinople reaffirmed the Treaty of July 1711, including the clause which bade him remove his troops from Poland. The time was now specified as 'within three months'.[4] In Charles XII's camp at Bender it was assumed that the journey home was soon to become a fact. The King, according to Feif's letter to Horn of 10 April, was putting everything in order to facilitate the return. For his own part he asked Horn to make sure that his brother – expected from Stockholm – would hurry lest he should arrive to find Bender evacuated by the Swedes.[5] Events were to show, however, that the Tsar did not intend to keep his promise to evacuate Poland, and the dilemma of Charles XII – how to get safely home – remained.

---

* Not to be confused with Yusuf Pasha, seraskier of Bender, who had been deposed in 1710.
† See above, p. 339.

The help which the Maritime Powers had given Russia to obtain a peace
which gave no stronger safeguards in respect of his own return than that of the
Peace of Prut occasioned the first significant change of course in Charles XII's
foreign policy. With Whitehall and The Hague working so much against his
interests, he became convinced of the desirability of listening to what offers
Louis XIV was willing to make Sweden. The War of the Spanish Succession
was drawing to its close as far as England was concerned,* and Charles felt
free to explore the possibilities which a renewal of Franco-Swedish friendship
might open. Mauritz Vellingk was empowered to sound Versailles on the
prospects of future cooperation between Charles XII and Louis XIV.[6]

II

This decision was influenced also by happenings in Germany and Poland. As
early as May 1712 Charles decided to test whether the withdrawal of Russian
forces as promised in the Peace of Constantinople had weakened the Tsar's
hold on Poland. He sent the major part of the Polish force at Bender, with a
considerable number of Cossacks – some five thousand in all – into the Commonwealth under the command of Grudzinski to gauge if a successful push
through Poland to Pomerania was feasible and also to assess what support for
Stanislaus existed once Augustus was bereft of Russian military help. Grudzinski managed to get as far as the Prussian frontier without having to fight
more than minor skirmishes; but there he was met by a combined Russo-
Saxon army and beaten at the battle of Krotoszyn on 28 June (N.S.) 1712.[7]
The Tsar thereupon used Grudzinski's march into Poland to justify the continued presence of his own troops. Discussions whether to connive at this
break of the Peace of April 1712 or to oppose it with force rent the Sultan's
advisers for several months.

The sending of one of Ahmed III's officials into Poland decided the issue:[8]
he went to ascertain whether Tsar Peter had fulfilled the peace terms of April
and returned to report not only that Russian troops were still stationed
throughout the Commonwealth but also that a new Swedish expeditionary
corps had at last landed on the island of Rügen and was marching into
Pomerania:† assuredly on its way for Poland and Bender. Jusuf Pasha, who
had been in favour of trusting Tsar Peter, was dismissed on 29 October and
on the same day war was declared on Russia for the third time. During the
month of November the Turkish army began to collect in Adrianople and the
Sultan took personal command of the campaign, a remarkable step if compared to his passivity in the earlier wars. The new Grand Vizier, Soliman
Pasha, was thought of as a subordinate in fact as well as in theory. Ahmed
was slighted in his *gloire* and pride by Tsar Peter's refusal to implement the
terms of the Peace of Prut, even after these had been reinforced by the Peace
of Constantinople.

* The news of the Anglo-French negotiations was common knowledge in the summer of 1711.
† See above, p. 339.

Charles XII's second big chance seemed to have come. Ahmed, as part of his defiance of Russia, decided to send a strong escort to Bender to enable the Swedish King to make contact with his own army. The secretary of the Swedish legation in Constantinople, Celsing, was sent to invite Charles to name the number of Turkish troops that he would need for his escort and to hand over a large sum of money to facilitate preparations for the journey.[9] Tsar Peter's representatives in the Turkish capital were imprisoned and those of Augustus – of whose business the Swedes knew little though they assumed that they boded no good – did not seem to make much progress in their negotiations.

That Prussia, or at least Ilgen, the chief minister, was keen to make a bargain with Sweden, was clear from the mission of Eosander* to Bender in the summer of 1712. Charles XII had himself approached Frederick I through Vellingk in May 1712 to suggest Prusso-Swedish cooperation; but when Eosander arrived the essence of his message was that his master was alarmed at the Tsar's military power and for that reason suggested a triple alliance of Prussia, Sweden and Augustus of Saxony. The price of such an alliance, it was broadly hinted, would be the transfer of some Polish territory to Prussia. The sacrifice of Stanislaus in Poland for Augustus's benefit was also implied. Frederick I was obviously becoming more adventurous as the war in the west was slackening, and Charles XII was sufficiently in need of allies to explore the possibilities of Eosander's mission, though the Augustus aspect of it alarmed him sufficiently to avoid early commitment.

Augustus was more directly busy in the south during the summer of 1712. He was anxious to prevent the Sultan sending Charles with an escort to Poland – a move which might well precipitate a pro-Stanislaus and anti-Russian rising – and for that purpose sent two emissaries to Constantinople, the Saxon officer von der Goltz and a representative of the Commonwealth, the palatine Chometowski. Both played on the theme of Augustus's willingness to join an anti-Russian league with the Sultan and the King of Sweden. The negotiations were, however, intended to postpone decisions, and when the Turks declared war on the Tsar on 29 October, Augustus's negotiators realized that they had suffered a setback.[10] Eosander was worse hit; Charles would obviously not be willing to pay a high price for a Prussian alliance now the Sultan was at war with Russia, and he returned to Berlin without the treaty he had hoped to achieve.

News which disturbed Charles arrived, however, hot on the heels of the harbingers of better times. The September landing of Stanislaus and Stenbock in Rügen, and Ahmed's determined stand against Russia, were followed by behaviour by his two stalwart collaborators which he at first found hard to grasp. Instead of pushing on from Pomerania to Poland, Stenbock and Stanislaus (and Vellingk) began to negotiate with Saxons and Prussians and entered into an armistice with the Saxon Field-Marshal Flemming. One reason for their decision was that the supply fleet for the expeditionary corps had been

* For his being used on an earlier mission to Stockholm, see above, p. 196.

destroyed by the Danes immediately after the Swedish landing at Rügen;*
but another was that Flemming tempted them with Augustus's cooperation
against Russia at the cost of Stanislaus giving up his Polish title. The price
seemed cheap, and Stanislaus set out for Bender to persuade Charles XII to
accept the sacrifice he himself was only too willing to make if Sweden by it
would gain allies against the Tsar.[11]

Charles's letters imploring Stanislaus to stick to the original plan for the
expeditionary corps arrived too late: the King of Poland was already on his
way to Turkey. Stenbock was told to restart the campaign, but when he moved
it was to the west – to Mecklenburg and Denmark. This was in itself useful
enough, but it took him in the opposite direction from where Charles XII
needed him and made it impossible for the King to utilize the Sultan's declaration of 29 October. It was a bitter blow.

Worse was to follow. Augustus, though his representatives had made little
impact on the Sultan, scored significant successes with Devlet-Gerei and the
new Seraskier of Bender, Ismail Pasha, in the summer and autumn of 1712.
Contacts with the two were made not only via Goltz and Chometowski, but
also by letters from Flemming and Sieniawski and by a mission of Jan Sapieha
to Bender.[12] Through all these channels Devlet-Gerei became convinced that
Charles XII was obstinately and unnecessarily opposing the plans for a large
coalition to bring the Tsar to his knees. The Khan had tired, as had most of
the Turkish and Tartar officials, of the prolonged stay of the Swedes and their
followers in Bender. The Swedish expeditionary corps, so long expected, had
not yet materialized in the late summer of 1712: was it not better to push the
'Iron-head' into collaboration with Augustus even against his will? The riddle
of the undoubtedly anti-Russian Devlet-Gerei's behaviour lies in his trusting
Augustus or rather those who spoke for Augustus, but his disillusionment
with Charles XII's power and desire to achieve a strong coalition against the
Tsar would seem to explain it.

The Khan did not suspect that Augustus had no intention of breaking his
alliance with Russia, though the Elector was naturally enough anxious to
reinsure against a repetition of the Prut campaign. His main concern was to
prevent Charles creating trouble for him in Poland, and when he failed in his
diplomatic efforts at the Porte to deny the Swedish King return via Poland, he
embarked on measures which he hoped would lead to Charles being captured
or immobilized by Tsar Peter's troops when he passed through Poland –
escorted by Ahmed's forces.

To the Khan and the Seraskier Augustus's representatives stressed the need
to make the escort for the Swedish King weaker than the one asked for: only
in this way, so ran their arguments, could the stiff-necked Swede be persuaded
to throw in his lot with the Khan, the Prussian King and Augustus. Augustus
was not eager to gain Turkish enmity by making the Swedish King his own
prisoner, but correspondence between his agents (intercepted by the Swedes

---

* See below, p. 362.

at Bender and read by the King) shows that the outcome envisaged from thei
arrangements with the Khan and the Seraskier was that Charles would befor
long be either in the hands of the Muscovites or of some of Augustus's Polis
friends.[13] In the anti-Russian mood of most Poles at this time, the Polis
followers of Augustus were not averse to a kidnapping of Charles o
Polish ground which would give them a trump card against all comers
Russian, Prussian, Saxon and Swedish. Nor was Saxon diplomacy prepare
to deny itself the advantage of a capture of the Swedish King if circumstance
seemed to demand it, though letting the Tsar do the dirty work still remaine
Augustus's own preference. No wonder that in such a maze of double-dealin
Charles began to hanker for the firmness of the old Franco-Swedis
alliance.

III

When certain information about a conspiracy against him got into Charles'
hands through intercepted correspondence,* at a time when he was alread
aware that Stenbock had abandoned the expedition to Poland, his dilemm
became acute. The King was convinced that given enough time, he coul
persuade the Sultan of the pernicious influence which Augustus had on th
Khan and on the Seraskier of Bender: he had the intercepted letters as proof
after all, and a secret correspondence with the Sultan's mother gave hin
hope that his enemies would draw the shorter straw.[14] But in the meantim
there was every prospect of his being forcibly deported to Poland with ar
escort smaller than the one stipulated and with the knowledge that even thi
would soon melt away so that 'friendly capture', in the efficacy of which
Devlet-Gerei sincerely believed, could be effected. Some of those at Bende
who had knowledge of the intercepted letters, the postmaster Naundor
for instance, believed that bribes ('2 millions of Dollars' are mentioned), wer
decisive in the affair; but though presents of money eased the collaboratior
planned it is clear that as far as the Khan was concerned the ideological moti
vation was by far the stronger one: he was convinced that Charles XII had t
be forced against his own will to cooperate with Augustus.

The effect of these developments on the Swedish King was plain to see
Naundorf, whose relation of the events of the *Kalabalik* was translated b
Robert Samber in a manuscript copy which has survived in the Rawlinsor

---

* Some Swedish historians of the 'anti-Charles' school, e.g. Fryxell, Sjögren, Nyström, argued
that such a conspiracy never existed; more recently Tenberg has doubted it, since the evidenc
usually quoted is based on Swedish sources only. Since that time, however, the researches o
Bonnesen into Augustus's policy in 1712 have substantiated the charges from Polish and Saxon
material, while two letters from the Sultan's mother to Charles XII, printed by I. Stafsing in 1960
explain the King's basic optimism. In view of the new material Tenberg's citations from diplomatic dispatches in the Dresden archives take on a greater significance, e.g. from a Saxon diploma
in Riga on 10 December 1711: '*Ihre Czarische Majestät flattiren sich den König von Schweden bal
[i.e. when Charles's escort has melted away inside Poland] persönlich zu sehen.*'

papers at the Bodleian Library,* puts it succinctly: 'These intercepted letters which discovered the Treachery obliged His Majesty to alter his resolution of departing homewards, and rather wait there the event of this Conspiracy.'[15] The situation was not easy. Communications with Constantinople and Adrianople were cut off by the Bender authorities. We learn from Naundorf that '8 Expresses' were sent to the Sultan and to Funck and Poniatowski, 'by several ways at once', but the only ones to arrive safely were those which went 'by the way of Germany' and these did not reach their destinations till after 'the Tumult' or 'the Fray' – the *Kalabalik* to give it the Turkish name by which it is generally known[16] – had been fought on 31 January/1 February 1713.

Charles XII's attempts to postpone his departure till he had certain news of Stenbock and Stanislaus proved offensive to the Porte since he demanded further sums to finance his departure: the 500,000 *Reichsthaler* which the Sultan had sent the King, he declared on 29 December 1712, had been used to pay off local debts and he was in need of another loan of similar size or at least of permission to wait till his army had reached Poland and could send money to him.[17] Faced with such ingratitude, the Sultan gave orders to the Seraskier of Bender on 18 January 1713 that he might forcibly abduct the Swedish King and bring him to Salonika from where a French ship would return him to his own dominions. A similar permission to employ force if Charles would not depart of his own free will through Poland was sent to the Khan on 24 January.[18]

Neither Devlet-Gerei nor Ismail Pasha were keen to use force. They had kept the Sultan and the Grand Vizier ignorant of their own negotiations with Augustus and there was always a chance that they might be found out. Moreover, Charles and his companions were popular with the Janissaries and the local population and force against them might rebound on those who ordered it.

By 1713 the Swedish camp was no longer as makeshift as in 1709, when Charles assumed that he and his men would soon be on their way to Poland. The tents of that summer were made warmer when the winter came by the addition of mud roofs; soon 'almost every one built him a house and settled himself as if he were to continue there for life.'[19] The Turks built Charles a house, in which he stayed for two years. Then, as the river Dniester flooded to a prodigious height', the whole Swedish camp had to be moved to Varnitza.† The King lived in a tent for some time but when the winter of 1712 approached he let a house be built for his own use which, with three other buildings (the Chancery, the house of von Grothusen, and the stables) formed a square. South of the stables were 'a great many barracks built half in and

---

* Naundorf's name is not given for the 'Narrative of the King of Sweden's movements 709–1714'; it has been identified and edited with an introduction by the present writer in *Tarı Araştırmaları* I, Ankara 1956, pp. 85–142.

† Where the Cossacks had their first camp, see above, p. 323: for the Swedish camps see illustration facing p. 205.

half out of the ground, the first for the Officers and the rest for the Subaltern and the common Soldiers'. This place and buildings, Naundorf explained 'were ordered like a camp and divided into several Streets, so that the squad rons and battalions now lodged every one by themselves. The officers apart ments had glass windows, the soldiers only leathern after the Turkish manner At the end of these houses there was a Corps du Guard or Watch House with a large ditch about it for security.' The Royal House, like the Chancer building, had strong brick walls 'after the Turkish fashion', and was buil with balconies on both sides of the entrance, 'upon which the trumpets use to sound to prayers every morning and evening'. It had six rooms on th ground floor. Naundorf described it:

The first room or entry was towards the West, the second towards the East, i which the Court Marshal* with the principal Officers dined, through this wa another chamber where the rest of the Officers dined; beyond this was the roon where his Majesty's Life Guards waited hung with a fine green cloath, in which w used to pray twice every day. The fifth room was the Anti-Chamber of his Majesty' Bedchamber hung with the same fine green cloath. The last was the King's ow room and Bedchamber which was the outermost towards the North. In this Roya Chamber there was a door to the North through which was a way to another littl building which was made for a Summer house whence was the finest prospec imaginable towards the North, East and West.

The view from the East side of the King's house was also famous 'for th delightful prospect it afforded'.[20]

The Turks called the Swedish settlement 'New Bender',† and Turkis houses, particularly coffee-houses and shops, grew up round the camp. Th Swedes were good customers and even when the Seraskier of Bender and th Khan tried to blockade the camp Janissaries and others managed to get figs bread, tobacco, brandy and meat to them and arranged that whole cartload of provisions should be 'seized' by the Swedes and paid for in secret.[21] Gun powder and bullets were also provided.[22]

Tension mounted between Charles and the Bender authorities from 1 January 1713 when the Khan sent a strong body of Tartars (thirty thousan the Swedes believed) into Varnitza. The King had been told of their approac and had collected his troops and officials in the square of the headquarter where provisions for six weeks were also stored and guarded. To stiffen Swed ish morale Charles with a small suite rode on 13 January 'through the middl of the Tartarian Army which stood like Organ pipes so close together on a sides'. He was not molested.[23]

In the parleys which followed Charles aired his Turkish to call representa tives of the Seraskier 'Villains and Traitors',‡ and was encouraged to make token stand which would force Devlet-Gerei and Ismael Pasha to ask new

* Gustav von Düben.   † Motraye referred to it as 'Carlopolis': *Travels* II, p. 5.
‡ [Naundorf] *Narrative*, p. 108: *Heyda damus kopokler*, etc.

rders from the Sultan when a French merchant, fresh from Adrianople,
ssured him that nothing was known there of the pass to which matters had
ome at New Bender.[24] The attempts of the Janissaries to make Charles XII
rust himself to their hands (they promised to save his life) were therefore
ebuffed; and when – through the same channels – the Swedes were warned
n Friday 30 January that the attack was to commence the following morning,
he night was spent making a 'Trench and Barricade of woods, carts, waggons,
tc., round our headquarters'.[25]

<h2 style="text-align:center">IV</h2>

he amount of fighting during the *Kalabalik* which began on Saturday 31
anuary 1713, and the loss of life which it entailed, has been grossly exag-
erated. The picturesque and picaresque aspects of 'the Fray' naturally com-
nended themselves to those who participated and those who – like Fabrice
nd de la Motraye (the latter dressed as a Tartar) – witnessed it.[26] The onset
f the battle was of course unsettling, particularly to those who had little
xperience of military action: 'the whole Hosts of the Tartars advanced
owards our Trench and made a halt within three or four Steps of it, which
as very frightful to see, being so great a number. At 10 o'clock in the fore-
oon there appeared several thousand Turkish Horse, after that several
housand Janissaries on foot, from Bender. These were drawn up in order, as
* they were to attack us presently.'[27] The charge was, however, postponed:
fter a salvo from their cannon ('so heavy that the earth shook with their
ring') which did little damage, Turks and Tartars retired. The explanation
or this was found by contemporaries either in the respect in which the Janis-
aries held the King and Colonel von Grothusen,[28] or in the superstition of
he enemy when the cold weather changed 'on a sudden and became as warm
s it had been in the Spring, and there appeared just over his Majesty's Room,
vhich was towards the North, three very fine Rainbows one over the other,
vhich struck the Turks with such amazement that they dropt the Attack for
hat time, saying that God had made a sign over the Swedes, and was with
hem that day, so that if they should attack them then they should all be
illed and utterly destroyed.'[29]

It is more likely, however, that the Seraskier and the Khan hoped to achieve
heir purpose without using real violence. They wanted to see whether the
rospect of battle would suffice to make Charles agree to leave under their
scort so that they could send him to Poland as arranged. The Poles and the
Cossacks at Bender had already put themselves under the protection of
Devlet-Gerei and Ismail Pasha – the former in the hope (now Stanislaus's
ower seemed null and void) of achieving reconciliation with Augustus, the
atter because it was clear that the Swedes could not hope to win a battle
gainst the Khan and the Seraskier. Some desertion took place from the
wedish camp on 31 January, but was stopped once the King informed a

delegation of officers, clergy and officials of the plot in which the Khan an
the Seraskier were implicated, taking the intercepted letters from his pocke
and assuring his listeners that he had a plan* for tackling the situation. To th
Poles and Cossack leaders who implored him to put himself under the prote
tion of either Devlet-Gerei or Ismail Pasha he also referred to the intercepte
letters which had cleared his eyes and warned him 'against the worst'.
Fabrice, who, incidentally, favoured cooperation with Augustus, had
similar reception.[31]

Neither to his visitors nor to his own men, in so far as they have left writte
evidence, did Charles confide his plan: it was assumed that he wanted to lea
them into a resistance so that the Swedes need not basely deliver themselve
up as prisoners, it being more honourable to be 'borne down by force'. Bu
the principal officers and officials must have known that his plan was to resi
sufficiently to ensure investigation of the whole matter by the Sultan, ye
without permitting a massacre of his men. This can be deduced from thre
happenings on Sunday I February which will be discussed in their chrono
logical context.

There were some hopes in the Swedish camp Saturday night that they wou
not suffer more than armed demonstrations of the type endured during th
day. Through 'perspective glasses' they inspected the 'abundance of canon
mortars, bombs and granadoes' which were ready for use against them an
watched the march on New Bender in the early morning by Tartars an
Turks, reinforced – they assumed because the Janissaries could not be relie
on – by men 'from the cities Aickerman and Ismael with drums beating' an
Moldavian Christians armed with muskets.[32] With the Janissaries, the Spa
and Lipkaner forces, 'there was', in Naundorf's words, 'such a vast number o
these Infidels that when we were on the top of the Royal house we could n
see over them.' He noted the colourful aspects – the thousands of 'little fla
of red, blue, yellow and other colours which the enemy carried' – and shivere
a little at 'a very large red Standard', planted on a hill, 'to signify that the
were to push the Swedes to the last drop of blood'. In the circumstances
seemed odd to him that 'His Majesty seeing all those preparations ordered i
Bravery the Trumpets to sound and Kettle drums to beat on the top of th
Royal house; to blow for action and summon the Enemy'; and less tha
strange that desertion began once more in the Swedish camp, particular
among junior officials and officers.[33]

To stop the rot Charles ordered a resolution to be made public throug
Hård, the commander of the drabants: 'that His Majesty did assure every on
from the highest to the lowest who should stand by him for two hours longe
and not desert should be rewarded by him in the kindest manner, but whoeve
should desert to the Infidels he would never see them more.'[34] It is wort
noting that nothing was said about a fight to the finish or about sacrificing lif
and blood; a moral rather than a military battle was envisaged. And when th

* Naundorf gives his words in German: '*Wir wissen schon was Wir thun*', see his *Narrative*, p.12

ght did begin* – after a second and third sounding of the Swedish trumpets
nd kettledrums for action – the Swedish generals and colonels cried out
Don't shoot, don't shoot' to men under their command, as did at least one of
ue King's drabants,† so that both officers and men let themselves be taken
risoners, apart from the relatively small numbers who moved back to defend
ue Royal House and the Chancery.³⁵ It could be argued that these officers
cted of their own accord in giving such advice, but in view of the King's
1anifesto (referred to above) and his post-*Kalabalik* approval of the behavi-
ur of the officers in question³⁶ we may deduce a deliberate policy of avoiding
nnecessary bloodshed while gaining the tactical advantage he needed to
revent the Khan's and the Seraskier's plans succeeding.

A strict line was therefore drawn between the deserters who gave themselves
p before the attack was launched and those who stood their ground to enable
ue King to report to Ahmed that Devlet-Gerei and Ismail Pasha had attacked
im. These two were careful to kill as few Swedes as possible. When Charles
1alloed' to the men in the Chancery building to join those in the Royal
Iouse, the 'cloud of arrows' which the Turks rained on them in their passage
it their marks so rarely that they seemed ill-aimed on purpose; the bombs
irected at the Royal House 'allways flew over the House and did no hurt',
·hile the cannon balls 'did not go through the walls, all the damage they did
·as to some of the timber on top of the House'. Again one is entitled to
uspect that the bombs and balls were not intended to do the maximum of
arm.‡

To those inside the House the struggle seemed a more serious matter and
·om their talks with friends and acquaintances, and their letters and diaries,
·e get stories – some of which originated with the Turks and Tartars – of
<ing Charles who 'pushed three Turks with his sword at once', killing all
1ree;¶ of the great losses which the Turks and Tartars met in their assaults
n the building, falling so thick 'upon one another before the House, which
ave them opportunity of jumping through the windows into it, but they were
ɔ well received by the Swedish swords that they were immediately thrown
ack slain, through the windows'; of the fate of those friends of fallen Turks
·ho came 'with a cart loaden with hay before them to take away this or that
reat man that was killed, but His Majesty immediately ordered some of his

* See [Naundorf] *Narrative*, p. 224, for the tension in the Swedish camp which made them long
·r the attack to begin: 'About eleven o'clock in the forenoon all the Turks and Tartars made the
·sault sword in hand with such a fury, making a hideous noise in their language of Alla, a Hilla,
lla, that is God is with Us, which they repeated continually, that it was impossible to resist them.'
† ibid., p. 125. Cp. the trick Naundorf gives as reason for his own capture: he had obeyed a
·y of 'Come out, come out, they that are in the House, we are to fall upon the Tartars. But all
ιat got out through the windows were mistaken being taken prisoners.'
‡ The King is said to have expressed surprise at the small effect of the attack – 'those vile
ascals don't know how to charge a cannon that they cannot make it pass so light a brick wall
; this which is in a manner new': ibid., p. 128.
¶ The basis for this story is that Charles, while trying to rid the Royal House of looters, was
ɔnfronted by three Turks: one of his officers, Roos, shot two and the King killed one with his
·ord.

men who were the best marksmen to fire at them who were behind the cart
which they did and seldom a shot failed for the Swedish blessing'; of the ma
who, when the stratagem of the hay cart miscarried, 'rolled a huge Vatt befor
him thinking by this means to carry off some of the Chief Turks who wer
slain, was not seen but now and then as he peeped to spy a Corpse, but upo
his peeping he got a Swedish pill and fell behind his machine'; of the King
wearying of the Turks who came to the door of the House to persuade hir
and his men to give in,* ordering some of his men 'to let fly at them whic
consequently was done to that Surprize that many fell upon the spot'.

After such stories it is with some surprise one examines the list of casua
ties: on the Swedish side were twelve or thirteen, on the side of the Turks no
more than forty.[37]

V

It would seem that Charles XII hoped that he and the men in the Royal Hous
could hold out till the morning of 2 February, when – we are told – h
promised his supporters that they would be given reasonable terms by th
Khan and the Seraskier. A bullet had grazed his nose and cheek and nicke
the lobe of his ear before he reached the House itself, and his hand was deep
cut between thumb and forefinger when he warded off a sabre stroke with hi
bare hand during the fight to clear the House of Turks bent on plunder. Th
afternoon's work of defending the building was tiring; the men were regale
with brandy though warned by the King not to drink 'too much in your hea
for fear of drunkenness'.[38] But just as the day was 'almost spent' the Turk
managed to put the wooden shingles of the roof of the Royal House on fire
Pitch, straw and other combustible material was thrown on to the roof and se
alight, and well-aimed arrow fire nullified Swedish efforts to push the burnin
bundles away with iron bars. There was nothing to quench the fire whic
spread rapidly through the loft and from there to the ground floor: the Kin
and Axel Roos[39] were the last to escape down the already burning staircas
with their coats over their heads.†

With the fire spreading through the six rooms, the Swedes, to avoid bein
burnt alive, made a sortie after removing the barricades before the doo
Escape to the undamaged Chancery building seemed a possibility as the Turk
fell back from the step of the Royal House. At this moment, however, th
King, running with sword in one hand and pistol in the other, fell to th
ground. He was caught by the Turks and his companions were also mad
prisoners. The time was about 8 o'clock in the evening. Charles was then take

---

* [Naundorf], *Narrative*, p. 129 relates that he had been told these Turks 'spoke very civily t
us in their language, thus, Loving Brothers, fear nothing, come over to us and we will protect yo
come out to us we will joyn you, fall upon the Tartars and destroy them. They called to the Kin
also, saying, Dear loving King, why will you not have recourse to us, none but we can save you o
you must die in this House.'

† Roos noted that Charles was now so parched that, in lieu of water, he drank a large glass o
wine: 'the first since he left Stockholm'. Grauers, *K.F.Å.*, 1966, thinks this should not be take
too literally.

ɔ Bender and lodged in the Seraskier's house. He was received with great
ivility and many apologies for what had happened.

The reason for the fall was believed, in Naundorf's words, to lie in Charles
ɔeing tired and weary': 'his Majesty having commanded all day from one end
f the house to the other his spurr accidentally intangling [him] he fell to the
round.'[40] A lieutenant threw himself on top of the King to protect him from
ɪjury; but the Turks, anxious to secure pieces of his uniform coat so that they
ɪight claim rewards for their share in his capture, were not otherwise hostile.
'he desire for plunder and ransom was evident also in the treatment of the
wedes captured throughout the *Kalabalik*. They were searched by Turks and
'artars and robbed of money, watches and other valuables; silver buttons
ere torn off civilian coats.* Those who had good clothes were stripped of
ɪem and given 'an old Tartar shirt with a vile rag, and over it an old Sheep-
ᴋin to ward off the cold'. Some borrowed money from Greeks or Armenians
ɔ buy themselves free; and Fabrice, Motraye and Jefferyes, at the King's
ɜquest, managed to obtain enough cash to free those who had not sufficient
redit to get out of captivity by their own efforts.[41]

It seems an irony of fate that orders from the Sultan, countermanding those
y which he had permitted Devlet-Gerei and Ismail Pasha to use force against
̵harles XII, arrived in Bender the very day after the *Kalabalik* had been
ɔught. These were dated 26 January and had been influenced by fresh news
f Sweden's position in Germany: the armistice concluded between Stenbock
nd Flemming on 19 November 1712 had been for two weeks only,† fighting
ad broken out once more in early December and on the 9th of that month the
wedes had won the battle of Gadebusch against Danes and Saxons. At the
'orte, the position of Funck and Poniatowski improved dramatically as
̵harles XII once more seemed a king within grasp of real power.[42]

In reality Stenbock had, by the negotiations with Flemming, by the armis-
ᴋce and by the direction of his march once it expired, lost whatever chances
e might have had to push through to Poland as planned: he could, with his
ᴋxteen thousand Swedes against the twenty-two thousand Saxons and Rus-
ᴋans Augustus had at his disposal in early October, have fought the Elector
•efore reinforcements arrived, or, avoiding an early battle, he could have
ᴋsked marching through Prussian territory into Poland. He has been strongly
riticized for failing to test either of these possibilities,[43] and a hypothesis that
e felt tied by his promises to the Swedish burghers to turn his back on the
astern theatre of war in order to attack Denmark has recently been put
orward as an explanation for his behaviour.‡

It seems more likely that Stenbock and Mauritz Vellingk (like King

---

* That women who were Swedish subjects were among the prisoners is clear from [Naundorf]
larrative, p. 133.

† The short period stipulated, after such lengthy negotiations, is curious and points to a lack of
ɪcerity on Augustus's part: he certainly achieved his objective of preventing Stenbock's push
ɔwards Poland while giving the Danes time to rally their forces.

‡ See above, pp. 341-2.

Stanislaus) were ensnared by the possibility of achieving an anti-Russian all
ance with Augustus. Stenbock may also have remembered what befell Charle
xii's army in 1708 when it became separated from its supply train. His ow
well-trained and well-equipped army had food and ammunition for a limite
period only (five weeks at the most)* since the Danish navy succeeded i
destroying the fully or partly loaded transport ships. He seems to have hope
for further supplies from Sweden and he was anxious to await the safe arriv:
of four thousand men who had not yet left Swedish ports.[44]

Certainty as to Stenbock's reasons for pushing west rather than east afte
30 September 1712 may never be reached, but it seems to me that Stanislau
and Stenbock were faced with a situation when they landed in German
which made them look upon the Polish expedition as a less feasible propos
tion than cooperation with Augustus to achieve an aim which they regarde
as identical with that held by King Charles: throwing Russia back from bot
Poland and the Baltic provinces. The skilled diplomacy of Augustus prevente
them from realising that the long-term advantages that might, or might no
be achieved were nullified by the damage done to the King's immediate pla*
and opportunities. Emotionally both were predisposed to listen to such ove:
tures: Stanislaus was anxious not to bring further suffering on Polan*
Stenbock – like Vellingk – was perturbed at the risk to Sweden's position i
the Empire if free play for Danish and Hanoverian, Saxon and Prussian dea
was given through the army's departure for Poland. Without intending to d
so, both of them moved closer to the policy of the Council: limited war an
negotiations which would lead to peace in one or more of the theatres of wa*
But whereas the Council put its hope in the mediation of the Maritin
Powers, Stenbock and Stanislaus (and Vellingk with them) preferred dire*
negotiations with the German princes, including the Elector of Saxony, on*
peace with one of Sweden's enemies impressed itself on them as being en
bodied in the logic of events. That they were in no small measure deceive
by Saxon diplomacy is clear: the success which Augustus achieved in t*
north with Stanislaus and Stenbock is, from the point of view of Charles x*
comparable to that Augustus gained in the south through his negotiation
again via middlemen, with Devlet-Gerei and Ismail Pasha.

The non-arrival of Stenbock's army in the eastern theatre of war, followe
by its capitulation to the Danes in May 1713, forced Charles xii to turn h
own mind to the theme of 'war and negotiations'. The reasons why he di
carded the solutions attempted by the Council and by Stenbock and Stanislau
will be discussed in the next chapter, as will be the policy he worked o*
between 1713 and 1714 to cope with Sweden's dilemma. But before the loss *
Stenbock's army, his Mecklenburg campaign did – though it contravened t*
expeditionary corps plan of Charles xii – have a brief but salutary effect on t*
King's fate.

---

* Supplies for three weeks seem to have been unloaded for most of the army, and we know th*
supplies for two weeks were collected on the island of Rügen for the whole army.

VI

tenbock's Mecklenburg campaign[45] was successful in its early stages given
ie view he now took of the role his army had to play. He relieved the pressure
n Stralsund and on Wismar. The battle of Gadebusch was a fine victory of
wedes numerically inferior both in cavalry and infantry* and cast lustre over
wedish arms once more. The important innovations by Cronstedt in
wedish artillery were revealed for the first time and became an object of
tense speculation all over Europe. The secrets which enabled Swedish field-
ns to be aimed more accurately remained closely guarded,† and though the
ctical advantage which the Swedish field-guns possessed at Gadebusch was
early visible, the means by which it was achieved were less obvious: a strong
t easily unfastened coupling-mechanism permitted horses to pull the gun
to firing position, muzzle to the front instead of to the rear. Time was no
nger wasted in turning movements; the gun pointed to the enemy and
tillery could now be used to march ahead of infantry, offering it a protection
hich moved with the men.[46]

The dramatic reversal which the Gadebusch victory produced at the Porte
as not revealed in words, but in deeds. The Seraskier of Bender kept quiet
 his new orders, and when Charles XII set out in a coach – for a destination
hich was not divulged – on 6 February 1713 he looked a helpless prisoner
ho had only been permitted to take with him, out of the goodness of Ismail
asha's heart, an escort of a hundred Swedes, among them (at his own
quest) those who had shared the fight in the Royal House five days earlier.
 Jefferyes he seemed an object of pity. 'I cannot express to Your Excel-
ncy', he wrote to the Secretary of State in Whitehall, 'what a melancholy
ectacle this was to me, who had formerly seen this prince in his greatest
ory and a terror to almost all Europe, now to see him fallen so low as to be
e scorn and derision of Turks and Infidels.'[47]

The impression of helplessness was increased by Charles having to be
rried. It was generally assumed that the King 'feigned himself sick' to avoid
o much contact with Ismail Pasha or to postpone his departure. We now
ow that Charles sustained an injury to his right foot by the fall on 1 Feb-
ary. The X-ray examination that was made of his body in 1917 revealed
idence of distinct breaks in two places which cannot be dated to any time
her before or after the *Kalabalik*. The King took to his bed, after having
od briefly at his interview with the Seraskier in the late evening of 1 Feb-
ary, and did not walk or ride for ten months.[48] But as he did not mention
y pain in his foot at Bender, nor refer to the injury ever (at least not to

* The Swedes had six thousand cavalry against seven thousand Danes and three thousand
xons and 7,800 infantry against 9,300 Danes.
† One of these was a screw setting which controlled the height of the shot, invented by Polhem
d adapted by Cronstedt.

anyone who has left a note of it),* the element of 'diplomatic' illness whic
may have been present to some extent has vastly overshadowed its medic
foundation and has merged with the assumed 'feigned sickness' which ke
him in bed long after the broken bones must have mended and which has no
been diagnosed as malaria from the reports left by Neumann.

That the King was conscious of having won a political victory over th
Khan and the Seraskier is intimated by Swedish eyewitnesses who found hi
'in as good a humour as in the days of his greatest luck and liberty', though h
naturally grieved at leaving behind in Bender so many Swedes, now under th
command of Axel Sparre.[49] From Fabrice he knew that the Seraskie
intended to send him to Adrianople,[50] and this was proof enough that Devle
Gerei and Ismail Pasha had failed in their plan to force him into Poland in
manner which could only benefit his enemies. This was confirmed during th
journey. An emissary of the Sultan met them who, when told of the *Kalabali*
pleaded that 'his Great Master was an utter stranger to these hellish co
spiracies'. An escort arrived, with 'some thousands of the greatest Spah
Persons of Distinction', to accompany Charles XII to Demotika near Adri
nople. On his arrival there, on 17 March, he was received with honour.[51]

Before the end of March Jefferyes could report from Constantinople;
found the scene as much changed in favour of the King of Sweden at th
place, as it had been managed in prejudice of him at Bender.'[52] Those respo
sible for the events of 31 January and 1 February were punished: Devle
Gerei was deposed and exiled to Rhodes and Ismail Pasha was sacked fro
his important post at Bender. To signalize a change in policy, the Gran
Vizier, Soliman Pasha, was removed from office and on 30 April followed
fourth Turkish declaration of war on Tsar Peter.

* The French ambassador in Constantinople mentions in a letter, however, that Charles
had to keep to his bed because of 'an injury to his knee'.

5

Plans in Maturity

fter the *Kalabalik* Charles XII realized that he had little to hope from changes
: the Sultan's court or from the more active policy against Tsar Peter which
ιey promised. He knew – before the Turks – that there was no likelihood
f Stenbock's being free to move to the east in time to achieve for Sweden any
:al influence on Turkish policy. The disappointments of previous years now
:ched themselves deeper on his mind: the Turkish wars with Russia of 1710
nd 1711 and 1711–12 had been wasted through the Council having, as he
ιw it, failed in their duty. Now it looked as if Stenbock, Vellingk and
tanislaus had let his last chance slip and that the war Ahmed had declared
n the Tsar in October 1712 would be similarly wasted even if it had, so to
ρeak, been 'recharged' after the *Kalabalik*.

The indifference Charles showed to Stenbock's fate after the surrender at
'ønning is striking when one remembers the years of their collaboration in
oland and the energetic way in which Stenbock had preached Charles's
ιause in the Council: it may be explained by the King's feeling let down to the
ρoint of betrayal when Stenbock turned west rather than east.[1]

The King's disillusionment with his own prospects is probably also the real
xplanation for the negative outcome of the attempts which the new Khan,
.aplan-Gerei,* and the new Grand Vizier, Ibrahim Pasha,† made during the
ιonth of April to get in touch with him to discuss the campaign against
·eter. Charles had been allocated the castle of Timurtash, close to Adrianople,
s a residence,[2] but he refused to call on the Grand Vizier and the Khan when
ιey invited him to do so. Charles's illness is usually accepted as the reason
>r this, though some blame his haughtiness, but we know that he did not
ontract malaria till the evening of 5 July;[3] and the broken bones in his ankle
id not preclude conversation – indeed, he is known to have sent a message
> Ibrahim that if the Sultan himself was present in the suite the Grand Vizier
ιad invited him to meet he would, in spite of his illness, join them.[4] In Bender
ιe rumour spread that the Sultan had been with Ibrahim, and had 'actually

---

* He was the brother of Devlet-Gerei, and had already been Khan between 1702 and 1707.
† His period of office lasted only three weeks; after his strangulation in prison the Sultan did
ot formally appoint a new Grand Vizier; but Ali Pasha – though at first only a *kaimakam* in
ιnk – exerted a strong influence on policy.

N

visited the King of Sweden three times in the night'[5] when it became know
that illness prevented Charles from paying his respects. It was not universal
believed at the time though it has been accepted in literary history.

The King's refusal to discuss plans made a bad impression on the Sulta
and to some extent Charles was kept, however politely, a prisoner while even
unfolded. When Stanislaus arrived at Bender on 18 February 1713 he wa
received with great honours,[6] but he and Charles were kept apart and conta
between the Swedish King and his representatives in Constantinople wa
under Turkish surveillance.[7]

Even before news of Stenbock's surrender at Tønning in May 1713 reache
the Sultan and his advisers, European developments had hastened t
conclusion of Russo-Turkish hostilities. The Peace of Utrecht, so long
negotiation, was signed on 11 April (N.S.) 1713 between France and a
Louis's enemies apart from the Emperor and the Empire; and it was assume
that French peace moves with the latter would follow shortly. And if the ne
Emperor, Charles VI,* got peace in the west before the Sultan had ended h
war with Tsar Peter, the complications of a war on two fronts might hav
to be faced. Even those who did not believe that the Emperor would speedi
close with Louis, nor that he would rush in to a war in the east, even if he d
get peace in the west, still urged a pacification with Tsar Peter and a clari
cation of the Porte's relationship with Augustus, so that Turkey might be fre
to embark on the reconquest of the Morea.†

It was known in Adrianople and Constantinople that Stenbock had n
been able to follow up his victory at Gadebusch. He had not attempted th
march through Prussia to Poland which – in the opinion of military experts
would still have been possible at the moment when the Danes and Saxo
were disorganized by their defeat and discomfited at the recent news of t
Sultan's declaration of war on Tsar Peter of October 1712, while Frederic
of Prussia was suitably impressed by the Swedish feat of arms.[8] Nor had l
pushed through to the west to free Bremen and Verden from Danish conque
and Hanoverian occupation. His plan, supported by Vellingk, was to mov
into Holstein and from there into Denmark to force Frederick IV to a separa
peace and thus to free Bremen and Verden. Once that had been done, l
wrote to Charles XII, he intended to make his way to Poland.[9]

This plan miscarried. It does not seem to have been well conceived in vie
of the considerable anti-Swedish forces in the area; strategic errors we
committed and time lost.[10] Tsar Peter was persuaded that he could be
Turkey in the north rather than the south. He obtained a promise fro
Hanover to remain strictly neutral and both Saxon and Russian forces we
to the help of Frederick IV, bottling Stenbock up in Holstein and forcing hi
to take refuge in the fortified town of Tønning where he was besieged fro

---

* He succeeded Joseph I as ruler of the Austrian Habsburg dominions in April 1711 and w
elected Emperor in the same year.

† This war, successful in its initial objective, began in December 1714, but Turkey suffered gre
losses through Austrian intervention 1716–18.

rly February 1713. When the Peace of Utrecht freed Danish and Saxon oops which had been in the service of the Maritime Powers, the destruction f Stenbock's army – whether it was mauled in a sortie, or forced to surrender seemed bound to follow. And quite apart from the knowledge that Charles ould not now command the army he had for so long expected, Stenbock's urning of Altona* on his march to Holstein had given Sweden an unenviable putation in North Germany which in widening ripples reached also to outhern Europe: Charles was seen as a ruler whose armies were losing the putation for decent behaviour which they had hitherto enjoyed.

II

n 5 June 1713 the negotiators of the Sultan and the Tsar made peace for wenty-five years at Adrianople: the Turks were anxious to deal with a revolt Mesopotamia and this made them relatively easy on Russia. The terms of ie Peace of Prut were repeated with only three changes, but all of these were onnected with Charles XII's interests. Tsar Peter now had to guarantee the ntegrity and independence of Poland' as well as to promise that his troops ould leave the territory of the Commonwealth;† and he had to declare that ussia would 'not in any way hinder' the journey of the Swedish King and his urkish escort through Poland. Finally, the independence of the Cossacks ving south of the Dnieper as well as of the whole Zaporozhian Cossack state as recognized in the new treaty. This was meant to solve the immediate roblem of Cossacks and Zaporozhians still at Bender and facilitate their eturn home; but Ali Pasha, being a more astute negotiator than Soliman asha, also hoped that the long-term advantage of a buffer belt of neutral erritory between Turkey and Russia would be achieved.[11]

When the Tsar hesitated to ratify the Peace, not finding the modifications f the Prut one to his liking, pressure was put on him – and on Augustus – y sending Stanislaus and the Polish troops at Bender to the very border of he Commonwealth with an escort of Turkish troops at the end of July.[12] A etachment of Swedish troops was also in the party, though Charles XII was ervous lest the delivery of the whole force into enemy hands were plotted nd sent his interpreter Savary to ask Stanislaus to be on his guard.[13] As soon s the Tsar indicated his willingness to ratify the Peace of Adrianople, the urkish escort was withdrawn and Stanislaus had to return to Bender.[14] On September the ratifications between Ahmed III and Tsar Peter were xchanged.

* The burning of Altona, justified as a reprisal for the burning of Stade by the Danes, was done destroy enemy magazines which Stenbock's army had not the means to carry with them. The act that a *Brandschatz* to save the homes of the inhabitants (who took refuge in Hamburg) was efused made an impression which was not erased by the 'revenge' destruction by the Russians of everal towns in Swedish Pomerania.

† This time a term of two months (as opposed to three months in 1711) was stipulated for the withdrawal of Russian troops.

Once the Russo-Turkish peace had been ratified and Augustus had indicated his willingness to regularize his relations with the Porte, King Stanislaus' position was weakening. The march to the Polish borders had shown the Turks that Stanislaus had little following in the Commonwealth now the Swedish army had failed to turn up; and Stanislaus, it was well known, was quite willing to abdicate the Polish throne if this would ease the problems of Charles XII. The Swedish King had indicated that, in certain circumstances he would accept Stanislaus's sacrifice: if Augustus was genuinely prepared to fight Tsar Peter, ways and means might be found for a compromise agreement – Stanislaus could, for instance, he designated as Augustus's successor in Poland and Charles would, in return, recognize Augustus as reigning King.[1]

Negotiations on these terms were set afoot by Charles in 1713–14, but events favoured Augustus, who was not slow to take advantage of them. The Mesopotamian revolt against the Sultan sparked off another in Syria which spread to Asia Minor; the Emperor made peace with Louis XIV;* and when Augustus signed his treaty with Ahmed III at the end of April 1714 he managed to slide out of two conditions which Ali Pasha had been anxious to obtain.[1] The Turkish desire for a Polish guarantee for that measure of Ukrainian independence which the Tsar had promised was ignored, and the question of Charles XII's return journey through Poland was referred to separate peace negotiations between Augustus and the Swedish King under Tartar mediation. A Tartar mission under Sefershah Bey did proceed to Poland at speed, but had great difficulty in pinning Augustus's representatives down even to a discussion of Charles's journey. By September the Bey realized that Augustus had never been willing to permit it. He was told that the question could not be discussed except in the context of Charles making a general peace with the whole anti-Swedish coalition and returned, disillusioned, to Constantinople.[1] By that time it was too late to remedy matters: Ahmed III had ratified the treaty of April by which he had recognized Augustus as King of Poland, and Charles XII had been kept away from the northern theatres of war over the summer of 1714.

Charles himself had given up the idea of a return journey through Poland as soon as the Sultan had made his treaty with Augustus and by June 1714 he had arranged for Stanislaus to make his home in Zweibrücken in the German territory Charles had inherited from his father as a personal possession. The plague epidemic had at last subsided and the frontier between Turkey and the Austrian dominions was open once more. The peace between the Emperor and France made a return through Habsburg territory acceptable to him. Preparations of all kinds were completed,† but the journey could not be started till the Sultan indicated his agreement to the change of route; this, in its turn, waited on Shefershah Bey's arrival from Poland. But knowing Ali Pasha's determination to open the campaign against Venetia as soon as

* The Peace of Rastadt signed on 6 March (N.S.) 1714, was known in Constantinople in early April.
† See below, pp. 383 ff.

•ossible,* Charles had no doubt that the Grand Vizier would welcome the eparture of the Swedes the minute the formalities in respect of the Tartar nediation report had been completed.

A return journey through Hungary and Austria, as well as being possible, vas now also desirable, and indeed necessary if Charles were to achieve ontrol of Sweden's policy in Germany. The diplomacy of Vellingk and von jörtz, the Duke-Administrator of Holstein-Gottorp's chief minister, had been ounteracting Denmark with some success in 1713 but by methods which did ot find favour with Charles. Görtz was motivated both by his determination ɔ regain the independence of Holstein-Gottorp (lost through Stenbock's nsuccessful campaign) and by a desire to secure the succession in Sweden should Charles XII die without heirs of his own body – of Charles Frederick,)uke of Holstein-Gottorp, the nephew of Charles. The kind of deal Görtz lanned, whereby Prussia would receive Wismar and Stettin in sequester ɔr the duration of the war in return for future help to obtain the Holstein-jottorp objectives, had the advantage from Vellingk's point of view that the ivil administration of these towns would remain Swedish and that help ıight be obtained to retain the rest of Pomerania. Charles, as well as his com-ıanders in Wismar and Stettin, refused to cooperate since they were all onvinced that Prussian troops, once in, could not easily be dislodged. The ɛquestration idea had, all the same, taken root. When Meijerfelt could no ɔnger hold out at Stettin against a large Russian army, the town was in Jovember 1713 handed to a Holstein-Gottorp diplomat who permitted a 'russian occupation. Separate arrangements between Prussia and Holstein-jottorp and Prussia and Russia regularized the sequestration, envisaged its xtension to other parts of Pomerania and promised future benefits all ɔund.[18]

Danish complaints made Tsar Peter cautious, however, in respect of upport for Holstein-Gottorp aims, and Görtz's policy suffered final ship-vreck when the Prussian King on 1/13 June 1714 signed a secret treaty with ₹ussia which promised Prussia outright annexation of Swedish Pomerania s far as the Peene river against Frederick William's guarantee† for Russian ınnexation of Ingria, Estonia and Karelia.[19]

Tsar Peter was similarly concerned to tie Hanover to the anti-Swedish ɔalition: not an easy task in view of Dano-Prussian–Hanoverian conflicting mbitions and mutual suspicions. It was from a fear of Danish expansion that ıe Elector of Hanover in 1712 had marched his troops into the duchy of 'erden; the Swedish authorities – seeing that Denmark had already con-uered the duchy of Bremen and the important town of Stade – were glad ıough to have a power regarded as friendly to Sweden, a guarantor of 'ravendal, prevent the complete loss of the western duchies. With Hanoverian

---

* Though war was declared before the end of 1714, the campaign proper opened in the spring ῾ 1715.
† Frederick William had succeeded Frederick I in Feb. 1713.

troops freed from the War of the Spanish Succession, however, Geor Ludwig – as determined as Frederick William not to be left out in the part tion of Sweden's German territories – felt strong enough to attempt to wre also the duchy of Bremen from Denmark. He hoped to obtain his objectiv with as little expenditure of military force as possible, and used his positio (since 2 August 1714) as King of Great Britain* to drive hard bargains. H was well aware of the tempting bait he now possessed: the British navy coul be used in such a way that victory would be assured for the anti-Swedis coalition. He could therefore afford to bide his time till his terms were me Danish unwillingness to deliver up Bremen without prior compensation i other Swedish territory limited Hanoverian commitment in 1714 to a 'Punc tuation' with Prussia of 11 November (N.S.) in which the two contractin parties agreed to oppose with arms any German state, and in particula Hesse-Cassel,† which should attempt to give Charles XII military suppor but Bernstorff was already planning the division of all Sweden's Germa possessions between Denmark, Prussia and Hanover, with the lion's sha for the latter.[20]

Tsar Peter did not dare to press Frederick IV too far in urging him to reli quish Bremen to George I for the common good. His own projected conques of Finland depended on Denmark and her naval power remaining in th anti-Swedish alliance.[21] He could not risk Frederick IV becoming dissatisfie enough to listen to the peace overtures and alliance suggestions which Charle XII was spreading far and wide in 1713 and 1714: the Tsar knew of thos which had been made to his own representatives as well of those which ha been tried on Augustus and Frederick William and deduced that Denmar had also been approached. For the moment therefore Peter rested conter with the way Prussia and Hanover had been drawn into the net of the ant Swedish coalition: they would, with Denmark, take care of the situation i Germany and leave him free to concentrate on Finland.

III

The Russian campaign against Finland[22] had been opened by the Tsar in 171 as soon as Stenbock's surrender seemed inevitable. His purpose was a twc fold one. Control of Finland would make Sweden's position less tenabl and force her to sue for peace. And at the peace-making his occupation c Finland would give him something to bargain with: land returned woulc he hoped, make the Swedes more willing to accept the loss of the Balti provinces and of those parts of Finland he had conquered – and meant t keep – in 1710.‡

The Swedes had a relatively small galley fleet which the Council had fel

---

* He succeeded Queen Anne in accordance with the 'Protestant Succession' laid down in 170
† For the reason for this emphasis see below, p. 394.
‡ See above, p. 334, for the conquest of Karelia and the fortresses of Viborg and Kexholm.

onstrained to use in the west for defence against Denmark and Norway.[23] Nor did Finland receive reinforcements in troops: these were needed for the German provinces. A strong squadron of Swedish men-of-war was sent to Finnish waters in May 1713, but could not prevent the Russian galleys making skilful use of their low draught. Helsingfors had been abandoned and set on re on 11 May; on 28 August Åbo was also given up. The Swedish army was forced north and west into Österbotten province. The 1714 continuation of the Tsar's campaign led to the loss of Österbotten also, and to a threat to Stockholm itself since the galleys might use the Åland islands as a staging-post for an attack on the Swedish coast.

The loss of Finland caused consternation in Sweden on other counts also. Refugees had to be absorbed into the economic life of the nation and the morale of the population was adversely affected by the Tsar's victories. The Council was concerned for the future. The problem of how to achieve peace agitated them, as did that of the succession in Sweden. Some favoured the young Duke of Holstein-Gottorp, now fourteen years old, as king if Charles should die: either because they considered him, as son of Charles's elder sister, to have the better right, or because they belonged to a group which centred round the Queen-Grandmother and expected to wield more influence than if Ulrika Eleonora succeeded Charles XII. The political intrigues of Görtz, and particularly the indiscreet negotiations of his colleague Bassewitz, for a Russian bride for the young Duke became known in Sweden and created a patriotic revulsion against a Holstein-Gottorp willing to trade away Swedish provinces in return for the Tsar's political support. Many rallied to the cause of Ulrika Eleonora, and her improved prospects brought about competition for her favour: the Council was anxious to associate her with itself and prevailed upon her to take a seat in the Council in November 1713;[24] a determined suitor, Prince Frederick of Hesse-Cassel, had already in 1711 embarked on a courtship by letters, gifts and go-betweens in Stockholm and in 1713 Conrad Ranck, a Swedish officer in Hessian service, was sent to Bender to seek Charles XII's consent.[25]

Ulrika Eleonora found herself wandering in a maze. She was keen to marry Frederick, but unwilling to do so till she had her brother's permission and determined to make sure that neither her married status nor his Calvinism would prejudice her chances in the succession stake. She realized that if Hedvig Sophia had lived, the elder sister would according to Swedish law have been closer to the throne, but Ulrika was ambitious enough to claim precedence before her young nephew. She was not yet aware that Frederick of Hesse hoped that the proposed marriage would make him King of Sweden rather than a Queen's consort; when she became aware of it she was too much in love to deny him his wish.

Ulrika was at the same time torn between her brother and the Council. She sympathized with the Council's desire for peace, and her letters to Charles XII are very open and moving on the Swedish need of an end to the

war;[26] but she was also moved by his appeals to their family bond and to th
role he envisaged for her as his 'regent' in Stockholm who should work i
cooperation with him to save Sweden. Her position inevitably became some
what ambiguous since the Council used her as a shield from the King's wrath
If Charles should return, they wanted the reinsurance of Ulrika's havin
agreed to any step to which the King might object.

Such a step was the calling in the autumn of 1713 of a Diet which sa
till April 1714.[27] The Estates were called partly to steady the country in
period of some alarm,* and partly to permit a testing of views and of willing
ness to support the war effort. In the event, the news of the *Kalabalik* create
great tension and strong groups, advocating specific policies, emerged
Considerable anti-Council feeling was evident in pamphlets and speeches an
a movement for giving full powers to Ulrika Eleonora gained frightenin
momentum once it was rumoured that the King had abdicated. Similarly
peace party, wanting to go further than the Council, became vocal: agains
the Council's policy of starting negotiations for an armistice, this claimed
right for the Estates to make definitive peace treaties.

In the end Horn had to use skill and finesse with a suspicious Ulrika† t
make her disavow her supporters in the Diet. The extremists in the Estate
were baulked by the argument that the King himself was actively engaged i
peace-making. Indeed, there is reason to believe that Charles's order
forbidding the Council to call a Diet, and to disband the Estates if these ha
met, were conveniently 'discovered' a considerable time after their arriva
to resolve a situation which threatened to get out of hand.[28]

IV

It is against this background of domestic tension and a complicated foreig
situation that Charles XII's planning for his post-Turkey policy must b
considered. The theme of war and peace was one that preoccupied hin
increasingly after the non-arrival of the Swedish expeditionary corps robbe
him of the chance to utilize either the 1710 or the 1712 Turkish break wit
Russia. Parallel with the development of his ideas on administrative an
economic reform‡ march his thoughts of Sweden's place in Europe and th
methods whereby she could retrieve the setbacks of 1709–14. His plannin
becomes mature: more profound and more flexible. Discussion with other
helped him, as it did in other fields. Foreigners and Swedes with knowledg
of European affairs broadened his outlook: the Swedish-born Ranck, wh
visited him on Frederick of Hesse's behalf in 1713, offered a new line o
approach to Sweden's problems in Germany. Poniatowski's French contact
in Constantinople pointed to useful cooperation with Louis XIV in the wes

---

* The fear that the Russians would fall upon the country was spreading, and stories that the
would bring child-eating Kalmucks with them found credence.

† Horn was the governor for the young Duke of Holstein-Gottorp.

‡ See above, pp. 342 ff.

s well as in the east. Swedish diplomatic correspondence from the capitals
f Europe, scrutinized and answered with intense concentration once the
King had been forced to ask his representatives to obey him rather than
he Council, also encouraged day-to-day attention on a European scale as
pposed to the earlier need to make decisions only in matters which immedi-
tely and directly affected the defence against the anti-Swedish coalition.[29]
Travellers who visited him at Bender again invited consideration of European
ffairs in general: Fabrice and de la Motraye were in some respects light-
veights, but they both helped to foster the King's interest in and improve his
nowledge of the political world remote from the eastern theatre of war.

The growing maturity of Charles in judgements on European politics and
n his own part in them is particularly noticeable in his conversations with
Axel von Löwen, who visited Turkey in April and May 1712. The two
onversed much on military matters,[30] naturally enough since Löwen had
ought in the War of the Spanish Succession between 1707 and 1711 (first
vith the Hessians and then with the Dutch). But they also discussed political
lecisions taken by the Swedish King in the past. Charles defended his Altran-
tädt demand that Augustus should give up the Polish crown not only on the
grounds that otherwise his own allies in the Commonwealth would have
uffered injustice and persecution, but also with the argument that such
lethronement was not unknown to history either ancient* or modern: had
ot the Allies at Gertruidenberg demanded that Louis XIV should help
lethrone his own grandson? Those who argued that only God had the right
o dethrone a ruler, might be countered by the equal sophistry of *'si Dieu ne
'auroit pas voulu, les hommes n'en seroient pas venu à bout'*; but for his own
art he made a distinction between an elected ruler, as Augustus in Poland,
and one who had succeeded by hereditary right, as Peter in Russia. It would
e fairer to blame him, the Swedish King held, for not having imposed such a
eace on Augustus in 1706 as to have rendered him incapable of creating
rouble later on: in that year Charles could have made himself master of
Saxony, *'lorsque personne ne le pouvoit empêcher'*; Augustus was the aggressor,
le bonheur des armes' was with the Swedes.[31]

The King also defended his refusal of Tsar Peter's offer of peace before
707. While agreeing that, as things had worked out, such acceptance might
eem the better course, this reasoning seemed to him superficial. For as peace
ould only have been bought at the price of leaving Russia territory on the
Baltic, the Tsar – with his *'penchant et genie pour la marine'* – would in a few
vears have constructed a formidable fleet which joined to that of the King of
Denmark† would have toppled Sweden *'tôt ou tard'*, the major stretches of
he country *'étant baignées par la Mer Baltique et ainsi exposées à être
avagées.'* To Charles XII the choice before him had seemed, and still seemed,

* He contrasted Alexander's treatment of Darius, whose dethronement was effected, with that
f Parius, who though defeated, kept his crown.
 † Denmark as a nation he could not bring himself to criticize; 'it did not recognize its own best
nterest', but the King of Denmark was 'the irreconcilable enemy' of Sweden.

like that before Henry IV of France, *'qui disoit que ses affaires et celles d'*
la France étoient dans un tel état que l'honneur l'obligeoit de vaincre ou d'
mourir'. He was well aware, he added, that his own troops had at time
sustained this maxim badly.[32]

But though this reveals that the memory of the Perevolotjna surrender stil
hurt, it was the positive measures to retrieve Sweden's fortunes which fille
the letters to Ulrika Eleonora. She was, once he had accepted Hedvig Sophia'
death, at one and the same time his last beloved link with the happy famil
life of the past* and the co-regent he desired, the only person with whom h
felt obliged to discuss policy freely and fully. In war, he stressed, there ar
swings of fortune. Sweden is down on her luck now, but if we work togethe
and trust in the efficacy of positive measures, God will lend his help and ou
situation will improve again. It was her task to comfort their grandmothe
and to show such courage that the Council might become less defeatist. H
tried to train her by keeping her informed in great detail of political an
military happenings relevant to his policy in Turkey; for if he should die, h
wanted her to 'be firm and of good heart', to display initiative and energ
in governing, above all not to give in to Sweden's enemies.[33]

The *Kalabalik* and the malaria attacks of 1713, and probably also th
embarrassment he felt at not being able to settle the question of her marriag
to Frederick of Hesse as speedily as she might have hoped for,† caused a sto
to these letters for a long time. He began several, but felt he could not writ
freely from Timurtash unless he had so safe and direct a messenger that h
could be reasonably sure that what he wrote her would be seen by her eye
only. At last, with the return, in September 1714, of Hans Henrik von Liewen‡
(who had arrived in March to report on the situation in Sweden and ha
brought a long cyphered letter for the King from Ulrika, but whose journe
home had been delayed by illness)[34] the correspondence was resumed.[3]
Charles complained that his own ability to write *en clair*, to say nothing o
writing in cypher or decoding the difficult *kansli* cypher she had used, ha
deteriorated; but the letter is, from the point of view of content, an admir
ably clear analysis of the policy he must now aim at and the tactics they mus
both adopt.

He begins by giving his agreement to her marriage and by expressing hi
joy, if she accepts Frederick, at the prospect of a brother-in-law with such

* The tone of the letters is emotional, expressing fear of her dying before him and leaving hin
the last one ('I pray to God that I'll be taken next,' 19 December 1710) and in need of reassuranc
(see, e.g. the one of 17 January 1711 in which he begs her to address him as 'Brother' as she use
to do). His own letters always begin 'Dear Sister' or 'Dearest Sister' and the phrase, 'though fa
away in my mind [I am] more with my Dear Sister than where I am', is typical of one aspect o
the correspondence.

† Frederick's desire to have the Swedish succession settled in his favour created difficulties an
Ranck returned to advise him to lower his sights, at least temporarily.

‡ Liewen penned verbatim records of his six conversations with Charles XII: translated int
Swedish (from their amusing amalgam of Swedish, High and Low German) and printed in *Hand*
lingar (Floderus) III, pp. 318–44, they afford valuable insight into the King's method of handlin
men and negotiations.

ne military reputation. He then tackles the problem which the Council's ersuasion of her to take part in its meetings has created for him. He cannot ccept that she is *of* the Council since she is *above* that body, as he himself is, nd therefore separate from it. He does not want her identified with those leasures of the Council of which he disapproves and explains that she and e are, in his opinion, as 'one Person, divided between two places': it would be s ludicrous to regard her and the Council as one and write to them on policy latters in one and the same letter as if he addressed that letter to the 'Council nd myself'. Finally he outlines his views on measures to be taken now there ; no longer any hope of working with or through the Porte. They can be ummarized and paraphrased as follows:

We must not make peace at the present time. I am empowering Vellingk to tart secret negotiations with Russia, Denmark and Poland as needs dictate, ut I do not mean them to lead to any speedy conclusion. They are basically ntended to keep our enemies from pursuing the war vigorously this summer. he enemies will soon discover that Vellingk has no full powers from me and hey will not risk signing without them; for if anything is missing in the natter of full powers, the resulting treaty is not valid. But one or more of the nemies may still be willing to negotiate, out of fear that the others might libble at the bait: none of the three will want to lose the opportunity of tarting negotiations which may eventually lead to peace.

All this does not mean, he continues, that I am against peace. I am in avour of a peace that is defensible in the eye of posterity but for it to be lefensible we must achieve a settlement that will endure for a considerable ime. We won't obtain a good peace if we rush into a general peace congress.* Ve must not treat with all our enemies at once and we must not show our-elves too keen. We must not let them know our real thought, which is to eparate our enemies one from the other by secret negotiations till better imes come. Better times won't come till we get more respect in Europe than ve now have. Such respect won't come till we are stronger in the military ense and display our willingness to use the sword in our own defence. I am igainst the mediation of other powers since I can see no advantages to be lerived from it. Most states are willing to see Sweden weaker than it was. Ve can't expect anyone to help us if we do not help ourselves first. I for one lo not vizualize our problems as being solved through the Maritime Powers. [do not agree with those who say the English are worse than the Dutch in :heir intentions towards us, but there is no reason to be *pleased* with England. [t is true that the situation has now changed so that French interests are :loser to those of Sweden, but nothing can as yet be settled. We must rely on ourselves first and foremost.

Having outlined his policy and the methods he intends to employ in general, he instructs her that she is to watch that the Council does not

* This refers both to the Council's desire for a mediation under the auspices of the Maritime Powers and to the general peace congress to which the Emperor had issued invitations at Brunswick in 1713; see below, p. 383.

sabotage his policy by undoing the new taxation system (which is for the benefit of the common man, on whose welfare the prosperity of the country in the long run depends) or by tampering yet again with the blockade of the Baltic provinces which is useful to Sweden.* The tone is easy and calm, but the desire to separate her from the Council and make her look at the situation with his eyes is obvious.

He ends with his disappointment that Liewen carried no portrait of her to Timurtash, and with a paragraph answering hers and their grandmother's reiterated wishes that he himself would soon marry. He tries a half-joking tone: if he had once promised to marry before thirty, he must now ask leave for postponement till he is forty. The figure seems to have reminded the King, now thirty-two years old, that the years are slipping by and there is some sadness in his: 'how fast the time goes, it runs away more quickly than we can believe, already so much of mine has disappeared.' The thought of the duties awaiting him when he reaches Swedish soil steadies him and produces a didactic: 'I have neither the time nor the opportunity for marriage. Even when I come home, there are too many things to be done to permit me to think of a speedy marriage.'[36]

V

To his fellow-officers he said less on his political plans, but to them he was at times more open on his own feelings on sex and marriage. All who knew him well had long since noticed that he was attracted to the prettier of the girls he met or even glimpsed, and wives of Swedish officers and officials had, during their visits to headquarters, commented on his interest in affairs of the heart – he was always keen to hear how this or that match was progressing.[37] In male company he was obviously freer: he liked gallant stories as long as they were 'not too coarse'.[38] In Turkey the very nature of the community surrounding the King, inactive when compared with the first nine years of the war, put down, willy-nilly, in a strange and exotic land, fostered curiosity in respect of the Turkish women and talk of amorous adventures in the past. Fabrice and de la Motraye give examples of the spicy stories which amused Charles.[39] Swedish sources confirm that the King after 1710 was not averse either then or later to listening to, or even eliciting, the reminiscences of others from the lists of love.†

Generally the King kept the conversation, when it turned to his own feelings in a light and bantering vein. The following exchange is typical. Some

---

* Charles does not specify in what way; presumably he expected her to realize that it (a) denied advantages to Peter, and (b) enabled Swedish privateers to supply the country with necessities, e.g. salt, as well as luxuries.

† See, e.g. Löwen, *Mémoires*, p. 73: '*A propos de ces choses – nous étions plusieurs, – le Roi nous examina sur le nombre des assauts. Le plus déterminéz les faisoient aler à cinque consécutive-ment. "Bagatelle", disoit le Roi, "quinze". Fabrice que le Roi goûtoit fort et qui avoit l'esprit vif répliqua: "Sire, c'est royal et passe le pouvoir de nous autres".*' Cp. ibid., p. 72.

German verses were read which refused to put Charles in the company of heroes since he, unlike them, had not loved. The King read the verses and defended himself with, '*L'amour est une foiblesse dont les grands hommes devroient être exemts.*' The whole company fell on him with the French verse:

> *Et si l'amour est une foiblesse*
> *c'est la foiblesse de grands coeurs.*

No one wanted to accept his challenge to respond to the German slight on him: there was no point in refuting his critics they argued since they were in accord with the world in general that:

> *Un héros que la gloire élève*
> *N'est que à demi récompensé*
> *Et c'est peu si l'amour n'achève*
> *Ce que la gloire a commencée.*

Charles hit back with one of his pet theories, that poets were out to flatter, but declared himself willing to give them the essence of a gallant answer if they would put it into verse: '*le sujet de la réponse doit être qu'ajant vaincu les fiers Saxons, nous avons craint de'être vaincu à notre tour par les charmes de belles Saxonnes.*'[40]

But that he adopted a thoughtful attitude to his own problem in relation to sex and marriage is clear from conversations he had with individuals. To Löwen for instance he spoke freely when he was questioned on the reasons why he remained chaste: '*L'inclination pour les belles femmes ne me manque non plus que à vous, mais je sais mieux la vaincre. Un pareil efort vous coûteroit trop, vous avez déjà pris goût à la chose que cependant vous devez modérer.*'[41] He returns several times to the theme that he knew himself to be of a passionate nature – and others also reckoned him to be of the 'cholerick temper',[42] one ingredient of which was passion – and that, if he once gave in to temptation he feared to become the slave of his inclinations in the way of a gambler who did not know where to stop. And loss of control was, he held, incompatible with his duties as King of Sweden while the war lasted. When it was pointed out to him that Caesar's love for Cleopatra did not interrupt his military ventures, he answered: '*Mais Marc Antoine y succomba et ce fut à perte; Henri 4.e, Roi de France, s'esposa et avoit trop de foiblesse pour ses maîtresses et étoit trop inconstant pour un vrai attachement, et dont je me sens capable si une fois je m'y mets, et je me suis proposé fermement de n'avoir aucun attachement de cette sorte pendant que je suis en guerre pour éviter toute distraction.*'[43] The '*vrai attachement*' remained his deepest longing,* but whether the name of Sophia Hedvig was still one that moved him, we can not say – he never spoke of this dream of his youth in so far as we know and he

---

* '*Je suis en garde contre moi-même, évitant de m'attacher, les passagères et les amours sales n'étant pas de mon goût, puisque je sens que j'aimerous constament*', he told Löwen, see *Mémoires*, p. 72. Cp. his comment to Feif in 1718, below p. 466*.

may have reflected that by the time peace had been restored between himsel and her brother she might well be of an age not considered 'marriageable'.

With a growing realization of himself, Charles became more sure in hi judgement of others. It cost him dear to get rid of the inculcated precept of hi childhood always to think the best of everyone. The first step was the hardes but when he had brought himself to send Lagercrona (always fighting an feuding with fellow-officers) away from Bender in September 1710[44] he foun his own feet. He still on principle disliked the teller of tales and made suc thorough investigations into the truth or otherwise of tales told that it wa jokingly remarked that the surest way to have one's merits brought to th King's attention was by having oneself slandered.[45] But for his own part h now felt free to criticize in confidential moments, specifically naming 'guilt men. He blamed Roos for not having formed '*un battaillon quarré*' whe things went wrong at the redoubts in the Poltava battle: if he had done so th pattern of the shots fired would have drawn Charles's attention* and secure help in time.[46] He blamed Gyllenkrook for not having been more forceful a Perevolotjna: since he knew the roads by which the army could be reunite with the King on Turkish soil, he might have given details to others.[47] H pointed out that Vellingk had let himself be cheated by Augustus in 1712 as i 1699;[48] and that Horn, to judge him on the evidence of his own letters t Bender, had forgotten the soldier's duty of daily work, neglecting both th *kansli* and the young Duke Charles Frederick in the long summers he sper on his estates. Nor was Cronhielm, his old tutor, exempt from the criticis of thinking more of his own concerns than of his duty as a Councillor.[49]

Charles tried to be fair (Lagercrona had some 'good qualities';[50] Velling had much esprit, was 'ingenious and active')[51] but the King was by 171 undoubtedly more cynical than in his early youth about people and the wa they reacted. Typical is his comment when he, in 1715, read Boileau's line on Alexander† in Löwen's copy of the *Satires*: '*C'est une liberté poétiqu outrée; s'il auroit reçu d'Alexandre l'argent que Louis 14 lui a donné, il auro prodigué ses louanges pour le premier de même que pour l'autre.*'[52] Charles wa incapable of putting himself sympathetically in the place of those he criticize in private, so that an element of unfairness sometimes struck the listener o the recipient of the letter: Ulrika, provoked by his condemnation of th Council, refuted with spirit that this body was 'asleep' to Sweden's re problems.[53]

The growth of the King's realistic judgement of men as well as of Sweden dilemma during the years in Turkey is, however, undeniable. He had face the loss of experienced advisers after Poltava. 'It is difficult', he wrote t Ulrika as early as December 1710, 'to find men of the right calibre to serv

---

* For Charles's ability to distinguish the Swedish pattern from that of enemy forces see Löwe *Mémoires*, p. 65.

† Voltaire's story that Charles, in Bender, had torn the copy of the Satires to pieces becau Boileau dared to criticize his hero Alexander may well be true, but Charles's strong disapproval much in Alexander's character can be seen from Löwen, *Mémoires*, pp. 41–2.

Js'.[54] He was on the look-out therefore for those who, whether Swedish or foreign, would prove capable helpers once attempts to exchange some of those he missed most in Russian captivity had failed. Experience between 1710 and 1714 robbed him of any illusions he might have had as to his own power while so far away. His answer, when he was asked to regulate the succession: 'They do not obey me while I am alive, why should I expect them to do so once I am dead?'[55] was probably compounded as much from knowledge of past royal wills set aside in Sweden and from a desire to shelve the issue as from personal pique. But some pique is clearly present in the anonymous 'they'. With disillusionment came shrewder insight. When Axel Sparre once told him that if he did not soon hurry home, Sweden might elect another ruler, Charles answered: '*Des entreprises pareilles demandent beaucoup d'esprit et de cœur*'[56] – qualities he did not espy in 'them'.

The mature Charles did not strike his entourage as either suspicious or cynical. Those who got to know him in Bender, and therefore speculated on his character, admired the way he rose above misfortune. He knew of the rumours which circulated in Sweden and elsewhere that he had gone mad; but he refused to counter them in any way.[57] He made, and explained, his own philosophy for kings he would be prepared to call 'great':

Le bonheur ne les rend pas grands, aussi peu que le malheur ne peut rien ôter à leur vertu. Et la fortune qui est une coureuse coquette ne doit pas décider de la vraie gloire, non plus que l'inconstance d'une femme infidelle devroit le faire de l'honneur de son mari. Les faux préjugéz du vulgaire, qui prend le faux pour le véritable, ne font aucune impression sur l'esprit de l'homme solide et juste qui sufit à lui-méme, et ne se soucie non plus de raisonnemens du public mal instruit et préoccupe que la lune qui va son chemin malgré l'aboiement* des chiens.[58]

It was these and similar sentiments which later were to earn him the title, during the siege of Stralsund, of 'philosopher-king' from Louis XIV's representative.[59]

The pride of these words, when written down, and the hint of a hope that he himself might be reckoned among the great which seems to lurk behind them, did not strike those who recorded them. They admitted that Charles was proud with equals, but so modest and friendly with everyone else (including themselves) that they marvelled at his egalitarian disposition. His praises – whether noted in diaries or letters at the time or recollected in old age – are so frequent and so unanimous that one becomes convinced of one thing: whatever the complex and mature Charles was really like, he exerted on those who met him a charm which was not there in his youth. He bound you to him, wrote Löwen, you'd follow him anywhere.[60] The soldiers had always felt attraction as well as respect for Charles XII; and the French officers – men

---

* The reference is to the first line of a Swedish poem by Georg Stiernhielm, which, without attempt at rhyme, runs: 'The moon in silence goes its round, Pays no attention to the barking of dogs, So also does the virtuous man, Lives in peace within his own sphere, Laughing at superficial splendour and Despising the gabbing tongues.'

like Maigret, Bousquet, Folard and many others – who took service in th
Swedish army after 1715 became strongly attached to him. After 170
civilians came no less under his sway. Men who had come on brief missions t
Turkey stayed, postponing departure again and again: Fabrice worked fo
Charles in later years as an unofficial diplomat; de la Motraye travelled to th
far north to meet him again; Görtz, who was on his way to him in Turkey i
1714, linked his fate for ever to his as soon as they met in Stralsund. Fe
warned Tessin not to come to Turkey when the older man suggested that hi
services might be useful in reconciling Council and King: 'All who come he
stay. Either they become so fond of Us, or We so fond of them, that they can
escape.'[61] Swedes who had not seen Charles for years exclaimed at th
gracious, yet open and free and easy manner of the King who returned t
Sweden's provinces in Germany at the end of 1714 and to Sweden itself a
the end of 1715.

BOOK SIX

Return to Europe

1

The Ride to Stralsund

Charles XII's preparations for the return to his own dominions had to be made on a diplomatic as well as a financial level. No new loan was forthcoming from the Turkish authorities,[1] but Ehrenskiöld obtained, from Viennese bankers and other private sources,* a sum large enough to cover the expenses which the King, his officials and his small army would incur during the journey from Turkey to Pomerania. There was enough to spare for a Swedish embassy of leave-taking, with customary costly presents, in Constantinople;[2] but not sufficient to repay all Turkish subjects who had advanced ready money to the King or his followers after the *Kalabalik*. When the party from Bender met Charles and his suite, a motley crowd of creditors and creditors' representatives came along too and those who could not be repaid – twenty-nine in all – decided to accompany their debtors to the far north to make sure of capital and interest.[3]

The route to be traversed and the question of Charles's status in the interval between leaving Turkish soil and reaching that of Sweden had been the subject of negotiations centred on Vienna. The Emperor was willing, and indeed anxious, to facilitate Charles XII's journey on several counts. The recent successes of the anti-Swedish coalition inside Germany had alarmed Charles VI and his advisers: their attitude towards Charles XII therefore changed from the censoriousness with which they had regarded his unwillingness to co-operate in the Brunswick congress (called in December 1712 by the Emperor to promote peace in the North)[4] to one in which they looked upon him as a serviceable brake on too rapid an expansion in the power of the North German princes. At Baden Villars had encouraged Prince Eugène to help the Swedish King reach his territories in the Empire before these were completely lost: the projected Catholic alliance between Vienna and Versailles, it was argued, ought to prefer a weakened Sweden to keep its foothold in Germany rather than permit an access of strength to the German Protestant rulers.[5] The Emperor, in his anxiety to secure the mediator's role in the Great Northern War, also assumed that by permitting Charles XII to return via the

---

* One hundred thousand *Reichsthaler* at nine per cent was borrowed in Vienna; other loans had to be taken up at higher interest, some at thirty per cent.

Habsburg dominions he could favour his own chances as opposed to those of the Maritime Powers whose separate peaces with France he still resented

Charles VI and Eugène would have preferred Charles XII to make a formal visit to Vienna or at least to permit himself to be received with royal honours by a representative of the Emperor. This the Swedish King was unwilling to do. He wanted to avoid commitments and promises in respect of a general peace congress and stipulated that his journey must be made incognito with no notice whatever being taken of it officially. Quite apart from the question of mediation, the awkward problem of Charles VI's title as King of Spain would have bedevilled any formal visit. Charles XII had never recognized the Archduke as Carlos III of Spain and, in view of the Emperor's claim to the title even after 1714, negotiations between them had to be carried out indirectly, via Fabrice.

Charles's insistence on permission to travel incognito (this or the King will choose another route, e.g. by sea in a French ship, was the gist of the messages to Vienna) brought speedy results: passes were issued that permitted Charles and his suite to travel incognito through Transylvania,* Hungary and the Austrian hereditary dominions, though Prince Eugène expressed his astonishment that Charles XII was willing to take the risk of travelling without an Austrian armed escort in a country 'where one can find men who for a 30 sol piece would fire a musket at him from a hedge'.[6]

II

On 20 September 1714 Charles left Demotika with a Turkish escort to see him and his party of 130 as far as Piteşti on the borders where the Sultan's province of Wallachia met Habsburg land. Here it had been arranged that the Swedes, with those Poles and Cossacks from Bender who wanted to join them, should make their rendezvous with the King they had not seen since the *Kalabalik*. At Timurtash, with its memories of malaria and weakness, Ahmed III's presents of farewell were ceremoniously handed over: fine horses, wonderful tents and a richly decorated and bejewelled saddle.

The route taken by the riders traversed the Balkan mountains by the usual passes,† the Danube was crossed at Ruscuk and on 8 October Pitesci was reached. Charles sent personal letters of thanks to the Sultan and the Grand Vizier with the escort that now left him; two days later those who had started from Bender, with horses for riding and for wagons provided by the Turks,[7] caught up. There were about 1,200‡ men in all who were divided into five groups, each under a major-general, with Sparre as commander-in-chief.[8] On 25 October the first group began its journey and the others followed with one day's interval between each departure.

* 'Siebenbürgen' in the documents of the period.
† Between Derwent-Selkva and Eszki-Stambol.
‡ In the Austrian dominions free daily rations were arranged for 1,500 men and 2,133 horses; the actual count reported to Vienna from the border posts was 1,162 men and 1,912 horses.

From the whole party Charles had chosen twenty-four officers to form a small suite of his own. Vienna had made only two conditions when the Emperor promised to respect his incognito: he was not to travel through Silesia and – lest Charles VI's honour should be tarnished by attempts to have the Swedish King kidnapped on Habsburg soil – Austrian commanders in Hungary and Transylvania would be told in a general way to keep a sharp look out for suspicious characters.[9]

The subject of a disguise for Charles had been debated among his advisers. It was desirable to prevent him being recognized. Protestant demonstrations or appeals would be an embarrassment since it was by the Emperor's courtesy that the Swedish King travelled. Attempts at capture by Russian, Saxon or Polish agents – though not considered likely – had to be taken into account. Fabrice joked that the problem was easy enough: if Charles borrowed Grothusen's black wig and Müllern's nightcap, if he used the best inns, imbibed freely and flirted openly, if he was seen wearing slippers, and if it became known that he slept long in the mornings – then nobody would guess his identity.[10]

Charles did his own picking and choosing among these and other suggestions and added some – like the name adopted – which bear his own hallmark. He did put on a dark wig, he chose a hat with gold braid and a brown uniform lined with white and he got his Chancery to make out a pass for Captain Peter Frisk. Some time during the ride he also grew a moustache and this either turned out darker than his hair or was coloured brown.[11] His plan was that he and two companions should move ahead of a second party of three, ordering horses for them and generally giving the impression that they were relatively unimportant men smoothing the path for those of higher rank. Count Ture Bielke was among those in the second* group and Fabrice tells in his *Memoires* that this officer was frequently thought to be the King of Sweden: not surprisingly as he was dressed in Charles XII's clothes, wore his gloves, and carried his sword and his *Etuis de Matematiques*.[12]

The trip ahead would be a tough one, at least for the King and his immediate companions once they had past Vienna. That far they planned to ride post, according to the arrangement with the Habsburg authorities, which would be tiring enough if one permitted oneself no rest-days; but after Vienna Charles aimed to ride at the fastest possible speed hoping he might reach Stralsund before anyone in North Germany knew he had left Turkey. The other officers and officials were also split into smaller groups which were to fan out along various routes after Vienna so that, if rumours of the King's departure from Turkey ran ahead of him, would-be seekers might be misled as to his own choice of road.[13]

To get himself and his officers into training, Charles spent two days

* The others were Poniatowski and Colonel Bousquet (a French officer in Swedish service since 1704). Bielke kept a journal of the return journey, from which the route and the distances covered each day is known. Rosen, of Charles's party in the early stages, has left some notes based on his own memories and those of Düring, but he wrote them down as late as 1762.

exercising on horseback in the neighbourhood of Piteşti: riding through gaps between posts that were staked ever closer together with cross-bars which were lowered again and again; picking up gloves thrown to the ground while in full gallop; and similar feats. The King had regained his health once he was permitted to move from Timurtash and its malaria-infested swamps back to Demotika,* and had ridden regularly for exercise on the outskirts of that town. There was no sign of weakness from his several leg injuries; and the fat which, to judge from Axel Sparre's portraits of him, he put on at times during the years in Turkey had been dieted and exercised away.[14]

On 27 October Captain Peter Frisk and his two companions, Captains Johann Palm and Erik Ungern – in reality the King's adjutant-general von Rosen and Major-General Düring – began their ride, estimated to last twenty-four hours, to the Rotenturm pass which gave access to Transylvania and through which many Turkish invading armies had passed into the heart of Europe. The two officers had been picked not only for their physical fitness, but also for their linguistic abilities: Rosen knew at least some of the dialects spoken in Wallachia and Düring's mother-tongue was German, which might help to hide the Swedish identity of the party. They took no guide and got off to a bad start, losing their way before they reached the pass and trying to retrieve it in pitch darkness† leading their spare horses. Guides were eventually found and, leaving Rosen as a link between them and the 'grand' party, Charles and Düring hurried ahead, riding at night in difficult terrain with the help of torchlights. In the morning of 30 October they rode through Rotenturm.

At Hermannstadt, a town three miles from the pass, the tired horses were left behind and the two men rode post-horses, accompanied by postillions, to Mühlbach in Transylvania. From there,‡ as throughout Hungary, the only means of transport was by post-coach. A little way inside the border, at Szilágy Somlyó, in the evening of 1 November, they met Field-Marshal Count Welczek, sent by the Emperor to see that Charles XII and his men were well cared for. The field-marshal did not penetrate the King's disguise, and from his later conversation with Poniatowski's party it seems as if Düring at least – and possibly Charles as well – had pretended to be somewhat the worse for drink.[15] From Welczek's own report we know that Poniatowski (officially travelling as Lieutenant-General Rosa) quickly admitted his real identity and that the field-marshal and his secretary assumed that 'Captain Bielke' who kept quietly in the background, and who only drank water at meals, was in fact Charles XII.

There was some relief at having, fairly positively, identified the King. His incognito would be respected, but in order to make sure he was not captured

---

* In November 1713; though he suffered another touch of fever in January 1714.

† The moon reached its first quarter on 3 November.

‡ The route chosen went from Mühlbach (Szaszsebes) over Karlsburg (Gyulafehérvár), Enyed, Kocsárd, Torda, Klausenburg (Kolozsvar), Korod, Berend, Zombor, Egregy and Bred to Zilah, the last Transylvanian post-stage: the surest details are by Ballagi, *K.F.Å.*, 1934, pp. 172–4.

THE WAR IN SWEDISH POMERANIA
AND NORWAY   1714–1718

N

Kongsvinger
Glommen
Kristiania
L. Øieren
Drammen
Hølen
Høland
Onstadsund
VÄRMLAND
Tønsberg
Moss
Holmedal
Kristianiafjord
Torpum
Kristinehamn
Frederikshald
Frederikstad
Hälleröd
Dinekilen
Strömstad
Västra Ed
Tanum
DALS-
LAND
BOHUS
Uddevalla
Vadstena
Marstrand
Gothenburg
Jönköping
S W E D E N
Varberg
JUTLAND
The Sound
Kalmar
Hälsingborg
Karlskrona
Kristianstad
Humlebæk
Lund
Copenhagen
Malmö
Ystad
ZEALAND
Trelleborg
BORNHOLM
(Swedish 1658–60)
SLESWIG
RÜGEN
Tønning
Kiel
Stralsund
Altefähr
RUDEN
HOLSTEIN
Stralsund
Tribsees
Greifswald
USEDOM
Travendal
Lübeck
Peene
Wolgast
Stade
Altona
Wismar
WOLLIN
BREMEN
Hamburg
Gadebusch
MECKLENBURG
SWEDISH POMERANIA
BRANDENBURG–PRUSSIA
Stettin
HANOVER
Weser
Elbe
Oder
Hanover

0   100
Kilometres

by his enemies or attacked by robbers a detailed description had been given
by Viennese authorities: look out for one who is tall, with a particularly slim
waist; his hair is *en brosse*; on the right side of his nose there is a small mark
from the injury he received at the *Kalabalik*; he limps a little when he walks;
be on guard if you see someone fitting this description who drinks wine with
lots of water in it for that may be Charles XII trying to throw you off the scent.[16]

Meanwhile the two companions continued undetected along the Hungarian
post-route over Debreczen, Buda and Raab to Vienna. They stopped nowhere
more than an hour or so at the staging-posts; but between stages (each of
some three to four hours) they slept on straw in the bottom of the coach: not
a regal coach, Fabrice mused in his memoirs – more fit for rats.[17] Tradition
claims Charles as a guest in many an inn along the route,[18] but with so many
officers of his suite travelling the same road, no certain identification is
possible. The two which dispute the honour in one of the Vienna suburbs
are far removed from the posting stage in Altstadt where Charles and Düring
must have arrived. It seems unlikely that the Swedish King made contact with
anyone in the Habsburg capital which he reached on 5 November:[19] he was
anxious to be on his way and wary of attempts to make him recognize the
Emperor's Spanish title, and he had purposely avoided Pressburg, where
Charles VI was staying at the time though it was on his direct route. Bitter
memories of disputed titles in Poland apart, Charles found it 'unbecoming'[20]
to recognize two Kings of Spain. He, as other European monarchs, had in
1700 recognized Philip V and Charles's pride would be hurt at any hint that
he were willing to 'buy' his way home at the price of such double-dealing.

From Vienna post-horses for riding were freely available in all directions
and speed could be increased since there was no need for postillions as guides.
The growing moon helped and the two averaged more than twenty-four
German miles every twenty-four hours, arriving at Stralsund on the night the
moon was full. The route chosen lay along as friendly territory as possible –
Bavaria (the ally of Louis XIV) and Hesse-Cassel: Linz, Passau, Straubing,
Regensburg, Nürnberg, Erlangen, Bamberg, Würzburg, Remlingen,
Esselbach, Dettingen, Hanau, Cassel.

It was in Cassel that Charles, according to his first Swedish biographer
Nordberg, came closest to being detected. A Swedish-born officer in Hessian
service, Brigadier Kagg, was at the post-house and had supper with the two
captains. His behaviour and his questions both before and during the meal
gave Düring the feeling that the King had been recognized. When the
Brigadier pointedly asked if Captain Frisk drank pure water in imitation of
his King, Charles is said to have found it wisest to empty a glass of wine. This
story may be less apocryphal than the dénouement, that at the moment of
departure, already in the saddle, Charles revealed his identity with a 'Goodbye
my dear Kagg, my greetings to the Landgrave.'[21]

After Cassel, Charles and Düring avoided Hanover territory* – as they had

* The second party took the Celle route and Bielke was again identified as the King.

hat of Saxony – but we do not know their exact route till they got to Ulzen near Mecklenburg. The usual post-road over Dömitz, Grabow and Parchim was followed through this duchy. At Triebsees they reached Swedish Pomerania and in the night of 10–11 November they knocked on the closed own-gate of Stralsund.

III

The King told the guard on duty that he came as a messenger with express etters for General Dücker, and asked to be brought to him. No one guessed Charles's identity. He wore – according to letters which were sent to Sweden he next morning – a big hat over a dark wig of the curled variety and his beard was 'quite long'.[22] He and his companion were kept waiting while non-commissioned and commissioned officers in ascending hierarchy were consulted as to the advisability or otherwise of disturbing the general. It was nearly 4 o'clock in the morning before Dücker received Charles XII in his bedroom. As soon as the first greetings were over, the King went to Dücker's *badstuga** to clean up but was so tired that he dozed off for a quarter of an hour, sitting at a table with his head resting on his arms. His boots had to be cut off. The surgeon who did this noted that the King's old wound had been chafed and bandaged it after treatment.

It was no wonder that Charles's feet were sore and swollen. The distance covered in less than a fortnight† – reckoned from Piteşti – was some 384 German miles. For 118 of these miles the King and Düring had travelled by post-coach, but the rest had been on horseback and it is unlikely that their boots had been taken off during the last 168 miles from Vienna to Stralsund which they had covered in six days and nights.[23]

The famous ride has captured the imagination of Europe, and particularly of the regions through which Charles and Düring travelled so speedily that they can have caught no more than glimpses of church towers and buildings and broad impressions of the changing landscapes. The many anecdotes connected with the ride have – with the possible exception of the Kagg story related above – proved without foundation: the King did not make secret calls to any one at the court of Vienna; it was not his cape, but Düring's, which was lost in Germany, cut into hundreds of pieces and proudly displayed as parts of 'Charles's woollen Turkish *habba*';[24] he did not stay the night at his or that German inn which later proudly put inscriptions to that effect beneath the prints of the Swedish King which they displayed on their walls. We know for a fact that he sent Count Welczek a valuable ring in appreciation of his services to the whole Swedish party,[25] and also that he conveyed his gratitude to the Emperor, via Sweden's diplomatic representative in Vienna.[26]

But the very legends surrounding the ride tell us something of the excitement and glamour which still clung to Charles's name: was a new act in the

---

* It is possible that this was a sauna-bath of the type in common use in all Swedish dominions.
† 13 days 4½ hours is the closest estimate.

heroic drama to begin? At a less superficial level, the Protestants of Germany took heart and reckoned with a possible protector against the Catholic front of Louis XIV and Charles VI. The Protestant Chamber of Estates of the Regensburg Diet had formally conveyed their thanks for Charles XII's services to their Silesian brethren – a letter which the King treasured because it linked with him the work of Gustavus Adolphus;[27] and it was generally held that he would not stand idly by if resurgent Catholicism should endanger the religious settlement of 1648.

From a more exclusively political point of view Charles's return occasioned intense speculation as to the shape of events to come. Would he, as was expected in Vienna, out of gratitude for the various ways in which his journey had been facilitated and his men fed and lodged, cooperate in the Emperor's Brunswick Congress to restore peace in the North? Would he, as George I and Frederick William hoped, outbid the anti-Swedish coalition and acquiesce in cession of land they coveted from Sweden's provinces in Germany in return for alliances of diplomatic rather than military support? Would he, as the Maritime Powers assumed, prove softer in respect of the Baltic blockade now he could judge Sweden's plight at closer quarters? Would he prove accessible, as individual Jacobites held possible, to cooperation with them against George I as King of Great Britain now that that King, as Elector Georg Ludwig, was moving so close to Sweden's enemies?

Among the declared military opponents, Frederick of Denmark, Augustus of Saxony and Peter of Russia, there was uneasiness and wariness: at the prospects which Charles might have of buying support, direct or indirect, for Sweden's cause; at the way in which he might make use of their conflicting ambitions; at the conviction that he would stiffen Sweden's will to resist.

In Sweden there was, above all, a deep emotional relief that the King had returned to his own. There had been talk of Charles's return since the spring of 1714, but in the event the news which on 17 November reached Stockholm by express, of his arrival in Stralsund preceded any letter which told of his departure from Turkey. It was received with 'indescribable joy everywhere' wrote Rhyzelius – a newly appointed drabant-chaplain who was waiting in Stockholm to join the army. He saw many who cried with joy;[28] joy and relief alike were given expression in the services of thanksgiving which were arranged at court by the Queen-Grandmother and in the churches through out the country.

Even the critics of the King's policy were pleased to have him home: at least he was now at hand to take charge himself and they would be rid of the fearful responsibility and of the conflict between what they and he saw as first priorities. And this conflict had in any case diminished: with the prospect of the King's return Horn and the Council had begun to trust less in the Maritime Powers and their mediation and more in the methods by which Charles hoped to achieve a reasonable peace. It is noteworthy that as early as April 1714 Horn reckoned with help from 'the King of France and our other allies' nside the Empire so that Denmark might be forced to evacuate Holstein-Gottorp and restore what she had conquered of Sweden's German provinces. He visualized no sacrifice of territory in Germany, since the sequesters and occupations would be terminated once Frederick IV and Augustus were defeated. But Russia, which could not be got at by land or sea in the way Denmark could, would have to be pacified. Horn hoped that Charles would now realize that he had better leave the Tsar St Petersburg 'for this time' since the luck of war had gone against Sweden: the town could be reconquered in the future.[29]

The weakness of Horn's reasoning lay in thinking that Tsar Peter, after his great military successes, would be satisfied with such a limited conquest as St Petersburg and surrounding districts; but his general attitude is close enough to that of Charles to show how much of a rapprochement with the King's own views had taken place with the news of his prospective return. The will to defence had been reanimated as soon as the King had been forced to give up his attempts to fight Russia in collaboration with the Turks. The importance of the Porte's relations with Russia was not underestimated by Horn. 'Can anyone, after God, but the Turks get St Petersburg back for us?' he mused.[30] But Charles's policy of having a hand in that reconquest Horn – and the majority of his colleagues – had never relished. With the apple of dissension removed from Charles's grasp, the Council looked forward to harmony and cooperation with their King. There was some uneasiness as to whether any of them would be 'out of favour'; but they trusted both in the King's well-known 'mildness' and their conviction that they had acted for the best of motives to the best of their ability in difficult circumstances.

IV

Sweden assumed that the ride to Stralsund was but one stage on the journey to Stockholm and that Charles would shortly proceed by ship to Karlskrona and from there hurry to the capital.[31] The King, however, had other plans. His first concern on his arrival had been to get out of his disguise. He would not present himself to the troops in Stralsund, or let himself be generally seen, till he could do so as himself in the style of clothing with which he had become associated. As soon as he awoke in the morning of 11 November, a tailor was called to measure him for a plain blue coat, a white waistcoat and a pair of buckskin breeches. This uniform, and a pair of new boots, were ready within twenty-four hours. While he waited, Charles stayed indoors and wrote letters destined for Sweden 'all the afternoon'.[32] The officers in his suite from Piteşti began to arrive: Rosen already on 13 November, Poniatowski and Bielke on the 15th; the rest a little later.* On that day Fabrice also arrived to find the King, returning from a parade of inspection, 'poking

* The five army groups naturally travelled more slowly; the last one reached Pomerania in March 1715.

his nose into my coach'. Motraye, Fabrice's travelling companion, an
Jefferyes were not far behind.[33]

From all corners visitors now began streaming into Stralsund. The Duke
Administrator of Holstein-Gottorp came to make his compliments and t
explain and excuse his and his ministers' policies in the years of Charles'
absence. His chief helper, von Görtz, had set out on a mission to Demotik
for this very purpose in the summer of 1714, and had already reache
'Hermannstadt in Siebenbürgen' when he met Fabrice – on his way to Vienn
to help prepare for Charles XII's journey – who persuaded him to return. N
good would come from such a late visit, Fabrice argued: the King was on th
point of breaking up from Turkey, much better to stay in Vienna for a while
be as helpful to Swedes in transit as possible, and then catch up with busines
in Stralsund. Not long after his own arrival, Fabrice had the pleasure o
introducing Görtz to Charles.[34] The King declared himself satisfied with th
Holstein-Gottorp explanations and excuses, and soon turned the talk t
positive measures for the future. In these discussions Görtz participated an
the Duke-Administrator in February 1715 accredited him to Charles in th
hope that he would use his gifts to win the King's confidence and enable hir
to work, in so far as was feasible, for the candidature of the young Duke i
the Swedish succession and for the recovery of Holstein-Gottorp lan
occupied by Denmark.

The rival party, that of the Hessians, also made an early appearance i
Stralsund. Frederick of Hesse had indeed planned to promote his marriage t
Ulrika Eleonora by a visit to Stockholm in the summer of 1714, but had bee
advised by Vellingk that he might succeed more speedily if he waited fo
Charles XII's return and negotiated directly with him. Vellingk himself was i
Stralsund when the King arrived, and arranged an invitation for the Hess
prince. On 1 December Charles rode out with all his 'generals and cavaliers' a
Frederick and his suite neared the town. The two professional soldiers got o
well together; the King soon broached the subject of the other's suit: he ha
better hurry to Stockholm and claim Ulrika Eleonora before winter and ic
made the voyage difficult. Quite apart from wishing to please his sister an
grandmother who had waited so long for specific consent (as expressed in
properly negotiated contract of marriage) Charles was keen to obtain th
military and moral help of a brother-in-law. Frederick had a heroic reputatio
from the War of the Spanish Succession. He had been a volunteer with Princ
Eugène in Italy in 1701, and, as lieutenant-general for the Hessian corps i
Dutch service since 1702 he had worked with Marlborough in many cam
paigns and shown great courage in attack. His actions brought him letters o
congratulations from the Emperor Leopold and from Queen Anne; hi
chivalry to prisoners taken brought him letters of thanks from Louis XIV. Hi
military and his political experience, to say nothing of his optimistic tempera
ment, made him a collaborator on whom Charles was to place much relianc

But Frederick's hopes that his wife's right to the Swedish succession, if no

is own, should be settled before the marriage were dashed. His earlier
o-betweens with Charles XII had let him know that the Swedish King was 'all'
or Ulrika Eleonora and 'nothing' for the young Duke of Holstein-Gottorp;
ut this was based on impressions which Düben in 1712 and Ranck in 1713
ained at the King's headquarters from talk with officials. The Hessians could
ake comfort from Charles's stipulation that Ulrika Elonora's children must
e brought up in the Lutheran faith of the mother rather than the Calvinist
ne of the father in order to preserve their right of inheritance to the crown;
ut as for the marriage contract itself, the King insisted that it must be
modelled directly on that between Hedvig Sophia and the Duke of Holstein-
Gottorp, in which the succession issue had not been broached.[35]

Charles XII has often been criticized for not settling the succession during
is lifetime. Had he done so, it has been argued, the loss of momentum in the
var effort might have been avoided; and Ulrika Eleonora might not have had
o forswear absolutism as the price for her victory over young Charles
rederick of Holstein-Gottorp.[36] The situation in 1718 was, however, rather
more complex* than this contention would admit. In any case Charles was
gainst a decision on emotional as well as political grounds. When in Turkey,
e had regarded Ulrika as his co-regent and continued to desire the closest
ollaboration with her and her husband as a team; but he assumed that
Ulrika – if her hopes of children were fulfilled – would become increasingly
reoccupied with her role as a wife and mother. At the same time the young
Duke was growing from child to young manhood and with Charles's approach
o Sweden his desire to see his beloved elder sister's child grew. So did concern
or the boy who had neither mother nor father, especially after the young
Duke became isolated by the death of the Queen-Grandmother (his great-
randmother) in 1715. To Charles it seemed that it was now up to him to
ain Charles Frederick and care for him as he had once done for Max of
Württemberg. He could not bring himself, even before he met the boy, to
oose between the sister and the nephew. The sister was closer to him, but it
ent against the grain to exclude the nephew from the family circle. Family
nity would also suffer if he gave either side the least inclination that he
voured one more than the other in the matter of succession; and after his
turn to Sweden and his meetings, first with the young Duke and then with
Ulrika Eleonora, he could not bear to do anything that disturbed the harmony
hich he so passionately desired within the family.

Even worse, from the political point of view, would be the effect of
premature choice in the succession issue. As long as both parties, the
rincipals as well as those who favoured their candidatures, had hopes of
ucceeding, both could be expected to collaborate with Charles in the war
fort. If the succession was laid down, some would be gained but others
ould be alienated. A choice would also give a handle for Sweden's enemies

---

* For the opposition to absolutism as a result of Charles XII's reforms in administration and
xation, see below, pp. 518 ff.

to negotiate with the candidate spurned and his supporters. The negotiations of Bassewitz in 1712–13 were an object-lesson in the value of the succession as a factor in diplomacy and one which impressed itself with increasing force when Ulrika Eleonora's hopes of a child were, if not extinguished, at least diminished by the miscarriages she suffered between 1715 and 1718.

As Charles XII, in December 1714, showed himself determined not to permit the linking of Frederick's marriage to Ulrika with the issue of the succession, the Hessians accepted the position. The Prince left for Sweden before the end of the year, the betrothal was announced on Ulrika's twenty-seventh birthday, and the marriage took place in March in the apartments of the Queen-Grandmother in the presence of the Council, court officials and the young Duke of Holstein-Gottorp, who had – as the only male member of the royal family in Sweden – received Frederick on his arrival in Stockholm. The marriage contract was ratified in Stralsund by Frederick's father, the Landgrave Charles, who at the same time signed a treaty with Sweden which put Hessian troops at the disposal of Charles XII.[37] The German threat to their own expansion which Hanover and Prussia had contracted to oppose could be interpreted as having materialized.*

V

There were other signs before the end of 1714 of the direction in which Charles XII was moving. Lieutenant-General Erik Sparre was sent to Versailles to suggest, now that the War of the Spanish Succession was over, a resumption of the old Franco-Swedish alliance. Charles was willing to guarantee the recent Peace of Baden between France and the Empire as well as renewing the Peace of Westphalia, against a fresh French guarantee of the Peace of Oliva of 1660 to uphold Sweden against Poland and Russia. More significant than these mutual guarantees embodied in a treaty signed in March 1715, was the clause by which Louis XIV promised Charles XII a yearly subsidy of 600,000 *riksdaler* for as long as the war lasted.[38] Here was a contribution more valuable than men and one which gave hopes of being able to pay not only the Hessian troops but also others who wanted to take service with the Swedes. And, indeed, individual Frenchmen began to enlist with Charles XII once it became clear that the Northern War would go on. Their experience, particularly of siege warfare, was considered valuable enough to make Swedish officers look out for likely candidates. The praise of Charles sent back to France by Louis XIV's ambassador to the King at Stralsund, Henri-François Colbert, Comte de Croissy (an officer by profession) also contributed to increase the number of Frenchmen in Charles XII's new officer-corps.

It did not at first seem inevitable that the war would continue inside the Empire. The only non-Swedish troops in Pomerania were Prussian ones.

* See above, p. 370

Augustus had withdrawn his own soldiers and his Russian auxiliaries to Saxony and Poland after the Tsar had given his blessing to the sequester arrangement with Prussia. Through the offices of the Hessian Landgrave Charles now tried to end the sequester. With the prospect of French money to come, and with Stanislaus settled in Zweibrücken, it was possible to offer the Prussian King payment of all costs incurred and to promise that Pomerania would not be used as the base for an attack on either Saxony or Poland.[39]

Charles also tried to rally the Emperor to his side by accepting his mediating role at the Brunswick congress on condition that Charles VI declared (even if only verbally and secretly) that the purpose of this congress was to negotiate in what manner Sweden's occupied and sequestered provinces in the Empire should be restored to her'. The moral support of such a declaration would have been invaluable for Sweden. The argument was used that it was the right and duty of Charles VI as head of the Empire to see that one prince of it, Charles XII, was not robbed of his land whether by conquest, occupation or sequestration when he was far away. The attack on each and every one of the Swedish provinces in Germany had, Charles the Emperor was reminded, come from princes of the Empire, while no offensive had been started from any of the Swedish provinces.[40]

In theory such a solution had its attractions for Charles VI; but in practice Vienna realized that it was impossible ot make Georg Ludwig of Hanover or Frederick William disgorge their share (however obtained) of Swedish German territory without recourse to force. Such force the Emperor, well aware of Georg Ludwig's access in power since 2 August 1714, was not prepared to use. In January 1715 the Hanoverian representative in Vienna was told that his master's alliance with Augustus and arrangements with Frederick William were known and belied his pacific words, but words of disapproval had little effect.

Vienna's attention was increasingly turned away from Germany: the Turkish declaration of war against Venetia in December 1714 spelt danger as well as opportunities for the Habsburgs in the east. This very war helped to put an end to the rapprochement between Louis XIV and Charles VI. Was it not likely that Louis was playing them false, encouraging the Turks to attack in the east and collaborating with Charles XII in Germany to enflame the Empire once more? Braubach has shown how much fear (unfounded, but still potent) of French attempts to forge a northern coalition of Sweden, Hesse, Saxony and Prussia* influenced Prince Eugène and Charles VI's Austrian ministers in the spring of 1715. Annoyance with Charles XII grew: was it not disobedience in a prince of the Empire to make a condition for participation in the congress of Brunswick called by his Emperor? Louis XIV's alliance offers were therefore rebuffed and the prospective partitioning of Sweden's German provinces was reluctantly accepted. Imperial diplomacy

* French attempts to mediate terms between Sweden and her enemies caused these suspicions.

would make the best of a bad job so that Habsburg interests were promote
in the process: Stralsund and Wismar must become free imperial cities.[41]

When Prussia's declaration of war against Sweden, on 1 May (N.S.) 171
was known in Vienna, it was realized that Hanover's could not be far behind
'We shall have to enter this competition in the North', the Emperor tol
Prince Eugène in June 1715, 'we must work with England so that we als
receive our *Avantage*'.[42]

Long before this Charles had realized that he was not likely to obtain
negotiated pacification in Germany, that he would sooner or later be attacke
in Pomerania and that Stralsund was likely to suffer a siege.

2

The Siege of Stralsund

Charles XII's decision to stay in Stralsund and await attack was variously motivated. Though he had a natural longing to see his sister and the rest of the family, and implored them to send recent portraits,* he was convinced that he would be of more use in Stralsund than in Stockholm.

The defence of Sweden was in good hands. Since 1714 General Taube – a trusted veteran of the pre-1709 war, exchanged from Russian captivity – had been in command of the army stationed on the east coast to ward off possible attacks by Russian troops. He was energetic and able but had (as Stenbock before him) found himself at loggerheads with the Council. When he argued that the army ought to be kept together during the autumn and winter of 1714, the Council overruled him on grounds of economy and the soldiers were dispersed to their home districts.[1] To strengthen Taube's hand Charles made him *överstathållare* ('stadholder') in charge of the capital and ordered him to work in close cooperation with Prince Frederick of Hesse. His brother-in-law's authority and military experience, coupled with Taube's knowledge of the lie of the land both in military and domestic policy matters, made a splendid combination and eased the King's mind about the eastern front. Prince Frederick corresponded regularly with Charles, and the way in which he 'reasoned as a soldier' against the civilian outlook of most of the Council was welcomed. Shocked at finding Stockholm and the whole east coast undefended, the Prince's reaction to councillors' complaints that the country lacked *nervus belli* was similar to that of Charles: let us do something about it, there is no point in being defeatist.[2]

The King's one worry in respect of his brother-in-law was Frederick's insistence, through Vellingk, that he receive recognition in titles and rank for the responsibility he shouldered. He hoped to be made Charles's viceroy in Sweden and *generalissimus* over the whole Swedish army: positions from which his wife's victory in the succession stake might be confidently predicted. The command given him in mid-April 1715 over the troops stationed in Sweden he did not think sufficient and by mid-September he

---

* The first portrait that arrived of Ulrika Eleonora was not to his liking ('too old, too thin and worried looking') and another had to be dispatched: see Charles's letter of 2 May (N.S.) 1715.

obtained from Charles the coveted position as '*generalissimus* over Our forces of horse and foot',[3] though the King still refused him the 'viceroy' which came too close to Ulrika Eleonora's prerogative.

Charles further argued that as long as he remained in Stralsund, the attention of Sweden's enemies – including that of Tsar Peter – would be directed to Germany rather than to an invasion of Sweden itself.* It seemed sensible therefore to hold out in Swedish Pomerania for as long as humanly possible A strongly conducted defence might cost his enemies dear enough to make one or other of them listen to terms. And even if it proved impossible to prise anybody out of the coalition on terms acceptable to the King, the defence of Stralsund would, in his opinion, still serve a useful purpose: the glory of Swedish arms – so tarnished by the surrender at Perevolotjna – would to some extent be restored even if the town had to give in. If reinforcement came from Sweden and luck returned, it was by no means certain that the town would have to be surrendered. Perhaps the fight could be carried on in Germany rather than in Sweden?

Finally, the respite gained in time could be used for positive measures to develop the sinews of war necessary to obtain a 'durable peace' that did not sacrifice the great-power position. Charles was near enough to Sweden to encourage and supervise the work on economic, financial and administrative reform, yet in closer touch with the changing conjunctures in the European political scene than if he transferred himself to Stockholm. He was prepared to cede Swedish territory for a given number of years to Hanover or to Prussia, or to both, if in return he could receive military help against the anti-Swedish coalition. Both were potentially dangerous: Georg Ludwig because he now had access to British naval power and Frederick William because in the flush of ambition on his succession in 1713 he was determined to convert the sequestration of Stettin into a permanent possession of as much of Swedish Pomerania as possible. Charles visualized that the extent and period for which cession were made to either would be in ratio to the help given and to the number of enemies the recipient was willing to fight, but it must not exceed thirty years and the support must be specific enough not to permit the recipient to wriggle out of the obligation while swallowing th bait: there would be no formal handing over either in Bremen or Verden, o in Pomerania, till the troops promised were fighting under Swedish command Outright cession of any Swedish territory to Georg Ludwig or Frederick William he would not contemplate since the amount of military help the could put at his disposal was not worth the sacrifice of giving up land 'fo ever'. Even cession for a period of years was risky enough.[5]

To any one of his three declared enemies – Tsar Peter, Augustus of Saxon and Frederick of Denmark – Charles was prepared to give land in outright cession on condition that the recipient undertook a firm obligation to help

---

* In this he was proved right: 'the Russians seem to be asleep', Frederick reported in August 1715: see Holst, *Frederick I*, p. 54.

obtain for Sweden a suitable equivalent in land from the remaining enemies: again the only obligation reckoned safe enough would be a joint war against the rump of the coalition, and cession was not to be made permanent till the equivalent had been secured.[6]

Charles realized that his ability to gain terms on these lines would depend on the work of reorganization of Sweden's resources and would take time. The wheel of fortune might work in his favour. The death of one of his opponents would obviously ease his position; but he could not reckon on this. The only certain path out of the slough of despond lay in self-help, to enable him to take advantage of what opportunities offered and make Sweden, in the long run, strong enough to fashion opportunities for herself.

II

The reconstruction of the military effort started as soon as Charles XII arrived in Stralsund. Men were called to Pomerania who could be trusted with the detailed working out of ideas already touched upon in correspondence now they had the authority of the King closer at hand. Important among them was Ehrenpreus, with whom the farming out of customs-dues was arranged so that advance payment of the year's income in one lump sum should be achieved, the profit to the *entrepreneurs* (a term used in preference to 'tax-farmers') being fixed at six per cent and deducted before the money was handed over. Ehrenpreus persuaded the King that another source of cash income should be exploited: contraband goods were now allowed into Sweden on payment of a special levy of eight per cent, thus satisfying the country anxious for imports whether originating from friend or foe while also helping the King. The Bank's reluctance to lend money to the Crown was overcome by the issue of bills similar to the French *caisses* and the English Exchequer bills: these were made legal tender to be discounted at six per cent. Ways and means were concerted to stop the export of ready money which had in recent years been leaking out of Sweden; and the issue of the so-called *nödmynt* (literally 'necessity money') was decreed to help the scarcity of ready money. In these the intrinsic copper value of individual coins bore little relation to their nominal 'silver' value.[7]

Even in decisions motivated by the immediate crisis, long-term aims were kept in view. Charles, going through the draft protectionist tariff he had demanded from the College of Commerce, insisted on a lower export-duty on bar-iron than the European market would have accepted, while increasing that on unworked iron steeply* so that the Dutch middlemen might find it harder to cream the profit from Sweden's most valuable ore.[8] In February 1715 a new privateering ordinance was promulgated[9] in the hope of decisively discouraging the Maritime Powers from trading with Russian-occupied

---

* The duty on bar-iron was raised from ten per cent to twenty-five per cent only, that on unworked iron from twenty per cent to eighty-four per cent.

Swedish ports. Its toughness brought protests, but Jefferyes (who was the bearer of them) was told in Stralsund that Sweden was only now taking measures which the Maritime Powers themselves had used freely in their wars against France. As for compensation for ships already arrested, he was reminded that Sweden had not as yet received compensation for ships brought up by England between 1689 and 1713.[10]

In the discussion of ways and means and future prospects which took place between the King and his Swedish advisers the Duke-Administrator's representative, von Görtz, gradually became prominent. His value lay in contacts at many courts and in his interest in financial matters. He expressed his willingness, for one year in the first place, to raise loans abroad to be covered by Swedish obligations. He outlined a system for the funding of the national debt, comparable to the way in which the South Sea Company in 1710–11 had come to the help of the English government when the expenses of a long war had caused severe financial strain. His rise to the position of chief economic adviser was rapid; by February 1716 he described himself as the *'Directeur des Finances et du Commerce'* of Sweden,[11] a title reminiscent of Colbert's role as *contrôleur général des finances*.

The growing participation of Görtz in discussions which affected Sweden caused anxiety to Frederick of Hesse. He and Ulrika – deeply in love with her husband and susceptible to his suggestions – saw in it a threat by the Holsteiners to her succession. They pleaded with Charles to permit Frederick to come to Stralsund in the hope that the Prince could then act as a counterweight to the Holstein-Gottorp influence on the King, and their appeals that Charles ought to leave the dangerous Stralsund for Sweden were in part motivated by their desire to keep a close eye on Görtz who, as the Duke-Administrator's accredited diplomat with Charles, would follow.[12] Their fears of Görtz were groundless, both in 1715 and later, in so far as any direct attempt to make the King favour the Holstein-Gottorp succession was concerned. Görtz was a shrewd judge of character and realized how much even the rumours of rivalry and competition within the family over the succession-issue pained Charles XII. He therefore completely ignored the subject and concentrated on practical help for Sweden.

Here he developed methods of his own for 'handling' the King. It was best he wrote to a friend, not to bother Charles XII with too many details at a time when he was preoccupied with military and diplomatic problems: if the King was given the general outline of any plan and allowed to ask enough questions to put him in the picture, he would support what followed and accept responsibility whether it succeeded or not.[13] This remained Görtz's way even when diplomatic activity was added to his financial ventures. He was never able to commit Charles, nor to go beyond the limited powers he was given for specific missions. He always felt that he was walking the tightrope between the world as he found it and the King's outlook on that world. He tried to persuade Charles to accept solutions which seemed sensible, or necessary, to him; but he had no illusion where the power of decision lay and felt unsure enough of his own position to fear that a single false step might topple him from the King's favour.*

He remained one helper among many, but one who impressed himself strangely and strongly on contemporaries in Sweden and in Europe at large. He became a hated character in Sweden. For the Hessians he stood for Holstein-Gottorp influence; for the old administrators he symbolized the break-away from regular channels and the institution of an arbitrary cabinet government. And because he was instrumental in financing the war effort, he seemed to most Swedes the incarnation of the evils of war. The anti-Görtz verses of the 1716–18 period were inspired by his political enemies,[14] but they were appreciated by all who wanted a scapegoat for the long war and were restrained by their feelings of loyalty and fairness from blaming the King who did his duty and worked so hard. It is significant that the charge of which Görtz's political enemies found him guilty and had him executed after Charles XII's death was that of his 'having alienated the late King's affection from his people'.† In Europe Görtz's contacts with the Jacobites made him the centre of a complicated web of intrigues between 1716 and 1717, and his negotiations with the Russians on Charles XII's behalf on the isolated island of Lövö in the Åland islands group kept Europe on tenterhooks between 1717 and 1718: what deal with Tsar Peter was the wily Görtz concluding? Quite apart from his actions, his appearance made him a dramatic figure. He was tall and imposing with a regal bearing, and his false eye, made of enamel,‡ fascinated those who met him. It is not strange that the image of 'Charles XII and Görtz'¶ should have imprinted itself on the last years of the King's reign, though it is a somewhat misleading one.

To counter the danger, as Ulrika and her husband saw it, of Görtz working himself into Charles XII's confidence for the purpose of furthering the young Duke of Holstein-Gottorp's chances, Frederick of Hesse sent Ranck to Stralsund in March 1715 to take care of Hesse interests. Ranck's letters, in cypher and signed Martin L'aisné, to Frederick have been discovered in Marburg[15] and form one important source of information about the military happenings of 1715. Taken with the reports and letters of Croissy, with the dispatches of Jefferyes, with the memoirs of Löwen and other officers, and with Charles XII's own letters, they enable us to follow the siege of Stralsund in great detail.

III

To help with the defence of Sweden's last possessions in the Empire, Charles called military experts from Sweden to help him. First of all, Meijerfelt, now governor-general of Scania, was sent for and given the charge of fitting out

---

* See below, p. 506.   † It is now admitted that his execution was a judicial murder.
‡ It replaced the eye he had lost in a student duel.   ¶ See illustration facing p. 461.

the fleet so that communications between Stralsund and Sweden could be kept open; a task he completed with a speed and energy which earned him Charles's gratitude and admiration.[16]

Cronstedt of the artillery was promoted to major-general and given control of the reorganization of the fortifications at Stralsund, Rügen and Wismar. The outer defences of Stralsund were strengthened, artillery parks strategically placed, batteries made to guard inlets by sea, and ammunition ordered in great quantities from Sweden.[17] The total forces at Charles's command grew, with the Hessians, to twelve thousand men, but the proportion of native Swedish troops was low. Sometimes, much to Charles's delight Swedish officers, who had escaped from Russia, turned up: Roland,* for instance, had to demonstrate the methods by which he had escaped (via Archangel and Spain) and recount his adventures twice over while the morning service was long delayed.[18]

Sweden's declared enemies were in no hurry to begin the attack before they had increased their numbers by the German rulers of Prussia and Hanover The Tsar and Augustus of Saxony did not want to move prematurely from their own stations in the east. Frederick of Denmark, busily negotiating with George of Hanover-England about the role of the British navy in the coming operations, delayed putting his own fleet into the water. It was Frederick William I of Prussia, encouraged by Russia and Saxony, who set the ball rolling.

Charles XII, though he had protested against the sequestration of Swedish Pomerania up to the Peene, was anxious to avoid provoking the Prussian King by any action which contested that king's right to hold temporary sway over the territory covered by the sequester. But he was determined not to let Frederick William cross the Peene river, and early in February 1715 ordered twenty Prussians stationed in Wolgast, a small town on the left bank of that river, to leave the place as it was outside the sequester area. The small number of Prussians involved obeyed without the Swedes having to use violence; but Frederick William, who was already preparing to occupy the strategically situated islands of Wollin and Usedom,† used the incident to justify an aggressive policy. He was encouraged by Tsar Peter and Augustus, for though these rulers (out of concern for their relationship with Frederick IV of Denmark) had not dared to ratify the document‡ by which they had given Prussia hopes of Swedish territory beyond the Peene, they were keen for someone to get the war against Charles in Stralsund moving.[19]

In March, with the excuse that Charles might use the islands as a stepping stone for an invasion of Poland across Prussia, Frederick William occupied and fortified Wollin and moved troops also into the Swedish forts on Usedom Charles protested at the infringement and when no notice was taken of his protest landed a superior force to that of the invaders on Usedom on 11/1

---

* Cp. above, p. 17.   † See map, p. 387.
‡ The 'recess of Schwedt' of 1714; cp. above, p. 370.

April. He waited for the Prussians to open hostilities, and then dislodged them from the forts of Swineschanze and Peenemünde Schanze. Still hoping to avoid an open break with Frederick William, he transported the Prussian troops to Wollin and refrained from any attempt to remove Prussian forces from that island. His efforts (via the Landgrave) to make Prussia relinquish Stettin to Hesse, on payment of the 400,000 *Reichsthaler* stipulated in the sequester, had failed,[20] but there was still a faint possibility that Louis xiv's offer to guarantee the sum might result in Stettin being handed over to a genuinely neutral power till the end of the war.[21]

Frederick William had, however, already crossed his Rubicon and committed himself to the anti-Swedish coalition. He therefore used Charles's reconquest of Usedom as the curtain-raiser to his official entry into the war: the Swedish civil government in Stettin was sacked; the Gottorp battalions in the town were expelled; the Swedish diplomats on Prussian soil were asked to leave; ultimatums impossible to accept were sent to Charles xii and military cooperation with the anti-Swedish coalition began.[22]

In the meantime negotiations between Hanover and Denmark had also progressed. On 15/26 June 1715 Frederick iv received, if not written promises of the active cooperation between his fleet and that of Great Britain which he desired, at least verbal assurances that British men-of-war would be used in the Baltic in 1715 to support the siege of Stralsund.[23] This was to be done under the cloak of protecting British commerce. Such protection was a genuine concern of Great Britain, as of the Dutch Republic: without naval escorts neither British nor Dutch merchantmen would risk sailing to Russian-occupied Swedish Baltic ports.[24] The British Admiralty was not keen to have its fleet entangled in the Northern War and took care that Norris, in charge of George i's squadron, should not have ammunition in quantities to tempt him into a shooting war. But individual British statesmen knew something of their King's Hanoverian commitments and connived at his use of the British navy,[25] while Dutch statesmen were unpleasantly surprised at the role of 'the enemy of Sweden', which George tried, unsuccessfully, to foster also in their squadron, and Norris – under pressure both from the Hanoverian representative of George i and from his King's allies – compromised as best he could.[26]

The wildest rumours flew around. Monteleón, the Spanish ambassador in London, imagined that Great Britain intended to conquer a place on the Baltic; and the Swedish minister, Gyllenborg, thought this not unlikely. He pointed to British success at Gibraltar and reminded his superiors that Elsinore had been coveted in Cromwell's time.*[27] It is certain that most of George i's British ministers sympathized with their King's desire to acquire Bremen and Verden for Hanover,† and that they trusted that any clash

---

* So had the duchy of Bremen, see Michael Roberts, *Essays in Swedish History* (1967), p. 160.
† An entry for British manufacture in Germany was envisaged if these duchies became part of Hanover; the direct communications by sea with Great Britain which such an expansion of Hanover would give had strategic advantages also, given the dynastic connexion.

between British men-of-war and those of Sweden could be passed off as those 'reprisals' for the privateering ordinance which Norris had been permitted to execute. It is equally certain that they did not want a full-scale war between Great Britain and Sweden, since this would damage British trade *vis-à-vis* the neutral Dutch and might also encourage the Jacobites and win them a Swedish alliance.[28]

The role played by Norris's squadron of 1715 has been much debated.[29] It is obvious that its mere presence had an inhibiting effect on Swedish naval strategy during the campaign for Stralsund. Charles XII wanted to prevent a clash with British men-of-war lest he give George I an excuse to bring Great Britain into the anti-Swedish coalition, and gave strict orders to Swedish naval commanders to be circumspect. He himself took great care to distinguish between Georg Ludwig the Elector and George I the King, and refused to listen to appeals on behalf of the Jacobites.[30] But the extent to which the British squadron was able to bottle up the Swedish fleet in Karlskrona in 1715 came as a shock to Charles. In retrospect it seemed as if the English, rather than the Danes and the Russians, had been his most serious naval enemies in 1715.[31] In July the projected Bornholm expedition of Norris helped to frustrate reinforcements for Stralsund.[32] In September, when Norris sailed out of the Baltic with the English merchantmen, he left behind – on George I's orders – eight of his best ships to act under the command of the Danish King 'to prevent Swedish supremacy in the Baltic': an act which gave positive help in the conquest of Rügen and thus made possible the fall of Stralsund.[33]

IV

The whole operation against Stralsund was indeed influenced as to timing by the exigencies of George I's double role as Elector and King. The army of coalition, to consist of Danes, Saxons and Prussians, had gathered for combined attacks on Stralsund and Rügen from early July onwards; but the junction with the Hanoverians was postponed time and again. The diplomatic preparations for cooperation were complete. Prussia and Denmark had on 7 April (N.S.) agreed that the objectives of the campaign – Stralsund as well as Rügen – should become Danish property in compensation for Bremen and Verden going to Hanover.[34] On 14 April (N.S.) Hanover and Prussia confirmed this arrangement and George I promised to take part in the siege of Wismar. It was the direct negotiations between Denmark and Hanover which took time since George I could not risk giving written promises in respect of the cooperation of the British navy. And even when, by the treaty of 26 June (N.S.), Frederick IV had declared himself satisfied with George I's verbal promises of naval help, the earnest of them in action was delayed and caused disputes. Not only was George keen to obtain Bremen and Verden at the lowest possible cost, he was also extremely reluctant to give any handle to the opponents of Hanoverian policy in Parliament at a time when the Jacobite rebellion made his position difficult.

Nevertheless, the risk of losing Bremen and Verden pushed him forward step by step.[35] By late June Prussian and Danish troops had encircled Wismar on the land side while Danish warships established a blockade.* By early July Prussian, Saxon and Danish troops had closed in on Stralsund from the south-east and south-west. In face of the numerical superiority of the enemy – twenty-eight thousand Danes and some twenty-seven thousand Prussians and Saxons – Charles decided not to dispute the river-crossings[36] and withdrew behind the outworks of Stralsund. The King was not fit at this time. A fall from a horse which had rolled heavily on top of his rib-cage had hurt him sufficiently to keep him indoors for some time in May, and his recovery was fairly slow. The King coughed blood, Jefferyes reported to London.[37] But it was the vast circumference of the front to be covered if the enemy were to be denied the crossings of the Peene, to the west, and of the Recknitz and Trebel rivers in the east which decided the withdrawal.

This withdrawal did not necessarily spell an early fall for Stralsund. It would be impossible to take the town without command of the sea approaches, and while waiting for Frederick IV and George I to achieve this the enemy land forces dug in. The Swedish seaward defence was strong. The islands of Rügen, Ruden and Usedom had good batteries and a Swedish naval squadron commanded the local water, the Greifswalder Deep. The first Danish attempt, on 7/18 July, to enter the Deep was foiled when a superior Swedish fleet of big ships arrived from Karlskrona, also escorting recruits and supplies. A second was made when Frederick IV, convinced that Norris would come to his rescue if need be, risked sending the major part of his fleet, twenty-one large men-of-war, to fight Sparre's twenty of the line off Rügen. The ensuing battle on 28 July/8 August, which Charles watched from a vantage point on the island 'till the ships were so shrouded in smoke one could hardly distinguish the flags', was claimed as a victory by both sides.[38] It was in effect a draw and both badly mauled fleets retired to Copenhagen and Karlskrona respectively for repairs. It was now that the eight British ships left with Denmark, 'the best' of Norris's fleet, proved their worth. Frederick IV joined them to his big vessels still fit for service and proceeded to cruise between Bornholm and Rügen to give cover for low-draught Danish ships sent to the Deep. Swedish men-of-war, with munitions and supply ships, had already put to sea in response to Charles's command, but sighting the combined Anglo-Danish squadron retired to port. Reiterated orders to come out whatever the risk reached them, but contrary winds proved one hindrance to leaving harbour[39] and the superior enemy another and seemingly greater one.†

---

* Some 5,000 Danes and 3,500 Prussians took part in the siege: 2,300 Hanoverians joined the besiegers on 2 November. The Swedish garrison counted 4,000.

† Not till Hopson and his squadron were preparing to sail home, after the fall of Rügen, did the Swedish fleet sail out. It arrived too late to save Stralsund; its men and supplies were diverted to Wismar.

On 14/25 September a reinforced Danish squadron forced its way into the Greifswalder Deep. On 5/16 November Rügen fell.

The benefit Frederick estimated he had received from the junction of George I's ships with his own is clearly indicated by his consent to hand over the whole of Bremen and Verden to the Elector of Hanover on 4/15 October: George I had proved that he was both able and willing to use the British fleet for what Norris in letters to Whitehall discreetly called 'the other purposes' – that is those which went beyond 'the security of our commerce' – of his master.[40] Frederick was the more anxious to reward George promptly as he hoped to secure British naval cooperation in the 1716 season for a joint allied descent on Scania. Only by an invasion of Sweden could all Charles's enemies – among whom Hanover counted since its declaration of hostilities on 4/15 October 1715 – hope to set the seal on their German conquests, but for Frederick this descent was of more vital concern than to anyone else since that alone would help him reconquer the peninsular provinces.

In October 1715, when Frederick made his concessions to George, it did not look as if his own first rewards – the plum of Stralsund and Rügen – would be long in falling to his lap. But in the event autumn storms, the time needed to prepare the allied landing on Rügen, and Saxon and Prussian jealousy of Denmark caused delays.

The allied attack on Rügen began on 1/12 November with a large flotilla of transports – 640 in all – and both Frederick IV and Frederick William I on board the naval escort. By this time some of the lesser Swedish positions were already lost. During July and August Charles XII, reasonably recovered in health, had rushed from island to island to inspect the defences and encourage the defenders, so busy, according to Ranck, that he hardly had time to read his letters.[41] In view of his inferiority in numbers he had no wish to sacrifice his troops needlessly. He permitted the Prussians to take Wolgast between 27–29 July (N.S.), and though because of its strategic importance Peenemünde had been asked to defend itself to the uttermost that fort had to give in on 22 August (N.S.)[42] and thus contributed to a weakening of the defences of the Greifswalder Deep.

With the enemy in at least temporary control of the Deep after 14/25 September, Charles realized that he would have to risk a major body of troops to keep the islands of Rügen and Ruden in Swedish hands – without them the Swedish fleet which he still hoped would arrive before winter set in might not be able to reverse the position.

As soon therefore as he learnt that the allied force had embarked, he sent Löwen to defend Ruden and went himself to Rügen with eight hundred foot and two thousand horse. He ranged his men and eight guns – a pitiable force when compared to an enemy at least five times that number – at Palmerort, the most likely landing place. Seeing Charles XII well entrenched, the Danish and Prussian Kings decided to take no chances. The weather was in any case bad and after two days at anchor they moved to Gross-Stresow where they anded unopposed on 4/15 November.[43] The Swedish army had to rush across the length of the island to catch up. When Charles arrived in the evening, he found the allies well dug in with *chevaux-de-frise* and heavy artillery. It was essential to attack, however, if Rügen were not to be given up without a fight. Having reconnoitred as best he could in the dark, the King decided to use a column formation as a battering-ram on the spot he considered weakest in the enemy bridgehead. The guns were placed in two batteries to support the men – nearly all Germans – and at 3 o'clock in the morning of 5/16 November the action began.

The impetus of the attack carried both infantry and cavalry forward through the outer defences to the earthen wall of the enemy position. Even after the Danish infantry had repulsed the foot-soldiers, they bravely rallied for a second assault. Charles, whose horse had been shot under him, put himself at the head of the infantry, but almost as soon as the second attack got under way a musket bullet hit him in the chest. Finding himself wounded and incapable of command, he gave orders for retreat. The superiority of the enemy in numbers gave no prospect of success; the Swedes had already lost four hundred killed* and two hundred wounded and he realized that the battle for Rügen was lost.[44]

The survivors made their way to the fort of Altefähr. Ranck later expressed surprise that the enemy had not pursued the wounded King: the horses of the cavalry were but 'poor farmhorses', and if the allies had shown less 'phlegm' they could easily have caught their quarry.[45] But not till two days later, long after Charles was back in Stralsund, did the enemy reach Altefähr, whose commander surrendered,[46] against orders, without a fight.† The defeat at Gross-Stresow necessitated the evacuation of the Mönchgut peninsula but the officer in charge, Stenflycht, got his men into Stralsund[47] and Axel von Löwen avoided capture by sailing his men to Sweden.[48]

V

Throughout the late summer and early autumn, defender and attackers had struggled feverishly for position. 'We push our fortifications', wrote Ranck on 6 August (N.S.), 'and the enemy their lines, forward at such speed that the like has never been seen before': the two must soon meet. Swedes of an optimistic frame of mind put their trust in the autumn rains which might halt enemy preparations, or in the King of France who might force a peace on the northern coalition by threatening to fall into the Empire with French troops.[49]

---

* Among the dead were Colonel von Grothusen and the brave General von Daldorff who had thought victory unlikely enough to promise, on the eve of the battle, that if the Swedes won he would ride to the moon and bring it back in his teeth.

† The garrison of 1,100 were mainly Germans, but also included remnants of the French dragoon-regiment formed in 1706 (see above, p. 215) which had taken part in the Gross-Stresow battle. According to the custom of the time, the non-Swedish prisoners took service with the victors.

But on 1 September (N.S.) Louis XIV died, and the rains did not stop the enemy. On 22 October/2 November the serious bombardment of the town and the citadel began.

Charles XII had to some extent shared the hopes of the optimists, but his innermost thoughts can be deduced partly from letters he sent to Ulrika Eleanora by 'safe hands' and partly from the new defence works linking all three approaches to the citadel which were building under Eosander's* leadership. The King realized that 'we are not now in a position to do the enemy any damage' and suggested that the besiegers of Stralsund might give up 'for this year' when winter came.[50] But he was at the same time preparing for a stout defence and for reinforcements from Sweden – in the spring of 1716 if not in the autumn of 1715 – which might make full use of the big new works with room for treble the number of men he had at his present disposal and with sites for a hundred guns.[51] A general inspection of all regiments in Sweden was in progress on Charles's orders to fill vacancies and check that the drill was up to standard.[52] If things went as the King hoped, the coming year would see a break-out from the Stralsund position and a modest offensive. In any case he assumed that the siege could be prolonged and thus save Sweden from invasion.[53]

Stralsund was well provided with food and fodder for the winter,† and there was sufficient ammunition and supplies to hold out till the spring. Until the fall of Rügen morale was high among the troops, who varied in number (depending on detachments sent outside the citadel) from seven to ten thousand, and fair among the eight thousand citizens, though they knew themselves surrounded by enemies who never numbered less than thirty thousand and sometimes as much as fifty thousand (their numbers also fluctuating according to detachments sent elsewhere).

During the siege the French soldier Croissy, whose slight and elegant 'courtier' figure did not impress Ranck till he became convinced of the Frenchman's bravery,[54] saw much of Charles XII. He had arrived in May 1715 and accompanied the King on inspection rides and 'promenades'. He was full of praise: 'Charles much better looking than on the portraits we have seen; he is so approachable and so free in conversation that I am not the least bit shy in speaking to him; indeed, the range of his conversation makes me feel I am talking to a philosopher rather than a King.' He is sure Charles liked him: 'as for me, I love him with all my heart'. In this, he argued, he was not alone, for the remarkable thing about the Swedish King is that he disproves the old saying that no one is a hero to his servants: those who have been with him longest admire him most.[55]

Löwen also found much to admire in Charles as a person during the siege, though he was free in his criticism of the way the defence of Stralsund had been handled. When he met Charles at Ystad in December 1715 he expounded

* On Prussia becoming Sweden's enemy, Eosander (for whom see above, p. 196) had gone into Charles's service.

† The harvest from Rügen had filled its stores.

the reasons for Swedish failure to hold Pomerania: the fleet should not have risked battle with the Danes, but stayed anchored off Rügen; Charles should have listened to his advice and put in more men to keep Usedom, the key to the whole defence; he ought also to have supported him and Dücker and the *'façons de Brabant'* ridiculed by others who had not their experience of siege-warfare in the Low Countries and favoured the old *'gå-på'* spirit which needlessly lost men. When he recapitulated *'circonstanciellement toutes les fautes commises à Stralsund'*, Charles listened *'avec une grande patience et condescendance'*. He answered, half-jokingly to turn away wrath – though Löwen took him as seriously as Gyllenkrook ever did – *'que comme il ne s'entendoit point à la défense de villes, il l'avoit voulu aprendre par lui-même ... et que l'expériance, même sans succès, rend entendue qu'un[e] autre fois il seroit meilleur ingénieur qu'il ne l'avoit été ce foi-ci'*.[56] Charles admired Löwen, for his fine defence of Ruden as well as for his successful escape with his men; and Löwen, looking back on the years he spent with the King, writes in a vein which might be dismissed as hagiographic but for the occasional outspoken criticism, never firmer than when reviewing the siege of Stralsund where he judged Eosander, the theorist, to be the worst offender.

Löwen's memoirs are full of Stralsund anecdotes illustrating what he most liked about the King: his concern for others; the way in which he accepted unpalatable truths and the blows of fate; his spirit *'magnamine et juste'* and *'son âme noble et droite'*:

> *On se pouvoit fier sur lui comme sur un ferme rocher, et comme il est permi de nommer hommes les plus grands rois, on peut dire que c'étoit un roi bien honnêt homme et ami à toute épreuve. Sa parole étoit sacrée et celle d'un vrai roi, et sa fidélité inviolable, et dans la guerre pourvu qu'on y alât bravement, il vous tenoit quitte de tout ce qui en arriva. Il est vrai qu' en s'exposant et se fatiguant à l'excès lui-même, il nous n'épargnoit pas et nous mettoit souvent sur les dents. Mais ses manières gracieuses et afables nous faisoi[en]t tout suporter avec patience, et il savoit s'atacher les coeurs d'une manière qu'on ne sauroit exprimer.*[57]

VI

Charles himself was badly shaken when he got back from Rügen and found that the Prussians and Saxons had made a significant breakthrough[58] at a spot where the natural sea defences had been thought sufficient.* A Prussian officer† who knew the town and its surroundings well had told the Saxon commander-in-chief, Count von Wackerbarth, of a sandbank which when the tide was at its lowest could be used to circumvent the defences. On this information a plan was made, involving feints to draw the attention of the Swedes elsewhere and heavy gunfire to hide the noise of men marching

---

* Löwen blames Eosander for neglecting (against advice) the defence of this particular spot: guns had been removed from it to strengthen other parts of the citadel.

† The traditional story, given by Lamberty, Voltaire, Nordberg and others, that a Swedish officer revealed the route has been disproved: Wackerbarth's informant was the Prussian Lieutenant-Colonel von Köppen.

through water, which had for its purpose the conquest of Stralsund for Augustus of Saxony with Prussian connivance. The Danes, in their eastern sector of the siege works, were left in ignorance of the venture.[59] The citadel was not captured and to that extent the Saxo-Prussian plan misfired; but by 25 October/5 November the Swedes had lost the important Frankentor sector of their outer defence works and suffered heavy losses in their vain attempts to retake it: some two hundred killed and five hundred taken prisoners against no more than fifty dead and eighty wounded on the enemy side. From this moment onwards, provided the tension between the Danish and Saxon commands did not prevent cooperation,* Charles could expect a storm on the inner defences.

In public the King still kept up his belief that naval and military help would come from Sweden in time to prevent the fall of Stralsund,[60] but private worries – illuminated at quite an early stage of the siege by Feif writing to Tessin[61] for plans and drawings for Stockholm castle 'that Charles might have something to drive away sad thoughts'† – obviously increased. He began to send key personnel to safety: Görtz had left for Hamburg on 9/20 November and Poniatowski was sent to Sweden on 3/14 December.[62] He also responded positively to those Prussian and Saxon overtures for peace which were part and parcel of the complicated double-dealing within the coalition. But on 7/18 November, unbeknown to the Saxons, Frederick William of Prussia, impressed by Dano-Hanoverian naval collaboration, signed a secret treaty with Frederick IV for the division of Swedish Pomerania with the Peene as boundary, accepting a Danish governor-general on Rügen. This, together with a public Saxo-Danish–Prussian agreement to leave the partition of Pomerania 'to the future', restored cooperation among the besiegers[63] and rendered the concessions Charles was willing to make of small importance.

The terms the King put forward are, however, of some interest in showing the limits of his sacrifices at a time when he was pressed to the utmost. His public suggestion – via Croissy – for a conference to be called by the guarantors of the Treaty of Westphalia to discuss the restoration of peace in the Empire, he could not expect his enemies to treat seriously since in effect it meant a French mediation. But secretly he let Croissy and others, such as his second-in-command at Stralsund, Dücker, know that he was willing to make deals with his besiegers: Prussia was to receive Stettin in perpetuity, but without any surrounding territory; Augustus would be recognized as King of Poland; and the sequestration of Wismar would be permitted. In return he demanded an end to the siege and a promise that Stralsund and Rügen would remain Swedish.[64]

---

* This tension arose from the Saxons wanting to keep Frederick IV to a partition treaty of September 1711 which had given Western Pomerania, with Stralsund and Rügen, to Augustus. Since that time, the entry of Hanover and Denmark's need of British naval power had transformed the situation, see above, pp. 402 ff.

† The King desired Tessin to keep this secret, lest he give offence by 'amusing himself' while the country was in financial difficulties and military danger.

When these terms were refused, Charles realized that there was no longer any point in his remaining in Germany. The enemy was coming ever closer to the citadel. The Swedes were forced to give up the outworks of the Tribsees Tor, and those of the Frankentor (where Düring was one among many who lost his life) remained in enemy hands when Charles's counter-offensive failed. The water in the moats froze.

The King had been urged ever since his return from Rügen to make an escape to Sweden while he could. Soon, it was feared, enemy ships and/or the freezing of the waters might make escape impossible. Postal communication with Sweden was becoming difficult: Ranck commented that the post-yacht had to be dispatched 'as secretly as a murder'.[65] Danger from the bombs and cannon balls 'which fly through the town as feathers'[66] the hardened officers took as philosophically as did Charles himself,* but the increasing purposelessness of the defence oppressed the majority of the officer-corps. The general comparison was with the *Kalabalik*, and Ranck wrote to Frederick of Hesse that he would much prefer 'two voyages to the Indies to this kind of party'.[67] The responsibility for Charles's safety weighed heavily on the senior officers, especially during the counter-offensive he led on 7/18 December. It was with intense relief they learnt on 10/21 December that the King had handed over supreme command to General Dücker and had given orders for the capitulation of Stralsund as soon as he himself had got away.[68]

Charles left in the knowledge that the besiegers would give honourable terms in view of the stout defence and hoped that the native Swedish officers and soldiers would be permitted free march to Wismar which still held out.† This was not obtained, but the terms of the capitulation of 12/23 December which Dücker signed permitted these troops (about a thousand in all) to leave Stralsund with banners flying and field-music playing, with the prospect of being released in four months' time against payment for their keep to Frederick William of Prussia.‡ The King's drabants and civilian officials were freed immediately, as were all volunteers. The non-Swedish troops were made prisoners-of-war and divided among the besiegers in ratio to the number of troops each ruler had put into the siege; most of them took service with their captors,[69] as was to be expected.

On 11/22 December Charles left Stralsund in an open rowing boat which battled its way through ice floes and enemy fire to one of the Swedish ships lying off Rügen. His page went with him, also two adjutants, Colonel von Rosen of the ride to Stralsund, and, in memory of Düring who had been an even closer companion during that ride, Düring's brother. The *Snappup*, the

---

* It was during this siege that Charles spoke of the warrior's death to the music of gunfire being preferable to the long-drawn-out sick bed with doctors, notaries and '*parens en pleur*' (Löwen, *Mémoires*, pp. 25–6), a simile possibly prompted by mental comparison between the death of Gustavus Adolphus, which he often lauded, and memories of the suffering of his own father.

† This citadel fell in April 1716, see below, p. 420.

‡ For their fate see *Bidrag S.N.K.H.*, VII, pp. 238 ff.: Swedish money did not arrive in full by the time arranged, Prussia did not stick to the terms of the capitulation and Charles XII authorized escape. Some got back to Sweden, others went to Poland to join the anti-Augustan forces.

brigantine in which Charles and his party sailed away from Germany, met hard weather – snowstorms and bad visibility – but had a fast passage and met no enemy ship.

There has been speculation both then and since whether the Prussians and the Danes connived at Charles's reaching Sweden in safety.[70] Frederick IV's historiographer royal claimed that it would have been an easy matter to send ships to capture Charles, 'but that the King of Denmark did not wish to do so'.[71] The lateness of the season seems, however, a more likely explanation than any sudden reluctance on Frederick's part to take his Swedish cousin prisoner: he had made arrangements with Frederick William that Charles, if captured at sea, should fall to Denmark's lot, if on land to Prussia's, and had promised rewards and promotion without end to the officer who should effect capture. The youthful hero of the Danish–Norwegian war at sea, Torden-skjold, had cruised off Stralsund with the fastest and finest Scandinavian ship of the era, the *Hvite Ørn*,* captured from the Swedes in 1714. Lack of provisions and damage sustained in a minor action had forced him to leave for Copenhagen some days before Charles put to sea.[72] It was 'fate' or God's will rather than any secret and unwritten clause of the capitulation agreement which permitted the skipper of the *Snappup* to land the King and his followers at Skåre,[73] near Trelleborg in Scania, at 4 o'clock in the morning of 13/24 December.

* 'White Eagle'.

3

The Norwegian Campaign of 1716

From Skåre Charles walked the short distance into Trelleborg in pouring rain and found a coach to drive him to Ystad, some five miles away. Here he was met by Count Bonde with letters and news of the family. The news was both sad and disturbing. The Queen-Grandmother had died in her eightieth year on 24 November and the King was naturally grieved, as he wrote to his sister on 14 December, that he should not have arrived in time to pay his last respects to 'so dear a Grandmother'.[1] The implications of the struggle for precedence at her funeral on 6 December between Frederick of Hesse and young Charles Frederick of Holstein-Gottorp were alarming: the Prince of Hesse had insisted that he, as the husband of Ulrika Eleonora, ranked higher than the fifteen-year-old great-grandson of the dead Queen, who – at the suggestion of his advisers – stayed away from the funeral rather than accept the Prince's ruling. Frederick, in his letter to Charles XII, put his own conduct in the best possible light:[2] the King, anxious to re-establish family harmony, chose to ignore the topic. In his letters to Ulrika Eleonora from Ystad he preferred to concentrate on what they had in common.

There had been some discussion during 1715 whether Charles Frederick should be declared of age when he became fifteen: the age at which Charles XII had been declared a major. The King, while in principle regarding an early majority as preferable to a regency, suggested delay in Charles Frederick's case. The Duke's lands were occupied by the Danes and would not benefit him; his paternal uncle, the Duke-Administrator, might take it to indicate Swedish distrust of him and his ministers, as the customary age in the House of Holstein-Gottorp – as in most Germany princely families – was eighteen. Charles XII had expressed pleasure when both his sister and nephew accepted his point of view.[3] Now, to minimize friction, he invited both Prince Frederick and the young Duke to come to him in Scania as soon as possible. His remedy was a simple one. In Stralsund he had refused to give Ranck any opening for reports of 'intrigues in Stockholm and here to split the Great Ones' (i.e. the royal family) by the expedient of saying he would not listen as he was sure they were 'without substance'.[4] Back in Sweden he consistently adopted the view that if he pretended to disbelieve all evidence of a split, the split might in time heal.

His letters to Ulrika Eleonora between 1715 and August 1716 (when they did at last meet) have four main themes: he thanks her for her letters, 'my best joy while I have been away' and for her support of the Stralsund siege, especially for money sent which was used to buy food for the town and thus helped it to hold out that much longer;[5] he regrets that he cannot, as he would wish, hurry to Stockholm and surprise her instead of being forced by circumstances to send written and all too brief messages;[6] he explains the military situation with the directness and openness he had begun in Turkey and discusses his plans in so far as this is compatible with security needs;[7] he tries to promote family unity* by praising her husband's services to him and by recommending the young Charles Frederick to her when he has to return to Stockholm while the Prince of Hesse remains. I shall miss him, is the gist of these letters, but I hope he'll prove a joy and comfort to you now you are 'all alone'.[9]

Charles XII's failure to return to Stockholm has often been criticized and taken as a sign either of indifference, or of downright fear to face the capital. His letters to Ulrika tell another story, of a longing to come back but of the duties that mount up and prevent him from leaving the south. That he had at first expected his stay in Ystad to be relatively short, while he awaited news from Germany of the terms of the capitulation,[10] is clear from the fact that Tessin was asked by Feif to prepare quarters for the King in Stockholm, bearing in mind that on account of his old leg injury, he preferred not to have too many stairs to mount.[11] But circumstances dictated a change of plan.

II

Throughout the autumn of 1715 Frederick of Hesse had preached an attack on Norway as soon as the danger from Tsar Peter should be over for the season, so that the King of Denmark's attention could be diverted from Germany. The Swedes had received valuable information from an officer-deserter on local Norwegian conditions, and a winter or early spring offensive might well pay dividends.[12] Charles had in principle agreed to the venture and the Prince of Hesse had been quite impressed with the quality of the soldiers he had inspected on the King's behalf for the prospective campaign.[13] The troops in Sweden amounted to forty thousand at this time, and more could be raised as soon as the money situation improved. The navy, Charles impressed upon Ulrika from Stralsund, had first call on any money available because of Sweden's essential need of it in the given situation.[14] Whatever the campaigns of the future, whether in Denmark–Norway, in Germany or against Russia, the necessary transport could only be safeguarded by a strong fleet. Even in southern Norway, where troops could march across a common frontier, no long-term success would be possible without naval support.[15]

* He tried to do so even after death; at his own funeral the Prince of Hesse and the Duke of Holstein rode in the same coach: Tessin having stressed this as being the late King's command.[8]

In Ystad Charles XII moved into the house which he had briefly occupied in 1700 when waiting to embark for the Baltic provinces. Here Frederick of Hesse found him on 23 December.[16] The campaign in Norway was discussed, but the unusually hard frost of the Christmas–New Year period seemed also to offer a chance of attacking Frederick IV of Denmark more directly: across the ice which lay thick over the Sound and the other waters between Sweden and the Danish islands. The idea of repeating the feat of Charles X – but in the opposite direction* – was tempting. Frederick IV had hardly any troops in Zealand, his forces being in the Holstein-Gottorp parts of Sleswig and Holstein, outside Wismar, on Rügen and in Pomerania. If the ice would hold, the Swedes could march towards Copenhagen and force Frederick to sue for peace. In all secrecy preparations were made. The Prince of Hesse began to gather the troops stationed in Scania together and Charles XII took care of the paper-work in his room. The visit of the young Duke and his governor, Arvid Horn, to Ystad was a fairly short one since the King expected soon to be on the move once more and Charles Frederick was too untrained to be taken as a volunteer on such an improvised campaign. Horn was glad of the opportunity to put himself right with the King. He was received with the utmost friendliness and grace,[17] but it was their common concern for the young Duke's education and training which formed the core of his conversations with Charles, not future policy. With Charles Frederick himself, the King rode every day in the neighbourhood of Ystad, but there were no festivities since the court was in mourning.

Charles XII's delight in being home and among his own was palpable. He seemed older to those who met him again after many years; less supple, and bothered by a cough, but so friendly and talkative that they were amazed when they thought back to the shy and reserved youth who had left Sweden fifteen years earlier.[18] Some of the high spirits bubbled over in the answers to Stockholm problems submitted, which seemed to invite a mock-serious treatment: how many courses were fitting to uphold the dignity of the ladies of his late grandmother's court in these hard times? The King was willing to restore the thirteen dishes thought suitable, but suggested – with some embellishments – that early matrimony might transfer the expense of keeping some of these ladies from him to their husbands.[19] But even such minutiae were a sign of being in touch and Charles let Ulrika know with what joy he contemplated the quick and speedy communication with Stockholm: he no longer felt 'shut in', or 'shut away'.[20]

Troops gathered at Landskrona and one detachment crossed the ice to occupy the small island of Hven. Swedish prisoners-of-war in Denmark escaped and joined Charles's army once more. In Copenhagen nervousness grew and orders were given to saw through the ice to help protect the capital: similar measures were taken all along the east coast of Zealand. But

* Charles X's army had in 1654 marched across the ice from Jutland to the islands and threatened Copenhagen.

between 9 and 11 January 1716 heavy storms broke up the ice in the Sound and the Danish venture became impossible.

Work continued, however, on the Norwegian campaign and it is possible that the 'march across the ice' was mooted more as a cover for it than as an operation seriously intended.[21] Food was collected for six weeks, maps were studied and on 15 February Charles turned aside Ulrika Eleonora's offer to visit him with all kinds of excuses: his quarters, though the best in Ystad, were far too uncomfortable for her; she ought not, for her health's sake, to travel at this time of year; he would come to Stockholm in the summer; he was really so busy with his duties that he had to suppress his own wishes and – most important – the war commanded him and dictated his time-table: he would have to go from Ystad 'for a while to visit his regiments'.[22]

III

The Norwegian campaign which began in February 1716[23] was intended not only to create a diversion in the west, and hope of sustaining part of the Swedish troops in enemy territory; but also to exert some pressure on George I and delay, if not prevent, the coalition's plans for a descent on Scania in 1716. Charles felt some contempt for both his 'new' enemies. 'I would not have deigned to use the methods Frederick William employed to grab Stettin, even if they gained me a hundred towns', he commented to Löwen. And towards George I he had a particular animosity: here was an ally who under the guise of help had turned enemy to promote Hanover's territorial expansion, and as an enemy he had made skilful and deceitful use of the resources of Great Britain to serve his particular interests as Elector.[24] Compared with these two, Tsar Peter was honest and straightforward. There was some comfort in the thought that Augustus's treachery had not profited him much: he now had so much trouble in Poland that the hope of being able to foster Stanislaus's cause did not seem a forlorn one to Charles in the New Year of 1716.[25]

It was disgust with George's duplicity which made Charles contemplate measures which favoured the Jacobites before the fall of Stralsund. Early in December 1715 Croissy judged the Swedish King willing to join France if the Regent decided to support James III openly on behalf of Louis XV.[26] Since the Regent decided against such backing, the question of Franco-Swedish cooperation did not materialize. For the Jacobites, however, Charles XII seemed the ideal promoter of their cause and they worked with great persistence from 1715 onwards to obtain his moral and military help. To summarize their secret plan of campaign of 1716: the Swedish King would – as a Protestant and a known supporter of Protestantism – endear James to the English people and gain the Stuarts more adherents than Catholic France.[27] James's Catholicism proved a stumbling block to the Protestant Charles XII and in spite of strong pressure from the Jacobites and from men in his own service, he remained adamant that he would not commit himself and returned money which the Swedish diplomat in Paris, Sparre, had accepted from Jacobite sources in 1715.[28] But since George as Elector was his declared enemy, Charles was not averse to limiting Hanoverian use of British resources by making the King of Great Britain fear that Swedish support for the Jacobites might become a fact. Both Charles's Norwegian campaigns, that of 1716 as well as that of 1718,* have therefore as one of their objectives the tying of some of George I's naval forces to the coast of Great Britain, in order to weaken the impact of British naval help to Sweden's enemies in the Baltic.

The chief purpose of the 1716 winter campaign was to paralyse the war effort of the King of Denmark. Frederick IV was the kingpin of any invasion of Sweden. If he could be discouraged sufficiently by the prospect of losing Norway, he might be persuaded to leave the coalition altogether. Without his fleet command of the Sound could not be achieved and his transport ships would be essential to land the troops of the coalition on the Swedish coast. Surprise was essential and strict secrecy was maintained. Troops movements and the collection of food and supplies were explained as essential for the Hesse inspection of the forces; but Swedish ships were forbidden to leave harbour lest such innocent-sounding news might alert the Danes.

The plan of campaign was as follows: Charles was to take command of some three thousand men gathering in Värmland and attempt to march straight to Kristiania; four thousand men, collecting in Vänersborg under General Mörner, were to cross the border in the neighbourhood of Moss and – bypassing the two forts of Frederiksten and Frederikstad – join Charles in the Norwegian capital. A cavalry force of eight hundred men was to make a feint further south, at Svinesund, to keep the Norwegians guessing as to the direction of the main attack. Its leader, General von Ascheberg, was also given the task of keeping communication open by building a bridge at Svinesund. Finally the Jämtland regiment was ordered to fall into the Røros region to prevent Norwegian forces stationed in the north from marching to support the capital through the eastern valleys.

On 16 February Charles, accompanied by Poniatowski and Rosen, left Ystad and rode north by day and night to Karlstad where troops were inspected between the 19th and the 22nd. Charles then continued to Holmedal where he met with Frederick of Hesse. Here a proclamation to the Norwegian people was prepared: the Swedish invasion was intended to force Frederick IV 'to think of peace' and no harm would come to the local population which was asked not to leave their homes. The Swedish soldiers were warned that no plunder or theft would be tolerated and they were ordered to treat the Norwegians 'as they would their own countrymen'. Orders were now sent to Mörner and Ascheberg to start moving. Charles with his corps pushed ahead as fast as he could, crossing the border on 26 February in the hope of out-flanking the Norwegian defenders of Kristiania.

* See below, pp. 424 ff., and 492 ff.

The troop movements on the Swedish side of the frontier had not gone unnoticed, but since the direction of the Swedish attack could not be known, the defence had been split into four sections: one remained in the capital as a reserve and three separate corps covered the invasion routes over Frederikshald, Kongsvinger and Høland. The force at Høland, about a thousand strong, was in the direct path of Charles's men and at the news of the Swedish approach – rumoured to be in strength – its commander, Kruse, withdrew leaving but a small party at Høland as look-outs. In the evening of the 27th a Swedish advance guard of 650 troopers – including the King and the Prince of Hesse – surprised the Høland party and took it prisoner; but while the Swedes rested after the hard ride over the snow-covered hills* they were in their turn surprised by Kruse, who with two hundred men had returned to investigate musket-fire heard in the distance. A brief and hard fight developed in which Poniatowski and Frederick of Hesse were both wounded – the latter so seriously that he had to be transported back to Sweden – and Charles only escaped being taken prisoner by Rosen's presence of mind. Kruse was, however, outnumbered when more Swedes arrived and was taken prisoner. The Swedes regarded him as exceptionally brave and treated him with great respect.

Kruse has been criticized for not bringing the whole of his force back, since he would then have outnumbered the Swedes,[29] but he had no means of knowing the size of the army he might have to face, and as early as 28 February the Swedish infantry caught up the advance guard. Charles prepared to continue at once to Kristiania, but a snowstorm lasting several days delayed the Swedes at Høland and gave the Norwegians time to organize the defence of the capital: Lützow moved from Frederikshald and with Sehested and the reserve posted nearly seven thousand men in two strong positions north-east of Kristiania, at Bagåsen and Gjelleråsen, while the local inhabitants helped to fell trees and make obstacles in the path of the invaders. Lützow's move had, however, opened the road for Mörner's advance and Charles, after a brief testing of the enemy strongholds, hurriedly outflanked them and moved south to join up with Mörner.† The weather was cold, the Norwegians unfriendly and the troops had to sleep most nights under open sky round camp fires. On 8 March the two corps met and moved on Kristiania. Clever use was made of the terrain and winter conditions: the frozen Bundefjord was crossed at a spot where the islands of Blekø and Hovedø sheltered the Swedes from the guns of Akershus fort and Kristiania was occupied during 10 and 11 March without a fight.

The Norwegian military and civilian authorities dared not risk a battle since a defeat would deliver the whole country into the hands of the Swedes.

* The route went over Trosterud, Rómsjø, Skarabølsseter to the lake of Mjermen; the Kongtorps hills were then traversed and the horses waded in snow to their bellies, leaving the riders to pull and push at times.

† The route went over lake Øjer, then through Enebakk and Spydeberg to Hølen, eleven kilometres north of Moss.

The government left Kristiania for Drammen and took up a new strong position at Gjellebekk. Before the move Akershus was provisioned and supplied so that the fort could be expected to hold out till the spring. Snipers from the fort incommoded the Swedish occupiers, but Charles could not begin a siege till artillery arrived by sea from Gothenburg, Mörner having been forced to leave the heavy guns behind since the snow was deep and he was short of horses. A defeat of the Norwegian army was the main objective of the Swedes; but attempts to outflank the Gjellebekk position failed;* and on 22 March Charles, having reconnoitred in person, decided that a full-scale attack would cost more men than he could afford to lose.

The attitude of the civilian population was worrying. The clergy refused to read Charles XII's proclamations to their parishioners and food requisitioning on any large scale was resisted by the peasants, who seemed deaf to promises and threats alike and often joined the armed forces as volunteers. Smaller units of Swedish soldiers were not denied food by the women-folk left on the farms – the tradition of peasant hospitality to strangers operating as strongly as fear. In the many anecdotes[30] which have survived locally the politeness of the King and his content with peasant fare are often contrasted with the haughty manners of his officers.† Plans had been made for magazines to be sent from Sweden; but the movement of supplies, by land or by sea, proved slow. The whole campaign had been hurriedly improvised and the lack of solid preparation began to tell. The Jämtland regiment could not carry out its task, being halted by deep snow: more important, Ascheberg had moved into Norway late – on 12 March only – and moved out again after a fortnight on a report (which proved false) that Danish reinforcements had landed at Frederikshald. His letter to Charles, explaining why he was unable to carry out his allotted task of building the bridge across Svinesund was intercepted; and it was not till 9 April that the King had news of his retreat when a peasant-courier‡ got through with letters from the Prince of Hesse.

Charles immediately sent a trusted officer, Delvig, with five hundred troopers to Sweden to move supplies of food and ammunition, get the bridge built and the artillery transport speeded up. He was also to remind the fleet of its orders, given already in December 1715, to cruise in such a way that communications between Denmark and Norway should be interrupted. The bridge was built within ten days and Delvig returned to the King, but the fleet was slow in fitting out and the Danes won the race for command of the sea approaches to Norway. This forced Charles XII to relinquish his hold on Kristiania. In the night of 18–19 April the Swedes left the capital to reach the

---

* One was led by Löwen (who was taken prisoner and not released till after Charles's death) attacking from Hadeland and Ringerike supported by another attempt on Ravnsborg; the other by Schlippenbach from Bærum with Nieroth in support against Krokskogen.

† Stories told of specific heroines, e.g. of Anna Colbjørnsdatter at Norderhov, have not stood up to modern research; but the tale of Charles who did not spurn the peasant 'flat-bread' buttered with the thumb and was rewarded by finding his lunch in one piece while the 'Swedish' bread demanded by his officers had crumbled is thought to have a factual base.

‡ For this courier, Halvard Bryngelson, see below, p. 478.

river Glommen before Danish reinforcements landed at Frederikshald and/or
Norwegian pursuers could catch up with them. Forced marches got them to
the broad river in time to construct rafts from timber stacked along its banks.
On 21 April, at Onstadsund, they crossed to comparative safety and could
afford to rest for some days.

Charles had no intention of evacuating Norway and thus removing his
pressure on Frederick IV, especially after he received news that Wismar had
fallen* and that the enemy coalition was preparing its descent on Scania.
Communications with Sweden were safe thanks to Delvig's bridge (completed
on 26 April) and Charles made his headquarters at Torpum, a manor-house
three-quarters of a mile from Frederikshald, while waiting for ships of the
Gothenburg squadron to arrive with supplies of all kinds. Till then food
remained scarce; Motraye, who visited Charles at Torpum on 13 May to
discuss the projected Lapland journey to be sponsored by the King, noted that
the royal breakfast was 'herring and bread only'.[31] The army was dispersed
between Frederikshald and Frederikstad, with some detachments on the far
side of Svinesund. At the end of April galleys and low-draught vessels successfully made contact with the King's army, having kept in shallow waters to
avoid battle with the big Danish ships patrolling outside. A well-planned
enemy attack on the Swedish bridge was defeated on 22 May, and Swedish
control of the waters of Svinesund was completed by the conquest of
Sponviken fort.

The logical next step was to conquer Frederikshald with its fort, Frederiksten. The fort was, however, built on a sharp bluff, difficult to take by storm
and Charles did not have the heavy artillery necessary for a siege. He therefore
planned to take town and fort by surprise in the night of 22 June. The Swedes
knew that most of the garrison (falsely estimated as less than eight hundred)†
slept in the town and hoped that by a night attack – to be carried out by
1,500 men – many of these would be netted in Frederikshald while Swedish
troops would make their way into the fort with those of the enemy who
hurried to defend it.

We know a good deal of Charles's plans and of their costly failure from
Major-General Hamilton's letters to Feif. The Swedish preparations had
become known and the element of surprise was lost. Frederikshald was taken
between 1.30 and 4 o'clock in the light summer night, but the storm on
Frederiksten was beaten off and the most influential burghers agreed to the
commander shooting the town into flames to force the Swedes to leave. The
musket-fire from the fort was accurate. Many officers and men were killed,
including three major-generals: Schomer, Delvig and Schlippenbach. The
King, unhurt but for a grazed cheek, asked – and was refused – a brief armis-

---

* On 8/19 April the Swedish commander surrendered the town to a mixed force of Danes,
Prussians and Hanoverians who occupied it on 12/23, partly because of shortage of food and of
illness among his 3,500 men but also because he wanted to prevent Russian participation in the
occupation of Wismar, cp. below, p. 423*.

† In reality it counted 1,500 men.

ce to remove the wounded Swedes from the burning town. Those who were
t had to fight their way out, across a bridge where they came under cross-fire
:om the fort and from an armed barge in the fjord, leaving behind five
undred dead and wounded. Charles wrote to Ulrika about the 'loss of several
rave officers, whom Fate would not permit a longer life' in a restrained and
esigned manner;[32] but those who watched him at close hand noted his grief.[33]

Worse was to come a few days later when on 24 June and 26 June Torden-
kjold skilfully used favourable conditions in Dynekilen to destroy a large
;wedish transport of food and ammunition on its way to the King. Torden-
kjold had brought galleys and shallow-draught ships from Denmark to deny
he Swedes the advantage of the leads. His squadron had more firepower
han the relatively few escorts sent with the Swedish convoy; he captured
.ome and others were scuttled to avoid capture.[34]

IV

The setbacks of 22–26 June necessitated the evacuation of the Frederikshald
listrict. Most troops were sent back to Sweden though some were left as a
:emporary guard for Svinesund bridge.* On the border between Norway and
Sweden the building of the fort of Sundsborg was started on 21 August to
prepare for the next round. Frederick of Hesse had long urged Charles to
:ome back to take command in face of the Scania invasion threat;[35] but the
King argued that there was time enough. He did not expect the invasion to be
launched while Danish barges and galleys were still off the Norwegian coast;
indeed, he assumed it would be postponed till George I's men-of-war had
returned from convoy duties for British shipping to the eastern Baltic,† and
thought there was a sporting chance that the whole plan might disintegrate.[36]

In the meantime he had plenty to do. He could direct the defence preparations from where he was. Corn and supplies for the army of defence in the
Malmö region were concentrated. He decreed that Lund, Landskrona and
Hälsingborg would be abandoned if the invasion took place. The bishop and
the university would evacuate their treasures from Lund to Malmö; those
leaving Hälsingborg would go to Engelholm. If the enemy landed, Landskrona
and Hälsingborg would have to be burnt but Kalmar must be defended. The
most likely spot for an enemy landing he calculated as between Ystad and
Trelleborg. The western parts of Sweden were closer to Zealand which would
make provisioning easier, but as these were more heavily fortified than the
areas further east he was inclined to believe that no landing would be risked
west of Ystad.[37] He was on the alert for news and sent skippers out to reconnoitre what kind of vessels moved through the Sound: it was important to
receive the first possible indication of the mass movement of transport-ships
which presaged the imminence of invasion. Intelligence from abroad was

* They stayed till 10 August to keep the enemy guessing as to Swedish plans.
† See below, p. 424 for George I's orders to Norris as to the use of the British fleet.

collected and sifted for hints of the timing of enemy plans,[38] and Charles XII'
diplomatic offensive to wreck these plans was intensified when Görtz reache
the Dutch Republic on 2/13 July.*

Charles saw his own role as that of the disturber of the invasion plans who
by remaining on the Norwegian border for as much of the summer as possible
kept Frederick IV and George I guessing. He urged his brother-in-law to mov
to Scania ahead of himself. Frederick of Hesse had made a slow recovery from
his February wounds, but devoted nursing by Ulrika Eleonora and a cure a
Medevi spa had made him fit by mid-July and in early August he reached
Kristianstad to begin work once more.

A meeting with Ulrika Eleonora had been much discussed during the
summer, and Vadstena – one of the palaces of the late Queen-Grandmother –
was picked on as not being too distant for Ulrika and more or less en route
for the King's own move south for the time when he thought invasion
possible. The meeting with his 'dear sister', Charles wrote to Frederick, might
have to be shorter than he would wish – perhaps the military situation would
permit only a single day – but he was not prepared to sacrifice this opportunity to see and speak to Ulrika unless Frederick summoned him urgently
to Scania. If this should happen, he implored Ulrika to remain at Vadstena
that he might take the next opportunity of a visit – Stockholm was too
distant.[39]

Neither Frederick,† nor the war, put obstacles in the way and brother and
sister spent the Thursday and Friday of 30–31 August together. Charles did
not bring adjutants with him and we have little factual information of his
stay at Vadstena except from Ulrika's letters to her husband[40] and a reference
to the emotional impact of the meeting which she penned in her 1740 comments to Nordberg's history of Charles XII.[41] We know that the King left
Major-General de la Gardie in command of the border troops on 26 August
and rode over Strömstad, Uddevalla and Vänersborg to Hjo on lake Vättern.
He was rowed across the lake in heavy rain, rode the last few miles completely
alone and was able to take Ulrika 'by surprise' as he had wanted to do since
December 1715. His cape was dripping wet, we hear from one of Ulrika's
ladies-in-waiting, and the little court was thrown into a joyful confusion at
his unannounced arrival.

There may have been a childish element in Charles's wish to take 'by
surprise', but privacy was probably the dominating motive. Charles knew that
the reunion with his only remaining sister would affect him deeply. Ulrika
noted that they both cried and that Charles found it hard to control his
emotion when they talked of their parents, of Hedvig Sophia and of the
family life they had once shared: his voice thickened and the tears were never
far away when the mother's name was mentioned. They got on surprisingly
well together considering the readjustments, partially achieved by corres-

* See below, p. 425.
† The Prince of Hesse was most anxious for the meeting to take place: quite apart from the
pleasure it would give his wife, he reckoned on its promoting her interests in the succession.

ondence, necessary after an interval of sixteen years in which the 'baby' ister had become a mature woman. Charles won Ulrika's heart during their ong talk alone on Thursday evening by praising her husband and his brave ervices to Sweden.[42] The next day had to be a more public one. They listened o the Friday sermon preached by one of the court chaplains, and Charles nust have seen something of Ulrika's ladies-in-waiting (all old acquaintances) ince he sent greetings to them by name in his first letter from Lund.[43] At 10 'clock in the evening of 31 August, after supper, the King took his leave and over Jönkoping reached a main road to Scania.

Tradition has it that the horse on which he rode away from Vadstena was Brandklipparen, the grey horse which had carried his father in the battle of Lund in 1676: presumably Ulrika Eleonora had taken it to Vadstena for this symbolic purpose. This is probably a pretty legend though Brandklipparen's long life is well documented: the horse was one of those Charles XII took with him on campaign in 1700; it survived all the battles including Poltava but was captured at the *Kalabalik*; it was bought back from the Tartars and sent to Sweden in 1716.[44] Charles did not go straight to Lund, since he wanted to inspect the coastal fortifications in the Hälsingborg area. This was done between 2 and 6 September and he then settled at Lund, which with its good communications with both western and eastern south Sweden was the ideal headquarters if enemy landings should materialize.

It seems an irony of fate that Charles should arrive in Lund just about the time Tsar Peter let his allies know that the invasion of Sweden was not to take place. The plans of the coalition had been well prepared and concerted.[45] Tsar Peter had brought together the more than forty thousand Russian troops he had promised for the venture and had a fleet of men-of-war and transport vessels lying off Danzig. Frederick IV had some thirty thousand troops ready and had commandeered the whole of the Danish merchant fleet for his share of the transport to Sweden. The two rulers had a conference at Hamburg between 28 May and 3 June (N.S.) in which the proportions of cavalry to infantry for the Scania attack were settled. A strong Russian raid on Sweden from the east Baltic was also agreed on to force Charles XII to fight on two fronts.

Problems however, multiplied throughout the summer. Tsar Peter was already suspicious and hurt at the refusal of the Danes, Prussians and Saxons to permit his army a share in the occupation of Wismar,* and this refusal was in itself proof of growing fear of the Tsar's power.[46] His troops had interfered in the Commonwealth unrest in 1715 and 1716; he had made himself the arbiter between Augustus and the Poles in April 1716 – calling both parties to him in Danzig to listen humbly to his decision;[47] he had, in the same month, married his niece to Duke Charles Leopold of Mecklenburg-Schwerin who was assumed to have Russian support in the claim he now put forward for

---

* See above, p. 420: Repnin had to accept this decision since the Tsar's allies threatened to prevent him forcibly from sending Russian troops into the town.

Wismar; his influence – backed by his military might – seemed to jump eve
further west in Germany;[48] in 1714 he had married another niece to the Duk
of Courland.

At the same time George I found himself in a difficult situation in Londo
There had been criticism of the way in which he had used the British fleet i
1715 and – faced with Jacobite rebellion* – he resisted Russian and Danis
pressure in the spring of 1716 for specifically aggressive orders for Norr
in writing.[49] Verbal promises only were made, and though these were late
shown to be sincerely meant, they helped to make the Tsar doubtful c
George's intentions. In the event, the Hanoverian influence over the Britis
navy was stronger and more direct in 1716 than in 1715. Norris arrived i
the Sound as early as 7 June with nineteen battleships (carrying 1,070 guns
more than a month before the Dutch squadron which had no other purpos
than convoying its merchantmen. Moreover, this Dutch squadron, and th
whole merchant fleet of both the Maritime Powers, were kept waiting in th
Sound for yet another month since Norris had orders not to proceed int
the Baltic proper till he could go as part of the anti-Swedish armada. Dela
in achieving this junction was due to Frederick IV having to wait for thos
of his ships that had been sent to Norway, and it was 8 August before Norri
could join his squadron to the Danish fleet of eighteen men-of-war and th
Russian one of twenty-four large ships.

Finally, the smaller Dutch squadron of six men-of-war (and a total of 30
guns only) undertook, with a small detachment of Norris's squadron, th
'official' task of convoying Anglo-Dutch shipping to the east Baltic, whil
Norris and George I's allies stationed their armada off Bornholm to bottl
the Swedish fleet up in Karlskrona and thus facilitate the descent on Scania.[5]

In spite of this impressive naval junction and of the corresponding military
junction of Russo-Danish forces in the King of Denmark's territories preparatory to the invasion attempt, Tsar Peter abandoned the plan on 19 Septembe
(N.S.). He argued that the season was too far advanced and suggested postponement till 1717. Both George and Frederick IV were shocked and did thei
best to persuade the Tsar to change his mind. The King of Denmark could
not afford to offend Danish mercantile interests by commandeering thei
ships for transports two years running, especially after a postponement which
did not make sense to him.[51] The Elector of Hanover, who had found in
Stanhope an English minister willing to cooperate in the northern policy,†
wanted to act while he could and was terrified at the prospect of Tsar Peter's
landing-troops for the Scania venture of 1717 being quartered in Mecklenburg,
so close to his own Electorate, for the winter.[52]

Peter remained adamant, however. He had reconnoitred the Swedish
defences and found them strong; he was worried at the time wasted while the

---

* The rebellion was defeated by February 1716, but Jacobite agitation remained significant.

† To the extent of writing to an English diplomat of his annoyance at 'the refusal of the Dutch
Commodore's coming into the line of Battle to force the Swedes into Port': quoted by Hatton,
Diplomatic Relations, p. 124.

▪alition fleet (including Norris) had waited for the return of those Danish ▪arships which had taken part in the Norwegian defence against Charles XII; ▪d he was disappointed that no chance to destroy the Swedish fleet had ▪aterialized. The Tsar was also alarmed at the conflict with his son Aleksey ▪hich culminated in the latter's flight from Russia to Vienna – a blow to ▪ternal authority which might well produce public repercussions. He was ▪ncerned lest the Prussian refusal (of late May) to send troops for the Scania ▪roject foreshadowed a break-up of the coalition, and he was profoundly ▪spicious of George I.[53] He knew of that ruler's alliance with the Emperor, ▪d assumed that the negotiations proceeding in Hanover between Stanhope ▪nd Dubois[54] might have for their real purpose French help for George to ▪hieve a separate peace with Sweden. He was not disinclined to enter the ▪ce for such a peace himself.

The desirability of a separate peace between Charles XII and Tsar Peter had ▪en a main theme of Cederhielm's clandestine correspondence with indivi-▪ual Swedes (including the King) once he had returned to Russia as a ▪risoner-of-war.[55] Görtz had, as we have seen, worked along similar lines ▪hough for a different purpose during the years after Poltava,* and in the ▪mmer and autumn of 1716 in the Dutch Republic, when his main task was ▪ borrow money against safe-conducts for Dutch shipping in the Baltic, he ▪egan those diplomatic soundings of interested parties which were the ▪ssence of Charles XII's peace-offensive. The Russians and the Jacobites fell ▪ Görtz's share, while Fabrice and other Germans were used for contacts ▪ith George I; and there are strong indications that Görtz and Poniatowski† ▪s early as 1716 helped to create dissension inside the anti-Swedish alliance by ▪ainting a tempting picture of the fruits that would fall to the ruler who came ▪rst in the race for peace.[56] At the same time the Jacobites, disappointed in ▪rench help, urged a separate peace between the Tsar and the Swedish King ▪n the hope that their joint support for a Stuart restoration would follow. ▪t was indeed Jacobites in the Tsar's entourage, e.g. his medical adviser ▪rskine, who facilitated Görtz's contacts with Kurakin, Shafirov and ▪stermann.[57]

V

▪sar Peter's suspicions of his allies were not justified, though understandable ▪n view of the Wismar incident. The deal between Stanhope and Dubois was ▪ot anti-Russian and it was indeed Russia's 'betrayal' of the Scania project ▪hich convinced George I that he would have to come to terms with his old ▪nemy France.[58] Poor Frederick of Denmark–Norway, who had not inten-▪ionally delayed the naval junction, was in mingled rage and despair at being ▪obbed of what had seemed the certainty of victory over Sweden. Hanoverian

* See above, p. 369.
† He went to Germany on diplomatic missions in the summer of 1716.

diplomacy in Copenhagen did what it could to improve Dano-Russia
relations in the hope that Frederick IV might permit the Russians winte
quarters in Denmark in the interests of a 1717 invasion,[59] but Frederic
refused, fearing a Russian plot to make him a vassal of the Tsar by virtua
occupation of Denmark on the pattern of Poland. The cracks in the allianc
opened wider in October when the Russian troops sailed from Denmark t
Mecklenburg.* The split into a Dano-Hanoverian camp and a Russc
Prussian one became a fact when in November the Tsar and Frederic
William I signed a treaty of mutual guarantee of the land they had taken fror
Sweden in case 'one of their former allies' should come to Charles XII's help.[6]

To this splitting of the coalition against him Charles XII had contribute
significantly by his Norwegian campaign of 1716. It was this campaign whicl
had forced Frederick IV to send seven of his big men-of-war and four frigate
to Skagerak under Vice-Admiral Gabel at the end of March, a squadroi
which was not free to return to Copenhagen till 7 August. If Charles XII ha
abandoned the campaign after he was forced out of Kristiania, Fredericl
would have been free to effect the naval junction with George I and the Tsa
at a much earlier date. The allied timetable had therefore been delayed by th
direct action of the Swedish King, and it was this tampering with the time
table which had operated most strongly on the Tsar's decision of 9 Septembe
to abandon the invasion.

Hardly less important was the moral effect of a campaign which could shov
no victory on land or at sea. The anti-Swedish coalition had looked upoi
Charles XII as in ignominious flight from Stralsund, had hoped to be abl
to dictate peace-terms to him once the invasion preparations were complete
and – if he refused – to overcome with relative ease his military oppositior
to the invasion. They knew how war-weary Sweden was and were wel
informed on the lack of money and supplies in 1715. They reckoned or
domestic disorders if the King were foolhardy enough to step up the wai
effort. Charles's achievement in 1716 and the willing helpers he found came
therefore as an unpleasant surprise.

The main fleet at Karlskrona, at the King's command, had fourteen big
men-of-war and five frigates ready with men and supplies to support Wismar
as soon as the sea was open. Just as it left Karlskrona on 20 April/1 May 1716,
news of Wismar's fall arrived in Sweden, and the next task set it by Charles
XII, an attack on the Danish fleet off Copenhagen (down to thirteen of the line
since Frederick had been forced to send naval help to Norway) became
impossible when George I sent Norris to the Sound more than a month earlier
than the Dutch squadron for the express purpose of defending Frederick IV's
navy.[61] The Karlskrona fleet scored a partial success in its third task: the
Tsar ordered twelve men-of-war away from the Swedish east coast to Reval
when Admiral Wachtmeister turned from the western Baltic to seek battle
according to the King's orders with Peter's fleet, and Russian galleys also

* For their departure in the summer of 1717, see below, p. 451.

ught the safety of port.[62] Tsar Peter became convinced that Charles was
t yet beaten to his knees and that the Swedish will to resist was stronger
an the allies had assumed.

This conviction was strengthened by news which came of energetic measures
remedy the shortage of money and promote economic growth. Between
ecember 1715 and his departure for the Continent in April 1716, Görtz was
tive in fashioning new organs for the direction of economic policy and in
tablishing collaboration between bureaucrats in sympathy with the King's
olicy.[63] It was clear that a new spirit was animating Stockholm: before
ng the magazines might be filled and Swedish manufacture and trade feel
e benefit of reorganization.

Most obvious, however, was Charles XII's own will not to give in, demon-
rated by the campaign in Norway with the minimum of time and resources
r planning and preparation. This raised grave doubts in the Tsar's mind as
the probability of success for the Scania invasion project. How could the
llies, he asked the Danish officers with whom he discussed the project, make
ure of food and forage in Sweden for a lengthy campaign? How could they
revent Charles ravaging the country before retreating further north? How
ould they force him to stand and deliver battle? Peter still had a healthy
espect for Charles as a commander. 'I know his way of making war', he said
Frederick IV, 'he would give us no rest and our armies would be weakened.'
Ie mentally compared Charles's fate when he invaded Russia and the risk
e himself would be running if he now invaded Sweden: the southern prov-
nces of the Swedish peninsula had been Danish until the 1650s; he was sure
hat Charles would not hesitate to ruin them according to *raison de guerre*
order to save the essential Sweden 'of the North' – the Sweden of Gustavus
asa and Gustavus Adolphus. Given the lateness of the season, with winter
oming, he could not bring himself to take the risk against such an adver-
ary.[64] That the Scania invasion of 1716 was called off was, therefore,
ssentially a by-product of the Norwegian venture of 1716 and all it implied.
he obvious military failure of the Norwegian campaign has discouraged
nterest in it and obscured its significant measure of success in the wider
uropean context.

4

Headquarters at Lund

The allied abandonment of the Scania invasion plan in 1716 meant tha
Charles XII's stay in Lund would become a long one. He could not be sur
that the plan would not be revived in the 1717 season and his presence in th
south of Sweden remained essential. Lund was, however, central enough t
serve as the best headquarters in the diplomatic and administrative sense a
well as in the military one: not too distant from Stockholm and yet clos
enough to the Continent to permit speedy contact. Lund thus became th
King's base until he departed for his second Norwegian campaign in Jun
1718.[1] He left it (apart from very brief trips) only twice – between 25 Augus
and 22 September 1717 when he inspected troops, magazines collected a
Strömstad and new fortifications at other places on the frontier with Norway
and between 10 March and 16 May 1718 when he combined another round c
inspections with a family reunion at Kristinehamn.*

The kind of life Charles made for himself in Lund, given that the war sti
dictated both its framework and much of its content, is therefore indicativ
of some of his peace-time interests and tastes in maturity. The house which h
used, belonging to one of the professors at the university, was a building o
two floors only so that stairs should not bother his leg. To give the feelin
of space he enjoyed, some of the rooms were enlarged, and some at least wer
redecorated in the Swedish colours of blue and yellow. Charles's collectio
of guns and of paintings, mainly portraits, were hung on the walls. Two nev
stables were built and a well with a pump of the most modern constructio
was sunk in the yard. It was said to have cost 'a lot of money', but the wate
was judged exceptionally fine. The garden was planted with fruit-trees and
flowering shrubs: the King's favourite vegetables – spinach, parsley and water
cress – were cultivated, and two pools were dug and furnished with fish fo
the table.

This house with its modest grounds was referred to as 'the Court', but it
staff was minute† and there were few guards or security measures. Adjutant
and some of the drabants were on duty in the anteroom to the King's

* See below, pp. 453–4, for this reunion between 21 March and 3 April.
† Feif asked Tessin for a butler, a master-cook, two helpers and six lackeys from Stockholm
letter of 21 December 1715.

chambers and attempts were made to keep beggars, vagabonds and stray dogs away from the Court since the noise which was the common objectionable denominator in all three cases was deemed disturbing to those busy with paper-work. The only grand outward sign of Charles's residence was the golden intertwined double C which adorned the new well.

The influx of officers and ministers, the housing of important foreign visitors (including Voynarovsky's wife who arrived to keep an eye on her husband's semi-voluntary investment in Charles's cause),[2] the comings and goings of couriers and diplomats, and even of spies discreet enough to keep on good terms with the Swedes,[3] created problems of accommodation. Many householders resented having 'guests' quartered on them and some professors of the university protested that they could hardly find room and/or peace to write their lectures. There is evidence from the magistrate's records that efforts were made to smarten Lund up so that it would at least look neat and tidy; but its essentially small-town character is underlined by at least one warning issued to the burghers from Charles XII: if they persisted in letting their pigs stray into the yard or gardens of the Court, their animals would be assumed to constitute 'free gifts' and be handed over to the hospital by the King's servants.[4]

Charles's working day[5] quickly settled into a routine pattern. Feif reported to the King early in the morning (often at 3 o'clock in the light months of the year), they worked together on memoranda and correspondence for several hours and continued in a long afternoon session. Inspection of troops or other military duties sometimes filled the forenoon between 7 and midday; but if these were not on the agenda the morning was taken up with conferences, with fitting in sittings for portraits, and with meetings with all kinds of experts, both on domestic and foreign affairs. Such men were usually invited to Lund to see the King, but it was not difficult for visitors with practical suggestions for the improvement of any aspect of Swedish life to get access to Charles XII even if they came to Lund on their own initiative. Secret diplomatic decisions were usually taken late at night. When Görtz stayed at Lund between November 1717 and April 1718 it was noted that he usually walked from his own lodgings to the Court 'after dark'.[6]

II

For relaxation Charles rode regularly and enjoyed conversations and discussions with his visitors and with the university professors. Lund had suffered from the invasion of 1709 and the campaign that followed as well as from the plague year that reached the town in 1712: the university (or 'Academy' as the King preferred to call it)[7] had less staff and students than before the war – twelve professors* and fewer than two hundred students. From the

---

* Theology had three, Philosophy seven, Law one, Medicine one.

beginning of his stay the King tended to look upon 'the Academy' as a plac
where he could drop in to obtain contact with new ideas in learning. His fir
visit, on 20 September 1716, was meant to be a formal one, but spotting
blackboard with algebraic equations the King asked the professor of mathe
matics, Quensel, to lecture on them. Later he asked for permission to b
present at a disputation where Professor Döbeln defended a thesis on th
nature of sensual perception, and he frequently came to listen to th
philosophy lectures given by Professor Rydelius.[8] There were of course som
purely official occasions – as when the university celebrated the King
birthday on 17 June 1717 with speeches and poems[9] – but the informal co
tacts are the more significant ones since the academic subjects in which Charle
showed an interest are also those which for preference he discussed wit
visitors better qualified than himself.

Mathematics was high on the list, and here the King had a chance to tal
over a subject which was part and parcel of his own life as a commande
with experts of the calibre of Polhem and his assistant, Svedborg (late
ennobled as Swedenborg). We know a little about their talks on the topi
with Charles.[10] The King did not value 10 highly as a base for calculation
since it led so speedily to fractions. To him 8 or 16 seemed more suitable
both being divisible more than once and having the advantages, respectively
of being the cube of 2 and the fourth power of 2. When he suggested that 6.
the second lowest multiple of the two, might prove a serviceable base
the experts objected to the cumbersome multiplication table which woul
follow: 64 times 64 equalled 4,096! Charles thereupon toiled the whole nigh
through to find ways of simplifying the work which a base of 64 would entai
and though the critics stuck to their point, Svedborg, who after 1718 becam
such a harsh enemy and even pathological hater of Charles XII,* alway
admired the King's insight into mathematics and judged him more gifted i
this discipline than any layman or professional he had ever encountere
including the great Leibniz.[12] Polhem reckoned Charles the equal of th
famous English professor, John Wallis, in working out highly complicate
calculations in his head.[13]

With Polhem and Svedborg the discussion of applied science sometime
led to talk of problems and experiments. We know, for instance, that th
freezing points of different liquids were touched upon, since Svedbor
recounts the King's story of a Polish winter so cold that the Hungarian win
froze solid and he was able to cut it like a cake with his sword and distribut
the pieces to the soldiers.[14]

Charles's interest in the philosophical theories of his day is testified b

---

* Swedenborg's picture of Charles XII as the ruler of false modesty who loved only himself an
desired to become the absolute master of Sweden and the world has obviously influenced th
'legendary' Charles XII; though his equation of Charles with a Lucifer who (as a punishment fo
having declared war on God) was himself punished by a *conjugium infernale* to a wife mo
terrible and stubborn than himself, is equally obviously affected by Swedenborg's own emotiona
and spiritual troubles.[11]

ourteen 'theses' on *Anthropologia physica* he wrote in Lund in the autumn of 1717, stimulated by discussions with the learned Hein, a visiting Hesse counsellor who had studied under Christian Thomasius, one of the central figures of the German philosophy of the Early Enlightenment. The King let Feif translate his theses into German and planned to send them to Hein for comment, but Feif persuaded him to desist. He argued that Hein might let Thomasius see them and that Thomasius in his turn might print them with his own commentaries, claiming Charles XII as his own disciple. It would not redound to Sweden's honour, the Secretary – choosing his words carefully – argued if her King took sides in rival philosophical schools: he must leave that kind of word-play to the professional philosophers.[15] It is possible, and even probable, that Feif's advice was in part motivated by a fear that Charles, by so open an interest in such issues as the definition of bodily and spiritual *vellyst* (i.e. *Leidenschaft, volupté*), would render himself suspect with the Swedish Church. There was nothing anti-Church in the theses, which by modern philosophers have been judged a typical summary of early eighteenth-century enlightened thinking on the way human beings reacted to stimuli,[16] but by strict clergymen the theses might well have been thought insufficiently religious in that they made no mention of either God or Bible.

There was indeed speculation after 1715 about Charles's attitude to religion. Many held that his praise of Moslem virtues (their abstinence from intoxicating drinks, their laws of hospitality, the way some of them acted with as much loyalty to their given word as any Christian) amounted to an admiration of Islam not fitting in the head of a Christian state:[17] a few reckoned him indifferent to religion. Most Swedes regarded this as 'foreign calumnies', but Charles's tolerance was a fact which impressed itself on those who knew him in his maturity. Swedish clergymen attracted by the Pietist movement argued that the King was in sympathy with them and that he aimed to lend them strong support against their more intolerant brethren, and there is some evidence on which to base such claims.[18]

His court chaplains, Nordberg and, after 1717, Rhyzelius, were convinced that his personal devoutness persisted throughout his life and were at pains to refute accusations that the King became progressively 'less religious' as he got older. Rhyzelius, who had been made chaplain to the Drabant corps already in 1713, but who did not meet the King till October 1716 in Lund, was in close contact with him during the last two years of his life and has left memoirs which deal with this period.[19] We look in vain to them for any detailed information about Charles XII's personal attitude to religion, outspoken though they are, since Rhyzelius's concern for the confidential nature of his position as the King's confessor precluded discussion and speculation. What we can glean from them is, however, indicative of a more than formal adherence to the faith in which the King had been brought up. Charles began the day with a prayer and some reading in the Bible; he prepared himself conscientiously

for the times, about four a year, when he went to confession;* and thoug
the chaplain had many a disagreement with Charles XII over the war – whic
he preached it was the King's religious duty to bring to a speedy end – th
former never doubted the latter's genuine desire to submit to the will of Go
and to live in such a way that he could account to God for his stewardshi
of Sweden.[20] An unexpected source complements this picture. A Norwegia
farmer who in 1716 wrote down what he noticed of Charles XII's behaviou
during a stage of the campaign when the King seemed most un-regal (hi
uniform was dirty and tattered, he was halt) made a point of mentioning tha
he read the Bible before going to sleep, and a Norwegian clergyman note
that the King prayed on his knees night and morning.[21]

Given the King's reserve about his spiritual life, this is as much as we ar
ever likely to learn about it. There is much evidence from Rhyzelius an
others of Charles's attitude to the less personal aspects of worship. The Kin
admired the cut of Rhyzelius's cassock, a rather wide one, and the new styl
caught on among the clergy in general; he discussed with the Lund theologian
semantic problems and biblical interpretation;[22] he appreciated Bisho
Svedberg's visit to Lund in November 1717 for sentimental reasons, bu
commented that the sermon he preached was not as brilliant as those h
remembered him giving before the late King. The fact that Svedberg ha
chosen for his text 'Heavenly signs in sun and moon' may have influenced thi
judgement, for Charles – a typical child of the Early Enlightenment – wa
averse to anything that smacked of superstition.

It is indicative of Charles's interest in theological disputation, which wa
closely linked to interpretation of Sweden's distant history and linguisti
development, that Svedberg found on the King's table not only his ow
recently published *Schibboleth* but also the even more recent counterblas
to it (which he himself had not yet read) by Urban Hjärne, and had som
trouble persuading Charles to lend it to him.[23] The concern for the purity an
status of the Swedish language was constant with the King and became mor
consciously motivated as he got older. He followed the Lund professoria
lectures – all given in Latin – with ease, but when one struck him as outstand
ing, he suggested that it might be printed in a Swedish version so that Swede
could learn that complex ideas could be expressed also in their native tongue.[2]
That this did not imply any contempt for or decline of joy in the othe
languages with which he was familiar is clear from various factors: hi
frequent and long letters in German to Frederick of Hesse whenever the wa
situation kept them apart can be instanced,[25] and so can the delight he foun
in the company of 'Luxembourg', an intelligent hunchback (often referred t
as 'Charles XII's dwarf') who was part of General Mörner's entourage – he wa
famous for his knowledge of French and Italian verse and had his nicknam
from the uncanny facial resemblance he was said to bear to the French general.[2]

---

* See below, p. 484†, for Rhyzelius's concern that Charles put off the confession planned for 2ç
November 1718 since he had no time to prepare properly.

III

Charles's 'escape' remained, as before, the planning for future building, the hope of expressing himself in architecture and of impressing his own style on the capital. On 1 November 1716 Feif wrote to Tessin that the King would like to see him and suggested (as from himself) that the real reason – Charles's desire to discuss building plans with him – might be discreetly hidden behind Tessin's own request to be permitted to come to Lund to discuss other business: the affairs of the Academy* might provide an excuse, or the preparations for the ceremonial state funerals with which the King wanted to honour the memories of his elder sister and grandmother as soon as there was money to spare for these to be staged with some grandeur.[27] Even before this date the King had asked that drawings and projects saved from the *Kalabalik* and sent to Stockholm for safety should be dispatched to Lund.[28]

Tessin's illness, and an ever-increasing burden of work in the capital† prevented any meeting with Charles XII till the spring of 1718,[29] but their correspondence about plans received and pored over was lively from December 1716 onwards. The King liked the general views and plans of the palace and other buildings submitted, but reminded Tessin that the new Chancery building must, for reasons of administrative convenience, be placed as close to the castle as possible.[30] He was particularly interested in the grandiose stable and carousel building, since this had been worked out along lines suggested by himself in Turkey, showing his preference for pure lines, rich materials and 'beautiful large colonnades'.

The King and Tessin did not always see eye to eye on all aspects of architecture. As an artist who admired Bernini and who had indeed studied under him, Tessin found Charles's dislike of sculpture in church architecture hard to take;[31] and the King's alternative to Tessin's plan for razing the Brunkeberg hill, namely to plant it with trees and use it as a contrast to the Royal Palace sector of the capital,[32] was not one which commended itself to the architect who wanted open space to make the surroundings of the palace impressive. Problems were also created by the King's concern, noticeable from the Turkey period onwards and possibly explicable from a sense of being 'on view' there, or even a near-prisoner as after the *Kalabalik*, that Tessin should make it possible for him to walk round each floor of the palace and also to move from palace to stable and to various quays without having to be in public view. The architect objected that the old castle-church would be in the way. The King retorted that either the church would have to be moved or Tessin would have to build another palace wing to enclose the church and thus enable him to walk 'en suite round the whole of the palace'.

Wide views were also important to Charles XII after Turkey: not even a

* Tessin had in 1714 been made Chancellor of Lund University.

† As well as being Chamberlain of the court he was increasingly used in higher administration, see below, p. 440.

statue of Charles XI, which Tessin suggested placing in the centre of the palac
court, would the King allow in that particular spot since it would spoil th
'beautiful prospect' from the palace to the Djurgården natural park and to h
favourite islands.[33] Tessin and Feif poked gentle fun at the King's desire fo
secret stairs in the palace (so that he would not always have to use the publ
doors) and covered private roads (so that he could ride away or go on boar
an *escaloupe* without being watched): sad for him, they joked, that th
world had lost the age-old secret of making rings which permitted the weare
to vanish into thin air at will.[34]

The slightly obsessive preoccupation with his own ability to move freel
and secretly is less noticeable after Charles XII's return from Turkey. In th
letters to Tessin from 1715 onwards the emphasis is on specific commissior
in which the King is anxious to have his personal preferences and ideas take
into account. The whole trend is towards simplicity, as might be expectec
but also towards a compromise with tradition based on Charles's experienc
during the war years and influenced, to some extent, by idiosyncrasies h
himself had developed. New standards and flags had to be ordered for sever
regiments and new uniforms, for royal servants as well as for the drummer
and trumpeters of the Lifeguards, had to be agreed.[35] The King did not muc
care for elaborate banners and standards on active campaign, preferring th
serviceable painted wooden ones. He respected the need of them for ceremoni
purposes but suggested some breaks with past designs. Heavy embroider
did not appeal to him; the double C, intertwined – but without cipher – wit
two laurel boughs beneath, was sufficient he suggested for standards, provide
the damask was good and the workmanship fine.[36] In the large flags whic
incorporated the Swedish lion or the Swedish crowns he was anxious tha
the balance between inset and background should be improved: for this, an
for reasons of economy also, the flag itself might be of cloth and the inset onl
of silk.[37]

The concern to save money is also noticeable in his suggestion that roya
servants should have plain suits for travelling and that their more elaborat
uniforms be kept for ceremonies and functions.[38] That reasons of econom
did not outweigh those of security is seen from Charles's own sketch an
comments for a badge for Chancery couriers:* this, to be worn on the chest
should comprise the royal crown, initial and cipher, and be made of gold les
it be easy to copy.[39] The desire to save money may at first sight also seem to
dictate the King's decision that trumpeters of the Lifeguards should have gol
or silver braid on their uniforms where drummers would have to be satisfie
with silk,[40] but there is a telling comment by Feif in one of the letters to
Tessin in 1718 which indicates that Charles XII ranked the drum low even o
utilitarian grounds: 'on campaign His Majesty cares for drums even less tha
he does for flags'.[41] As for drum-flags, Feif quoted the King as saying, 'w

* The postal reforms which were successfully carried out at this time were, at least in par
motivated by the need for speedier and safer communications between Stockholm and the King'
headquarters: see N.Forsell, *Svenska postverkets historia*, I (1936), pp. 146 ff.

an fight without them'. The King's prohibition against the colour green, hitherto used,[42] may also have some personal significance, green having become identified with Russian uniforms. His wish to have the Swedish lion represented with feet resting on solid earth, 'contrary to what is customary',[43] may, at least subconsciously, have been motivated by thoughts which were not wholly in the realm of aesthetics. The delight in simple and good design, and the insistence that the pattern of anything for which he felt responsible should not clash with his own idea of what was fitting, is noticeable also outside his relationship with Tessin. When Rhyzelius became his confessor the King suggested that new communion plate should be made, but asked to have the drawings for approval for the double set, chalice and paten for ordinary use and covered smaller vessels for active campaign, submitted to him.[44] The result* is of a characteristic Caroline style, bold and clear form, simple but effective decoration.

The question of the golden mean between extravagance and meanness was one that Charles came back to again and again in his correspondence. He himself delighted in giving presents of gold ducats, and many anecdotes have survived about this trait in his character, but he was well aware of the need to conserve money lest the war effort should suffer and took care to characterize the stories current in Sweden of the former opulence of Piper and Grothusen as 'mendacities'.[45] On the other hand he disliked gold and silver art treasure and trophies being melted down for coinage[46] – such sacrifices would be as meaningless and unnecessary within the new financial system he envisaged as would the melting down of church-bells for cannon in a Sweden rich in metal. He could hardly bring himself to credit the stories he elicited by his own questions in 1717, from a traveller recently arrived from the capital, that the ladies-in-waiting in Stockholm had to bring their own table silver to court. Tessin was immediately ordered to provide silver knives, spoons, forks, salt-cellars and other tableware, and Charles suggested that if Tessin could lay his hands on enough money the ladies should also be provided with *confiturer*, the silver dishes filled with bon-bons and other confectionery which he remembered as being popular.[47] 'It is certain', Feif once summed up, 'that His Majesty prefers people to live in an honourable manner and that too obvious parsimony seems to him indecent.'[48]

When the financial situation eased slightly, thanks to foreign loans and reorganization at home, Charles did not only think of the war effort and the prisoners-of-war in Russia: Swedish diplomats abroad were asked to engage foreign experts in the applied arts. From January 1718 the call went out to Amsterdam as well as to Paris for skilled engravers and painters.[49] The secret planning for buildings and decoration and for the promotion of the arts in general was meant to erupt into open preparation much in the same way as the military offensive of 1718 followed the secret reorganizations of the

---

* The set is now in Historiska Museet, Stockholm. It was lent to the Victoria and Albert Museum during the Swedish silver exhibition of 1963: see catalogue entry no. 51.

Lund period. In this Tessin, with his strong desire to found an Academy o Art,* must be seen as the driving force, strongly supported by the King, and the meeting of the two in March 1718 – when once more they studied plan and discussed projects – was a muted fanfare to what they both hoped would be the start of a new period of happy collaboration: a resumption of tha broken off in 1700.

IV

Money was one of the preoccupations of Charles throughout the Lund period, both on the personal level and the national one. That concern had begun as soon as he set foot in Sweden in 1715, since the cash he had brough from Stralsund for current expenses was stolen soon after his landing. A valise containing his papers and money disappeared, and though the bag itself and the papers were retrieved the ducats were not: one of the first letters penned from Ystad was an appeal to Stockholm for 'hand-money' for the King.[50] Charles's personal expenditure was, however, on a modest scale and it was the finances of the realm which remained the pressing problem. The King reckoned that he needed eighteen barrels of gold (equivalent to forty million *riksdaler*) to prepare a strong enough army and navy to enable him to carry out his new offensive. The task of achieving as much as possible of this target was handed over to Görtz. Working directly under the King, Görtz was able to cut across the demarcation lines which divided the various Colleges and committees, and on arrival in Stockholm at the end of 1715 he set about constructing a new organ of government, the *upphandlingsdeputation* (literally, the 'loan-deputation') to run a new financial system.

The essence of this system, strongly influenced by ideas current in Europe in an age which has been labelled that of the 'financial revolution',[51] was to repay old loans – which had taken the form of anticipations of government income – from money raised by 'obligations', loans to the state redeemable after four years on which an interest of six per cent would be regularly paid. It was hoped that the *obligationer* would tempt Swedish subjects who had transferred money abroad or had tied it up less profitably at home, and the interest was put high enough to attract also some foreign investors. The long-term aim was to achieve a funded debt, and the English example is particularly noticeable in the planning stages when Görtz attempted to persuade Swedish merchants to take charge of the 'obligations' – the *upphandlingsdeputation* was formed once his offer had been refused.[52]

The emergency or 'necessity-money', of little intrinsic value, was part and parcel of the new system. It used to be held that the copper *mynttecken* (i.e. coin-tokens) and paper *myntsedlar* (i.e. coin-tickets) conceived of as *obligationer* which carried no interest, were issued because the 'obligations' failed to produce quick results, but it is now realized that they were essential

* This was not founded till 1735.

to what Görtz called the *gezwungene Credit* though during the period of his imprisonment in the Dutch Republic more of them were issued than he thought advisable.[53] In some respects the *nödmynt* were thought of as a short-term expedient, particularly by the King. It was feared that the small intrinsic value of the coins would make it easy for forgers to duplicate them and the successive series of coins* was originally part of a plan to withdraw the previous issue as soon as a new one appeared.

This could not be carried out in practice, partly because the Crown needed to keep the largest possible amount of money in circulation and partly because people got attached to each issue as it appeared and feared that the next would retain less of its nominal value: the amount of *nödmynt* in circulation between 1716 and 1718 (estimated as at least thirty-four million *riksdaler*) was large enough to cause inflation.[54] To limit this, control from the centre grew, particularly when the harvests of 1717 and 1718 proved poor ones: prices of basic necessities and most goods were then fixed, and import and export was supervised and directed in ways which to contemporaries seemed unprecedented and hateful. There were mutual recriminations. Those in favour of reform blamed the merchants and the diehards for putting private interests above the public good, while others deplored and vilified government measures: the drawing in of the 'good' copper money was particularly disliked. But though there were many complaints of the 'Görtz system', the fact that the 'necessity-money' enjoyed greater confidence in 1718 than in 1716 is proof of considerable success in strengthening the economy.[55]

Complaints were particularly vocal in Gothenburg, where the privateers feared that the passes Görtz was empowered to issue for neutral ships would interfere with the town's opportunity to make profits. Between August 1716 and February 1717 Görtz issued fifty-two passes in the Dutch Republic and more followed† when he was released from imprisonment in August 1717.‡ The policy of passes, already recommended by Polhem in 1715, had several advantages. Dutch mercantile interests put up surety money against abuse of the passes (since these did not permit the holder to sail to Russian-occupied Swedish ports). This gave short-term financial help. Sweden's relations with the Republic improved, Dutch imports of cargoes which were badly needed – corn, salt, herrings, tobacco and wine – increased dramatically,[56] and a wedge was driven between the Maritime Powers which resulted in the States General's refusal to become partners to that blockade of Sweden which Britain imposed in February 1717 and maintained for two years. British fears of Dutch commercial successes in Sweden in their turn helped to restrain George I's Baltic policy in 1717 and 1718,[57] and the prohibition of Swedish imports to Britain proved ineffectual in respect of the most important one,

* These were named by the King in characteristic manner: *Kronan* (the Crown) in 1715; *Publica Fides* in 1716; *Wett och Wapen* (Law and Arms) in 1717; *Flink och Färdig* (Quick and Ready) in 1718; others were named after Roman and Greek gods; cp. below, p. 470.

† The actual numbers were 47, 1716; 161, 1717; 750, 1718; and 153, 1719.

‡ For the February arrest and the August release, see Hatton, *Diplomatic Relations*, pp. 147–59.

iron. This British manufacturers could not do without, and British merchants had to buy from Dutch middlemen who, during the blockade – as Lindeberg has shown – bought what amounted to the total consumption of both the Maritime Powers in Sweden and resold the British 'share', at a profit, to Britain. The Swedes registered an increase in the price of iron of thirty per cent.[58]

In his primary purpose of obtaining large loans in the Republic to finance the buying of men-of-war Görtz was less successful. He did sign a contract on 19/30 September 1716 for a large loan to materialize in 1717,[59] but could find no banker ready to risk investment* in Sweden's future at a time when the Scania invasion plan was still thought to be on. He continued to Paris in the hope of persuading the French government to issue the subsidies for 1716, due under the 1715 treaty, in French *billets d'état*. The Regent expressed his willingness to pay but, concerned for the success of his negotiations with George I, found excuses for delay. The financier Hogguer, who had both Swedish and Swiss family ties, actively promoted Görtz's search for ships and brought him into contact with moneyed Jacobites anxious to purchase Swedish military help. Similar overtures came also from London, transmitted via the Swedish envoy Gyllenborg who sympathized with the Jacobite cause. Görtz, well aware of Charles XII's decision not to give military support and of his refusal even to accept a letter from the Pretender pleading his cause, ordered Gyllenborg not to commit himself, but he led both Gyllenborg and Jacobites on both sides of the Channel to believe that if they dealt with him, Görtz, only and kept everything secret from King Charles, something might eventually be done for James III.

He made much play with the general full powers which he had from the King dated 23 October 1716, realizing that there was little likelihood of the hopes he had awakened ever being fulfilled but anxious not to let slip an opportunity he glimpsed of buying large warships to strengthen Sweden's fleet for the 1717 season. He reckoned he could repay the Jacobite money he proposed to 'borrow' with interest as soon as funds became available (either from the French subsidies or from the Dutch loan) accompanying repayment with regrets that Charles XII was unable to help them 'at present'. After all, Sparre had at one stage, in 1715, accepted Jacobite money which Charles had insisted on repaying as he would have no part in a 'plot'.†

Görtz was already on his way to England to sign a contract with Jacobites for a loan of £60,000 – which the Jacobites concerned were determined to make specific enough to prevent it being interpreted as anything but subsidies for military support – when information about George I's decision to have

---

* Dutch investment in Sweden was assessed, probably too highly, as amounting to forty thousand gulden in 1717 by an English diplomat at The Hague: see Hatton, *Diplomatic Relations*, p. 163, note 2.

† Cp. above, pp. 416–17. The money which Görtz obtained 'privately' in France in 1716, some 175,000 livres, was also repaid by the Swedish Crown though payment, with interest, was not complete till 1755.

him arrested made him move from Calais to the Dutch Republic. Correspondence between Gyllenborg and Görtz during 1716 had been intercepted and was published in London as a justification for the arrest of Gyllenborg in January 1717, an arrest which created a great stir and much discussion about diplomatic immunity.[60]

It is now known that neither George I nor the British government believed that a Swedish invasion of Great Britain was imminent or even agreed to by Charles XII, and that the arrest was made in the hope of unifying the country behind George I's Baltic policy. The coup was crowned with success in so far as Parliament accepted a total prohibition of trade with Sweden in February – neither imports from, nor exports to, that country would be permitted – but George's hope that Britain might be persuaded to declare war on Charles XII and thus enable him to use the British navy with greater freedom was doomed to disappointment.[61] George's request that his ally, the Dutch Republic, should arrest Görtz and examine his papers for incriminating correspondence met with only partial compliance: the arrest was effected, by private pressure, in the town of Arnhem and approved by the province of Gelderland, but Görtz's papers were never opened and the States General kept as aloof as possible from the whole affair for fear of Swedish commercial reprisals.[62] Throughout his arrest Görtz was able to keep in touch with diplomatic contacts among Russians, Prussians and Saxons in the Republic through intermediaries who were allowed to visit him, and if any harm resulted from his restricted freedom between February and August 1717 it was to Sweden's financial affairs.

V

There were, however, others who could run the day-to-day administration of the *upphandlingsdeputation* and the *kontributionsränteri* once the new system had been set in motion. Görtz was thought of as the head of the former, in the sense that he was frequently consulted by its members, the most important of whom was the Holsteiner von Dernath, but in accordance with Charles XII's encouragement of individual responsibility we find a division into spheres of activity among the four who, apart from the accountant and the secretary, made up the group.* The *kontributionsränteri* handled much of the practical work in connection with the decisions of the *deputation*, both in respect of 'obligations' and of 'necessity-money'.[63]

A new generation of Swedish administrators, interspersed with older men, like Tessin, who were anxious to promote Charles's ideas, came to the fore from 1715 onwards. The reform-plans of 1712–13 were now put fully into effect, modifications or novelties being introduced as required. The division into 'expeditions' worked well and there is evidence that the *ombudsman* of

---

* Von Otter was detailed to look after the war effort, Thegner to take care of trade and Von Höpken to handle the correspondence with the King and other government agencies.

each department met his colleagues for discussion of business as laid down in the King's scheme for reorganization. The physical distance between Charles and his 'ministers' (some of whom were heads of department) in Lund (or wherever the 'Court' stayed for any length of time) and Stockholm did, of course, tend to lessen the importance of Stockholm in so far as decision-making was concerned: it is symptomatic that von Dernath and Höpken of the *upphandlingsdeputation* spent long periods* at Lund in the early stages of the financial and economic reconstruction. This was, however, unavoidable in the war situation; and rumours that Charles XII intended – when peace came – to move his capital to the south of Sweden were without foundation.†

Experience showed, however, that quite apart from the office of the 'ombudsman in chief' there was need for some central authority to check that orders and regulations were carried out not only by the administration (that was the field of the *högste ombudsman*) but also among the population at large. In January 1718 Tessin was designated *högste ordningsman*, to be in charge of 'order' in the broadest sense in cooperation with local authorities. His task, aided by two assistants, was to see that regulations which concerned trade and manufactures were kept and that hospitals and poorhouses were well run; but quite apart from the 'police' aspects of his job, he was specifically instructed to work also for the improvement of agriculture and for the economic prosperity of the towns.[64] The King's death brought to an end this experiment, as it did to much of the administrative reorganization, the one exception being the office of *högste ombudsman* which was continued under the title *Justitiekansler*. During Charles XII's lifetime Leijonstedt, the holder of the office, was very active, both at his own initiative and when discreetly reminded by the King of problems that needed investigation.[65]

For the wider objective of stimulating Sweden's economic life, Charles had no shortage of advisers both outside and inside the administration proper. Polhem was the most energetic of all of them: rich in inventions immediately benefiting mining and the metallurgical industries; prolific in projects which needed shorter (such as the establishment of salt-refineries) or longer (such as the Göta canal and the Motala canal) periods of preparation. Charles XII was especially fascinated by the canal plans. With the Baltic provinces in Russian hands, Sweden no longer had easy access to masts which could be transported cheaply by sea. The woods near lake Vänern and Vättern had fine enough trees, but transport was the problem; Karlskrona, the naval base, could be supplied by the Motala project and Gothenburg through the Göta one if they were put into effect. Finance would not permit simultaneous progress. The Göta project seemed the more important, as one of the war aims of Frederick IV was that Sweden should renounce that

* The winter of 1716–17 and the autumn of 1717.
† But his reform of the postal services was no doubt influenced by the need to speed up contact with Stockholm: see Feif's letter to Tessin of 10 March 1718.

exemption from Sound dues which she had held since the 1650s.* A canal from Vänern to the Göta river (which had to be made fully navigable) would provide an alternative route for Swedish exports. In January 1718 Charles signed a contract with Polhem for the massive undertaking to be carried out within five years.[66] The canal was begun with great energy but was halted when Charles died. No till the twentieth century did the Göta canal become a reality.

Among the administrators Feif, with his manufacturing background, was particularly active in spite of the amount of paper-work that fell to his share. He virtually handled the King's correspondence for the whole of the war effort on the military side, diplomacy alone falling outside his sphere. He encouraged his wife to start tapestry weaving in silk and wool on a small scale to convince Charles XII that as good damask could be made in Sweden as abroad. It was Charles's own mother who had, for charity reasons, founded an orphanage where tapestry was first woven at Karlberg; now mercantile enterprise in this field, as in many others connected with textile manufacture, was begun in the hope of cutting down the spending of money abroad.[67] Ideas for the improvement of agriculture also passed from Feif to Tessin.[68]

The work of reconstruction was helped by good harvests in 1715 and 1716. Sweden, with Finland as well as the Baltic provinces in Russian hands, had a population which was smaller than at the beginning of Charles XII's reign: famine years before the war and the plague of 1710–12, as well as losses in battle,† had reduced the number of inhabitants by at least fifty thousand.[69] The resources in manpower were now utilized for the purpose of supporting the war effort. The burden of that war effort was more evenly and fairly distributed than ever before. Not only was the tax on property of 1713 maintained, but by January 1718 Charles, against much opposition evidenced by delaying tactics, had achieved the introduction of the money land tax he had urged as far back as 1712.[70] Nine-tenths of Sweden's exports now consisted of copper and iron, and both raw materials were manipulated by the central authority in such a way that they brought the maximum of income. In 1717 and 1718 they were bought from the producers for the Crown at fixed prices and since they were greatly in demand, in particular the iron, on the European market, they were made to carry very high export duties to be paid by the buyer.[71] With the help of this income, and with the 'forced credit' at home implicit in the use of 'necessity-money', Sweden managed to pay for the import of necessities (chief of which, since the loss of Livonia, was grain), to re-equip the navy and the expanded army and to build magazines which would permit a new military offensive to avoid a dictated peace.

* For his obtaining this see below, p. 512.   † For these losses, see below, pp. 516–17.

BOOK SEVEN

The Last Venture

1

Diplomatic Preparations

The chief concern of Charles XII in the period when the new army was being fashioned and supplied was to prevent his enemies launching an offensive against Sweden comparable to the Scania project, at the same time taking care that the work in progress was not drained of its slowly mounting strength by having to meet Russian small-scale attacks from the Baltic provinces or from Finland.

These dangers were surmounted by skilful diplomacy of an intricate kind which has occupied specialist historians for decades and about which there is still disagreement. The web of 'ostensible' letters, written for the express purpose of keeping one or other of the many enemies guessing, for long made interpretation of the evidence hazardous,[1] but with the examination complete not only of Swedish material but of the diplomatic archives of the whole anti-Swedish coalition[2] – as well as of Sweden's would-be-allies, in the military sense, the Jacobites and Alberoni of Spain, and of her formal allies though not co-belligerents, Hesse and France[3] – the threads of the negotiations can now be more clearly distinguished.

Basically there existed for Sweden two possibilities and each had its strong advocates who pressed Charles XII to accept the solution they judged the best one. Many Swedes were of the opinion that what must be safeguarded above all was Sweden's position in the Empire: it was this, as Sparre put it in a letter of 1715, which made Sweden a European power.[4] It would be best therefore to make some sacrifices to Tsar Peter of Russia and expend more effort against the would-be despoilers of Bremen, Verden and Swedish Pomerania. It was this reasoning which made men like Gyllenborg sympathizers with the Jacobite cause: if Charles XII sided with James III he could unseat George I in Great Britain and then it would be an easy task to cope with him as Elector of Hanover. With Hanover out of the coalition, Frederick William I of Prussia could next to be forced to make peace, though in his case it was realized that some sacrifice of land in Pomerania would have to be made.[5] Görtz and the Holstein-Gottorp administration in general naturally favoured the retention of Sweden's power position in Germany. Without that it was impossible to visualize the restoration of Holstein-Gottorp independence *vis-à-vis* the King of Denmark. Charles XII would have to hold both Bremen and Verden to the west of Frederick IV's possessions and Wismar to the east to be able to act as a shield for Duke Charles Frederick. In respect of Swedish Pomerania, the Holstein-Gottorp interest was less intense,* though obviously the safe bridgehead of Stralsund and Rügen was desirable so that the Swedish forces in the Empire might be reinforced at speed.

Where the Holstein-Gottorpers and those who were mainly concerned with Sweden's position in the Empire parted company was over peace with Denmark. In Görtz's opinion, Frederick IV ought to be made to pay for his entire role in bringing about the war in 1700: compensation for the Ducal family for occupation of Holstein-Gottorp land in Sleswig and Holstein would, he hoped, be on the agenda at the peace. But from Charles XII's point of view, and that of the majority of Swedes, peace with Denmark–Norway, if it could be obtained without sacrifices, would bring considerable advantages. If Frederick IV left the coalition, Sweden would no longer see so much of her war potential tied to the western part of the peninsula and could more readily grapple with Hanover or with Russia, the two major enemies. Through Müllern, Charles XII on 11 January 1716 let Görtz know of his conditions for peace with Denmark–Norway and urged him to work for a settlement on the simple basis of the restoration of the *status quo*. If Frederick IV would restore the lands of the Duke of Holstein-Gottorp and renounce any intention of keeping Swedish land in Germany, Charles would sign a separate peace.[6] Görtz loyally followed the orders received, but was rather relieved to discover that the terms were totally unacceptable to Denmark.[7]

The chief exponent of the 'peace-with-Denmark' school was Frederick of Hesse. If he had dared, he would have suggested Swedish sacrifices to obtain it.† As it was, he concentrated on the great advantages of peace with Frederick IV: no further campaign in the difficult terrain of Norway would be necessary; a frontal attack on the Russian-occupied Baltic provinces would be possible; the war would cease to be so crushing a burden on Sweden itself – once more war would nourish war. Ever since he came to Stockholm Frederick had been in favour of a concentration of Swedish forces, naval and military, against Russia, and his letters and memoranda to Charles are full of projects for a descent on Livonia. If Denmark–Norway could be satisfied (and here there is an implicit hint at sacrifices by Charles XII either on behalf of Holstein-Gottorp or directly, in the form of Swedish land in Germany since without any *quid pro quo* Frederick IV could not be expected to fall in with the Prince of Hesse's plans), then the collaboration of the Danish fleet would render the venture against Tsar Peter feasible.[8]

It was natural that the Prince of Hesse should be less concerned with Sweden's position in the Empire than Charles XII and his diplomats and

* Görtz, as we have seen between 1709 and 1714, was less averse than many Swedes to satisfying the Prussian King by sizeable sacrifices; see above, p. 369.

† At the peace with Denmark in 1720 which he helped to negotiate the Duke of Holstein-Gottorp's land in Sleswig and Holstein was sacrificed in principle.

officers. Frederick could expect to become the Landgrave of Hesse if he outlived his father, and would have a footing in Germany in his own right. He was therefore not averse to the idea of buying friendship with Denmark, Hanover and Prussia by the partitioning of the Swedish German provinces, nor was he at all reluctant – in view of the rivalry between himself and Charles Frederick of Holstein-Gottorp for the Swedish succession – to see sacrifices made to Denmark at the expense of the young Duke.

As an alternative, or as a complement, to peace with Frederick iv, he preached peace between Sweden and the Elector of Hanover. Again, naval help from Britain might result from giving up Bremen and Verden and the assistance would, once more, facilitate the attack on Russia.

In his willingness to see Sweden reduced in Germany, Frederick of Hesse could reckon with some sympathy from Swedish administrators in the domestic field. By the terms of the Peace of Westphalia Sweden had been precluded from the slightest change in the constitutional or social life of the provinces which she gained in 1648. The very treaty which made Bremen, Verden, Pomerania and Wismar her possessions guaranteed all rights to Estates and town magistrates and for this reason Swedish absolutism of the 1680s had not been transplanted to the Empire. The German provinces carried too little of the burden of their own defence, so ran the argument of many Stockholm bureaucrats.[9] Even for those Swedes who had no particular sympathy with such a view, the overriding economic importance of recon-quering Sweden's Baltic provinces gave powerful support to the second basic alternative: the idea of peace-with-all-the-rest so that we may concentrate on getting back Ingria, Estonia and Livonia. Livonia was particularly regretted: it had been the 'corn-barn' of the nation and Riga had been the 'jewel in the Swedish coronet of East Baltic towns'. But Swedish as well as Baltic-born Swedish noblemen were also concerned for their land property in all three provinces and would prefer to see Tsar Peter chased away from as much of the Finnish Gulf and the Baltic as possible.[10]

Against the policy of big sacrifices in Germany in the hope of undoing the damage done by Russia stood those who thought it senseless to give up much in the west without certainty of recouping what was wanted in the east. Far better, these argued, to come to terms with Tsar Peter and give up some land to him, at least 'for this time'. If he would return Finland and Livonia, might he not be permitted to keep Karelia and Ingria, and even part of Estonia? Narva ought not, it was held, to be ceded in view of its trade which had improved so strikingly since English merchants were given privileges there in the 1690s.[11]

This policy, identified with Görtz, was not his alone. Horn had been in favour of it as far back as 1714.* The Swedish major-general in Hessian service, Conrad Ranck, stressed in March 1716 to Frederick of Hesse that though peace with George i or Frederick William i would be useful, it would

* See above, p. 391.

be a 'master-stroke, if Charles XII could obtain peace with the Tsar: then the
rest of his enemies 'would fall to their knees from sheer surprise'. In February
1717 he reiterated his opinion that an agreement with the Tsar was the 'most
important move in the present game of chess'.[12] The Landgrave, throughout
1716, favoured Swedish–Russian negotiations and helped to promote contact, but Frederick of Hesse, just because Görtz became progressively identified with the Russian peace negotiations, became their most outspoken
opponent. He feared that Görtz, as part of a deal with the Tsar, would stipulate Russian support for the succession of Charles Frederick of Holstein-
Gottorp in Sweden. That might put an end to his wife's prospects and to his
own ambitions to become King of Sweden – either jointly with her, on the
pattern of William and Mary in Great Britain or, preferably, through her
transferring her rights to him. He began to warn Charles against Görtz.
Delicacy forbade him coming into the open with the accusation that Görtz
was using his influence to settle the succession on the Duke of Holstein-
Gottorp, but he was as explicit as he dared: from hints that 'the Holsteiners
and particularly Görtz' were gaining too much influence with Charles XII, he
progressed to warnings that they were fomenting 'many pernicious intrigues'
at home and abroad and must be regarded as 'enemies of Sweden'.[13]

II

In this maze of conflicting advice Charles XII went his own way, listening and
learning from all, building his own system along the lines which he had
confided to Ulrika Eleonora in 1714. One reason why that system has been
so hard to fathom is that the King had to keep it a secret from all lest the gain
he expected to reap – freedom to fashion and train the new army – should be
forfeited. He would have liked to confide in Frederick of Hesse and Ulrika
Eleonora, but their obsession with the succession-issue made them incapable
of an unbiased attitude to his diplomatic offensive. His admiration for
Frederick's military gifts and willingness to work hard remained great, and
he rewarded his part in the successful defence of Gothenburg against an
attack in the summer of 1717 by Tordenskjold on the naval vessels and the
magazines of the town[14] with promotion in November to *generalissimus* over
the whole Swedish fleet.[15]

But Charles was less optimistic than the Prince of Hesse about the
feasibility of a frontal attack on the Russian-occupied Baltic provinces. He
knew the tenacity of Tsar Peter's resolve to keep what he had gained and
thought Russian coastal defences so strong that any Swedish invasion would
be extremely hazardous. Naval assistance from Danish or British men-of-war
would of course be of great help in landing a Swedish expeditionary corps,
but it could not significantly solve the problem of assaulting what was in
effect a Russian citadel stretching from Finland to Courland. In any case, it
was unlikely that such naval support could be bought without cession of

Swedish land, and gambles which had for their prerequisite sacrifice of territory while giving no certainty of compensation had little attraction for Charles.

He eagerly grasped every chance of contact with his enemies, with the object of assessing his chances of achieving separate peace arrangements. He argued, on the analogy of Louis XIV's separate peace with Queen Anne's government in 1710–11, that once the first peace was won the 'tolerable' peace with the rest would follow. The idea of 'equivalents' so prevalent in his peace negotiations between 1716 and 1718 was also in part modelled on what he had learnt of the negotiations for the Peace of Utrecht.[16] The Landgrave Charles of Hesse was particularly useful in obtaining contacts both with Russian and Hanoverian circles in 1716 and 1717, though his son's antipathy to any negotiations in which Görtz had a hand limited his usefulness from the autumn of 1717 onwards.

To some extent Hesse mediators were therefore replaced by French negotiators. The Regent, safe in his personal alliance with George I and knowing that Stanhope needed France for his 'southern peace plan',* felt freer in the North in 1717: outstanding subsidies were paid to Charles XII,[17] and a French ambassador, de la Marck, was sent to Lund and received with as much state as the little town could muster – twenty-four carriages were sent to meet him on his arrival in May.[18] Officially de la Marck came to mediate between George I and Charles XII in the matter of Gyllenborg's arrest, which had brought the retaliatory arrest of Jackson, the British resident in Stockholm. This objective was speedily accomplished. The Swedish King, anxious to minimize friction between himself and Great Britain and maximize that between the British nation and George I, declared himself only too willing to disavow any connexion with the Jacobites in a personal letter to the Regent, and George I, who for some time insisted on a disavowal from Charles addressed to him as King of Great Britain, was forced by British and Dutch pressure to accept the expedient of communication via France.[19] De la Marck stayed on, however, to carry on the less public part of his work begun as soon as he arrived in Lund: to offer French help in achieving a peace on terms which did not weaken Sweden excessively in Germany.[20]

The view from the summit, and therefore the control, remained with Charles in spite of the use he made of would-be mediators. To the Landgrave's disappointment, the formal negotiations which proceeded along channels he had helped to open up were entrusted to Vellingk and to Görtz and his helpers.[21] The Regent's offices were accepted with alacrity but it was Swedish diplomatic representatives abroad, instructed by Müllern, who confided to their French colleagues that particular piece of the jigsaw puzzle which was handed into their care at any given time.[22] Several trusted foreigners and in particular Poniatowski had a share in these negotiations, and even some who were outside the Lund circle proper but well known to

---

* See Hatton, *Diplomatic Relations*, pp. 159 ff. for this plan to reconcile Charles VI and Philip V, which it was hoped would be rewarded with Imperial investiture for Bremen and Verden.

Charles were permitted a part in the peace-offensive, Fabrice being most prominent in this group.[23]

From the material which has survived from all the interested parties – not excluding those individuals* who with more or less encouragement from Charles XII's enemies tried to get in touch with the Swedish King or his representatives – the moves in Charles XII's diplomacy between 1716 and 1718 can be reconstructed and his short-term as well as his long-term objectives clarified.

The most obvious motive behind his peace offensive was to gain time to mount the military offensive which, in his opinion, would be the only sure way to achieve a tolerable peace. He did not expect to obtain such a peace either with George I or with Peter the Great, his two main enemies, until Sweden was in a position to bargain from strength: here was the strongest bond between him and Görtz. Charles would have echoed the sentiment (or the emissary may have echoed that of the King) which Görtz expressed already in 1716: 'If first we begin to give land away, our greedy enemies will not leave us our shirt.'[24] Nor did the King believe that it would be possible to implement the 'equivalent' policy till he could show that he was of some consequence in the military sense. While confined to Sweden he could exercise at best a negative influence, keeping his enemies from concerted action by diplomatic tactics and strategic placing of the military resources at his disposal. He could not exert a positive pull on events till he was able to move a strong force outside Sweden.

He therefore agreed with Frederick of Hesse that he must move the war effort away from Sweden as soon as possible. He disagreed, however, on the direction of the thrust, as Hesse's favourite frontal attack on the lost Baltic provinces would leave the dangerous combination of Frederick IV and George I free to control the war in the west. The King's solution to Sweden's dilemma was a well-prepared military campaign against Norway as the first stage in a move to the Continent. Such a campaign could be expected to lead to tolerable peace terms being obtained from Denmark–Norway and Hanover, possibly also from Saxony and Prussia, and would not be without effect on the Tsar who might be attacked in his Baltic citadel from the rear once a Swedish army stood on German soil once more.[25]

With the projected offensive against Frederick IV went estimates of what could be regarded as a sensible and durable peace if the second Norwegian campaign proved successful. The *status quo* would form the base, but the expense and effort of the new campaign, necessitated by Denmark's refusal of the terms of 1716,† entitled Sweden to compensation: a minor rectification of the Norwegian–Swedish frontier so that a strip of Norwegian territory – up to the Glommen river – would be incorporated with Sweden was envisaged. This new frontier would render invasions from Norway, of the kind that had

* Among these can be noted Townshend and Cadogan in Britain; see Hatton, *Diplomatic Relations*, p. 153.
† See above, p. 446.

been mounted in 1709 to coincide with the attack on Scania from Denmark, more difficult or even impossible for the future. The cession of Bornholm by Frederick IV would also be welcomed. The naval campaigns of 1715 and 1716 had shown the importance of the waters round that island and its possession by Sweden would help secure communications with the German provinces.[26]

If Frederick IV was brought to make peace, Charles did not regard the Elector of Hanover as an important enemy: British opposition to his commitment in the north was growing and it was British naval help to the anti-Swedish coalition as a whole, and to Denmark in particular, which had damaged Sweden in 1715 and 1716. Relations between George I and Tsar Peter remained cool, even after Russian troops left Mecklenburg in the summer of 1717.[27] The Tsar was hurt at George's refusal to put the British navy at Russia's disposal for an attack on Sweden from Finland, and George was made uneasy by the Tsar's toleration and even encouragement of Jacobite contacts.[28]

Given the defeat of Frederick IV and the isolation of George I, Charles XII looked upon Augustus of Saxony as a spent force. His position in Poland was weak and his German Electorate was in no mood to pay for his whistling of any aggressive tune. Stanislaus from Zweibrücken continued to press for a Swedish peace with Augustus whereby his own position might be regularized – hoping that Courland, for instance, might fall to his share – but Charles was for various reasons disinclined to enter into serious negotiations at this stage. He argued that Augustus was in no position to harm Sweden, and that it would therefore be dishonourable to forget his treaty obligations to the Poles, in favour of their liberties *vis-à-vis* Augustus, and to the Ukrainians, where Orlyk had every right to expect him to keep his agreement with the late hetman Mazepa. He remained hopeful that, when the chips were down, more would be gained for Stanislaus than Courland.[29]

Prussia was a more redoubtable opponent, mainly because of the military and diplomatic support Frederick William I could offer Tsar Peter; but by himself the Prussian ruler presented no military danger and the problem of what would have to be sacrificed to him could safely be left to be settled as events unfolded. Negotiations with him would serve a useful purpose – as with all other members of the coalition – in that it would help to *augmenter la jalousie* within the enemy ranks,[30] but there was little sense in tying oneself to terms prematurely. If things went well, some Swedish diplomats argued, loss of land to Frederick William might be avoided altogether.[31]

Specific peace-terms would have to be presented to the Tsar and to George I, both to keep them apart and to test where the best conditions could be obtained.[32] George I, as long as Frederick IV of Denmark-Norway remained in the coalition, was potentially as great a danger to Sweden as the Tsar, though Russia occupied far more Swedish territory. As early as July 1716 Charles XII told Görtz that he would be willing, if Tsar Peter offered good terms in exchange (i.e. guaranteed help to obtain 'equivalents' for Sweden), to let

Russia keep Karelia and Ingria as far as Viborg on the Finnish side and Narva on the Baltic. Neither town must be included in the cession and Görtz must not reveal these ultimate concessions too speedily. The terms were confirmed in May 1717, but the King vetoed a suggestion by Görtz that the Tsar might be tempted with the offer of Wismar.[33] The Tsar's starting offers transmitted separately through Görtz and Poniatowski, were pitched low – the restoration of most of Finland with retention of all other conquests – yet the mere willingness to treat was eagerly grasped. After Görtz's release from Arnhem he met the Tsar at 'Het Loo', the favourite palace of the late King William III, at the end of August and agreement was reached that a formal peace conference should be held between Sweden and Russia as soon as possible. The Åland islands group, inaccessible for would-be spies, was suggested as a suitable venue, and Görtz was furnished with a pass from Tsar Peter to afford him safe travel to Lund for consultation with Charles XII.[34]

This news, diligently spread by the Swedes, caused alarm to Frederick IV and George I who interpreted it, rightly, as the outcome of their own refusal, justified by their dislike of Russian selfishness, to put large Danish and British fleets at the Tsar's disposal in the summer of 1717 to enable him to invade eastern Sweden. It created uneasiness among the rest of the coalition, which was skilfully exploited by Görtz during a leisurely return journey which took in Berlin, Dresden and Warsaw. He had neither desire nor orders to conclude negotiations: it was enough to sow the seeds of dissension and wait to harvest the crop when it suited Charles XII. Görtz used his eye if not his tongue to good purpose when he travelled through Riga, Reval, Helsingfors and Åbo to Sweden, where he arrived – escorted by a Russian man-of-war – on 22 November. On 3 December he reported to Charles XII, and was relieved to find that his 'mishap' in getting arrested had been forgiven.[35]

Russian pressure to have the conferences opened had little effect in Sweden, though excuses put forward had a plausible air. The Tsar's representatives, Ostermann and Bruce, were ready to start negotiations in January 1718, but the Swedish delegation, led by Görtz and Gyllenborg,* did not arrive at Lövö till 19 May 1718.

III

The mere knowledge that Russo-Swedish official peace-talks were scheduled had repercussions of the kind hoped for at Lund. The monarch who felt hardest hit was George I. His aim had been to get both Sweden and Russia out of the Empire and he had not taken seriously hints from Hesse and Sweden that Charles XII would come to terms with Russia. George knew that Tsar Peter would not make peace without Reval as well as Riga and thought it impossible that Sweden should accept such terms. He did not express himself as forcibly as his secretary Robethon – inherited from William III –

---

* The former envoy to George I, recalled to Sweden after his release.

who declared Charles XII '*une Furie déchaînée de l'Enfer, auprès de laquelle le Zar est un Ange*';[36] but he found himself disturbed at the weakening of his own diplomatic position *vis-à-vis* Charles. He had less to bargain with than the Tsar and was loth to give up any part of Bremen and Verden. Nor was he keen to accept cession for a term of years in place of the outright possession he aimed at. Charles XII told de la Marck, probably with the intention that the remark should be passed on, that a Suedo-Russian peace would weaken George I's military position by robbing him of his excuse for sending British fleets into the Baltic.[37]

There was some cautious optimism at Lund towards the end of 1717. Görtz boasted that he had given Charles XII money and diplomatic freedom for the next two years if that space of time were needed to mount the offensive by land and sea.[38] Von Müllern and von Kochen (the second-in-command in the department for foreign affairs) as well as Vellingk and other key diplomats began to feel that if they played their cards right and had a modicum of luck in the military field, the Tsar might eventually have to be satisfied with Ingria only and George I with a small part of Bremen and Verden.[39] Part of this optimism was for public consumption, an element in propaganda warfare launched at home and abroad, but there was also some genuine hope that much could be gained by playing George I and the Tsar off against each other.

In December Görtz wrote to Fabrice, who had been in London since August of that year,* suggesting that the Elector of Hanover might care to send an official representative to Lund so that conferences there might counterbalance those which were to take place with Tsar Peter's representatives in the Åland islands. As for terms, Sweden tried to throw the ball into George I's court in December 1717: he might indicate through his emissary what help he would give Charles XII in return for the mortgage of Bremen and Verden for a given number of years; if he could offer foolproof guarantees for military help, preferably naval, then it might be possible to negotiate for the outright cession of some parts of the duchies.[40]

George I welcomed the Swedish offer to get even with the Tsar in the race for peace, but he was unwilling to risk too public a commitment in the first instance and sent Fabrice to Lund as an unofficial go-between without full powers.[41] If things worked out well, Fabrice could be reckoned of the Hanoverian camp:† if things went badly, his trip could be explained as a private one occasioned by his friendship with the Swedish court.

It was at the end of February 1718, after a cold and miserable journey, that Fabrice arrived in Scania. He met Görtz outside Lund – en route for Stockholm – and had brief conferences with Charles XII and Müllern in Lund. The King and his court were preparing for that family reunion at Kristinehamn which Charles XII had promised himself and Ulrika Eleonora as soon as

---

* See his *Memoiren*, p. 162.
† His father W.L.von Fabrice – the 'Fabrice le Père' of Swedish diplomatic correspondence – was a Hanoverian councillor and a cousin of Bernstorff.

weather conditions offered easy travel northwards from Scania by sledge. Fabrice joined the party, returning to Lund in mid-April.[42]

There were many opportunities for sounding the views of both Lund and Stockholm courtiers and advisers during the two weeks (21 March to 3 April) that the reunion lasted. Every one of the royal family had brought their own most important helpers. Frederick of Hesse was supported by Hein and by the Swedish Major-General Leutrum whom the Landgrave had bought free of Prussian captivity and sent to help his son counteract Görtz's influence. Görtz was there and thought of by the Hessians as in attendance on the young Duke Charles Frederick, though he was generally regarded as one of the 'ministers' of Charles XII rather than a 'Holsteiner' as such.

For Charles one purpose of the reunion must have been – though we have no evidence in the form of any remark by him – to further family unity. The way in which he divided his spare time points to this. He spent a good deal of it with Ulrika, who noted (long after the King's death) that even at this 'last meeting' her brother 'had water in the nose' when he mentioned their parents, and particularly their mother, in conversation with her.[43] He took a great interest in his nephew, nearly eighteen, who had completed his studies at Uppsala and was going to join the army on the campaign to Norway. With memories of his own youth and the toughening which he had felt in need of after the cosseting and fussing of the older generation, he took Charles Frederick out on long rides and encouraged him to risk the ice which covered the lakes of the neighbourhood: at least once it broke under both of them, but so near the shore that they were in no real danger. The young man's training as a soldier was already beginning under his uncle's tutelage. From Hein's report to the Landgrave we learn that the King had to give up much of each day to work, particularly to consultations with Görtz,[44] but there was also time to see old friends, especially Tessin, whom he had not met since 1700 and with whom he could at last talk about building plans and other favourite projects.

Görtz was the first to break up, leaving Kristinehamn to prepare for that splendid entry with which Charles XII wanted him to impress the Tsar's negotiators at the opening of the Lövö conferences.* On 2 April Frederick of Hesse and the young Duke left on an inspection of border posts close to Norway. Early in the morning of 3 April Ulrika Eleonora and her suite took the road to Stockholm. Charles XII accompanied his 'dear Ulla' for several miles before he hastened to catch up brother-in-law and nephew at Eda Fort in Värmland. He did not return to Lund till 10 May.

In the meantime Fabrice, who had arrived with stiff terms from George I (just listen to offers, was the Elector's official opening gambit) met with equal firmness (Tsar Peter is anxious to make a deal, we do not need any accommodation with Hanover) and became more conciliatory. He could not commit George, but he suggested that the Elector would, in the last resort, be willing to take part of the duchies on mortgage for a given period if only the

---

* He took sixty-seven servants and a fine service of silver plate for this express purpose.

remaining parts were given in outright cession. Hopes rose that Fabrice could persuade George to send a Hanoverian diplomat suitably instructed and empowered so that bargaining could begin on the military help – preferably naval – to be stipulated in return for those portions of Bremen and Verden to be ceded in perpetuity.[45] That such equivalents to be conquered with his help should be gained at the expense of Denmark–Norway had already been made clear to George through Ranck and Vellingk in 1716: Bornholm and Norway east of Glommen had been mentioned as suitable areas of compensation, singly or in combination, according to the scale of Swedish cessions to Hanover.[46]

The Kristinehamn visit had delayed Fabrice's negotiations and George had become increasingly anxious. The Russo-Swedish talks were due to open any minute according to his information from the Tsar's court; and he was worried by the attempts of Poniatowski – Charles's roving 'foreign minister' in Europe between November 1717 and May 1718 – to disrupt the formation of the Quadruple Alliance,[47] no doubt in an effort to lessen Hanover's bargaining power over Bremen and Verden. He therefore decided, early in March 1718, to send the Hanoverian diplomat Schrader to Lund to support or supplant Fabrice. His orders were as stiff as those with which Fabrice had left London, since George I had no intention of committing himself till he could see more clearly the impact of Russia's negotiations with Sweden. The arrival of Schrader was, all the same, a feather in the cap of Charles XII and negotiations were continued with Schrader and Fabrice throughout the spring months.[48]

It used to be assumed that these Lund conferences were not seriously meant, that they were feints arranged by Görtz as opposed to his 'real' negotiations with the Russians,[49] but it is now realized that both sets of negotiations were genuine in so far that Charles XII was as anxious to find out what terms George I could be made to offer as he was to know those which Tsar Peter would in the last resort accept. There was indeed a close connexion between the two sets of negotiations from the Swedish point of view. They did not run parallel: when one set of negotiations languished, or were made to languish, the other was revived, not only to play each set off against the other but also to prolong the breathing-space which permitted Swedish military preparations to be completed while paralysing cooperation inside the coalition. It was something of a diplomatic triumph for Charles XII, who gave the order for start, stop and restart, that he still had control of both sets of negotiations even after the military offensive against Denmark–Norway was opened in the autumn of 1718. He retained it, indeed, till the day of his death, and though it can be argued that by that time the cleverness of his diplomatic assistants could not for long hide the 'feint' element that persisted in both sets of negotiations, Charles was then negotiating from strength* and in a position to elicit better terms as his military offensive developed.

---

* For both George and Peter being willing to continue the negotiations after Charles's death, see below, pp. 459‡.

IV

It was partly to give the Hanoverian negotiations a chance to get off the ground that the start of the Lövö conference had been delayed, but the Swedes were also anxious to see if they might profit from the flight of Peter's son Aleksey from Russia. Görtz reckoned it the mistake of his life that he had not seen the possibilities which this opened early enough.[50] When Charles XII on 26 November 1717 was prevailed on to send orders to Poniatowski that he should offer Aleksey a place of refuge in Sweden, the authorization came too late: the Tsarevich had already agreed to return to Russia.[51] Some delay was also due to the amount of work Görtz had to catch up with in Stockholm after his long absence, and a last minute postponement was involuntary: heavy storms prevented Görtz, Gyllenborg and their suite, embarked in two magnificent galleys, from joining the Russian delegation* till 8 May 1718. Negotiations proceeded at a snail's pace, though with a great show of activity, since Sweden wanted the alternative set of negotiations with George to proceed far enough to be used as a lever at Lövö. Combining Swedish reports with the Russian ones (recently examined and discussed by S. Feygina)[52] the progress at Lövö can be charted in the minutest detail, though for our purposes only the main lines will be drawn.

Görtz explained in the first session that he possessed no full powers and had only come to listen to Russian terms and report these back to Charles XII. He asked for a specific Russian peace project, more for European consumption than for the objective he confided to his opposite number: to turn the Swedish King's mind towards peace. The propaganda element inseparable from the Åland islands conference for the Swedes, as well as the simultaneous negotiations with George I, necessitated 'ostensible' and 'real' letters from Görtz to Charles XII. The 'ostensible' letters were those which were read by the King and by those in the know of foreign affairs at Lund, von Müllern in particular, and in Stockholm. The 'real' letters were marked '*pour les propres mains du Roy*' and were handed to Charles XII discreetly, during a ride or a walk, by von Kochen when no one else was watching.[53] These 'real' letters were burnt and Charles never discussed their contents with anyone. One complete draft of a 'real' letter has, however, been found among Görtz's papers and historians have thus been able to compare this, of 30 July 1718, with an 'ostensible' report dated two days previously, and to show that when Russian peace terms are mentioned in the 'ostensible' letter Görtz strongly advises the King to accept them even though they are not as good as hoped for, while in the 'real' letter he virtually asks Charles to disregard the 'ostensible' one and proceeds to evaluate the situation in terms of 'hanging on': it would be shameful to accept harsh terms at the moment when 'glorious possibilities' seem to open for Swedish arms.[54]

* This had arrived on 30 April/11 May at Lövö.

Before this comparison was made, historians postulated a strong contrast between the King's objectives and those of Görtz, depicting Charles as bent on war at all costs, refusing terms which his negotiator at Lövö thought sensible, and seeing Görtz as an adviser desperately trying to persuade the King to make peace with Russia and Russia alone. We now know that Görtz, like Charles, reckoned with the coming military offensive as the only means to improve Russian and Hanoverian peace terms and we have enough information from Görtz's private reflections as well as from his correspondence with Swedish officials and diplomats to establish this beyond doubt.*

But at the time of the Lövö negotiations the discrepancy between the 'ostensible' and 'real' letters to the King created some problems which were intensified by Görtz's private letters to Müllern and de la Marck widely exaggerating the Russian offers for purposes of spreading alarm and despondency among Sweden's enemies by their implication of a speedy peace with Suedo-Russian cooperation to follow.[55] The 'ostensible' letters – carefully leaked to the Russians – encouraged the Tsar to carry on the Åland island negotiations in spite of the several adjournments† which Görtz asked for to 'work on Charles XII', but Müllern and others were puzzled by them: how could Görtz suggest that the King should accept conditions which were lower than offers Görtz himself had reported from the Tsar at an earlier date? More significantly, Frederick of Hesse became convinced that Görtz was in favour of making an unnecessarily hard peace out of concern for separate Holstein-Gottorp interests. Throughout the summer and autumn of 1718 the Prince of Hesse and Ulrika were cast in gloom at the prospect they themselves conjured up of Görtz selling Sweden's Baltic provinces for the price of Russian military support to settle the Swedish succession on Charles Frederick of Holstein-Gottorp.

The question of a wife for the young Duke and speculation on the Duke's chances in the succession struggle, formed part of all diplomatic exchanges of the period, but no such deal as suspected by Frederick of Hesse did take place at Lövö and it was not till the fourth and most desperate session with the Russians that Görtz did more than hint at the advantages which might be derived from a future union between the Duke and the Tsar's daughter (at this time nine years old) to cement the political alliance. Even then the topic was only lightly touched upon. The suggestion, which cropped up also in the talks with George I – though with a different bride – must be seen as one bait among many to keep the negotiations afloat.[56]

Charles XII had done what he could to minimize Hesse distrust of Görtz.

* E.g. his letter to Kochen of 6 June 1718: '*Cependant je ne laisse pas d'être du sentiment que c'est justement dans le temps qu'on est au plus fort en négociations, que'il faut faire le plus grand effort, la crainte faisant plus d'empression sur les ennemis, que toute autre consideration et tout trait de politique.*'

† The first session lasted from 20 May to 2 June; the next from 9–22 July; the third (after Ostermann's absence to consult the Tsar and a visit by Görtz to Stockholm) lasted from 1–18 August; the fourth session from 6 November to 12 November after Görtz and Ostermann had both consulted their masters.

He permitted Frederick to send an observer* to Lövö in Görtz's suite, and when Hesse agitation grew, he agreed that Conrad Ranck should take a full share in the Lövö negotiations on behalf of the Landgrave. Ranck had always been in favour of a settlement with Russia rather than with Hanover, and in the summer and early autumn of 1718 he conferred first with the Landgrave, then with the King of Prussia and, finally, also with Tsar Peter and Shafirov at St Petersburg before proceeding to Lövö to await the opening of the fourth session,[57] due to start as soon as Görtz landed with Charles XII's answer to the Russian 'final offer' worked out during the August session.

This 'final offer' had gone a considerable way to meet the Swedes. The initial positions, with Charles XII willing to consider no more than the cession of Ingria and Tsar Peter insisting that he would return Finland only – and Finland without Viborg at that – had been unpromising, but in secret sessions between Görtz and Ostermann negotiations on equivalents, and on a Russo-Swedish military alliance after the conclusion of their separate peace, had covered a lot of ground. Might Mecklenburg serve as a compensation for Sweden's cession of Livonia to Duke Charles-Leopold?† Would Charles consider the reinstatement of Stanislaus in Poland worthy of sacrifices in Swedish land? How many troops and ships would the Tsar be willing to put at the Swedish King's disposal for the conquest of Norway and the reconquest of his provinces in the Empire? Could the frontier of Finland be redrawn to bring the Kola peninsula and Archangel on the Swedish side?

In the end Tsar Peter firmly refused any change of the Russo-Finnish border to Sweden's advantage and added the demand of Kexholm (with its strong fort on the Ladoga) to that of Viborg and baulked at giving even auxiliary help against Frederick IV of Denmark–Norway or Frederick William of Prussia. But he declared himself willing to support Charles XII's war effort in 1719 against Hanover and Saxony–Poland with twenty thousand men, eight large men-of-war and a number of transport-ships for the Swedish expeditionary corps intended for the Empire. Russian soldiers and ships were to serve under Swedish colours, that is Tsar Peter would be an auxiliary rather than an ally, unless better Swedish terms for the alliance – such as a guarantee for the Russian succession as laid down by Tsar Peter – could be arranged in time for the 1719 campaign.[58]

The Tsar was also prepared to comply immediately, as an earnest of his good faith, with a request that Görtz had cleverly put forward as of importance to himself: if Peter would consent to the exchange of Field-Marshal Rehnskiöld and General Mörner's son, he, Görtz, would gain valuable allies against those who opposed him in Sweden: both of them he was sure, would help him to persuade the King of the need for peace with Russia. The exchange against two Russian generals in Swedish captivity was agreed on, and Görtz's long delay between the third and fourth sessions of the conference – ten

* Frederick's secretary, Harmers.
† For theꞏTsar's influence over Mecklenburg, see above, pp. 423–4.

weeks elapsing between them – is in part explicable by the pressure he wanted to exert to make sure that Rehnskiöld, whose freedom was greatly desired by Charles XII, should land in Sweden before he himself returned to Lövö. On 19 October the exchanges were effected: a few days later Rehnskiöld met Görtz briefly in Stockholm before hastening to Charles XII's headquarters.[59]

The Tsar and his negotiators had naturally become suspicious of Swedish intentions as the Åland congress dragged on from session to session. Ostermann at an early stage advised his master to break off and let the dice of war decide the issue, and Peter was worried enough to reinsure with George I to the extent of breaking off connexions with the Jacobites and with Alberoni and assuring the King of Great Britain of his loyalty.[60] But he remained reluctant to break off the negotiations with Sweden, even after his position at home and in Europe had become easier through Aleksey's being enticed back to Russia, where he died in prison in circumstances which have never been fully clarified. The reason for this reluctance is not difficult to find. The Tsar knew of Swedish negotiations with George I via Fabrice and others, and though George's position strengthened *vis-à-vis* Sweden throughout the summer and autumn of 1718* this only increased Peter's fear that George I might steal a march on him in the race for a separate peace with Charles XII.

The Russian hope for progress in the Tsar's own negotiations with Charles XII received a setback as soon as Görtz arrived on Lövö on 6 November and transmitted his King's answer to the 'final demand': Peter's help must be given also against Frederick of Denmark–Norway so that Danish territories could be attacked from Germany and guarantees for this help, as well as for that against Saxony and Hanover, must be devised. Tempers rose on the Russian side of the table, but Ranck, with some success, worked to smooth over problems and Görtz, in secret talks with Ostermann, brought out his trump card: was it not time to think seriously of the advantages which both powers might derive from King Charles's nephew choosing a bride from the House of Romanov? The conference was adjourned to permit Görtz, who promised to return within one month, to consult with the King of Sweden,† already embarked on his Norwegian campaign. On 12 November Görtz and Ranck left Lövö, leaving behind Gyllenborg and the secretarial staff, among them Görtz's trusted secretary Stambke.

The sands of time might be running out, since Ostermann threatened rupture of the conferences if Charles XII's 'final answer' did not prove acceptable enough to the Tsar to lead to an armistice, but the fact remains that the congress had not been broken,‡ was still in being and would be so at least until Görtz returned.[61] The next step, as always, had to be decided on by the King after consultation not only with Görtz but with all

* See below, p. 460.
† Görtz had done so between the first and second and between the third and fourth sessions; between the second and third his confidential secretary Stambke had been sent to headquarters.
‡ It is significant that neither Charles's death nor Görtz's arrest caused the Tsar to abandon the conferences: these were broken off by Frederick of Hesse in 1719.

his ministers informed of the particular stage his various negotiations had reached.

Logically the next step – as both Görtz and Müllern agreed before Görtz left Stockholm for Norway – would be an intensification of the negotiations with George I. These had never been abandoned, but little progress had been recorded since Fabrice's return to London in June 1718. Since then George had scored successes both as King and Elector: Admiral Byng had destroyed Alberoni's proud Mediterranean fleet off Cape Passaro; the Quadruple Alliance had been signed with France and the Emperor;* and Dubois, Stanhope's friend, had got into the saddle in Paris, thus giving George greater security against Jacobite support from France.

To guard against danger from the North (for Great Britain as well as for Hanover) George hastened to respond to Tsar Peter's overtures by a joint mission of Norris and Jefferyes to Russia, while at the same time pursuing negotiations for a triple alliance between Hanover, Saxony and the Emperor lest the dreaded Russo-Swedish collaboration for 1719 should materialize. But he was not easy in his mind in spite of Bernstorff's brave front to Fabrice,[62] and once Charles XII's Norwegian campaign had started there was every prospect that he would be willing to negotiate further if only in the hope of averting a Swedish invasion of Scotland or Bremen and Verden: the twelve British men-of-war which Fabrice had been told to ask for might yet join the Swedish navy and facilitate the crossing of Charles's army to the Continent.

The list of those with whom Charles could hope to enter into fruitful negotiations contained powerful figures quite apart from Tsar Peter and George I. The Emperor Charles VI had obtained a glorious peace at the expense of the Turks at Passarowitz on 21 July (N.S.) 1718, extending his dominions further south than ever before. His prestige was high and he was burning with ambition to pacify the North and make his power felt in the Empire. This gave scope for playing on Imperial resentment at the arrogance of Hanover and Prussia and their encouragement of Russia, and Swedish diplomacy† had already begun to exploit such possibilities.[63]

The growth in power and prestige of George I and Charles VI must to some extent be seen as limiting factors on Charles XII's freedom of action, and historians have often assumed that 1718 spelt 'the end of the line' for him.[64] But, given his attitude to exchanges and equivalents to uphold the great-power position, George I's greater security and the Emperor's reawakened concern for the Empire offered Sweden valuable alternatives to Russo-

---

* The alliance was so named as the accession of the Dutch Republic was expected. Dutch refusal to sign was connected with northern affairs, see Hatton, *Diplomatic Relations*, pp. 161 ff. Eventually a fourth partner, Victor Amadeus of Savoy, was found.

† C. Nordmann, in his book of 1962, considers that Charles XII's greatest mistake was not to ally himself with Charles VI in 1714–15. Whether such an alliance could have been obtained at a time when the Emperor's military attention was turned towards the south-east is an open question: the argument is reminiscent of Syveton's 'if only Charles had joined Louis XIV' in 1706, Haintz's 'if only Charles had partitioned Poland with Prussia any time between 1702 and 1708', and Hassinger's 'if only Charles had grabbed the last chance to tie Prussia to his side in 1713'.

Ulrika Eleonora the
younger, Queen in 1718,
from a painting by
J. Starbus, *c.* 1720

Duke Charles Frederick
of Holstein-Gottorp,
from a painting by D. von
Krafft

CAROLVS·XII·R·SVELE·   BARO·GOERTZ·

Charles XII and Baron Görtz,
from an engraving

Charles XII in 1715,
from a painting by T. Wedekind

Swedish cooperation: Charles could join George, Augustus and the Emperor – with France's approval – in an attack on Russia for the purpose of regaining the major part of the Baltic provinces. Negotiations along these lines would at the very least serve to soften Tsar Peter's peace terms.

The diplomatic offensive, coupled with news of Sweden's military preparations, had in any case paid off handsomely. A certain gauge of Charles's increased stature on the eve of his military offensive is the number of rulers and statesmen who took the initiative in contacting him. Frederick William of Prussia dispatched an emissary, Schomer, to Sweden; Augustus of Saxony asked to be permitted to send a representative; delegates from the Polish Republic arrived secretly to petition Charles's help against Augustus; Alberoni, wishing to revenge himself on George I, pressed Spain's alliance on him; James Sobieski offered him his daughter in marriage; and the Jacobites continued to weave their European-wide webs, never giving up hope of capturing Charles XII.[65]

Most significantly, of course, the roads were still open for negotiations with Tsar Peter as with George I. It was time for the military offensive to explore which path would lead to a tolerable peace with any one member of the anti-Swedish coalition. Charles reckoned that one peace achieved, the rest would follow on the pattern of Louis XIV's experience between 1711 and 1713.

2

Military Preparations and Planning

Charles XII aimed at augmenting the Swedish operational army to about sixty thousand men[1] before a military offensive was embarked upon and to make the naval detachments at Stockholm, Karlskrona and Gothenburg strong enough not only to defend the country but to act as escorts for a fleet of transport-ships large enough to land considerable forces on the continent of Europe. The army would have to be equipped and trained for the Norwegian as well as the continental campaigns, though some of Charles's advisers – notably Frederick of Hesse and Meijerfelt – were against a Norwegian campaign and would have preferred to direct the Swedish attack to Germany without a preliminary or complementary diversion to the west. Magazines, particularly for the Norwegian campaign, were considered essential by the King for the success of his overall plan for the offensive and would have to be collected in strongly fortified positions. From experience gained, Charles was anxious also to improve the administration of the army and the navy and to increase the flexibility of operations through novel methods for cooperation between the various specialized branches of the military forces at his disposal.

The targets aimed at were in the main reached. By October 1718 the Swedish army consisted of some sixty-five thousand men, though the numbers mentioned abroad tended to be higher either through conscious exaggeration by the Swedes or inaccurate guess-work by foreign diplomats.[2] A transport-fleet of 145 ships, capable of carrying 17,500 men and four thousand horses, was ready by the summer of 1718. The Stockholm naval squadron now comprised both sailing vessels and galleys, though its shallow-draught ships were still short of the fifty Charles XII had ordered* to be built in the old yards which had seen little naval construction since the founding of the Karlskrona base.[3]

The Gothenburg squadron of frigates and galleys had been successfully defended in a five-hour battle against Tordenskjold's bold attack on 3 May 1717 and had been expanded by fresh building since that date. It had also been divided between Gothenburg and Marstrand to protect the new forts

* From Stralsund of 7/18 March 1715.

and magazines building at Sundsborg and at Strömstad, on the entrance to Dynekilen fjord. This was a consequence of the naval activities of Tordenskjold, assisted by British men-of-war detached from the squadron which George I sent to the North under the command of Admiral Byng in April 1717 'to attack the Swedish ships wherever he meets with them ... to seize all vessels which come out of any of the Ports of Sweden, as well as Ships of War and Transports and Merchantmen, and to take all Ships of other Nations which would go into the Ports of Gottenburg or any other part of Sweden'.[4] On 8 July Tordenskjold, relying on Richard Lestock's five large ships securing his rear, attacked Strömstad with vigour but was driven back. His later bombardments of the fort had little effect and the joint cruising of his successor,* Rosenpalm, and Lestock for the rest of the season was in deep waters and could not prevent a relatively free traffic between Gothenburg, Strömstad and Sundsborg. As a precautionary measure, however, part of the Gothenburg squadron was stationed at Marstrand to discourage Danish–Norwegian naval activities in the western *skärgård*.

The British blockade in 1717 had some effect in Sweden all the same. It bottled up the Gothenburg privateers at a time when they had developed into a cooperative, so to speak, with the Crown. Under the leadership of Lars Gatenhielm, they formed themselves into a joint enterprise, sharing risks and profits, and were permitted – against money securities – to charter naval frigates and to enlist sailors and soldiers in their crews.[5] The spring of 1717 had been a successful one, and the autumn was to prove likewise, but during the months that George I's navy cruised off the coast they soon learnt the wisdom of keeping in port.†

The objectives of George I and Frederick IV at sea were not, however, achieved in 1717. Frederick had planned to conquer Gotland, protected by the British fleet, but the non-arrival of the Dutch squadron (due to the States General's determination not to be drawn into a naval war in the Baltic)[6] meant that Byng had to use the major part of his fleet to convoy trade. The British blockade of Swedish exports had relatively little impact as Swedish iron was sent via Königsberg, with the connivance of merchants of that town, at times when enemy warships were active.

In 1718, George I, by promising the Dutch Republic a share in the trade advantages which he would stipulate for the British as part of his eventual peace settlement with Sweden,‡ obtained a measure of cooperation. The States General refused to participate in the blockade, but offered to convoy the whole of the Dutch and British trade while Norris – once more in charge of the British squadron – and the Danes should 'observe' the Swedes.[7] With Charles XII's invasion of Norway a probability and that of Hanover a possibility, however, the Dano-British forces had to be split to keep an eye both on

---

* Tordenskjold lost his command after the two consecutive failures of May and July 1717.

† A similar pattern can be observed for 1718 – successful spring and autumn activities, quiet in the summer.

‡ For the eventual non-fulfilment of that promise, see Hatton, *Diplomatic Relations*, pp. 203–5.

the western approaches near Gothenburg and Strömstad and the exit from
Karlskrona whence it was rumoured that the Swedish fleet was ready to sail
for Germany.[8]

Such rumours were consciously fostered by Charles XII who had ordered
some regiments to move in the direction of the main naval base to lend
credence to them.[9] It is possible that the timetable of Charles's offensive in
Norway was postponed till after the departure of Norris's squadron from
the Sound. The start of the Norwegian campaign had, according to Frederick
of Hesse, been promised for August 1718,[10] and it may well be that Norris's
presence, unencumbered by convoy duties, contributed to Charles XII's
decision to delay since too soon a disclosure of his hand would permit a
dangerous concentration of Dano-British vessels in the Strömstad area. This
cannot be said for certain, since other considerations may have played their
part in postponement – the stage of the Åland islands negotiations or the bad
harvest. Indeed, a misunderstanding may have existed between those who
believed the whole campaign was due to start in August and the King who
had given orders for the action against Trondhjem to start – as it did – in that
month:* Charles, well aware of the danger implied in Dano-British naval
collaboration, is likely to have timed his southern invasion of Norway for
after Norris's departure. But if Norris's presence did contribute to a later
start for the Norwegian campaign, its main effect was not in the military but
in the psychological field, in reinforcing the dislike of the Prince of Hesse,
who remembered the winter campaign of 1716, of a late venture into that
country in 1718 and strengthening his determination to break it off if he were
given the chance.†

The Karlskrona squadron, whatever Charles XII tried to make his enemies
believe, was not completely fitted out in the summer of 1718. Von Liewen
and Claes Sparre had worked energetically since they took over from Wachtmeister (who had asked to be relieved in 1714); and the *generalissimus* position
accorded to Frederick of Hesse in November 1717 had helped to oil the
administration and financial works for the final spurt. Interesting innovations
were started, among which may be mentioned an organization modelled on
the British navy and the creation of a strong force of 'marines'.[11] The King
planned for a large navy (since he did not want to count on cooperation with
either that of Tsar Peter or that of George I), but Poniatowski's attempts to
purchase naval vessels abroad had stranded on the scarcity of big ships in
Europe[12] and on Sweden's lack of foreign currency: the Dutch money
promised for 1717 materialized only in part and Tsar Peter, in return for his
1717 recognition of French mediation rights in the Great Northern War,
obtained the Regent's pledge not to renew the Franco-Swedish treaty when
it expired in April 1718. French subsidies consequently stopped and the
opportunity of anticipating their not very regular payments as a lever for
private loans lapsed.[13]

---

* See below, p. 477.   † ibid., p. 511.

Given the size of the Swedish navy (estimated as twenty-two of the line in 1718) it was deployed to the best advantage: the Stockholm squadron with its transport fleet kept Tsar Peter guessing as to the thrust of a possible attack; the Karlskrona main fleet – supported by the move of soldiers to the south – had made the whole anti-Swedish coalition uneasy; the Gothenburg–Marstrand detachments maintained that control of local waters which was so vital for the impending Norwegian campaign.

II

It used to be generally believed that Charles XII's army in 1718 consisted of old men and young boys, a real scraping of the barrel; but recent research into the muster rolls of the regiments has disproved this.[14] There were only seventy-three men over fifty-five and only thirty boys between fifteen and seventeen among the vast total of soldiers, non-commissioned officers, and non-fighting personnel.* The medical examination of men and the veterinary one of horses was stiff enough to send home man and beast not found perfectly fit. Nor were too short recruits accepted.[15]

Categories of men were, however, called up who used to be regarded as exempt. Tessin protested that apprentice gardeners were taken from the royal gardens, and Charles's reply that this loss might in the long run be preferable to his finding fully qualified Russian gardeners in charge only partly mollified the older man.[16] There was certainly some general resentment at men being called to the colours who had not previously been reckoned as soldier-material: lazy students; young servants of the nobility or farmworkers on manorial estates; able-bodied organists and vergers, even men from farms with staging-post duties.[17]

The main bulk of the recruits came, as before, via the *indelingsverk*. To the many regiments set up to replace those lost at Poltava and Perevolotjna were now added some achieved by a cooperation of three, five or even seven *hemman* units. But to these provincial regiments were added a considerable number of regiments paid by the Crown and consisting either of Swedish or non-Swedish subjects.

The troops – thirty-seven infantry and twenty-three cavalry regiments – were not all equally well clothed (contracts placed abroad did not produce cloth for uniforms as speedily as expected), but the troops destined for stage one of the offensive were given priority above those which formed the reserve in Sweden. In matters of equipment and drill all were treated alike. The Swedish armament industry had produced sufficient pistols, muskets, and swords of the Charles XII model. The cavalry squadrons perfected their close square, 'knee to knee', with fast attack using *armes blanches* after the one and only salvo; the infantry practised their intricate evolutions, their limited

* Six per cent were older than forty (of these less than one-fifth were over fifty); 17·6 per cent were younger than twenty-one (of these more than half were under twenty); cp. below, p. 516.

controlled firing and their *gå-på* tactics – whether the arm was the pike or the sword – along lines evolved during the war years abroad.

One change came with the absorption of the Drabant corps (which had been reduced to eight officers and thirty men by 1716) into a joint Royal Drabant and Lifeguard squadron.[18] The old corps had been composed exclusively of officers serving as privates. Now privates and non-commissioned officers were admitted since good officers were in short supply. The men were hand-picked; Charles made a special point of asking that, height and intelligence having been taken into account, men 'not notable for their thirst' might be chosen. His preference for bachelors in this corps, the rule rather than the exception in such guards elsewhere in Europe, caused some caustic comment and he was obliged to defend himself: he did not ask that all soldiers should remain in the unmarried state, just these particular guards, and they could always resign when they felt inclined for matrimony. As for himself he took the opportunity to tell Feif he still hoped to enter into marriage* when God gave peace.[19]

The greatest changes of these years came in the development of artillery and in the cooperation between different sections of the army. The expansion of the artillery, and particularly of siege-artillery, was such that historians who have not looked beyond the Norwegian campaign of 1718 have found its size inexplicable. There was certainly need for a restocking of the artillery park. Much had been lost at Stralsund and Wismar; some of that in Sweden itself had been melted down for coinage during Charles XII's absence; and fresh losses were incurred during Tordenskjold's attack in Dynekilen in June 1716.[20] Luckily Cronstedt, a Prussian prisoner-of-war after Stralsund's capitulation, managed to escape and rejoin Charles XII in October 1716.[21] With his assistant Schaffer he worked out plans which received the King's approval in February 1717. Görtz obtained French experts in novel methods of casting and within a surprisingly short time heavy artillery sufficient for two simultaneous sieges, and quantities of cannon capable of being mounted on barges to serve as firing platforms, were produced and an artillery-corps of 3,380 men trained. Charles XII was present at many of their exercises, and took an interest also in the technical aspects of Cronstedt's innovations: the rank of *Friherre* (baron) conferred on the latter in August 1718 was regarded as a compliment to the whole corps. The largest cannon ever cast in Sweden – eighteen 48-pounders – were marvelled at,[22] and field-pieces capable of Cronstedt's famous *Geschwinder Schott*† were manufactured in quantities to give each

---

* This is the last recorded comment we have of Charles on his own hopes of marriage and the words Feif remembered, printed in Nordberg, *Anmärckningar*, pp. 50–1 are therefore worth quoting: 'As for myself, when God gives peace, I also will marry. But I will seek a wife not for reasons of state, but one whom I like well and believe I will love for ever so that I need not keep what the French call maitresse: in simple Swedish a whore.' Ulrika (see her letter to her husband cited by Holst, *Ulrika Eleonora*, p. 146) noted on 1 Sept. 1717 that she had found her brother not 'uninclined' to marriage and William Coxe was told by Poniatowski's son that his father was aware of Charles XII's plan to marry: see *Travels*, 5th ed., I, p. 49.

† This fired twelve to fourteen shots a minute, a ten-fold acceleration, due partly to the use of an *enhetspatron*, i.e. combined bullet and charge.

regiment thirty-two 3-pounders and sixteen 6-pounders, to be drawn by four and eight horses respectively. These pieces were incorporated with the regiment and their crews did not form part of the artillery corps as such.[23]

During his earlier campaigns Charles had frequently divided the operational army under his command into 'columns' for particular ventures, but the regiment had remained the only permanent unit, the 'columns' being decided on by the King when required, with adjutants giving the necessary orders to effect a temporary collaboration. Now, building on previous experience and visualizing the coming offensive as a whole, reorganization was decreed from Lund in November 1717 and completed by the late summer of 1718.[24] Regiments were combined, by twos and threes, into brigades called *indelningar*. Care was taken that each brigade contained the same 'type' of soldier, that is the brigade, whether an infantry one or a cavalry one, consisted of either Swedish native troops raised in the traditional manner, or of nationally recruited Swedes 'for the emergency', or of mercenary non-Swedish regiments. Each brigade had a commander, who – if he happened to be a colonel – left his regiment to the complete control of his next-in-command for the duration of his brigade-posting. The usual rank for a brigade commander was lieutenant-general. The resulting brigades became the basic unit for larger army-groups arranged as and when the war effort required. These were called *tilldelningar* (i.e. divisions) if they consisted of infantry and cavalry brigades only, and *hufvudtilldelningar* (i.e. main-divisions) if they also comprised artillery regiments. The specific requirements of each arm of the war on land was safeguarded by an inspector-in-chief of full general's rank for infantry, cavalry and artillery respectively.

Charles XII now arranged for a permanent staff to assist himself as commander-in-chief. Seven 'directors', each with his own duties, were attached to the King. Four might be regarded as heads of military 'departments': one to deal with legal issues; one with responsibility for the commissariat (food, medical services, and all money-matters); and two for the training and equipment of, respectively, the infantry on its own and the cavalry and artillery combined. Three were to help the commander-in-chief run the campaign: one to work out the complicated marching-'tickets'; the second to arrange camps and quarters in accordance with the march-routes; the third to assist with the tactical planning of battles and with the responsibility for the smooth supply of ammunition and arms during operations.

Evaluation of the reorganization of Charles XII's army has differed. Seen in the narrow context of the Norwegian campaign only, it has been judged 'top-heavy', with too many non-fighting personnel, and with too elaborate arrangements for brigade and division collaboration,[25] but by military historians who have taken the wider plans as well as the then state of European army organization into account it has been considered ahead of its time in conception and execution and has received great praise.[26] Contemporary

military observers, such as the Frenchman Folard who served with Charles's
last army,[27] were impressed not only with the *gå-på* spirit and discipline but
also with the smoothness and flexibility of the organization, and helped in
their writings to carry Charles XII's ideas into the mainstream of European
eighteenth-century thinking on the art of war.*

III

The magazines in the new fortifications had not been easy to fill. Arms and
ammunition fashioned from Swedish raw materials had caused little difficulty:
there were good craftsmen in all the main centres of production and those of
Stockholm were particularly busy between 1716 and 1718.[28] But the harvest
of 1716, though promising to be well above average, had in some parts of the
country been ruined by prolonged periods of rain late in the summer. That
of 1717 was a complete failure in Norrland and Dalecarlia and a poor one in
the rest of Sweden: that of 1718 was hardly better. The Crown did what it
could. It had never been its custom to hinder agriculture by robbing a farmer
who could not pay his dues of horse and cow (though the animals became
'Crown property' in theory until his debts had been paid), and to prevent
famine on the scale of 1695–7, Charles decided in 1717 to let grain already
stored in the magazines be distributed for seed-corn against the borrower
agreeing to replace what he had received on the scale of one barrel being
repaid by a barrel and a half.

It was the 1718 poor harvest which decided the King to issue, from Strömstad on 15 September, maximum prices for the necessities of life, grain, salt
and herring, with orders to the *upphandlingsdeputation* that prices on other
commodities and goods should be fixed commensurate with that list. He
could not leave Sweden at the mercy of speculators when famine threatened.
To stop black-marketeering high fines were decreed for anyone who deviated
from the prices laid down, the fine to be divided between the person who
reported the transgression and the magistrate who levied the fine. To encourage
imports all merchants who shipped food and necessary goods were assured
that the state would pay the difference between the maximum price laid down
and the price they themselves had had to pay abroad. Distilling of spirits was
also temporarily prohibited to conserve grain.[29]

The measures taken by the government to overcome the bad harvests of
1717 and 1718 were only partially successful,† and in these circumstances it
is understandable that there were some gaps in the magazines collected for
the campaign. Six months of food, drink and a good quantity of fodder for the
horses had been the target. Vast quantities of grain, lentils and peas, salted
or smoked meat and herring had been stored, but the grain was depleted since

* See below, pp. 525–6.
† In districts where both salt and flour was in short supply, as e.g. in Dalecarlia, illnesses
connected with undernourishment caused a sharp rise in the death rate in these years.

the borrowers of 1717 had not been able to repay in 1718; the stock of spirits (of which the soldier's daily ration was $\frac{1}{32}$ of a given measure, a *kanne*, a day) was below what was estimated as necessary; and there was some doubt whether the contractors for the brewing of beer would be able to fulfil their obligations in view of the bad harvest. The most serious shortage was, however, in fodder, though there were hopes of getting more supplies before the opening of stage two of the offensive.[30]

One effect of the bad harvests was that the peasants, who were the principal carters of items to be stored in the magazines, began to grumble in some areas close to the Norwegian frontier. The west coast population had been known to swear and curse at the war before now, but that was regarded merely as a safety-valve ('I must go and have a look at the people of that region', the King commented on one occasion)[31] since they had suffered during the four months' Danish occupation of 1709 and the Norwegian invasions of 1710 and 1711 and they had, anyhow, been Swedish subjects for little more than half a century. The story that someone in the west had expressed a wish that the first bullet of the new campaign would hit Charles XII is well founded though it cannot be pinned down to any particular person;[32] and in Jämtland (a province that had been Norwegian till 1654) several peasants refused to transport goods for the magazines being collected for the corps destined to attack Trondhjem. They had horses and carts enough to comply with their orders, and their refusal worried Charles XII sufficiently to make him decree corporal punishment for persistent offenders lest disobedience be encouraged. Such punishment of civilians was against Swedish custom and was felt to be harsh, but it got supplies moving once more and is the only example in the reign of its kind.[33]

Peasant discontent was not general, though weariness with the war was probably as widespread as among other classes of society. The tradition of 'preferring one king to many', the one central paternalistic authority to that of the oppression of the local big-wigs, was strong, and Charles XII had given proof time and again of his concern for social fairness and justice. In small, but significant, matters this had been seen in the weighting of the 'luxury-tax' of 1716:* each class was taxed on 'unnecessary luxuries' but left free of tax, or taxed lightly, on those that might be termed 'necessary luxuries'. The nobleman was not taxed on his carriage, which was thought part of his way of life, but was taxed on his coffee, tea, chocolate, tobacco and sumptuous clothes and wigs: all farmers, farm-labourers, private soldiers and corporals were exempt from the tax on tobacco, and for the social categories in between the tobacco-tax operated on a scale fixed according to status and income. In more important ways the King's sympathy for those he regarded as carrying too heavy a burden compared with the rest of the community had been shown by his insistence on a new land register since 1712 and his introduction in 1718 (on the register's completion) of the principle that taxes and

---

* This tax was not particularly productive, as people tended to avoid the taxed articles.

dues on land hitherto paid in kind should be simplified and paid in money, with a single land-tax as the end objective of the reform.

That Charles's motivation was basically one of concern for the country's prosperity as a whole has already been stressed, but his genuine concern for the peasants who seemed to have the roughest of deals was often expressed.[34] That the reform helped the farmers and was disliked by the other Estates is demonstrated not only by the bureaucratic delays in producing the land register, but also by the fact that the three higher Estates put it into reverse, against the vote of the Fourth Estate, in 1723. The reform of the lower courts had also been of a kind which benefited local interests and gave the ordinary man readier access to justice, and much was hoped from the commission, with the King's old tutor Cronhielm at its head,* for codification of the laws of the land. The local self-government encouraged by various reforms connected with the 1712 tax structure has been judged the foundation of 'modern Sweden'.[35]

Nevertheless, opposition to the King's policy was growing, quietly but persistently, among other classes and particularly among the administrators. The way foreigners were trusted by Charles was felt as a grievance and by implication as a lessening of trust in those who had, to a larger extent than the King realized, made sacrifices for the war effort over many years. They had put up with deductions from their salaries; had, if unwillingly, accepted the principle of taxation as a percentage on property, but when – to finance the new military offensive – Charles XII at the opening of the 1718 campaign, decreed a capital levy of 6 per cent as a civilian contribution to the war effort[36] this seemed the last straw. Did the King want to reduce them to a classless society? The pace of reform inside the administration seemed too fast for many. Everything was in constant flux, they complained. And was there not a danger that the special wartime innovations, such as the *upphandlingsdeputation*, might survive the war and permanently put the older administrative organs into a limbo of non-importance? Görtz might, with perfect sincerity, stress how keen he was to get out of the 'galley' of hard work in which he had involved himself, but he was not believed and the impression he gave of thinking the Swedes more stupid than himself rankled.[37] The list of foreigners, and especially Holsteiners, was recited. Von Dernath was powerful indeed and the accountant of the *deputation*, Ecklef, and its secretary, Rothlieb, were fellow-Holsteiners. Satirical poems about them and about the newfangled money – called 'Görtz's gods' because of the Roman names Charles had given to many of them† – abounded,[38] and discussions began among serious patriotic men as to whether absolutism was either necessary or desirable in a country like Sweden with an old and proud tradition of *monarchia mixta*.

This discussion was not a simple return to the 'nobility-versus-Crown' strife of the seventeenth century. The prophets of change, of a move away from

---

* Its task was completed in 1734.   † Mars, Jupiter, Saturn, Phœnix.

absolutism, were men of the lesser nobility as well as men of the high nobility.*
They were inspired, in part, by French constitutional experiments in the
years immediately after the death of Louis xiv, but they were most strongly
motivated by a disillusionment with Swedish absolutism. If this was what it
led to, 'cabinet government' and a lessening of influence for officials who had
served their country faithfully and according to their lights, then it was time
for change. There was no plotting against Charles xii in the ordinary sense,
though plots were rumoured and 'evidence' sent to the King by a clergyman
named Brenner: 'evidence' which the King always burnt and made light of
when anyone touched on the subject. Brenner was not well balanced, Charles
reminded his advisers: he had been forbidden to preach at Bender because
he was so odd and, anyhow, the King did not want to listen to tale-bearers.[39]

But planning for the future among small groups of influential men was a
fact. Charles had no heir of his own body. The chance to do away with
absolutism would come if he should die during the new military offensive.
Then the would-be reformers would have the opportunity to play off Ulrika
Eleonora against Charles Frederick: whoever proved willing to forswear the
abolutist form of government and return to the 'good old days' when Council,
Colleges and Diet had a real say in affairs would gain the crown.[40] Among
the more influential of these planners for a specific future contingency were
some of those who took charge of the 'revolution' after the death of Charles
xii: the Ribbing brothers (both in Tessin's *högste ordingsman* department
and as such in contact with provincial feeling), one of whom was by an English
diplomat dubbed the Pym and Hampden of Sweden,[41] and – if more uncer-
tainly – Arvid Horn.

The long period between 1716 and 1718 when army officers had been
stationed in Sweden, in frequent contact with their relatives and connexions
in Council and administration, ensured that the new ideas permeated the
higher ranks of the army as well as the higher bureaucracy. There was no
question of present disloyalty or of anti-war feeling as such among the
officer-corps, but the line of their future conduct was becoming clear: we are
patriots and the defence of Sweden must go on even if Charles should die –
provided our terms are met.

IV

There were some officers, and among them the *generalissimus*, who dis-
approved of the Norwegian campaign they knew Charles planned for 1718.
They had bad memories of that country from 1716. It was hilly and sparsely
populated and their past experience made them think of it as unsuitable for
battles of a traditional kind. Strategy might differ in the Low Countries,
where siege warfare was natural in densely populated areas, and in the
vastness of Poland and Russia where the enemy had to be chased long

* Cp. below, p. 519, for some distinction between the plans of higher and lesser nobility.

distances, but tactics in battle were essentially similar. All commanders, whether they fought in western or eastern Europe, aimed at the ideal battle where the enemy – whatever form of attack was favoured by terrain and circumstances – would be if not annihilated at least decisively defeated. But how could the normal tactics be deployed in a country like Norway with hills and lakes and narrow passes even in the eastern part of the country? A winter campaign was particularly deplored by Meijerfelt, who with the frankness customary in Charles XII's circle of trusted officers sent his King a memoranda setting out objections to the venture: it would cost too much in men and effort; success would not bring many advantages; was it not better to wait till conjunctures became favourable and jump straight to the Continent?[42]

Frederick of Hesse had similar opinions and was, as well, worried at the implications of directing the offensive against Denmark–Norway in the first place. Might it not blunt the attack on the Continent? Secretly he feared that the direction of the offensive meant a gain in power for Görtz and that the Holsteiner's interest in forcing Frederick IV to restore Holstein-Gottorp to Charles Frederick was exerting an undue influence on Charles XII's planning. His own German point of view made him inclined to think the Emperor, after his victory over the Turks, as the more important enemy of both Sweden and the German princes. In the aide-memoire* which he penned in October 1718 of points to be raised in a future conversation with Charles XII the desirability of containing the Emperor is stressed in number 5 of the 12 points listed.† The others cover the misdeeds of Görtz and the *upphandlings-deputation*, and show that Frederick at this time was moving close to the Swedish opposition against the 'foreigners' – Görtz is deceiving the King, trade is being hamstrung, the true servants of Charles are neglected while the *deputation* is 'intriguing' to little benefit for the country, the man-in-the-street complains that Görtz and the *deputation* use money like water and the honest administrators are sad that 'a foreigner governs all'.[43]

But though Frederick of Hesse shared a hatred of Görtz and the *deputation* with many Swedes, he and his wife differed from the opposition in their attitude to absolutism. Ulrika Eleonora was, like Charles XII, brought up in the absolutist tradition and only under great pressure from her husband did she, after her brother's death, yield the principle of it. In practice she was soon found intractable and exchanged for Frederick, who – with no shadow of hereditary claim to the Swedish crown – could be more easily controlled. Ideally, Frederick would have preferred to maintain absolutism, but his contact with dissatisfied Swedes in the last year of Charles XII's reign convinced him that he could not obtain the crown for Ulrika Eleonora without

* This document from Riksarkivet was first examined by Stig Jägerskiöld who assumed its date to be April 1718; it has been printed (in Swedish translation) by Holst in his biography of Frederick (p. 96) and demonstrated to be of October 1718.

† Frederick's fear of the Emperor was such that he, via Leutrum, advised Charles to make peace with Russia (and/or Prussia) and send fifty thousand men to Germany to fight Charles VI.

some sacrifice in theory which he hoped could be limited in practice: only if Charles were persuaded to name Ulrika as his successor could he hope to maintain absolutism intact.

Before the military offensive started, the possibility that Charles XII might die without pronouncing the name of the one whom he wished to succeed was considered fairly remote: more men died from wounds in battle than were killed instantly. But Frederick, with advice from the Landgrave and help from Hein, did from May of 1718 plan what steps his wife ought to take in the event of Charles dying without choosing between her and Charles Frederick – planning which has been taken, too easily, as 'proof' of Frederick's intention to have his brother-in-law murdered during the campaign. With the succession unsettled and the prospect of Frederick himself leaving for the Norwegian campaign (which he, as will be recalled, regarded as 'promised' for August) it is not strange that he and Hein should give Ulrika written advice how she ought to act if Frederick sent news of her brother's death: as soon as the customary praise of the dead King had been given in Council, she was to proclaim herself Queen and let herself be crowned before the Diet was called, thus circumventing the intrigues of those at home and abroad who favoured Charles Frederick's candidature and robbing the Estates of an opportunity to suppress absolutism. To mollify legitimate discontent, she should at her coronation make a public declaration of her intent to listen, soon, to the advice of the Estates on how to remedy past mistakes and help the country back on its feet. She ought to cooperate with one or more of the Council and she must be ruthless in arresting those she and her advisers suspected of plotting against her.[44]

The plausibility of the theory that Frederick of Hesse arranged for Charles XII's murder will be discussed below.* The documentary 'evidence' in this indictment against him is the memorandum of May 1718 and some of his letters which Ulrika Eleonora copied. One to 'le Comte M.W.' (presumably Mauritz Vellingk) and one to a 'Monsieur le Gnal'. Both letters show some disillusionment with Charles XII and his obstinate refusal to listen to reason (i.e. the King will not admit Görtz's 'guilt' and will not give up the Norway campaign), but there is nothing in them which can be interpreted as a desire to do away with his brother-in-law. Indeed the pious hope is expressed that home truths, repeated as he intends to repeat them for Charles, however unpopular this will make him, will in the end – like raindrops on a stone – make an impression.[45]

In an atmosphere which must to some extent have saddened him, for he was genuinely fond of his brother-in-law, Charles XII finalized his plans for the military offensive. Lieutenant-General Karl Gustaf Armfelt, who had served with Catinat in Italy against Eugène and was used to mountainous country, and had since defended Finland with great courage, was chosen as commander for the army group that was to march from Jämtland in early August into Norway to surprise Trondhjem.

* See below, pp. 507–8.

In Trondhjem he would be close enough to Scotland to put some fear into George I, but since Charles XII's written orders to Armfelt delivered to him at Strömstad in June 1718 have been lost, we have no proof of the King's future plans if Armfelt had succeeded in conquering Trondhjem. The presence of equipment of a type normally issued for naval ships among the baggage for the Jämtland army (bread carriers and leather water-bags, for example) has led historians to assume that, with ships taken from Trondhjem harbour, a good part of Armfelt's 7,500 men were meant to continue to Scotland to raise a Jacobite rebellion. The fact that Charles XII had agreed to support a project for a trading and privateering venture based on Madagascar and led by Jacobites[46] has been thought to lend credence to this theory on the basis of in-for-a-penny-in-for-a-pound. It seems unlikely that Charles, in the political circumstances of the time, when he had resisted so many previous appeals from the Jacobites, should have endangered his relations with Great Britain to the extent of fomenting rebellion. He had, in Turkey, given Queen Anne, via James Jefferyes, a promise that he would not help the Jacobites,[47] and like most monarchs he regarded it as part of his royal *gloire* not to break his word once given. Like Louis XIV in relation to William III and Anne, Charles might take the view that he was released from his promise if the population of Great Britain rose against a ruler who was his enemy, but George was his formal enemy only in his capacity as Elector and the rebellion of 1715 had shown very limited support for James Edward Stuart. That Charles XII had made contingency arrangements for a force of Poles and Swedes ('some thousands' were mentioned) to be used in Scotland is clear from the notes which General Schwerin made of conversations he had with the King in the trenches before Frederiksten. Such planning was probably influenced by Alberoni's project of a descent in favour of the Jacobites: collaboration with Spain had been discussed though no decision had been reached or commitment made.[48] But to the present writer – for reasons which will be discussed below – it seems most probable that Charles had in mind a feint at an invasion of Scotland.*

It is possible that a part of the Jämtland corps, if successful at Trondhjem, might have been asked to proceed to Bergen† which would indeed be a glittering prize: a port rich in ships which had flourished greatly in the European wars of 1689–1713.[49] It was from Bergen that previous Swedish attempts, under Charles XII's grandfather, to hold Trondhjem had been defeated. And Bergen had the inestimable advantage of being 'centrally' situated in Europe. With favourable winds a ship could reach the Netherlands in two days and two nights, the German coast in hardly more time, France, Portugal and Spain within the week. Command, however temporary, of Bergen would help Sweden's imports (particularly of salt) and would establish rapid communications with the south of Europe and with Alberoni if need be.

* See below, pp. 492–3.

† Charles told Schwerin of his intention to occupy all Norway south of Trondhjem: see below, p. 493.

That Bergen was less than two days from Scotland was also of some import-ance, since the element of frightening George I into 'sense' (from the Swedish point of view) was a significant factor in Charles XII's planning.

V

One task clearly allotted to the Jämtland army was to hold Norwegian forces in the north of the country lest they march down the broad eastern valleys to reinforce the Danish–Norwegian troops in the south and weaken the chances of success for the army Charles XII intended to march into southern Norway. This main army numbered thirty-six thousand combatants:* twenty-one thou-sand infantry and thirteen thousand cavalry. It had been divided into three groups. The largest, of fifty-nine squadrons of cavalry and twelve battalions of foot soldiers, collected at Strömstad. It was to be under the command of Frederick of Hesse, to whom the King in September 1718 confided his plan of campaign of three separate army groups, two of which should operate in the field while the third would tackle the Norwegian fortresses.[50] The second group, nearly equal in size to the first, which the King himself intended to command, gathered at Västra Ed in Dalsland and consisted of thirty-three squadrons of cavalry and twenty-two battalions of infantry. Charles was to join it at the last minute to preserve secrecy as to the direction of his first thrust. The third group, a much smaller one, consisting of cavalry and infantry in the proportion of ten squadrons to five battalions, was stationed in Värmland by the Holmedal magazine, under the command of Lieutenant-General von Albedyhl, but since the King later moved this force (a little over three thousand in all) into cooperation with sections of smaller groups strung out along the Värmland border, it seems likely that the Värmland postings were mainly intended to keep the Norwegian defenders guessing.[51]

The further plans, for stage two (the continental one) of the campaign, can be deduced only from indirect evidence: from the transport-ships gathered; from the masses of siege artillery already mentioned; from the high pro-portion of cavalry to infantry in the new army – cavalry which could not be deployed in Norway in its entirety; from equipment such as four-wheeled wagons unsuitable for Norwegian roads; from the posting of those sections of the army not taken along to Norway; from various plans discussed at head-quarters and among the King's political advisers as to the way the offensive would unfold and, perhaps most poignantly, from the words of the King at Frederiksten to General Schwerin:† 'In Germany there was once a thirty years war: it would be possible to carry on one that lasted forty years as long as we made peace with one enemy after the other and in the end got a tolerable and secure Peace.'[52]

An overriding concern and part of the King's planning for the offensive

---

* Forty thousand if those serving in transport are included.

† Schwerin reported these words, *inter alia*, in 1728 in response to a request from Frederick I on behalf of the Diet and the Chancery for material relating to Charles XII's last *dessein*.

as a whole was to fashion, out of an army that consisted of raw recruits as well as of veterans, which had non-Swedes as well as native-born Swedes, one which could measure up to that which in 1700 had moved to the continent of Europe, and, more important, could be expected when fighting in Germany to stand up against troops which had been seasoned in the War of the Spanish Succession under great commanders. In this sense the Norwegian campaign can be seen as a testing and training ground for the second stage.

Charles never tired of explaining to his officers that they are the ones who must build morale and encourage their troops by example to *gå-på*, to teach the soldiers not to show their natural fear of risking their lives. Two letters expressing his attitude are known. One, found as recently as 1938 in the Wrangel-archive near Wesenberg in Estonia, is dated just before the King's own offensive began, from Strömstad 16 October 1718 and is addressed to Lieutenant-General de la Barre, Armfelt's second-in-command for the Trondhjem venture, at a time when the King was disappointed with the Jämtland army* and alarmed at reports which reached him of bad discipline among officers and men. He impresses on de la Barre that a second-in-command is responsible nearly as much as the general in charge and that both of them must be active and ubiquitous: it is no good relying on the regimental officers and their written reports for it is 'those that command the army and not those that command the regiments who are responsible for carrying out the orders from headquarters'. He lists the ways in which the new regulations have not been followed and suggests means for improving arrangements for advance-guards, billeting and feeding of troops. The tone is sharp at times, with echoes of the King's lasting hatred of the 'Perevolotjna attitude': to retrieve the damage done by the weak opening of the campaign, Barre and Armfelt must carry on in the manner ordered and by the methods prescribed even if the result should be 'that not a man survives'; command must be exercised seriously and quietly, without entering into any *raisonnement* with those whose duty it is to obey and without taking account of or asking those who are allotted specific tasks whether they have courage or wish to tackle the job.[53]

The second letter is briefer and was written during the King's own offensive, on 20 November 1718, to Lieutenant-General Giertta, in charge of a cavalry detachment starting an allotted task in the offensive.† The King had no reason to be dissatisfied with Giertta whose men had so far done well and the letter was indeed only a repetition of oral orders this officer had received. But in a postscript Charles added: 'Our parties must be told to act in the old manner, to attack the enemy without pausing to reflect whether the enemy is stronger or weaker. They must break through with sword in hand.'[54] Giertta was an old drabant: he knew what 'the old manner' meant. It was Charles's hope that the new army would learn to adopt it as their own proud tradition.

* See below, p. 485.   † ibid., p. 483.

3

The Norwegian Campaign of 1718

The first stage in the operations against Norway had begun before the army of forty thousand started moving. The Jämtland corps had a timetable of its own.[1] Armfelt had been ordered to move on 4 August, but heavy rains made the roads difficult and he started eleven days late, on 15 August. In the south, command of the Idefjord was contested throughout the summer: and since Dynekilen fjord was closed by Sundsborg on the Swedish side and Frederikshald on the Norwegian side, the naval battles which this tussle entailed were fought with artillery and small vessels which had been laboriously transported overland* (in each case to avoid the enemy positions or fleets). The Norwegians hoped to cross to the Swedish side of the fjord and disturb the preparations for the invasion: the Swedes desired access to a network of roads leading to Kristiania.

Charles XII himself was present with the artillery, and from his stay in this neighbourhood and the many visits of inspection south to Strömstad in Bohuslän and north to Holmedal in Värmland, anecdotes have been gathered which tend to show him in the light of one who enjoyed the simple life and was keenly interested in ordinary folk. Similar stories abound on the Norwegian side from the 1716 as well as the 1718 campaign and are in part explicable by the similarity in temperament of the people on both sides of the border who had, of course, till the 1650s been fellow-Norwegians. Officers who accompanied Charles on inspections in Sweden in 1718 noted with astonishment, and even some distaste, how much he enjoyed visiting farms where he had stayed on previous occasions. He gossiped with an old woman as if she were a close friend, one of them noted; he remembered the names of all the children and spent an evening rocking the cradle of the new baby, happier than in the grandest company.[2] Acquaintances from earlier years were also well received. Surgeon Schultz, who had served with the Guards from 1703 till he was taken prisoner at Perevolotjna, had been freed from captivity through an exchange arranged by Charles XII, and called at Strömstad in 1718 to give thanks. '*Wir kännen Euch wieder*', was the King's first words to him, at which – so Schultz tells us in his memoirs – he lost all

---

* Svedborg had helped the Swedish transport by certain inventions of a technical nature.

memory of past troubles and became willing to follow His Majesty anew. He
made the Norwegian campaign as one of the King's doctors and may have
regaled him with curious tales from Russia, such as that rare clock he had
seen in Tsar Peter's palace in St Petersburg which could tell from what
quarter the wind came and how strong it was.[3]

Inscriptions on chairs and benches said to have been used by Charles XII
in 1716 and 1718, like the narrow wooden form from Östervallskog's parish
in Värmland ('K. Charles rested here for the night, 1716') now in the Swedish
Historical Museum, or the simple chair he is supposed to have used during
the siege of Frederiksten in 1718 and which is kept in the Norwegian Folk-
museum, may or may not express a literal truth, but the wooden painted
bowl which bears the legend 'Charles XII drank from this bowl at Halward's
in Klefmarken at Dal' is probably authentic since it belonged to a young
peasant who for his services as a messenger to and from Kristiania in 1716[*]
was rewarded with the farm of Klevemark in Värmland by the King. Inscriptions and anecdotes tell us something of the way in which the population on
both sides of the frontier interpreted one side of Charles's character: none
of the big-wigs' pride they detested and despised; well-mannered as peasant
tradition evaluated manners; frugal and self-disciplined; generous with others.
Such stories, like young Alstrin's comment in 1707,[†] put one in mind of the
fact that Charles's Vasa roots were not long pulled up from the land and
hint also of peasant tenacity and shrewdness imposed by long experience of
the vicissitudes of nature and fortune.

II

The battle for Idefjord remained so inconclusive during the summer that
Frederick IV could assume that he had nothing to fear till the winter. Then
Charles might repeat the pattern of the 1716 campaign, for in the border
country between Sweden and Norway the most favourable times of the
year for warfare were either the dry high summer (indeed the August that had
been 'promised' by Charles) or the late winter when lakes were frozen and
roads firm. The Danish King did not feel strong enough to take the offensive
against Sweden on his own. He had tried to arrange a concerted attack
with Tsar Peter and George I, whereby Peter would invade Sweden from
Finland while western Sweden would be opened up by a strong Dano-
Norwegian attack actively supported by George I's navy. Such plans, mooted
from the end of 1717 onwards, had come to nothing. George, busy in the
Mediterranean,[‡] could not spare a large fleet for the North in 1718. Tsar
Peter, cognisant of the fact that Charles's main army was collecting on

---

* The hazards involved are seen from the 'double-play' he had to engage in with the Norwegian
authorities: to get important letters through he permitted them to read and make extracts of the
less important ones.

† See above, p. 217.

‡ ibid., p. 460.

the Norwegian border, estimated the chances for an invasion from the east as good but decided against it to keep the Åland islands negotiations going.

The position of Frederick IV was further complicated by Sweden's splitting the coalition into an 'English' and a Russian side. His military experts generally regarded joint Dano-English–Russian cooperation at sea, and the addition of Hanoverian and Prussian land-forces to those of Denmark–Norway and Russia, as essential for a real defeat of Sweden, but political considerations demanded that the King make a provisional choice of main ally in case Charles XII succeeded in his quest for a separate peace with either Tsar Peter or George I. In August 1718, Frederick consulted twenty-eight of his foremost political and military advisers as to the best course to take, and chose George. The break-off from the Danish side at this time of tentative negotiations for a marriage between the Tsar's daughter Anna and the Danish crown-prince Christian (which had been initiated by Russia) is indicative both of the distrust which Frederick still felt of the Tsar and of his continued reliance on British naval help.[4]

It was of course hoped that the moment for a definitive choice might never come, but for the time being Frederick was in no state to launch an offensive. Plans for defence for Norway had been worked out in 1717, and when news arrived of Armfelt's crossing the frontier, these were put into effect. Reinforcements were sent both to Trondhjem and to eastern Norway, and by October Lützow, in command of all southern forces, had twenty-nine thousand men at his disposal, roughly half of which were tied down by garrison duties in fortified places. Lützow's task was not easy. The border was long, it was hard to assess just where the Swedish breakthrough (or breakthroughs) would come, and the scarcity of good roads as well as the configuration of the terrain prevented troops being moved speedily from one place to another. He divided his operational army into two corps; a larger one, under command of Lieutenant-General Count Sponeck, covered the Svinesund–Tistedal front and worked hard on land and sea on defence works intended to delay the Swedes if they approached from the south-east or east. The second corps, led by Major-General Gaffron, had for its main purpose the defence of Kristiania and was stationed to the north-east of the capital so as to intercept Swedes coming from the Värmland area.

Charles XII's strategy in 1718 has been judged exemplary by military historians.[5] His aim was as few losses in men as possible and, as usual when he started a campaign of movement, his first step was to manœuvre the enemy out of the best defended positions. By stringing his army-groups out on a long front, yet organizing them in such a way that they could easily be redeployed, he kept the enemy guessing. By concentration at Strömstad he engendered a conviction in Norway that this area was the most likely spot from which the offensive would be launched. The activity on the Idefjord during the summer may well have served a similar purpose, being a feint rather than a serious attempt to break through.* What Charles achieved by starting the offensive from Dalsland in the night between 29–30 October with his own group, inferior in numbers to the Strömstad one, while asking Frederick of Hesse and Field-Marshal Mörner to hold their horses, was to make the enemy defence works untenable within a few days. With Charles on the eastern side of the Idefjord the Norwegians scuttled their vessels on the fjord on 1 November, the same day that Charles with an advance guard of nine hundred troops took up his headquarters on the Tistedal river. Their route had gone via Fossanebru on the border over Berby and Præstebakke to the flat plateau known as Ideslætten. They had met hardly any resistance: the soldiers posted to protect the pass leading down to Ideslætten had retired to Frederiksten as soon as they were attacked by the Polish cavalry, whose strange 'Kalmuck' cries they found bloodcurdling.[6] The rest of the King's group, joining him from Hallerød, had not found much opposition either but had been kept busy repairing bridges and cutting down wooden barricades.

On 5 November Sponeck accepted the consequences of Charles's strategic success. He abandoned the Svinesund–Tistedal line, fearing encirclement if he stayed east of Glommen since he heard that the Swedes were moving also from Värmland. Sponeck was much criticized by Lützow for this decision, and some historians have agreed that he should have accepted battle on the Tistedal river. He was, they have pointed out, deceived by exaggerated rumours as to the size of the Värmland corps and misinformed as to the direction of its march-route. But modern authorities hold that Sponeck made the right choice: to risk battle against a superior enemy was not justified in the circumstances and his plan – to reform west of Glommen, trusting that the Swedes would be held up and weakened by a prolonged siege of Frederiksten – was sensible enough.[7]

III

Sponeck's withdrawal west of Glommen opened the road for the Strömstad group to move forward without serious opposition. There were those who had argued (e.g. Maigret in a letter to Görtz in April 1718) that it would not be too expensive in men to cross Svinesund supported by the guns of Sundsborg fort,[8] but thanks to the strategy actually employed bridges could now be constructed which permitted Frederick of Hesse's forces to cross in complete safety to the Frederikshald side of the fjord. The Prince made his headquarters at Torpum, where Charles had stayed in 1716.

An enemy stand could be expected west of Glommen, and we know from Norwegian sources that Sponeck's troops were strung out along its western bank, from Frederikstad in the south to Næs in the north with orders to shorten the line as soon as the river froze to the stretch between Onstadsund

---

* Haintz holds, however, that it was Charles's lack of success on Idefjord which postponed the campaign from August to the end of October.

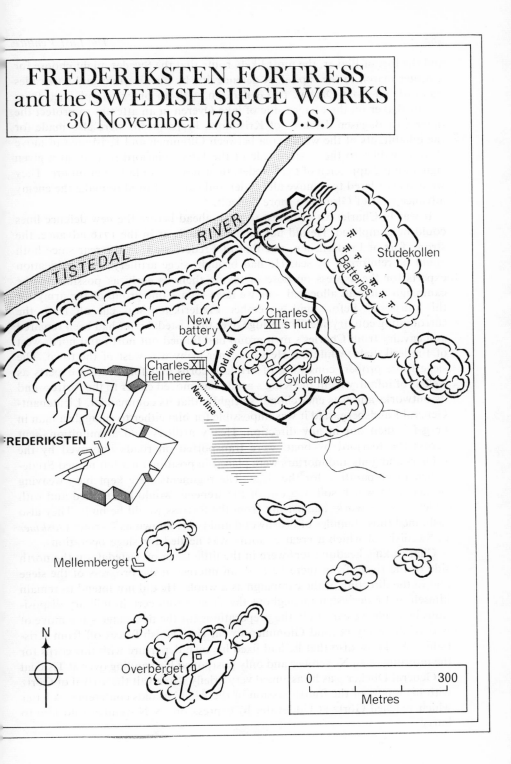

FREDERIKSTEN FORTRESS
and the SWEDISH SIEGE WORKS
30 November 1718 (O.S.)

TISTEDAL RIVER

Studekollen

Batteries

New battery

Charles XII's hut

Charles XII fell here

Old line

New line

Gyldenløve

FREDERIKSTEN

Mellemberget

Overberget

N

0   300

Metres

and the fort of Blaker, the most likely route that the Swedes might choose for a winter march to the capital. A defence line by fortifications and barricades was ordered from Drøbak to Gjelleråsen, with an outer one planned from Fet to Blaker on the eastern side of lake Øyeren in an attempt to protect the innermost Bagåsen defences of Kristiania. Preparations were also made for the inhabitants of the whole area between Glommen and Kristiania to move their valuables to the western side of the Kristianiafjord so that, at a given signal on the approach of the Swedes, their houses could be put on fire. They were also ordered to remove all fodder and stores of food to make the enemy advance west of Glommen more difficult.

It was in Charles XII's interest to push ahead before the new defence lines could be completed. He did not intend to leave, as in the 1716 advance, the strong fort of Frederiksten, nor that of Frederikstad, in the rear since both could be reinforced by sea. He had brought siege artillery and fortification experts for the express purpose of taking them as early as possible in the campaign and had allocated – as we have seen – one group of the army for this purpose.[9] Before mid-November Frederiksten was cut off from the surrounding countryside. The bridge over the Tistedal river had been repaired and cavalry from Charles's own group had fanned out north and north-west of Frederikshald, while the Hesse-Mörner army was west of the town. The siege force proper, consisting of artillery corps and fortification experts as well as of infantry from the King's army, had moved closer to the fortress and its outworks and was encircling it so tightly that its commander, Lieutenant-General Landsberg, said it was impossible for him either to smuggle a man in or get a man out in any direction. Heavy artillery and ammunition, sent across the Idefjord by boat, were transported on roads improved by the soldiers and guns and mortars were placed in position on a hill named Stude-kollen in preparation for the siege. The regiments were kept busy weaving baskets into which soil dug out of the trenches would be emptied and with which defence works against fire from the fortress would be built. They also fashioned those bundles of brushwood and twigs known as fascines (*faskiner* in Swedish) of which a great quantity was needed for siege operations.

Charles XII's headquarters were in the little town of Tistedal, on the north side of the river; from there he took an interest in the progress of the siege and in the directing of the campaign as a whole. He did not intend to remain himself at Frederiksten throughout the siege. From certain military dispositions he made we can study the preparations for the next stage – the move of part of the army beyond Glommen to cut the Danish forces off from Kristiania. We know also that he had fixed his own departure with this corps for the morning of 29 November and only postponed his handing over at Tistedal to General Dücker – as he assumed very briefly – to await the arrival of Görtz with his report of the fourth session of the Åland islands conference. A letter which reached Görtz at Uddevalla by express on 28 November told him to hurry.

To prepare the advance west of Glommen Charles used the Värmland corps which, on its first entry into Norway had found its allotted task of clearing the enemy from the fortified places and passes along the border an easy one: there had hardly been any opponents to chase away since Sponeck had ordered evacuation all along the line. The corps was next ordered to rid the whole of the middle eastern section of Glommen, with lake Øyeren, of enemy troops, to get what supplies it could and begin milling grain and baking bread in preparation for advance, and to move the clergy to the western side of Glommen lest they should become leaders of peasant resistance to the occupation.[10] The only fort east of Glommen which by mid-November still held an enemy garrison was Blaker. Its commander refused to capitulate and, as we now know, it was at this fort that the Dano-Norwegian defence hoped to anchor one end of its outer defence line to cover Kristiania. The fort was, however, a weak one and it was assumed that it would soon surrender unless reinforced with cannon. To prevent this one of the Värmland corps commanders,* Leutrum, stationed some five thousand men around it, while another, Giertta, with his cavalry occupied those places at which Glommen could be crossed. The activities of the Värmland corps – the 'third' army if one reckons the King's as one and the Hesse–Mörner one as another – served a two-fold purpose: it safeguarded the quarters of the other two armies and it widened the area known to be cleared of enemy troops much further north. It was also allocated a place in Charles XII's plan for the next stage of the operations, in that his orders to Leutrum to attack Blaker fort 'sword in hand' were timed† to synchronize with the start of the 29 November venture and would therefore free both Leutrum and Giertta with their respective corps for participation in the move across Glommen.

The officer chosen to lead the new venture was Colonel Stenflycht. He had been taken prisoner at Stralsund, but had escaped to Poland and worked with the anti-Augustan forces there. On the pacification of the Polish civil war in 1717,‡ he made his way to Sweden. Charles sent for him on 14 November 1718 and asked him to reconnoitre west of Glommen with a small cavalry force of Swedes and Poles, about a hundred in all, and report back with information as to how best to cut the enemy army off from the capital: he was to keep his trip absolutely secret. Stenflycht reported back on 26 November to Charles in the approaches. The next move was then fixed for the 29th in the morning: Stenflycht – again with the utmost secrecy as to the purpose of the operation – was to get a corps of about a thousand officers and troopers ready and Charles would join them as a volunteer. 'We did not get hold of the Danes this side of the river', Stenflycht reports Charles as saying,[11] implying that it would be necessary to come to grips with the enemy army on the western side. Whether Charles intended to surprise Kristiania once more,

---

* For the recall of General Albedyhl, originally in command of the Värmland corps, see below p. 486.

† This was effected on 1 December.

‡ See above, p. 423.

as in 1716, and then, with his superior numbers marching across Glommen in strength, challenge Lützow to battle cannot be deduced with certainty from Colonel Stenflycht's report, though it seems the likely deduction to make. What is certain is that the next stage of the operations was planned to take place on the western side of Glommen and that the King was to be a member of Stenflycht's party.

The deduction of active campaigning as contrasted with reconnaissance work for this new stage of the offensive is strengthened by the fact that Charles arranged to take holy communion in the evening before his scheduled departure with Stenflycht. The tradition in Sweden, as in the other Scandinavian countries, was not one of frequent communion: participation in it was regarded as particularly solemn and important for the religious life of the individual or strongly linked to the great commemorative feasts of the Church. That Charles roughly followed this pattern during the 'peaceful' years at Lund is clear from the notes which Rhyzelius (who had become the King's *biktfader* in succession to Nordberg in October 1717) made of the times when he prepared the King for communion by confession and administered the sacrament to him: four in all.* But it was also military tradition, established long before Charles's own time, and faithfully followed by his father, to be confessed and take holy communion before the opening of the campaigns or when battle was expected.

It is significant that when Charles XII postponed the operation for a few days he also postponed the communion. The reason he on 26 November gave Rhyzelius, whom Feif had called to headquarters on his behalf, was that there was 'too much of a racket just now' and both the King and Cronstedt (when Rhyzelius asked him to intercede with Charles)† intimated that the King had not yet had an opportunity to prepare himself properly for the solemn occasion.[12] One is entitled to suggest, it seems to me, that the King wanted to postpone confession till after his talks with Görtz. We know from Rhyzelius himself that he always took the opportunity of Charles XII's confession to probe the King's conscience on his attitude to war and peace and that theological and political 'disputation' sometimes were part of the preparation the chaplain felt that the King ought to submit to before communion. In the busy army life such preliminaries could no doubt be cut short by Charles XII, and the preparation the King hinted at for himself was probably peace of mind. This he could hardly have until he had evaluated the diplomatic situation in the light of Görtz's news and given the necessary orders for the next stage of the diplomatic offensive. He would want to confess and ask God's forgiveness for mistakes made after Görtz's visit, not before. Then he would be ready for Rhyzelius's offices and the next stage of the military campaign.

* On 14 June and 1 November 1717, on 10 March and 10 June 1718.
† Rhyzelius received Feif's letter on the 24th; he reported to the King in the morning of the 25th and was told 'to wait till tomorrow'. In the evening of the 25th he went to the siege-works in the hope of speaking once more to Charles but found him too busy and saw Cronstedt instead: when he returned in the early morning of the 26th the communion was postponed.

IV

Although the offensive had opened so well and the strategical success had been such a striking one, Charles XII had worries. The most serious one concerned the Jämtland army. Armfelt and his 7,500* men had manœuvred well against a force under Budde which was not greatly inferior in numbers, but, within sight of Trondhjem, he had run into serious difficulties of supply. The weather was bad, food brought along had been consumed and it was not easy to get stores from the magazines in Jämtland moved across the mountains. Some regiments were less well fitted out than regulations decreed: boots and socks became worn and morale suffered as sickness began to spread. In the circumstances the quick success against Trondhjem which Charles had hoped for was out of the question and Armfelt retraced his steps somewhat to get safer contact with his base.

A German officer, Marcks von Württemberg, was sent to report on the situation to the King in late September and reached Strömstad at midnight one (unspecified) October evening. He was immediately admitted to the King's room and – as he later recalled[13] – was questioned behind locked doors for seven hours about the northern campaign. It would seem that Charles received an exaggerated idea of the lack of discipline in Armfelt's army and conceived a fear that the general planned a retreat to Jämtland. Whether this was due to his own misconstruction of what Marcks had to say, or whether Marcks (who in his 1728 report recalls that 'I mentioned our muddles') misjudged the situation due to lack of familiarity with the terrain so far north or with Swedish and Finnish temperament is difficult to say† – probably a bit of both came into play. Next morning he was sent straight back to Armfelt to tell him that retreat to Jämtland was absolutely forbidden and that the attack on Trondhjem and its two forts, Kristiansten and Munkholmen, must be attempted 'if at all possible'. Speed was urged on Marcks and indeed he covered the distance, which he estimated at one hundred (continental) miles, in ten days.

The King's sharp reaction in the letter he wrote to de la Barre on 16 October has been cited above‡ and is indicative, possibly, of some tension in himself on the eve of the military offensive and, more certainly, of the important role which the Trondhjem campaign played in the strategic planning of his offensive. That the rocket was, in large measure, undeserved is clear now the difficulties with which the Jämtland army had to cope have been investigated. In the circumstances it says much for the loyalty and devotion to duty of both Armfelt and de la Barre that they seem to have accepted it in good part. They were both experienced soldiers, toughened in the fighting in Finland, and showed great tenacity and courage in attempting to carry out

---

* This was the number of combatants; with non-fighting men his army counted nine thousand.
† He had, however, served for ten years with the army in Finland.
‡ See above, p. 476.

the orders Marcks brought them. The problem of supply was largely overcome and Armfelt marched on Trondhjem once more while de la Barre and his cavalry patrolled in terrible weather to seal off the invasion area. The bravery and skill of the Jämtland army have been praised by Norwegian and Swedish historians alike.[14] But the fact remained, and weighed heavily on the King, that the surprise on Trondhjem had failed and that the outcome of the venture would remain in doubt since the Norwegians had been given time to plan their defence.

In the event, several warships reached Trondhjem from the south before Armfelt came within sight of the town on 4 November and several battalions of troops succeeded in getting through Østerdal and Gudbrandsdal during his temporary absence so that the defenders became superior in numbers to Armfelt's army. The general did not feel able to attack in these circumstances. He based his further plans on Charles XII's 'if possible', encamped south of the Nida river, and waited for the roads to become hard enough to permit transport of heavy artillery from Jämtland that he might begin a regular siege of the town. He was still there when, at the end of December, news reached him of Charles's death with orders from the Prince of Hesse that he withdraw his army to Sweden.*

Another officer who attracted at least implied disapproval from Charles XII was Albedyhl, the original commander of the largest group in the Värmland corps. His lack of initiative in the early stages of the campaign was noted and in mid-November he was ordered to let his men join those already under Major-General Leutrum's command while he himself reported to headquarters. It is not known whether he was reprimanded by the King, but the demoting implied must have been obvious and humiliating: the obverse of the ruling whereby Charles rewarded exceptional services in the field by promotion to encourage officer initiative and responsibility.

The morale of the soldiers in the new army preoccupied Charles during the siege of Frederiksten. It was not an ideal time of the year for campaign. The weather was bad, and many of the troops were raw and unused to rough living conditions in tents and home-made huts. A period of quiet, before battle proper is joined, is always difficult for those in command and Charles's participation in the siege operations was, as Rehnskiöld and Mörner intimated in their letter to the Council in Stockholm after the King had been killed, in part explicable by his desire to get the war moving. 'Night and day', they wrote, 'in rain and cold, His Majesty insisted on being present in the approaches, so that everything might run that more smoothly and work proceed at greatest speed.'[15]

That the King was driven also by some need of his own seems indicated by the rest of their sentence: 'although we with constant and humble prayers

---

* Various circumstances – the late arrival of the news; dispositions made in anticipation of a prolonged stay which now forced the retreat along a difficult unsupplied route; terrible weather conditions with forty-eight hours intense cold at a time when the troops marched over high mountains – all combined to make the withdrawal a catastrophe. Two-thirds of the force perished.

begged him to desist'. Such restless absorption with the work in hand cannot be fully explained by Charles's own answer to those of his generals who (in less solemn terms than those employed in the letter written after his death) asked him to rest and offered to relieve him and be as eagle-eyed in their attention to duty as he himself could be: 'I am younger than you; I can stick the work.' There must have been some inner turmoil he wanted to quell, but its nature can only be guessed at and the guesses made are probably more indicative of the guesser's temperament than of Charles's. For those who felt the immediate shock of his death, every action or glance they remembered from the King's last days seemed pregnant with meaning. He had seemed sad and preoccupied, he had burnt papers and had such an odd expression when he did so. He had looked back in a special way when he left headquarters in the afternoon of 30 November and the way he had swung his hat, twice, in greeting to the generals who saw him off seemed a salute of farewell. Several officers had premonitions of Charles XII's death and one said – or at least it was firmly believed that he did so – to those close to him as the King rode off: 'Whoever wants to see the King alive, look his fill now – we shan't see him again.'[16]

Historians have built, as they must, on the material available. Was Charles seeking death and did he burn papers which he wanted no one to study? The prosaic truth is that he burnt, according to his invariable custom, another screed from the clergyman* who regularly sent him unbidden reports of intrigues and plots.[17] Did Charles have a premonition of his own death? Does not the fact that he put on a new uniform on the Sunday afternoon before going to the trenches once more prove either one or the other of these hypotheses?[18] The prosaic truth is that Charles, according to his valet, put on a new uniform every fortnight[19] and though it probably was not 'new' in the literal sense every time, it frequently was so since the King was hard on his clothes during campaigns. Sometimes when the going was tough, circumstances forced him to look slovenly. We know that he was tattered and dirty and even looked unappetizing in his rough campaign of 1716, from the laconic comment of a Norwegian clergyman who noticed that the royal nose was dripping and there was at least one hole in his uniform – made by Kruse.[20] But this was not an attitude to his uniform and to the example which his uniform ought to be for his men that he adopted by choice.

The idea of a premonition or a voluntary seeking of death implied in the 'new uniform' is further weakened by the fact that Charles put it on, not in the afternoon before riding away to his death, but in the morning of 30 November before he went to service for the first Sunday in Advent. He had spent the six days between 24 and 30 November in the siege-works, and the better part of the five nights as well: during his brief rests in the hut made for him in those works he had hardly bothered to undress. It is not strange therefore that he acquiesced when Neumann suggested clean clothes before

* See above, pp. 17–18, 471, 487.

the sermon and even asked for 'a completely new set'.[21] The jacket and breeches, boots and spurs, gloves and linen which can still be seen in *Livrustkammaren* in Stockholm was then brought him.

My own guess at the reason for the King's driving himself hard and for that preoccupation which was noted by too many independent witnesses to deserve light dismissal, is as fallible as other deductions and as liable to stricture of the kind I have indicated. But I have felt bound to attempt some deductions and have made three which seem reasonable to me in the light of the evidence of the events of 24–30 November 1718 seen against the background of the King's career and character.

One is the way in which Charles XII wanted to use the opportunity of the siege,* particularly after the troops digging the trenches had come under fire from Frederiksten fort, to inculcate the spirit which he wanted to become characteristic of the new army: disregard for personal danger when duty bids. If the King was seen to do so, it would be easier for others to follow his example.

The second is that the King, having castigated de la Barre so strongly, wanted (since he had to work across the grain of his inclinations in such reprimands) to prove, if only to himself, that he did not ask more of his fellow-commanders than he did of his own body and brain; that in being ever-present and ever-watchful at the siege for as long as he remained at Frederiksten, he was following the precepts he had laid down for de la Barre: the responsibility rests with he who commands the whole army, there is no excuse for him slacking in the slightest.

Finally, it seems to me, that Charles XII was in some measure drugging himself with ceaseless activity at a time when he did not want to ponder too deeply the risks involved in the military offensive. He had weighed the chances and was basically optimistic about the outcome, but he must have known that the army he was attempting to mould was the last one Sweden had to offer to fight for its just cause. The last throw of the dice of war, under God, was about to begin and the period of waiting was nerve-racking.

V

The officer in charge of the technical part of the siege-works was the Frenchman Maigret, trained under Vauban, and the general in charge of the troops employed was von Schwerin. The garrison of Frederiksten was not large, only some 1,400 men, but the fortress was well constructed and maintained and protected by three outworks – Mellemberget (also called Stortaarnet after its great tower) and Overberget to the south-east and Gyldenløve to the east.† The Swedish siege-works were planned so as to facilitate the eventual

* Conversations with the late General Petri, whose knowledge of the history of the Swedish Caroline army was unrivalled, put me on the road to this deduction.
† See plan, p. 481.

storming of the fortress, and as the northern aspects of it offered some advantages (particularly that of natural shelter below the brow of a hill for infantry collecting for attack) the approaches and trenches were directed in in the first place towards Gyldenløve.

The batteries placed on Studekollen gave some protection against the minor fire-power of Gyldenløve, while the outwork itself and the configuration of the terrain rendered the early stages of the siege relatively risk-free. With the approaches completed, the first trench proper was opened in the night of 24 November. From combined Swedish and Norwegian sources (such as Landsberg's report to Frederick IV and the journal of the Frederikshald magistrate sent to the Kristiania authorities),[22] we know that the main digging took place at night with improvements to the breastworks during daylight hours. Relatively few soldiers could be employed in digging at any one time, two to four hundred were used for each shift, and digging parties were arranged on a rota basis drawn from different regiments to spread the risk, and probably also to create nuclei of soldiers who had survived a dangerous assignment in as many regiments as possible. In the first night a distance of 861 steps* was achieved; in the second ninety; in the third sixty-six. On the following day, 27 November, Gyldenløve (with its garrison of thirty men) was easily taken, the King being among the first of the two hundred grenadiers to climb the storm-ladders. After that day he used a small hut behind Gyldenløve as a substitute for his rooms at Tistedal, had his meals brought there by his servant, and rested there off and on.[23]

The trench works now proceeded in a half-circle round Gyldenløve before straightening out parallel with the fortress and casualties, which had been very light – amounting to twenty-seven only for the first four nights – began to rise. This was due to the soldiers coming within range of the guns of Frederiksten and even, as they approached closer,† to musket-fire from its walls. They were also exposed to fire from Mellemberget and Overberget: in the words of the Frederikshald journal 'we offered them the sweetmeats of our Cartouches and Mortars'. The cannonade and bombardment was 'continuous', according to the same source throughout the day,[24] and at night 'lightbombs' were used and Landsberg fixed flares‡ on the walls of the fortress to illuminate the Swedish trenches and those who worked in them. In the fifth night fifty-five men were killed or wounded, while in the sixth the losses were thirty: a reduction possibly due to the *'faux attaque'* which we know was in progress on 30 November when fifty men were positioned on a protected place to make a deliberate noise with spades and stones in order to draw fire away from the trenches.[25]

Such losses, though bad for morale among the diggers, were in themselves insignificant; and the siege was progressing rapidly and successfully. By the

* The Swedish military 'step' was at the time equivalent to 75 centimetres (as against the present one of 80 centimetres).
† In the fourth night two hundred steps progress was made, in the fifth 180, in the sixth 210.
‡ These were made by igniting 'wreaths of tar' fixed to long poles.

morning of 30 November the trench parallel with Gyldenløve, the so-called
'old line', had been completed, as well as the communication-trench to the
projected next parallel, the 'new line', work on which was due to start in the
evening of 30 November. A road, which would serve for the removal of some
of the artillery from Studekollen to a spot in front of Gyldenløve, was very
close to completion and 30 November had been given as the date for this
move.

The projected 'new line' was but 250 steps from the counterscarp of the
fortress and sapping proper would be the next stage of the operations. Maigret
assured Charles XII on 30 November that the fortress would fall within the
week, and Landsberg's report makes it clear that he did not expect to hold
out much longer.[26] The optimism of the one and the pessimism of the other
were based on the same premises: the very situation of Frederiksten made
it an easy target for the heavy Swedish artillery. The fort was on the top of a
steep bluff rising above the town of Frederikshald. It presented to a would-be
attacker a formidable front of high walls and cunningly contrived counterscarp, but the very height of these walls, insufficiently anchored on hard cliff
foundations, could not for any length of time withstand Cronstedt's bombardment, Maigret's skill in the use of parallel trenches with their scientifically
worked out angles, and the Swedish great superiority in numbers. Cronstedt's
artillery park on Studekollen had eighteen big cannon (six of them were
howitzers for 36-pound balls and six mortars for 75-pounders). When these
were moved from Studekollen into their new positions, the outcome of the
siege was only a matter of time.

The thin layer of soil on the bluff meant that instead of digging deep
trenches into the earth, the Swedes had to build upwards from shallow
trenches with baskets filled with earth (*skanskorgar*, literally 'fortification-
baskets') and fascines. Even where the soil was deepest, in front of Gyldenløve,
a depth of half a metre was the norm. Since the height of the breastwork
towards the enemy was fixed at one and a half metres above the normal level
of the top-soil, and since the breastwork itself had to be very thick at its
base to afford protection against enemy fire, enormous quantities of fascines
and fortification-baskets were needed. Some three thousand of the former
and six hundred of the latter were used each day of the siege, but with the
amount of the soldiers available for their manufacture, collection and
distribution this created no problem for the attackers.

The one danger envisaged was a break-out by the enemy garrison which
would bring the Swedes unnecessary losses, and strong detachments were
held in readiness after 28 November to meet such a contingency. The need to
cut losses, for the sake of morale, in the digging parties was also appreciated.
The 'new line' which was to be started in the evening of 30 November would
give the diggers – and the sappers who would soon start their part of the siege
operation – greater protection from Overberget and Mellemberget than the
'old line' and Charles was therefore impatient to see it completed. The

lieutenant in charge of the work in the late afternoon of 30 November noted that the King, on arrival at the siege-works, was impatient for the men to begin digging: Why are they dawdling? he asked, even before 6 o'clock, the agreed time, had come.*

Later that evening, some time after 9 o'clock, Charles xii was watching from the 'old line' trench, with his heels dug into the earthen part of the breastwork. His arms, on top of the parapet, took most of his weight; one elbow was crooked to give support for his head. Kaulbars, his adjutant, and Maigret were standing below, their heads roughly level with the King's boots. Other officers were close by in the trench, among them General Schwerin, forming a 'royal party' of some nine or ten in all. The King had insisted, against advice, on climbing into a position which the others declared dangerous since it exposed his head and shoulders above the breastwork. He told them he wanted to 'observe the situation'. They assumed he wished to look at the fortress for signs of any break-out as well as taking a peep from above at the work on the 'new line', but became uneasy when he stayed aloft longer than was needed for a rapid survey of the situation. It seems inescapable, therefore, that Charles had yet another motive for putting himself in the exposed position. It does not seem likely that he was seeking death as has sometimes been averred. Probably he wanted to advertise his presence to the digging party and to strengthen their courage by taking risks equal to theirs: the 'old line' was more exposed to flank-fire than the 'new', but they were under direct fire from the fortress.

The officers asked the King to climb down. '*Var inte rädd*',[27] they heard him answer, an exhortation not to be afraid which – since we do not know the intonation of the phrase – has for us an element of ambiguity which it cannot have had at the time. For *rädd* can have a touch of 'frightened' or 'cowardly' according to the tone of voice in which it is uttered. Though the whole phrase can also sound half apologetic, in excuse of foolhardiness, implying no more than the 'do not worry about me' of routine response to routine requests, on the other hand the three words can be given a strong message of reassurance by a small difference in inflection. But none of those who were in the trench give us in their reports any indication of how they interpreted the words which are the last recorded ones from Charles xii, though Kaulbars noted that the King was in 'a good mood' and talked of this and that as he looked over the top of the trench. A few minutes later the King was dead – shot through his head from temple to temple – and with his death the Norwegian campaign was abandoned.†

VI

The outcome of the campaign, as of the whole military offensive, had Charles xii lived, is impossible to conjecture. The Norwegian defence authorities

* See below, p. 501.
† For the reasons for this, and for the continuation of the war in the east, see below, pp. 511–13.

estimated that he would have met difficulties as he progressed beyond Glommen, but the arguments they use relate to peasant guerrilla warfare and the difficulties of climate, terrain and supply without evaluation of the respective strengths of soldiers and artillery. [28] Charles himself* was optimistic about his chances. During the diplomatic offensive he stressed to his advisers that he need not make sacrifices in Swedish territory lightly: he could cope with Hanover and Saxony alone and even with Denmark–Norway at a time of the year when George I's fleet was not supporting Frederick IV. Swedish diplomats and high officers, who based their assessments on talks either with the King or with persons close to him, reckoned with a successful Norwegian campaign in 1718 and a crossing in 1719 to Jutland, simultaneous with attacks on Zealand and landings in Germany. With Norway held, and George to some extent intimidated by threats of help for the Jacobites, Denmark could be knocked out of the war and Bremen and Verden could be reconquered. Some thought that Hanover would be put under contribution as Saxony had been in 1706–7, and it was generally held that sixteen thousand Hessians would join Charles's fifty thousand for the third stage of the offensive against Sweden's remaining enemies in the Empire, Prussia and Saxony. Stanislaus might even become King of Poland in reality as well as name once more, and Tsar Peter would in any case be forced to moderate his claims. [30]

Charles's military dispositions certainly fit in well with such speculations. He had given orders for both the Karlskrona and Gothenburg fleets to be ready to move in the spring of 1719 as soon as there was no ice in the sea, to give him, as Charles put it, 'the advantage' of the Danes. [31] Transport-ships had been collected in Bohuslän as well as in other ports along the Swedish coast. The voyage from the Swedish west coast to Jutland could be done within six to eight hours in good weather conditions and in Jutland few Danish troops were stationed. From Jutland the road was open into Germany by land. Danish documents show that Frederick IV did not expect an attack on Denmark, either on Jutland or the islands, early in 1719. He counted on Charles XII's army weakening itself so much by the winter campaign in Norway that he himself could risk – with George I's help – an invasion of Scania and Bohuslän to attack the Swedes in the rear. [32] The element of surprise, so essential for the post-Norway stage of the military offensive, was therefore present, and contingency planning was complete from the Swedish side also for stages beyond knocking Frederick IV out of the war.

Conversations which Charles XII had with Schwerin and also with Rehnskiöld when the field-marshal, now sixty-eight years old, joined him before Frederiksten, reinforce the impression left by the military dispositions for 1719. The field-marshal was not, as has been sometimes suggested,† a broken man after his years as a prisoner-of-war in Russia: his military

---

* Görtz, in a letter to a friend, expressed himself '*théologiquement, politiquement et mathématiquement*' sure of the outcome – if only the King would not take risks with his own life. [29]

† E.g. in F.S.Bengtsson, *The Life of Charles XII*, p. 473.

Charles XII in 1717, from a painting by D. von Krafft

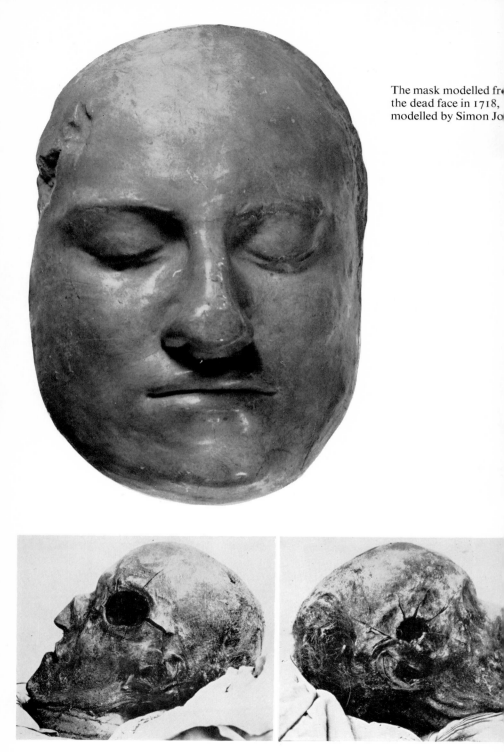

The wound in the left temple; and in the right temple. Copies of photographs taken at the opening Charles XII's coffin in 1917

service in Bohuslän in 1719 is proof to the contrary. Charles had obviously longed to have him back, to have someone from 'the old days' who could share responsibility with him in the new offensive. We know nothing about the personal side of their reunion, though we know that Rehnskiöld arrived on 21 or 22 November and that at least once, on 28 November, he had 'a long talk' with Charles in the approaches.[33] The only direct information we possess of the subjects they discussed is that immediately after seeing Rehnskiöld the King told Schwerin that he did not expect the Åland islands conference to succeed at this stage: clearly Sweden's relations with Russia must have been debated between the field-marshal, so recently a prisoner with the Tsar, and the King.[34]

Whether Charles was open with Rehnskiöld about a possible descent on Scotland we do not know. Schwerin had the impression that such a descent would be made if the Trondhjem venture succeeded:* the Swedish troopers sent would take their saddles and reins but no horses, the Poles would bring their own mounts.

A guerrilla venture to test what element of Jacobite opposition remained in Scotland, or cooperation with Alberoni in the Spanish projected invasion of George I's dominions, may have formed the background for this project. We know, however, that Charles had not committed himself in any way to Alberoni, and it seems more likely that he planned a feint to tie British naval forces to local coasts in expectation of a full-scale Swedish invasion at the time when Charles planned his own invasion of Denmark or Germany. Rehnskiöld must have been told – as was Schwerin – that Charles did not intend to keep Norway though he wanted to move the Swedish frontier to Glommen, 'the natural frontier' as he termed it. In the meantime, however, he planned to conquer the whole of Norway south of and including Trondhjem to have something to bargain with at the peace-making. The attack on Denmark would follow early in 1719: its purpose was to force Frederick IV out of the war and to retrieve Stralsund and Rügen for Sweden as well as the lost lands of the Duke of Holstein-Gottorp.

Within the context of this projected stage two of the military offensive the King's intentions at the end of 1718 are more pacific in tone than the general speculations on peace-terms thrown out in the diplomatic correspondence.'† These had been 'inspired', in the sense that only the firmest of fronts could be publicly shown lest the enemy demands stiffen: we are entitled to accept the more realistic appraisal of what Sweden could and could not do which Charles XII showed in his conversations with Schwerin as the truest version of his plans. Tsar Peter's staunch support of Frederick William I during the Åland island conference and his unwillingness to sacrifice Frederick IV seem to have influenced the King. Sacrifices – even without equivalents – must, he argued, be made to Prussia to diminish the number of enemies in east Germany: he declared himself willing to follow French advice and buy

---

* See above, p. 474. † ibid., pp. 451 ff.

R

Prussia out of the war by ceding Frederick William part of Pomerania with Stettin. Saxony was now less dangerous an enemy and he hoped to see Stanislaus restored in Poland. The talks with Russia would be continued but he did not intend to leave Sweden unprotected and thus tempt Tsar Peter into attacking her. A strong force under Liewen would be left in Sweden when the main army went to the Continent and to prevent the Tsar coming to Frederick IV's help he intended to send some regiments from Norway in the early spring of 1719 'to act against Russia'.*

The King's reference to a long war 'in Germany', cited above,† is ambiguous in so far that it is not explicit against what powers the war was to be fought. Did Charles think of a struggle with the Emperor along Frederick of Hesse's lines? There were rumours among officers and officials that the King might become the protector of North Germany and its Protestants in a manner reminiscent of Gustavus Adolphus's plans for a division of 'imperial' power between the Habsburgs and Sweden or at least for an alternation of Catholic and Protestant emperors.[35] There was also talk among diplomats that Charles, once he brought his new army to the Continent, might ask compensation from those powers, including the Habsburg state, which had not kept their promises and guarantees of 1706 and 1707.[36]

But such speculations would seem to derive from that 'vested interest' in a western theatre of war which was so noticeable before the Russian campaign. The King's thoughts in 1718 circled, as Schwerin's letter shows, round the objective of getting peace with Sweden's declared enemies in Germany. Nothing is said in the report about Russia – possibly because Schwerin at the time of writing in 1728 was in Russian service and therefore chose to be particularly discreet on this aspect of the King's plans – but Charles must have visualized that peace in Germany would enable him to exert at least a back-door pressure on Tsar Peter and thus achieve better terms at the peace-making. The King may have been half-jocular, half-serious, as in so many of his remarks, when he spoke about a possible 'forty years war' in the Empire; but there is no doubt about the seriousness of his final words to Schwerin on the subject of the tolerable and secure peace he hoped to achieve piecemeal: 'for it would be much more harmful to Sweden to agree to a hard and insecure general peace than to accept a long war conducted outside the frontiers of Sweden proper.'[37]

---

* This somewhat enigmatic expression, taken in conjunction with the 'some regiments', makes it clear that a full-scale offensive was not planned; possibly an attempt to reconquer Finland or to stay Russian operations by feints was contemplated.

† See p. 475.

4

The King's Death: Murder or an 'Honest Enemy Bullet'?

One of Charles's last pleasures must have been to have Rehnskiöld at headquarters and his generals and male relations around him in the late morning and early afternoon of 30 November: to go to service together, to eat together, to talk of this and that. The distance between the King's headquarters at Tistedal and those of the Hesse-Mörner army at Torpum was no more than three-quarters of a mile and visits were not difficult. We know that for this Sunday many had come to Tistedal from Torpum and some had stayed the Saturday night: possibly a reunion in Rehnskiöld's honour and the same time an opportunity for Charles XII to brief the Torpum group on his future plans. Mörner, at least, was staying at Tistedal for we hear that Charles, when he got in from the trenches, went to Mörner's room* and finding him abed walked up and down talking to him while the general dressed.[1] And since Charles Frederick of Holstein-Gottorp did not return to Torpum in the late afternoon of 30 November it seems as if he was on some extended stay, possibly to be at hand to greet Görtz or even to be taken along on the Stenflycht venture and be trained by Charles in the art of war as once Max of Württemberg had been.

The King, we are told, had noticed with pride how well the young Duke of Holstein-Gottorp had developed during the campaign[2] and this also must have given him joy. The kind of boy he would like him to be is discernible from a question he repeatedly asked of Liewen in 1714[3] in Turkey: was the Duke weak? Was he too much fussed and mollycoddled by the women-folk at court?†

Charles Frederick of Holstein-Gottorp has often been portrayed in an unflattering light: the comments of the French ambassadors about his weak physique, his backwardness, and his low intelligence have been taken at face-value without reference to the fact that the diplomats in question were 'Hessian' by inclination and by orders from Paris.[4] A different view is taken by historians at work on material hitherto ignored. Their more favourable

---

* From Stenflycht's memoirs we can fix the time he and the King left the siege-works, 2 o'clock at night, and know that the King dealt with paper-work in his own room on arrival.

† Liewen rather side-stepped the question but reported that the Duke was handsome and could be toughened.

impression is reinforced by our knowledge of the intelligence and energy with which the Duke worked for the Holstein-Gottorp cause in later years.[5]

All in all the Sunday must have been a success of sorts and made Charles happy. Much emphasis has been put on the 'deep thoughts' in which the King sat in Mörner's chamber, bestirring himself off and on with an exclamation 'as to himself' which – posthumously – was remembered as '*Håll*', i.e 'Hold'.[6] Many of those present at Tistedal must have been inclined, as is normal when one suffers bereavement, to invest everything remembered from the King's last day with solemnity and significance. Historians anxious to establish a premonition of death, or a murder theory, have tended, however, to make use of the contemporary evidence too uncritically, reading into the exclamation the meaning of either 'Hold on to life' or 'Stop – stay – the hand of the murderer'. It seems more likely that Charles XII, with little sleep for several nights running (his generals had asked him to rest *at least half the night*),* was tired enough to keep dropping off to sleep when he sat down and that, not being particularly comfortable on the hard chair, he kept waking up, and that the exclamation may have been '*Hä*', the Scandinavian equivalent then as now of 'Ho', and one which we know the King was apt to use. In any case Charles XII was clearly in a cheerful mood when he returned to the siege-works in the late afternoon. Maigret, who received him there, noted that he arrived '*d'un humeur fort gay*', and conversed at length about the siege.[7]

II

The general atmosphere at the Tistedal headquarters among the officers below general's rank cannot be judged to have been a cheerful one. With Görtz expected the division into 'Holsteiners' and 'Hessians' made itself felt, and past discussion as to the wisdom or otherwise of the Norwegian campaign revived. When Rhyzelius arrived from Torpum on 25 November he found most of his acquaintances fed up with war in the wild and wet and cold Norway – far from the type of campaigning ground that gave glory and a European reputation as well as offering more civilized conditions.[8] Some even talked mysteriously of 'one shot that might make an end to the campaign' but declined to explain themselves when challenged. Several witnesses had heard Cronstedt, a strong 'Hessian', prophesy on 20 October that the King would die within one calendar month, and on being chaffed on 30 November, he is reported to have answered: 'The day is not yet at an end.' This reported saying has been used to lend credence to the rumour that Cronstedt, on his death-bed, confessed that he loaded the gun that killed Charles XII though the shot was fired by someone else, the then corporal of drabants Stierneroos. The confession is not well authenticated (indeed, the clergyman who is supposed to have received it gave evidence on oath that there was no truth in it),[9] but even if the confession were genuine neither

* My italics; quotation from the Rehnskiöld-Mörner report referred to above, pp. 486–7.

Stierneroos nor Cronstedt were anywhere near the spot where the King fell on 30 November and both were devoted to him.

Some confessions are well authenticated, but prove little. Sicre, the Frenchman who had come into Polish–Swedish service in Bender in 1712 after having been shipwrecked off Chios, and who was Frederick of Hesse's adjutant in 1718, opened the windows of his house wide during an illness in Stockholm in 1722 and shouted that he had murdered Charles XII.* Since he had been in the trenches on the night of 30 November and in the royal party his confession 'stuck', though he was horrified and astonished on his recovery to be told of what he had said. So must Fabrice have been who, during an attack of melancholia, confessed that he had murdered the King, though in 1718 he was far from the Norwegian wintry scene. It is worth noting that Voltaire, who knew both Fabrice (from whom he in London learnt much about Charles XII's period in Turkey)[10] and Sicre† was sceptical about the murder-theory.

At the time of the King's death no one presumed his having been murdered: none of the officers who were close to him in the siege-works; not Duke Charles Frederick who as the nearest blood-relation broke the sad news to the Council in Stockholm; not Rehnskiöld and Mörner in their report as field-marshals; not the enemy at Frederiksten who – noticing the stop in the siege – deduced that one of their shots had killed someone of importance. They guessed either the Prince of Hesse, or Rehnskiöld, or the young Duke: 'immediately everything became so quiet not only the whole night through, but even the next day'.[11] When it became known, through Swedish deserters, that it had pleased God to remove the King of the Swedes it was reckoned that he had been hit by a 'cartouche from the left'.[12] Later, competition set in among members of the garrison as to who had rid Norway of 'so terrible and strong an enemy'. There is a tradition, oral till written down in 1808, of the soldier from the west of Norway, John Vedlo, who while on guard-duty on the fortress spotted 'something shining and moving' in the Swedish trenches, shot and later realized that he had killed Charles XII.[13]

Similar stories abound, but Archdeacon Coxe, the historian and traveller who visited Frederikshald in 1784 spoke to an old man in his nineties who – in the version which Coxe published in his *Travels through Poland, Russia, Sweden, Jutland, Norway, Livonia, Courland, etc.* – seemed determined to claim no credit: he himself had served at Overberget on 30 November and not a shot had been fired from that outwork – all the shooting came from the main fortress.[14] This statement (now known to be erroneous)‡ became well

* Authorities differ whether the illness was one of mental depression or delirium induced by fever.

† Voltaire uses the proper French form, Siquier, but since this officer accepted a swedified spelling while in Charles's service I have thought it pedantic to revert to Siquier.

‡ Landsberg, the commander of the fortress, gives details in his report of the amount of shot from both outworks and in particular from Overberget on the night of 30 November. Of the royal party in the trench Carlberg noted heavy shooting from Overberget and so did Kaulbars who tried to protect Charles XII from it by a ruse: when the King first decided to look over the parapet,

known all over Europe since Coxe's *Travels* were translated into French and
German, and was later to become one of the corner-stones for the theory that
Charles XII had been murdered. For if no shot had been fired from Overberget
on 30 November 1718, and the King was shot through the temples, was it not
more likely – it was argued – that the shot came from the small communication trench at an angle to the 'old line' by someone who secretly crept into
it with the object of murdering Charles? Even if the King could be assumed
to have turned his head to the right, could he have turned it so much that
a shot from the fortress would have produced the effect observed when the
coffin was opened and his wound examined?

That examination of Charles's body, in 1746, brief and ocular though it
was, had already laid the first important corner-stone of the murder-theory.
It was noted that the wound in the right temple was much smaller than the
wound in the left one: if the bullet had entered from the left, one would have
expected the wound in the left temple to be smaller, as entry wounds produce
smaller cavities than exit wounds. Fuel was added to fire of the murder
rumours already current: an entry cavity on the right and an exit one on the
left fitted the assassin in the communication-trench, aiming a pistol or musket-
shot at Charles at close quarters.[15]

In the eighteenth century it was sometimes believed that the King had been
murdered by a sword, possibly because of a confused report of the dream
Neumann had in 1720: Charles, becoming aware of his assassin, began to
draw his own sword out of the scabbard.[16] The theory of a murder by the
sword was neither widespread nor long-lived, but Neumann – hearing in his
dream Charles tell him that 'someone came creeping along' – has remained
one of the witnesses called on to support the thesis of a murderous shot from
the communication-trench. Controversy on this point is still alive and a case
has been painstakingly built up, with motives deduced, for the murder of
Charles XII.[17] The majority of those historians who accept this case hold
Frederick of Hesse morally responsible. His hand could not have fired the
shot as he was at his own headquarters at Torpum at the time, but someone
who acted for him was supposed to be the murderer. His adjutant Sicre, who
was in the siege-works at the material hour, is usually picked on as the King's
assassin by those historians who are convinced of the 'Hessian guilt'.

The reason for the Prince of Hesse having his brother-in-law murdered,
whomever he picked for the foul deed, has been found in his ambition to have
the succession devolve on Ulrika Eleonora and himself in preference to
Charles Frederick. He was – so runs the main political argument in favour of
the murder-theory – forced to pick this particular moment in time because he
knew that Görtz would be joining the King very shortly. A letter from his
wife had informed him that Görtz left Stockholm for Norway on 24
November; and he assumed – to continue the 'pro-murder' reconstruction

Kaulbars supported him under the armpits and contrived to let him drop to a safer level whenever
he heard the cannon from Overberget fire. It was when Charles discovered this that he kicked
footholds and climbed higher up in the trench.

of the Prince's reasoning – that the deal Görtz brought from the Åland islands was one which involved the succession being settled on the young Duke of Holstein-Gottorp. Before the Suedo-Russian conferences at Lövö had been fully explored, it was thought that a peace embodying such a clause had been drafted by an all-mighty Görtz who was on his way to demand the King's signature. Even after this belief has been shown to be untenable respectable scholars have still stuck to the 'Hessian guilt' because they hold that Frederick of Hesse may not have been aware of the real state of affairs. Even the biographer of Frederick of Hesse in 1953, who argued that Frederick was as flexible as Görtz in the question of peace-negotiations, felt he could go no further in exonerating the prince than to say that his guilt has not been proved.[18] The recent scholarly analysis by Thanner of the 'revolution' in Sweden after the death of Charles XII presupposes that the guilt of Frederick and of Sicre is proved by the very clockwork precision of Frederick's steps after Charles's death.[19] Other modern historians have other suspects and other motives: the discontent among the higher officers with the King's war policy was so strong, Palmstierna holds, that a likely murderer would not be hard to find, and he points his finger at Cronstedt, Stierneroos and even at Rehnskiöld.[20]

III

When a general who has won fame in battle is killed on active campaign rumours that he has been murdered usually ignite spontaneously, and even when historians have agreed that there is not enough substance to make them burn for long they tend to flicker in legend. After 1632 it was strongly rumoured that Gustavus Adolphus had been murdered, but it would be hard to find a historian today who took stories to that effect seriously. In the case of Charles XII, just because historians have had to deal with very intricate evidence of a ballistic, medical and diplomatic nature – whether in the end they come down in favour of the murder-theory or not – the folk legends surrounding Charles's death have been kept alive.[21] Even those which at first sound preposterous have been minutely examined and some of them have been thought to offer if not credible evidence at least significant corroboration for the murder-theory.

A case in point is the folk legend about the silver (or brass) button which served as the missile that killed the King. Charles XII was, so ran stories which cropped up in different places in the border districts between Norway and Sweden, immune to ordinary bullets. It was a fact that four bullets had found his body and not killed him. The one aimed at him in the Narva battle had fallen into the folds of his neck-cloth and had been shaken out at night; the one at the Bender *Kalabalik* had only grazed his cheek: the one that hit him in the chest at Stresow did not penetrate to his heart; and the damage done by the one which struck his foot on his birthday, 17 June 1709, did not find a vital organ. On these facts legend began to embroider: it was a mysterious force which prevented the 1702 bullet from passing through the King's jugular vein; that same force deflected the 1713 bullet and weakened the impact of the 1715 one. The only one that managed to do him some damage – even if 'only in the foot' – had to be fired on the magic date of the King's own birthday. Clearly something more than an ordinary bullet was needed to get rid of him, and a version of the continental silver-button projectile as a murder weapon spread, in which the great King Charles was killed in the trenches of Frederiksten with a button cut from his own uniform.

Many buttons were picked up near the fortress, some silver, some of brass and some were said to be the murder-button. Different stories attribute this *kulknapp* (i.e. button-bullet) as being fired by either a Norwegian or a Swede. Like all legends it has played on people's minds if they were in the mood or state for autosuggestion. A soldier from Västergötland who fought in the Norwegian campaign confessed on his death-bed that it was he who had killed Charles XII with a button cut from the royal uniform.[22]

One of the many button-finds have interested a team of historians who in 1940 brought out a book of essays attempting to prove the murder-theory. The button is a brass one, similar in quality to the big brass buttons favoured by Charles XII, and is now exhibited in Varberg Museum. Shooting experiments with similar buttons convinced the medical expert of this team that damage of the kind Charles suffered could be inflicted by a projectile fashioned from such a button if used in circumstances which fitted the murder-theory as to direction and distance,[23] but his experiments have not been well received by his colleagues in the medical profession.[24]

The group of legends second in popularity to that of the *kulknapp* is one of equally ancient lineage in European and other folklore. Stories abound in mythology in which the hero – whether soldier or messianic – mysteriously cheats death. It is therefore not surprising to meet folk traditions from Norway and Sweden which deny that Charles XII was killed at Frederiksten. Somehow he got away, and – according to different versions of the story – left for America or 'other foreign parts' where he lived to a ripe old age. In other versions he stayed in Sweden. In 1728 there was a rumour in Scania that Charles XII and one of his colonels had been seen riding through the provinces. When Mallet visited Scandinavia in 1755, he noted that the 'lower classes' still believed that Charles XII was alive.

Such legends have no bearing on the murder-theory, though some of them – for instance the one which avers that Charles XII was taken to Stockholm and kept a secret prisoner there all his life – do say something about public attitudes towards the situation in Sweden after 1718.[25] And the rumours among soldiers after they had returned from the Norwegian campaign that the 'Princess', that is Ulrika Eleonora, had got someone to murder Charles XII on her behalf hint at popular suspicions of Ulrika usurping the throne. These have never, to my knowledge, been investigated and may be incapable of investigation. I would suggest, however, that they may be traced back to the fact that when Frederick of Hesse, as *generalissimus*, and the generals decided on 1 December 1718 in a council of war to abandon the Norwegian campaign – though not the war – they told the army that the siege of Frederiksten had to be given up because Russians and Danes were invading Sweden.[26] They hoped in this way to speed the withdrawal to Sweden where both the Prince and the officers urgently wanted to repair to the capital for political reasons. The campaigning season proper, as most of them understood it, was several months off and in the meantime there was work to do. Frederick of Hesse wanted to help Ulrika confirm her power, and to fashion the war effort according to his own ideas. The politically committed officers wanted to play their part in bringing absolutism to an end and many shared with Frederick an urge to topple the Görtz system. But, it seems to me, their lie to the soldiers rebounded on Frederick and his wife when the army got back and found no enemy in the country. Here, in my opinion, we have the first kernel of the 'Hesse guilt' which was to burst into such hectic blossoming and which caused at least two openings of Charles XII's coffin. The one in 1799 was motivated more by Gustavus IV's slightly morbid desire to see what Charles XII looked like, but the ones of 1859 and 1917 were definitely linked with the murder issue, as was that of 1746 in all probability.

IV

At about 4 o'clock on 30 November Charles, accompanied by General Schwerin, his adjutant Kaulbars and some other officers rode to the siege-works of Frederiksten. It was already getting dark; the date according to the new style was 11 December. The King had been present at an early evensong and had held a conference with his generals at which we are told he had 'given them his orders'.[27] Though we know nothing of the contents of these orders, and they probably dealt only with the day-to-day progress of the siege and other routine matters, it is possible that the King had gathered the generals together to reveal something of stage two of the Norwegian campaign in which he himself expected to be engaged shortly.

In the late afternoon of 30 November Charles was impatient to see the 'new line' started. The soldiers in the working party, four hundred of them, were to report at 6 that evening. Charles was in good spirits, as Maigret noted, but he seems to have fussed till the digging party had fallen in and work begun. Maigret first staked the new line; two hundred soldiers then followed him through the 'old line' and the communication trench, carrying their spades and picks and a bundle or two of twigs, the fascines, for protection during work. Each dropped to the ground at a spot indicated for him by Maigret and at a given signal started digging at speed, with the fascines strategically placed to obtain greater safety against the enemy's fire. As the first party got dug in, the remaining soldiers came along with more fascines and with fortification-baskets to be filled with earth so that the new trench could be built up as well as dug down. The soldiers of the second advance lay down behind the fascines, holding the baskets to be filled and putting them into position, then returned for more baskets, filled and unfilled. Carlberg walked along the new line to encourage the men.

The slant of the new line was less open to flank fire from Overberget and Mellemberget, but it is clear that fire from the fortress must have become increasingly accurate now the soldiers were within the range of musket-shots: seven of them were killed and fifteen wounded between 6 o'clock and the time (about 10 o'clock) the work was interrupted – a heavy rate of casualties when one takes into account that in the two previous full nights' work the casualties (dead and wounded) had been fifty and thirty respectively. This throws into relief Carlberg's report that the men's shock at seeing their comrades fall beside them was considerable on the 30th – inciting sympathy for the dead but also a determination to dig faster lest they themselves should fall victim to the next bullet or ball.[28]

At 8 o'clock Charles retired to his hut near Gyldenløve for a short while, to eat the supper which Hultman brought him. The two swapped the small jokes bred of everyday familiarity. 'Your food is so good I'll promote you master-cook', teased the King. The servant was quick in repartee, 'I'll have that in writing, Sire.'[29]

After supper Charles returned to the trenches to watch and to encourage the soldiers by his presence and example. The officers accompanying him into the 'old line', apart from Schwerin, Maigret and von Kaulbars, were Captain Knut Posse of the Lifeguards, Captain Schultz of the fortification corps, and Captain André Sicre. A little later Carlberg joined the royal party from the 'new line'.

Carlberg, then a young lieutenant of twenty-two, later wrote a report[30] – based on notes made immediately after the events of 30 November – which he handed to the historian Wargentin in 1777. To this can be added a report which Maigret wrote at the request of Gedda, a Swedish diplomat in Paris, in 1723.[31] Kaulbars also committed to paper a report on the night in question which was found in 1898 though it was – until the identification of the author by Nils Ahnlund in the 1940s – known as the 'anonymous relation'.[32] Some cross-checking even for 30 November is possible from the papers which reached the Chancery as a result of the questionnaire sent in 1728* to officers who might possess letters and memoranda deriving from Charles XII or have information about his last campaign.

From these reports (and other documentary and cartographical material) the sequence of events in the moments before the King died can be recon-

---

* It is to this questionnaire we owe Schwerin's report already referred to above, p. 494. The request was motivated by a desire to gather material for the author chosen to write the history of Charles XII: the historiographer royal after 1719, Wilde (originally charged with the task), did little; Rosenadler who took over made slow progress, but the material was put to good use by the King's old chaplain Jöran Nordberg whose history of Charles's reign was published in 1740.

structed, though no report or letter is specific on the actual time of death.
This, however, from a comparison of them all can be set at about 9.30 p.m.
Charles decided to climb up high enough to watch the soldiers in the new
line – and to be seen by them – and as he said to his party, 'to observe the
effect of the strong musket and cannon fire'. He kicked two footholds* some
ninety centimetres from the bottom of the trench ('5 quarters' in the measure-
ment of the day).[33] Maigret, Kaulbars and Carlberg – who joined the royal
party straight from the 'new line' and found Charles XII already poised with
his head and shoulders above the breastwork – were closest to the King.
Maigret recalled his own head as being just about on the level with the heels
of Charles's boots and Carlberg noticed that the King's head, resting on
his left arm, was turned somewhat towards the fortress. The night was thick
and cloudy; the moon was not yet up, but the flares burning on the fortress
and the frequent lightbombs gave some illumination. Certainly the King
could be seen by the soldiers working on the 'new line' and the word that he
was there, taking as great risks as they, might be expected to spread and
possibly hearten them in their work. The night was cold, the King was
wrapped in his cloak and he wore his hat, turned up and buttoned into
position, on the regulation left side of his head we may assume.

Some seven minutes after Carlberg's arrival, just before 9.30, the King was
hit. He died instantaneously. 'There was not the slightest movement,' Carlberg reported, 'except that his hand fell away from his left cheek and his head
slid slowly into his mantle but without the least tremor of his body which
stayed as before.'[34] Maigret recalled that the King's feet lost their grip but
the body remained in position, supported by the breastwork.[35] It was Kaulbars – who carried the foremost responsibility for the King's safety that night
– who first realized that his master was dead. He sensed that the King's head
sank down, no longer supported by the hand under the cheek-bone (the hand
was left under the head) and he heard a rattle in the throat 'occasioned by the
blood'. The sound of the shot entering the King's body also alerted him and
others. It was, when he tried to describe it, 'the same sound which occurs
when one slaps two fingers sharply against the palm of one's hand'.[36] Maigret
thought of the sound as similar to that made 'by a stone thrown with great
force into mud'.[37] Several of the eyewitnesses recall that not a word or a
sound came from the King and when they later observed the wound they were
not surprised: the shot seemed to Maigret to have been as big as a pigeon's
egg: it had gone in above the left ear and out close to the right ear. Carlberg
thought it natural that with such a head-wound death should have been
instantaneous enough to freeze the slightest movement.†

Kaulbars spoke first. 'Lord Jesus, the King is shot', he told Carlberg, 'go
tell General Schwerin and fetch him here.'

The General's reaction was that typical of all the officers present: mingled

---

* See above, pp. 491 and 497‡.
† The instantaneousness of the death was confirmed by the medical examination of 1917.

shock and acceptance expressed in 'Lord Jesus'. He hurried to the scene, made certain that the King was dead and ordered him laid down in the trench while Carlberg and Posse were sent for a stretcher. Soldiers were posted at the entrance to the 'old line' – which gave the only access to the 'new line' – to give the officers time to think. Two soldiers' cloaks were put over the stretcher to keep the identity of the body hidden for some time at least, and Sicre removed the King's hat, through which the bullet had passed, and put his own wig and gold-braided hat on the corpse. Carlberg and Schultz were put in charge of the party of twelve carriers of the Guards and sworn not to tell them it was their King on the stretcher. But on their way back towards Studekollen they missed the road and stumbled down the steep hill towards the river. The stretcher heeled over, cloaks, gold-braided hat and wig fell off and, as the clouds parted for a moment, the moon shone on Charles xii's dead face and his soldiers recognized their burden. They were bidden to stop their lamentations and to say nothing of what they had seen on pain of dire punishment.

At Studekollen Carlberg was met by orders to carry on to headquarters in Tistedal where Schwerin had preceded the stretcher. The distance was about half a mile further. The road was well known and the moon was up. At 1 o'clock in the morning of 1 December the stretcher was put down close to the King's house; the bearers were sent away and Schultz went to consult with Schwerin. Carlberg remained with the stretcher, and later recalled that it was with tears in his eyes and an aching heart that he watched the features of Charles xii stiffening in death on his bier. Lackeys and lifeguards came to help carry the body into a room on the ground floor where Schwerin and Neumann, the King's surgeon, were waiting. The young Duke of Holstein-Gottorp, Field-Marshal Mörner, General Dücker and other high officers collected in the room. 'We laid down our beloved King, dead and bloody', was the memory which remained with Carlberg, and personal grief fairly shouts from the letters, dated 1 December, which Duke Charles Frederick, Rehnskiöld and Mörner had to force themselves to write to Stockholm.

A late arrival who did not reach Tistedal till daylight on 1 December was the Prince of Hesse. Sicre had hurried to Torpum with news of Charles's death, carrying the King's hat, through which the shot had passed. This has been thought sinister: did he not carry proof to the Prince that the foul deed was done? In fact as will be shown below,* it is Charles's hat which establishes the direction of the shot as from the left beyond all reasonable doubt and thus undermines the murder-theory to the extent that, in my submission, it vanishes; and the reason for Sicre's burden on his road from Frederiksten to Frederick of Hesse must be sought elsewhere. Some authorities have assumed that he wore the hat in place of his own which with his wig had been used to disguise the dead King;[38] but it is also possible that he 'carried' it in the sense that he brought it along lest it should be lost. There seems an element

* Cp. below, p. 508.

of 'keep-sake' in the circumstance that the Prince of Hesse, when he dispatched Sicre to Stockholm* that same night with news of Charles's death, sent the hat along to be given to Ulrika Eleonora.

The rest of the uniform was also carefully preserved. The King's body was prepared, first for the temporary coffin which was borne by relays of soldiers to Idefjord and thence transported to the other side of the waters, and then embalmed by Neumann at Uddevalla and put into a more worthy casket for the journey by road to the capital. And special arrangements were made so that the carriage used should jolt the body as little as possible.[39]

While Neumann and his helpers worked at Uddevalla, one of the newly arrived artists, a Frenchman named Simon Josse who had accompanied the campaign, in preparation for future commemoration of it, sculptured a fine mask of the King. This has become known as a death-mask though it was not in fact modelled on the face. Four or five copies of this mask[†] are still in existence, one in the Fitzwilliam Museum at Cambridge. It used to be believed that the mask was made by the famous Hedlinger at Karlberg, where the King's body rested till the solemn funeral on 28 February 1719, even after measurements taken at the 1917 examination of the body had shown that the mask was not a death-mask in the true sense, being slightly too short to fit Charles XII's features. The art-historian who recently identified the sculptor of the death-mask with great ingenuity has made the interesting observation that the King's wounds are represented on the mask in such a way that a shot from the right may be deduced. He has, on this basis, put forward a hypothesis that the artist was making a 'Holstein' attempt to encourage rumours of a 'Hesse' murder and that the death-mask was thus a part of conscious political propaganda.[40]

The hypothesis is a fascinating one, but does seem to press the material too far. By its very nature we cannot expect from the sculptured mask a naturalistic impression of the entrance and exit wounds of the injury and even a mask modelled on the dead face would not have included the full area of the damage. Artistic and aesthetic considerations may have influenced the sculptor. But Mr Stenström probably has a point in judging the artist as having accepted the explanation – current among some of the private soldiers in the army – that the King had been shot from the right.[‡] This explanation seems to have arisen among men who, probably not all equally well informed about the layout of the siege-works, had heard about the relative sizes of the two wounds in the King's head and did not, *a priori*, connect them with any thought of murder.

We shall probably never know whether the artist, who himself died in 1719, and has left no personal papers, believed that Charles XII was murdered,

* Sicre arrived at Torpum 'before 10 o'clock' on 30 November; he reached Stockholm on 5 December.

† See illustration facing p. 493.

‡ The artist cannot have got this impression from Neumann, who in his report writes that the King was shot from 'the left side'.[41]

nor is it at this stage of our knowledge ascertainable if 'Holstein' partisanship influenced him directly or indirectly. If it did, it cannot have come from
any high level. Young Charles Frederick was not worldly wise and was so
heartbroken that he refused the approaches (not in themselves well-
authenticated) of senior officers to further his own chances in the succession-
stakes.[42] That he cooperated to the best of his ability with Frederick of Hesse,
even to the extent of approving the arrest of Görtz and other 'Holsteiners'
in the Swedish administration. That this did not arise from cowardice
is shown by the young Duke's voice raised at the council of war on
1 December for the continuation of the Norwegian campaign according to
the lines laid down by the dead King.

Nor is it easy to accept the accusations of some historians that Charles
Frederick consciously acted treacherously towards Görtz. Görtz had been
arrested without his knowledge. Secretly and hurriedly Frederick of Hesse
had in the night of 30 November sent a couple of officers to arrest Görtz
'in the King's name'. They caught up with him on 2 December at Tanum
vicarage on the Swedish side of the frontier and took him straight to Stockholm and prison. Once the arrest was effected, Charles Frederick – pitted
against the wily and experienced Frederick of Hesse – was easily convinced
that his uncle knew best, that there had been intrigues which he in his youth
and innocence could not fathom, that the arrested men were in Swedish
service anyhow and that he ought not to rock the boat and work against
Ulrika, now Queen of Sweden.[43]

The one person who might have instigated Holstein propaganda as early
as January–February 1719 would have been Görtz, but he had been effectively
silenced not only by his arrest but by his arrest in the name of a King already
dead. He had felt rather uneasy as he approached headquarters lest his
enemies should have blackened him enough to lose him Charles's confidence.
A draft letter, protesting his entire loyalty to the King, was found in his shirt
when he was searched at Tanum vicarage.[44] The other 'Holsteiners' were
arrested in Stockholm on the very night Sicre arrived after conferences with
Taube and Ulrika, before any news of the death of Charles was made known
or even rumoured. They guessed it from their being thrown into prison. 'Now
the King is dead', von Dernath is creditably reported to have said to the officers
who came to arrest him.[45] 'Holstein' power and 'Holstein' utilization of the
murder-theory did not gather strength till the end of the 1720s.

V

The main clues needed to investigate the 'assassin's bullet' versus the 'blind
shot' have now been laid before the reader. There was some popular acceptance of a shot from the right, though all the officers present in the trench on
30 November reported the shot as coming from the left. This belief in a shot
from the right gained general credence after the opening of the coffin in 1746

and has persisted to the present day, strengthened by the (too uncritically accepted) tradition via Coxe that no shot had been fired from the outworks on the night in question. Indeed, until 1859, when the Danish historian Paludan-Müller raised doubts[46] about the murder-theory, this theory was the accepted view among scholars of Charles XII's death. The lines in the commemorative poem by Olaus Rydbeck (the younger) read at Uppsala University in 1719 were analysed and oft quoted:

> And was the one who aimed a Dane,
> And did the bullet come from thence?*

After 1859 the battle was joined between those who agreed that Paludan-Müller had a point and those who refuted his findings. An enormous amount of material had to be examined: topographical studies were made, ballistic experiments carried out and the documentary source-material of all kinds (some of it discovered after 1859) tested and re-tested. The search for the culprit was from a number of names bandied about (which reasons of space forbid us to examine here) – narrowed down to Sicre, shooting on behalf of Frederick of Hesse. Since Sicre can now be shown from Carlberg's and Kaulbars's reports to have been one of the royal party, the earlier assumption that he had been lying hidden in the communication-trench waiting to shoot the King must be regarded as untenable. Frederick's ostensible 'motive' must also be said to have disappeared since letters between himself and Ranck show that he was well aware of the fact that Görtz brought nothing conclusive from the fourth Åland islands conference.[47] There was therefore no 'need' for him to kill Charles before Görtz arrived.

It seems utterly incredible that Ulrika Eleonora, whose terrible grief at the news Sicre and Taube brought to her on 5 December is well documented, and who had even refused to follow Hein's advice on how to secure the succession if it involved any bloodshed in the capital, should have connived at her brother's murder.[48] And the most critical perusal of Frederick's letters to Ulrika Eleonora from the Norwegian campaign fails to provide a single clue that might support the supposition that he was planning murder: he has accepted the campaign though he does not like it, he is whiling away spare time in reading philosophy and theology – this is the tone of his share of the correspondence. Her letters to him are full of concern for his safety but also for the safety of her brother.[49] The relationship between Charles and his *'generalissimus'* was one of great trust from the King's side; it is worth noting that the Prince of Hesse was one of the few (possibly the only one) to whom Charles as early as September 1718 confided his plan of campaign for Norway in any detail.† From all we know it seems unlikely, to put it no higher, that

---

* In the original,
> *Må skytten tå war Dansk, och kulen ther ifrå?*
> *Jag intet thera tror: Ty falskt skiöt ingen tå,*
(The last half-line runs, in literal translation, 'For false shot none then').
† See above, p. 475.

Frederick, with his devoted service as Charles's comrade-in-arms, should have planned his brother-in-law's death, however alarmed he was at Görtz's influence, epsecially as our evidence forces us to the conclusion that he was less worried about Görtz in late November 1718 than he had been in October 1718.

Frederick's innocence (however cold-blooded his planning for using the opportunity of Charles's death), and indeed the impossibility of the murder-theory is, in my opinion, convincingly established by ballistic experiments carried out by the police-surgeon G. Hultkvist. A shot from the left was increasingly accepted among scholars after the 1917 commission of experts decided that this was indeed the direction of the shot as established on medical evidence. One difficulty remained: no amount of ballistic experiments, whether on living animals or human corpses, with shot of the kind indicated by the commission's findings could produce a large entrance cavity and a smaller exit one. Hultkvist, pondering this problem, remembered the King's hat which had been forgotten by previous ballistic experts, perhaps just because Sicre had removed it. He then repeated his experiments through a double layer of hair-felt comparable to the thickness of Charles's turned-up hat and achieved results which were identical with those of 30 November 1718, that is, an entrance-wound similar in size to that which the King had suffered, with an exit-wound smaller in circumference.[50]

With Hultkvist's experiments the shot from the left is, as far as I am capable of judging, proved ballistically. Those who hold to the murder-theory stress that we have no certain knowledge of how Charles XII wore his hat on that particular night, but I find it difficult – not to say impossible – to accept that he would wear it in any other way than according to regulation: with the brim turned up and buttoned to the left side.[51] When you have lived in uniform as long as Charles did, you would instinctively notice if you had accidentally put your hat on in the wrong way, and quickly remedy the mistake.

There remained, and remains, a lack of certain knowledge whence the shot from the left was fired and what kind of shot it was. It can only have been shot from the outworks or the fortress. We know that shooting was lively both from Overberget, Mellemberget and Frederiksten – Carlberg noted this and it is confirmed from an independent report by the commander of the fortress.[52] The distance from the fortress was some three hundred steps, from Mellemberget about 450 metres and from Overberget about 600 metres. What kind of shot could have carried that far with the impact with which Charles was hit? Ballistics experts still argue this, but the combined results of topo-graphical and ballistics experts indicate that a cartesch ball from Overberget could certainly have killed the King, and that the turn of his head to the right renders Overberget the most likely source of the shot, though a cartesch or falconet ball from the fortress is not ruled out.[53] In much of the documentary evidence a cartesch ball is mentioned as the probable cause of Charles XII's death. The Danish commander of Frederiksten thought it a likely possibility;* and in the letters from the Swedish headquarters which were sent to Stockholm and abroad it is stated as the killing projectile.[54]

Conversely, experiments with bullets from a distance of twenty-five metres (that is, from the communication-trench of the murder-theory) have not produced results commensurate with the wounds inflicted on the King, and buttons made up to resemble those of the *kulknapp* legend burst when fired at speed. From the common-sense point of view a pistol-shot from the communication trench seems out of the question, since at that distance it would have left traces of gunpowder on the King's face which would have been noticed by one or other of those who wrote their reports. A musket-shot from the communication-trench would have to be well aimed, and French survivors of the siege – interviewed by Fersen who in the 1740s was investigating the murder-theory – told him that before the moon was up the night was so dark and thick that they thought it impossible for accurate aim to have been taken even with the help of the illuminations from the fortress. These helped the besieged rather than the besiegers.[55] And, again from the common-sense point of view, does it seem likely that the officers with Charles xII in the 'old line', all experienced soldiers, should not have recognized by sound or flash a projectile from the right at close quarters? None of them saw a flash and all assumed the shot to come from the left.[56] Sicre, when questioned by Voltaire, said he could have killed Charles xII, if he had so wanted, but he revered him as a hero and had such respect for him that it would have been an impossibility for him ever to want to harm him.[57]

It may never be possible to establish whether the shot came from the outworks or from the Frederiksten fortress, but it seems to me inescapable that it did come from either Mellemberget, Overberget or the fortress and not from the communication-trench or the 'new line', which had not progressed far enough to permit a shot to the King's left temple. It follows that Charles xII was not murdered but killed by a blind shot, or as he himself might have said, by an 'honest enemy bullet'.

* See above, p. 497.

Epilogue

After Charles XII's death Frederick of Hesse, having compromised with the anti-abolutist forces[1] to achieve Ulrika Eleonora's proclamation and coronation, had a relatively free hand to carry on the war as he thought best. He had, at the council of war held at Tistedal on 1 December 1718, found the generals willing to abandon the Norwegian campaign. With some it was not popular; with others it took second place to the coming political struggle for constitutional government, whether of the Council or the Estates. Frederick, seeing the way the wind blew, bowed to the inevitable and stressed his own long service in a constitutional state *par excellence*, the Dutch Republic, as an added motive for choosing Ulrika in preference to Charles Frederick. Neither the generals nor Frederick had any thought of giving up the war effort. Frederick distributed the ten thousand *daler* in good silver coin which arrived for the war-chest from the *upphandlingsdeputation* just after the King's death among the generals,[2] as a reward for their 'fatigues' in the campaign;[3] but what he was buying* was their consent to him as Charles's successor as a war-leader, not their consent to abandoning the defence of Sweden.

That Sweden remained at war for two and a half years after Charles XII's death is at one and the same time ample proof that he was throughout his life at one with the nation in wishing to resist the anti-Swedish coalition that had attacked the country, and that he had between 1716 and 1718 created a war potential of momentum enough to survive even the dismantling of the Görtz system and the reversal of reform in many spheres of economic and social life.

But it is undeniable that the momentum of Charles's military offensive was blunted by the halt which the constitutional struggle and the combined Swedish and Hesse desire to break with the Görtz system implied. And when the offensive was resumed it was along lines long ago staked out by Frederick of Hesse: peace with other enemies so that a concentrated effort could be made against Russia. In achieving peace with George I, Frederick William of Prussia and Frederick IV of Denmark–Norway, he showed considerable acumen and skill,[4] but the terms of those peace-makings were

* The sums were subtracted from the salaries of the officers in question in 1723.

those which fitted his own views of Sweden's future rather than those Charles
had held of a tolerable peace.

The commercial advantages for British merchants were not too high a
price to pay for British naval help,[5] but the 'guarantees' which for Charles XII
had always been so important were not obtained, nor were there any guarantees given in return for the outright cession of Bremen and Verden in their
entirety against money payments which had to be used to buy peace with
Denmark–Norway.[6] The sacrifice to Prussia of Swedish Pomerania to the
Peene – that is up to and including Stettin – was also made without any
corresponding arrangements of 'equivalents' for Sweden.[7] George I's diplomatic help was made freely available to Frederick and the fact that Frederick
IV of Denmark–Norway had his terms pressed as low as possible must
certainly be reckoned one of the gains from the peace with Hanover.
Stralsund, with Rügen and Wismar, were returned to Sweden against a money
payment and at a sacrifice which was logical enough now Frederick of Hesse
gave up the Swedish great-power position in Germany, but which Charles XII
would not have contemplated: the complete sacrifice of the interests of the
ducal House of Holstein-Gottorp.* For Frederick of Hesse it was no hardship
for Sweden solemnly to promise Frederick IV that she would not oppose the
reabsorption into the Danish Crown of the Holstein-Gottorp lands in the
duchy of Sleswig when possession in perpetuity was guaranteed to the Danish
Crown by Great Britain and France in 1720.[8]

It is easy to exaggerate the manner in which Frederick of Hesse, now His
Royal Highness as consort of Queen Ulrika Eleonora, and soon – in 1720 – to
be Frederick I of Sweden,[9] was influenced by Hesse interests and hatred of
Holstein in the peace settlements of 1719 and 1720 as well as by his hope of
securing the Swedish crown – should his marriage to Ulrika fail to produce a
direct heir – in the Hesse line.[10] By and large, given that he was German
enough to prefer the sacrifice of Sweden's position in the Empire to her loss
of the Baltic provinces to Russia, he tried to uphold the interests of the
country to which he had tied his own fortune. He fought hard, though in vain,
for Sweden's freedom from Sound-dues and his firmness stiffened George I's
and the Regent's resolve to beat the Danish terms down in other respects.
More significantly, Frederick's every action, after February 1719 when the constitutional compromise had been worked out, served to channel the Swedish
war effort and the help from his ally, George I, against Tsar Peter. The European
situation seemed to favour his plans, and for a while it looked as if a powerful
coalition – Great Britain, France and the Emperor Charles VI – would join
Sweden in a war with Russia to make sure of a peace in the North which
would regain the major part of Sweden's Baltic provinces for her.[11] But the
guarantees, on which Charles XII had been so adamant, of military help in
return for cession of land had not been obtained, and though George I was

---

* Rosén has in his *Svensk Historia* (1961), p. 612, emphasized that with the Holstein alliance
gone, the 'corner stone' of the Swedish great-power position had been removed.

sincere enough in 1719 when the prizes of Bremen and Verden were handed to him, the naval cooperation which Frederick envisaged with Norris's squadrons in 1719 and 1720 did not materialize in the way he and his Swedish advisers had assumed it would.[12] George's policy remained one of cautious help for his new ally, Sweden, as it had been cautious after 1717 in respect of his then ally Denmark–Norway; in both cases such caution was dictated by issues closer to British than to Hanoverian interests.

And when the European situation changed in 1720 and 1721 – when the Emperor became less keen on a crusade against Tsar Peter[13] and when France as well as Great Britain felt the impact of the bursting of the South Sea Bubble and the crash of Laws' system[14] – conjunctures moved in Sweden's disfavour and she was left to face Russia alone.[15] The result was the Peace of Nystad of June 1721, virtually dictated by the Tsar. The Baltic provinces were lost in their entirety, and the Finnish districts of Karelia (including Viborg) and Kexholm were ceded to Russia. The rest of Finland was restored and Sweden, to feed her people, was permitted to import from her former granary a large quantity (fifty thousand rubles worth) of grain annually without the payment of export duty.[16]

II

Charles XII's share of responsibility for the loss of Sweden's great-power position has been the matter of continuous debate.[17] His reputation has fluctuated with changing political conditions and his life and work has been reinterpreted in contemporary political rather than historical terms. When Sweden, or Europe, has felt threatened by Russia's might, Charles's name has been conjured with as one who – if given enough support – would have contained the 'Russian menace'.

In the agitation of the 1860s, when Poland was seething against Russia and many Swedes hoped to free Finland (lost in its entirety to Russia in 1808–9), the anniversary of Poltava in 1862 produced a mammoth meeting with Polish, Hungarian and Italian speakers and a collection was taken which brought in eleven thousand *riksdaler* to build a statue of Charles XII.[18] It is the first and only one Sweden has raised to him and is well known to every visitor to Stockholm in its prominent position near Jakobskyrkan. It shows him in a most uncharacteristic and dramatic pose: with arm stretched and finger pointed towards the enemy of the east, Russia.[19] Similarly, the dislike of Russian power once the russification-policy in Finland tore at heart-strings never broken produced renewed interest of a contemporary political kind in Charles in the 1890s.*

And conversely, the twentieth-century Swedish acceptance of the status of a smaller power and sincere belief in the virtues of international cooperation

---

* Though it also gave impetus to the research of the 'New School' in Caroline historiography; see above, p. xiii.

without recourse to war has made Charles XII a 'warrior-king' of whom the progressive classes in society have been ashamed: again, a reaction with unhistorical over- or undertones. The sympathy with liberal or socialist movements in Russia has – oddly – produced an admiration for Tsar Peter which in itself is perfectly justifiable though the converse hatred and contempt of Charles XII, who stood in Russia's way, is not.

Added to such rather obvious hazards is the lack of sympathy which an age that has long outgrown absolutism has felt for an absolutist king, an age for which the duty of defending territory, acquired on the whole by the sword, with the sword is largely repellent. The very fact that Charles in his lifetime was used as a symbol of hatred for absolutism by the English pamphlet propaganda etched itself on the minds of nineteenth-century liberals. We know of no Swedes who, like Southey, suffered nightmares about the 'evil Charles XII',[20] but we can count many who reckoned him wicked just because he was an absolute king. Similarly, the very reasonable objections of contemporary statesmen in England (a country with which eighteenth- and nineteenth-century Swedish liberals felt the deepest sympathy) to Charles XII's tenacity in his defence of Sweden, have been remembered through the ages and created a guilt feeling about the 'warrior King', postulating also a too artificial distinction between Charles and Sweden which when all is said and done carried on the war for two and a half years after his death. Rather than examining the reasons for English (and later British) statesmen finding Charles XII and his wars a nuisance to their own equally rationally conditioned policies, the Swedes have accepted the well-turned phrases of Bolingbroke and the witticisms of Pope on the utter unimportance of wars taking place so far beyond the civilized world.

Added to the difficulties which ideological, as opposed to historical, evaluations have created is the problem posed by having to deal with a ruler of undoubted influence whose character in much is enigmatic. The large amount of non-controversial research on aspects of the reign carried out between the 1930s and the 1960s does not seem to have lessened this problem appreciably. The youngest generation of Swedish scholars, if they are at all interested in the reign of Charles XII, have begun re-fighting the battles between the 'old' and the 'new school' in Caroline research.[21] The achievement of a picture in depth, which puts Charles XII into perspective and makes him part of the history of Sweden and of Europe, in the sense of the 'trends of the age' has not yet been achieved, though I am sure it will be by those more qualified than I to do so. Some of these trends, as I see them, ought, however, to be indicated before I commit myself on Charles's personal short-term impact.

The most obvious long-term trend is the growing power of Russia. With its diplomatic isolation broken by participation in the war of the Holy League, with a leader as dynamic as Peter, it was only a question of time before the powerful resources of Russia, especially in manpower, would be properly utilized. In the long run could Sweden, with $2\frac{1}{2}$–3 million people, however well administered and however well defended, hold a Russia of more than ten million back from the Baltic? This is not to say that Russian advance was 'inevitable'. The 'accident of history' might have decreed otherwise. Tsar Peter, ill and worn at times towards the end of the war, was thought more likely to die before Charles XII; if this had happened, then the story might have had a different ending. And Russia did not, in spite of a tendency by Russian historians to assume this,[22] fight alone. She was helped, enormously, by the war on Polish soil (in its turn largely dictated by Charles being forbidden by the Maritime Powers to fight Augustus in the Empire) between 1701 and 1706, and by George I's associating Great Britain, however deviously and indirectly, with the anti-Swedish coalition between 1715 and 1718, and in particular by the very important use of the British navy in the Baltic in 1715 and 1716.

Another long-term trend, which has not been much appreciated by historians,[23] is the way in which the German powers, including the Emperor, welcomed the undoing of the 1648 settlement. The struggle between the house of Habsburg and Louis XIV for the interpretation of 1648 between 1660 and 1714 (a struggle in which Louis was, on the whole, victorious)* had its counterpart in the struggle to chase Sweden out of the positions she had gained in 1648. But in Sweden's case, since her rulers had become German princes in perpetuity, with a seat (in contrast to France) in the German Diet, the struggle was one that had brought to the front not only the Emperor but all those North German princes who had seen the ambitions of their own states either curtailed or circumscribed by the rise of Sweden. Hesse, friendly to Charles XII, no less than Prussia and Hanover which became his enemies, was, as we have seen, affected by this trend. The house of Habsburg, however much individual Emperors might fear the growth of power of the North German princes through the spoils they expected from the partitioning of Sweden's holdings in the Empire, was basically in sympathy with ousting the alien conqueror of 1632–48.

Yet a third trend which affected Sweden's fate is the way in which ambition and opportunity combined to make German princes in Charles's reign ruling monarchs outside the Empire, so that at one and the same time their powers as German princes were immeasurably enhanced while the complex bonds of Imperial government and loyalties hindered Sweden's efforts to come to grips with enemies who were in theory 'German' enemies only: Augustus of Saxony and Georg Ludwig of Hanover are both of inestimable importance in relation to Sweden in the age of Charles XII since Saxony and Hanover could not be touched (except at great risk or given favourable conjunctures) while the Polish–Lithuanian Commonwealth and Great Britain nourished the war effort against Sweden.

Finally, the past relationship of Sweden with the west of Europe laid down

* For this see Hatton, 'Louis XIV and his fellow-monarchs', *Louis XIV*, ed. J. Rule.

a pattern which it was difficult to break during the reign of Charles XII, though there were those among his advisers who urged him to break it. The union of the Maritime Powers in 1688 had created a dilemma for Sweden which she found it difficult to solve: was the combined naval strength of England and the Dutch Republic more of a menace to Sweden's economic prosperity than the aggression of Louis XIV on land? The balancing policy which Sweden had adopted since the 1648 peace had by 1681 led her to cooperation (at least in the diplomatic sense) with those who opposed France going beyond the treaties of 1648 and 1659; but from 1688 onwards her initiative was paralysed by the equal balance between the two camps centred respectively round Louis XIV and William III. Danger to the house of Holstein-Gottorp, ever the anchor-pin for Sweden's policy of containing Denmark's natural desire for reconquest of seventeenth-century losses, moved Charles XII into the William camp – in the diplomatic sense anyhow – in 1700; but in the military sense he remained uncommitted as long as the War of the Spanish Succession lasted. This uncommittedness of Sweden, in the Nine Years War as well as in the war of 1700–13, brought distrust from both sides,* and diplomatic commitment to Louis XIV in 1715 was ended, against Sweden's desire after Louis's death, by the Regent of France, when he found George of Great Britain a more useful ally than Charles XII.

There is, therefore, a sense in which one can speak of Sweden as forfeiting international goodwill in a competitive age by too 'selfish' a policy: she did not want, or could not afford, the ties of firm alliances and lost the (admittedly uncertain) advantages which such alliances might have brought. The element of necessity is here probably slightly stronger than volition: Charles IX did not want to commit himself in the Nine Years War because he had to solve the problem of a reconstruction of the country's resources which would permit defence of the great-power position; Charles XII did not want to commit himself in the War of the Spanish Succession because the resources skilfully channelled to that defence only sufficed if concentrated solely on the task in hand.

III

Charles is popularly reckoned to have ruined his country. This, at least, is one aspect of the history of the reign where independent research – maintaining neutrality between 'old' and 'new' schools – has been able to clarify the actual state of affairs. Historians have penetrated behind the official local reports of the time, which were darkly coloured to protect local resources, and have brought to light the actual statistical material so abundantly available.

We now know that the loss of men due to the war was surprisingly small: certainly less than thirty thousand and of these some eight thousand – possibly

* See Hatton, 'Gratifications and foreign policy', in *William III and Louis XIV* (edd. R. M. Hatton and J. S. Bromley), pp. 68–94.

more – eventually returned from those made military prisoners in Russia or taken away from Finland as civilian booty to be sold as slaves.[24] Some of the military prisoners whom the Danish King sold as galley-slaves to Venice also returned.[25] The decline of the population of Sweden during Charles's reign was greater than this figure, and is variously estimated between sixty and one hundred thousand: but the larger part of these losses are attributable to the famine and consequential epidemics between 1696 and 1700 and to the plague years of 1710 to 1712 – for neither of which can Charles be held personally responsible. Sweden therefore, in 1718, was not a land bereft of men: at the 1750 census (the first modern one undertaken) the number of males of the age to have served in Charles's army was surprisingly large and only slightly smaller than that of females in the same age groups.[26]

Similarly, the number of derelict farms has been shown to have stood at under three per cent at the time of Charles XII's death, and even here derelict farms are found mainly in places (e.g. the island of Öland) which had been hard hit by the plague or in those which had suffered both from the plague and the war, as Scania and the west had.[27]

The stresses of the long war, the tiredness associated with such a prolonged effort, were noticeable in Sweden in spite of the way in which the economy of the country had been stimulated. For this the bad harvests of 1717 and 1718 carry some of the blame; but undoubtedly the very effort to mount the military offensive must have been a taxing one, psychologically as well as economically, in a period of bad harvests. To some extent this improved with better harvests in 1719 and 1720. The Görtz system had alienated many burghers and some of the well-to-do had taken their money abroad. Charles XII and his advisers were too prone to think that all complaints of difficulties were unfounded. Research into the financial circumstances of Stockholm craftsmen have shown that though they had plenty of work, none of them had anything like fortunes saved up.[28] Studies of the wealthier classes of society in respect of their fortunes have not been undertaken, but those of individual families tend to give a picture of hard work and of great energy, the lady of the house coping well when her husband was at war, managing the estate with skill.[29] But there was undoubtedly resistance to unpopular measures, particularly of a financial nature, by local administrators: the case-study by Olander for Skaraborg's *län* shows that officials, from the *landshövding* downwards, ignored decrees which did not suit them.[30] Central administrators whom Charles sometimes thought lax in their duties or lukewarm in their concern for the public good were – as far as one can judge from the evidence available – either too tired or too cautious to take risks and show the initiative and energy which the King so admired and tried to inculcate in civilian as in military life. He had grown to manhood in the army and did not, it seems, realize that the *esprit de corps* which shared physical danger breeds is not a characteristic of civilian life except under siege conditions which make soldiers and civilians in some sense one.

Again, Charles failed to realize the growing civilian administrative resentment against the 'foreigner'. His army – though national in a way which was unparalleled in Europe, thanks to the reforms of Charles xi – had room for men born abroad, particularly in the last years of his reign when he lacked officers and there were plenty to be had from a Europe at peace but for the Great Northern War. Officers from the west of Europe, particularly French ones, were added to the familiar Germans who tended, however, to serve with their own nationals in the Swedish army. Some of the French officers were specialists – Major Maigret and his chief assistant Colonel Bousquet were both fortification officers – but we know that two captains in a regular Swedish regiment in 1718 could not speak Swedish.[31]

In the army, the common European outlook on the art of war and the qualities which made for a good officer, enabled these foreign officers to be accepted and absorbed in a way which proved impossible in the administrative machine. There were in Sweden many administrators of non-Swedish family by origin; most of Charles's foreign office experts were of Baltic-German descent – Vellingk, von Müllern, and von Kochen among them – but the absorption of their families from provinces which had become Swedish in allegiance in the late sixteenth and early seventeenth centuries had been a gradual process. The rapid influx of Holstein-Gottorp nationals, especially into the *upphandlingsdeputation*, and the amount of power they were supposed to wield relative to their numbers, caused irritation, suspicion and resentment. It bred a determination to get rid of the foreigners when opportunity offered, since the hated Görtz system was identified with them. Görtz himself was, unjustly, held responsible for all changes which were disliked in the administrative and financial life of the nation. That he was accused, and executed, for having 'alienated the King's affection from his own subjects' is indicative of this. There were those who genuinely, if erroneously, believed that Görtz was lining his own pockets at the expense of the nation; but those in the higher administrative positions must have known that all available money, including part of Görtz's private fortune, went towards the war effort; and the majority of the councillors and officials must – unless they chose to suppress this – have remembered enough of the King's tenacious attempts at reform from Turkey to realize that they were making Görtz the scapegoat for policies initiated and desired by Charles xii.

But reforms from the King, ably helped by Görtz and others, came too thick and fast for the older administrators to gain confidence in the 'new system'. Beyond this, most changes made by Charles xii in the administrative machine were part and parcel of changes which hit the higher social classes in their pockets. The King's efforts to share the burden of the war more fairly, and in particular to lighten that carried by the Fourth Estate, were resented by the three higher Estates. Significantly, all such reforms, as well as the administrative changes, were undone after Charles xii's death.

It has been suggested that an individualistic attitude towards life among the well-educated administrators of Sweden was making itself felt in the early eighteenth century; and this may be one of the reasons why the civilian officials, as opposed to the military ones, were less willing to accept the kind of sacrifices which Charles thought it natural for 'everyone' to bear. The contact with European political thought, ably demonstrated by Thanner,[32] meant that from 1715 onwards a group of intellectuals among the officials, often of high noble rank and counting among them also some sons of the Church,* began to discuss constitutional reform. Uppsala, with its university and close proximity to Stockholm, became a centre for this group. They looked back to the good old days before absolutism had been introduced in Sweden, arguing that *dominatus regius absolutis* was a foreign one, read Saint-Pierre and absorbed the theories of the polysynod either in French, German, or English, and had a complete constitutional blueprint ready to overturn absolutism as soon as a chance offered, looking upon themselves as a 'liberty party'.

This group was essentially an élite, representing the Council of the Realm idea, and by its side we can distinguish another group – the one to which most officers belonged and the more middling rank of the administrators. This group also thought of reform, but of reform which would neither go back to 'Council' government, nor keep absolutism, but go forward to 'Estates-government', where a less oligarchic rule would ensue in which the big majority of the lesser nobility joined with like-minded members of the Estate of Burghers and Clergy to control the higher nobility and erode its entrenched position.

It was between these two groups that the struggle of the 'Age of Liberty' was played out,† and since eyes were already turned to the struggle for power at home during the last years of Charles XII's reign, it may be said that to an increasing circle of educated Swedes what the King was fighting for was already becoming irrelevant. The great-power position abroad, the one which he had been born to defend, was to them not a live issue: the war ought to be got rid of as sensibly and tolerably as possible, but above all speedily, and sacrifices of territory outside Sweden would be tolerated as a means to that end.

IV

The growing difference in aims and objectives between this group and Charles XII is, in one sense, paradoxical, since the King was as interested in the pursuits of peace as they were and as influenced by the Early Enlightenment ideas in general as they: in law reform, in the practice of toleration, in the care for the arts and sciences, in the application of scientific knowledge to mining and manufacture, in the promotion of trade. The administrators who

---

* E.g. Bishop Erik Benzelius and Jesper Svedberg, the Uppsala *domprost.*

† For a brief survey of this in English see Hatton, *New Cambridge Modern History*, Vol. VII, ch. 7.

knew Charles well in the post-1715 period stressed what a splendid ruler he would make for Sweden when peace came; with his energy, his fervent absorption in new ventures and new techniques, his concern not only for the well-being and prosperity of the country, but for the intellectual life of the nation. Many regretted him for that very reason long after his death[33] when Frederick I, tamed by his fight with Council and Estates, withdrew into a life of private pleasures in which the hunt and his mistresses counted most. But the parallel between Charles XII and the 'opposition' which formed against him ready to act on his death must not be taken too far: the essence of that opposition was the constitutional undoing of absolutism, irrespective of who the King was, in the interests of oligarchy whether narrow or wide, and the very paternalism of Charles XII which had been demonstrated by his reforms after 1712 made him anathema, in principle, to them.

Personal devotion to Charles was not absent in the intellectual élite, and was noticeably present among the officer section of that loose group which comprised the 'Estates' party as opposed to the 'Council' party. Indeed, there are indications that many officers belonged to the 'opposition' only in the sense that they felt obliged to be politically active after the death of Charles lest Council government should be re-established. The Duke of Holstein-Gottorp might have formed a focus for this group. He would have proved a 'Swedish' King as opposed to a foreign-dominated Queen (for no one doubted that Frederick would be the power behind the throne): the contrast between Charles Frederick speaking Swedish in the council of war on 1 December 1718 while Frederick of Hesse spoke German was not lost on them. Knowing the hatred many officers as well as civilians had of the Görtz régime, the young Duke had in private expressed his willingness to give up the 'ministers' system, that is he would sacrifice the 'cabinet government' of Charles XII; but when the decisive moment came, he was both too young and too emotionally shattered by his uncle's death to act.* The family tradition in grief showed itself once more: Charles Frederick shut himself in his room and could not bear to speak to anyone. The letter he wrote to the Council in Stockholm as 'nearest blood relation' he was hardly able to finish. Having reported the 'utterly regrettable and for the whole Realm of Sweden so infinitely sad happening that His Royal Majesty, my highly respected and highly beloved Uncle died yesterday', he excused himself for the briefness of his communication. 'This nearly unbearable Sorrow touches my heart more than anyone else. I can write no more.'[34]

Personal distress is also evident in Rehnskiöld's and Mörner's letter to the Council when they reported on the outcome of the council of war on 1 December and on the events which had led up to Charles's death, but mixed with it is a sorrow that Charles should have died so young (for to them Charles at thirty-five years of age seemed young) and at a time when the tide

* In later years he became the candidate of the 'Holstein' party in Sweden which had as one of its objectives his succession to the throne, since Frederick had no children by Ulrika.

was at last turning in his favour. They grieve that the enemies of the Realm have shot dead 'this inimitable King'; they speak of his courage, wisdom, grace and mildness; they recall the way in which he never spared himself in his love for his subjects and his determination to protect Sweden against the 'violation of the enemies and their base trickery to ruin us through and through'. How sad it is, they add, that he should be killed far too early in life, just at the moment when there was every hope of a 'desirable issue' from the long war-years and of some relief from the 'unutterably heavy fatigues he had born in the past'. At the end of their letter the restraint breaks down:* 'We shall miss him when success comes, to see him lie dead before our eyes is grief indeed.'[35]

No one who knew either the military or the political situation at the end of 1718 assumed, as many historians have done, that Charles XII had come to the end of his tether as far as opportunities or possibilities were concerned;[36] and indeed, the more we learn about the period, the more we appreciate that if anything could have brought the military offensive to yield the 'tolerable' peace it would have been a longer life for the King. He was a strategist and tactician of proved merit, in one of the most inventive periods of his career, with that indefinable gift of command that inspired confidence and encouragement, terror and awe. As long as he lived Sweden could postpone discussion of the domestic issues which had been raised, in part by the war effort and in part by his own refusal to marry till peace came. The succession struggle acted as a catalyst for the overturn of absolutism; but it is impossible to tell if this could have been avoided, given the temper of the time, even if Charles had left sons.

On the personal side, having followed his life from cradle to grave, one cannot but echo the grief of his field-marshals that he died so young. Rhyzelius, writing his own memoirs, divided the ages of man into four. *Infantia* 'Childhood', he reckoned up to the age of seven; from seven to fourteen was *Puerita*, 'Youth'; then came *Adolescentia*, from fourteen to twenty-one, defined as 'More Mature Youth'; after twenty-one was *Juventus*, 'Maturity'. Part of Charles's *Adolescentia*, as well as all the years of *Juventus* which fate allowed to him, was spent on a job he had not chosen but for which he had been trained since childhood and for which he showed such aptitude that he became a general of renown. But that life did not offer him all he had hoped for was clear to him and to those who knew him best. 'He would have been a great King, had he lived', the young Tessin remembers his father as saying – and the elder Tessin was probably in as good a position as any to judge Charles's potentialities as a peace-time monarch. 'He did not know himself', a remark of the younger Tessin's, points to a family tradition that the King as a person had lacked opportunities for fulfilling more than some facets of his character and personality.[37]

* Rehnskiöld, we are told, was one of those generals who couldn't hold back his tears when Charles's body was brought to Tistedal on 30 November.

Charles himself considered he had missed something by not marrying and having a wife and children of his own. Whether his postponement of what he hoped would prove the happiness of 'a wife who loved me and not the King' was due only to the responsibilities the war laid on his shoulders cannot be decided. It might be argued that his is a typical case of an early orphaned boy, deeply attached to his mother who, transferring affection to his sisters, would have remained a bachelor all his life, however much he talked of wanting to marry. But the slightly obsessive absorption with duty of one who has to shoulder immense responsibilities at an early age may be a more fitting analysis of his case. Some self-doubt is natural in face of daunting odds. What if he should fail to defend Sweden as his father had taxed him with doing once the country were attacked? If he did fail, he seems to have argued, he could only hold his head up if he had shown stoic self-discipline and devoted all his time and all his energy to the task. '*On peut cesser d'être heureux*', he once commented to Löwen, '*ce qui ne dépend de nous, mais on ne doit cesser d'être juste*'.[38]

Charles XII's self-discipline made people who did not know him well think of him as without emotion. Rosenadler, who at the King's funeral on 28 February 1719 delivered his *personalier*,[39] stressed this in a simple and dignified oration which tried to characterize Charles as he had seemed to those who could not accept such a superficial judgement. It is not a fulsome speech or a high-flown one, and two phrases are oddly moving: Charles XII had been *barhiertat*, openhearted, a word which in Swedish also carries a slight connotation of being vulnerable from sheer sincerity of purpose; and he had a '*liksom fortrolig väsen*' – a 'sort of confiding disposition', a phrase which hints at a rather excessive trust in the goodness of men.

V

On the political level – with which Rosenadler was not concerned – Charles XII was, as this biography has tried to show, less open and trusting than sometimes thought and used all the wiles at his command which he deemed within his concept of honourable behaviour. His feints were as skilfully deployed on the diplomatic as on the military field; secrecy and enigmatic answers became second nature to him. Minor secretaries as well as grand officials could read the signs off his face when it was and when it was not safe to broach a particular political problem. He had the dynasty's predilection for bold solutions derived from Sweden's situation in which the great-power position had to be built up and defended by military efforts which tested the country to the uttermost and could not easily be remounted in the same generation. Hence the Grand Design – which failed. He also learnt, I would submit, that realistic appraisal of what was possible and what was not possible which we are more likely to associate with Gustavus Adolphus and Charles XI. He learnt it in a hard school, in the years in Turkey when his political calculations were shown to rest on insufficient foundations or false premises; that he learnt it to good purpose the diplomatic offensive and the military planning of 1716–18 show.

One aspect of Charles XII's policy which was brought to a successful conclusion was his struggle for Protestant rights in Silesia. The King who, in Cederhielm's judgement, 'did not want to force any man's religion', felt a moral obligation to fulfil Sweden's guarantee of such rights under the Treaty of Westphalia. Here he picked up the mantle of Gustavus Adolphus which Charles X had let fall; and just because there existed a treaty right* his persistent efforts proved effective. Motraye waxed indignant at Voltaire's comment in 1731 that Charles XII's work for the Silesian Protestants had not amounted to much and stressed the great and beneficial changes in respect of freedom of worship which he had witnessed with his own eyes in Silesia in 1714. Vigilance remained necessary: in January 1718 Charles XII sent a memorial to Stiernhöök at Vienna on recent minor contraventions of the Altranstädt agreement to the detriment of the Protestants, and negotiations on this issue were still in progress at the time of the King's death.[40]

Charles XII lived to roughly the same age as his predecessors on the Swedish throne who, like him, were fated to spend their reigns as commanders in the field: when he was killed in 1718 he was thirty-six years old, the same age as his grandfather Charles X who had died in 1660, and only two years younger than his great-grand-uncle Gustavus Adolphus who fell in battle in 1632. None of the three lived to see the end of the war into which they had been drawn. Of all three, Charles XII had to sustain what his field-marshals called the unutterably heavy fatigues' of war for the longest period: eighteen years as opposed to the eleven of Gustavus Adolphus and the four of Charles X. In some ways Charles XII's task was much harder than theirs; they were after all swimming with the tide in that Sweden's great-power position was building during their reigns and they were able to make use of favourable opportunities offered by temporary weakness of one or other of their enemies; when Charles XII was faced with the task of defending the great-power position, the tide was running strongly against Sweden in that every state that had ever suffered from the aggression (however motivated) of his predecessors combined to overwhelm her.

Charles XII has probably been underestimated as a general because of a lack of specific information about him as a strategist and tactician. The theatres of war in which he fought were not central ones, like those in which Gustavus Adolphus fought between 1630 and 1632, while Charles X's Polish and Danish campaigns were inextricably interwoven with Brandenburg and Dutch military efforts. Sweden's lone struggle in the Great Northern War did not – as did her wars of 1630–48 and 1655–60 – entail fighting beside one of the western nations and this has militated against Charles XII's contribution to the

* Conversely, Charles XII's appeal to Louis XIV to mitigate his treatment of Protestants in France had no appreciable effect, and his efforts for the repeal of the 4th clause of the Treaty of Ryswick, so detrimental to Protestant interests in the Empire, proved unavailing.

art of war being examined and analysed in its European context. Finally
the pacific inclinations both of Europe and Sweden between 1721 and 1740
meant that no officers trained by him made their marks as commanders: there
was no direct school of pupils. Frederick II's contemptuous gibe that Charles
XII should have had the courage to commit suicide after the loss of Stralsund
has left its mark (while his praise has been forgotten),[41] as has the boast of
Maréchal de Saxe that he, given Charles's opportunities, would have made
short work of the Polish troubles.[42]

An attempt to put Charles XII as a commander into the wider context of
the art of war through the ages, was made in Sweden in 1918 with the publication by the General Staff of a history of the Great Northern War in four folio
volumes with a separate set of maps and sketches. This is marred (as is the
much later study by Porfiriev of Tsar Peter as a commander)[43] by a conviction
that the chief figure examined is unique in his application and adaptation of
classical battle patterns and that he, alone, aimed at that absolutely decisive
battle (the *Vernichtigungsschlacht* of Germany military terminology) which
the linear tactics, supposedly reigning supreme on the rest of the battlefields
of Europe, ignored.

In Sweden this thesis has long ago been abandoned as realization of the
inter-European character of the art of war has grown and as proofs have
accumulated that Swedes learnt from the rest of Europe during the reigns of
Charles XI and Charles XII: in arms-production, in organization and in
tactics. Indeed, the embarrassment now felt at the claim that Charles XII was
the great exponent of a war of movement as opposed to a war of the lines – in
the face of such obvious exceptions to linear warfare in the west as Marlborough's and Eugène's campaign of 1704 – is acute enough to have brought
the volumes of *Generalstaben* into some disrepute. Yet this work remains invaluable. The Bennedich-Stille[44] examination of the King's strategic aims is
still the basis from which historians must start and its technical clarification of
the King's battles is definitive. One could wish that military historians would
make greater use of the maps and sketches which offer no linguistic hindrance
to research: it would be interesting to know what they thought of Charles XII's
own estimation of the battle of Holovzin as the finest one of his career.

The specifically Swedish contribution to the art of war, built up under
Charles XI and continued and developed by Charles XII, can now be distinguished as that of pioneering national armies provincially based and well
supplied, so that individual looting became unnnecessary and organized
looting, the *praeda militari*, a great rarity, the Crown at the same time
achieving control over supply and finance so that the fortunes made by
contractors and financiers in the armies of the west have no counterpart in
Sweden.* Indeed the *indelingverk* of Charles XI, until recently thought a

* This may in one sense have become a weakness: there was no vested interest in war which
could keep the momentum going during Charles XII's years in Turkey. Cp. for the effect of the
reduction on the ambitions of the high nobility Hatton, 'Gratifications and foreign policy'
William III and Louis XIV, p. 93.

retrograde step, has now been shown to possess distinct advantages and flexibilities[45] of which Charles XII could and did take full advantage.

Of Charles XII's individual contribution, his demand for artillery that could keep up with and play its part in speedy campaigns and attacks gave Cronstedt, that '*trollkarl*' (i.e. magician) among engineers as contemporaries admiringly labelled him, the impetus to unfold his genius; and Charles's consistent and conscious sponsorship of Cronstedt's technical innovations certainly led to important changes in European artillery development in the eighteenth century, the Danes, Russians and Germans being quick to copy the 'Cronstedt system' in the 1720s and 1730s. Less obvious, but possibly more significant, is the legacy of Charles XII which can be traced in the works of those French military commentators, principally Folard, who either from direct observation or from discussions with officers who served under Charles XII have assessed the novelties he introduced in organization to produce flexible deployment of his forces and the cohesion and impact which his improved drill and the *gå-på* tactics of the *armes blanches* gave in attack. Through them something of Charles's military thinking and methods were transmitted to the generals who transformed warfare in the age of the French Revolution.[46]

The King's tactical innovations can be studied in the changing drills and regulations published (but kept secret from foreigners) in his lifetime or committed to print in the post-1718 years: notably in the 1731 *reglement*. The contemporary Swedish officer's appreciation of them comes across vividly and proudly in the diaries and letters of the war. Schönström noted with admiration the line and column turns for the cavalry; Posse wrote to his brother in March 1708 with near-wonder about the 'fifty different kinds' of evolutions, charges, counter-marches and formations which Charles XII (truly a general 'gifted beyond belief', a King 'above all others') had thought out: they filled forty sheets of large paper and the whole army now practised them, perfecting the art of obeying silent commands – the lowering of a single flag sometimes sufficed to set a complicated manœuvre into operation. Even enemy officers who fought the Swedish armies of Charles's time expressed admiration. Löwen quotes one of them as saying to him in later years: '*Quelle infanterie que la votre! Quelle contenance! Quel silence! Quelle obéissance!*'[47]

Folard, a veteran of the War of the Spanish Succession, served with the Swedes in the relatively inactive years of 1716 and 1717; but he took part in the preparations for the Norwegian campaign to come and observed the training of the new army. He marvelled at an ingenious bridge constructed for it, 'the finest he had ever seen', and tried to make a contribution of his own by working on ideas to improve the Swedish naval artillery.[48] He talked to officers of the earlier years of the Northern War and was a member of that inner circle which after dinner discussed the art and science of war with Charles XII. '*Je n'ai jamais tant profité que dans ses conversations*', he wrote in that many-tomed *Histoire de Polybe ... avec un commentaire ou un corps de*

s

science militaire which he had planned to dedicate to the Swedish King.[49] In the battle between Ancient and Moderns Folard had no hesitation in coming down on the side of Charles, his 'modern hero', whom he ranked above Alexander the Great *'par ses actions, par ses vertus, par sa valeur et par ses grandes qualités pour la guerre'* – indeed as one of the greatest of all times: 'there never was one like him'. On reflection he came to the conclusion that it was in the variety of tactical means whereby Charles XII achieved his many successful river crossings that his *'vive force'* was unsurpassed.[50]

As a strategist Charles XII was influenced both by family temperament and by Sweden's geographical position and political problems. He shared intelligence and an aptitude for war with Gustavus Adolphus and Charles X; he also shared their liking for radical solutions to problems in the military and political field. Like Gustavus Adolphus he may have toyed, but only after 1715, with the thought of making himself a kind of protector over Protestant Northern Germany; before that time he had been too busy trying to follow Gustavus's precept of making the ditch between Sweden and Russia so wide that 'the bear could not jump over it easily'. Hence the Grand Design which failed. Like Gustavus and Charles XII he became involved in the problems of the Polish–Lithuanian Commonwealth and developed his own blue-print for a solution of those problems along lines that would suit Sweden's commercial interests and his own ideas of a 'national' religiously tolerant Poland. Like Charles X (though under different circumstances) he found he could not cope with the enmity of Denmark without an invasion of Norway, but his own plan for containment – the removal of the frontier to Glommen – was a less aggressive one than the incorporation of the Trondhjem district attempted by his grandfather.

But while it is essential to look at Charles XII within the context of past Swedish commitments, which indeed caused the Great Northern War, it is permissible to glance also at what distinguishes the whole generation that fought so hard to defend the great-power position during the long war. Here we meet an attitude towards a task which is not easy to define, but so easy to observe that a word still in current usage – at least among the older generation – has been coined for it: to be a *karolin*.* It embraces the virtues which were needed to hold out for twenty-one years against the coalition that attacked Sweden in 1700: endurance, loyalty, and an acceptance of responsibility without sentimental or pompous trappings. Indeed, the sharp but not sour quip, the barb of which is directed against yourself as much as against the circumstances in which you find yourself, or the witticism intended to dispel tension or lower the emotional temperature, are as characteristic of the Caroline attitude as are the stoic virtues. So is the fact that it contains not a trace of glorification of war. It springs from the defender's attitude and not from that of the aggressor, though its acceptance of the duty to fight to defend one's country is strong enough to inhibit any reflection that to one's

---

* i.e. to be of the Caroline age in a figurative sense; the plural of a *karolin* is *karoliner*.

enemies, that country is seen as the robber-baron of the past. The Caroline style – which the generation created – made the long and hard war easier to bear. If judgement there has to be on Charles and the rest of the original *karoliner* then it should be, as Folard was the first to suggest, not in respect of the victories they won but 'according to the enemies which they faced and the obstacles which they met in their war'.[51]

Abbreviations used in Selected Bibliography and Notes

A.A.H.   See Main Documentation, Unpublished 2 d.
A.E.   See Main Documentation, Unpublished 2 c.
Add. M.S.   Additional Manuscript collection in the British Museum.
B.M.   British Museum, London.
Bidrag S.N.K.H.   See Bibliography: non-Swedish contributions of importance.
Bref.   See Main Documentation, Printed 1.
Brinkmanska Archivet   See Contemporary diaries, journals, letters and
    reports, Feif's letters to Tessin.
D.B.L.   *Dansk Biografisk Leksikon.*
F.E.B.   Foreign Entry Books; See Main Documentation, Unpublished 2 a.
Generalstaben   See Bibliography: Army and Navy.
Handlingar   See Main Documentation, Printed 7.
Handlingar (Floderus)   See Main Documentation, Printed 6.
Handlingar (Malmström)   See Main Documentation, Printed 8.
H.A.   *Historisk Arkiv,* Stockholm.
H.H.   *Historiska Handlingar,* see Main Documentation, Printed 2.
H.T.   *Historisk Tidskrift,* Stockholm.
(Danish) *H.T.*   *Historisk Tidsskrift,* Copenhagen
(Finnish) *H.T.*   *Historisk Tidskrift,* Helsinki
(Norwegian) *H.T.*   *Historisk Tidsskrift,* Oslo
K.F.Å.   *Karolinska Förbundets Årsbok* – the yearbook which prints most
    specialist articles (*Scandia* is next on the list) by historians doing research in
    the period 1654–1721. The standard of the work accepted is very high;
    much attention is given to Russian and Polish research and the old gibe
    of a 'nationalist' outlook seems to a non-Swede like myself unjustified.
K.K.D.   *Karolinska Krigares Dagböcker,* ed. by A. Quennerstedt, 21 vols.
    1901–18 – a series in which journals, letters and diaries of officers and
    officials in-the-field have been published.
Kungl. Bibl.   Kungliga Bibliotek, Stockholm.
L.U.Å.   *Lunds Universitets Årsbok.*
L.U.B.   Lunds Universitets Bibliotek.
P.H.T.   *Personhistorisk Tidskrift.*
P.R.O.   Public Record Office, London.
R.A.   Riksarkivet, Stockholm.
R.A. Anglica   See Main Documentation, Unpublished 1.
S.B.L.   *Svensk Biografisk Leksikon.*
S.P.   State Paper collection of the Public Record Office; see Main docu-
    mentation, Unpublished 2 a.
U.U.Å.   *Uppsala Universitets Årsbok.*
U.U.B.   Uppsala Universitets Bibliotek.

Selected Bibliography*

MAIN DOCUMENTATION

Printed

1   The letters of Charles XII, published by E. Carlson, *Konung Karl XII:s egenhändiga bref*, 1893, abbreviated as *Bref*, which also includes drafts of and changes in official letters to illustrate the King's personal share in them. Letters which have come to light since 1893 are referred to in the notes.

2   Charles XII's correspondence with the Council, published in *Historiska Handlingar rörande Skandinaviens historia* (abbreviated as *H.H.*), vols. 1 (1700–1), 2 (1701–2), 3 (1703–5), 4 (1706–9), 5 (1710), 7 (1711), 9 (1711–12), 10 (1712), 11 (1713), 14 (1714), 15 (1715), 1816, and following years with a good index, of 1919, by E. Naumann.

3   Collections of official decrees collected by A. A. von Stiernman and published posthumously in vols. 5 and 6 of *Samling utaf kongl. bref, stadgar och förordningar etc. angående Sveriges rikes commerce, politie och œconomie utigenem från åhr 1523 in til närwarende tid* (1775).

4   Collection of decrees, resolutions and letters concerning the Swedish army, collected by S. Gahm Persson and published as *Kong. Stadgar, Förordningar, Bref och Resolutioner angående Swea Rikes Land-Milice till Häst och Fot*, vol. 4 (1814).

5   Collection of miscellaneous documents by E. M. Fant, *Handlingar til Uplysning af Svenska Historien*, IV (1802)

6   Collection of miscellaneous documents by T. Floderus, *Handlingar Lörande till Konung Carl XII:s Historia*, vols. I–IV (1819–1826), abbreviated as *Handlingar* (Floderus).

7   Collection of documents, princaipally Danish and Austrian diplomatic dispatches, published by A. Fryxell, *Handlingar rörande Sveriges historia ur utrikes arkiver*, vols. II–IV (1839–43), abbreviated as *Handlingar*.

* More documents, printed and unprinted, books and articles have, of course, been used than here listed; the criteria for inclusion have been (a) to mention those from which quotations have been taken; (b) to bring a few important books – and in special cases articles – before the reader who may want to pursue a particular topic. References to further monographs and articles are given in the notes at the end of the volume. The Selected Bibliography has been divided into MAIN DOCUMENTATION (a) PRINTED, (b) UNPUBLISHED; CONTEMPORARY DIARIES, JOURNALS, LETTERS AND REPORTS; COLLECTIONS OF LETTERS AND MEMOIRS; WORKS WHICH INCLUDE MUCH DOCUMENTATION, PARTICULARLY LETTERS, OFFICIAL AND PRIVATE; HISTORIOGRAPHICAL STUDIES; METHODOLOGICAL STUDIES OF SOURCE-MATERIAL; BIOGRAPHIES OF CHARLES XII; BASIC WORKS; ECONOMIC AND FINANCIAL HISTORY; ART AND INTELLECTUAL LIFE; RELIGION AND CHURCH; POLITICAL IDEAS AND POLITICAL PROPAGANDA; SOCIAL IDEAS AND TENSION; RECENT BIOGRAPHICAL STUDIES; THE SWEDISH EMPIRE; ADMINISTRATION AND LAW; ARMY AND NAVY; FOREIGN POLICY; NON-SWEDISH CONTRIBUTIONS OF IMPORTANCE. Place of publication, unless otherwise stated, is Sweden.

8   Collection of documents, principally French diplomatic dispatches published
     by C. G. Malmström, *Handlingar rörande Sveriges historia under åren 1713–20*
     (1854), abbreviated as *Handlingar* (Malmström).
9   Collections of documents illustrating the situation in Sweden at the time of
     Charles xii's death: L. Thanner's editions of *Handlingar angående revolutionen
     i Sverige 1718–19, H.H.*, 36: 1 (1954) and *Handlingar till Sveriges politiska
     historia 1718–19, H.H.*, 37: 1 (1961).
10   Collections from dispatches from Sweden or Charles xii's headquarters, or of
     orders to diplomats accredited to Sweden: *British Diplomatic Instructions*,
     vol. I: *Sweden 1689–1727* (London 1922); *Recueil des Instructions données aux
     Ambassadeurs et Ministres de France*, vol. II: *Suède* (Paris 1889); *Sbornik
     Imperatorskago Istoritjskago Obstsjevsktva*, vols. 39 and 50 (St Petersburg);
     Historical Manuscript Commission: *Stuart Papers*, 7 vols. 1903–23; *The Des-
     patches of Sir Robert Sutton, ambassador in Constantinople* (1710–14), (Camden
     Third Series vol. LXXVIII, London 1953, ed. A. N. Kurat.)
11   Individual series of letters (by non-Swedes) or reports of an official nature:
     a) Bolingbroke: *Letters and Correspondence of Henry St John, Lord Viscount
     Bolingbroke*, ed. T. Parke, 4 vols. (London 1798).
     b) Fabrice: *Anecdotes du sejour de Roi de Suède à Bender, ou Lettres de Mr le
     Baron de Fabrice pour servir d'éclaircissement à l'histoire de Charles XII*
     (Hamburg 1760).
     c) Jefferyes: *Captain James Jefferyes Letters from the Swedish Army 1707–1709*,
     ed. R. M. Hatton, *H.H.* 35: 1 (1954). *Kapten Jefferyes bref till engelska regerin-
     gen från Bender och Adrianople 1711–1714, från Stralsund 1714–1715*, ed. E.
     Carlson, *H.H.* 16: 2 (1897).
     d) Marlborough: *Letters and Despatches of John Churchill, first Duke of
     Marlborough*, ed. G. Murray (London, vol. IV, 1848 ed.)
     e) Marlborough: *Correspondence with Heinsius*, ed. by B. van't Hoff (The
     Hague, 1951).
     f) D'Avaux: *Negotiations ... d'Avaux* (for 1693 and 1697–8) ed. F. A. Wijnne,
     3 vols., the last in two parts (Utrecht, 1882–3). Cp. Main Documentation
     Unpublished 2a for the years missing in this collection.
     g) [John Robinson]: *An Account of Sueden* (London, 1694), to be read with
     R. M. Hatton, 'John Robinson and the Account of Sueden', *Bulletin of the
     Institute of Historical Research*, 1955.

Unpublished

1   Swedish (and non-Swedish) scholars have utilized the unprinted material from
     R.A., Kungl. Bibl., L.U.B., U.U.B., and other collections to such an extent
     that I have thought it most correct to refer to a document as quoted in a well-
     known work rather than to give the original reference. The only exception is to
     the Anglica section of the R.A. where I have used some letters which – as far
     as I have been able to ascertain – have not been used by other scholars:
     abbreviated R.A. Anglica.
2   Non-Swedish archives.
     a) In the Public Record Office, London (abbreviated P.R.O.): State Papers
     Foreign Sweden, (S.P.95) vols. 10–16 especially; Denmark (S.P.75), vol. 24;
     France (S.P.85) vols. 161 and 162 in particular; Hamburg (S.P.88), vol. 17;

Foreign Ministers in England (S.P.100), Sweden vols. 60–63; Foreign Entry Books (S.P.104), Sweden, vol. 13; Foreign Office Papers (F.O.95), vols. 576–8; the papers of d'Avaux from Stockholm.

b) In the British Museum, London (abbreviated B.M.): Add.MS. 7075 (Stepney Papers); 27457 (Miscellaneous: C.2.); 28899, 28903, 28907 (Ellis Papers); 35105 and 35106 (Robinson Correspondence); 35885 (Hardwicke Papers); 37985 (Blathwayt Correspondence); 40796 (Vernon Letters); 41178 (Miscellaneous; f.135); Harley Loan Papers 29/45.*

c) In the Archives des Affaires Etrangères, Paris (abbreviated A.E.): Correspondence Politique Suède, Supplements, vols. 6 and 7.

d) Algemeene Rijksarchief, The Hague, Archief Anthonie Heinssius (abbreviated A.A.H.): 140 (Rumpf letters of 1689), 1190 (Haersolte letters of 1707).

e) Brydges Papers, Huntington Library, San Marino, California (for news from the Netherlands sent to the paymaster-general in London).

CONTEMPORARY DIARIES, JOURNALS, LETTERS AND REPORTS

Adlerfelt's journal for 1708–9, ed. by S.E.Bring under the title *Karl XII:s krigsföretag 1700–1706* (1919).

Agrell's diary 1707–13, ed. by A.Quennerstedt: *K.K.D.* V.

Alstrin's letters to J.Upmarck: *H.T.* 1884.

Amira's memoirs, ed. by N.Jorga under the title *Storia dal Soggiorno di Carlo XII in Turchia, scritta dal suo primo interprete Allessandro Amira* (Bucharest 1905).

Barck's letters to Hermelin, 1702–8, 2 vols. ed. by C.von Rosen (1914–15) under the title *Bref från Samuel Barck till Olof Hermelin.*

Benzeliuz's anecdotes, ed. by H.Lundgren as *Anecdota Benzeliana* (1914).

Bielke's Mémoires (in French) ed. by G.Hallendorff under the title *Ture Gabriel Bielkes hågkomster af Karl XII* (1901).

Browallius's diary, ed. by H.Almquist: *P.H.T.* 1916.

Carlberg's report on 30 November 1718: edition in *K.F.Å.* 1920.

Cederhielm's diaries, journals, letters received and 'defence': *K.F.Å.* 1915, ed. by G.Carlquist; *K.F.Å.* 1925, ed. by F.Wernstedt; and *K.F.Å.* 1960, ed. by S.Waller.

Cederhielm's letters to his brother, ed. by A.Quennerstedt in *K.K.D.* VI (1707–22) and VIII (1700–1 and 1706).

Chancery diary, 1709–14 (*Kanslidagbok*);† ed. A.Quennerstedt: *K.K.D.* IV.

Charles XI's almanac-entries: the 1896 ed. by Z.Nordin, the 1918 one by S.Hildebrand; with publication of originals found since 1918 in *H.T.* 1947 and 1951.

Charles XI's letters to Nils Bielke, ed. by O.Malmström: *H.H.* 18: 2.

Fabrice, *Memoiren*, ed. and translated into German by R.Grieser, *Die Memoiren des Kammerherrn Friedrich Ernst von Fabrice* (Hildesheim 1956).

Feif's letters to Horn, ed. by M.Bohnstedt: *P.H.T.* 1921.

Feif's letters to Polhem, ed. by S.E.Bring: *K.F.Å.* 1911.

Feif's letters to Tessin, ed. by G.Andersson in *Handlingar ur Brinkmanska archivet på Trolle-Ljungby*, vol. I (1859), abbreviated as *Brinkmanska archivet.*

---

* I gratefully acknowledge permission to quote from these papers.
† Often known as von Kochen's diary, but it is not wholly by him.

Folard's memoirs, scattered in his *Nouvelles Decouvertes sur la Guerre*, and the 6 vols. of his *Histoire de Polybe*, etc.

Görtz's letters from prison at Arnhem in 1717, ed. by T. Westrin: *H.T.* 1898.

Görtz's explanation of his relationship to the Jacobites 1716–17: ibid.

Gyllenbrook's memoirs, ed. by N. Sjöberg under the title *Axel Gyllenkrooks relationer från Karl XII:s krig* (1913).

Gyllenkrook's 'relation', ed. by S. Bring in *H.H.* 34: 2 (1952).

Hermelin's letters to Barck 1702–9, ed. by C. von Rosen under the title *Bref från Olof Hermelin till Samuel Barck* (1913) with additional letters by N. Herlitz in *K.F.Å.* 1914, pp. 125–148.

Hogguer's memoirs published by F. Pouy as *Memoirs du B: on Hogguer, financier-diplomat concernant la France et la Suede 1700 a 1767* (Amiens 1890).

Hultman's memoirs, in *Handlingar* (Floderus), I.

Kagg's diary, ed. by A. Lewenhaupt: *H.H.* 24.

Kochen's 'relation' of the *Kalabalik*, ed. by S. E. Bring: *K.F.Å.* 1948.

Lagerberg's diary from his mission to Devlet-Gerei: *Dagbok under vistelsen hos tartar-chan Dowlet Gherey 1710–11* (1896).

Leutrum's journal from the Norwegian campaign of 1718 ed. by A. Quennerstedt: *K.K.D.* XII.

Lewenhaupt's journal, 'relation', 'justification' and 'points met', ed. by S. E. Bring in *H.H.* 34: 2 (1952).

Liewen's report of six conversations with Charles XII in Turkey, in *Handlingar* (*Floderus*), III.

Löwen's *Mémoires* (in French) with German introduction and notes in Swedish, ed. by F. Adler and S. Bonnesen: *K.F.Å.* 1929.

Lyth's diary, ed. by A. Quennerstedt: *K.K.D.* II.

Maigret's report on 30 Nov. 1718: in *K.F.Å.* 1920 edition.

Motraye, Aubrey de la, *Travels through Europe, Asia and parts of Africa*, II (London 1732); *Remarques historiques et critiques sur l'Histoire de Charles XII de M. de Voltaire* (London 1732).

[Naundorf], 'Charles XII in Turkey: Narrative of the King of Sweden's movements 1709–14. A Robert Samber translation identified', ed. by R. M. Hatton, in *Historical Studies* I (Ankara 1956), pp. 83–142.

Neumann's report of his attendance on Charles XII as a surgeon and of his dream of 14 April 1720: *H.H.* 4, pp. 188–91.

Nordberg, *Anmärckningar vid Karl XII's historia* (Copenhagen 1754) and his 'Passages' ed. by C. Hallendorff, *Studier öfver den äldre Karl XII:s historiografien* (1899).

Onjuchowska (Pani); recollections of Charles XII written down by T. Bulgarin in 1807, reprinted in *Ögonvittnen*, ed. H. Villius (1962).

Petre's diary, ed. by A. Quennerstedt: *K.K.D.* I.

Pihlström's diary, ed. by E. Carlson: *H.H.* 18:4.

Piper's and Rehnskiöld's entrybook for letters 1709–15, ed. by P. Sörensson, *H.H.* 21: 2.

Piper's diary 1709–14, ed. by E. Carlson: *H.H.* 21 (1906).

G. A. Piper's diary, selections printed in *För skola och Hem* (1902), but used by me as printed from the original in G. Petri's regimental history, III.

Poniatowski, S. *Mémoire ou plutot une relation du palatin de Masovie des événements de sa vie depuis de chez lui, faire sur la requisition de sa famille 1734, 22 de janvier.* The Swedish translation, of the part relevant to the Charles XII period, with editorial notes, has been printed in *H.T.* 1890, pp. 181–288 under the title *Stanislaus Pontiatowskis berättelse om sine öden tilsammans med Karl XII*, and it is to this edition that the references given under Poniatowski's memoirs are given; *Remarques d'un seigneur polonais sur l'historie de Charles XII* (The Hague, 1741).

Posse's diary, ed. by A. Quennerstedt: *K.K.D.* I

Posse's letters to his brother 1700–8: *H.T.* 1882, pp. 81–94, 159–171.

Rehnskiöld's journals 1702–6 ed. by A. Quennerstedt: *K.K.D.* IX.

Rehnskiöld's and Piper's entrybook from 1709–15, ed. by P. Sörensson in *H.H.* 21:2.

Reuterholm's journals and memoirs, ed. by S. Landahl, *H.H.* 36: 2 (1956).

Reuterholm's letters to J. Cronstedt 1706–7, ed. by L. Wahlström: *P.H.T.* 1908.

Reuterholm's table-talk: see Browallius's diary.

Rhyzelius's memoirs, ed. by J. Helander under the title *Biskop A. O. Rhyzelii Anteckningar om sitt lefverne* (1904).

Roland (C. von) memoirs, ed. by S. E. Bring under the title *Minnen från fångenskap i Ryssland och Karl XII:s krig* (1914).

Roland (E. von) memoirs, ed. by S. Tunberg: *K.F.Å.* 1917.

Roos's 'relation', ed. by S. E. Bring, *H.H.* 34: 2 (1952).

Savary's* 'relation' from Turkey, ed. by G. Carlquist, *K.F.Å.* 1913, pp. 223–307.

Schönström's memoirs, ed. by C. Hallendorff under the title *Karl XII. En karolins berättelse* (1915).

Schmalensee's memoirs, ed. by T. Kocken: *K.F.Å.* 1957, pp. 117–52.

Schultz's memoirs, ed. by G. Löfgren: *K.F.Å.* 1948, pp. 71–103.

Schwerin's report of 1728, ed. by T. Westrin; *H.T.* 18.

Siltmann's journal, ed. by A. Quennerstedt: *K.K.D.* III (1907).

Siltmann's letters, ed. by S. Jägerskiöld, *K.F.Å.* 1936

Stålhammar's letters to his wife 1700–8, ed. by A. Quennerstedt: *K.K.D.* VII.

Stenbock's letters to his wife (and his wife's letters to him) ed. by C. M. Stenbock under the title *Magnus Stenbock och Eva Oxenstierna*, 2 vols. 1913–14.

Stenbock's letters to Charles XII, 1702–5, ed. A. Quennerstedt: *K.K.D.* XII.

Theyls (W.), *Mémoires* [from Turkey] (Leyden 1721).

Ulrika Eleonora's diary for 1709, ed. by E. W. Dahlgren: *P.H.T.* 1915.

Ulrika Eleonora's 'memoirs' ('Anmärkningar' of 1740) ed. by M. Swederus: *Stockholms Magazin* 1780.

Weihe's diary, ed. by E. Carlson, *H.H.* 19: 1.

Weismantell's diary 1709–14, ed. by S. E. Bring, *H.H.* 28: 1 (1928).

Wisocki-Hochmuth's diary, ed. by A. Quennerstedt: *K.K.D.* II.

COLLECTIONS OF LETTERS AND MEMOIRS

a) M. Crusenstople. *Karakteristiker ur Samtidas Förtroliga Bref och Anteckningar häntade af Författaren till Almanackens Biografi* [no date] in which A. O. Hermelin's

---

* One of Charles XII's interpreters who returned to Sweden with him and from whom Folard and Motraye had information.

protocol from an important conference of June 1702 should be noted, as also a memorial by Piper of Sept. 1702.

b) ed. H. Villius, *Ögonvittnen*. *Karl XII*, 1962 in which eyewitness accounts, e.g. those by Pani Onjuchowska and Søren Hagerup, are more easily accessible than in the original editions. The personal dislike of most of the contributors for Charles xII makes for lively reading in the editorial introductions, but in the case of one letter printed, that by Giertta from *H.T.* 1898, there is a total misreading of the letter: Giertta, who blames the failure at Poltava on the King not being able to lead the army, is interpreted as 'not being able to prevent himself from criticizing the King as a commander'.

c) Letters from private soldiers, ed. by E. Ingers: *K.F.Å.* 1914, pp. 208–37.

WORKS WHICH INCLUDE MUCH DOCUMENTATION, PARTICULARLY LETTERS, OFFICAL AND PRIVATE

1   Adlerfelt, G. *Historie Militaire de Charles XII, roi de Suède,** *I–IV* (Amsterdam 1740).
2   Nordberg, J. *Konung Carl den XII:s historia*, I–II 1740. The German edition of 1745–51 contains the largest amount of documents.
3   Moser, F. C. von. *Rettung der Ehre und Unschuld des ... Georg Heinrichs, Freyherrn von Schlitz, gennant von Goertz* (1776).
4   Loenbom, S. *Kong. rådets och fält-marskalkens, herr grefwe Magni Stenbocks lefwerne*, 4 vols. (1757–65).
5   Rosen, C. von. *Bidrag till kännedom om de händelser som närmast föregingo svenska stormaktsväldets fall* (1701–4), 2 vols. 1936.

HISTORIOGRAPHICAL STUDIES

1   By K.-G. Hildebrand, in *H.T.* 1954 and *H.T.* 1955.
2   By G. Jacobson in *K.F.Å.* 1941.
3   By E. Olsoni in *K.F.Å.* 1956.
4   O. Haintz, 'Karl xII von Schweden im Urteil der Geschichte', *Preussische Jahrbücher* (Berlin 1936).

METHODOLOGICAL STUDIES OF SOURCE-MATERIAL

Villius, H. *Karl XII:s ryska fälttåg. Källstudier* (1951).
Westin, G. 'Dagböcker som källor for Karl xII:s ryska fälttåg: *K.F.Å.* 1953.
A. L. Lewenhaupt's, 'berättelse', in *Festschrift* for F. Lindberg 1963.
Tengberg, E. *Från Poltava till Bender* (1952).
Jonasson, G. 'Planläggningen av rysska fälttåget år 1701', *K.F.Å.* 1966.

* The original manuscript (without such added material) for 1700–6 has been ed. by S. E. Bring under the title *Karl XII:s krigsföretag 1700–1706* (1918); note also the 'official history' of Charles xII's war by G. Adlerfelt, published anonymously 1706 as *Wahrhaffter Entwurff* etc.

BIOGRAPHIES OF CHARLES XII

1 classical: Voltaire, *Historie de Charles XII* (1731) to be read in conjunction with H. Brulin's article in *K.F.Å.* 1940.
2 revolutionary: Beskow, B. von, *Karl den Tolfte. Et Minnesbild* (1868–69).
3 the soldier among his men: Bengtsson, F. S., *Karl XII⁸ Levnad*, 2 vols. 1936 and many later editions. An abbreviated English translation *The Life of Charles XII* (London 1960).
4 the King and the war: Haintz, O. *König Karl XII von Schweden*, 3 vols. (1936, 1951, both with sec. ed. of 1958, 1958). Citations are to the 1958 ed.

BASIC WORKS

1 Fryxell, A. *Karl den Tolftes historia*, vols. 21–29 of *Berättelser ur svenska historien* (1856–59).
2 Carlson, F. F. *Sveriges historia under Carl XII:s regering* vols. I and II (1910 ed. of 1881–85 work carrying the story down to 1706); vol. III (1910) by E. Carlson (to 1710).
3 Hjärne, H. *Karl XII. Omstörtningen i Österuropa 1697–1703* (1902).
4 Schirren, C. von, *Zur Geschichte des nordischen Krieges* (Kiel, 1913).
5 The 'Old School' contributions by a.o. C. Annerstedt, C. O. Nordensvan, C. Adelsköld, C. Bratt and, more weightily, Arnold Munthe, *Karl XII och ryska sjömakten*, 3 vols. 1924–27, to be read in conjunction with S. Backman's review of vol. I in *K.F.Å.* 1927.
6 The collective work of the 'New School' ed. by S. E. Bring, *Karl XII* (1918) with contributions by H. Hjärne, G. Carlquist, N. Herlitz, H. E. Uddgren, A. Stille, P. Sörensson, S. Schartau, E. Naumann, J. A. Lagermark.
7 Jagerskiöld, S. *Sverige och Europa 1716–1718* (1937).
8 The collective work, ed. by N. Ahnlund, *Sanning och Sägen om Karl XII:s död* (1940).
9 Ahlmström, W. *Arvid Horn och Karl XII 1710–1713* (1959).
10 Kentrschynskyj, B. *Mazepa* (1966).

ECONOMIC AND FINANCIAL HISTORY

Heckscher, E. F. *Sveriges ekonomiska historia från Gustav Vasa* II:1 (1936); *Svenskt arbete och liv* (1941).

Hildebrand, K.-G. 'Ekonomiska syften i svensk expansions-politik 1700–09', *K.F.Å.* 1949.

Olander, G. *Studier över det inre tillståndet i Sverige, under senare delen av Karl XII:s regering* (a case-study of Skaraborg's *län* 1715–18), 1946.

Bjurling, O. *Sweden's foreign trade and shipping around the year 1700* (Lund, 1961).

Åstrom, S.-E. *From cloth to iron* (2 parts, Helsinki, 1963, 1965).

Lindeberg, G. *Svensk ekonomisk politik under den Görtzka perioden* (1941); *Krigsfinansiering och krigsshushållning i Karl XII:s Sverige* (1946).

538 *Bibliography*

Åmark, K. *Sveriges statsfinanser 1719–1809* (1964) has much material for the Charles XII period, revising older authorities at times.

ART AND INTELLECTUAL LIFE

Strömbom, S. *Svenska kungliga porträtt* (1943).
Josephson, R. 'Karl XI och Karl XII som esteter', *K.F.Å.* 1947.
Karlson, W. *Stat och Vardag, Stormaktstidens herremanshem* (1945).
Hans Järta's lecture of 1846, printed in *K.F.Å.* 1912.
Elfstrand, P. 'Karolinsk ikonografi', *K.F.Å.* 1945.
Tigerstedt, E. N. *Svensk litteraturhistoria* (1948).

RELIGION AND CHURCH

Pleijel, H. *Svenska kyrkans historia*, V (1935);
    Der Schwedische Pietismus in sienen Beziehungen zu Deutschland (1935).
Lindgren, B. *Bidrag till den svenska pietismens historia*. I: *Pietismen i Stockholm 1702–21* (1897).
Hildebrand, K.-G. 'De gamla fältprästerna', *Fulhälsning ... ärkestiftet* 1943, pp. 129–141.
Almquist, H. 'Study of the Swedish prisoners-of-war in Russia', *K.F.Å.* 1947.
Normann, C. *Prästeskapet på karolinska tiden* (1952).

POLITICAL IDEAS AND POLITICAL PROPAGANDA

Lagerroth, F. *Frihetstidens författning* (1915).
Hjärne, E. *Frän Vasatiden till Frihetstiden* (1929).
Grauers, S. *Sveriges Riksdag* IV: *Riksdagen under den karolinska tiden* (1932);
    'Några bidrag till oppositionens historia under Karl XII', *K.F.Å.* 1921.
Thanner, L. *Revolutionen i Sverige efter Karl XII:s död* (1953).

SOCIAL IDEAS AND TENSION

Strindberg, A. *Bondenöd och stormaktsdröm* (1937).
Hallendorff, C. *Ridderskapet och adeln och dess riddarhus* (1926).
Huly, O. T. 'Om hälso-och sjukvärd under Karl XII:s rysk-polska fälttåg', *Lychnos* 1938;
    'Pesten i Sverige 1710,' *Hygienisk Tidskrift*, 1915.
Rosén, J. *Det engelska anbudet om fredsmedling 1713. En studie i politisk propaganda* (1946).
Haverling, S.-E. 'Huvuddrag i svensk och antisvensk propaganda in Västeuropa på 1710-talet', *K.F.Å.* 1952.
Wright, H. G. 'Some English writers and Charles XII', *Studia Neophilologia*, Uppsala 1942–43.

RECENT BIOGRAPHICAL STUDIES

Lundh-Eriksson, N. *Hedvig Eleonora* (1947).
Åberg, A. *Karl XI* (1958).
Holst, W. *Frederik I* (1953).
 Ulrika Eleonora, Karl XII:s syster (1956).
Josephson, R. *Nikodemus Tessin d.y. Tiden-Mannen-Verket*, 2 vols. 1930–31.
Grauers, S. *Arvid Horn*
Lewenhaupt, A. *Karolinen Edvard Gyldenstolpe* (1941).
Schürer von Waldheim, M. *Prins Maximilian Emanuel af Württemberg* (1913).
Biederstedt, R. *Johann Friedrich Eosander, Gründzüge einer Biographie* (1961).
Kentrschynskyj, B. *Mazepa* (1966).
Uddgren, H.E. *Karolinen Adam Ludwig Lewenhaupt* I–II (1909, 1945).
Olsson, S. *Olof Hermelin, En karolinsk kulturpersonlight och statsman* (1953).
B.Sallnäs. *Samuel Åkerhielm* d.y. (1947).

Biographical data
Lewenhaupt, A. *Karl XII:s officarare*, 2 vols. 1921.
Elgenstierna, G. *Den introducerade svenska adelns ättartavlor*, 9 vols. 1925–36.
S.B.L. (has reached the letter F.); for the rest see *Svenska Män och Kvinnor*.

THE SWEDISH EMPIRE

Schartau, S. 'De svenska Östersjöprovinserna vid det stora nordiska krigets utbrott,'
 I.Livland, II. Estonia, III. Ingermanland: *K.F.Å.* 1924–26.
Soom, A. *Der Herrenhof in Estland im 17 Jahrhundert* (1954).
Isberg, A. *Karl XI och den livlandska adeln 1684–1695* (1953).
Sepp, E. 'Estland under det stora nordiska kriget och det svenska östproblemet',
 Svio-Estonica 1936.
Back, P.-E. *Herzog und Landschaft. Politische Ideen and Verfassungsprogramme in
 Schwedisch-Pommern* (Lund 1955).
 'Striden, om nebenmodus. En studie i Karl XI:s pommerske finanspolitik', *K.F.Å.*
 1958.
Peters, J. 'Unter der schwedischen Krone', *Zeitschrift für Geschichtswissenschaft*,
 1966.
Åstrom, S.-E. *From Stockholm to St Petersburg. Commercial factors in the political
 relations between England and Sweden 1675 to 1700* (Turku, 1962).
Pirimaë, H. I have only been able to consult this Estonian scholar's important work
 in the excellent summary by A.Loit in *H.T.* 1964.

ADMINISTRATION AND LAW

Wedberg, B. *Karl XII på justitietronen* (1944).
Munthe, A. *Kansliet under det karolinska tidevarvet* I (1935).
Steckzén, B.*Krigsskollegii historia*, vols. II–III (1937).

Gerentz, S. *Kommerskollegium och näringslivet* (1951).
Bååth, L. M. and Munthe, A. *Kungl. Statskontoret 1680–1930* (1930).
Eden, N. et al. *Kammarkollegiets historia* (1941).
Stiernman, A. A. von. *Alle riksdagars och mötens besluth etc.*, III (1733), with a good index by C. U. Leyonmarck of 1820.
The protocols of the Four Estates: the Nobility, the Clergy, the Burghers and the Peasants, have all been published for the greater part of the period dealt with; for full references to the long titles see, e.g. S.E. Bring, *Bibliografisk handbok till Sveriges historia*.

ARMY AND NAVY

Generalstaben [ed. Bennedich] *Karl XII på slagfältet*, 4 vols. 1918–19.
Wikander, J. *Översikt över Sveriges krig under 1700-talet* (1920).
Tengberg, E. *Karl XII och Ryssland* (1958).
Lybeker, O. et al. *Svenska flottans historia* (1943).
Traung, O. *Lars Gathenhielm. Kaperiverksamheten under Karl XII tiden* (1952).
Grauers, S. *Ätten Wachtmeister genom seklerna*, II (1946).

Regimental histories, e.g. those by:

Petri, G. *Livgrenadjärregementets historia*, III (1958).
Bensowa, E. *Kungl. Skaraborgs regementets historia*, II (1944).
Pihlström, A. *Kungl. Dalregementets historia* (1902–10).
Wernstedt, F. *Kungl. Svea livgardes historia*, IV (1954).
Schreber von Screeb, T. 'Kong Maij:tz Drabanter 1695–1718,' *K.F.Å.* 1936, pp. 43–152.
Ågren, S. *Karl XI:s indelningverk för armen* (1922).
Munthe, L.W. *Kungl. Fortifikationens historia* 3 vols. (1902–19).
Jacobsson, T. *Artilleriet under Karl XII:s tiden* (1943).
Lilliehöök, L. Articles in *Artilleri-Tidskrift* 1945 and 1946.

FOREIGN POLICY

Rosén, S. *Den svenska utrikespolitikens historia* II: 1 (1952).
Jägerskiöld, S. *Sverige och Europa 1716–1718* (1937).
Brulin, P. *Sverige och Frankrike åren 1700–1701* (1905).
Jonasson, G. *Karl XII och hans rådgivare* (1960).
Rystad, G. 'Ryssland eller Polen', *Scandia* (1961–62).
Herlitz, N. *Från Thorn till Altranstädt. Studier över Carl XII:s politik 1703–1706* (1916).
Backman, S. *Från Rawicz till Fraustadt. Studier i det store nordiska krigets diplomati 1704–1706* (1940).
'Karl XII's polska detronisations-politik', *K.F.Å.* 1947.
Hildebrand, K.-G. 'Karl XII och den östeuropäiske frågan' *Svensk Tidskrift* 1937.
'Sverige och England 1707, *K.F.Å.* 1937.
Stille, A. *Studier öfver Danmarks politik under Karl XII:s polska krig* (1889).

Nilsson, S.A. 'De svensk-turkiska förbindelserna före Poltava', *Scandia*, 1953–4, to be read with B.Kentrschynskyj, *Mazepa* (1962), and E.Tengberg, *Karl XII och Ryssland.*

Tengberg, E. *Från Poltava till Bender. En studie i Karl XII:s turkiska politik* (1953).

Sörensson, P., *Sverige och Frankrike 1715–1718*, 3 parts, 1909, 1916, 1921.

'Kejsaren, Sverige och de nordiska allierade från Karl XII:s hemkomst från Turkiet till alliansen i Wien', 4 parts, *K.F.Å.*, 1926, 1927, 1928, 1929.

Steinius, S. 'Sachsen och Preussen i den nordiska krisen 1709', *K.F.Å.* 1949.

Almquist, H. *Holstein-Gottorp, Sverige och den nordiska ligan i den politiska krisen 1713–1714* (1918).

Lundberg, B. *Sverige och Preussen. Frhn krigsutbrottet 1715 till freden 1720*, 2 parts, 1913–14.

Schartau, S. *Förhållandet mellan Sverige och Hanover 1709–1715.*

Bonnesen, J. *Studier över August II:s utrikespolitik 1712–1715* (3 parts, 1918–24, the last part available only in duplicated form in Swedish university libraries).

Carlson, F.F. *Om fredsunderhandlingarne åren 1709–1718* (1857).

NON-SWEDISH CONTRIBUTIONS OF IMPORTANCE

Bidrag til den Store Nordiska Krigs Historie, 9 vols. published by the Danish general staff, chief editor A.P. Tuxen and – for vol. 9 – K.C.Rockstroh (Copenhagen 1899–1932).

Lewitter, L. 'The Russo-Polish Treaty of 1686 and its antecedents II; *Polish review*, 1964, pp. 21–37.

Konopzynski, W. *Polskai Szwecja od pokoju Oliwskiego do upadku Rzeczypos-politej 1660–1695* (Warsaw 1924), the part from 1700 translated in 'Karl XII och Polen', *K.F.Å.* 1924, pp. 54–126.

Feldman, J. *Polska w dobie wielkiej wojny północnej* (Krakow 1925), used in the summary by K.-G.Hildebrand, *K.F.Å.* 1936, pp. 153–86.

Um die Polnische Krone. Sachsen und Polen während des Nordischen Krieges 1700–1721, edd. J.Kalisch and J.Gierowski (Berlin 1962), with important contributions by the editors, Piwarski, Koroljuk, Lemke and others.

Gierowski, J. 'From Radoszkowice to Opatów – the history of the decomposition of the Stanislaw Leszczyńsky Camp', *Poland at the XIth International Congress of Historical Sciences* (Warsaw 1960).

* Nikiforov, L.A. *Russko-angliyskie otnosheniya pri Petre I* (Moscow 1950).

Tarle, E. *Severnaya voyna i shvedskoye nashestviye na Rossiyu* (Moscow 1958).

Shutoy, V.E. *Bor 'ba narodnykh mass protiv nashestviya armii Karla XII 1700–1709* (Moscow, 1958).

Feygina, S. *Alandskiy Kongress* (Moscow 1959).

Wittram, R. *Peter der Grosse* (Göttingen 1954).

Peter I. Tzar und Kaiser (2 vols. Göttingen 1964).

Hassinger, E. *Brandenburg – Preussen, Schweden und Russland 1700–1713* (München 1953).

Mediger, W. *Mecklenberg, Russland und England–Hannover 1706–1721* (Hildesheim 1967.

* In Russian titles I have adopted the transliteration in use at the School of Slavonic and East European Studies, University of London.

Gerhard, D. *England under der Aufstieg Russlands* (Munich, Berlin 1933).

Braubach, M. *Prinz Eugen von Savoyen*, vols. III–V (Munich 1964).

Sumner, B. H. *Peter the Great and the Ottoman Empire* (Oxford 1949).

Chance, J. F. *George I and the Northern War* (London 1909).

Kurat, A. N. *Isvec kirali XII. Karl, in Turkiyede kalisi ve bu siralarda Osmali Imparatorlugu* (1943) utilized in German (unpublished) translation by W. Björkman, deposited in U.U.B.

Syveton, G. *Louis XIV et Charles XII* (Paris 1900).

Nordmann, C. *La crise du Nord au début de XVIIIe siècle* (Paris 1962).

For reference to the main European works on international relations in the period see R. M. Hatton, *Diplomatic Relations between Great Britain and the Dutch Republic* (London 1950).

'Gratifications and foreign policy', *William III and Louis XIV*, edd. R. M. Hatton and J. S. Bromley (Liverpool 1967).

'Louis XIV and his fellow-monarchs', *Louis XIV*, ed. J. Rule (Columbus, Ohio, 1968).

Notes

BOOK I, CHAPTER I: THE PERSON AND THE PERSONALITY

1   See S. Strömbom, *Svenska kungliga porträtt*, I (Stockholm 1943), section (pp. 3–18) 'Karl XII'; P. Elfstrand, 'Karolinsk ikonografi', *K.F.Å.* 1945, pp. 162–7; R. Josephson, 'Karl XI och Karl XII som esteter', ibid., 1947, pp. 41–9.

2   Alstrin's letter to Upmarck, 18/28 May 1707: *H.T.* 1884.

3   Protocol of the 1799 viewing by Fredenheim, printed by V. Djurberg, *K.F.Å* 1916, pp. 276–8.

4   See the drawing by Paul Myrén, reproduced in *Dagens Nyheter* 30/8, 1917.

5   See A. Stille, 'Karl XII och Porten', in Bring, *Karl XII*, p. 396.

6   Compare, e.g. the article by A. Nyström with that by S. Clason and A. Stille in *Dagens Nyheter* 16/7 and 5/8, 1917. That this must to some extent have been inevitable was born in on me when I asked General Petri – who had been present at the 1917 opening – his impression of Charles XII's features: 'He looked as I had always pictured him in my mind.'

7   To judge from the King's relative baldness, this portrait – in the possession of Major Schürer von Waldheim in 1924 – must date from the post-1714 period; it has been reproduced in *K.F.Å.* 1917, p. 26.

8   A copy of this Latin description, dated 14 Dec. 1714 from Rawicz, was sent to Hermelin and is now in R.A.; it has been printed in Swedish translation by N. Herlitz, *K.F.Å.* 1922, pp. 207–9.

9   The portrait of Charles XII by King Stanislaus, now in the Skattkammar collection, from 1711 or 1712 (and therefore not done from life), would seem to hint at the same trait since there is a marked difference in treatment of the two eyes; it is reproduced in Bring, *Karl XII*, p. 368.

10 A. de la Motraye, *Travels*, II, 6 describes this habit in 1712: the King, with his right hand, 'combs' through his thinning hair; the engraving has been reproduced in O. Kuylenstierna, *Karl XII* (1925, 2nd ed.), p. 188.

11 C. G. Creutz's letter to his wife, 30 Oct. 1707 in *K.F.Å.* 1911, p. 169, where the portrait is reproduced, p. 168.

12 This was painted at Bauske in 1701; an interesting comparison between this and the Löwen portrait painted in Elbing in December 1703 is made by S. Bonnesen, 'Ett hittils okänt Karl XII:s porträtt', *K.F.Å.* 1929, pp. 1–4.

13 Creutz's letter of 30 Oct. 1707, *K.F.Å.* 1911, p. 169.

14 Elfstrand, *K.F.Å.* 1945, p. 165. The Löwen portrait of the King in profile from 1714 has been judged a near caricature, showing a particularly heavy jowl,

small eyes and a coarse nose: it is now in the Nationalmuseum, Stockholm. The Löwen miniature of 1714, now in the Skattkammar collection, also shows a fairly heavy jaw and so does the mask modelled from the dead face, see illustration facing p. 493.

15 Feif's letter to Tessin, 30 Feb. 1712, in _Brinkmanska archivet_; cp. Strömbom, p. 372 for Sparre's letter to the Queen Grandmother.

16 Elfstrand, _K.F.Å._ 1945, p. 166; G. W. Lundberg's article in _Svenska Dagbladet_ 29/3, 1931; cp. Motraye, _Remarques_, pp. 59–60, for a contemporary explanation that Krafft had painted the King without permission: hence the anger and the slashing.

17 _Dagens Nyheter_ 28/7, 1917: 'Vid Carl xii:s öppnade kista'.

18 Nordberg, II, 'portrait' at the end of vol. II (pp. 685 ff.).

19 Browallius's diary, 2 Feb. 1736, from Reuterholm's table-talk.

20 R. Josephson, _Tessin_, I (1930), 148.

21 Rhyzelius's memoirs, 2 Jan. 1718, tells how he taught Charles to respect the four top buttons of his clergyman's gown: by having them sown on very firmly; cp. Hultman's memoirs, _Handlingar_ (Floderus) I, 126–7.

22 Browallius's diary, 2 April 1735, reporting Reuterholm's story how Örnstedt cured the King of tugging at his lace-cuffs: he pointedly remarked that they were paid for with his own money.

23 Juel's letter of 12 Jan. 1698: _Handlingar_, IV.

24 Campredon's letter of 15 April 1717, printed in _Handlingar_ (Malmström) I, 42: but note from Charles's letter to Ulrika, 25 Jan. 1717: _Bref_, that he used herbs as a tea against colds and coughs.

25 ibid., letter of 25 Jan. 1717.

26 Bielke, _Mémoires_, p. 43.

27 _Ibid._ p. 43; for orders to procure fine linen for the King's shirts and good quality stockings when he was in Turkey see the letter of G. von Düben to T. Funck of 27 April 1712: _H.T._ 1889, pp. 372–3.

28 Schönström's memoirs, p. 44; cp.: Bielke, _Mémoires_, p. 63 (attributing the discarding of the furs to Charles's sensitivity to being teased for looking plump).

29 This cap has been preserved in Kungl. Livrustkammaren, see photograph in _Sveriges Historia genom tiderna_ (ed. H. Maiander), III, 185.

30 Nordberg, II, 'portrait'.

31 See, e.g. the Löwen miniature of 1703 mentioned in note 9 above.

32 See, e.g. frontispiece, from 1707.

33 Nordberg, II, 685; Fabrice, _Memoiren_, p. 25: '_die schönste Augen der Welt_'.

34 Alstrin to Upmarck, 18/28 May 1707: _H.T._ 1884.

35 Nordberg, II, 'portrait'.

36 Bielke's _Mémoires_, pp. 6–7, gives this phrase as '_Hvad gör Ni?_' – 'What are you doing?' – but the more usual rendering is '_Hvad säger Ni?_'

37 Feif, reporting a conversation with Charles xii to Horn, in letter of 17 Dec. 1710: _P.H.T._ 1921: cp. the letters of Charles xii to Hedvig Sophia and Ulrika Eleonora in _Bref_.

38 Schrönström's memoirs, p. 44.

39 See, e.g. the comment in 1700 by a Saxon diplomat on Charles's 'limited intelligence', cited by C. Bratt, _Karl XII som härförare_ (1931), p. 15.

40 Alstrin's letter to Upmarck, 4/14 May 1707: _H.T._ 1884.

41 The expression used by apothecary Lambert in 1708 is 'my heart froze'; the
    equivalent on the personal level to the political phenomenon observed by
    Fabrice in Turkey, *'il est adoré dans ce pais-ci, et craint en même tems'*, letter of
    4 July 1710: *Lettres.*

42 We have similar evidence from many other sources, e.g. from the official H.H.
    von Liewen whose verbatim report of six conversations with Charles XII in
    Demotika in 1714 are printed in *Handlingar* (Floderus) IV, 318–44, and from
    the young officer Petre who relates conversations with the King in the trenches
    at Poltava in his diary, printed in *K.K.D.* I, 260 ff.

43 For his service abroad see the introduction by Fritz Adler (in German) in
    K.F.Å. 1929 to the Löwen *Mémoires* (in French); also the Löwen papers
    deposited in R.A.: Sigrid Leijonhufvuds samling, vol. 24.

44 Feif's correspondence with Horn, Tessin and Polhem has survived; see Biblio-
    graphy under 'Contemporary diaries, journals, letters and reports'.

45 Hultman's memoirs: *Handlingar* (Floderus) I, 59–60; for the marches of the
    Caroline army see S.Landtmanson, 'De senaste karolinska musikfynden',
    K.F.Å. 1913, pp. 389–405.

46 Nordberg, I, 7.

47 First pronounced by E.G. Geijer, this judgement has gained wide currency.

48 Rhyzelius's memoirs, p. 80.

49 Schürer von Waldheim, *Maximilian*, p. 93.

50 These letters are printed in *Bref*; those to his grandmother have been largely
    lost and relatively few of those to his elder sister have survived.

51 See, e.g. E.Carlson, the editor of the *Bref*, p. xxxvii.

52 For such routine phrasing see F. Redlich, *De Praeda militari. Looting and
    Booty 1500–1815* (Wiesbaden, 1956), pp. 39 ff.

53 They have been printed in *Stockholms Magazin*, 1780 by M.Swederus, pp.
    568 ff., under the title 'Ulricae Eleonorae Anmärkningar', from now on cited
    as Ulrika Eleonora's memoirs.

54 Though the Danish diplomatic reports, printed in *Handlingar*, II–IV, are built
    on good contacts at court.

55 For Tessin see R.Josephson's 2 vol. biography published in 1930 and 1931:
    Nicodemus Tessin d.y.-Tiden–Mannen-Verket.

56 Add. MS. 35885, ff. 1–2 (and Add. MS. 31022, f. 211), 'Character of the King
    of Sweden 1707'. Raby, its author, was not (vide *Ögonvittnen*) accredited to
    Charles XII in 1704.

57 First printed in *Nytt sockenbibliothek*, 1862 from T.Bulgarin's memoirs; the
    place has been identified by A.Quennerstedt, *Vårt Land*, 8/12, 1903 and the
    story repeated in the same author's *Ur Karl XII:s lefnad*, I (1916), pp. 172 ff.

58 For the Browallius diary, ed. by H.Almquist and printed in *P.H.T.* 1916, see
    Bibliography under 'Contemporary diaries, journals, letters and reports'.

59 For Reuterholm's journal and memoirs, ed. by S.Landahl, printed in *H.H.*
    36: 2, see ibid.

60 For Reuterholm's letters to J.Cronstedt, 1706–7, printed in *P.H.T.* 1908,
    see ibid.

61 For Carl von Roland's memoirs, ed. by S.Bring, Stockholm, 1914, see ibid.

62 For this controversy see A.Nyström, 'Ett interessant Carl XII dokument',
    Dagens Nyheter 16/7, 1917 and S.Clason and A.Stille, 'Carl XII hermafrodit?

En vederläggning', dated 21/7, printed in the same paper, 5/8, 1917.
63 Ulrika Eleonora's memoirs, pp. 570–1; Juel's letter of 8 Dec. 1697: *Handlingar*, IV.
64 Nordberg, II, 'portrait'; Schönström's memoirs, p. 45.

BOOK I, CHAPTER 2: THE FAMILY

1 For Swedish foreign policy in this period see G.Landberg, *Den svenska utrikspolitikens historia*, I: 3 *1648–1697* (1952) pp. 176 ff.; K.Zernack. *Studien zu den schwedish-russischen Beziehungen in der 2. Hälfte des 17. Jahrhunderts*, I (Giessen, 1957) pp. 56 ff.
2 A.Åberg, *Karl XI* (1958), pp. 63–111.
3 L.Laursen and C.Bøggild-Andersen, 'Ulrikke Eleonore', *D.B.L.*; W.Holst, *Ulrika Eleonora d.y. Karl XII:s syster* (1956), p. 8.
4 S.P. 95, vol. 10, Allestree's letter of 3 March 1677.
5 The authors of 'Ulrikke Eleonore', *D.B.L.*, regard the story that Charles XI complained of his bride's looks having been overpraised (frequently cited in Swedish works) as apocryphal.
6 See, e.g., S.P. 95, vol. 11, Warwick's letter of 18 Nov. 1682 and Torcy's 'Compte-Rendue' in *La Mission extraordinaire du Marquis de Torcy ... en 1685* (ed. J.Marchand, Paris, 1951), p. 105.
7 S.P. 95, vol. 11, Robinson's letter of 31 March 1680.
8 ibid., Robinson's letter of 14 April 1680.
9 O. Malmström, *Anteckningar rörande Drottning Ulrika d.ä. och Karl XI:s Hof* (1898), pp. 117–18; N.Lund-Eriksson, *Hedvig Eleonora* (1947), has emphasized the shared interests of the two queens and put the tension into perspective; cp. Holst, *Ulrika Eleonora*, p. 10.
10 The position is illustrated in S.Bolin and J.Carlsson, *Historisk Atlas* (2nd ed. 1947), p. 21. For a lucid exposition of the problem see *Bidrag S.N.K.H.* I (ed. A.Tuxen, Copenhagen, 1899), pp. 4, 11 ff.; for a brief survey in English see P. Torntoft, 'William III and Denmark-Norway, 1697–1702', *The English Historical Review*, 1966, pp. 2 ff.
11 See G.Rystad, *Johan Gyllenstierna* (1957), and authorities there cited for discussion of this problem; cp. the appendix in Zernack, op. cit., pp. 158–62.
12 See Åberg, pp. 97–9.
13 O.Sjögren, *Carl XII och hans män* (1904), p. 10.
14 Hedvig Sophia in 1681, Charles in 1682, Gustav in 1683, Ulrik in 1684, Frederick in 1685, Charles Gustavus in 1686, Ulrika Eleonora in 1688.
15 Add. MS. 37985, Warwick's letter of 29 April 1681.
16 ibid., letter of 15 June 1681.
17 ibid., letter of 27 June 1681.
18 ibid., letter of 26 July 1681.
19 ibid., letter of 7 Sept. 1681.
20 ibid., letters of 26 April, 3 May and 8 June 1682.
21 ibid., letter of 17 June 1682.
22 Charles XI's almanac-entry, 17 June 1682.
23 Scheel's letter of 17 June 1582: *Handlingar*, II.

24 Letter to Queen Christina, 21 June 1682, printed in *P.H.T.* 1908 ('Om Carl XII:s dop').

25 The assumption, in Swedish and non-Swedish works, that the early baptism indicated a fear that the infant might be too weak to survive is therefore not justified.

26 Add. MS. 37985, Warwick's letters to Conway of 22 June and to Blathwayt of 4 and 12 July with list of god-parents f.208a; for the ceremony see the article in *P.H.T.* 1908, cited above.

27 For a discussion of this decision see S. Stolpe, *Queen Christina of Sweden* (London, 1966), pp. 48 ff.

28 The high numerical numbers in a dynasty begun in the early sixteenth century is usually explained by foreign observers as a 'Gothic' attempt to lend 'antiquity' to the Vasa line.

29 This is typical of the 'old school' of Caroline historiography; e.g. Nyström, Sjögren, Carlson.

30 S. Göransson, *Den europäiske konfessionspolitikens upplösning 1654–1660* (1956).

31 Ulrika Eleonora's memoirs, pp. 569–70.

32 Cp. text, p. 420.

33 P. Meijer-Granquist, *Carl X Gustaf* (1910), pp. 8–9. Cp. the famous portrait by S. Bourdon.

34 For some softening of the generally accepted aggressive aspects of his Polish policy see B. Kentrschynskyj, 'Karl Gustav inför krisen i öster 1654–1655', *K.F.Å.* 1956.

35 The journal covered 1638 to 1640; for the gift (translated from Latin into Swedish) see Nordberg, I, 9.

36 This son fought for the Allies in the War of the Spanish Succession and fell in battle in 1708.

37 Åberg, *Karl XI*, e.g. p. 151.

38 For the so-called 'quarter-reduction' (*fjärdepartsreduktion*) see S. Dahlgren, *Karl X Gustav och reduktionen* (1964).

39 For the work of the *reduktionskommission* see O. Lindqvist, *Jakob Gyllenborg och reduktionen* (1956); for that of the *formyndarräfst*, see A. Munthe, 'Till förmyndarräfstens historia', *H.T.* 1936 and R. Blomdahl, *Förmyndarräfstens huvudskede* (1963), with ensuing discussion between H. Schück and the author in *H.T.* 1964 and 1965.

40 S.P. 95, vol. 13, Duncombe's letter of 28 March 1689/90.

41 ibid., Duncombe's letter of 5 March 1689/90 and 16 April 1690. Cp. the Danish diplomatic reports of the period printed in *Handlingar*, II, e.g. Meyer's letters of 9 and 23 Sept. 1682.

42 It used to be held that the high nobility kept aloof from service if they could; but material which permits a revaluation is now available: see K. Ågren, 'Gods och ämbete', *Scandia*, 1965, pp. 227–46 and U. Sjödell, 'Les Anecdotes de Suède', ibid., pp. 141–72.

43 For a survey of this work with full bibliography see M. Roberts, 'Charles XI', *Essays in Swedish History* (London, 1967), pp. 226–68.

44 S.P. 95, vol. 12, Robinson's letter to Warre, 16 Dec. 1689.

45 See Lundh-Eriksson, p. 252, that this was '*I himmelen, i himmelen där Herren Gud själv bor*' by Laurinus.

46 Hedvig Eleonora told the Danish ambassador Sehested this, see his letter of 28 Jan. 1699: *Handlingar*, IV.

BOOK I, CHAPTER 3: THE CHILDHOOD OF A PRINCE

1 G.Utterström in *Historiska Studier tillägnade Nils Ahnlund* (1949), pp. 238–77.
2 For a description from 1697 by the Dane Gyldencrone see *K.F.Å.* 1923, 229–30; for Fabrice's finding it beautiful in 1707, see his *Memoiren*, p. 29; for Motraye's praise after frequent visits 1716–21 see his *Travels*, II, 194.
3 See Torcy's comments from 1685 in Marchand, op. cit. Cp. Tessin's views, text, pp. 433–4.
4 These have been immortalized in Erik Dahlberg's *Suecia Antiqua et Hodierna*, the plates of which were first printed in 1717. For its various issues (and the 1924 edition) see article in *Nordisk Familiebok* under 'Suecia'.
5 W.Karlson, *Stat och Vardag. Stormaktstidens herremanshem* (1945).
6 A. Strindberg, *Bondenöd och Stormaktsdröm. Studier över skedet 1630–1718* (1937), pp. 211–304, weaves the 'Gothic' movement into the political history of the reign of Charles XI.
7 Robinson to Trumbull, 2 Oct. 1695: H.M.C. *Downshire MS.*, I, 557.
8 Add. MS. 27457, Duncombe to Blathwayt, 9 July 1692.
9 Luxdorph's letter of 15 June 1695: *Handlingar*, III.
10 See. apart from diplomatic reports, Horn's diary from 1684–5 printed in *K.F.Å.* 1946, pp. 112 ff.
11 The dating is not certain; historians' estimates vary between six months and two years: since the infant Gustav is not depicted it must be before 1683.
12 Stockfleth's letter of 18 April 1685: *Handlingar*, II.
13 ibid., letter of 27 Dec. 1684; for her grief at his death ibid., letter of 30 May 1685.
14 Åberg, *Karl XII*, p. 173; cp. Charles XI's letter to Nils Bielke of 8 July 1685 in the collection ed. by O.Malmström, *H.H.* 18: 2.
15 Stockfleth's letters of 9, 13, 16, 20, 27 and 30 May 1685: *Handlingar*, II.
16 ibid., letter of 25 July 1685.
17 Charles XI's almanac-entries for 27 Sept. and 12 Oct. 1685.
18 ibid., entries for 17 Dec, 1686 and 1 Feb. 1687.
19 Stockfleth's letters of 5 and 26 March 1687: *Handlingar*, II; for Hjärne's position and standing see the article by O.Strandberg in *Svenska Män och Kvinnor*, III.
20 Meyer's letter of 30 Aug. 1682: *Handlingar*, II.
21 See Elfstrand, *K.F.Å.* 1945, pp. 158–9.
22 There is some evidence that her power was generally resented; at the time when a marriage between Charles XII and the Danish princess Sophia was discussed at court it was stressed that Sophia must not bring 'another Marshalk'; cp. Charles XII's letter to Ulrika Eleonora of 12 Aug. 1707: *Bref.*
23 See letters quoted from the Danish Rigsarkiv in the article on 'Ulrikke Eleonore' in *D.B.L.*
24 E.g. Stockfleth's letter of 18 Aug. 1686: *Handlingar*, II.
25 Undated letter by Stockfleth of autumn 1688: *Handlingar*, II, pp. 404 ff.

26 Stockfleth's letters of 25 Aug. 1688, 27 March and 28 June 1689: *Handlingar*, II.
27 ibid., letter of 10 Nov. 1688 (pp. 408–9).
28 ibid., letter of 18 Dec. 1686.
29 The two signatures can most easily be compared in *Sveriges Historia genom Tiderna*, ed. H.Maiander, III (1948), p. 128 (Charles xi's of 1687) and p. 187 (Charles xii's of 1715).
30 Printed as nos. 1 and 2 in *Bref*.
31 For Charles xii's education see G.Carlquist (in *Karl XII*, ed. Bring, 1918), pp. 45–56; O.Kuylenstierna, *Carl XII* (1926) – both with drawings and exercises reproduced and instructions and reports summarized.
32 Undated letter from Stockfleth of 1688: *Handlingar*, II, 404.
33 For Lindschöld see the biography by E.Ingers (1908).
34 Nordberg, I, p. 9; cp. S.P. 95, vol. 13, Duncombe's and Robinson's letters of 14 and 17 June 1689 for the King's appreciation of Lindschöld.
35 See Hatton, 'Gratifications and foreign policy' (in *William III and Louis XIV*, edd. R.M.Hatton and J.S.Bromley, Liverpool, 1967), pp. 92–3; for his exemplary family life see A.Lewenhaupt, *Karolinen Edvard Gyldenstolpe* (1941), pp. 7 ff.
36 For the royal family's grief, see Ulrika Eleonora's memoirs, pp. 571–2.
37 Charles xi's almanac-entries for 1689 to 1693.
38 Nordberg, I, 19.
39 These, dated 28 March 1690, are now in Kungl. Biblioteket.
40 The expeditions and duties are best reconstructed from Charles xi's almanac-entries for 1691 and 1692.
41 S.P. 95, vol. 11, Sir Edward Wood's letter of 13 March 1677/8.
42 In 1707 Cederhielm considered the King's German 'perfect' (see his letter to his brother of 18 July 1708 printed in *K.K.D.* VI; but in 1716 Charles felt in need of an amanuensis, for Poniatowski acting as one see Charles's letter to Frederick of Hesse of 8 June 1716: *Bref*.
43 Löwen's *Mémoires*, p. 33.
44 Schönström's memoirs, p. 51.
45 See A.Quennerstedt's articles in *Vårt Land* 25/11 and 26/11, 1897.
46 See, e.g. O.Sjögren, *Carl XII och hans män* (1904), p. 15; O.Kuylenstierna, *Carl XII* (1925), p. 24.

BOOK I, CHAPTER 4: THE HEIR APPARENT

1 Browallius's diary, 24 Jan. 1736, based on Reuterholm's table-talk.
2 Robinson's and d'Avaux's dispatches complement each other in giving information about Charles xi's work: Robinson had good connexions in the Chancery and d'Avaux had confidants at court.
3 Åberg, *Karl XI*, pp. 122 ff.
4 Ulrika Eleonora's memoirs, p. 670.
5 D'Avaux's comment of 1697 on Charles xii cited by E.Godley, *Charles XII of Sweden* (London, 1928), p. 12; for similar comments on Charles xi see, e.g. the same ambassador's letter of 13 Jan. 1964, F.O. 95, vol. 577.
6 Quoted by A.Lewenhaupt, *Karolinen Edvard Gyldenstolpe* (1941), pp. 15–16.

7   Löwen, *Mémoires*, pp. 26–27; cp. Add. MS. 41178 (ff. 135a–136a) Robinson's letter of 22 Dec. 1700, for the King's health improving as soon as he became his own master.

8   This, bound with the journal of 1692, is now in Kungl. Biblioteket; it has been printed in O. Kuylenstierna, *Karl XII*, pp. 27–30.

9   S.P. 95, vol. 13, Robinson's letter of 27 Nov. 1689.

10   The journal is printed in Kuylenstierna, *Karl XII*, pp. 31–5.

11   S.P. 95, vol. 13, Duncombe's letter of 11 Jan. and 5 March 1689/90.

12   A good reproduction in Åberg, *Karl XI*, facing p. 96; cp. R. Josephson, *K.F.Å* 1947, pp. 15–17, for this magnificent series which occupied much of Ehrenstrahl's time between 1673 and 1689.

13   S.P. vol. 14, Robinson's letters of 22 Aug. 1694 and 7 Sept. 1695; cp. Holst, *Ulrika Eleonora*, p. 16.

14   N. Lundh-Eriksson, *Hedvig Eleonora*, p. 243.

15   Add. MS. 7075, Robinson's letter to Stepney, 19 Aug. 1691.

16   For the party see Charles XI's almanac-entry for 3 Feb. 1692 and O. Bergström's article in *P.H.T.* 1907, pp. 21–9.

17   Add. MS. 36407, Robinson to Stepney, 6 Feb. 1691/2; for Charles XI's sobriety see [Robinson] *Account of Sueden*, p. 79.

18   There are constant references to the ups and downs of her health in Danish and English diplomatic reports.

19   Stockfleth's letter of 30 April 1690: *Handlingar*, II.

20   ibid., letters of 4 June and 6 Dec. 1690.

21   Luxdorph's letter of 27 July 1692 and Juel's letter of 8 Feb. 1693: *Handlingar*, III.

22   ibid., Juel's letter of 19 July, 1693.

23   Ulrika Eleonora's memoirs, pp. 570–1. Cp. Kuylenstierna, *Carl XII*, pp. 40–1 and Lund-Eriksson, *Hedvig Eleonora*, pp. 173–4.

24   Juel's letter of 2 Aug. 1693: *Handlingar*, III.

25   ibid., letter of 16 Aug. 1693.

26   S.P. 95, vol. 14, Robinson's letter of 16 April 1695.

27   Luxdorph's letter of 2 Dec. 1693: *Handlingar*, III; cp. reports in d'Avaux's dispatches that the King refused to remarry 'for the sake of his children', and that only the death of Prince Charles might make him do so, e.g. those of 26 June 1693 and 13 Jan. 1694: F.O. 95, vols. 576 and 577 respectively.

28   Luxdorph's letter of 21 Oct. 1693 and Juel's letter of 30 Nov. 1695: *Handlingar*, III.

29   ibid., Luxdorph's letter of 14 March 1694.

30   Holst, *Ulrika Eleonora*, p. 16; Charles XI's almanac-entries give details of all family outings: the princesses and the Queen-Grandmother sometimes came hunting and in the winter the princesses frequently came along to see the fishing nets taken up from under the ice.

31   Luxdorph's letter of 19 May 1694: *Handlingar*, III.

32   ibid., letter of 23 May 1694; S.P. 95, vol. 14, Robinson's letter of 23 May 1694.

33   ibid., Robinson's letter of 2 June 1694.

34   For information about the Prince's prowess being given to diplomats from this trip see S.P. 95, vol. 14, Robinson's letter of 21 Feb. 1694: 'Last night the court returned hither, and we are told that among the hunting exploits the

chiefest was, that the Prince (who is not yet twelve years old) kill'd one Bear, two Wolves and a Hare. The Bear the King caus'd to be opened, and the Bullet was found to have gone through his Heart.' Cp. Charles XI's almanac-entry for 5 Feb. 1694 and his noting the exact age at which the Prince shot the bear: 11 years, 7 months, 19 days.

35 Charles XI's almanac-entries, for 1693–7; cp. d'Avaux's comment in letter of 19 May 1697 that the new King must be brave since he had taken part in the cavalry exercises of the army of Charles XI, exercises which were not without danger: Wijnne, II.

36 Letter of 27 January 1692: *Handlingar*, III.

37 Stockfleth's letter of 5 April 1684: ibid., II.

38 Luxdorph's letter of 5 January 1695: ibid., III.

39 ibid., Nostitz's letter of 9/19 July 1690.

40 ibid., Juel's letters of 1 July 1693 and 16 Feb. 1695.

41 For Princess Sophia see article on 'Sophie Hedevig' by L. Laursen and C. Bøggild-Andersen in *D.B.L.*

42 Juel's letters of 27 Feb. 1695 and 20 May 1695: *Handlingar*, III; S.P. 95, vol. 14, Robinson's letters of 1 Jan. 1694/5 and 6 April 1695.

43 L. Stavenow, *Sveriges politik vid tiden för Altonakongressen*; S. P. Oakley, *William III and the Northern Crowns during the Nine Years War, 1688–1697*, unpublished Ph.D. thesis, London, 1961.

44 A.A.H. 140, Rumpf's letter of 28 May 1689.

45 For this period see Landberg, op. cit., and A. Lossky *Louis XIV, William III and the Baltic Crisis of 1683* (Berkeley and Los Angeles, 1954).

46 That this was realized by foreign diplomats is clear from, e.g. Duncombe's comment that Charles XI and his advisers intended ('next to their owne interest') to 'recover a just ballance for the common good and safety of Europe': see his report of 1692 printed in *The English Historical Review*, 1924, 574 ff., ed. by F. F. Chance.

47 E. F. Heckscher, *Sveriges ekonomiska historia frän Gustav Vasa*, I: 2 (1936), 562–4.

48 A. Attman, *Den ryska marknaden i 1500-talets politik 1558–1595* (1944), and the same author's 'Freden i Stolbova 1617. En aspekt'; *Scandia* 1949–50 (1950), pp. 36 ff.

49 For an excellent historiographical study of recent works on the transit-trade from Poland, Russia and the Far East see A. Loit, 'Sverige och Östersjöhandeln under 1600-talet', *H.T.* 1964, pp. 302–37.

50 Hatton, 'Gratifications and foreign policy', *William III and Louis XIV*, passim.

51 Heeckeren to Heinsius, 22 Feb. 1696: Heim, *Heinsius Archief*, III, 182–3.

52 Luxdorph's letter of 27 May 1696: *Handlingar*, IV.

53 ibid., letter of 25 Nov. 1696.

54 V. Djurberg, *Ett kungligt cancerfall* (1922).

55 Luxdorph's letter of 3 April 1697, reporting Cronhielm: *Handlingar*, IV.

56 ibid., Sehested's letter of 28 Jan. 1699, reporting Hedvig Eleonora.

57 See A. Isberg, *Charles XI och den livlandska adeln* (1953).

58 Luxdorph's letter of 23 Dec. 1696: *Handlingar*, IV.

59 The best diplomatic reports on the progress of Charles XI's illness are by

d'Avaux who had good sources of information: see his letters 13 Jan., 20 and 27 March, 3 and 10 April 1697 in F.O. 95, vol. 578.

60   Benzelius's memoirs (pp. 669–72), based on what Charles XI's confessor Jöran Wallin had told him.

61   Luxdorph's letter of 3 April 1697: *Handlingar*, IV.

BOOK II, CHAPTER I : SOVEREIGN RULER

1   For the influence of the concept of 15 as 'responsible' in civil law, see T. Höjer, *K.F.Å.* 1942, pp. 7–8.

2   Hjärne's letter to Hermelin of 27 June 1707: *H.T.* 1882.

3   Luxdorph's letter of 20 March 1697: *Handlingar*, IV; cp. d'Avaux's dispatch of 3 April 1697: Wijnne, II.

4   For Bielke's position at this time see the entry by G. Wittrock in *S.B.L.*, and the same author's article in *K.F.Å.* 1917, pp. 40 ff.

5   Luxdorph's letters of 17 and 28 April 1697: *Handlingar*, IV.

6   S. Bergh, 'Stockholm's slotts brand 1697', *K.F.Å.* 1916, pp. 76–119.

7   Cited in J. Rosén, *Den svenska utrikespolitikens historia*, II: 1 (1952), p. 38.

8   See, e.g. S.P. 95, vol. 15, Robinson's letter of 29 Dec. 1697.

9   M. Höjer, *Om Carl XII:s myndighetsförklaring och 1697 års riksdag* (1866), p. 11.

10   See, e.g. Luxdorph's letters of 28 April and 30 June 1697: *Handlingar*, IV.

11   Hatton, 'Gratifications and foreign policy', *William III and Louis XIV*, pp. 88–94.

12   Carlson, I, pp. 2 ff.

13   Carlquist (in Bring, *Karl XII*), p. 66.

14   For the misery caused by the bad harvests there is much information in the diplomatic reports, see, e.g. d'Avaux's letter of 17 April 1697: Wijnne, II.

15   Add. MS. 28899, Robinson's letter of 15 May 1697.

16   Bergh, *K.F.Å.* 1916, p. 119.

17   For reproduction of some of these plans see Josephson, *Tessin*, II, 85 ff; for their being admired see A. E. Suède, Suppl. vol. 7 (memorandum of 31 Dec. 1704) f. 126b: '*Ce sera un des plus beaux Edifices qu'on puisse voir, si le projet sur lequel on travaille se peut executer.*'

18   N. Lundh-Eriksson, op. cit., pp. 218 ff.

19   *Sveriges Ridderskap och Adels Riksdags-protokoll* (1900), pp. 189 ff.

20   This information, from Luxdorph's letter of 10 Nov. 1697 (*Handlingar*, IV), is confirmed by a letter from Oxenstierna's daughter of the same date cited by G. Jonasson, *Karl XII och hans rådgivare* (1960), pp. 66–7.

21   T. T. Höjer, 'Carl XII:s Myndighetsförklaring, Några synpunkter', *K.F.Å.* 1942, pp. 7–37.

22   G. Jonasson, op. cit., pp. 48 ff.

23   Luxdorph's letter of 3 Nov. 1697: *Handlingar*, IV.

24   See Gyldencrone's journal of 1697 in *K.F.Å.* 1923, p. 218; for Voltaire's interest in Piper's role see H. Brulin, *K.F.Å.* 1940, pp. 12–13, Voltaire's letter to Thieriot.

25   Quoted by Höjer, *K.F.Å.* 1942, p. 35.

26 Juel's letter of 30 July 1698: *Handlingar*, IV (with specific mention of Wallen-stedt and Piper).

27 Cp. Louis XIV asking d'Avaux in a letter of 9 May 1697 if it is essential by Swedish law that Charles XII should reach eighteen before he is declared of age: F.O. 95, vol. 578; for Charles XII arguing that early majority is preferable to a regency; see his letter to Ulrika Eleonora of 28 May 1715: *Bref.*

28 Luxdorph's letters of 16 June 1697: *Handlingar*, IV.

29 ibid., letter of 27 Nov. 1697.

30 M. Höjer, op. cit., pp. 20 ff.

31 G. Adlerfelt, *Karl XII:s krigsföretag 1700–06* (ed. S. E. Bring, 1919, with the journal for 1708–9), hereafter cited as Alderfelt; p. 8 describes the ceremony.

32 S.P. 95, vol. 15, Robinson's letter of 22 Dec. 1697. For the French agent La Picquetière being asked by 'some senators' for French practice and referring them to *Theatrum Europaeum* for Louis XIV's coronation, see that agent's letter in A. E., Suède, Suppl. vol. 6, ff. 263a and b.

33 Luxdorph's letter of 1 Dec. 1697: *Handlingar*, IV.

34 ibid., letter of 18 Dec. 1697; S.P. 95, vol. 15, Robinson's letter of 15 Dec. 1697.

35 The daughter was Maria Elisabeth, the son Christian August; for their arrival see ibid., Robinson's letter of 11 Dec. 1697.

36 This representative, Baron Jens Juel, was delayed on his journey by podagra, but his secretary Paulsen reached the capital in time to witness the ceremony, see Gyldencrone's journal in *K.F.Å.* 1923.

37 S.P. 95, vol. 15, Robinson's letter of 11 Dec. 1697.

38 ibid., cp. the description of the coronation by Paulsen in *K.F.Å.* 1923, p. 216; for the festivities arranged by Luxdorph see his letter of 15 Dec. 1697 in *Handlingar*, IV.

39 Carlquist (in Bring, *Karl XII*), p. 71.

40 Juel's letter of 9 Feb. 1698: *Handlingar*, IV, p. 165.

41 Carlquist (in Bring, *Karl XII*), p. 71, quoting d'Avaux and Luxdorph.

42 S.P. 95, vol. 16, Robinson's letter of 4 Dec. 1697.

BOOK II, CHAPTER 2: THE ADOLESCENT

1 Juel's letter of 19 Jan. 1698: *Handlingar*, IV.

2 ibid., letter of 18 Dec. 1697 and 9 Feb. 1698.

3 ibid., letter of 5 Jan. 1698.

4 ibid., letter of 19 Jan. 1698; Add. MS. 35106, Robinson to Blathwayt, 14 June 1699.

5 ibid., Robinson's letter of 14 June 1699; cp. Juel's letters of 19, 22 and 29 Jan. 1698: *Handlingar*, IV.

6 ibid., Juel's letter of 1 Jan. 1698.

7 ibid., letter of 22 June 1698 for this incident.

8 ibid., letters of 19 Jan., 16 and 25 Feb. and 5 March 1698.

9 Carlson, I, pp. 127 ff.

10 For the anti-absolutist bias in the Bonde family see the analysis by U. Sjödell, 'Kring de Bondeska Anekdotane', *Scandia*, 1965, pp. 141 ff.

11 This and other underlinings are noted by A. Quennerstedt, *Vårt Land*, 25/11 and 26/11, 1897.

12   Nordberg, *Anmärckningar* (1754), pp. 17–18.
13   For an article by B. Boëthius putting Jacob Boëthius's opposition to absolutism into perspective see *S.B.L.*
14   Carlson, I, p. 75, note 2.
15   Cp. F.O. 95, vol. 577, d'Avaux's letter of 22 Apr. 1694, that the Swedes are harder on Calvinists than on Catholics.
16   Add. MS. 28899, Robinson's letter of 15 May 1697.
17   *Calendar State Papers Domestic* (ed. E. Bateson, 1943), p. 37, Blathwayt to Williamson, 8/19 Aug. 1698.
18   S.P. 95, vol. 15, Robinson's letter of 3 Aug, 1698; Juel's letter of 30 April 1698: *Handlingar*, IV.
19   ibid., Luxdorph's letter of 8 Dec. 1697.
20   ibid., letter of 21 April 1697.
21   See Juel's and Luxdorph's letters for information gathered from Countess de la Gardie and Mrs Clodt, from Hjärne, Gyldenstolpe, Bielke, Dahlberg, Stenbock, Tessin and others.
22   Luxdorph's letter of 30 June 1697: *Handlingar*, IV.
23   ibid., Juel's letter of 4 Dec. 1697.
24   ibid., Juel's letter of 7 July 1697.
25   ibid., Juel's letter of 24 March 1698.
26   ibid., Juel's letter of 16 March 1698.
27   ibid., Luxdorph's letter of 18 Dec. 1697; Juel's letter of 29 Jan. 1698.
28   ibid., Luxdorph's letter of 18 Dec. 1697; Juel's letters of 29 Jan., 25 Feb. and 16 March 1698.
29   ibid., Luxdorph's letter of 9 Oct. 1697.
30   ibid., Luxdorph's letter of 13 Nov. 1697.
31   Ulrika Eleonora told her husband in 1736 that her mother on her death-bed had extracted a promise from Charles XI that Hedvig Sophia should not be married into the Holstein-Gottorp family if it could be avoided: see Holst, op. cit., p. 28. A contemporary report by d'Avaux gives the truer version: Charles XI promised that Frederick should stay away from the Swedish court till Hedvig was older and could make up her own mind, see letter of 2 Feb. 1695: F.O. 95, vol. 575.
32   Juel's letter of 27 April 1698: *Handlingar*, IV.
33   ibid., Juel's letter of 16 March 1698.
34   ibid., Juel's letters of 29 Dec. 1697 and 30 March 1698.
35   ibid., Juel's letters of 4 May 1698. Cp. R. Josephson, *K.F.Å.* 1947, pp. 35 ff.
36   Luxdorph's letters of 13 Nov. and 4 Dec. 1697: *Handlingar*, IV.
37   ibid., Juel's letter of 9 Feb. 1698.
38   ibid., Luxdorph's letter of 11 Dec. 1697 reporting Bielke; cp. letter of 5 Jan. 1698 and Juel's letters of 22 Dec. 1697 and 5 Jan. 1698.
39   ibid., Juel's letter of 5 Feb. 1698.
40   ibid., Luxdorph's letter of 5 Jan. 1698; this must be the portrait referred to by Greg in his letter from Copenhagen of 5 Feb. 1698: 'our princesse here sat very lately to have her picture drawn which otherwise she does not love to do and therefore the king her father was present himself the first time to see it begun'. I am grateful to P. Torntoft for bringing this letter, in S.P. 75, vol. 24, to my attention.

41 Luxdorph's letter of 5 Feb., Juel's letters of 25 and 30 March 1698: *Handlingar*, IV.

42 ibid., Luxdorph's letter of 13 Nov. 1697. Cp. Juel's letter of 25 March 1698.

43 He told this to a lady at court, Miss Lewenhaupt, who told Juel's wife, see Juel's letter of 15 Nov. 1698: *Handlingar*, IV; Hedvig Eleonora made a similar revelation to Barck in 1705: see his letter to Hermelin of 11 March of that year.

44 Luxdorph's letter of 5 Feb. and Juel's of 2 March 1698: *Handlingar*, IV.

45 For this reason – as well as her tender years – the match between Ulrika Eleonora and her cousin, Prince Christian August of Holstein-Gottorp, which was rumoured in diplomatic reports seems not to have been seriously discussed.

46 Juel's letter of 25 May 1698: *Handlingar*, IV.

47 ibid., Luxdorph's letter of 8 Dec. 1697: Juel's letters of 15 Jan., 2 March and 2 April 1698.

48 ibid. Luxdorph's letter of 5 Feb. 1698; Grüner's letter of 4 Feb. 1698.

49 ibid., Juel's letters of 13 July and 2 Nov. 1698; Luxdorph's letter of 5 Feb. 1698; Grüner's letter of 28 Jan. 1699 – the last being the most specific on the joint hope of Hjärne, Wachtmeister and himself to find a medicine to '*corroborare partes Genitales quae etiam verenemque excitare possunt*'.

50 ibid., Grüner's letter of 19 Nov. 1698, Düben having reported some 'raillery' between himself, Klinckowström and the King. The article in *Dagens Nyheter* of 21 Feb. 1926 on Charles XII's marriage offers is somewhat misleading on the tone of the conversation, ignoring the '*railleri*' aspect.

51 Juel's letter of 16 March 1698, reporting a talk with Gyldenstolpe: *Handlingar*, IV.

52 ibid., Luxdorph's letter of 5 Feb. 1698; cp. letter of 28 Jan. 1699 for Hjärne having assured Grüner that the King was not impotent.

53 Reuterholm's memoirs, *H.H.* 36: 2, p. 87; cp. Motraye, *Travels*, II, 343, that during his stay in Stockholm people pointed out to him a 'pretty living proof' of Charles XII's youthful amour.

54 Juel's letters of 6 April and 7 July 1698: *Handlingar*, IV.

55 ibid., Juel's letters of 2 March and 6 July, reporting talks with Miss Lewenhaupt.

56 B. Wedberg, *Karl XII på justitietronen* (1944), pp. 42–3.

57 Juel's letters of 15 and 19 Oct. and 26 Nov. 1698 (based on letters from Düben); *Handlingar*, IV.

58 ibid., letters of 14 and 17 Dec. 1698 for Charles's comments; and letters of 13 and 16 April and 10 May 1698 for the attitude of the court.

59 For the 1701 and 1702 attempts by the Queen-Grandmother and by named Swedes of influence see A. Stille, *Studier öfver Danmarks politik under Karl XII:s polska krig 1700–1707* (1889), pp. 7–11, based on Grüner's dispatches.

60 ibid., Juel's letter of 14 Dec. 1698 and Grüner's letter of 28 Jan 1699.

61 D'Avaux's dispatch of 23 March 1698, Wijnne, III: 1.

62 ibid., D'Avaux's dispatch of 6 March 1698.

63 Juel's letter of 9 Feb. 1698: *Handlingar*, IV.

64 For the exaggeration see S. Bonnesen, 'Gåsgalgane i Ystad', *K.F.Å.* 1931; C. Wallin, ibid., 1952, pp. 121–8 has printed an eyewitness account of the (much discussed) goose-riding: Charles XII was indeed present, but took no part in it; local women as well as men did take part in this traditional

Scanian pastime that seems so gruesome to modern readers and which – see
J.H.Plumb, *The First Four Georges* (London 1956), p. 15 – was common also in
England. For the rest see the entries of 2 May, 18 June and 17 Nov. 1698 in the
diary of the King's page Kagg in *H.H.* 24; for reports based on talks with
Düben, Piper and Wallenstedt as well as on general gossip see Juel's letters o
4 and 25 May, 18, 22 and 29 June and 13 July 1698: *Handlingar*, IV; and
d'Avaux's dispatches of 18 May, 1 and 15 June 1698: Wijnne, III: 1.

65   Löwen, *Mémoires*, p. 27.
66   D'Avaux's dispatch of 19 May 1697: Wijnne, II.
67   For the presents see Juel's letters of 7 May and 17 Aug. 1697: *Handlingar*, IV
68   These have been used by Holst, *Ulrika Eleonora*, pp. 29 ff.
69   Juel's letters of 9 July and 14 Sept. 1698: *Handlingar*, IV.

BOOK II, CHAPTER 3: THE REINS OF OFFICE

1   Juel's letters of 15 and 26 Oct. 1698; Grüner's letter of 16 Nov. 1698: *Hand-
    lingar*, IV.
2   ibid., Juel's letters of 25 Oct., 2 and 16 Nov., 14 Dec. 1698.
3   Tessin to Cronström, 7 April 1697, cited by R.Josephson, *K.F.Å.* 1947, p. 33.
4   ibid., pp. 31–7.
5   Kagg's diary, 28 May 1698: *H.H.* 24; Sehested's letter of 31 May 1699
    Handlingar, IV.
6   Kagg's diary, 16 Nov. 1698: *H.H.* 24.
7   Hans Järta, 'Karl XII och hans tidehvarf', *K.F.Å.* 1912, pp. 295–6, for the King's
    initiative in respect of foreign actors and singers in 1699 and 1704; see Joseph-
    son, *Tessin*, I, 186 ff., for plans for opera and other entertainments in the post-
    1716 period.
8   For the design of this statue see R.Josephson, *K.F.Å.* 1947, p. 30; for
    Hårleman's study-trip abroad see Järta's lecture of 1846 printed ibid., 1912,
    p. 297.
9   Some of the sketches of ships are reproduced in Bring, *Karl XII* (p. 375); for
    the King having played the architect and designed a house see Feif's letter to
    Tessin of 30 Feb. 1712: *Brinkmanska archivet*.
10 Ulrika Eleonora's memoirs, p. 575; R.Josephson, *K.F.Å.* 1947, pp. 35–6.
11 Holst, *Ulrika Eleonora*, p. 30 for 1699; for 1697 see Luxdorph's letter of
    8 Dec. 1697: *Handlingar*, IV.
12 Kagg's diary, 27 and 28 July 1690: *H.H.* 24.
13 For the plays performed see R.Josephson, *Tessin*, I, 147 ff.
14 Kagg's diary, 23 Sept. 1699: *H.H.* 24.
15 Holst, op. cit., p. 31.
16 Kagg's diary, 10 Aug. 1699: *H.H.* 24.
17 Lundh-Eriksson, op. cit., p. 231; Motraye, *Remarques*, pp. 12–13; for a report
    in 1698 that Charles had determined not to partake of strong drink see
    d'Avaux's dispatch of 23 March: Wijnne, III.
18 The authority for this is Hultman, his servant after 1707.
19 Most observers, Swedish and foreign, after 1700 mention this: see, e.g. Raby's
    'Character' of 1707 in Add. MS. 35885, f.1 and Robinson's 'Character' of 1710

printed in G. Burnet *History of my own times,* II (1724), 535. S. Grauers, *K.F.Å.* 1964, pp. 145 ff., in a valuable article examining the royal accounts for 1700–2 notes the cost of wine and brandy 'for the King's use' and doubts whether Charles XII was a total abstainer. There were rumours in Germany in 1709–10 that Charles had begun to drink wine, but Fabrice – on arrival in Turkey – found them to be false, see his letter of 4 July 1710: *Lettres.*

20 Juel's letter of 1 Jan. 1698: *Handlingar,* IV.

21 D'Avaux's letter of 29 Jan. 1698, Wijnne, III: 1.

22 Add. MS. 35105, Robinson's letter of 4 Dec. 1698.

23 Juel's letter of 16 March 1698: *Handlingar,* IV, reporting Hedvig Eleonora's conversation with his wife.

24 For his pension from 1698 see Å. Stille, *Bengt Oxenstiernas politiska system och Sveriges förbindelser med Danmark och Holstein-Gottorp 1689–1692* (1947), p. 139, note 2; for Juel's arranging that Charles XII should be told of this see Juel's letter of 16 March 1698: *Handlingar,* IV.

25 ibid., Juel's letter of 9 Feb. 1698; cp. text, p. 127.

26 ibid., Juel's letter of 14 Dec. 1698.

27 ibid., Juel's letter of 18 June 1699.

28 Add. MS. 35105, Robinson's letter of 4 Dec. 1690.

29 Luxdorph's letter of 9 Oct. 1697: *Handlingar,* IV.

30 Horn's memoirs, with comments by Gustav Horn, *Arvid Bernard Horn* (1852), pp. 6–7.

31 Grüner's letters of 4 and 11 Feb. 1699: *Handlingar,* IV.

32 T. Lenk, 'Flintlåstillverkningens införande i Sverige. Armémodellerna', *K.F.Å.* 1937, pp. 226 ff.

33 *See Bidrag S.N.K.H.,* I, 233–8 for details.

34 For Hein's mission see C. Hallendorff, *Bidrag till det store nordiska krigets förhistoria* (1897), pp. 38 ff.; S. Svensson, 'Czar Peters motiv för kriget mot Sverige', *H.T.* 1931; R. Wittram, *Peter I. Czar und Kaiser,* I (1964), 203 ff.

35 Add. MS. 35106, Robinson to Blathwayt, 26 Aug. 1699; E. Olmer, 'Om ryssfruktan i Sverige för 200 år sedan', *H.T.* 1903, pp. 295–317.

36 Dahlberg's letter to the King of 1 July 1697, cited by Olmer, loc. cit., p. 297.

37 ibid., pp. 299, 315, citing Lillieroot's letters of 14/24 and 17/27 July 1697; cp. Juel's letters of 6 and 26 Nov. 1698: *Handlingar,* IV.

38 Olmer, *H.T.* 1903, p. 297; cp. S. Backman, 'Karl XII och den ryska sjömakten av Arnold Munthe', *K.F.Å.* 1927, pp. 82–3.

39 K. Piwarski, 'Das Interregnum 1696/7 und die Politische Lage in Europa', *Um die Polnische Krone, Sachsen und Polen während des Nordischen Krieges 1700–1721* (Berlin, 1962).

40 S. Backman, 'Karl XII:s polska detronisations-politik', *K.F.Å.* 1947, p. 95.

41 Olmer, *H.T.* 1903, p. 303, quoting Vellingk's letter of 3 June 1698.

42 See Carlson, I, 195; S. Backman, *K.F.Å.* 1947, pp. 92 ff.

43 Both S. Steinius, 'Sachen och Preussen i den nordiska krisen 1709', *K.F.Å.* 1949, pp. 49 ff., and Hassinger, op. cit., pp. 21 ff., have pointed to the need for a modern study in depth of Augustus's Polish policy as well as for a more substantial investigation into his Saxon policy than the pioneer work of P. Haake, *August de Starke,* of 1926. The essays published in 1962 by Polish and Russian historians in *Um die polnische Krone, Sachsen und Polen während des Nordischen*

Krieges, edd. J. Gierowski and J. Kalisch, have gone some way to fill this gap though Gierowski also emphasizes the need for further research.

44   For Augustus's embassy to Sweden see J. Rosén, *Den svenska utrikespolitikens historia*, II: 1 (1952), 66 ff. and authorities there cited.

45   See Juel's letter of 26 Oct. 1698; Sehested's of 7 Jan. 1699 and Grüner's of 4 Feb. 1699: *Handlingar*, IV.

46   Olmer, *H.T.* 1903, p. 309 for this being done via Rafał Leszczyński in Nov 1699 on his advice.

47   For this embassy see T. Westrin, *H.T.* 1908, pp. 170 ff.; H. Almquist, 'Scener från Ryssland år 1699', *K.F.Å.* 1937, pp. 7–79; Wittram, I, 211–14, with Russian references.

48   The historical discussion whether Tsar Peter or Augustus was the 'real' architect of the anti-Swedish alliance is in one sense irrelevant given the desire of both, and of Frederick IV of Denmark–Norway, to profit from the death of Charles XI. In the context of the European situation – with both the Tsar and the Elector of Saxony having alternative plans for expansion – I regard Frederick IV as being the corner-stone of the formative years of the alliance.

49   Add. MS. 35106, Robinson's letter of 2 Aug. 1699; Grüner's letters of 17, 30 Aug. and 2 Sept.: *Handlingar*, IV.

50   Most recently by G. Jonasson, op. cit., of 1960, pp. 112–25.

51   There was also a hope that if Denmark could be forced to keep the peace, Augustus and Tsar Peter might refrain from opening hostilities. Note that Hassinger (op. cit., pp. 31 ff.), the most recent non-Swedish scholar to examine the outbreak of the war, considers Charles XII's policy firm, but not aggressive.

52   D'Avaux's letter of 24 July 1697: Wijnne, II.

53   There had been considerable fear in Stockholm that the Duke of Holstein-Gottorp who died at the end of 1694 should have come to terms with Denmark which prejudiced Sweden's 'back-door' entry; cp. d'Avaux's report, on 19 Jan. 1695, of joy at the accession of Duke Frederick IV who is 'entièrement' pro-Swedish: F.O. 95, vol. 577. For Christian Albrecht's relationship to Denmark see Å. Stille, 'Efter Altonakongressen', *K.F.Å.* 1940, pp. 53–79.

BOOK II, CHAPTER 4: ON THE BRINK OF WAR

1   For the orders of 15 July 1697 see Jonasson, op. cit., p. 112.

2   Starhemberg's letter of 24 Oct. 1699: *Handlingar*, III.

3   ibid., Pentenrriedter's letter of 6/16 Dec. 1699.

4   Add. MS. 28899, Robinson's letter of 6 Aug. 1699.

5   For Pufendorf's years in Sweden see O. Malmström, *Samuel Pufendorf och hans arbeten i Svensk historia* (1899), pp. 8 ff.; cp. the introduction to B. Steckzén and N. Wingers, *Erik Dahlbergs Bataljplaner* (1922), for the unsuccessful attempts in 1694 to make him re-enter Charles XI's service.

6   M. Ranft, *Die Merkwürdige Lebensgeschichte derer vier berühmten Schwedische Feldmarschalle, Grafen Rehnschild, Stenbock, Meyerfeld und Dücker* (Leipzig, 1753), p. 51.

7   S. Olsson, *Olof Hermelin* (1953), p. 182.

8   Charles's comment to officers who came to condole him on his father's death is quoted in Löwen, *Mémoires*, p. 26: Löwen's own father had been one of those

present and remembered the King saying '*qu'il ne seroit jamais l'agresseur, ce qu'il estimoit la chose du monde la plus injuste et contraire à la vraie gloire*'.

9   S.P. 95, vol. 15, Robinson's two letters of 20 July 1698; Add. MS. 35106, Robinson's letters of July 12 and 19, 1699.

10   See J. Konow, 'Carl Gustaf Rehnskiöld i Holland', *K.F.Å.* 1957, pp. 69–74.

11   Grüner's letter of 5 Feb. 1699: *Handlingar*, IV.

12   Holst, *Ulrika Eleonora*, p. 43.

13   For the Danish efforts see Torntoft, *The English Historical Review*, 1966, pp. 5–14.

14   Add. MS. 35106, Robinson's letter of 16 June 1700.

15   See N. Herlitz (in Bring, *Karl XII*), p. 117.

16   F. Wernstedt, 'Några detaljer från arméns mobilisering och uppmarsch vid stora nordiska krigets utbrott', *K.F.Å.* 1926; see also the regimental histories by F. Wernstedt, E. Bensow, G. Petri and others listed under 'Army and Navy' in Bibliography and R. Sjöberg (ed.), *Den svenska armen genom tiderna* (1949).

17   See S. Ågren, *Karl XI:s indelingsverk för armén* (1922); A. Åberg, 'Rutger von Ascheberg och tilkomsten av den karolinska armén', *K.F.Å.* 1951.

18   G. Jonasson, *Karl XII och hans rådgivare* (1960), pp. 113–20, though I can not accept his interpretation that the transport was motivated solely by Charles XII's feeling of obligation towards the Duke of Holstein-Gottorp: Sweden's need of the Holstein alliance as well as Charles's personal dislike for and independence of the Duke are equally demonstrable.

19   Add. MS. 35106, Robinson's letters of 30 Sept. and 4 Oct. 1699.

20   For the correspondence of Ferdinand Wilhelm, Duke of Württemberg-Neustadt with Heinsius (Archief Heinsius 585) see Torntoft, loc. cit., pp. 14–15.

21   For orders (on William III's behalf) to continue to do so see Add. MS. 35106, Blathwayt's letter of 6/16 Oct. 1699.

22   E. Hassinger, *Brandenburg-Preussen, Schweden und Russland 1700–1713* (München, 1953), pp. 38 ff.

23   See Carlson, I, 263 for Swedish ships trying to prevent this transport from Marienburg to Riga.

24   N. Herlitz (in Bring, *Karl XII*), p. 114.

25   Sehested's letter of 7 March 1700: *Handlingar*, IV.

26   N. Herlitz (in Bring, *Karl XII*), p. 114; the treaty is in Dumont, VII: 2, p. 474 ff.

27   Add. MS. 28903, Robinson's letter of 21 Jan. 1699/1700.

28   See H. Almquist, *K.F.Å.* 1937, p. 25, note 1 for a promise to do so on 10 Nov. 1699; the resident appointed, Andrey Chilkov, arrived in Stockholm in July 1700.

29   Alderfelt, *Histoire Militaire*, I, 87 stresses the friendly reception also at the royal headquarters in Zealand; a drabant has left a detailed description (Olof Stiernhöök's journal) of Chilkov's farewell audience: *K.F.Å.* 1913, pp. 352–5.

30   Hassinger, op. cit., p. 51, n. 76 quoting Tsar Peter's comment to a Prussian diplomat.

31   English, French and Danish diplomatic reports agree on this point; the evidence from Swedish sources supports it; new material for the 1697–1700 period brought to light, e.g. in R. Josephson's recent article in *K.F.Å.* 1961 on Tessin's assistant Törnquist (ennobled Aldercrantz in 1712), reinforces it.

32 Bodleian Library, Oxford, Orig. MS. Add. D.23 ff. 67a–68a, undated letter from Robinson (of 1709) to Bishop Burnet, printed in Burnet's *History of his own times*, II (1724), pp. 535–6.
33 S.P. 95, vol. 15, Robinson's letter of 9 July 1698.
34 For Leopold's own promotion of the 4th article see H.von Srbik, *Wien und Versailles, 1692–1700* (München, 1944), pp. 220, 268 ff.
35 Sehested's letter of 15 March 1699: *Handlingar*, IV.
36 The following instances are taken from B. Wedberg, *Karl XII på justitietronen* (1944) in which the records of the Supreme Court have been examined to ascertain the King's own points of view.
37 In *Ögonvittnen* (1960, ed. by H.Villius), pp. 40–5, a case which illuminates this trait has been printed from the 'Rådsprotokoll i justitieärenden' in R.A. of 26 Oct. 1698.
38 Bielke, *Mémoires*, pp. 3–4.

BOOK III, CHAPTER I : THE DANISH CAMPAIGN

1   Add. MS. 35106, Robinson's letter of 26 Aug. 1699.
2   See Cederhielm's memoirs printed in *K.F.Å.* 1915, p. 11, for the secret meetings of Piper, Polus, Åkerhielm and himself (in Åkerhielm's lodgings) both in southern Sweden and in Zealand.
3   See K.-G.Hildebrand, 'Ekonomiska syften i svensk expansionspolitik 1700–1790', *K.F.Å.* 1949.
4   Vellingk's letter of 20 April 1700.
5   This would be in accordance with Charles XI own expressed intentions if he were ever forced to go to war: see, e.g. d'Avaux's letter of 24 April 1697, F.O. 95, vol. 578.
6   E. Holmberg, 'Sjö-expeditionen mot Arkangel 1701', *K.F.Å.* 1918; N.F.Holm, 'Kampen om ryska ishavsvägen på Karl XII:s tid', *Forum Navale* 1948, pp. 16 ff.
7   Cited in N.Herlitz (in Bring, *Karl XII*), p. 114.
8   *Generalstaben*, II, 272–95.
9   Torntoft, loc. cit., pp. 15–16.
10 See *Bidrag S.N.K.H.*, I, 239 ff. for Danish disappointment when Frederick IV's fleet was unable to come to grips with the Swedish one in the early summer.
11 S.P. 95, vol. 15, Robinson's letter of 29 March 1697/8.
12 See E.Hornborg, *Sveriges sjöförsvar* (1944), pp. 29–32, for a summary of the recruitment system, with references to larger works by G.Unger; see also O.Lybeker *et al.*, *Svenska flottans historia* (1943).
13 S.P. 95, vol. 15, Robinson's letter of 29 March 1697/8.
14 Harley Loan Papers in B.M. 29/45, Miscell., has a letter from John Drummond in Amsterdam of 22 Sept. 1704 stressing how new this traffic is: before the last war Swedish and Danish ships seldom went to Cadiz and 'never within the Mediterranean'.
15 See especially A.Munthe, *Karl XII och den ryska sjömakten*, I–III (1924–27), and E. Hornborg, *Finlands hävder*, III (1931).
16 For a brief explanation of this system see E. F. Heckscher, *Svenskt arbete och*

liv (1941), pp. 146–7: it became obsolescent during Charles XII reign and was tacitly abandoned though never formally abolished.

17 G. Jonasson, *Karl XII och hans rådgivare*, pp. 116–17, has examined the Chancery discussions with the Duke of Holstein-Gottorp which preceded this answer.

18 Kagg's diary, 3 April 1700, noting the date from which war is regarded operative: *H.H.* 24.

19 U. Brandell, 'Förandringar i den svenska statshushållningen under det stora nordiska krigets tidigare år', *K.F.Å.* 1941, pp. 65 ff. for the navy's need of cash.

20 Kagg's diary, 14 April 1700: *H.H.* 24.

21 Charles XII's letter to Ulrika Eleonora of 23 April 1700: *Bref.*

22 Holst, *Ulrika Eleonora*, p. 42.

23 ibid., p. 57.

24 ibid., p. 42.

25 Add. MS. 40796, Stanhope's letter to Vernon, The Hague, 23 April/4 May 1700.

26 Add. MS. 35106, Robinson's letter of 16 June 1700; for the Anglo-Dutch expedition see *The Journal of Sir George Rooke*, ed. O. Browning (Publications of the Navy Record Society, London, 1897).

27 For the problem of rank see Add. MS. 40796, Stanhope's letter of 19/30 April 1700 and Add. MS. 35106, Robinson's letters of 21 and 30 June 1700.

28 ibid., Robinson's letters of 16, 17, 20 and 28 June 1700.

29 S. Grauers, *Wachtmeister*, II, 237–8; G. Jonasson, 'Kriget mot Danmark år 1700', *K.F.Å.* 1962, stresses the importance of the navy's role in the campaign.

30 Add. MS. 35106, Robinson's letter of 14 July 1700; Jonasson, *K.F.Å.* 1962, pp. 143–4.

31 N. Herlitz (in Bring, *Karl XII*), p. 122.

32 Add. MS. 35106, Robinson's letter of 25 July 1700 reporting visit of the 23rd.

33 ibid., Robinson's letter of 25 July 1700.

34 Stuart's journal is published in *Krigsvetenskapsakademiens handlingar* (1916), pp. 39–118; for the Danish decision not to oppose the Swedes in strength see *Bidrag S.N.K.H.*, I, 437 ff.

35 Add. MS. 35106, ff. 104a–105a, enclosed in Robinson's letter of 27 July 1700; for the draft of the relation, by Åkerhielm, see G. Jonasson, *K.F.Å.* 1962, pp. 131 ff.

36 N. Herlitz (in Bring, *Karl XII*), pp. 124–5.

37 Add. MS. 35106, Robinson's letter of 7 Aug. 1700.

38 Cederhielm's diary of 9–19 August, ed. by F. Wernstedt, is in *K.F.Å.* 1925, pp. 65 ff.; Åkerhielm's report has been printed by G. Jonasson, ibid., 1962, pp. 171–2.

39 Cederhielm's journal in *K.F.Å.* 1925; G. Jonasson, ibid., 1962, pp. 161 ff.

40 Add. MS. 35106, Robinson's letter of 27 July 1700: Stuart had been wounded at the landing, but stayed till the Swedes were securely established.

41 G. Jonasson, *K.F.Å.* 1962, pp. 166–7, has shown that the older interpretation which dated Charles XII's decision till after the receipt of a second and stiffer letter from Rooke cannot be maintained.

42 Add. MS. 35105, Robinson's letter of 28 July 1700. G. Jonasson's argument in

Karl XII och hans rådgivare (1960), pp. 142–3, that Charles, under pressure from the Duke of Holstein-Gottorp, adopted the worst solution does not seem to be convincing: the Chancery argument for sending the major part of the army to Livonia leaving only a token force to act with the guarantors would have carried grave military risks.

BOOK III, CHAPTER 2 : NARVA

1   Wittram, I, 224 and n. 60 for the treaty of 3 July 1700 (known in Moscow on 8 August); see also B. H. Sumner, *Peter the Great and the Ottoman Empire* (Oxford, 1949), pp. 18–22.
2   For a discussion of the Tsar's motivation and reasons see Wittram, I, 229 ff.; cp. A. Isberg, 'Erik Dahlberg och Tsar Peter', *Svio-Estonica*, 1962.
3   Add. MS. 35106, Robinson's letter of 14 Aug. 1700.
4   ibid., Robinson's letter of 24 Aug. 1700.
5   ibid., Robinson's letter of 29 Aug. 1700.
6   See G. Jonasson, *Karl XII och hans rådgivare*, pp. 168–73, 182–6, 192–7.
7   Oxenstienerna's review of the foreign situation of 5 March 1702, printed in Nordberg I, p. 215; cp. Stille, *K.F.Å.* 1914, p. 35.
8   Add. MS. 35106, Robinson's letter of 24 Aug. 1700.
9   Jonasson, p. 172 for letters to Gyllenstierna and the Duke of Holstein-Gottorp.
10 Add. MS. 35106, Robinson's letters of 22 Sept. and 16 Oct. 1700.
11 ibid., Robinson's letter of 12 Sept. 1700.
12 ibid., Robinson's letter of 29 Aug. 1700, quoting Polus and Åkerhielm during talks in the south of Sweden: help was eventually given in cloth and gunpowder rather than in cash; cp. Jonasson op. cit., pp. 210 ff.
13 Add. MS. 35106, Robinson's letter of 16 June 1700.
14 For Franco-Swedish relations at this time see H. Brulin, *Sverige och Frankrike under nordiska kriget och spanska successionskrisen åren 1700–1701* (1905), pp. 60 ff.; Y. Erdmann 'Die französische Ostpolitik und J. R. v. Patkul in den ersten Jahren des Nordischen Krieges', *Jahrbücher für Geschichte Osteuropas* 1961, pp. 321 ff.
15 Add. MS. 35106, Robinson's letters of 22 Sept. and 16 Oct. 1700; Brulin, pp. 186 ff.
16 N. Herlitz (in Bring, *Karl XII*), p. 128.
17 Nordberg, *Ammärckingar* (1754), pp. 5–6, based on Dahlberg's letter to Hermelin from Riga of 10 December 1700.
18 But the Riga reception did contrast with the splendid manner in which other countries, e.g. Brandenburg, received the Tsar in spite of his incognito.
19 Löwen, *Mémoires*, p. 34.
20 See the examination by A. Isberg, 'Johann Reinhold Patkul och Livland åren 1699–1701', *K.F.Å.* 1960, pp. 71–97.
21 Cited in Carlson, I, 287.
22 See Hassinger, op. cit., p. 49 for the contemporary quote *'on ne sait jamais qu'il veut tromper'*.
23 For Augustus's policy see C. Hallendorff, *Konung Augustus Politik åren 1700–1701* (1898).
24 Jonasson, op. cit., p. 181; for G.H. von Welz's mission ibid., pp. 132 ff.

25 Brulin, op. cit., pp. 99 ff.
26 N. Herlitz (in Bring, *Karl XII*), p. 130.
27 Rehnskiöld's letter to Oxenstierna of 6 Sept. 1700, cited in Carlson, I, p. 389, note 3.
28 Jonasson, op. cit., p. 209.
29 Browallius's diary, 1 May 1735.
30 Cederhielm's memoirs, *K.F.Å.* 1915, p. 85 ff.
31 Cederhielm's diary, *K.F.Å.* 1925, pp. 74–5.
32 ibid., p. 77.
33 ibid., p. 76.
34 ibid., p. 77.
35 For Guiscard's negotiations after his arrival at Reval on 20 Nov. 1700 see Brulin, op. cit., pp. 129 ff.; see also Jonasson, op. cit., pp. 188 ff.
36 See S. Olsson, *Olof Hermelin* (1953), pp. 235 ff.
37 Cited in *Generalstaben*, II, p. 304.
38 Carlson, I, 406–7.
39 ibid., p. 412.
40 Rehnskiöld to Wrede, cited ibid., p. 412, note 2.
41 See A. Isberg, 'Propaganda och fakta om slaget vid Narva', *K.F.Å.* 1963, for modifications needed to *Generalstaben*, II, 332 ff.
42 See, e.g. C. M. Posse's letters to his brother of 15 Oct. and 10 Nov. 1700: *H.T.* 1882.
43 Wittram, I, p. 241; for Swedish dead and wounded see *Generalstaben*, II, 353.
44 Carlson, I, 419, note 1.
45 Stenbock's letter to Oxenstierna, 28 Nov. 1700, cited *Generalstaben*, II, 355.
46 ibid., II, 354–5.
47 Wittram, I, 240.
48 Bratt, op. cit., pp. 18–19, has emphasized Rehnskiöld's share.
49 Add. MS. 28907, Robinson's letters of 19 Dec. 1700 and 26 Jan. 1701.
50 Schönstrom's memoirs, p. 44. For glimpses of the King during the battle see, e.g., Posse's letter to his brother of 9 Dec. 1710: *H.T.* 1882.

BOOK III, CHAPTER 3: THE CROSSING OF THE DVINA

1 Carlson, I, 422–3; for the thanksgiving in the army see, e.g., Posse's 'relation' enclosed in letter to his brother: *H.T.* 1882, pp. 91–2.
2 For William III's appreciating a battle-plan of Narva sent by Stuart see Add. MS. 28907, Robinson's letter of 20 March 1700/1; the expression that Charles was an 'extraordinary young man, as well as a Grand Prince', is found in F.E.B 104, vol. 13, letter of Secretary of State of 14 Jan. 1700/1.
3 Hatton, 'Louis XIV and his fellow-monarchs', *Louis XIV*, ed. J. Rule (Columbus, Ohio, 1968).
4 H. von Srbik, *Wien und Versailles*, pp. 124–36.
5 See M. A. Thomson, 'Louis XIV and the origins of the War of the Spanish Succession', *William III and Louis XIV*, edd. R. M. Hatton and J. S. Bromley, (Liverpool), 1967.
6 Hatton, *James Jefferyes's Letters* (in *H.H.* 35: 1, 1954), pp. 6–7.
7 For the negotiations leading to this treaty see Jonasson, op. cit., pp. 221–7.

8 See, e.g. Barck's letters to Hermelin of 16 Aug. 1702 and 19 Sept. 1706; Hermelin's letters to Barck of 6 Nov. 1706 and 26 Jan. 1707; Charles xii's letter to Ulrika Eleonora of 2 Sept. 1714: *Bref*, though he (vide Löwen's *Mémoires*, p. 37) always retained his admiration for the English nation and judged their church 'la plus raisonnable'.

9 The original plan for 1701 can be seen from Stuart's letter to Oxenstierna of 14 June 1701: C.von Rosen, *Bidrag till kännedom om de händelser som närmast föregingo svenska stormaktsväldets fall* (1936), I, 10, note 6.

10 Carlson, I, 445–7.

11 For measures to keep the soldiers in good health (rules of hygiene, medicines, etc.) see O.T. Hult, 'Om hälso-och sjukvärd under Karl xii:s rysk-polska fältåg', *Lychnos*, 1938, pp. 95 ff. with a French summary, pp. 136 ff.; G.Petri, 'Karl XII som fältherre', *K.F.Å.* 1937, pp. 141 ff.; cp. the regimental histories, e.g. E. Bensow, *Kungl. Skaraborgs Regimentets Historia*, II, 341 ff.

12 For the Birsen treaty of 26 Feb./9 March 1701 see Wittram, I, 243–7.

13 Hassinger, op. cit., pp. 47 ff.

14 See A.Stille, *Studier öfver Danmarks politik under Karl XII:s polska krig* (1889), pp. 14 ff.

15 G.Jonasson, 'Karl XII:s baltiska militärpolitik år 1701', *Scandia*, 1963, pp. 264 ff., and the same author's 'Planläggningen av rysska fälttåget år 1701', *K.F.Å.* 1966.

16 See, e.g. Uddgren, in Bring, *Karl XII*.

17 Charles xii's letter to Ulrika Eleonora of 20 Feb. 1701; for the incidence of sickness see O.Nordensvan 'Svenska armén åren 1700–1709', *K.F.Å.* 1916, pp. 129 ff.

18 Magnus Stenbock's letters to his wife; Philström's diary, *H.H.* 18: 4, p. 98.

19 ibid., pp. 98–9. Reuterholm in his memoirs, pp. 15–16, tellingly sketches Stenbock's gifts and character.

20 E.g. Charles xii's letter to Ulrika Eleonora of 20 Feb. 1701: *Bref*.

21 ibid.

22 For the winter quarters at Lais see Quennerstedt, *Ur Carl XII:s Levnad*, I, 29–60.

23 For the Dvina crossing see *Generalstaben*, II, 378 ff.

24 Letter of 10 July 1701, cited ibid., p. 379.

25 Löwen, *Mémoires*, pp. 53 ff.

26 Churchgoing was not compulsory, but officers were asked to encourage their men to attend whenever there was an opportunity.: see, e.g. Bensow's regimental history.

27 K.-G.Hildebrand, 'De gamla fältprästerna', *Fulhälsning ... ärkestiftet* 1943, pp. 129 ff.

28 Compare, e.g. the two letters quoted in Carlson, I, 50 note 1 from 1702.

29 Steinau's report of 10/20 July 1701, copy in R.A. (Store Nord. Krig, vol. 95), used by *Generalstaben*.

30 *Generalstaben*, II, 381 and note 3.

31 ibid., II, 397.

32 G.Rystad, 'Ryssland eller Polen?', *Scandia*, 1961–2, pp. 298 ff.

33 G.Jonasson, *Scandia*, 1963 and *K.F.Å.* 1966.

34 Carlson, II, 4–5; K.-G.Hildebrand, 'Karl XII problem', *H.T.* 1934, p. 400 and

K.F.Å. 1949, pp. 23–5; cp. Hassinger, p. 54 for Prussian fear at rumours that Sweden wanted the *dominium directum* over Courland, leaving the *dominium utile* for the Duke.

35 Holmberg, *K.F.Å.* 1918, pp. 121 ff.

36 For the negotiations see Jonasson, *Karl XII och hans rådgivare*, pp. 210 ff.: the treaty was signed 27 Sept. 1701 and led to the Maritime Powers paying 200,000 *rdr* in lieu of help according to the treaty of 1700. The Republic also promised to arrange a loan for Sweden of 30,0000 *rdr*.

37 See Jonasson, op. cit., pp. 229 ff., with some corrections to S.Backman, 'Karl XII:s polska detronisationspolitik', *K.F.Å.* 1947.

38 'The suggestion ought to be made to the Poles that they might get rid of their troublesome warlike king': Jonasson, op. cit., p. 239.

39 Rehnskiöld's letter to Oxenstierna 29 Aug. 1700, cited by Jonasson, ibid.

40 Printed in A.A.Stiernman, *Samling utaf kong. bref*, etc., V (1766), 887 ff.; see Backman, *K.F.Å.* 1947, pp. 100–1 for the receipt of letters on 6 and 12 May from Wachschlager which influenced the King.

41 The Cardinal's letter and Charles XII's answer are printed in Nordberg, I, 169 ff. and 171 ff.; cp. von Rosen, I, 13 ff.

42 Cederhielm's journal, *K.F.Å.* 1915, p. 90.

43 Backman, *K.F.Å.* 1947, pp. 94 ff.

44 See, e.g. A.Munthe, *Karl XII och den ryska sjömakten*, I (1924), 105 ff.

45 For Polish dissolution, moral and political, see J.Feldman, *Polska w dobie wielkiej, etc:*, IV, 51 ff., especially the quote by Backman, *K.F.Å.* 1947, p. 112; cp. K.G.Hildebrand, 'Polen 1704–1709', ibid., 1936, pp. 153–86, giving a summary of Feldman's conclusions; cp. Hassinger, op. cit., pp. 22 ff.

BOOK III, CHAPTER 4: INVOLVEMENT IN POLAND

1 For the victory at Rauge see H.E.Uddgren (in Bring, *Karl XII*), pp. 226–7; for the defeat at Erastfehr see Schlippenbach's own report printed in Adlerfelt, *Histoire Militaire*, I, 102 ff.

2 For Radziejowski being in the know see Hassinger, pp. 37–8.

3 Diaries and letters stress the King's refusal to abandon his tent for a house.

4 The one by the French diplomat du Héron from May 1702 is printed in Fant, *Samlingar*, I (1798); the one (also in French) by the Dutch Haersolte von Cranenburgh from the Heinsius Archief has been twice printed, first by van der Heim, *Het Archief van den Raadpensionaris Antonie Heinsius*, III (1880), appendix; and then in *K.F.Å.* 1959, pp. 99–104, with an introduction by W. Holst; cp. the slightly earlier one by Bonnac printed in C.von Rosen, *Bidrag till kännedom, etc.*, I, 15, note 4.

5 The style which Charles XII popularized (and which was known to French diplomats as 'à la Titus') became known as a 'Schwedenkopf' in Germany.

6 *K.F.Å.* 1959, p. 99; for a later dislike of green for similar reason see text, p. 435.

7 See Strömbom, *Kungliga Porträtt*, numbers 16, 19, 21 and 21.

8 *K.F.Å.* 1959, p. 99; that Charles XII, or his staff, was not as indifferent as diplomats assumed to the quality of his headgear see Düben's letter of 27 April

1712, asking for six new hats to be sent 'of the type and quality the King prefers': *H.T.* 1889, pp. 372-3.

9   *K.F.Å.* 1959, p. 99; cp. du Héron, May 1702; cp. Raby's 'Character' of 1707, Add. MS. 35885. ff. 1-4.

10   ibid., f. 1b.

11   Motraye, *Travels*, II, 171.

12   See, e.g. G. von Düben's letter to T. Funck of 27 April 1712: *H.T.* 1889, pp. 372-3.

13   D. Almquist, 'Johan Eriksson Ehrenskiöld', *K.F.Å.* 1948, p. 28.

14   Du Héron, May 1702; Haersolte: *K.F.Å.* 1959, p. 100.

15   S. Grauers, 'Med Karl XII i fält under de första krigsår', *K.F.Å.* 1965 and ibid., 1966, 'Karl XII:s hovhållning under kriget i Polen 1702-1705'; cp. E. Thormann, 'Konung Karl XII:s "Fatabur i fält" åren 1700-1706', ibid., 1941, for the fine table linen used in the campaign years.

16   The clergyman Søren Hagerup, reprinted *Ögonvittnen* (ed. H. Villius), p. 182,

17   Nordberg, II, 'portrait'; du Héron, May 1702; Haersolte: *K.F.Å.* 1959. p. 100.

18   Du Héron May 1702; cp. Hagerup, *Ögonvittnen*, p. 182.

19   Schmalensee's memoirs from 1704, *K.F.Å.* 1957, p. 123.

20   Schultz's diary for 18 Oct. 1706, *K.F.Å.* 1948, p. 76, commenting (since the King and his generals spent the night in the open with the medical orderlies): '*es stehet zu zweiffelen dasz eine solche ungleiche Cammeratschafft je mahls susammen geläget haben*'.

21   Nordberg, II, 'portrait'.

22   ibid., 'portrait'; Motraye, *Remarques*, p. 32 gives a less charitable explanation of Charles's inattention during the sermons which he himself had witnessed: the King was indifferent to religion after the setbacks of 1709.

23   Haersolte, *K.F.Å.* 1959, pp. 100-1; cp. du Héron, May 1702.

24   Haersolte, *K.F.Å.* 1959, p. 101.

25   ibid., p. 101.

26   ibid., p. 100.

27   ibid., p. 100.

28   ibid., pp. 100, 104.

29   ibid., p. 103.

30   ibid., pp. 100-1.

31   But Charles sometimes signed himself 'your friend', see, e.g. the letter to Giertta in 1718, printed in *H.T.* 1895, p. 341.

32   Hassinger, op. cit. p. 57.

33   For such a letter of 14 March 1700 see Jonasson, p. 231 and note 8.

34   This letter must be seen against the background of the negotiations (discussed by Jonasson, pp. 223-7) to obtain Swedish troops for the Allies in 1701-2.

35   Cederhielm's diary, *K.F.Å.* 1915, p. 91.

36   Reuterholm's memoirs *H.H.* 36: 2, pp. 9, 84; cp. ibid., p. 92.

37   Lewenhaupt, *Gyldenstolpe*, p. 142.

38   See Piper's diary for 1709-14 in *H.H.* 21: 1.

39   Hermelin's letter to Barck of 20 Dec. 1707, with similar expressions in letters of 3 June, 24 Aug., 12 Nov. 1702; cp. Reuterholm's letter to Cronstedt of 16 Feb. 1707: *P.H.T.* 1908.

40 Barck's letter to Hermelin of 7 Jan., 18 Oct. 1705, 19 Sept. 1706, 21 Dec. 1707; cp. letters of 28 June and 16 and 23 Aug. 1702.

41 Such bias has been diagnosed in respect of Lewenhaupt, Creutz and Gyllenkrook by G.Westin, 'A.L.Lewenhaupt's berättelse om fälttåget i Ryssland 1708–09. Några synpunkter', *Historiska Studier tillägnade Folke Lindberg* (1963), pp. 96–106.

42 For the negotiations see von Rosen, II, 2 ff.; and Erdmann, loc. cit., 321 ff.

43 Haersolte: *K.F.Å.* 1959, p. 104.

44 For the answer see von Rosen, I, 18 ff.

45 See Backman, *K.F.Å.* 1947, pp. 97 ff. for the mission of James's secretary Jan Jacob Kiki; for the correspondence via Cederhielm see Jonasson, pp. 251 ff.

46 Cederhielm's papers, *K.F.Å.* 1915, p. 90.

47 ibid., p. 91; cp. Hermelin's letter to Barck of 3 Dec. 1702 for the King (half-jokingly) having said the Swedes would have to fight ten years with the Poles and twenty with the Russians.

48 Nordberg, *Anmärckningar* (1754), pp. 20–3.

49 G.Jonasson, at present engaged on a continuation of his examination of the different attitudes of the King and the Chancery in respect of policy. Cp. Hassinger, p. 48, for Prussian disbelief at the time in Augustus's sincerity.

50 Reuterholm's memoirs, *H.H.* 36: 2, p. 13.

51 Cederhielm's papers, *K.F.Å.* 1915, p. 92.

52 Our knowledge of the meeting is built on the memoirs of Poniatowski (who was in attendance on the Sapiehas), printed in *H.T.* 1890, pp. 183–4; cp. Carlson, II, p. 70–1 for correspondence between Charles XII and the Sapiehas before the meeting.

53 See Hessinger, op. cit., p. 29, quoting Alvensleben from 1703.

54 Löwen, *Mémoires*, p. 35.

55 Herlitz in Bring, *Karl XII*, p. 151.

56 Oxenstierna's memorial is printed in Nordberg, I, 215; for a fine analysis of its four alternatives see A.Stille, *K.F.Å.* 1914, pp. 23–54.

57 For Hermelin's protocol and Piper's memorial see Crusenstolpe, *Karakteristiker*, pp. 133–44; for Cederhielm's comments see *K.F.Å.* 1915, pp. 87 ff.; for Poniatowski see *H.T.* 1890, pp. 183 ff.; for Poniatowski's service with Charles XII see R.Laache, *Karl XII og hans trofaste Grev Poniatowski* (Oslo, 1959).

58 Crusenstolpe, *Karakteristiker*, p. 134.

59 See *Generalstaben*, II, 406 ff., for the military movements which preceded the battle of Kliszów; cp. von Rosen, I, 49 ff.

60 ibid., p. 408 and n. 3.

61 Cited by F.Bengtsson, *Karl XII^s Levnad*, I (1948 ed.), 238.

62 Haintz, I, 64.

63 Vellingk's report, cited in *Generalstaben*, II, 440.

64 Charles XII's letter to Hedvig Sophia (undated) from 1702: *Bref*, no. 8 (the second one sent on the topic); cp. ibid., p. 56, for his asking Ulrika Eleonora to comfort 'sister Hedevig'.

BOOK III, CHAPTER 5: THE GRAND DESIGN

1 For Patkul's fate after Kliszów see H. Hornborg, *Konspiratören Johann Rein-hold Patkul* (1945), pp. 193 ff.; for his negotiations see documents printed by N. Herlitz 'Patkul mot Karl XII 1703–1705', *K.F.Å.* 1915, pp. 178–97 and Erdmann, loc. cit., pp. 336 ff. and authorities there cited.

2 For these see Cederhielm's diary, *K.F.Å.* 1925, pp. 78–166; von Rosen, I, 67 ff., and II, 22 ff.; Hassinger, pp. 75 ff.

3 Stralenheim's letter from Vienna to Cederhielm of 25 Sept. 1702: *K.F.Å.* 1915, p. 75; for the effect of this information see *H.H.* 19: 2, p. 229.

4 Charles XII's letter to Piper, printed in Nordberg, I, 284 and *Generalstaben*, II, 402.

5 For contributions levied in Poland see A. Flodén, 'Kontribution och revision under Stora nordiska kriget. Några anteckningar kring Jacob Burenskiölds verksamhet i Polen 1702–4', *K.F.Å.* 1962, pp. 173–98. Z. Łakociński, *Magnus Stenbock w Polsce* (Wrocław 1967) was published too late for me to make use of it.

6 Flodén, *K.F.Å.* 1962, gives a case-study of the close examination of accounts and of Polish complaints; cp. Hermelin's and Cederhielm's correspondence for 1702–6.

7 Reuterholm's Journal, *H.H.* 36: 2, p. 15.

8 Browallius's diary, 21 Oct. 1735.

9 Charles's letter of 29 Aug. 1702 cited in note 4 above.

10 For these negotiations see von Rosen, II, 27–56.

11 Hermelin's (cyphered) letter to Barck 21 Nov. 1702; Cederhielm's diary 24 Oct. 1702, *K.F.Å.* 1925, pp. 152–3.

12 For the 1703 campaign see R. Antoni, 'Fälttåget i Polen 1703', *K.F.Å.* 1914, pp. 53–124.

13 The date is usually given as 20 September – building on Adlerfelt – but S. Grauers, *K.F.Å.* 1966, p. 95, has found evidence which shows that the 19th – the date given in Kagg's diary, *H.H.* 24 – is the correct one; for the injury see V. Djurberg, *K.F.Å.* 1911, pp. 85–96.

14 See Norwegian folk traditions from Romerike ed. H. Refsum (Norwegian) *H.T.* 1932, p. 219; cp. Søren Hagerup (*Ögonvittnen,* ed. H. Villius, p. 182) in 1716 likening the King, with his flying cloak and loping gait, to a large winged bird.

15 Add. MS. 7075, Robinson's letter of 16 March 1702/3 (N.S.); cp. Hermelin's letter to Barck, 6 March 1703; for Robinson's mission see Hatton, *Jefferyes Letters*, pp. 7–8, 11 and authorities there cited.

16 ibid., pp. 8–11.

17 See, e.g. Haintz, I, 72; Olsson, *Hermelin*, p. 428.

18 Carlson, II, 174 ff.; von Rosen, I, 104 ff. The Electoral Prince remained a Protestant till 1717; for Papal hopes that support of Augustus in Poland might promote conversions in Saxony see H. Lemke's contribution to *Um die Polnische Krone*, pp. 292 ff.

19 For the Pultusk battle, see Antoni, *K.F.Å.* 1914, pp. 82–7.

20 Charles XII's letter to Rehnskiöld, end of April: *Bref,* pp. 240–1.

21 ibid., p. 241; editor's comment p. xxix and n. 9 to p. 175.

22 W.Konopczynski, 'Carl XII och Polen', *K.F.Å.* 1924, pp. 74–5, has stressed the victory for Augustus implied in the Lublin Diet.

23 For these moves see Antoni, *K.F.Å.* 1914, pp. 88 ff. and H.E.Uddgren (in Bring, *Karl XII*), pp. 241 ff.

24 For the negotiations leading to the treaty of 6/16 Aug. 1703 see von Rosen, II, 39 ff.; for those leading to the July one see Hassinger, pp. 90 ff.

25 See Hermelin's letter to Barck of 23 Aug. 1703 for tar issue; Hassinger, pp. 122 ff. for Danzig one. For the wider issues involved see K.Hautala, *European and American tar in the English market during the seventeenth and early eighteenth centuries* (Helsinki, 1963), and H.Bauer et al., *Danzigs Handel* (Danzig, 1925).

26 Hermelin's letter to Barck, 2 June 1702.

27 Charles's letter of 29 August 1702, cited in *Generalstaben*, II, 402.

28 See M.Schürer von Waldheim, *Maximilian*, pp. 12 ff.

29 ibid., p. 24; cp. Hermelin's letter to Barck, 23 May 1703.

30 Wisocki-Hochmuth's diary, *K.K.D.* II, 196.

31 See Biederstedt, *Eosander*, pp. 13 ff. for his 1703–4 visit to Stockholm; cp. the negotiations carried on from Swedish headquarters (Hermelin negotiating in Danzig with Alvensleben), Olsson, *Hermelin*, pp. 365 ff.

32 Holst, *Ulrika Eleonora*, p. 68.

33 Biederstedt, *Eosander*, pp. 85 ff.

34 The pioneer work into the 1703–4 negotiations between Charles and the Cardinal is by N.Herlitz, *Från Thorn till Altranstädt* (1916), pp. 109 ff.; see also Konopczynski, *K.F.Å.* 1924, pp. 79 ff. and Feldman (in Hildebrand's résumé), ibid., 1936, pp. 153–86.

35 Lewenhaupt, *Gyldenstolpe*, p. 145.

36 Note from Hassinger, p. 17, that the Prussian King dissuaded Charles XII from using a Polish–Swedish force to free the Sobieskis because of the danger of war with the Emperor. The Swedish King did, however, send an escort to ensure the third Sobieski brother, Alexander, a safe passage to Swedish headquarters.

37 For these visits in 1703 see Olsson, *Hermelin*, p. 406, note 10; cp. Hassinger, op. cit., p. 32 for the Emperor's fear already in 1700 that Charles XII might support the cause of the Silesian Protestants.

38 See the Russian historian V.D.Koroljuk 'Der Eintritt der Rzeczpospolita in den Nordischen Krieg' (in *Um die polnische Krone*, edd. J.Kalisch and J.Gierowski) building on Raczynski and Jarochowski; cp. Hassinger, p. 165. N.Herlitz, op. cit., p. 225, points out that we have no evidence to show that Charles XII knew of this document.

39 Reuterholm's journal in *H.H.* 36: 2, pp. 148–9; S.Grauers, *Horn*, I, 47 ff.

40 Reuterholm's journal in *H.H.* 36: 2, p. 148.

41 Nordberg, I, 525 ff.; Feldman (résumé by K.-G.Hildebrand), *K.F.Å.* 1936, p. 166 ff.

42 For the 1704 campaign see H.E.Uddgren (in Bring, *Karl XII*), pp. 250–64; Herlitz, op. cit., pp. 261 ff.; Haintz, I, 100–4.

43 Charles XII's letters to Horn of 14 and 24 Feb. 1704: *Bref*; Grauers, *Horn*, I, 95 ff.; Reuterholm's journal, *H.H.* 36: 2, pp. 149–51.

44 ibid., pp. 151–6.

45 For the Baltic theatre of war in 1703 and 1704 see H.E.Uddgren (in Bring,

Karl XII), pp. 246–50, 264–70; Wittram, I, 257–62 building on H.Sepp, F. Biemann and Russian authorities.

46 See Koroljuk's contribution in *Um die polnische Krone*, pp. 138 ff.
47 See Schmalensee's memoirs, *K.F.Å*. 1957, p. 125; Poniatowski, *H.T.* 1890, p. 193 claims that he answered, on Charles's behalf, the pleasantries shouted across by the Saxon party; Nordberg, I, 545, makes Klinckowström, the King's page, give the answer.
48 Uddgren (in Bring, *Karl XII*), p. 263.
49 See N.Herlitz, 'Patkul in 1705', *K.F.Å*. 1921, p. 126 for the Tsar's telling the Prussian diplomat Kaiserlingk that he would rather carry on war for ten years more than give up his foothold on the Baltic.
50 See Hassinger, pp. 141 ff.
51 The most thorough investigation of the Suedo-Polish relations in this period is S.Backman, *Från Rawicz till Fraustadt*, (1940), pp. 129 ff.
52 Haintz, I, 126.
53 For the Gemäuerthof battle see N.Herlitz, 'Slaget vid Gemeuerthof', *K.F.Å*. 1913, pp. 146–83; cp. *Generalstaben*, II, 500–6.
54 See the portraits reproduced in Schürer von Waldheim, *Maximilian*, comparing, e.g. those facing pp. x and 33; cp. Lewenhaupt, *Gyldenstolpe*, pp. 169–70 that Edvard Gyldenstolpe grew a Polish moustache and had a portrait made before he shaved it off.
55 J.Feldman's favourable judgement of Stanislaus (see the résumé by K.-G. Hildebrand in *K.F.Å*. 1936, pp. 160–1) whose good work was hindered by his less able Swedish ally has not been accepted by the present generation of Polish historians: the contributors to *Um die polnische Krone* depict Stanislaus as a weak-willed tool of the Swedes.
56 The peace-treaty is printed in Nordberg, I, 617 ff.; for a fine analysis of its economic aspects see K.-G. Hildebrand, 'Ekonomiska syften i svensk expansionspolitik', *K.F.Å*. 1949, pp. 25–32; cp. the same author's discussion, ibid., 1936, pp. 182–4, with corrections of Kopnoczynski, Haintz and Grauers.
57 ibid., 1936, pp. 184–5; ibid., 1949, pp. 32–40; D.Almquist on 'Några karolinska kanalprojekt', *K.F.Å*. 1935.
58 See Schulenburg's letter to Prince Eugène, printed by Zechlin, *Die Schlacht by Fraustadt*, pp. 86 ff.
59 For the Fraustadt battle see *Generalstaben*, II, 442–73; Haintz, I, 138–41.
60 Charles xii's letter to Rehnskiöld of 7 April 1706: *Bref*; another letter of congratulation ibid., of 2 May 1706.
61 For Rehnskiöld being called to the King's headquarters on 6 August 1706 and staying there on the 7 and 8 see his journal, *K.K.D.* IX, p. 195. It is possible that Charles xii consulted Rehnskiöld on 26–27 July when, according to the journal, the King unexpectedly paid him a visit.

INTERLUDE: CHARLES XII IN SAXONY, 1706–7

1 See Hermelin's letter to Barck, 16 May 1703, for Charles xii saying he felt he 'had come home' when he heard German spoken.
2 See diaries and letters of the period, e.g. Schmalensee's diary, *K.F.Å*. 1959, p. 3

and Charles XII's letters to Ulrika Eleonora of 24 March and 9 June 1704, 12 April and 15 May 1705 with one to Hedvig Sophia of the same date: *Bref*; cp. the journal of the Lifeguard hautboist, W. Lennart for 1705, ed. by S. Roth, 'Een lijten tijderächningh', *K.F.Å.* 1927, pp. 75–6.

3 Charles XII's letters to Ulrika Eleonora of 4 Jan. 1705 and to Hedvig Sophia of 18 Jan. 1705: *Bref.*

4 This expression, used in jest, is found in a letter to Ulrika Eleonora of 23 Dec. 1706: *Bref.*

5 ibid., mentioning the regulations passed forbidding marriage while serving with the army abroad. There is a significant passage in an earlier letter to Ulrika of 10 Dec. 1703 in which he explains why he can't take time off to visit Stockholm: when he had been away from camp a few days a rumour spread that 'he had fled and gone to Sweden'.

6 E.g. when Hultman, who had served the Gyldenstolpes before entering royal service in 1694, arrived in 1707, see Lewenhaupt, *Gyldenstolpe*, pp. 177–8.

7 See Charles XII's letter to Hedvig Sophia of 3 Nov. 1704: *Bref.* The Holmström lines are printed ibid., note 3.

8 Alstrin's letter to Upmarck, 8/18 May 1707: *H.T.* 1884.

9 Bielke, *Mémoires*, pp. 11–12; Nordberg, II, 689. In Charles XII's letter to Ulrika Eleonora of 9 June 1704: *Bref*, he tells of his great unhappiness at losing Hård, but does not mention his own share in the 'carelessness in exercise' which caused the accident.

10 Alstrin's letter to Upmarck, 8/18 May 1707: *H.T.* 1884, based on information from three clergymen at headquarters: Vallerius, Nordberg and Aurivillius.

11 Jefferyes's letter of 4 July 1708: *H.H.* 35: 1.

12 Against Philip IV of Spain.

13 Nordberg, *Anmärckningar* (1754), pp. 30–2, based on what Piper told him in Russia.

14 Heremelin's letter to Barck of 3 Dec. 1702.

15 Hermelin's letter to Barck 12 Oct. 1703.

16 Voltaire, *Charles XII* (1731 ed.), p. 169.

17 For Voltaire's contacts see H. Brulin, 'Handskriftsmaterialet till Voltaire's Charles XII', *K.F.Å.* 1940, pp. 7–37.

18 Motraye, *Remarques historiques* (London, 1732); Poniatowski, *Remarques* (London, 1741); Nordberg, preface to 1740 edition and *Anmärckningar* (Copenhagen, 1754).

19 Löwen, *Mémoires*, p. 27 recalling a conversation at Ystad in 1715; cp. N. Tengberg, *Om frihetstiden*, p. 34 and Holst, *Ulrika Eleonora*, p. 114 for similar slightly earlier remarks.

20 See, e.g. Reuterholm's letter (fragment) to Cronstedt of 1707: *P.H.T.* 1918, p. 130. The importance of propaganda was, however, fully realized, see Olsson, *Hermelin*, pp. 311 ff.; cp. S.-G. Haverling, 'Huvuddrag i svensk och antisvensk propaganda i Västeuropa på 1710-talet', *K.F.Å.* 1952, pp. 80 ff.

21 S.P. 80, vol. 17, Robinson's letter of 6/17 July 1706, reporting conversation with Piper of the 4th.

22 For the Altranstädt treaty see Nordberg, I, 706 ff.; S.E. Bring, 'Fördraget i Altranstädt', *K.F.Å.* 1909 and H. Kretzchmar, 'Der Friedenschluss von Altranstädt 1706/7' (in *Um die polnische Krone*, pp. 161 ff.).

23 See J.Wimmer, 'Die Schlacht by Kalisz am 29 Oktober 1706' (in *Um die polnische Krone*, p. 184); for Mardefelt's report see Nordberg, I, 743 ff.

24 Brydges Papers, vol. 3, Huntington Library, Senserf to Brydges, 12/23 Nov. 1706 from Rotterdam. Cp. ibid., for Drummond's letter of the same date.

25 Charles XII's letter to Ulrika Eleonora of 23 Dec. 1706: *Bref*; for the royal cousins getting on well see Reuterholm's letter to Cronstedt 30 Dec. 1706: *P.H.T.* 1908.

26 Cederhielm's memoirs, *K.F.Å.* 1915, pp. 95–6; for the stay in general see A. Günther, 'Das Schwedische Heer in Sachsen', *Neues Archiv für Sachsische Geschichte u. Altertumskunde* (Dresden, 1904), pp. 231–63.

27 Reuterholm's letter to Cronstedt of 28 June 1707: *P.H.T.* 1908; Peter Upmarck's letter to his mother 21 Aug. 1707: *H.T.* 1891, p. 200.

28 Günther, loc. cit., p. 245.

29 Lewenhaupt, *Gyldenstolpe*, p. 169 based on Edvard Gyldenstolpe's requests to have miniatures and jewellery with the King's portrait sent from Sweden; Fabrice, *Memoiren*, p. 26, for the Electress Sophia asking 'thousands of questions'.

30 For his Bible and Bible reading see, e.g. Raby's 'Character', Add. MS. 35885; for his punishment of blasphemy see Nordberg, *Anmärckningar* (1754).

31 Bielke, *Mémoires*, p. 42.

32 It is clear from Raby's 'Character' that his (incognito) visit to the Swedish headquarters took place in winter; for the poem 'An Epistle to the King of Sweden from a lady of Great Britain' in 1717 see H.Wright, 'Some English Writers and Charles XII', *Studia Neophilologica*, 1942–3, pp. 117–18: "Shou'd he (i.e. the Pretender) like thee on Shives of coarsest Bread rudely with dirty Thumbs his butter spread.'

33 Alstrin's letters to Upmarck of 4/14 May, 8/18 June and 7 Sept. 1707; *H.T.* 1884.

34 Nordberg, *Anmärckningar*, pp. 56–7.

35 Reuterholm's journal, *H.H.* 36: 2, pp. 63–4, and Hermelin's letter to Barck of 9 July 1707; cp. Hjärne's letter to Hermelin of 29 June 1707; *H.T.* 1882.

36 Hjärne's letters to Hermelin of 24 April and 22 June 1707; *H.T.* 1882; Hermelin's letter to Barck of 16 Jan. 1707.

37 Bielke, *Mémoires*, p. 56.

38 Creutz's letter to his wife, *K.F.Å.* 1911, p. 169 (of 30 Oct. 1707).

39 ibid., p. 169.

40 R.Josephson, *K.F.Å.* 1947, p. 41.

41 For the Swedish painter J.D.Swartz who studied abroad 1700–8 see article in *Svenska Män och Kvinnor*.

42 H.Villius, *Ögonvittnen. Karl XII*, p. 6; cp. E.Hornborg, 'Karl XII i närbild', *Handelsbladet* 24/2 1962.

43 Cp. S.Grauers's review of *Ögonvittnen* in *H.T.* 1962, p. 34 in which he stresses that even the documents printed can bear other interpretations than those of the editor and the contributors.

44 For a discussion of this problem see C.de Folard, *Histoire de Polybe, etc.* (1727) III, 258 ff.

45 C.Nordmann, *La crise du nord au début du XVIIIe siècle* (Paris 1962), p. 45,

note 49, with references which seem lightweight in respect of Görtz. For Reuterholm's (undated) letter of 1707 to Cronstedt: *P.H.T.* 1908, p. 135.

46   Schürer von Waldheim, *Maximilian*, pp. 74–5.

47   Fabrice, *Memoiren*, pp. 26 ff.

48   See text, pp. 90 ff. Motraye, *Remarques* (1732), pp. 26–7 reports Neumann, who had been in long attendance on Charles XII, for the King's body 'being perfect in every way': when his corpse was embalmed in 1718 the only damage found was incipient hæmorrhoids, due Neumann thought to the many years of hard riding.

49   Löwen, *Mémoires*, p. 73.

50   Tessin's memoirs, cited by Josephson, *Tessin*, p. 169; Fabrice, *Memoiren*, pp. 60 ff.; Motraye, *Travels*, II, pp. 6–7 and 343; Bonnac in a letter to Louis XIV cited by von Rosen, I, 15, n. 4, commented on this trait as early as 1701 (presumably from hearsay): '*il ayme à entendre des discours les plus libres qu'on puisse tenir sur les femmes, et les contes les plus grossiers qu'on fasse sur leur sujet*'.

51   Löwen, *Mémoires*, pp. 72–3.

52   Bielke, *Mémoires*, p. 41.

53   Charles XII's letter to Hedvig Sophia of 4 January 1705: *Bref*.

54   S.P. 95, vol. 10, Allestree's letter of 13 March 1677 on conversation reported to him by a Guards officer as well as discussions whether confession and communion could remove the guilt.

55   The best review of Swedish–Prussian negotiations is by Hassinger, op. cit., pp. 208 ff. Haintz, I, 206–10, blames Charles XII for not offering Prussia enough Polish territory and other advantages to make her a firm ally; Hassinger, p. 209, n. 155 agrees with Haintz that Swedish offers were not enough to lead to a '*tragfähiges*' (lasting) alliance, but does not consider this a major political blunder till 1713.

56   R.A., Anglica, Leyoncrona's letter of 29 October 1706; cp. S. Schartau, *Förhållandet mellan Sverige och Hannover 1709–15* (1903), pp. 9 ff.

57   See Adlerfelt, *Histoire Militaire*, III, 145 ff.; F. Goll, *Der Vertrag von Altranstädt. Österreich und Schweden 1706–07* (Prague, 1879).

58   See Lewenhaupt, *Gyldenstolpe*, pp. 174–5, building on Stralenheim's letters to Edvard Gyldenstolpe, and N. Holm, 'Stralenheim und Zobor', *K.F.Å.* 1960, pp. 98–104.

59   See Lewenhaupt, *Gyldenstolpe*, pp. 164 ff. for these troubles; cp. Hermelin's letter to Barck of 13 April 1707.

60   See Haintz, I, 170; cp. *Acta Pacis Westphalicae*, edd. M. Braubach and K. Repgen, I (Münich 1962), pp. 198 ff, for Sweden not being strong enough to get her ideal terms through.

61   G. Syveton, *Louis XIV et Charles XII. Au camp d'Altranstadt: La mission du baron de Besenval* (Paris, 1900); reckoning it Charles XII's worst mistake not to come to terms with France; cp. Olsson, *Hermelin*, pp. 460 ff.

62   For this mission see G. Kiss, 'Franz Rákóczi, Peter der Grosse und der Polnische Thron um 1707', *Jahrbücher für Geschichte Osteuropas*, 1965, building on the envoy Raday's dispatches; for an earlier mission of 1704 see K. Benda, *Le projet d'alliance hungaro-suedo-prusienne de 1704* (Budapest, 1960).

63   For this visit see S.P. 88, vol. 17, Robinson's letter of 17/28 and 19/30 April

1707; Reuterholm's letter to Cronstedt, 20 April 1704: *P.H.T.* 1908; Hermelin's letter to Barck, 20 April 1707; Poniatowski's memoirs, *H.T.* 1890, pp. 197 ff.

64 Löwen, *Mémoires*, pp. 38–9.

65 Marlborough to Godolphin of 29 April 1707 (O.S.), printed from the Coxe copies (Add. MS. 9099) by K.-G. Hildebrand, 'England och Sverige 1707', *K.F.Å.* 1937, p. 197.

66 ibid., p. 185, n. 3, printing an extract from Marlborough's letter to Godolphin of 11 July 1707 (O.S.) (original at Blenheim). This can be reinforced from a significant 'inner Cabinet' minute from the end of 1707 (in a series to be printed shortly by H. Snyder in the Cambridge *Historical Journal*) to the effect that England must try to get into 'nearer measures' with the King of Sweden: I am grateful for a preview of Professor Snyder's article.

67 R.A.: Anglica, Leyoncrona's letters of 27 March and 26 July 1709; for earlier negotiations see Hatton, *Jefferyes Letters*, p. 45 and note 1, and Archief Heinsius 1190, Haersolte's letters from 19 March 1707 onwards.

68 Robinson's letter to Harley of 15/26 March 1706/7, printed by Hildebrand *K.F.Å.* 1937, p. 193 from the original in the P.R.O.

69 Brydges Papers, vol. 3, Huntington Library, Marlborough's letter of 18 May 1707.

70 Bielke, *Mémoires*, pp. 44 ff.; Nordberg, *Anmärckingar*.

71 For the Anglo-Dutch mediation during the conference of 26–30 July 1707 see Robinson's letters in S.P. 88, vol. 17; for the negotiations in general see E. Carlson, *Föredraget mellan Karl XII och kejsaren i Altranstädt 1707* (1907).

72 See Hermelin's letter to Barck of 4 May 1707 for Charles XII having spoken to Marlborough in this vein.

73 For these see Robinson's letters in S.P. 82, vol. 24; cp. J. Milne, 'The diplomacy of Dr John Robinson at the court of Charles XII of Sweden 1697–1709', *Transactions of the Royal Historical Society* (London, 1948), pp. 90–2.

74 The mediators, Robinson and Haersolte, sent express a document as requested by the Swedes promising *sub spe rati* the guarantee of the convention: S.P. 88, vol. 17, Robinson's letter of 20/31 Aug. 1707. It is possibly this letter which has made Milne conclude (loc. cit., p. 85) that England guaranteed the 1706 treaty.

BOOK IV, CHAPTER I: PLANS AND PREPARATIONS

1 For Russian fears that the Swedes would do so see Stig Backman, *Från Rawics till Fraustadt* (1940), pp. 433 ff.; for the revolt see Wittram, I, 172 ff.

2 For Neugebauer's letters to Piper in 1704 and for his arrival at the Swedish headquarters early in 1705 see H. Almquist, 'Patkul och Neugebauer-Rysk värvning och ryssfientlig agitation i Europa 1702–1705', *K.F.Å.* 1938, pp. 7–83; and the same author's 'En avslöjad anonym. Martin Neugebauers plan till et svenskt fälttag mot Moskva (1706)', ibid., 1939, pp. 7–14.

3 See part 4 of Robinson's memorial of March 1707 printed from the Blenheim archives by K.-G. Hildebrand, *K.F.Å.* 1937, p. 188.

4 There was also strong resentment at Sweden's treatment of Danzig, see Olsson, *Hermelin*, pp. 386–7.

5 See Hertlitz (in Bring, *Carl XII*), pp. 211–12 for the allied defeat not being

unwelcome to the Swedes; one Swedish Chancery official expressed relief to a French agent: Olsson, *Hermelin*, p. 489, note 60.

6 For the Hungarian mission to Charles XII in 1707 see G. Kiss, 'Franz Rákóczi, Peter der Grosse und der Polnische Thron um 1707', *Jahrbücher für Geschichte Osteuropas*, 1965, pp. 344–60.

7 ibid., for Russian invitations to Rákóczi; cp. Wittram, I, 285 and Hassinger, pp. 206 ff. for other invitations.

8 Lewenhaupt, *Gyldenstolpe*, p. 165, based on Edvard Gyldenstolpe's recruiting experiences in 1707.

9 The pioneer study of these convoys has been made by S. Grauers, 'De militäre transporterna över Östersjöen under den stora nordiska krigets första skede 1700–08', *Historiska Studier tillägnade Folke Lindberg* (1963), pp. 79–95.

10 S. Waller, 'Den svenska huvudarméns styrka år 1707', *K.F.Å.* 1957.

11 For soldiers and volunteers of all nations, 'even a hermit', see Reuterholm's letter to Cronstedt, 25 October 1707: *P.H.T.* 1908.

12 See regimental histories for this practice.

13 Uddgren, *Lewenhaupt*, II, 115 ff.

14 See Cederhielm's memoirs, *K.F.Å.* 1915, p. 96–7.

15 See the studies of the 'Caroline sword' in *K.F.Å.* 1927 and 1932.

16 T. Lenk, 'Flintlåstillverkningens införande i Sverige. Armémodellerna', *K.F.Å.* 1937, pp. 226–41.

17 Cp. Cederhielm's memoirs, *K.F.Å.* 1915, p. 94 for his and Piper's advice that the main army ought not to go into Saxony since this would permit the world to 'look into their cards, both the strong and the weak ones'.

18 Petri, *Livgrenadjärregementets historia*, III, 211 and Wernstedt, *Livgardets Historia 1660–1718*, p. 445; for the army being as well clothed and equipped as ever a Swedish army had been see Hermelin's letter to Hjärne of 13 April 1707: *H.T.* 1882.

19 Many of the diarists and memoir-writers give details of the rations, see, e.g. Schönström's memoirs, p. 43.

20 Gyllenkrook's memoirs, pp. 39–40, 43.

21 Hjärne's letter to Hermelin of 27 July 1707: *H.T.* 1882.

22 B. Sallnäs, *Samuel Åkerhielm d.y.* (1947), pp. 17 ff. based on unprinted memoirs: the King asked him to stay when in April 1713 he arrived on a mission from the Council; after service in the Chancery-in-the-field he transferred to the war department, accompanying Charles XII on his later campaigns.

23 See Reuterholm's journal, *H.H.*, 36: 2, pp. 63, 144; Browallius's diary of 26 Nov. 1735.

24 Reuterholm's letter to Cronstedt of 9 July 1707: *P.H.T.* 1908; Jefferyes's letter of 16 Aug. 1708, *H.H.* 35: 2; Hermelin's letter to Barck 20 Dec. 1707; see also Olsson, *Hermelin*, p. 494.

25 Löwen, *Mémoires*, pp. 35 ff.

26 Hermelin's letter to Barck of 11 Oct. 1707; Hjärne's letter to Hermelin of 24 April 1707, *H.T.* 1882.

27 Gyllenkrook's memoirs, p. 56; for characterizations of the two men see Reuterholm's letter to Cronstedt of 16 Feb. 1707: *P.H.T.* 1908; for bad relations between them Schönström's memoirs, pp. 28–9.

28 S.P. 91, vol. 6, Jefferyes's letter to Whitworth of 27 July/7 Aug. 1709 printed by

Hatton, *Jefferyes Letters*, p. 78, note 1; Charles XII confirmed Piper's opposition to the Russian campaign in conversation with Löwen, see *Mémoires*, p. 40.

29   Charles XII's letter to Rehnskiöld of 7 Jan. 1704: *Bref.*

30   H. Villius, *Karl XII:s ryska fälttåg* (1951); G. Westin, 'Dagböcker som källor for Karl XII:s ryska fälttåg', *K.F.Å.* 1953; S. Waller, 'Josias Cederhielm's Dagboksanteckningar och Brev 1700–1709', ibid., 1960.

31   Petri, op. cit., III, 228–9.

32   See N. Herlitz, 'Svenska papper på villospår', *K.F.Å.* 1914, pp. 126–33; S. Backman, ibid. 1927, p. 79, note 1; Villius, pp. 8–9.

33   E. Tarle, *Severnaya voyna i shvedskoye nachestviye na Rossiyi* (Moscow, 1958).

34   C. Hallendorff, 'Karl XII och Lewenhaupt', *U.U.Å.* 1902; A. Stille, *Carl XII:s fälttågsplaner 1707–09* (1908); the same author's chapter 'Tåget mot Ryssland' in Bring, *Karl XII*, pp. 290 ff.; C. Bennedich, 'Karl XII:s krigföring 1707–09', *K.F.Å.* 1911.

35   F. F. Carlson cited by K.-G. Hildebrand, *H.T.* 1955, p. 26; cp. E. Carlson, III (a continuation of I and II by F. F. Carlson), 98 ff.

36   *Sbornik*, vol. 50, p. 220.

37   Jefferyes's letters of 9 July and 1 Sept. 1708, *H.H.* 35: 1; cp. von Siltmann's letter of 5 Aug. 1708: *K.F.Å.* 1937, p. 167.

38   For Eneman's sermon of 6/16 Aug. 1709 see D. Krmann's *Historia ablegationes ad regem Sueciae Carolum XII* (Budapest, 1884), pp. 582–3, reprinted in E. Carlson, III, note 573; for the pietism of the Swedish prisoners-of-war see Almquist, *K.F.Å.* 1947, pp. 5 ff.

39   Add. MS. 22198, Robinson's letter to Raby of 14 April 1708.

40   Marlborough's letter to Boyle of 5 July 1708: 'Whatever may be thought fit hereafter, I do not see any necessity for the payment of it' (i.e. 'the yearly allowance of £2,500'); cp. his letter to Sunderland of 1 Nov. 1708 that he is 'of the opinion that we need not be overhasty in that matter but stay a little to see what turn those affairs will take': *The Letters and despatches of John Churchill, First Duke of Marlborough* (ed. G. Murray, London, 1845), IV, 96 and 287.

41   B. Kentrschynskyj, *Mazepa* (1962), pp. 287 ff.

42   For this mission see Olsson, *Hermelin*, pp. 514 ff.; Jefferyes's letters in *H.H.* 35: 1 of 21 Dec. 1707, 26 Dec./5 Jan. 1707/8 and 14 Jan. 1707/8 building on information from Cederhielm; Reuterholm's letters to Cronstedt of 22 and 29 Nov., 6 Dec. 1708: *P.H.T.* 1908.

43   For this diplomacy see S. Backman, *K.F.Å.* 1949, pp. 113–20.

44   Olsson, *Hermelin*, p. 515; K. G. Hildebrand, 'En relation om Mazepa våren 1707', *K.F.Å.* 1935, pp. 157–66.

45   Hermelin's letters to Marck 29 Nov. and 13 Dec. 1707; S. Nilsson, 'De svensk-turkiska förbindelserna före Poltava', *Scandia*, 1953–4.

46   Carlson, III, pp. 103–4.

47   A. Stille, *Karl XII:s fälttägsplaner 1707–1709* (1908), accepted by a majority of present day historians, e.g. Petri, *K.F.Å.* 1937, p. 148; Haintz, I, 189. For a contemporary estimate that the Baltic provinces could not form a base, see Schönström's memoirs, p. 2.

48   Hermelin's letter to Barck of 29 Nov. 1707; Reuterholm's journal, p. 15.

49   Orlyk's relation, cited by B. Kentrschynskyj, *Mazepa*, p. 231.

50   E. Carlson, 'Krasnokutsk-Gorodnoe-Kolomak', *K.F.Å.* 1947.

51 Petri, *Livgrenadjärregimentets historia*, III, 253–4.
52 B. Kentrschynskyj, 'Propagandakriget i Ukraine 1708–1709', *K.F.Å.* 1958, pp. 102 ff.
53 E. Tarle, op. cit., p. 169. Note in the service-report of Gustav Soldan (*K.F.Å.* 1910, pp. 273–4) that he – who knew Russian well and had the task of translating intercepted letters – was in 1706 ordered to learn something about printing and to buy a Russian printing-press (which he did in Elbing) that 'the King might issue Russian patents and manifestoes'.
54 O. Klopp, *Der Fall des Hauses Stuart*, etc. XII, 360 ff.
55 Neugebauer's memoir, printed by F. F. Carlson, *H.T.* 1888, pp. 275–9, assumed to be by Mühlenfels; for identification of writer see H. Almquist, *K.F.Å.* 1939, pp. 7 ff.
56 Löwen, *Mémoires*, pp. 56 ff. K. G. Hildebrand, *H.T.* 1939, pp. 212–15 cites a letter of 8 Nov. 1707 which may be deduced as giving Piper's support (and hence the King's) for the dethronement of the Tsar; but the letter (written by the Swedish diplomat at The Hague) may well have had a diplomatic purpose.
57 Schönström's memoirs, p. 48. Cp. Hermelin's letter to Barck of 20 Dec. 1706 for Charles saying that he would never interfere with the due processes of law.
58 S.P. 88, vol. 17, Robinson's letter of 22 Aug. 1708.
59 Cederhielm's memoirs, *K.F.Å.* 1915, pp. 96–7; F. Hjelmquist, *Kriget i Finnland och Ingermanland 1707 och 1708* (1909); cp. Haintz, I, 197 for a summary of the historical discussion on the place of the Lybeker corps in Charles XII's strategy. G. Petri, 'Karakteristiska drag i Karl XII:s fältherrekonst', *K.F.Å.* 1937, explains the factors which necessitated operational responsibilities being left with local commanders.
60 For a revision of older views see Uddgren, *Lewenhaupt*, II, pp. 115 ff.; cp. G. Petri's 'Reviderade domslut', *K.F.Å.* 1950, pp. 206–9.

BOOK IV, CHAPTER 2: ACROSS THE RIVERS

1 Jefferyes's letter of 2 Nov. 1707, *H.H.* 35: 1; for the condition of Poland – ravaged also by the plague – see J. Gierowski, op. cit., p. 541.
2 Bielke, *Mémoires*, pp. 46–7.
3 For the peace offers see Hassinger, op. cit., pp. 202 ff.; Syveton, op. cit., 112 ff.; Olsson, *Hermelin*, pp. 473 ff.
4 See, e.g. Fryxell, Carlson, Munthe.
5 Löwen, *Mémoires*, pp. 34–5 reporting conversation with Charles XII in 1712, the King emphasizing in particular Tsar Peter's '*penchant et genie pour la marine*'.
6 Jefferyes's letter of 14 Jan. 1707/8; *H.H.* 35: 1.
7 Petri, III, 219.
8 Jefferyes's letter of 14 Jan. 1707/8, *H.H.* 35: 1.
9 ibid., Jefferyes's letter of 26 Dec./5 Jan. 1707/8.
10 Bielke, *Mémoires*, pp. 47–8; Jefferyes's letter of 21 Dec. 1707: *H.H.* 35: 1.
11 ibid., letter of 21 Dec. 1707.
12 For the mission see Nordberg, I, 833 ff.; cp. S. Nilsson, 'Rasjids Krönika', *K.F.Å.* 1954, pp. 89–91.
13 Hermelin's letter to Barck, 29 Nov. 1707.
14 Schmalensee's diary, *K.F.Å.* 1957, pp. 121 ff.

15   Letter of 17 April 1708 to his father, printed (in Swedish translation from the original French) by Lewenhaupt, *Gyldenstolpe*, pp. 182–3.
16   Jefferyes's letter of 20 January 1707/8, *H.H.* 35: 1.
17   Schmalensee's journal for 1708, *K.F.Å.* 1957, p. 130. The accusation that Charles XII ordered the man to be shot goes back to Hultman's memoirs, *Handlingar* (Floderus), I, 20 and also to the diary of Norsbergh in *K.K.D.* III, 191.
18   Bielke, *Mémoires*, p. 49; Nordberg, I, 834.
19   Nordberg, I, 834 ff.; Hultman's memoirs, *Handlingar* (Floderus), I, 21; Gyllenkrook's memoirs, p. 42.
20   Jefferyes's letter of 20 Jan. 1707/8, *H.H.* 35: 1.
21   Petri, III, 224, notes that the hope of cutting off Menshikov's retreat was not realized.
22   For Russian defence preparations see Wittram, I, 288 ff.
23   Jefferyes's letter of 15/26 Feb. 1707/8, *H.H.* 35: 1.
24   Petri, III, 225.
25   Jefferyes's letter of 11 March, 1708, *H.H.* 35: 1; see also Petri, III, 226–7.
26   Jefferyes's letter of 11 March 1708, *H.H.* 35: 1.
27   Nordberg, I, 849.
28   For exercise in the new drill see, e.g. Colonel Posse's diary, *K.K.D.* I, 304: Charles XII being with the regiment on 27 and 28 April 1708 'from four in the morning till seven at night'.
29   Jefferyes's letters of 27 March (O.S.) and 27 June (O.S.) give precise dates; those of 3, 12 and 22 May (O.S.) tell of preparations for the march, *H.H.* 35: 1.
30   For Polish affairs at this time see J. Gierowski, 'From Radozkowice to Opatów, *Poland at the XIth International Congress of Historical Sciences* (Warsaw, 1960), pp. 217 ff.
31   Jefferyes's letter of 21 March 1708, *H.H.* 35: 1; S.P. 82, vol. 24, Robinson's letter of 2/13 April with extract of Hermelin's letter of 16/27 March 1707/8 to himself and copy of his own letter to Marlborough on the subject of recognition and guarantee, stressing that he had 'rather softnd in the translation' Hermelin's reference to the King of Sweden's concern; for earlier pressure from Hermelin via Leyoncrona in London see letters quoted in Olsson, *Hermelin*, pp. 495–6.
32   ibid., Robinson's letters of 19 June and 10 July (both N.S.) 1709, the latter reporting via Hermelin Charles XII's 'great satisfaction'; cp. Nordberg, I, 850 and Jefferyes's letter of 27 June (O.S.) 1708, *H.H.* 35: 1.
33   Uddgren, *Lewenhaupt*, II, ch. 2.
34   Jefferyes's letters of 27 March, 3 and 12 May (all O.S.) 1708, *H.H.* 35: 1; Gyllenkrook's memoirs, pp. 46 ff.
35   Jefferyes's letter of 18 April 1708, *H.H.* 35: 1.
36   Pani Onjuchowska's relation, see above, p. 545, note 57.
37   Jefferyes's letter of 26 May (O.S.) 1708, *H.H.* 35: 1; for the revolt see B. Kentrschynskyj, 'Peter I och uppröret vid Don 1707–1708', *K.F.Å.* 1963; cp. Wittram, I, 290 and authorities there cited.
38   Jefferyes's letter of 26 May (O.S.) 1708, *H.H.* 35: 1; cp. H. Almquist, 'Ryska fångar i Sverige och svenska i Ryssland 1700–1709', II, *K.F.Å.* 1943, pp. 38 ff. for his journey over Viborg and Stockholm; this and other articles ibid., 1942 and

1946 deal with the fate of the prisoners-of-war and negotiations on exchanges.

39 Jefferyes's letter of 26 May (O.S.) 1708, *H.H.* 35: 1; cp. S.A.Nilsson, 'De svensk-turkiska forbindelserna fore Poltave', *Scandia*, 1953-4, pp. 128 ff.

40 Gyllenkrook's memoirs, p. 43 quoting Sparre and Lagercrona.

41 See Bielke, *Mémoires*, pp. 56-9, for the detailed prophecies of Coryander and for those of 'Les Prophets': Ankarhielm and Nordenhielm.

42 Gyllenkrook's memoirs, p. 48.

43 Hermelin to Barck, undated, late April 1708 (II, p. 152).

44 Gyllenkrook's memoirs, p. 44.

45 Lambert's observation from 1708; cp. a similar comment on the King's behaviour in Turkey by Fabrice, *Memoiren*, pp. 48-9.

46 Wittram, I, 293.

47 *Generalstaben*, III, 559-60; Petri, III, 231-2.

48 Hermelin's letter to Barck 16 June 1708; Cederhielm's letter to his brother of the same date in *K.K.D.* VI.

49 Cederhielm's letter to his brother of 16 June 1708, *K.K.D.* VI.

50 Wittram, I, 293, quoting Menshikov's letter of 16 June 1708 and Tsar Peter's of 23 June: '*Der Feind hat euch getauscht*'.

51 ibid., pp. 290 ff.; V.E.Shutoy, *Bor'ba narodnykh mass protiv nashestviya armii Karla XII, 1700-1709* (Moscow, 1958); Tarle, op. cit., pp. 138 ff.

52 Hermelin's letter to Barck 29 Nov. 1707.

53 Adlerfelt, *Histoire militaire*, III, 281.

54 Jefferyes's letter of 27 June (O.S.) 1708, *H.H.* 35: 1.

55 Posse's diary: *K.K.D.* I, p. 309.

56 Jefferyes's letter of 27 June (O.S.) 1708, *H.H.* 35: 1.

57 For the battle see *Generalstaben*, III, 580 ff.; to be read in conjunction with the Russian authorities summarized in *K.F.Å.* 1932-3, pp. 16 ff.; Petri, III, 235 with good sketch map.

58 Jefferyes's letter of 4 July (O.S.) 1708, *H.H.* 35: 1.

59 ibid., letter of 9 July (O.S.) 1708; cp. for the 'wonderful but expensive victory', comment of Hermelin in his letter to Barck of 5 July 1708.

60 Tengberg, *K.F.Å.* 1948, p. 103.

BOOK IV, CHAPTER 3: THE BLOWS OF FATE

1 Jefferyes's letter of 9 July (O.S.) 1708, *H.H.* 35: 1.

2 Cederhielm's letter to his brother of 18 July 1708, *K.K.D.* VI.

3 There is no material which will permit an answer, though Carlson, III, notes 393 and 394, blames Charles for having left Lewenhaupt too little time for preparations: it will not do, however, to assume that the first Lewenhaupt heard of his task was by the King's letter of 26 May (which reached him on 3 June) – he had been briefed already in March, see Bennedich, *K.F.Å.* 1911, p. 66.

4 Jefferyes's letter of 17 July (O.S.) 1708, *H.H.* 35: 1.

5 For the campaign see F.Hjelmquist, *Kriget i Finnland och Ingermanland 1707 och 1708* (1912); A.Munthe, *Karl XII och den ryska sjömakten*, II, 398 ff.; E. Tarle, *Russkiy flot i vnesnaya politika Petra I* (in the collected works edition,

vol. XII, Moscow, 1962); cp. Haintz, I, 240 for information via the Prussian diplomat in Moscow, Keyserlingk; and Wittram, I, pp. 294–5.

6   S.P. 82, vol. 24, Robinson to Boyle, from Hamburg, 4 Sept. (N.S.) 1708.

7   Jefferyes's letters of 17 July (O.S.) and 3 Aug. (O.S.) 1708, *H.H.* 35: 1; cp. Hermelin's letters to Barck of 15, 19 and 24 July 1708.

8   Jefferyes's letter of 3 Aug. (O.S.) 1708, *H.H.* 35: 1; cp. Hermelin's letters to Barck of 15 and 19 Aug. 1708.

9   Jefferyes's letter of 3 Aug. (O.S.) 1708, *H.H.* 35: 1.

10 For this see H.Almquist, *K.F.Å.* 1938, pp. 23 ff.

11 Jefferyes's letter of 3 Aug. (O.S.) 1708, *H.H.* 35: 1.

12 Cederhielm's letter to his brother, *K.K.D.* VI, 104.

13 Jefferyes's letter of 3 Aug. (O.S.) 1708, *H.H.* 35: 1.

14 Rehnskiöld's letter to Charles XII of 11 Dec. 1707: *K.K.D.* XI, 112–13.

15 Jefferyes's letter of 16 Aug. (O.S.) 1708, *H.H.* 35: 1.

16 ibid., letter of 16 Aug. (O.S.) 1708.

17 Cederhielm's letters to his brother of 10, 17, and 23 Aug. 1708: *K.K.D.* VI.

18 Jefferyes's letter of 16 Aug. (O.S.) 1708, *H.H.* 35: 1.

19 Bennedich, *K.F.Å.* 1911, pp. 65, 68–70.

20 A. Stille, *Carl XII:s fälttågsplaner 1707–1709* (1908), pp. 64 ff. was the first historian to explain these manœuvres in terms of Charles XII waiting for Lewenhaupt to catch up with him.

21 Uddgren, *Lewenhaupt*, II, 131 ff.; for their arrival see Lewenhaupt's memoirs (based on journal) *H.H.* 34: 1, and Petre's diary, *K.K.D.* I, p. 151.

22 Petri, III, 246–7.

23 Jefferyes's letter of 1 Sept. (O.S.) 1708, *H.H.* 35: 1; von Siltmann's report of 9 Sept. 1708, summarized by S.Jägerskiöld in *K.F.Å.* 1937, pp. 167–8; for the Malatitze attack see Petri, III, 247–8 building on an unpublished account by Meijerfelt; see Carlson, III, 154–6, for the Russians celebrating Malatitze as a victory.

24 Petri, III, 249; Gyllenkrook's memoirs, p. 53.

25 Jefferyes's letter of 1 Sept. (O.S.) 1708, *H.H.* 35: 1.

26 Petri, III, 249, stresses also Tsar Peter's boldness and skill in the attack on Roos's isolated column.

27 Jefferyes's letter of 1 Sept. (O.S.) 1708, *H.H.* 35: 1.

28 ibid., letter of 1 Sept. (O.S.) 1708; cp. Carlson, III, 157.

29 Jefferyes's letter of 12 Sept. (O.S.) 1708, *H.H.* 35: 1; cp. Posse's diary, *K.K.D.* 1322 ff.; Carlson, III, 157–9.

30 Jefferyes's letter of 12 Sept. (O.S.) 1708, *H.H.* 35: 1.

31 ibid., Jefferyes's letter of 12 Sept. (O.S.) 1708.

32 See Bennedich, *K.F.Å.* 1911, p. 103.

33 Stille, op. cit., pp. 90 ff.; Bennedich, *K.F.Å.* 1911, p. 103; Petri, III, 252.

34 P.S. to Jefferyes's letter of 12 Sept. (O.S.) 1708, *H.H.* 35: 1.

35 See Schönström memoirs, pp. 48–9.

36 Jefferyes's letter of 12 Sept. (O.S.) 1708, *H.H.* 35: 1.

37 Uddgren, *Lewenhaupt*, II, 132 ff. shows that headquarters realized Lewenhaupt might not yet have reached the Dnieper; cp. Stille, op. cit., p. 90, for the return of the messenger.

38 His relation has been used by Petri, III, 253–4.

39   Eyewitness cited by P.Engdahl, *K.F.Å.* 1930, p. 212.
40   Jefferyes's letter of 18 Sept. (O.S.) 1708, *H.H.* 35: 1; cp. Cederhielm, quoted by Carlson, III, 161 and 164; for details see Schmalensee's journal, *K.F.Å.* 1957, pp. 131–2.
41   Schönström's memoirs, p. 58; Gyllenkrook's memoirs, p. 61.
42   For Lagercrona's mission see ibid., pp. 63–5; Poniatowski's memoirs, *H.T.* 1890, pp. 172 ff.; Nordberg, *Anmärckningar* (1754), pp. 33–8.
43   Cederhielm's letter to his brother of 11 Sept. 1708: *K.K.D.* VI.
44   Gyllenkrook's memoirs, pp. 66–7.
45   Jefferyes's letter of 18 Sept. (O.S.) 1708, *H.H.* 35: 1.
46   For the 'official' version see, e.g. Meijerfelt's 'relation' cited by Petri, III, 254 and Schmalensee's journal *K.F.Å.* 1957, p. 132; for the importance of Severia see Petri, III, 259 and B.Kentrschynskyj, *Mazepa*, pp. 321 ff.; cp. Stille, op. cit., pp. 40 ff.
47   Jefferyes's letter of 18 Sept. (O.S.) 1708, *H.H.* 35: 1; cp. Gyllenstierna's report, cited by Carlson, III, 169.
48   G.A.Piper's memoirs cited by Petri, III, 257.
49   Jefferyes's letter of 7 Oct. (O.S.) 1708, *H.H.* 35: 1.
50   ibid., letter of 7 Oct. (O.S.) 1708.
51   The germ of this contention, e.g. by Carlson, III, 167–8 and note 401, can be seen in Weihe's diary, *H.H.* 19:1, p. 11, where he notes that the misfortune of Lewenhaupt's army (in which he served) would not have happened 'if the King had waited for us'.
52   E.g. C.Hallendorff, 'Carl XII och Lewenhaupt året 1708', *U.U.Å.* 1902, pp. 141 ff.
53   Bennedich, *K.F.Å.* 1911, pp. 109–10 for orders to Lewenhaupt.
54   Wittram, I, 300; for the battle in general see the Russian authorities cited ibid., note 111; from the Swedish side Lewenhaupt's memoirs, *H.H.* 34:2, pp. 182 ff. and Weihe's diary, *H.H.* 19:1, pp. 5 ff.o Jefferyes's letter of 28 Oct. (O.S.) 1708, *H.H.* 35:1; Uddgren, *Lewenhaupt*, 11, 144 ff.
55   Weihe's diary, *H.H.* 19: 1, p. 10.
56   Jefferyes's letter of 7 Oct. (O.S.) 1708, *H.H.* 35: 1.
57   Tarle, op. cit., pp. 220 ff.
58   Jefferyes's letter of 7 Oct. (O.S.) 1708, *H.H.* 35: 1.

BOOK IV, CHAPTER 4: THE FIGHT FOR THE UKRAINE

1   B.Kentrschynskyj, *K.F.Å.* 1958, p. 102 ff.; C.Nordman, 'Ett Mazepa manifest', *H.T.* 1958, pp. 61 ff.
2   Ensign Piper's memoirs, cited by Petri, III, 261.
3   B.Kentrschynskyj, *Mazepa*, p. 328, with discussion of various estimates, some exaggerated, for propaganda purposes.
4   K.-G.Hildebrand, *K.F.Å.* 1949, p. 33; B.Kentrschynskyj, *Mazepa*, pp. 340–2.
5   Poniatowski's memoirs, *H.T.* 1890, p. 201; for the crossing see *Generalstaben*, III, 624–44; Weihe's diary, *H.H.* 19: 1, and Cederhielm's letter to his brother of 10 Nov. 1708; *K.K.D.* VI, 16 ff.
6   B.Kentrschynskyj, *Mazepa*, p. 326.
7   E.g. Schönström's memoirs, p. 17; Petre's diary 11 May 1709: *K.K.D.* I.; cp.

Weihe's diary, *H.H.* 19:1, pp. 18 ff. where he notes *i.a.* that the sheep were too fat to eat.

8   Cp. Posse's more reasoned comment that he felt he had come among barbarians because he did not know the language, 'being without conversation': letter to his brother of 27 Nov. 1707: *H.T.* 1882.

9   Lyth's diary, *K.K.D.* II, p. 63.

10   Posse's diary, *K.K.D.* I, 334; Pihlström's diary, *H.H.*: 8, p. 15.

11   A. Stille, *Carl XII:s fälttågsplaner 1707–1709*, pp. 159 ff., and the same author's chapter in Bring, *Karl XII*, pp. 312–14.

12   E. Carlsson, 'Krasnokutsk-Gorodnoe-Kolomak', *K.F.Å.* 1947, pp. 175–212.

13   Haintz, I (1958 ed.) 255, note 3.

14   Ensign Piper's memoirs, cited by Petri, III, 268–70. Other diarists, e.g. Petre, *K.K.D.* I, 24 Dec. 1708, tell us that the King and the Prince of Württemberg avoided frost danger to nose, ears and feet by rubbing with snow.

15   Adlerfelt, *Histoire Militaire*, III, 389, 399. The safeguarding of Mazepa's fortune, essential for the Ukrainian war effort, was part of this aim; see Schmalensee's journal, *K.F.Å.* 1957, p. 134.

16   Posse's diary, *K.K.D.* I, 338; Schultz's diary, *K.F.Å.*, 1948, p. 81; cp. Schmalensee's journal, ibid., 1957, p. 133 for the tap of the barrel of 'the strong brandy' freezing when in use and having to be thawed.

17   For there being no sermon on account of the cold either on 24 or 25 Dec. see Posse's diary: *K.K.D.* I, 337.

18   Meijerfelt's (unpublished) relation, cited by Petri, III, 272; for the Veprik action ibid., 271–3; Bensow's regimental history, pp. 376–9.

19   E.g. Cederhielm's letter to his brother of 31 March 1709, *K.K.D.* VI, on the loss of *'l'élite et la crème de tout beaux officiers'*.

20   Gyllenkrook's memoirs, p. 81.

21   Lewenhaupt, *Gyldenstolpe*, p. 93; Waldheim, *Maximilian*, p. 92.

22   Löwen, *Mémoires*, pp. 25–6.

23   Charles XII's letter to Ulrika Eleonora,

24   Hermelin's letter to Barck of 24 Sept. 1708 stresses the uncertain post; this is repeated in letters of 11 Nov. and 4 Dec.

25   See Siltmann's and Jefferyes's journals.

26   Nordberg, I, 889; cp. Gyllenkrook's memoirs, pp. 90–4.

27   See Carlsson, *K.F.Å.* 1947, pp. 203–4 with quotations from Petre's diary, *K.K.D.* I, 182–3, which illustrate the help given by the officers, also the King's orders to arrange housing for the refugees.

28   E. Tengberg, 'Karl XII i Ukraine våren 1709', *K.F.Å.* 1948, pp. 120–3.

29   B. Kentrschynskyj, *Mazepa*, pp. 352–9.

30   Tengberg, *K.F.Å.* 1948, p. 110; Wittram I, 292, stresses that the Russians failed to interrupt the post routes.

31   P.S. to Hermelin's letter to Barck of 31 March 1709, mentioning that these goods came from Turkey.

32   Nordberg, I, 905; for a deduction of the contents of the letter, since lost, from the answer (printed by Nordberg, I, 913 ff.) and from the Grand Vizier's instructions in respect of the answer see S. A. Nilsson, 'Rasjids krönika', *K.F.Å.* 1954, pp. 92–3.

33   *Generalstaben*, III, 644; Haintz, I, 257.

34 N. Herlitz, 'Den polska frågan 1708–1709', *K.F.Å.* 1914, pp. 170–1.

35 Charles XII to Stanislaus of 31 March 1709, cited (from copy in R.A.) by B. Kentrschynskyj, *Mazepa*, p. 406.

36 The Russian peace-terms at this time went beyond just this town (for what is known of them see E. Tengberg, 'Meijerfelts mission efter Poltava. Några Anteckningar', *H.T.* 1952, pp. 270 ff.) and it can be assumed that Jefferyes's phrase indicated the minimum gain with which the Chancery-in-the-field assumed the Tsar might be satisfied.

37 Jefferyes's journal enclosed in letter of 27 June (O.S.) 1709, *H.H.* 35: 1, pp. 69–70.

38 Ensign Piper's memoirs, cited by Petri, III, 276, 281.

39 See, e.g. Petre's diary, *K.K.D.* I, 269.

40 Gyllenkrook's memoirs, pp. 95 ff.

41 Jefferyes's letter of 27 June (O.S.) 1709, *H.H.* 35: 1; cp. Weihe's diary, *H.H.* 19: 1, p. 39; Adlerfelt, *Histoire Militaire*, IV, 52 ff. For a critical examination of the views of Stille and Bennedich, see E. Carlsson, 'Det svenska högkvarterets planläggning av slaget vid Poltava', *K.F.Å.* 1947, pp. 130 ff.

42 ibid., 1946, E. Tengberg, 'Några anteckningar kring slaget vid Poltava'; ibid., 1948, H. Villius, 'Peter den stores beslut å gå över Vorskla'; ibid., 1947, E. Carlsson, 'Det svenska högkvarterets planläggning av slaget vid Poltava'; ibid., 1949, W. Kleen, 'Poltavaslagets strategiska inramning'; ibid., 1958, G. Petri, 'Slaget vid Poltava'.

43 These are listed in Jefferyes's journal enclosed in his letter of 27 June (O.S.) 1709, *H.H.* 35: 1, pp. 69–75.

44 ibid., cp. Schmalensee's journal, *K.F.Å.* 1957,

45 Jefferyes's letter of 27 June (O.S.) 1709, *H.H.* 35: 1.

46 Possibly 22,000 Swedes only, see *K.F.Å.* 1947, p. 142; for the Russian losses see Tengberg, *Karl XII och Ryssland*, pp. 10 ff.

47 For this mission, working through Mazepa, see S. A. Nilsson's article in *Scandia*, 1953–4 and B. Kentrschynskyj, *Mazepa*, pp. 407–8.

48 Hermelin's letter to Barck expresses expectation as early as 31 March 1709.

49 Siltmann's journal, *K.K.D.* III, entries 11 April and 9 May 1709.

50 S. A. Nilsson, 'De svensk-turkiska förbindelserna före Poltava,' *Scandia*, 1953–4, pp. 134 ff.; cp. B. Kentrschynskyj, *Mazepa*, pp. 389 ff.

51 Jefferyes's letter of 27 June (O.S.) 1709, *H.H.* 35: 1; Adlerfelt, *Histoire militaire*, IV, 69; for Russian diplomacy at the Porte at this time see B. H. Sumner, *Peter the Great and the Ottoman Empire* (1949), pp. 59 ff.; cp. Wittram, I, 300–7 with authorities cited in note 118.

52 S. A. Nilsson's article in *Scandia*, 1953–4, pp. 142 ff.; cp. B. Kentrschynskyj, *Mazepa*, pp. 409–12.

53 For the Polish situation see J. Gierowski, 'From Radoszkowice to Opatów – the history of the decomposition of the Stanisław Leszczyński camp', *Poland at the XIth International Congress of Historical Sciences* (Warsaw, 1960), pp. 257 ff.

54 B. B. Kentrschynskyj, *Mazepa*, p. 411.

55 Jefferyes's journal enclosed in letter of 27 June (O.S.) 1709, *H.H.* 35:1.

56 Tengberg, *Karl XII och Ryssland*, pp. 23–6, shows the 'postponement' aspect – the wait and see policy – of the Turks to have been stronger than Nilsson in his

Scandia article assumed and therefore judges the Swedish position to have been more favourable than the 'no-hope' Nilsson postulated.

57 Jefferyes's letter of 27 June (O.S.) 1709; *H.H.* 35:1, pp. 67–8; Petre, *K.K.D.* I, 284, notes that the belief was general 'among the ordinary soldiers' that Stanislaus was 'within ten miles of the main army'.
58 Jefferyes's journal, *H.H.* 35: 1, p. 75.

BOOK IV, CHAPTER 5: POLTAVA AND PEREVOLOTJNA

1 For the older view see A. Stille, *Carl XII:s fälttågsplaner 1707–1709*, pp. 183–4; for a revision see E. Tengberg, 'Några anteckningar kring slaget vid Poltava', *K.F.Å.* 1946; E. Carlsson, 'Det svenska högkvarterets planläggning av slaget vid Poltava', ibid., 1947; H. Villius, 'Peter den stores beslut att övergå Vorskla', ibid., 1948.
2 Lewenhaupt's memoirs, *H.H.* 34: 2, p. 395; Djurberg, *K.F.Å.* 1912, pp. 103–8.
3 Hultman's memoirs, *Handlingar* (Floderus), I, 37–41, giving condensed versions of the stories as told to the King.
4 Jefferyes's journal, *H.H.* 35:1, p. 75; for the King's orders to Rehnskiöld see Petre's diary, *K.K.D.* I, 282; Poniatowski's memoirs, *H.T.* 1890, p. 204 notes the decision reached; see also extract from Meijerfelt's (unpublished) journal printed by E. Carlsson in *K.F.Å.* 1947, pp. 144–5.
5 E. Carlsson has stressed this, *K.F.Å.* 1947, pp. 145–8; cp. the criticism of W. Kleen, ibid., 1949, pp. 143–6.
6 Adlerfelt, journal entry for 18 June 1709.
7 Tengberg, *K.F.Å.* 1946, pp. 76 ff.; though Villius ibid., 1948, p. 148, does not exclude the possibility that the Russian decision was taken as late as 19 June.
8 Jefferyes's letter of 27 June (O.S.) 1709, *H.H.* 35: 1; cp. for Russian peace feelers Nordberg, I, 906 ff.
9 For Piper's views see E. Tengberg, 'Meijerfelts mission', *H.T.* 1952.
10 For the general desire in both armies to have an end to the war see the dispatches of the well-informed Keyserlingk in Moscow for 1708–9 (published by B. Krupnicki in 1939, and utilized by Tengberg, *K.F.Å.* 1948, pp. 124–6).
11 Jefferyes's letter of 27 June (O.S.) 1709, *H.H.* 35:1, pp. 68–9.
12 Schönstrom's memoirs, p. 20.
13 Jefferyes's letter of 27 June (O.S.) 1709, *H.H.* 35: 1, p. 68; cp. E. Tengberg, 'Meijerfelt's mission after Poltava', *H.T.* 1952, p. 271.
14 Löwen, *Mémoires*, p. 34; cp. Hassinger, op. cit., p. 120 for a Prussian diplomat's report that Charles XII assured him he would never break his word 'unless I were given the greatest of provocations'.
15 For numbers engaged and the battle in general see, apart from the articles cited above in footnotes 1 and 5, G. Petri, 'Slaget vid Poltava', *K.F.Å.* 1958, pp. 125–61; E. Tengberg, *Karl XII och Ryssland* (*H.A.* 7, 1958), pp. 27–50. Russian studies into the battle have, for the most part, been made available by translations: N. L. Jonakov's study of the campaign of 1708–9 is available in typescript in Krigsarkivet, Stockholm; E. I. Porfiriev, *Peter I* appeared in 1958 in Swedish; and the researches of the younger historians have been summarized in J. Hedberg and G. Medwedjev, 'Artilleriet – en avgörande faktor i Poltavaslaget', *K.F.Å.* 1961, pp. 105–34, and W. Granberg, 'Redutterna i

slaget vid Poltava enligt ryska källor och rysk krigsvetenskaplig litteratur', ibid., pp. 91–104.

16   Jefferyes's journal, *H.H.* 35: 1, p. 75, for the quotation; Tengberg, 'Karl XII i Ukraine våren 1709', *K.F.Å.* 1948, pp. 120 ff. for the significance of the Cossack fast coming to an end.

17   See, e.g. Poniatowski's memoirs, *H.T.* 1890, p. 204, stressing also, however, the calmness once the battle was begun; cp. the 'relations' by Lewenhaupt, Creutz and Gyllenkrook in *H.H.* 34: 2.

18   Petre's diary, 6 June 1709: *K.K.D.* I.

19   Siltmann's report, cited by F.Bengtsson, *Karl XII:s Levnad*, II (1948 ed.), p. 206.

20   Schmalensee's journal, *K.F.Å.* 1957, p. 137.

21   Lewenhaupt's memoirs, *H.H.* 34: 2, p. 238.

22   Piper's diary, *H.H.*:21, p. 41, on Menshikov's passing on this comment by Rehnskiöld.

23   For the King's words, see Bielke's *Mémoires*, p. 73; Tengberg's assumption, *K.F.Å.* 1946, p. 86, that the criticism was directed at Rehnskiöld's failure to grasp the significance of the 'great ouvrage' is weakened by the fact that both Charles and his field-marshal knew the topographical features of the battle area well.

24   See the Hedberg-Medwedjev article on the importance of the artillery, 'the decisive factor' at Poltava, in *K.F.Å.* 1961, pp. 124 ff.

25   Weihe's diary, *H.H.* 19: 2, p. 60.

26   Gyllenkrook's 'relation', *H.H.* 34: 2, p. 317 for congratulations.

27   Lewenhaupt's 'relation', *H.H.* 34: 2, p. 237; Granberg's interpretation, *K.F.Å.* 1961, p. 126, that the King all along intended to postpone stage two of the battle till the afternoon – when the artillery should have reached him – does not seem to me convincing: the orders by which Charles attempted (in vain) to call more troops and artillery to him (Schönström's memoirs, p. 28 and Adlerfelt, *Histoire militaire*, IV, 741) I see as a response to Roos's disappearance.

28   G. Petri, 'Slaget vid Poltava', *K.F.Å.* 1958, pp. 125–61, a fine tactical study of the battle from Swedish source material – utilizing the researches of Carlsson, Tengberg, Villius, Klein, Jonakov and Porfiriev – has a section labelled 'The hours of waiting in the Mal. Budischtjewood'.

29   Petri, *K.F.Å.* 1958, p. 148; for the role of Mazepa, the Cossacks and the Zaporozhians in the battle (more active than often admitted) see B.Kentrschynskyj, *Mazepa*, pp. 429 ff.

30   Creutz's 'relation', *H.H.* 34:2, p. 277; Gyllenkrook's 'relation', ibid,. p. 318; Lewenhaupt's 'relation', ibid., p. 240.

31   ibid., Gyllenkrook's 'relation', p. 318. For a possible difference of opinion (indicated by Lewenhaupt's 'relation', ibid., pp. 240–1) between the King and Rehnskiöld in respect of where best to form the infantry line, see Petri, *K.F.Å.* 1958, pp. 149–50: his conclusion is that if one existed, Charles bowed to the field-marshal's decision.

32   Wittram, I, 314; for Lewenhaupt's estimate see his 'relation', *H.H.* 34:2, p. 243.

33   ibid., p. 245.

34   Roos's 'relation', ibid., pp. 335–6.

35   Creutz's 'relation', ibid., pp. 279–80; Lewenhaupt's 'relation', ibid., p. 247.

36   E. Carlsson, 'Karl XII och kapitulationen vid Perevolotjna', *K.F.Å.* 1940 pp. 147–51, building on Meijerfelt's (unprinted) memoirs; the part dealing with the period 17 to 28 June has since been published by H. Villius, *Karl XII:s ryska fälttåg. Källstudier* (1951), pp. 263–8.

37   For the Swedish figures see *Generalstaben*, III, 868–73; for the Russian ones Wittram, I, 315.

38   Schürer von Waldheim, *Maximilian*, pp. 86–7, building on F. W. Bardili's biography of 1730.

39   Piper's diary, *H.H.* 21, p. 2, quoting Rehnskiöld's comment to him: 'Ess ist alles verlohren'.

40   S. E. Bring, the editor in 1919 of the original manuscript and of the journal for 1708 and 1709, deals in the introduction with the fate of the manuscript and with the eighteenth-century publication of the *Histoire Militaire*.

41   The conscious planning – as well as the leadership of Charles XII – has been emphasized by E. Carlsson, *K.F.Å.* 1940, pp. 128 ff., with analysis of the earlier views of Carlson and Stille.

42   Schönström's memoirs, pp. 31, 39–40.

43   Ensign Piper's memoirs, cited by Carlsson, *K.F.Å.* 1940, p. 119.

44   Creutz's 'relation', *H.H.* 34: 2, pp. 281–2.

45   Carlsson, *K.F.Å.* 1940, pp. 153 ff, reconstructing Gyllenkrook's mission to find such places from a comparison of Meijerfelt's (unprinted) 'relation' with Gyllenkrook's memoirs and 'relation'.

46   B. Kentrschynskyj, *Mazepa*, pp. 436–7.

47   For Lewenhaupt talking alone with the King ('for some hours') see Schmalensee's journal *K.F.Å.* 1957, p. 138. For Lewenhaupt's side of the story see his 'Points', *H.H.* 34: 2, pp. 398 ff.; for that of Charles XII see his letter to Ulrika Eleonora of 14 Dec. 1712: *Bref.* Cp. Bielke, *Mémoires*, p. 77 and Gyllenkrook's memoirs, pp. 133–4. To the mood of the army diaries and letters of those who were present at Perevolotjna give significant clues: Aggrell, *K.K.D.* V; Siltmann, *K.F.Å.* 1937; Weihe, *H.H.* 19: 1; Petre, *K.K.D.* I, etc.

48   See Norsbergh, who was rowed over in the same boat as the King.

49   Poniatowski's memoirs, *H.T.* 1890, p. 207.

50   Agrell's diary, *K.K.D.* V., 17.

51   Stavenow's review of Carlson, III, in *H.T.* 1910, pp. 39 ff.; F. Lagerroth 'Kapitulationen vid Perevolotjna', *Social Demokraten* 8/11, 1926; Tarle, *Karl XII och Poltava* (Swedish translation of 1951), pp. 46 ff.

52   Gyllenkrook's 'relation', *H.H.* 34: 2, pp. 327–8.

53   Even Lewenhaupt's 'relation' admits this by implication, *H.H.* 34: 1, pp. 264 ff. cp. Tengberg, *Karl XII och Ryssland*, p. 61.

54   Note from Lewenhaupt's 'Points', *H.H.* 34:2, pp. 399–400, that he denies having given Siltmann the trumpeter with which the Prussian made his way to the Russians; cp. Siltmann, *K.K.D.* III, 333 ff., that he left with a 'tambour Swedish servants and all my baggage' to speak to Menshikov on behalf of the 'Swedish generals', but that Creutz arrived before long to carry on direct negotiations.

55   Lewenhaupt's 'Objection answered', *H.H.* 34:2, pp. 403 ff. Tengberg, *Karl XII och Ryssland*, pp. 51–66, stresses the personal responsibility of Lewenhaupt

more than Uddgren in his biography and Petri in 'Reviderade domslut', *K.F.Å.* 1952.

56 Charles xii's letter to Ulrika Eleonora, 12 Dec. 1712: *Bref.*
57 Bielke, *Mémoires*, p. 78, for rumours to this effect; he himself prefers the 'terrible confusion' as an explanation.
58 The prospect of being permitted 'a turn home' on parole also played a significant part in the capitulation negotiations: see Weihe's journal, *H.H.*, 19:1, 68 ff.; for Lewenhaupt's promises that they would 'soon be free', see Roland's memoirs, p. 58; for Lewenhaupt's saying the capitulation was according to Charles xii's orders see Lyth's diary, *K.K.D.* II, 74.
59 Kentrschynskyj, *Mazepa*, p. 438.
60 Schmalensee's journal, *K.F.Å.* 1957, p. 139; Roland's memoirs, pp. 58–9.

BOOK V, CHAPTER I : GRIEF AND GRIEF OVERCOME

1 For the trek through the 'desert' see Norsbergh's diary, *K.K.D.* III, 217 ff.; Agrell's diary, ibid., V, 60 ff.; Poniatowski's memoirs, *H.T.* 1890, pp. 207 ff.; Hultman's memoirs in *Handlingar* (Floderus), I, 52 ff. with addition printed by W. Lebedin in *K.F.Å.* 1944, p. 45.
2 See the fragment of Bielke's memoirs (left out of his *Mémoires*) printed by S. Leijonhufvud in *K.F.Å.* 1929, pp. 114–15; cp. B. Kentrschynskyj, *Mazepa* p. 450.
3 These letters are printed in *H.H.* 4, 155 ff.; the concept of the letter to the Council showing (*a*) what Charles took out of the draft submitted to him and (*b*) what he added has been printed by E. C.[arlson] in *H.T.* 1888, pp. 280–2.
4 For this revolt see Kentryschynskyj, op. cit., pp. 452–3, putting the entry in the Chancery diary (*K.K.D.* IV, 5: 11–12 July 1709) into perspective.
5 In a (hitherto) unprinted lecture on 'Karl xii efter Poltava' Professor S. A. Nilsson has shown that it was this flooding of Russian troops into Poland which forced Charles xii to give up his plan to return home as soon as he was able to ride once more – I am grateful to Professor Nilsson for lending me the manuscript of this lecture.
6 Bielke (by implication): in *K.F.Å.* 1929, pp. 114–15.
7 Gyllenkrook's 'relation', *H.H.* 34: 2, p. 327.
8 Charles xii's letter to Ulrika Eleonora of 14 Dec. 1712: *Bref.*
9 In spite of strong pressure from Stockholm.
10 W. Holst, *Ulrika Eleonora* (1956), p. 66; cp. Ulrika Eleonora's diary for 1709: *P.H.T.* 1915, p. 7.
11 See Neumann's report of the operation in *H.H.:* 4, p. 189; Bielke's memoirs in *K.F.Å.* 1929, pp. 116–17; Djurberg's article, ibid., 1912, pp. 120–1; cp. the moving account which Motraye, *Travels*, II, 346, gives based on information from Swedish officers.
12 Holst, *Ulrika Eleonora*, p. 19.
13 ibid., pp. 56 (Hedvig), 263 (Ulrika). Cp. ibid., p. 66 for the Queen-Grandmother retiring to her bed with grief when Hedvig Sophia died.
14 Bassewitz had this from Roepsdorf; cp. text, p. 520.
15 Charles xii's letter to Ulrika Eleonora of 9 Aug. 1707: *Bref.*
16 ibid., letters of 12 June, 25 July, 19 Dec. 1710, 17 Jan. 1711.

17   ibid., letters of 19 Dec. 1710 and 17 Jan. 1711.
18   Several of the diaries and letters of the period comment on these facts.
19   See the 'Fältkonsistorieprotokoll' from Bender, ed. by S.E.Bring in *K.F.Å.*
      1917, pp. 81 ff.; cp. Chancery diary *K.K.D.* IV, 15: Charles XII paying for
      and being present at a wedding where the bride was Swedish.
20   For this expedition see E.Wrangel, 'Den första svenska orient-expeditionen
      och Cornelius Loos' teckningar', *K.F.Å.* 1931, pp. 113–71; S.Hedin, *Resare-
      Bengt* (1921), pp. 173 ff.
21   R.Josephine, 'Karl XI och Karl XII som esteter', *K.F.Å.* 1947, pp. 57 ff.
22   Wrangel, *K.F.Å.* 1931, p. 168.
23   Agrell's Diary, *K.K.D.* V, 229–30; apart from this criticism Agrell is full of
      praise, especially for the fine drawings brought back.
24   Motraye, *Travels*, II, 347–8, with Motraye's comment that the King forgave
      harmless vanity but disliked a 'malicious lye'.
25   Wrangel, *K.F.Å.* 1931, p. 171.
26   ibid., pp. 116 ff. and authorities there cited.
27   Drummond's letter to Harley from Amsterdam, 22 Sept. 1704: B.M.Harley
      Loan 29/45.
28   Wrangel, *K.F.Å.* 1931, p. 118.
29   The complete manuscript, ed. by K.U.Nylander, was printed in 2 vols. in 1889
      on the occasion of a congress of orientalists in Stockholm.
30   Fabrice, *Memoiren*, p. 29; the letters from his mission (the first of which was
      written on 25 June/6 July 1710) to the Duke-Administrator of Holstein-
      Gottorp, to Görtz and other ministers are printed in *Anecdotes du Sejour du
      Roi de Suède à Bender ou Lettres de Mr Le Baron de Fabrice pour servir
      d'eclaircissement à l'Histoire de Charles XII* (Hamburg 1760) – hereafter cited as
      Fabrice: *Lettres*. They are important source-material for Holstein and Swedish
      policy between 1710 and 1714.
31   Fabrice, *Memoiren*, pp. 63–4.
32   ibid., pp. 44–5.
33   Voltaire, cited by R.Grieser in the introduction to Fabrice, *Memoiren*, p. 5; cp.
      Motraye, *Travels*, II, 343 and Löwen, *Mémoires*, pp. 33 ff.
34   Jefferyes's letter of 18 May 1711 (reporting audience with Charles of 30 April),
      H.H. 16: 2.
35   Motraye, *Travels*, II, 6, for dining at Grothusen's, and the same author's
      Remarques, p. 40, for having met the Swedes who gave him information at
      Fabrice's table; cp. Fabrice, *Memoiren*, p. 61.
36   ibid., pp. 48–9.
37   Löwen, *Mémoires*, p. 26 writes that Charles XII had sent him to take such
      service.

BOOK V, CHAPTER 2: WAR IN DEPENDENCE ON THE
PORTE

1   See e.g. Hultman's memoirs: *Handlingar* (Floderus), I, 58.
2   'Narrative of the King of Sweden's Movements 1709–1714', ed. by R.M.Hatton
      for *Historical Studies* I (Ankara, 1956, from Rawlinson MSS. 132, Bodley

Library, Oxford; hereafter cited, from the identification made, as [Naundorf] *Narrative*), p. 103; cp. for the reception Chancery diary, *K.K.D.* IV, 8 ff.

3 Fabrice, *Memoiren*, 43–4.

4 [Naundorf] *Narrative*, p. 105; cp. Fabrice, *Memoiren*, pp. 68–9.

5 [Naundorf] *Narrative*, p. 104.

6 Piper's diary, *H.H.* 19: 1, pp. 9 ff.; Chancery diary, *K.K.D.* IV, 14 ff.

7 Kolmodin, 'Mazepa i Turkiet', *Svenska Dagbladet* 16/1, 1925; B. Kentrschyn-skyj, *Mazepa*, pp. 464–7.

8 ibid., p. 463.

9 Agrell's diary, *K.K.D.* V, 30 ff.

10 Chancery diary, ibid., IV, 15; Djurberg, *K.F.Å.* 1913, pp. 113–14.

11 For Nilsson's (so far unpublished) research on the contested problem of the Gyllenkrook expedition see note 5 to preceding chapter.

12 Carlson, III, 285 and note 583; Wittram, I, 317–18.

13 Extract of Jefferyes's letter to Whitworth, printed in *Sbornik*, vol. 50, p. 216; for original (differing only in spelling and place-names) see S.P. 91, vol. 6, enclosure to Whitworth's letter of 27 June/7 Aug. 1709; Jefferyes's letter of 13 July (O.S.) 1709, *H.H.* 35: 1, p. 76.

14 See, e.g. S.P. 82, vol. 24, Robinson's dispatch of 9/20 Aug. 1709 from Hamburg; Brydges papers, vol. 3. Huntington Library, Hallungius to Brydges 16/27 Aug. 1709 from The Hague.

15 Jefferyes's letter of 13 July O.S. 1709, *H.H.* 35: 1, p. 77.

16 See, e.g. Schmalensee's journal, *K.F.Å.* 1957, p. 141; cp. Wittram, I, 321–2, with full references in note 126; and Carlson, III, 292–4.

17 See, e.g. Siltmann's letter of 21 July (N.S.) 1709: *K.F.Å.* 1937, p. 171.

18 Among the better informed, however, as, e.g. in Moscow, it was assumed that Charles, having 'with between two and three thousand men got over the Nieper, 'tis thought by this time he has got safe into Poland': Whitworth's letter of 27 July/7 Aug. 1709, *Sbornik*, vol. 50, p. 212.

19 For this treaty and the secret article of 10/21 October see Wittram, I, 324–5.

20 See A. Stille, 'Danmarks politik gentmot Sverige 1707–1709', *L.U.Å.* 1898, pp. 81 ff.

21 V. Steinius, 'Sachsen och Preussen i den nordiska krisen 1709', *K.F.Å.* 1949, pp. 41 ff.; Hassinger, pp. 233 ff.; Wittram, I, 327–8.

22 B. Kentrschynskyj, *Mazepa*, pp. 458–9.

23 ibid., p. 460, based on Ferriol's letters to Torcy.

24 For this expedition see Nordberg, II, 20–2; Carlson, III, 287–8 and note 589.

25 For Krassow's retreat, 5–11 Oct. 1709, see Steinius, *K.F.Å.* 1949, pp. 84 ff; for Stanislaus's position see J. Gierowski, loc. cit., pp. 230 ff.

26 They arrived with the French regiment of Krassow's corps, under Colonel Zülich, to Bender in 1711.

27 See A. Ballagi, 'Zur Geschichte der Heimkehr Karls xii und des schwedischen Heeres durch Ungern', II (extract from the Hungarian work of 1922), *K.F.Å.* 1934, pp. 146–8.

28 For the offers of ships from the Maritime Powers, France and Turkey see Müllern's letter to Horn (partly in cypher) of 26 April 1710, printed in G. Horn, *Arvid Bernard Horn* (1852), pp. 136 ff.

29 ibid., p. 137, letter of 26 April 1710.

U

30   For Swedish diplomacy at the Porte see the Swedish typescript translation by
     W. Björkman (available in Uppsala University Library and other main Swedish
     libraries) of A. N. Kurat, *Isvec kirali XII. Karl' in Turkiyede kalisi ve bu sira-
     larda Osmanli Imparatorlugu* (Istanbul, 1943); S. Grauers, 'Ett turkisk forsk-
     ningsbidrag om Karl XII i Turkiet', *K.F.Å.* 1954, pp. 104–20 summarizing
     Kurat's findings; the pioneer Swedish research by A. Stille, 'Karl XII och
     Porten 1709–1714' (in Bring, *Karl XII*), supplemented by E. Tengberg, *Från
     Poltava till Bender. En studie i Karl XII:s turkiska politik 1709–1713* (1953), and
     specialist articles by N. Jorga, E. Refik, K. V. Zetterstien, S. Jägerskiöld, G.
     Jarring and others. Cp. the memoirs of Charles XII's interpreters, that of
     Savary in *K.F.Å.* 1913; that of Amira published by Jorga in 1905.
31   For the Stockholm point of view see W. Ahlström, *Arvid Horn och Karl XII
     1710–1713* (1959); S. Grauers, 'Några bidrag till oppositions historia under Karl
     XII', *K.F.Å.* 1921; J. Rosén, *Det engelska anbudet om fredsmedling 1713 (L.U.Å.*
     1946).
32   Hassinger, op. cit., pp. 336 ff.
33   ibid., pp. 240 ff.; Steinus, *K.F.Å.* 1949, pp. 53 ff.; J. F. Chance, *George I and
     the Great Northern War* (London, 1909), pp. 11 ff.
34   A typical example in a letter to Drummond printed in *Letters and Correspon-
     dence public and private of Lord Viscount Bolingbroke*, I, (London, 1798 ed.
     G. Parke), 55–6: 'In short, my good friend, there is a certain point to which all
     human affairs may be carried, and no farther can they go; the wise man feels
     this, and stops in time; [if] we have wantonly overloaded fortune, she sinks
     under the burden and can or will assist such presumptious people no longer.'
     Cp. advice printed in *B.D.I. Sweden*, from August 1709 onwards.
35   See B. M. Harley Loan 29/45, Miscell., Drummond's letter to Harley of
     [undated] August 1710 reporting pressure by Augustus.
36   This has been shown by J. G. Stork-Penning, *Het Grote Werk* (Groningen,
     1958) and the same author's 'Het gedrag van de staten 1711', in *Bijdragen voor
     de Geschiedenis der Nederlanden*, 1963–4, pp. 193–229.
37   Grauers, *Horn*, pp. 196 ff.
38   R. Wittram, 'Peter der Grosse und Livland. Zur Kernfrage des Nordischen
     Krieges', in *Deutschland und Europa. Festschrift für H. Rothfels* (Düsseldorf,
     1951).
39   Charles's correspondence with the Council between 1709 and 1715 is printed in
     H.H. 4, 5, 7, 9–11, 14–15; the discrepancies between them have been illumin-
     ated with the help of other material by S. Grauers, *Arvid Horn* (1920), pp. 151–
     291; Wahlström, op. cit., passim; E. Tengberg, op. cit., passim; and briefly by
     D. Lundström, *Magnus Stenbock i Stockholm 1712 (H.A.:* 8, 1959), pp. 10 ff.
40   See, e.g. the journal of Tessin for 1710, *Nicodemus Tessin d.y:s memorial och
     anteckningar för åren 1702–1713 (H.A.:* 5, ed. S. E. Bring, 1955), pp. 20–48.
41   See H. Almquist, *Holstein-Gottorp, Sverige och den nordiska ligan* (1918).
42   S. Bonnesen, *Studier över August II:s utrikespolitik 1712–15*, I, 12 ff.
43   Charles XII was not the only Swede to resent the convention. Hassinger, op. cit.,
     pp. 283 ff. prints a memorandum by Cederhielm which he discovered as an
     enclosure to Keyserlingk's dispatch of 3/14 May 1711: why should the Allies
     help the enemies of Sweden, when Charles XII in his days of *'Glück und Sieg'*
     had taken care not to harm the Allies is the gist of it.

44 Charles XII's letter to the Council, 4 Dec. 1710: *H.H.* 5.
45 Stille, 'Karl XII och Porten' (Bring, *Karl XII*), pp. 359–60.
46 B.Spuler, 'Die europäische Diplomatie in Konstantinopel', *Jahrbücher für Kultur und Geschichte der Slaven*, 1935, pp. 361 ff.
47 *Sven Lagerbergs Dagbok under vistelsen hos Tartar Dewlet-Gherey 1710–11*, ed. M.Lagerberg (1896).
48 For the campaign see A.N.Kurat, 'Der Prutfeldzug und der Prutfrieden von 1711', *Jahrbücher für Geschichte Osteuropas*, 1962, pp. 22 ff.; cp. the same author's 'Prutfättåget och Prutfreden 1711', *K.F.Å.* 1939, pp. 106 ff.; cp. the same author's edition of 'Letters of Poniatowski on the Pruth campaign 1711', *Slavonic Review*, 1947.
49 Haintz, II, 104–5; though note that Kurat, *K.F.Å.* 1939, p. 111, emphasizes the dislike of the Turks of the Ukraine part of Charles XII's plan and their determination to control the war.
50 Charles XII's letter to Funck of 27 July 1710: *Bref.*
51 See Fabrice's letter of 24 Dec. 1710: *Lettres*, p. 39.
52 For the Baltic theatre of war see F. Arwidson, *Försvaret av Östersjö-provinserna 1708–10* (1936), pp. 153 ff.; cp. Wittram, I, 338–44.
53 Wittram, I, 386.
54 Poniatowski's memoirs, *H.T.* 1890, pp. 223, 226.
55 Nordberg, II, 182–3; Kurat, *K.F.Å.* 1939, pp. 108–10.
56 Kurat, *Jahrbücher*, 1962, pp. 26–7.
57 ibid., pp. 37 ff.; Wittram, I, 381 ff.
58 See Kurat in Björkman translation for full treatment of this problem.
59 For the peace-terms see Kurat, *Jahrbücher*, 1962, pp. 49 ff.
60 Charles's letter of protest dated Bender 20/30 July 1711 is in *Bref*, nr. 267; the memorial delivered by Funck on 27 July has been printed by Kurat, *K.F.Å.* 1939, pp. 167–9.

BOOK V, CHAPTER 3: THE BEGINNINGS OF REFORM

1 His family owned a sulphur-works and he himself had been engaged in the manufacture of hats before entering Chancery service in 1682; his interests are evident in letters from Turkey to Tessin, printed by G. Andersson in *Handlingar ur Brinkmanska archivet på Trolle-Ljungby*, I (1859), 133–46, and in those to Polhem, printed by S.Bring in *K.F.Å.* 1911, pp. 238–56.
2 Feif's letter to Horn of 27 June 1710: *P.H.T.* 1921.
3 S.Grauers, *Arvid Bernard Horn* (1920), xi–xii.
4 *P.H.T.* 1921, P.S. to Feif's letter of 27 June 1710.
5 ibid., Feif's letters to Horn of 27 June and 17 Dec. 1710, 14 Feb. and 26 March 1711.
6 *P.H.T.* 1921, pp. 102–3, undated letter (by editor, M.Bohnstedt, dated to Feb. or March 1711) from Feif to Horn. Horn's second wife, of the Piper connexion (see text, p. 520*), had died in 1708; his marriage to Gyllenstierna's daughter took place in 1710.
7 Feif's letter to Horn of 14 Feb. 1711, giving details of expenditure, following official requests of 2 April and 20 Sept. 1710; cp. D.Almquist, 'Johan Eriksson Ehrenskiöld', *K.F.Å.* 1948.

8   For these loans see B.Kentrschynskyj, *Mazepa*, p. 476; and T.Westrin, 'Anteckningar om Karl XII:s orientalske kreditorer', *H.T.* 1900, pp. 52 ff.
9   Charles XII's letter to the Council of 3 Feb. 1711: *Bref*, pp. 369 ff.
10   S.Loenboem, *Lefwernesbeskrivning öfwer Herr Nils Gyllenstierna* (1773), pp. 66 ff.
11   Feif's letter to Horn of 8 May 1711: *P.H.T.* 1921. In October 1711 Wrede gave up his position as president of *kammarskollegium* and *statskontoret*, but he continued influential till his death in 1712.
12   See D.Lundström. *Magnus Stenbock i Stockholm 1712*, pp. 21 ff.
13   For C.G.Dücker see article in *S.B.L.* by S.E.Bring.
14   Lundström, pp. 16–17; W.Ahlström, *Arvid Horn och Karl XII 1710–1713*, pp. 10 ff.; Rosén, in *L.U.Å.*, 1946, pp. 21 ff.
15   Charles XII's letter to Stenbock of 23 Feb. 1712, printed in S.Loenbom, *Kong. rådets och fältmarskalkens herr grefwe Magnus Stenbocks lefwerne* (4 vols. 1757–65) III, 288 ff.
16   Feif's letters to Horn of 10 April and 24 July 1712: *P.H.T.* 1921.
17   ibid., P.S. to letter of 26 March 1712.
18   ibid., letter of 10 April 1712.
19   For Russian participation see Wittram, II, 225;
20   Feif's letter to Horn of 24 July 1712: *P.H.T.* 1921.
21   In his speech of 3/14 July 1712, printed by Lundström, appendix 2; cp. ibid., pp. 51 ff.
22   ibid., p. 57.
23   E.Naumann, 'Om centralförvaltningen under Karl XII:s tid' (in Bring, *Karl XII*), p. 543.
24   See J.E.Almquist, 'Ett forsök under Karl XII:s regering till grundskatternas forenkling i samband med ny jordeboksmetod', *K.F.Å.* 1916, pp. 208 ff., for the possibility of C.G.Fröchlich having influenced some of the King's ideas; for the Feif and Silfwercrantz influence see D.Almquist, 'Feif's finansiella reformer', ibid., 1922, pp. 233–53; E.Ekegård, *Studier i svensk handelspolitik under den tidigare frihetstiden* (1924), pp. 109 ff.; cp. E.F.Hesckcher, *Sveriges Ekonomiska Historia*, I: 2, pp. 691–2, 702–3.
25   Feif's letter to Horn of 24 July 1712: *P.H.T.* 1921. For Feif having asked a friend to send him '*en secret des eclaircissements amples*' on the way French domestic and foreign affairs were managed see Campredon's letter of 27 October 1714: *Handlingar* (Malmström).
26   Naumann (in Bring, *Karl XII*), p. 551.
27   D.Almquist, 'Johann Eriksson Ehrenskiöld', *K.F.Å.* 1948, pp. 38 ff.; Ahlström, pp. 22 ff.
28   G.A.Axelson, *Bidrag till kännedomen om Sveriges inre tillstånd på Karl XII:s tid* (1888), p. 169; for the loan being paid off by 1710 see Ahlström, p. 83.
29   Ahlström, p. 25.
30   See D.Almquist, 'De karolinska mynttecknens ursprung', *K.F.Å.* 1936, pp. 187 ff.; cp. Ahlström pp. 17, 21 for royal suggestions and Council opposition.
31   See D.Almquist, *K.F.Å.* 1948, pp. 45–58, for details of the various loans and the expenses defrayed from them; cp. ibid. 1935, A.Munthe, 'Karl XII i Turkiet', for the accounts reproduced and discussed.
32   J.Almquist, *K.F.Å.* 1916, pp. 209, 213.

33 For Polhem see S.E.Bring's introduction to 'Några bref från Casten Feif till Christopher Polhem', *K.F.Å.* 1911, 233 ff.; Polhem's technical innovations in mining have been expertly dealt with by S.Lindroth, *Christoffer Polhem och Stora Kopparberget* (1951). Polhem's writings have been published in a 4 vol. edition 1947–54.

34 See S.Gerentz, *Kommerskollegium och näringslivet* (1951); cp. Heckscher, *Sveriges ekonomiska historia*, II: 2, pp. 682 ff.

35 Feif's letters to Polhem of 9 Feb. 5 and 21 March, 4 Nov. and 13 Dec. 1712 printed in *K.F.Å.* 1911, pp. 238–56.

36 ibid., Feif's letters to Polhem of 9 Feb. and 4 Nov. 1712.

37 Feif's letter to Horn of 30 February 1712: *P.H.T.* 1921.

38 V.Djurberg, 'Om regementsfältskären Melchior Neumann och Karl xii:s blessyrer' II, *K.F.Å.* 1913, pp. 62–3, identifying the manuscript as nearly identical with the Timoni article printed in the *Philosophical Transactions* of the Royal Society for 1714.

BOOK V, CHAPTER 4: THE KALABALIK

1 For Charles's diplomacy see E.Tengberg, *Från Poltava till Bender*, pp. 160 ff., and Kurat (Björkman translation summarized by Grauers, *K.F.Å.* 1954, pp. 104–02); for Russian attitude to the Prut peace see Wittram, I, 383–95.

2 See A.Stille (in Bring, *Karl XII*) p. 371 for the qualification in respect of putting the declaration into effect: 'unless the Tsar fulfils the peace conditions and hands over Azov'.

3 See Theyls, *Mémoires*, pp. 74 ff. for his role as a go-between in the negotiations between Shafirov and the Dutch diplomat Colyer; A.N.Kurat's introduction to *The Despatches of Sir Robert Sutton* (Camden, Third Series, 1953), pp. 7 ff. and Jefferyes's letter of 30 Feb. 1712 in *H.H.* 16: 2; cp. A.Åberg, 'Från Prut till Bender', *K.F.Å.* 1954, pp. 95 ff. complementing the researches of Tengberg, op. cit.

4 For the prospect of Charles xii's departure which this conjured up, see summary by Ahmed Refik of Grand Vizier's letter to the Khan of Crimea of 1 March 1712, *K.F.Å.* 1937, pp. 86–8 ('Johannes Kolmodins turkiska kvarlatenskap', by K.V.Zetterstéen); cp. N.Jorga's article ibid., 1911, pp. 198 ff.

5 Feif's letter to Horn of 10 April 1712: *P.H.T.* 1921; cp. Charles xii's letter to the Council of 14 July 1712, *H.H.* 10, on his longing to get 'closer to Our own lands'.

6 Charles xii's orders of 19 Nov. 1711 to Funck at Constantinople to get in touch with the French ambassador and tell him 'as from yourself' of royal displeasure with the Maritime Powers and the possibility of Franco-Swedish collaboration, though without support for French expansion in the Empire: *Bref*, p. 389 foreshadow this policy.

7 For the march of 1 May 1712 (as well as an earlier abortive attempt of March 1712), see S.Bonnesen, 'Jan Sapieha. Ett bidrag til historien om kalabaliken i Bender', *K.F.Å.* 1954, pp. 147–9.

8 For the Turkish mission of August 1712, accompanied by two Swedish officers dressed as Turks, see Kurat (Björkman translation), pp. 626 ff.; Stille (in Bring, *Karl XII*), pp. 376 ff.

9   Celsing's journal, *K.F.Å.* 1932–3, p. 123, notes his departure with the money from Constantinople on 1 Nov. and arrival at Bender on 10 Nov. 1712.

10 For these missions see Eosander's letters published by F.F. Carlson: *H.T.* 1896 and Goltz's report (in French) of his mission published by A.N. Kurat in *Tarih Vesîkalari* (Istanbul, 1958), pp. 5–41. Hassinger, op. cit., pp. 274 ff. reckons that Charles XII's refusal to agree to a partition of Poland at this time doomed the fate of Sweden: a conclusion which, in my opinion, fails to take into account the pro-Russian attitude of the Prussian crown-prince and the unwillingness of Augustus to leave the anti-Swedish alliance. Ilgen and Flemming may have been serious, their principals were less so.

11 F.F. Carlson, *Om fredsunderhandlingarna åren 1709–1718* (1857) pp. 40–4; for Eosander's role in the negotiations see Biederstedt, op. cit., pp. 61 ff.; cp. Haintz II, 186 ff.

12 S. Bonnessen, *K.F.Å.* 1954, pp. 127–87.

13 ibid., pp. 172 ff.; cp. the same author's *Studier över August II:s utrikespolitik 1712–1715*, I (1918).

14 See Bonnesen, *K.F.Å.* 1954, pp. 173–4, printing a letter from Sapieha to Sieniawski of 14 Jan. 1713; cp. Grothusen's letters to Funck of 18 and 20 Jan. 1713 printed by Quennerstedt, *Kalabaliken vid Bender* (1910), pp. 62–6. E. Tengberg's doubts (*Från Poltava till Bender*, pp. 221–38) as to the authenticity of the intercepted letters may – after Bonnesen's researches – be regarded as stilled. The letters from Ahmed's mother are printed as an appendix to J. Stafsing, *Kalabaliken i Bender* (1960).

15 [Naundorf] *Narrative*, pp. 107, 109–11; cp. Quennerstedt, *Kalabaliken*, p. 28.

16 According to Kolmodin, *K.F.Å.* 1920, p. 290, '*vak-a-sy*' is the correct phrase, but '*Kalabalik*' is too well established to be displaced. For accounts of *Kalabaliken* see Hatton's introduction to [Naundorf] *Narrative*, footnotes 5 (participants) and 41 (eyewitnesses).

17 See Grothusen's letter to Funck of 12 Jan. 1713, printed in Quennerstedt, *Kalabaliken*, pp. 58–9.

18 Sultan's letter to Khan, summarized by A. Refik in *K.F.Å.* 1937, pp. 90–2.

19 [Naundorf] *Narrative*, p. 105.

20 ibid., pp. 106, 112–13; cp. Hultman's description in a letter of 6 Feb. 1712, cited by Lendin, *K.F.Å.* 1944, pp. 124–5; see also the sketch reproduced from Krigsarkivet in A. Quennerstedt, *Kalabaliken*, p. 38, and the contemporary plans at end of that volume.

21 [Naundorf] *Narrative*, pp. 116–19.

22 ibid., p. 109.

23 ibid., p. 115.

24 ibid., p. 118 and note 42; cp. Kurat, *The Despatches of Sir Robert Sutton*, p. 163, note 1.

25 [Naundorf] *Narrative*, p. 119.

26 See Fabrice's letters of 31 Jan. and 15 Feb. 1713: *Lettres*, pp. 160–213; cp. those of 27 Jan., 4 and 20 Feb. 1713 printed in Motraye, *Travels*, II appendix, pp. 3 ff.; ibid., pp. 103 ff. for Motraye's account: for other authorities see Hatton's introduction to [Naundorf], *Narrative*, p. 94, note 41; Villelongue – whose account was used by Voltaire – was not present: H. Brulin, *K.F.Å.* 1948, p. 173.

27 [Naundorf] *Narrative*, p. 119.
28 Kochen's report, *K.F.Å.* 1949, pp. 199–200.
29 [Naundorf] *Narrative*, pp. 119–20.
30 ibid., pp. 123–4.
31 Fabrice's letters of 31 Jan. and 15 Feb. 1713: *Lettres*.
32 [Naundorf] *Narrative*, p. 120.
33 ibid., pp. 120–1.
34 ibid., p. 122.
35 Roos names all thirty in the Royal House, none of whom were killed in the *Kalabalik*: see Quennerstedt, *Kalabaliken*, p. 42. That the Swedes had orders not to shoot is confirmed by Agrell in his letter to Auseen of 23 March 1713: *Handlingar* (Floderus), IV, 343–4, and by Giertta's letter printed in *H.T.* 1898, pp. 70–4.
36 Bielke, *Mémoires*, p. 89–90, stressed this; Stafsing, *Kalabaliken*, p. 32, concludes, after examining Charles XII's correspondence with Sparre, that he is correct.
37 ibid., p. 33; Tengberg, op. cit., p. 259.
38 [Naundorf] *Narrative*, p. 129.
39 Roos's 'relation', used by Quennerstedt, Lendin and others.
40 [Naundorf] *Narrative*, p. 131. For a different explanation, that he was accidentally tripped by a Swede, see Kochen's 'relation', *K.F.Å.* 1949, p. 202.
41 [Naundorf] *Narrative*, pp. 132–3.
42 Tengberg, *Från Poltava till Bender*, pp. 261 ff., though note Åberg, *K.F.Å.* 1954, p. 103 that Sutton at least knew of the Gadebusch victory as early as 22 January. Charles had news of the victory already on 15 Jan.: see Quennerstedt, *Kalabaliken*, p. 25. Goltz's report, *Tarih Vesîkalari* 1958, p. 24, confirms that the report of a Swedish victory decked out '*par toutes les plus brilliantes coleurs de leurs menteuse eloquence*' had a strong effect at Constantinople.
43 Haintz, II, 183 ff.
44 To Charles he stressed his intention to continue the campaign into Poland once supplies and reinforcements had reached him.
45 The best treatment of the campaign in Haintz, II, 172–225.
46 For Cronstedt's activities after his escape from Russia and until Charles XII's return in 1714 see L. Lilliehöök, 'Karl XII's artilleri', *Artilleri-Tidskrift*, 1945, pp. 143–56, 203–16.
47 Jefferyes's letter of 8 Feb. 1713, *H.H.* 16: 2, p. 42; cp. Fabrice's letter of 18 Feb. 1713: *Lettres*, pp. 214 ff., and Motraye, *Travels*, II, 100 ff.
48 See Stille, in Bring, *Karl XII*, p. 396; by 4 February the King was also feverish (possibly from an infection to the cut in his hand?): his physicians ordered a blood-letting which left him weak, see Djurberg, *K.F.Å.* 1913, pp. 60–1.
49 Sparre's detailed letters to Charles XII during the time he was left in charge have been printed in *H.T.* 1900, pp. 57–99; for Soldan's work in buying back and salvaging papers of the commissariat and the Chancery see his service report: *K.F.Å.* 1911, pp. 275 ff.
50 Fabrice, *Memoiren*, p. 97 (editor's summary of letter of 4 Feb. 1713); cp. Fabrice's letter to Görtz of 15 Feb. 1713: *Lettres*, p. 221.
51 [Naundorf] *Narrative*, pp. 154–5; cp. Kurat (Björkman translation), p. 663, for route taken from Bender to Adrianople; cp. the summary in *K.F.Å.* 1941,

pp. 107 ff. by P. Reuterswärd of the 1938 study by Stoitschev of the Bulgarian M. Bimbelow in charge of the Turkish escort.

52   Jefferyes's letter of 26 March 1713, *H.H.* 16: 2.

BOOK V, CHAPTER 5: PLANS IN MATURITY

1   The failure to secure Stenbock's release (and that of his army) must be laid at the Council's door: Ahlström, *Arvid Horn och Karl XII 1710–1713*, pp. 166–92, has shown that the Councillors failed to carry out the agreement Stenbock made with Frederick in order to deny Charles XII an army and a general who could be used offensively in the east; but the King's indifference must be assumed since he took no initiative after his return to the Swedish dominions to have Stenbock freed. For the King's being '*dans une grande colère, surtout contre le Velt-Maréchal Stenbock*', thinking both him and Stanislaus taken in by Flemming, see Fabrice's letter of 18 Feb. 1713: *Lettres*, p. 218.

2   He stayed there from early April till early November 1713, having first spent a fortnight at the castle of Demotika, to which he returned in November.

3   Djurberg, *K.F.Å.* 1913, pp. 63 ff., building on Neumann's report.

4   For the problem of etiquette see C. Lind, *Karl XII i Turkiet* (1875) and Tengberg, op. cit., 276 ff.

5   [Naundorf] *Narrative*, p. 136.

6   ibid., p. 139, for reception.

7   Stille (in Bring, *Karl XII*), p. 395.

8   See Haintz, II, 201 ff.; 206–7.

9   Loenbom, op. cit., IV, 268 ff.

10   For the Stenbock campaign after Gadebusch see *Bidrag S.N.K.H.*, IV, 252 ff., and Haintz, II, 205 ff. building, *i.a.* on R. Koser's researches.

11   See K. Stählin, *Geschichte Russlands*, II, 109; Sumner, op. cit., pp. 69–70. The peace treaty (translated into Swedish by Zetterstéen) is printed by A. Refik in *K.F.Å.* 1919, pp. 153–61; for a French copy see enclosure in *The Despatches of Sir Robert Sutton*, pp. 180–1.

12   Stille (in Bring, *Karl XII*) p. 398 seems to overemphasize the positive objectives of the Turks in this expedition, e.g. the securing of buffer-territory in which the Poles at Bender might be resettled.

13   See J. B. Savary's memoirs (ed. G. Carlquist), *K.F.Å.* 1913, pp. 294–5.

14   [Naundorf] *Narrative*, pp. 140–1, gives details of Stanislaus's movements and of the explanations for them current among the Swedes at Bender.

15   Stille (in Bring, *Karl XII*), pp. 400–1 for the Tornskiöld mission; cp. F. F. Carlson, *Om Fredsunderhandlingarna åren 1709–1718* (1857), pp. 55 ff.

16   See Theyls, *Mémoires*, pp. 52 ff., for his share in obtaining this treaty.

17   Stille (in Bring, *Karl XII*), pp. 403–7.

18   See Hassinger, pp. 256 ff.; Haintz, II, ch. 9 (pp. 226–42); Wittram, II, 255–60.

19   ibid., pp. 260–5; Haintz, II, 293–4.

20   For the punctuation see Haintz, II, 300; for Hanoverian plans see W. Mediger, *Mecklenburg, Russland und England-Hannover 1706–1721* (Hildesheim, 1967), pp. 221–4 and the authorities there cited.

21   Wittram, II, 260 ff.

22   For this campaign see H. E. Uddgren, *Kriget i Finland år 1713* (1906); E. Horn-

borg, *Försvaret av de östre riksdelarna och Karl XII:s krigs-ledning 1701–14* (1936) and Wittram, II, 244–5, building on Russian authorities.

23 See Lagermark, in Bring, *Karl XII*, pp. 609 ff.; J.Häggman, *K.F.Å.* 1922, pp. 191 ff.; cp. extract from Council protocol on discussion whether more galleys could be built as Charles had ordered printed by G.Horn, *Arvid Bernard Horn* (1852) pp. 173–4: money was the rub.

24 S.Grauers, 'Några bidrag till oppositions historia under Karl XII', *K.F.Å.* 1921, p. 215 from the protocol of the Council in October and November 1713.

25 W.Holst, *Fredrik I* (1953), pp. 31 ff. He had been preceded early in 1712, ibid., p. 42, by an emissary of Ulrika's, Anders von Düben, in the same errand.

26 W.Holst, *Ulrika Eleonora*, (1956), pp. 94 ff. printing drafts of her letters to Charles XII of 10 Nov. and 16 Dec. 1713.

27 Grauers, *K.F.Å.* 1921, pp. 211–30.

28 S.Grauers, *Sveriges Riksdag*, IV (1932), 132–43.

29 Rosén, op. cit., pp. 127 ff.; the King's policy can be deduced from changes made in drafts submitted to him by von Müllern. The various notes submitted to the English government after Charles's break with the Council are particularly illuminating: S.P. 100, vols. 60–3.

30 Löwen, *Mémoires*, pp. 29–30, 53–61, 65–8.

31 ibid., pp. 31–3.

32 ibid., pp. 33–4.

33 Charles XII's letters to Ulrika Eleonora of 25 June, 30 July, 19 Dec. 1710, and 12 May, 19 June 1711, 4 Dec. 1712: *Bref.*

34 Liewen's report of his mission has been translated into Swedish (with a sample of the original mixture of Swedish, German and Low German) and printed in *Handlingar* (Floderus), III, 318–44; for Liewen's illness see Charles XII's letter to Ulrika Eleonora of 2 Sept. 1714: *Bref.*

35 Holst, *Ulrika Eleonora*, pp. 84 ff., prints letters which illuminate the marriage negotiations.

36 Charles XII's letter to Ulrika Eleonora of 2 Sept. 1714: *Bref.*

37 See, e.g. Schulenburg's report in *Leben und Denkwürdigkeiten Johann Mathias Reichsgrafen von Schulenburg*, I (1734), 306 of conversations with Rehnskiöld's wife and with Ulrika Düben; cp. Kristina Piper's letter to Ulrika Eleonora cited by Holst, *Ulrika Eleonora*, p. 54 and S.P. 88, vol. 17, Robinson's letter of 15/26 Feb. 1703 reporting Charles XII's talk with his wife about acquaintances.

38 Josephson, *Tessin*, I, 169.

39 Typical examples of the tone ('not too coarse') of the stories going the rounds is the one about the Swedish officers – who paid court to the wife of a Dutch merchant – making 'conquests in the Low Countries' (Motraye, *Travels*, II, pp. 4–6), and the 'Turkish sermon on love' (Fabrice, *Memoiren*, pp. 68–9): the latter may have sparked off the conversation quoted from Löwen's memoirs in text, p. 376†.

40 Löwen, *Mémoires*, pp. 70–1.

41 ibid., p. 73.

42 S.Stolpe, *Queen Christina*, pp. 43 ff., has an interesting section on seventeenth-century medical opinion on 'dry and hot' temperaments and 'cold and melancholy' ones.

43 Löwen, *Mémoires*, pp. 72–3.

44   Charles XII's letter to Ulrika Eleonora of 19 Dec. 1710; Feif's letter to Horn of 17 Dec. 1710: *P.H.T.* 1921; Fabrice, *Memoiren*, pp. 46–7; Bielke, *Mémoires* p. 3; Löwen *Mémoires*, pp. 50–1.

45   Schönström's memoirs, p. 45.

46   Löwen, *Mémoires*, pp. 61–2.

47   ibid., p. 62.

48   ibid., pp. 36–7.

49   Charles XII's letter to Ulrika Eleonora of 2 Sept, 1714: *Bref.*

50   ibid., Charles XII's letter to Ulrika Eleonora of 19 Dec. 1710.

51   Fabrice, *Memoiren*, p. 47.

52   Löwen, *Mémoires*, pp. 63–4.

53   Ulrika Eleonora's letter to Charles of 27 Nov. 1711 cited in *Bref*, p. 127, n. 1.

54   Charles XII's letter to Ulrika of 19 Dec. 1710: *Bref* (pp. 106–7).

55   Cited by H.Lindeberg, *Görtz. Ett offer för enevåldet* (1925); cp. the remark 'that the country will never lack a King' made to Löwen at Ystad, *Mémoires*, p. 27.

56   Löwen, *Mémoires*, p. 70; cp. Liewen's report of his second conversation with the King: *Handlingar* (Floderus), III, 325.

57   Löwen, *Mémoires*, p. 70.

58   ibid., pp. 42–3; cp. p. 49.

59   Croissy's letter to Torcy of 27 May 1715 (N.S.): A.E., Corr. Pol. Suède, vol. 10. Swedish translation printed by P.Sörensson in *K.F.Å.* 1910, pp. 315–16; Cp. Folard's comment on Charles's conversation on war in 1716 and 1717, '*Ce brave Prince en parloit aussi bien qu'auroit pu faire Caesair*': *Histoire de Polybe etc.*, V. 484.

60   Löwen, *Mémoires*, p. 55.

61   Josephson, *Tessin*, I, 167.

BOOK VI, CHAPTER I: THE RIDE TO STRALSUND

1   Stille (in Bring, *Karl XII*), p. 407.

2   Axel Sparre's letter to Charles XII from Bender 31 Match 1714: *H.T.* 1900, p. 77; D.Almquist, *K.F.Å.* 1948, pp. 52 ff.; Funck had died in November 1713 and Grothusen presented Charles XII at the leave-taking, giving also the desired exact information about the route to be followed.

3   Westrin, *H.T.* 1900, pp. 90 ff.; J.Kolmodin, 'Said Mehmed Effendi's berättelse om sin beskickning till Sverige år 1733', *K.F.Å.* 1920, pp. 256 ff.

4   For correct date of invitation see Haintz, II, 259 (from Schartau); for the congress see Hassinger, pp. 272 ff.

5   M.Braubach, *Prinz Eugen von Savoyen*, III (1964), 297, based on Villars's report.

6   Fabrice, *Memoiren*, p. 108; for the negotiations with Vienna see ibid., pp. 105, 108–9; Braubach, *Prinz Eugen*, III, p. 298.

7   Date of the King's departure from Swahn's manuscript diary quoted by Ballagi, *K.F.Å.* 1934, p. 152; for the Bender party being provided with horses see [Naundorf] *Narrative*, p. 142.

8   Bielke, *Mémoires*, pp. 91–2, gives details of the five groups.

9 Braubach, *Prinz Eugen*, III, 298; P. Sörensson, *K.F.Å.* 1926, p. 160; Ballagi, *K.F.Å.* 1934, pp. 150–1.
10 Motraye, *Travels*, II, p. 171; Fabrice, *Memoiren*, p. 113.
11 Bielke, *Mémoires*, p. 92; Ballagi, *K.F.Å.* 1934, pp. 163–4.
12 Bielke, *Mémoires*, p. 93; Fabrice, *Memoiren*, p. 107; the build of the two was similar and Bielke had in 1705 (see Schmalensee's memoirs, *K.F.Å.* 1957, p. 127) been taken for Charles XII.
13 Fabrice, *Memoiren*, pp. 106–7.
14 Bielke, *Mémoires*, p. 92, for the exercises at Piteşti; Fabrice, *Memoiren*, p. 104, for the periodic fasting in Turkey.
15 C. Burenstam, *Om Carl XII:s och svenska krigares hemfärd från Turkiet* (The Hague, 1872), pp. 72 ff.; Bielke, *Mémoires*, p. 93; A. Quennerstedt, *Ur Carl XII:s Lefnad*, II (1916), pp. 84–5; Ballagi, *K.F.Å.* 1934, pp. 160 ff.
16 Printed, from the Vienna Archives, by A. Fryxell in *Handlingar*, IV, 343–5.
17 Fabrice, *Memoiren*, p. 108.
18 See Ballagi, *K.F.Å.* 1934, pp. 173 ff. for such rumours and for the route taken after Szilágy-Somlyó (with map ibid., p. 197).
19 Quennerstedt's assumption (op. cit., p. 87) that he might have met Stiernhöök, his representative in Vienna, is weakened by Ballagi, *K.F.Å.* 1934, p. 184; for the King's arrival on 16 Nov. (N.S.): ibid., p. 185.
20 Burenstam, op. cit., p. 22. For the problem created for Charles XII by Charles VI's claim to the Spanish title see P. Sörensson, 'Keijsaren, Sverige och de nordiska allierade från Karl XII:s hemkomst från Turkiet till alliansen i Wien 1719', I, *K.F.Å.* 1926, pp. 162–3.
21 Quennerstedt, op. cit., p. 89.
22 [Magnus Gran's] first letter of 22 Nov. (N.S.) 1715, ed. and identified by S. Dalhgren, 'Några brev angående Karl XII:s ankomst till Stralsund år 1714', *K.F.Å.* 1924, p. 230; cp. Fabrice, *Memoiren*, p. 113.
23 Ballagi, *K.F.Å.* 1934, p. 187 and Fabrice, *Memoiren*, p. 108, agree on the average speed for the whole journey, the former giving 21·8 geographical miles and the latter '*bei bescheidener Rechnung 20 deutsche oder 100 englische Meilen in 24 Stunden*'. Fabrice's statement that the King and his companion arrived '*am 17. Tage*' may be due to a misreading of the manuscript by the editor. Jefferyes, in his letter of 4 Dec. (*H.H.* 16: 1, p. 62) gives the King's journey as 2,000 German miles in a fortnight, i.e. 28 Oct. (O.S.) to 11 Nov. Before Ballagi's researches secondary authorities usually gave 15 days: e.g. Quennerstedt, op. cit., p. 90.
24 Bielke, *Mémoires*, p. 93.
25 Quennerstedt, op. cit., p. 45.
26 Sörensson, *K.F.Å.* 1926, p. 163.
27 ibid., p. 167.
28 Rhyzelius's letter to Benzelius of 17 Nov. 1714 from Stockholm: *P.H.T.* 1926, p. 34.
29 Horn's expression in Council, cited from the protocol by G. Horn, *Arvid Bernard Horn*, p. 199.
30 ibid, p. 198 from same source; cp. Horn's letter to Charles XII of 2 May 1714 printed ibid., pp. 140–2.
31 Rhyzelius's letter to Benzelius of 17 Nov. 1714: *P.H.T.* 1926, p. 34.

32   [Magnus Gran's] second letter of 22 Nov. (N.S.) 1715: *K.F.Å.* 1924, p. 230;
     cp. the King's letters to the Queen-Grandmother and to Ulrika Eleonora of
     12/22 Nov. 1715: *Bref.*

33   Fabrice, *Memoiren*, p. 112; Motraye, *Travels*, II, 18; Jefferyes's letter of 4 Dec.
     1714, giving his own arrival as 28 Nov. (N.S.): *H.H.* 16: 1.

34   ibid., p. 113; for Görtz's journey and the motives behind it see H. Almquist,
     'Görtz' resa till Orienten år 1714', *K.F.Å.* 1911, pp. 206–32.

35   W. Holst, *Fredrik I* (1953), pp. 45–47; S. Jägerskiöld, 'Den hessiska politiken
     och den svenska tronföldjdsfrågan 1713–1718', *K.F.Å.* 1934, pp. 115–16.

36   The difficulties in settling the succession were well realized by contemporaries
     even when they favoured one candidate above the other, see, e.g. the analysis
     of the problem by the pro-Ulrika Eric von Roland printed in *K.F.Å.* 1917, pp.
     222–30.

37   Holst, *Fredrik I*, p. 46; cp. the same author's *Ulrika Eleonora*, p. 109, for a
     memorandum in her possession as to the usefulness of the Hesse alliance which
     would 'so-to-speak connect Bremen-Verden with Zweibrücken'.

38   P. Sörensson, *Sverige och Frankrike 1715–18* (1909), pp. 31 ff.

39   P. Sörensson, 'Utrikespolitiken efter hemkomsten' (in Bring, *Karl XII*) p. 418;
     cp. for Prussian attempts at gaining Swedish land by negotiation with Charles
     XII: B. Lundberg, *De diplomatiska förbindelserna mellan Sverige och Preussen
     1709–1715* (1893), pp. 158 ff.

40   P. Sörensson, I, *K.F.Å.* 1926, pp. 165–6.

41   Sörensson, III, *K.F.Å.* 1928, p, 227; Braubach, *Prinz Eugen*, III, 300–1,

42   ibid., quoting Charles VI's letter to Eugen of 27 June 1715.

BOOK VI, CHAPTER 2: THE SIEGE OF STRALSUND

1   For Taube's work see G. Petri, 'Den finska armén och försvaret av Norrland
     1714–1716', *Norrlands Försvar*, 1922, pp. 10 ff.

2   Holst, *Fredrik I*, pp. 52–3, quoting his letter to Vellingk; cp. the same author's
     Ulrika Eleonora, pp. 131 ff.

3   Holst, *Frederik I*, p. 53.

4   See, e.g. *Bref*, pp. 387–8, draft of 14 Oct. 1711 for Charles's concept of the
     provinces as the outer bulwarks of the empire which have to be defended at all
     costs: if they are lost they will not only endanger Sweden, but they will cost
     more to reconquer than to defend.

5   The concern to retain Sweden's vote in the Imperial Diet is particularly
     strongly expressed in the King's draft for a letter to Vellingk of 30 Apr. 1717:
     Bref, p. 420 ff.

6   See Jägerskiöld, op. cit., pp. 9 ff.

7   See G. Lindeberg, *Svensk ekonomisk politik under den Görtzka perioden* (1941),
     pp. 11 ff.

8   C. Danielsson, *Protektionismens genombrott och tulltaxrevisioner 1715 och 1718*
     (1930), pp. 102 ff.

9   Lindeberg, op. cit., pp. 40 ff. The ordinance has been frequently reprinted,
     most recently in O. Traung, *Lars Gathenhielm. Kaperiverksamheten under Karl
     XII:s tid* (1952), appendix III.

10   Jefferyes's letters of the spring of 1715, *H.H.* 16: 2, pp. 73 ff.

11 Quoted by F.von Moser, *Rettung der Ehre und Undschuld des ... Georg Heinrich von Schlitz, gennant von Goertz* (Hamburg 1774), p. 30.
12 S.Jägerskiöld, *K.F.Å.* 1934, pp. 116–18; Holst, *Fredrik I*, p. 58.
13 Görtz to von Dernath, cited ibid., p. 56.
14 G.Lindeberg, 'Några politska visor mot Görtz', *K.F.Å.* 1936, pp. 295 ff.
15 They have been printed by W.Holst, 'Karl XII i Stralsund. Stämningsbilder av ett ögonvittne generallöjtnanten Conrad von Ranck', *Ord och Bild*, 1939.
16 [M.Ranft], op. cit., pp. 327 ff., cp. Häggman, *K.F.Å.* 1922, p. 179, note 3.
17 L.Lilliehöök, 'Karl XII:s artillery', *Artilleri-Tidskrift* 1946, pp. 173–88.
18 *Minnen från fångenskapen i Ryssland och Carl XII:s krig. Carl von Rolands Biographie*, ed. S.Bring (1914), pp. 61–3.
19 Mediger, op. cit., pp. 189 ff.
20 Haintz, III, 11–12.
21 ibid., p. 13.
22 Wittram, II, 265, seems to accept (in contrast to Haintz) the Ranke argument that Frederick William genuinely desired a reconciliation with Sweden.
23 *Bidrag S.N.K.H.*, VII, 64 ff. The unpublished Bonn 1951 thesis of F.Genzel, *Studien zur Geschichte des Nordischen Krieges 1714–1720 unter besonderer Berücksichtigung der Personalunion zwischen Grossbritannien und Hannover*, has important new material showing Hanoverian intentions for the use of the British fleet; and Mediger, op, cit., pp. 234 ff., covers Hanoverian discussions with both Denmark and Prussia in great detail with telling quotations in his volume of notes.
24 R.M.Hatton, *Diplomatic Relations between Great Britain and the Dutch Republic 1714–1721* (1950), pp. 74, 78; for the decrease in Anglo-Dutch trade to these ports during the Swedish blockade before 1715 see Lindeberg, op. cit., p. 42.
25 Hatton, op. cit., pp. 76–8; J.J.Murray, 'Sjömakternas expedition till Östersjön 1715', *K.F.Å.* 1953, pp. 134 ff.
26 Mediger, op. cit., pp. 240 ff.; C.Nordmann, *La crise du Nord au début du XVIIIe siècle* (Paris, 1962), p. 175, note 15.
27 Hatton, op. cit., p. 76.
28 ibid., p. 79.
29 Apart from the authorities already mentioned in the footnotes to this chapter see J.F.Chance, *George I and the Northern War* (London, 1909) pp. 80 ff.; W. Michael, *England under George I* (London, 1936 translation of 1921 German ed.), I, 73 ff.; B.Williams, *Stanhope* (Oxford, 1932), pp. 232 ff.; L.A.Nikoforov, *Russko-Angliyskie otnosheniya pri Petra I* (Moscow, 1952), pp. 120 ff. The researches of Hatton, Murray, Nordmann, Genzel and Mediger have strengthened Michael's contention of Hanoverian influence on English policy; but Mediger's judgement, op. cit., p. 240 that it is not possible to say if the British fleet rendered any real help is, in my opinion, cautious to the point of being misleading.
30 Hatton, op. cit., p. 79; H.M.C. *Stuart Papers*, I (London, 1903) 372 ff. and 421.
31 The anxiety in Stralsund that the British fleet might cooperate with Sweden's enemies is vividly mirrored in Jefferyes's letters, *H.H.* 16: 1; for the paralysing effect on Sweden's naval activities when the cooperation ensued see G.Lindeberg, op. cit., pp. 46–7 and P.Sörensson, *K.F.Å.* 1929, pp. 196–7.

32 Hatton, op. cit., pp. 79–81.

33 Murray, *K.F.Å.*, 1953, pp. 192–8 shows that adverse wind and weather was not the only reason for the late exit of the Swedish fleet from Karlskrona.

34 Haintz, III, 19 ff.; Holm, *H.T.* 1881–2, pp. 2 ff.

35 Mediger, op. cit., pp. 243 ff., adds to what is already known about this process from *Bidrag S.N.K.H.* VII, 91 ff. and Genzel, pp. 70 ff.

36 Haintz, III, 25–30 takes issue with the argument of H. Voges that Charles XII ought to have risked a battle at this stage.

37 Jefferyes's letter of 24 May 1715: *H.H.* 16: 2, 107–20.

38 For the battle of Jasmund (called after the peninsula near which it was fought) see *Bidrag S.N.K.H.* VII, 107 ff.; for Löwen explaining to Charles XII the way wind and weather influenced the battle see *Mémoires*, p. 70.

39 D. D. Alridge regards Droysen's argument that bad weather kept the Swedes in port for the vital period as more justified than Murray, loc. cit.

40 Norris's letter to Townshend of 24 June (O.S.) 1715, quoted by Chance, op. cit., p. 86.

41 Ranck's letter to Frederick of Hesse of 16 Aug. 1715: *Ord och Bild*, 1939.

42 The Prussian General von Arnim's report of his victory, cited by Haintz, III, 34–5, shows the heavy casualties both of the defenders (whom Arnim gives as 300, correcting the generally accepted figure of 450) and the 1,000 Prussians who stormed the fort.

43 *Bidrag S.N.K.H.* VII, 182 ff.; Haintz, III, 43–5, with refutation of Voges's assumption that the movement to Palmerort was a feint.

44 The most detailed report of the battle by a participant is by Villelongue (found in a long 'relation' of his service with the Swedes sent as two letters to Voltaire in 1730), ed. by H. Brulin, *K.F.Å.* 1948, pp. 230–2; also *Generalstaben*, IV, 909–12 and Haintz, III, 47–9 (with criticism of Ranke's and Voges's judgements).

45 Ranck's letter to Frederick of Hesse of 20 Nov. 1715: *Ord och Bild*, 1939.

46 Villelongue (*K.F.Å.* 1948, p. 233), who formed part of the rearguard from Stresow, explains Lieutenant-General Marschalk's surrender as due to a concern for his and his family personal property in Rügen; he himself took the precaution to obtain a certificate (printed ibid., pp. 234–5) from fellow-officers that he had in vain tried to persuade Marschalk to follow orders.

47 For his route see Haintz, III, 48, note 1. For his saving the field-artillery see Lilliehöök, *Artilleri-Tidskrift*, 1946, p. 182.

48 Löwen, *Mémoires.*, pp. 47–8.

49 Ranck's letter to Frederick of Hesse of 16 Aug. 1715: *Ord och Bild*, 1939; for an appeal made to Louis XIV to fall into Rhenish Prussia see F. F. Carlson, *Om fredsunderhandlingarna*, p. 86.

50 Charles XII's letters to Ulrika Eleonora of 27 May/7 June and 20 Sept./10 Oct. 1715: *Bref.*

51 For the Stralsund fortifications and the new works see H. Voges, *Die Belagerung von Stralsund in 1715* (Stettin, 1922), pp. 3 ff. and R. Biederstedt, *Eosander*, pp. 42 ff.; Nordberg, II, 508 and 526–7 (including a report of Croissy's); Jefferyes's letters of 29 June and 2 Aug. 1715, *H.H.* 16: 2.

52 The order from Demotika for such inspections reached Sweden in October 1714; for the report submitted in April 1715 by the Councillor Count Jakob

Spens on the six districts that fell to his share see *K.F.Å.* 1939, pp. 51–74, ed. by N. Belfrage.

53 Charles XII's letter of 27 May/7 June 1715 to Ulrika Eleonora: *Bref.*
54 Ranck's letter to Frederick of Hesse of 16 Aug. 1715: *Ord och Bild* 1939.
55 Croissy's letter to Torcy of 27 May 1715, printed, from A.E., Correspondance Politique, Suède, vol. 132, by P. Sörensson in *K.F.Å.* 1910, pp. 315–16.
56 Löwen, *Mémoires*, pp. 48–9; Löwen's criticism of Eosander (ibid., p. 45) must be balanced by Biederstedt's biography, pp. 44–5.
57 Löwen, *Mémoires*, p. 52.
58 The best account of this in Haintz, III, 57–62.
59 The justification was that Denmark and Russia were not willing to give Augustus his fair share of the booty: see Virmont's letter to the Emperor of 21 Nov. 1711, cited by Sörensson, *K.F.Å.* 1926, p. 228, note 3.
60 Ranck's letters to Frederick of Hesse of 16 Aug. and 30 Nov. 1715: *Ord och Bild*, 1939.
61 Feif's letter to Tessin of 23 March 1715; *Brinkmanska archivet.*
62 Moser in his biography of Görtz holds that Görtz's first conversation with Charles XII on finances took place in Ystad in December 1715 and G. Lindeberg, op. cit., p. 2, accepts this; but unless the trip to Hamburg had some connexion with Swedish attempts to get finance it seems inexplicable that Görtz should have moved on to Sweden from Hamburg. Nordberg, II, 472, stresses Görtz's role as one who discussed 'useful and practical plans' already at Strelsund.
63 *Bidrag S.N.K.H.* VII, 208 ff.
64 P. Sörensson (in Bring, *Karl XII*), p. 420.
65 Ranck's letter to Frederick of Hesse of 20 Nov. 1715: *Ord och Bild*, 1939.
66 ibid., letter of 30 Nov. 1715.
67 ibid., letter of 30 Nov. 1715.
68 ibid., letter of 13 Dec. 1715; and editor's introduction.
69 For the capitulation negotiations and the terms obtained see *Bidrag S.N.K.H.*, VII, 214 ff., cp. Nordberg II, 538 ff.
70 The report of the captain who effected Charles's escape is printed in G. Unger, 'En legendbildning kring Karl XII:s hemresa frän Stralsund 1715', *H.T.* 1935, pp. 379–80: the *Hvalfisk* was boarded first and later transfer was made to the *Snappup* and at least two additions were made to the royal party en route, among them Feif.
71 A. Højer, *Friedrich IV glorwürdigstes Leben* (Copenhagen 1829).
72 Bergersen, *Tordenskjold*, I, 566.
73 The generally quoted landing-place at Stafsten (Stavsten) has been proved mistaken by L. Lindahl, 'Stavsten. Sanning och sägen om en historisk märkesplats', *K.F.Å.* 1934, pp. 102–10.

BOOK VI, CHAPTER 3: THE NORWEGIAN CAMPAIGN OF 1716

1 Charles XII's letter to Ulrika Eleonora of 14 Dec. 1715: *Bref* Cp. ibid., the affectionate letter he wrote to the Queen-Grandmother from Stralsund on 11 Nov. 1714 (nr. 6) thanking her for her care of Charles Frederick, for presents

sent (among them a bed and a miniature portrait of her) and promising to effect commissions asked for; cp. the expressions quoted from the King in Hermelin's letter to Barck of 20 and 23 April 1707, hoping that she would recover from an illness and live that he might see her again. For presents to grandmother and sister from Turkey see Düben's letter of 27 April 1712: *H.T.* 1889.

2 Holst, *Fredrik I*, pp. 64–5, quoting Frederick of Hesse's letter to his father.
3 Charles XII's letter to Ulrika Eleonora of 28 May 1715: *Bref.*
4 Ranck's letter to Frederick of Hesse of 15 Nov. 1715: *Ord och Bild*, 1939.
5 Charles's letter to Ulrika Eleonora of 24 and 31 Dec. 1715: *Bref.*
6 ibid., letters of 14 and 31 Dec. 1715; 24 Jan., 15 Feb., 24 June and 21 July 1716.
7 ibid., letters of 14 Dec. 1715, 24 Jan., 25 Feb. 1716.
8 Bring, 'Karl XII:s likfärd och begravning', *K.F.Å.* 1918, p. 230 and note 1.
9 Charles XII's letters of 14 Dec. 1715 and 24 Jan. 1716 to Ulrika Eleonora; *Bref.*
10 ibid., Charles XII's letter to Ulrika Eleonora of 14 Dec. 1715.
11 Feif's letter to Tessin of 21 Dec. 1715: *Brinkmanska archivet.*
12 Holst, *Fredrik I*, pp. 67–9, citing Frederick of Hesse's letters to Charles XII from Sept. 1715 onwards; cp. Charles XII's letter to Frederick of Jan. 1716 (undated) on the maps of Norway given him by this officer: *Bref.*
13 Holst, *Fredrik I*, p. 68.
14 Charles XII's letter to Ulrika Eleonora of 2 May (N.S.) 1715: *Bref.*
15 See his orders from Ystad of 23 Dec. 1715 to the civil and military authorities, cited in Petri's regimental history, III, 423–4.
16 Quennerstedt, *Ur Carl XII:s Lefnad*, II, 95.
17 Horn's relationship to the King after 1715 has not been covered in any detail since both Grauers's and Ahlström's studies stop in 1713; G. Horn, *Arvid Bernard Horn* (1852) has a gap between 1715 and 1723.
18 Rumpf's letter of 24 Jan./4 Feb. 1716, cited by Holst, *Ulrika Eleonora*, p. 140.
19 Feif's letters to Tessin of 21 Dec. 1715 and 14 Jan. 1716: *Brinkmanska archivet.*
20 Charles XII's letter to Ulrika Eleonora of 24 Jan. 1716: *Bref.*
21 This possibility is mooted by Petri, III, 427; but Charles XII's letter to Frederick of Hesse of Jan. 1716 (undated) points to a genuine plan to use 'the bridge to Zelandt' if at all possible: *Bref.*
22 Charles XII's letter to Ulrika Eleonora of 15 Feb. 1716: *Bref.*
23 For this campaign see J. A. Lagermark, *Karl XII:s krig i Norge 1716* (1883) and the same author's 'Kriget i västra Sverige och Norge' in Bring, *Karl XII*, pp. 615–33; *Bidrag S.N.K.H.* VII, 56 ff.; S. Steen, *Det norske folks liv og historie 1640–1720* (Oslo, 1930), pp. 410 ff.; Petri, III, 427 ff.; cp. I. M. Munch's article in *Norsk Militær Tidsskrift*, 1902, pp. 42 ff. where use is made of Norwegian reports and of intercepted Swedish letters.
24 Löwen, *Mémoires*, pp. 35–7.
25 S. Jägerskiöld, *Sverige och Europa 1716–18* (1937), pp. 83 ff.
26 Croissy's letters from Stralsund: *Handlingar* (Malmström), pp. 35 ff.
27 Edinburgh National Library, MS. 5129, ff. 3a–4b.
28 H.M.C. *Stuart Papers*, I (London, 1903), Bolingbroke's letter to Mar of 29 Sept. 1715 and James's letters to Bolingbroke of 23 and 29 Sept. 1715.

29   Hans Nobel's report to Frederick IV of 1716, printed in *Norske Samlinger* (Christiania, 1852), ed. C. Lange, pp. 137 ff.; *Bidrag S.N.K.H.* VIII, 85 ff.
30   For these see Refsum, *K.F.Å.* 1930, pp. 117 ff., and the same author's article in (Norwegian) *H.T.* 1932, pp. 210 ff.
31   Motraye, *Travels*, II, 249–50.
32   Charles XII's letter to Ulrika Eleonora of 24 June 1716: *Bref*.
33   Lagermark, in Bring, *Karl XII*, pp. 630–1.
34   *Bidrag S.N.K.H.* VIII, pp. 152 ff.; O. Bergersen, *Vice-Admiral Tordenskjold*, II, 593 ff.
35   Holst, *Fredrik I*, pp. 71–2.
36   Charles XII's letters to Frederick of Hesse of 8 June and 21 July 1716: *Bref*.
37   ibid., pp. 209 ff., letter of Aug. 1716 (no date).
38   ibid., letter of 11 Aug. 1716; cp. *K.F.Å.* 1927, p. 68, for the services of a certain Franc in such intelligence work.
39   Charles XII's letter to Ulrika Eleonora of 21 July and 5 Aug. 1716: *Bref*; cp. Holst, *Ulrika Eleonora*, pp. 146 ff.
40   ibid., pp. 147–8, printing Ulrika's letters to her husband of 1 and 8 Sept. 1716.
41   Ulrika's memoirs, pp. 570–1.
42   Holst, *Ulrika Eleonora*, p. 147, Ulrika's letters to her husband of 1 Sept. 1716.
43   Charles XII's letter to Ulrika Eleonora of Sept. 1716 (undated); *Bref*, p. 162.
44   Rumpf's letter of 11/22 Sept. 1716, cited by Holst, *Ulrika Eleonora*, p. 146, says that Charles left 'by ordinary post-horse accompanied by a groom with a torch'. For Brandklipparen being captured at the *Kalabalik* and later rebought see Hultman's memoirs: *Handlingar* (Floderus), I, 69: cp. Nordberg, II, 105; for Brandklipparen spending its last years at Engsö (the Piper residence) see H. Piper, *Engsö från medeltid till nutid* (1961), pp. 61 ff.
45   For the Scania plan see in particular E. Holm, 'Studier til den store nordiske krigs historie' (Danish), *H.T.* 1881 and 1882; K. J. Hartman, *Tsar Peters underhandlingar år 1716 on landgang i Skåne* (1887); J. J. Murray, 'Scania and the end of the Northern alliance 1716', *Journal of Modern History*, 1944; R. E. Lindgren, 'A projected invasion of Sweden 1716', *Huntington Library Quarterly*, 1944; Nikiforov, op. cit., pp. 126 ff. Feygina, *Alandsky kongress* (1959), pp. 96 ff.; Mediger, op. cit., pp. 312 ff.
46   *Bidrag S.N.K.H.*, VIII, 299 ff.; Haintz, II, 75–7; Wittram, II, 278–9; Mediger, op. cit., 283–90.
47   Wittram, II, 279–80; for the Polish conflict see J. Gierowski, 'Personal-oder-Realunion', in *Um die polnische Krone*, 279 ff.
48   Mediger, op. cit., chapter 4, has shown that Tsar Peter planned a virtual protectorate over Mecklenburg and argues that the Tsar's cooperation in the Scania plan – which envisaged an invasion of Sweden from the west as opposed to the invasion from the east which he really preferred – was motivated by his Mecklenburg ambitions. Here he differs from Wittram, who (II, 573, note 39) sees the Russian concentration of troops in North Germany as caused by the Tsar's desire to achieve a real blow at Sweden in cooperation with his allies.
49   The fullest account of the negotiations for the British navy in Mediger, op. cit., pp. 296 ff., with use of most previous authorities.
50   Hatton, op. cit., pp. 121–4.
51   *Bidrag S.N.K.H.*, VIII, 292 ff.

52 Mediger, op. cit., pp. 305–6.

53 *Bidrag S.N.K.H.* VIII, 289–309; Wittram, II, 290–2.

54 For these negotiations – which had begun at The Hague before the treaty between George I and the Emperor was signed on 5 June 1716 – see Hatton, op. cit., 127 ff. which complements the older studies of Wiesener and Bourgeois.

55 Cederhielm's report of '1709–1718', *K.F.Å.* 1915, pp. 100–7; for Cederhielm's efforts via foreign diplomats see documents printed by E. Hassinger in *K.F.Å.* 1938.

56 S. Jägerskiöld, *Sverige och Europa, 1716–18* pp. 27 ff. for Görtz's efforts; cp. ibid., pp. 45 ff. for the Swedish use of the Landgrave of Hesse in contacts with the Tsar.

57 ibid., pp. 42–3, 66, 67, 71, building on the Görtz-Vellingk correspondence and the H.M.C. *Stuart Papers*, III; see also Feygina, op. cit., pp. 153 ff. and M. Bruce, 'Jacobite relations with Peter the Great', *Slavonic and East European Review*, 1935–6, pp. 342 ff.

58 Hatton, op. cit., p. 127.

59 *Bidrag S.N.K.H.* VII, 302 ff. Mediger, op. cit., pp. 320 ff. has shown how persistently but unsuccessfully the Tsar attempted to use these negotiations to obtain a written promise from George I that the British fleet should be put under Russian command for an attack on Karlskrona to capture or ruin the Swedish fleet.

60 For the treaty of Havelberg of 16/27 Nov. 1716 see Haintz, II, 121–2 and Wittram, II, 293–4.

61 Hatton, op. cit., 120 ff., Mediger, op. cit., 239 ff.

62 For the Russian fleet moves in 1716 see Mediger, op. cit., pp. 214–312, 319–20, based on Russian material; for the Swedish see G. Unger's *Sjömaktens inflytande*, III, 63 ff.

63 G. Lindeberg, *Svensk ekonomisk politik under den Görtzka perioden* (1941), pp. 76 ff.

64 *Bidrag S.N.K.H.*, VIII, 294–309 for Shafirov's transmitting the Tsar's 'no' of 19 Sept., for the Tsar's letter of 12 Sept. (O.S.) to Frederick IV and for report of the Tsar's conference with Frederick IV on 3 Oct.

BOOK VI, CHAPTER 4: HEADQUARTERS AT LUND

1 A. Quennerstedt, *Ur Carl XII:s Lefnad*, II (1916), 133 ff. has much information on the Lund period from local records; see also Hultman's memoirs: *Handlingar* (Floderus), I, 180 ff.

2 Charles Frederick of Holstein-Gottorp commented in his letter to Ulrika Eleonora (cited in Holst, *Ulrika Eleonora*, p. 140) on the many Poles and Turks in Ystad; later on most were given lodgings in Karlshamn and only the more important ones lived in Lund, see Westrin: *H.T.* 1900, 28 ff.

3 Quennerstedt, op. cit., p. 152 mentions the Russian spy Henrik Holterling who duped the Swedes into believing he favoured their cause.

4 ibid., pp. 135–8; *K.F.Å.* 1947, p. 66; with photographs of details ibid., 1910, pp. 290–1.

5 See Feif's letter to Tessin of 1 Nov. 1716: *Brinkmanska archivet*; cp. Samuel Åkerhielm's memoirs cited by Sallnäs, op. cit. pp. 20 ff.

6   Quennerstedt, op. cit., p. 143.

7   Charles xii's letter to Frederick of Hesse, of Aug. (undated) 1716: *Bref*, p. 209.

8   Quennerstedt, op. cit., pp. 139–40.

9   ibid., p. 140 for details.

10   Mainly through information which Svedborg gave in a letter to Nordberg and which he utilized in his history of Charles xii: II, 598–602.

11   See *Emanuelis Swedenborgi Diarium Spirituale*, ed. J.Tafel (Tübingen, 1843–6).

12   K.-G.Hildebrand, 'Swedenborg', *Svenska Dagbladet* 30/11 1947.

13   Polhem had studied with Wallis when in England: see K.Hagberg, 'England och Sverige', *Svenska Dagbladet* 17/12, 1945.

14   K.-G.Hildebrand, loc. cit.

15   The manuscript for this 'Anthropologia physica' was kept by Feif and Nordberg printed it in his *Anmärckingar* (1754), pp. 52–60; it has been reprinted by Carlson: *Bref*, pp. 467–9; cp. Holst, *Fredrik I* (1953), p. 83–4.

16   C.Silje, *Karl XII som filosof* (1891); P.Engdahl, 'Karl XII. En studie över hans personlighet', *K.F.Å.* 1930, p. 250.

17   For Svedborg thinking so, see K.-G.Hildebrand, loc. cit.; Voltaire, *Histoire de Charles XII* (1731), 169.

18   H.Plejel, *Der schwedische Pietismus in seinem Beziehungen zu Deutschland* (1935), p. 101; cp. the same author's edition of H.Schröder's 'Levernesbeskrivning' in *Samlinger och studier till Svenska Kyrkans historia* (1940). For Charles xii's tolerance even in earlier years see Cederhielm's opinion, *K.F.Å.* 1960, p. 136.

19   A.O.Rhyzelius's, *Antäckningar om sitt lefverne* (hereafter referred to as Rhyzelius's memoirs) ed. by J.Helander in 1904; Rhyzelius's memoirs in so far as they deal with the 1716–19 years had been printed earlier in (Danish) *H.T.* 1867.

20   Rhyzelius's memoirs, pp. 77–83, 98.

21   Refsum, *K.F.Å.* 1930 for the first comment; for the second see 'Description of the King of Sweden in 1716' by Søren Hagerup, printed in Danish in *Journal for Politik, Natur og Menneskekundskap* (Copenhagen, 1808), reprinted by Villius, *Ögonvittnen*, pp. 181–2.

22   Rhyzelius's memoirs, p. 72; Quennerstedt, op. cit., pp. 141–2.

23   ibid., pp. 156–7.

24   ibid., p, 140.

25   In *Bref*, though note that the King felt he wrote it badly and needed assistance: he mentions on 8 June 1716 that he has called on Poniatowski as amanuensis: *Bref* (to Frederick of Hesse).

26   H. Piper, *Engsö från medeltid till nutid* (1961), pp. 58 ff. where stories of his presence at headquarters in Scania and on the Norwegian campaign are related. A Swede by birth, he was always known as Anders 'Luxemburg'.

27   Feif's letter to Tessin of 1 Nov. 1716: *Brinkmanska archivet*.

28   ibid., letter of 11 Aug. 1716.

29   Josephson, *Tessin*, I, 188, thinks Charles xii made excuses to postpone the meeting.

30   Feif's letter to Tessin of 13 Dec. 1716: *Brinkmanska archivet*.

31   R.Josephson, 'Carl XI och Carl XII som esteter', *K.F.Å.* 1947, pp. 54–6: Tessin thought Charles influenced by Islam conventions.

32   For the possible influence of views of Constantinople, discussed with his officer-
     artists, on this plan see ibid. 1931, pp. 57–60.
33   Feif's letters of 28 April, 19 Nov., 12 Dec. 1712 and 17 July 1713: *Brinkmanska
     archivet.*
34   R.Josephson, *K.F.Å.* 1947, p. 65.
35   For Charles's decreeing changes in the models of uniform submitted, see his
     letter to Frederick of Hesse of Jan. (undated) 1717: *Bref.*
36   Feif's letters to Tessin of 27 March 1717 and 25 Sept. 1718: *Brinkmanska
     archivet.*
37   ibid., letter of 20 Feb. 1718.
38   ibid., letter of 16 May 1717.
39   ibid., letter of 17 Dec. 1716.
40   ibid., letters of 27 March and 16 May 1717.
41   ibid., letters nr. 67 (undated) 1717 and 25 Sept. 1718; for the trumpeters being
     used for signals in the Caroline army see the article by O.Cederlöf, *K.F.Å.*
     1960, pp. 7–20 (with authorities cited p. 18, note 27) analysing the Lemke battle
     scenes painted to commemorate Charles XI's wars.
42   Feif's letter to Tessin of Feb. 1718: *Brinkmanska archivet.*
43   ibid., letter of 20 Feb. 1718.
44   Rhyzelius's memoirs, p. 80; an illustration of the set is in *K.F.Å.* 1947, p. 66,
     with photographs of details ibid., 1910, pp. 290–1.
45   Feif's letter to Tessin of 22 Aug. 1718: *Brinkmanska archivet.*
46   R.Josephson, *Tessin*, I, 184.
47   Feif's letter to Tessin of 4 and 15 July 1717: *Brinkmanska archivet.*
48   ibid., Feif's letter of 22 Aug. 1718.
49   S.Stenström, 'Karl XII:s Dödsmask och Simon Josse', *Livrustkammaren*, 1965,
     pp. 128 ff., from the Görtz and Preis archives in R.A..; W.Holst, *Carl Gustav
     Tessin* (1936) pp. 15 ff. tells of Tessin's son, sent abroad in 1714, being used to
     buy books, prints and paintings in France and Italy.
50   Feif's letter to Tessin of 21 Dec. 1715: *Brinkmanska archivet*; when new money
     arrived with Nordberg some of it was stolen from a drawer in the King's desk:
     see Löwen, *Mémoires*, for Charles's unwillingness to believe that an officer
     suspected of the theft was guilty: 'a colonel does not steal'.
51   P.G.M.Dickson, *The financial revolution in England. A Study in the develop-
     ment of public credit 1688–1756* (London, 1967), p. 7, stressing the influence of
     England's long wars with France on her financial revolution.
52   G.Lindeberg, *Svensk ekonomisk politik under den Görtzka perioden* (1941), pp.
     82–94; for Swedish capital having gone abroad from 1708 see Campredon's
     dispatches of 9 Feb. and 2 Mar. 1715, printed in *Handlingar* (Malmström).
53   D.Almquist, 'De karolinska mynttecknens ursprung', *K.F.Å.* 1936, pp. 187–
     213, supplemented by G.Lindeberg, op. cit., pp. 111 ff.
54   C.Nordmann, 'Les finances carolines et le Système de Görtz' (section III of
     'Monnaies et finances suèdoises au XVIIe siècle'), *Revue du Nord*, 1964, pp.
     469–88.
55   G.Lindeberg, op. cit., pp. 260 ff.
56   ibid., pp. 119 ff.
57   R.M.Hatton, *Diplomatic Relations between Great Britain and the Dutch
     Republic 1714–1721*, pp. 153–9 and 173–5.

58 G. Lindeberg, op. cit., 358 ff.

59 G. Lindeberg, *Krigsfinansiering och krigshushållning* (1946), pp. 34 ff., discusses the novel features of this contract by which the Dutch firm promised to bring two million *riksdaler* worth of silver into Sweden in return for certain concessions. S. Haverling, *K.F.Å.* 1952, pp. 92–3 has examined the pamphlet propaganda (mainly British) against the contract.

60 J. J. Murray, 'The Görtz-Gyllenborg arrests – a problem in diplomatic immunity', *Journal of Modern History*, 1956, pp. 325 ff. For Görtz's transactions with the Jacobites in 1716 and 1717 see his own explanation, printed by T. Westrin in *H.T.* 1898; the broader treatment in Jägerskiöld, *Sverige och Europa 1716–1718*, pp. 68 ff. and C. Nordmann, *La crise du nord au début du XVIIIe siècle*, pp. 84 ff.

61 Hatton, op. cit., pp. 147–9.

62 ibid., pp. 149–57.

63 G. Lindeberg, op. cit., pp. 96–106, discusses the work of the *deputation*; for von Dernath see the same author's article, *K.F.Å.* 1934.

64 R. Josephson, *Tessin*, I, 193 ff.; E. Naumann, 'Centralförvaltningen', in Bring, *Karl XII*, pp. 556–9.

65 ibid., pp. 548–9.

66 S. E. Bring, *Göta kanals historie* I (1930), 6 ff.

67 Feif's letter to Tessin of 12 Sept. 1717: *Brinkmanska archivet*.

68 ibid., letter of 25 Sept. 1718, passing on his own and Charles xii's suggestions.

69 For a discussion of this complicated problem see S. Schartau, ('Inre tillståndet'), in Bring, *Karl XII*, pp. 503–16, reducing the earlier estimate of a loss of 158,000 to 'certainly no more than 100,000'; E. F. Heckscher, *Sveriges ekonomiska historia*, I:2 (1936), 407 ff. estimates for the period 1699–1721 an average yearly decrease in the population as small as 0·5 *pro mille* and shows that there was no decrease at all up to 1715. The contemporary estimate (Campredon) was 80,000 lost through the plague and 30,000 through the war.

70 See J. Almquist's study in *K.F.Å.* 1916, pp. 224 ff.

71 G. Lindeberg, op. cit., chapters IX and X deal with copper and iron respectively; cp. his *Krigsfinansiering och krigshushållning*, pp. 68 ff.

BOOK VII, CHAPTER I: DIPLOMATIC PREPARATIONS

1 P. Sörensson, 'Utrikespolitiken efter hemkomsten' (in Bring, *Karl XII*), noted the importance of the secret correspondence of the King and in his *Sverige och Frankrike 1715–1718* (3 parts, 1909–21) brought the problem of 'ostensible' letters to the fore. K. J. Hartman, *Ålandska kongressen och dess förhistoria* (6 parts, Åbo, 1921–31); 'Om förhallandet mellan Karl xii och Görtz på utrikespolitikens område efter konungens hemkomst från Turkiet till hans död' (Finnish), *H.T.* 1929; 'Ålands-kongressen 1718 i dess viktigaste skede', *K.F.Å.* 1924; 'Kring Karl xii:s problemen i mina arbeten', ibid., 1934; *Karl XII och hessarna* (Åbo 1935), has been preoccupied with interpreting the 'ostensible' letters and with the 'camouflage' aspect of Swedish policy. For his stimulating but changing key-patterns see S. Jägerskiöld, 'Kring K. T. Hartmans arbete: Ålandska kongressen och dess förhistoria', *K.F.Å.* 1932–3 and K.-G. Hildebrand, 'Karl XII – problem', *H.T.* 1934; G. Petri, 'K. J. Hartman': ibid., 1936;

G. Lindeberg, 'K.J.Hartman, Forskarmetoder och forskargärning', *Scandia*
1936. J. Rosén, *Den svenska utrikes-politikens historia*, II: 1 (1952), 202–3
accepts one of Hartman's interpretations which proved unacceptable to
Jägerskiöld: see below, note 54.

2 The pioneer work is by S. Jägerskiöld, *Sverige och Europa 1716–1718* (1937), who
utilized Swedish, Danish, Prussian, Hanoverian, Hessian, Saxon, Mecklenburg,
Oldenburg, Austrian, French, British, Neapolitan and Polish archive material
as well as the Görtz papers still in existence. It can now be complemented by
S. A. Feygina, *Alandskiy kongress* (Moscow, 1959), which examines Russo-
Swedish relations for the whole period after Charles XII's return from Turkey
from Russian archive material. Note also the propaganda aspects of Swedish
policy after 1715 examined by S. Haverling in *K.F.Å.* 1952; Rosén, op. cit.,
pp. 44-57 has a brief but important independent analysis.

3 For these C. Nordmann, *La crise du nord au début du XVIIIe siècle* (Paris,
1962), is particularly useful though his general treatment of the negotiations
would have been helped by a knowledge of Feygina's research; for Alberoni
see the same author's 'Alberoni och Karl XII', *Svensk Tidskrift* 1953, pp. 226 ff.
The publication of the relevant volumes in *H.M.C. Stuart Papers*, I–VII, 1903–
34 should also be noted. Hesse policy has been examined by Jägerskiöld, op.
cit., and in 'Den hessiska politiken och den svenska tronföljdsfrågan
1713–1718,' *K.F.Å.* 1934; see also W. Holst, *Fredrik I* (1953), pp. 78 ff.

4 Erik Sparre's letter of 27 June 1716, printed by Westrin, *H.T.* 1898, p. 98.

5 Jägerskiöld, op. cit., pp. 320 ff.

6 Jägerskiöld, op. cit., p. 103 from Müllern's entry book in R.A.; for Charles
XII's ealier orders of 31 Oct. 1716 in favour of peace-negotiations with Denmark see the King's letter to Görtz: Moser, op. cit., 530 ff.

7 Jägerskiöld, op. cit., pp. 104–7; with correction of earlier authorities who
assumed that Görtz did not obey orders.

8 See the memorial of 10 Dec. 1716, which Frederick of Hesse sent to Charles
XII, printed by P. Sörensson in *K.F.Å.* 1917, especially pp. 210–12; cp. Holst,
Fredrik I, pp. 76–7 and ibid., pp. 78 ff. for Hesse efforts in favour of peace
with Hanover and/or Prussia.

9 There are quite a few examples of such Swedish opinions reported by foreign
diplomats; but note that Horn in 1724 said that even what remained of Pomerania brought Sweden more respect and standing in Europe than 'half of
Sweden': cited from the Council protocol by J. Peters 'Unter der Schwedischen
Krone', *Zeitschrift für Geschichtswissenschaft* 1966, p. 40.

10 For the importance of the possessions in the East Baltic see L. Thanner: *H.T.*
1956, p. 166; cp. the 'guarantee of privileges' issued by Ulrika and Frederick in
1719 and 1720: S. Dahlberg, 'Uppgörelsen med reduktionen efter eneväldets
fall', *H.T.* 1967, pp. 77 ff.

11 S.-E. Åström, *From cloth to iron*, I (1963), pp. 125–33; see A. Loit, *H.T.* 1964,
pp. 314 ff. for a summary of the thesis of H. Piirimäe of 1962 on the subject of
Narva's trade.

12 Cited by Holst, *Fredrik I*, p. 80 from the Marburg archives. For Ranck's
London mission of Jan. 1717, see Jägerskiöld, p. 121.

13 Holst, *Fredrik I*, p. 79 (from memo in Marburg by Frederick of Hesse of what
he had told Charles XII); cp. the same author's *Ulrika Eleonora*, pp. 133 ff.

14   For this attack see Charles XII's letter to Ulrika Eleonora of 6 May 1717: *Bref*; cp. O. Kuylenstierna, 'Peder Wessel Tordenskiolds trenne angrepp på Göteborg, Nya Elfsborg och Nya Värfvet åren 1717 och 1719', *Bidrag till Kännedomen om Göteborgs och Bohusläns fornminne och historia*, 1900, pp. 165 ff.

15   Holst, *Fredrik I*, p. 83.

16   For Charles XII's ideas on the peace-offensive see his letter to Frederick of Hesse of Jan. (undated) 1717: *Bref*, pp. 211–15; the written instructions given to Poniatowski in June 1716, discussed by Jägerskiöld, op. cit., pp. 45 ff.; and the oral ones to Görtz of Nov. 1716, cited by Moser, op. cit., pp. 530 ff.

17   P. Sörensson in Bring, *Karl XII*, p. 452.

18   Rhyzelius's memoirs, p. 76.

19   R. M. Hatton, *Diplomatic Relations between Great Britain and the Dutch Republic 1714–1721*, pp. 153–8.

20   For de la Marck's mission see *Recueil des Instructions, Suède*, pp. 278–90 and P. Sörensson, op. cit., II, 12 ff.

21   See Jägerskiöld, op. cit., pp. 128–35 for full powers sent to Vellingk for negotiations with George I and with Frederick William of Prussia and to Preis (Swedish diplomat at The Hague) to negotiate with the Tsar; ibid., p. 139 for the Landgrave not being trusted with the contents of the instructions for the Swedish negotiators.

22   The Vellingk papers in R.A. have been well utilized by F. F. Carlson, K. J. Hartman and S. Jägerskiöld in their studies of Swedish diplomacy.

23   Fabrice has rendered an account of his share in his *Memoiren*, pp. 117–27; cp. Mediger, op. cit., pp. 390 ff. for George I's peace-terms, to be submitted to Sweden via Fabrice and his father, of 24 Aug. 1716.

24   Moser, op. cit.

25   See Charles XII's letters to *krigskollegium* 15 Oct. 1716 and to *upphandlingsdeputation* 2 Nov. 1716, cited by Jägerskiöld, op. cit., p. 111.

26   See, e.g. draft of Charles XII's letter to Vellingk of 30 April 1717: *Bref*; cp. Görtz's plan of Nov. 1717 printed by P. Sörensson, *K.F.Å.* 1924, pp. 231–7.

27   W. Mediger, *Mecklenburg, Russland und England-Hanover 1706–1721*, p. 366, concludes that British–Hanoverian pressure (as well as the Tsar's failure to weaken the Anglo-French alliance) forced the removal of Russian troops from Mecklenburg; but the Tsar's hope by such withdrawal to win British naval help for his pet project of an attack on Sweden from the east and a French guarantee for his conquests should not be disregarded.

28   G. H. Jones, *The main stream of Jacobitism* (Cambridge, Mass., 1954), essential for the movement in general, needs to be supplemented for the relations of Jacobites with foreign powers with the works of Nordmann, Feygina and Jägerskiöld. We have brief articles in English by Murray (on the Jacobites and Sweden) and Bruce (on the Jacobites and Russia) and a more extended study which also included Spain would be welcome.

29   Charles XII's letter to Frederick of Hesse of Jan. (undated) 1717: *Bref*; cp. Jägerskiöld, op. cit., pp. 45–6 and 86 ff. For the Polish situation at this time see F. Gierowski, 'Personal-union oder Real-union', *Um die polnishe Krone*, pp. 254 ff. and Mediger, op. cit., pp. 193 ff. based on modern Polish research.

30   See Charles XII's letter to Frederick of Hesse of Jan. (undated) 1717: *Bref*, in connexion with the Schomer mission to Lund. The 'augmenter la jalousie'

motif is frequently encountered: see, e.g. Müllern's letter to Görtz 25 Oct. 1716, cited by Jägerskiöld, op. cit., p. 94.

31 ibid., pp. 174 ff.

32 Charles XII's letter to Frederick of Hesse of Jan. (undated) 1717: *Bref*; Görtz to Vellingk of Aug. 1717, cited by C. Nordmann, *Svensk Tidskrift* 1953, p. 270 from R.A.

33 Such opposition may have been influenced not only by the fear of the Tsar as a neighbour in Germany but also of the news – much spoken of at the time – of Peter's plan to dig a canal which would bypass the Sound: see Mediger, op. cit., pp. 174–5.

34 For these negotiations see Jägerskiöld, op. cit., pp. 160–7; and Feygina, op. cit.

35 For Görtz's negotiations on his way to Lund see B. Lundberg, 'Görtz i närheten av Berlin september 1717', *K.F.Å.* 1912, pp. 217–49; P. Sörensson, 'Görtz och sachsarne i september 1717', *K.F.Å.* 1922, pp. 117–68; Jägerskiöld, op. cit., pp. 175 ff.; for Görtz's reception: ibid., pp. 219–20.

36 Robethon's letter to St Saphorin of 1 Oct. 1717, cited ibid., p. 205.

37 The French ambassador's report cited in Sörensson op. cit., III, 31.

38 Görtz's letter to Charles XII of 14/25 Nov. 1717, cited by Jägerskiöld, op. cit., p. 209.

39 Vellingk's *'Pensées sur le parti à prendre'*: *H.H.* 12, 338 ff.; Jägerskiöld, op. cit., pp. 210–1, citing also von Müllern and von Kochen.

40 ibid., pp. 267 ff., citing Görtz's letters of 29 Nov. and 9 Dec. 1717 written at Charles XII's orders.

41 See J. F. Chance, 'The mission of Fabrice to Sweden', *The English Historical Review*, 1906; Jägerskiöld, op. cit., pp. 270–4.

42 Charles XII's letters to Ulrika Eleonora of 17 Sept. 1717 and 2 Jan. and 7 March 1718: *Bref*.

43 Ulrika Eleonora's memoirs, p. 507.

44 Holst, *Fredrik I*, pp. 89–90.

45 See Feif's letter to Tessin of 17 Feb. 1718: *Brinkmanska archivet*, suggesting that Tessin might arrive ahead of the main party so that he and the King would have some extra undisturbed time, 'the King intending to be at the meeting-place a day early'; for the eventual arrival of Charles XII later than the Stockholm contingent and for his talks and discussions with Tessin see Holst, *Ulrika Eleonora*, pp. 152 ff. and Josephson, Tessin, I, I, pp. 195 ff.

46 For the 1716–17 suggestions see Rosén, op. cit., p. 149; for the 1717–18 negotiations at Lund see Jägerskiöld, op. cit., pp. 274–9.

47 For the Quadruple Alliance negotiations see O. Weber, *Die Quadrupel-Allianz vom Jahre 1718* (Vienna, 1887) and Hatton, op. cit., pp. 166–205, showing *inter alia* that the alliance remained a triple one, since by the time the Dutch were willing to accede Stanhope had become convinced that the terms demanded – an equal share with the British in commercial advantages to be gained in the Baltic – was too high a price to pay for their entry.

48 Jägerskiöld, op. cit., pp. 279 ff.

49 Hartman – whose great service it was to kill the old-fashioned Charles XII–Görtz dichotomy – held this view. Not till Jägerskiöld's researches did the negotiations with George I receive their full due.

50 See Görtz's letter to Charles XII June (undated) 1718, quoted by Jägerskiöld, op. cit., p. 232, note 8.

51 P. Sörensson, op. cit., II, 151, with other correspondence on this subject; for the Tolstoy mission which secured Aleksey's return see Wittram, II, 377–81.

52 Feygina, op. cit., the Åland island negotiations proper being treated pp. 208 ff.; O. Andersson, *Lövö under fredskongressen* (Åbo, 1939), pp. 11–69, adds some local colour.

53 Jägerskiöld, op. cit., p. 468, based on von Kochen's evidence during the process against Görtz.

54 The letter of 30 July 1718 was printed in 1826 by P. G. Cederschiöld, *Bihang till Riksdagen i Stockholm 1719, innehållande protocoller och handlingar hörande till actionen emot Baron v. Görtz*, II, 133 ff. Rosén, op. cit., p. 202, is unable to accept Jägerskiöld's thesis of a difference in content between the official letter of 28 July and the private one of 30th and agrees with Hartman (*Ålandska kongressen*, III, 117) that Görtz in both urges the King to accept the Tsar's terms: the difference lies in the arguments deduced. In view, however, of the important P.S. to the letter of 30 July – which Rosén ignores – I find myself in agreement with Jägerskiöld's treatment of this issue (op. cit., pp. 343–8) though not with his interpretation of the problem of the King's answer via Kochen to the letters of 28 and 30 July.

55 These were successful enough to have impressed themselves on contemporaries: Löwen, *Mémoires*, p. 37, believed that if Charles XII had lived, Europe would have been astonished to see his and Tsar Peter's dogs 'hunt together'.

56 For Hessian fears of both a Russian and an English marriage for the Duke of Holstein-Gottorp see Jägerskiöld, *K.F.Å.* 1934, p. 120 and note 1.

57 Holst, *Fredrik I*, pp. 94–5. The Hartman thesis, in *Karl XII och hessarna* (1935), that the tension between 'Holsteiners' and 'Hessians' was a simulated one, fabricated by secret agreement between Charles XII and the Hessians to serve as camouflage for Swedish diplomacy, has been disproved by Holst and Jägerskiöld (op. cit., chapter IX).

58 Full details of the Russian terms in Feygina, op. cit., pp. 272 ff.; it is clear from her work that Görtz, playing both on the danger of peace with George I and on Charles's disinclination to any peace, softened Ostermann's attitude. Görtz's exaggerated and at times completely false reports of Russian offers bedevilled Swedish early research into the Åland congress. M. Poliyevktov, *Baltiyskiy vopros v russkoy politike posle Nishtadskogo mira* (St Petersburg, 1907) pp. 61 ff. and Hartman, *Ålandska kongressen*, III, 93 ff. were the first to stress the discrepancy between the Swedish and the Russian reports.

59 Note that Charles XII in orders to Görtz and Preis in 1717 made the freeing of Rehnskiöld one of the Swedish desiderata in negotiations with the Tsar: Jägerskiöld, op. cit., p. 133; see ibid., pp. 378–9, 398, 401–5, for the negotiations on the topic at Lövö, and Feygina, op. cit., pp. 270, 284, 287, 293.

60 This is clear from correspondence printed in H.M.C. *Stuart Papers*, VII, see, e.g. pp. 189 ff. Jerningham's letters of August 1718; Feygina, op. cit., p. 325, prints documents which show the Tsar's anxiety to keep the lines both to Charles and George I open.

61 ibid., pp. 314–27; Jägerskiöld, op. cit., pp. 462 ff.

62 Fabrice, *Memoiren*, p. 127: Bernstorff ordered him to send a courier to Sweden

to tell Charles XII that George I would not continue the negotiations 'as long as Herr von Goertz continued his Aland conferences'; for the Hanoverian–Swedish negotiations continuing through French channels see S.P. 78, vol. 162, letter of 8 Oct. 1718.

63 See Sörensson, III, *K.F.Å.* 1928, pp. 246–68.
64 For the anti-Russian plans from March 1718 see Mediger, op. cit., 402 ff. and Wittram, II, 406–7.
65 B. Lundeberg, *K.F.Å.* 1914, refers to D. G. Schomer's 1717 mission; for the Sobieski marriage offer see Th. Westrin, 'Det sista giftermåls anbudet till Karl XII', ibid., 1912, pp. 250–7; for the Spanish and Jacobite efforts see Jägerskiöld, op. cit., pp. 442 ff. and C. Nordmann, op. cit., pp. 84 ff., 160 ff. and 243 ff.

BOOK VII, CHAPTER 2: MILITARY PREPARATIONS AND PLANNING

1 Meijerfelt's letter of 6 Dec. 1716, quoting Charles's aim of 60,000 men, is cited in Lagermark, 'Rustningarna till Karl XII:s sista fälttåg', *H.T.* 1886, p. 213.
2 ibid., pp. 304 ff. has tables of all regiments; for exaggeration abroad see Jägerskiöld, op. cit., p. 283, note 4.
3 J. Häggman, 'Bidrag till den svenska krigsförvaltningents historia under det stora nordiska krigets senare skede', *K.F.Å.* 1922, pp. 179 ff. (with royal orders from Stralsund p. 193 and note 1): cp. Lagermark, *H.T.* 1886, pp. 277 ff.
4 Stanhope's letter to Leathes, 22 March 1717, cited from F. E. B. Holl., vol. 82 in Hatton, *Diplomatic Relations*, p. 154. For the clash which occurred on 17 July 1717 when four British men-of-war attacked and captured the Swedish frigate *Illerim* off Öland, see E. Holmberg, *K.F.Å.* 1915, pp. 19–20.
5 Olof Traung, *Lars Gatenhielm. Kaperiverksamheten under Karl XII:s tid 1710–1719* (1952), pp. 66 ff.; for the Dano-British operations see *Bidrag S.N.K.H.*, IX, pp. 65 ff. and Bergersen, *Tordenskjold*, II, pp. 744 ff.
6 Hatton, op. cit., p. 156.
7 ibid., pp. 173–5.
8 *Bidrag S.N.K.H.*, IX, 239 ff.
9 Petri, *K.F.Å.* 1937.
10 W. Holst, *Fredrik I*, p. 96.
11 See Häggman, *K.F.Å.* 1922, p. 173; cp. the same author's *Studier i Frihetstidens försvarspolitik* (1922), pp. 34 ff. for reversal of many of the innovations. For the division by order of 3 July 1717 of the navy into squadrons differentiated by blue, yellow and '*die Swedische bunte flagge*' see Traung, *Gatenhielm*, pp. 10 ff.
12 Ships were being reserved for the Anglo-French showdown with Philip V and Alberoni in the Mediterranean; this was one reason why Poniatowski found it difficult to obtain ships; for his mission and movements see B. Lundberg, *K.F.Å.* 1912, pp. 221 ff.
13 For the Franco-Russian treaty see Wittram II, 311 ff.
14 S. Kreuger, 'Bidrag till frågan om svenska armén under norska fälttåget 1718', *K.F.Å.* 1952, pp. 100–11, whose detailed researches have confirmed the results

of the sample investigation of A. Stille, 'Lefnadsaldern hos Karl xii:s sista här', *H.T.* 1901.

15 For the men see Charles's letter to Frederick of Hesse, Jan. (undated) 1717: *Bref*; for the horses see C.O.Nordensvan, 'Svenska armén åren 1709–1718', *K.F.Å.*, 1919, p. 233.

16 Feif's letter to Tessin of 3 Oct. 1717: *Brinkmanska archivet.*

17 Nordensvan, *K.F.Å.* 1919, pp. 227–8; cp. Petri, *Livgrenadjärregementets historia*, III, 454.

18 T.Schreeber von Schreeb, 'Kongl. Maij:tz Drabanter 1695–1718', *K.F.Å.* 1936, pp. 43 ff., has shown that previous assumptions (e.g. in Nordberg, II, 597–8) that the drabants were replaced by 'the Lifesquadron' is mistaken.

19 Nordberg, *Anmärckningar* (1754), pp. 50–1, based on what Feif told him.

20 L.Lilliehöök, 'Karl xii:s artilleri', *Artilleri-Tidskrift*, 1946, p. 343.

21 See article on C.Cronstedt by E.Naumann in *S.B.L.*

22 These are illustrated in O.Kuylenstierna, 'Det svenska artilleriet under Karl XII', *K.F.Å.* 1917; for earlier Swedish cannon-casting see, based on Swedish authorities, C.M.Cippola, *Guns and Sails* (London, 1965), pp. 52 ff.

23 For the artillery improvements and innovations of 1716–18 see Kuylenstierna, loc. cit., pp. 1–25; T.Jacobson, *Artilleriet under Karl XII:s tiden* (1943); L. Lilliehöök, 'Karl xii:s artilleri', *Artilleri-Tidskrift*, 1946, pp. 343 ff.; Petri's contribution to the Ahnlund *Festschrift.*

24 For further details see *Generalstaben*, IV, 944–56; Häggman, *K.F.Å.* 1922, pp. 182–205 and the same author's *Studier i Frihetstidens försvarspolitik*, pp. 27–119 where the reversal process throws much light on Charles xii's innovations.

25 *Bidrag S.N.K.H.*, IX, 283 ff., 374 ff.

26 G.Petri, reviewing the above volume in *H.T.* 1935, pp. 199–203.

27 For Folard's service with Charles xii see the biography by C.de Coynart, *Le Chevalier de Folard 1669–1752* (Paris, 1914), pp. 80 ff.

28 T.Söderlund, *Stockholms handverkare 1719–1721* (1943); pp. 24 ff.

29 S.Schartau, 'Om Sveriges inre tillstånd under Karl xii:s tid', in Bring, *Karl XII*, pp. 510–13 with, ibid., p. 558, illustration of a maximum price list.

30 For the magazines see Charles xii's letter to Frederick of 8 June 1716: *Bref* and Lagermark, *H.T.* 1886, pp. 278 ff.

31 Feif's letter to Tessin of 18 Feb. 1716: *Brinkmanska archivet.*

32 Z.Esberg's letter of 29 Oct. 1718 to Benzelius: *P.H.T.* 1926, 'Strödda politiska nyheter 1709–18 ur Erik Benzelius d.y:s brevvaxling', ed. S.Grauers.

33 Schartau, in Bring, *Karl XII*, p. 529; cp. A.Strindberg, *Bondenöd och Stormakts-dröm* (1937), pp. 305 ff. who concentrates on the peasant suffering during the war.

34 See, e.g. Charles's letter to Ulrika Eleonora of 12 Sept. 1714: *Bref*, p. 132.

35 P.Engdahl, *K.F.Å.* 1930, p. 246; cp. E.Naumann, 'Centralforvaltningen' (in Bring, *Karl XII*), pp. 559 ff.

36 For this so-called '6th coin', similar to that imposed in the Dutch Republic in 1672 – to be used to replenish the magazines – being much resented by the moneyed classes see N.Tengberg, *Om Frihetstiden* (1867), p. 31. For Charles's own motivation see *Bref*, p. 429 (order of 20 Nov. 1718).

37 See Browallius's diary, 25 Nov. 1735. For Stiernhöök maintaining that Görtz treated the Swedish diplomats 'as a Grand Vizier' see Jägerskiöld, op. cit., pp.

113–14; cp. Motraye, *Travels*, II, 340, though stressing that he himself had always found Görtz 'affable'. For Görtz's desire to get out of the galley, but 'with honour' see his letter to von Dernath of 10 Feb. 1718: Jägerskiöld, op. cit., p. 290.

38   G. Lindeberg, 'Några politiska visor mot Görtz', *K.F.Å.* 1936, pp. 205–315.

39   Feif's letter to Tessin of 11 Jan. 1716: *Brinkmanska archivet*; for P. J. Brenner and his later fate see article by E. Naumann in *S.B.L.*

40   L. Thanner, *Revolution i Sverige efter Karl XII:s död* (1953), pp. 48 ff.

41   Cited from Poyntz's letter of 1724 in C. G. Malmström, *Sveriges politiska historia från Karl XII:s död till statshvälfningen 1772*, I (1893), p. 27.

42   See Meijerfelt's letter to Charles XII (sent on 1 Nov.) printed by S. Jägerskiöld in *K.F.Å.* 1935, pp. 167–73.

43   Holst, *Fredrik I*, pp. 95–6.

44   ibid., pp. 90–1.

45   Holst, *Fredrik I*, pp. 92–3, prints both letters in Swedish translation.

46   C. K. S. Sprinchorn, 'Madagaskar och dess sjöröfvare i Karl XII:s historia', *K.F.Å.* 1921, pp. 241–79, analyses the economic and colonial motives for this support which continued after the death of Charles XII. T. Höjer, in *H.T.* 1937, pp. 57–62, has emphasized that in the whole correspondence only such motives are mentioned, while there is no sign of willingness to cooperate with Spain or the Jacobites.

47   For this promise given on 3 Feb. 1714 see Jefferyes's letter of 10 Feb. 1714, *H.H.* 16: 2, where the Swedish declaration is printed pp. 32 ff.

48   Fears of Swedish–Spanish collaboration is mirrored in the reports asked for and received from Paris in 1718, see, e.g. S.P. 78, vol. 162, letters from July onwards; the fullest treatment of Alberoni's negotiations with Swedes, Jacobites and Russians is in C. Nordmann, *La crise du nord au début du XVIIe siècle* (Paris, 1962), pp. 159 ff.

49   This suggestion has been made by A. Wattrang, 'Karl XII och försvaret av Finland', *K.F.Å.* 1954, pp. 124–5. For Bergen's position at this time see B. Lorentzen, *Bergen og Sjøfarten*, I (Bergen, 1959), 233–71.

50   Charles XII's letter to Frederick of Hesse of 9 Sept. 1718: *Bref*.

51   For the dispositions see G. Petri, 'Den svenska huvudarméns samling och immarsch i södra Norge 1718', in *Historiske Studier tillägnade Nils Ahnlund* (1949), pp. 215 ff.

52   Th. Westrin, 'Karl XII's sista planer', *H.T.* 1895, pp. 341–2, printing Schwerin's letter of 28 Nov. 1728. It is not an easy one to unravel since Schwerin recalls conversations both with Charles XII and with Rehnskiöld, and C.-F. Palmstierna, in *H.T.* 1939, p. 361, has assumed that the comment by Charles XII cited in the text was made to Rehnskiöld. S. Jägerskiöld, in *Sanning och Sägen om Karl XII:s död* (1941), p. 32 corrects a similar mistake of his own in respect of another conversation reported in the Schwerin letter.

53   This letter is printed with an introduction by P. Wieselgren in *Svio-Estonica* (Tartu, 1938), pp. 209 ff.

54   This letter is printed by Th. Westrin, 'Karl XII:s sista egenhändiga bref', *H.T.* 1895, pp. 340–1.

BOOK VII, CHAPTER 3: THE NORWEGIAN CAMPAIGN OF 1718

1 For this corps and its operations see G.Petri, *Armfelts Karoliner* (1919); *Bidrag S.N.K.H.* IX, 302 ff. and E.Hornborg, *Karolinen Armfelt* (1952); A. Wattrang, 'Karl xⅡ och försvaret av Finland', *K.F.Å.* 1954, pp. 121–6.

2 See, e.g. Reuterholm's journal, *H.H.* 36: 2, 751; cp. E.Bergman, 'Karl XII och Halvord Bryngelsson' *K.F.Å.* 1916, pp. 181 f.

3 Schultz's memoirs, *K.F.Å.* 1948, p. 98.

4 *Bidrag S.N.K.H.*, IX, 180 ff.

5 For the campaign in general see G.Petri, 'Den svenska huvudarméns samling och inmarsch i södra Norge, *Studier tillägnade Nils Ahnlund* (1949), pp. 215–37; J.A.Lagermark, 'Karl xⅡ:s sista fälttåg', *H.T.* 1897 and 1898; H.O.Wahl 'Felttogene 1716 og 1718', *Norsk Militær Tidsskrift* (Christiania, 1903); *Bidrag S.N.K.H.* IX, 230 ff. and G.Petri's review of this volume in *H.T.* 1935, pp. 199 ff.; P.G.Bergrén, 'Karl XII's galärtransport från Strömstad till Idefjorden och striderna därstädes år 1718', *K.F.Å.* 1920, pp. 153–95; L.Lilliehöök, 'Karl XII:s artilleri', *Artilleri-Tidskrift*, 1946, pp. 357 ff.

6 Frederikshald Magistrate's Journal 11 Nov. (N.S.) 1718, printed in *Samlinger til det norske Folks Sprog og Historia*, I (Christiania, 1835), 188.

7 For criticism see *Bidrag S.N.K.H.*, IX, 332–6; for the newer views see Petri, loc. cit.

8 Maigret's letter to Görtz, cited by Lagermark, *H.T.* 1898, p. 227.

9 Charles xⅡ's letter to Frederick of Hesse of 9 Sept. 1718: *Bref.*

10 Lagermark, *H.T.* 1897, p. 286.

11 Stenflycht's 'relation' (of 1728), printed, in Norwegian translation, from German by J.Wahl in *Norsk Militær Tidsskrift* 1902, pp. 391–406; the original in R.A. has an additional paragraph for 30 November published (in Swedish translation) by N.Ahnlund in *Sanning och Sägen om Karl XII:s död* (1941), p. 38.

12 Rhyzelius's memoirs, pp. 96 ff.

13 G.W.Marcks von Württemberg's report of 1728 printed in *K.K.D.* XII, 422–5.

14 E.g. *Bidrag S.N.K.H.* IX, 297; Hornborg's biography of Armfelt and Petri's history of the campaign cited in note 1 above.

15 Rehnskiöld's and Mörner's letter of 1 Dec. 1718, printed in *Norske Samlinger* II, ed. C.A.Lange (Christiania, 1860), 561 ff.

16 The authority for the papers being burnt is Carlberg (*K.F.Å.* 1920, p. 223); the rest is from Nordberg's manuscript additions to his own copy of Charles xⅡ's history now in Västerås Gymnasii och Stiftsbibliotek, either published by C. Hallendorf, *Studier öfver den äldre Karl XII:s historiografien* (1899) pp. 50 ff.; or unpublished (the story of the farewell remark) but cited by C.F.Palmstierna, *H.T.* 1939, p. 315.

17 A.Nyström, *Karl XII och sammansvärjningen mot hans envälde och lif* (1900); N.Ahnlund, *Sanning och Sägen* (1941), p. 86 thinks it likely that the papers were from Görtz.

18 The latest historian to suggest that Charles sought death is C.F.Palmstierna in *Carl XII:s död* (1940) p. 91.

19 Bielke, *Remarques*, printed with *Mémoires*, pp. 81 ff., gives 'every week' a new uniform.

20 Søren Hagerup's report, reprinted by Villius, *Ögonvittnen*, pp. 181–2; cp
    Refsum, *K.F.Å.* 1930, p. 124.
21 See Djurberg, *K.F.Å.* 1913, p. 96, quoting Neumann's report: *H.H.* 24, p. 191
    cp. Stenflycht's relation printed by N.Ahnlund in *Sanning och Sägen* (1941,
    p. 38.
22 For Landsberg's diary and reports see C.Paludan-Müller, 'Er Carl den Tolyte
    falden ved Snigmord', *Nyt Historisk Tidsskrift*, I (Copenhagen, 1846), cp
    Ahnlund, *Sanning och Sägen*, pp. 45–6.
23 For the location of this hut see Bring, *K.F.Å.* 1928, p. 162, note 1; cp. Hult-
    man's memoirs, *Handlingar* (Floderus), I, 126.
24 Magistrate's Journal for 6 and 8 Dec. (N.S.) 1718: *Samlinger*, pp. 190–1.
25 See the so-called anonymous relation (later identified as by Kaulbars) printed
    in *K.F.Å.* 1920, pp. 253–5.
26 [Maigret's] comment is in Motraye, *Travels*, II, 380; with name in *Remarques*
    (1732) p. 51; Landsberg's diary is quoted by Paludan-Müller; cp. the evidence
    of the officer Huusman to Coxe's Swiss translator Mallet in 1755 that the fort-
    ress could not have held out for long against 'the terrible fire' of the Swedish
    artillery: Coxe, *Voyage en Pologne, Russie, Suède, Dannemarck etc.*, III, 200,
    footnote by translator.
27 Motraye had this phrase from officers present in the trench: *Travels*, II, 341.
28 *Bidrag S.N.K.H.*, IX, 374 ff.
29 See S.Jägerskiöld, *Sverige och Europa 1716–1718*, pp. 87 ff., 127 ff., 267 ff.
30 See P.Sörensson, in Bring, *Karl XII*, pp. 452 ff.; S.Jägerskiöld, op. cit., pp. 210
    ff., 381 ff.
31 G.Petri, *H.T.* 1935, p. 202; S.Jägerskiöld, op. cit., p. 285 ff. Cp. the invention of
    a 'trolley' to wheel cannon ashore: A.Scholander, 'En säregen landstignings-
    kanon', *K.F.Å.* 1950, pp. 104–10.
32 *Bidrag S.N.K.H.*, IX, 400 ff.; cp. J.F.Chance, *George I and the Northern War*
    (1909), pp. 303 ff. for Danish hopes of cooperation with George I for 1719.
33 For his arrival see introduction to his journal of 1702–6 by A.Quennerstedt
    in *K.K.D.* XI.
34 See Schwerin's report of 1728 printed by Westrin in *H.T.* 1895, pp. 341–2, as
    also for the following information about Charles's plans.
35 Westrin, citing Hogguer's memoirs of conversations with Görtz; *H.T.* 1898.
36 ibid.; cp. Jägerskiöld, op. cit., pp. 280 ff.
37 Schwerin's report, *H.T.* 1895, p. 342.

BOOK VII, CHAPTER 4: THE KING'S DEATH: MURDER OR AN 'HONEST ENEMY BULLET'?

1   Nordberg's handwritten notes on the 'King's last day' entered in his own copy
    of his Charles XII's biography (see note 16 to chapter 3) are among those
    published by Hallendorf, *Studier*, p. 50; the Stenflycht manuscript printed by
    N.Ahnlund in *Sanning och Sägen om Karl XII:s död*, p. 38, gives important
    eyewitness information.
2   His development can be traced by a comparison of early letters to his governor,
    Horn (printed in G.Horn's biography of 1852), and those he penned to his
    aunt in his teens (cited or quoted in Holst, *Ulrika Eleonora*, p. 109 ff.). Per-

mission for him to be declared of age had been sought and granted from the Emperor early in 1718: Sörensson III, *K.F.Å.* 1929, p. 258.

3   Liewen's report of 3rd and 6th conversation: *Handlingar* (Floderus), III, 329 and 342.

4   See, e.g. Campredon's letters of 18 July 1716 and Jan. 1719: *Handlingar* (Malmström).

5   I am indebted to Dr S. Landahl for information about research in progress.

6   The '*Håll*' is in Nordberg's notes.

7   Maigret's letter to Gedda of 23 Dec. 1723: *K.F.Å.* 1920, p. 206.

8   Rhyzelius's memoirs, p. 96 for 25 Nov. 1718; for the conversation related by J. L. von Salza see C.-F. Palmstierna, *H.T.* 1939, p. 375. Comments by N. Ahnlund on the three versions of the Salza anecdote are in *Sanning och Sägen*.

9   For the 'Confession' see N. Ahnlund, 'Anklagelserna mot Karl Cronstedt', *Sanning och Sägen*, pp. 151–64.

10 For the Sicre illness and confession see N. Ahnlund 'Sicres bekännelse', ibid., pp. 119 ff.; for Voltaire's contacts with Fabrice see H. Brulin, 'Handskriftsmaterial till Voltaires Charles XII', *K.F.Å.* 1940, pp. 16–17 and the unpublished 1961 thesis (London) of J. D. Felix, *A Study of Voltaire's Historie de Charles XII with special reference to the author's sources and conception of history.* For Fabrice's confession see W. Coxe, *Travels* (4th ed. 1792), II, 95: he had the story from the 'celebrated botanist Miller', but at second hand.

11 Frederikshald magistrate's journal of 8 Dec. (N.S.) 1718: *Samlingar*, II.

12 C. Paludan-Müller, loc. cit., pp. 110–13.

13 T. Frødlich, *Fjon eller Masfjorden i Hordaland Fylke* (Kristiania, 1924), p. 68.

14 W. Coxe, *Travels through Poland, Russia, Sweden, Jutland, Norway, Livonia, Courland etc.* (4th ed. London, 1792, with new material based on journeys in 1784 and 1785), V, 25–7.

15 For the historiography of the shot from the 'right' see N. Ahnlund, 'Den äldste litteraturen', *Sanning och Sägen*, pp. 63–76. It is worth noting that Motraye (1723–32) who was in Sweden 1716 to 1721 and spoke to many of the officers present on 30 November stresses a shot from the left, while Voltaire (1731 and later editions) maintained a shot from the right, as did Nordberg (1740).

16 For the growth of the tradition that Charles drew his sword see N. Ahnlund 'Villospår', *Sanning och Sägen* pp. 173–9; cp. S. Bring, *K.F.Å.* 1918, p. 159 and note 4 for the statue by Zhendre depicting the dying King drawing his sword half-way out of the scabbard. Neumann's vivid description of his dream of 14 April 1720 is affixed to his 'report on his services as Charles XII's surgeon' published in *H.H.* 4, pp. 188–91; see Djurberg, *K.F.Å.* 1913, pp. 118–19 for this manuscript not being discovered till 1959.

17 See in particular L. Weibull, 'Carl XII:s död', *Scandia*, 1929, pp. 229–74; S. Bolin, 'Kring Carl XII:s död', ibid., 1930, pp. 151–84; A. Sandklef, C.-F. Palmstierna, N. Strömbom and S. Clason, *Carl XII:s död* (1940). Cp. S. Dahlquist, 'Till belysning av frågan om Karl XII:s död', *K.F.Å.* 1930, pp. 133–46, based on Schering Rosenhane's anti-Hessian comments.

18 Holst, *Fredrik I*, p. 100.

19 L. Thanner, *Revolutionen i Sverige efter Karl XII:s död* (1953), pp. 72–3.

20 C.-F. Palmstierna, *Carl XII:s död*, pp. 79 ff. in section 'Mordryktarne', and

the same author's 'Mordryktarne kring Frederikshald', *H.T.* 1939, pp. 360–418.

21 A. Sandklef in *Carl XII:s död* (1940), pp. 203–82; Ahnlund in *Sanning och Sägen om Karl XII:s död* (1941) pp. 181–234.

22 For the folk-legends on the button theory see N. Ahnlund, 'Folktraditionen', *Sanning och Sägen*, pp. 184–95; ibid., pp. 196–213 'Öxnevalla-sagner', where p. 196, the confession is cited.

23 See S. Clason 'Banesårets vittnesbörd om kulan' in A. Sandklef *et al.*, *Carl XII:s död* (where the *kulknapp* theory is supported also by Sandklef and Strömbom from non-medical evidence).

24 G. Hultkvist, 'Kulknappen', *Sanning och Sägen*, pp. 253–9; cp. ibid., pp. 261–6 (B. Göthberg Edlund's contribution) and pp. 225–31 (N. Ahnlund's contribution) for criticism of the Sandklef deductions in the *kulknapp* issue.

25 Folk-legends cited by N. Ahnlund, *Sanning och Sägen*, p. 190–2; P. H. Mallet, 'Voyage en Norvège' as appendix to W. Coxe, *Noveau voyage en Dannemarck, Suède, Russie, Pologne*, IV (Geneve, 1791), 189.

26 Landsberg's diary for 14 Dec. 1718 (N.S.) printed by C. Paludan-Müller, loc. cit.

27 Nordberg, 'Passages'.

28 Carlberg's report: *K.F.Å.* 1920, pp. 224–5.

29 Hultman's memoirs: *Handlingar* (Floderus), I, pp. 126–7.

30 The best edition (by S. E. Bring) of Carlberg's report (from a manuscript in Kungl. Biblioteket) is in *K.F.Å.* 1920, pp. 222–37; for earlier partial or complete editions see ibid., pp. 213–21; for the composition of the report see Djurberg's article, ibid., 1913, pp. 96–7.

31 Maigret's letter to N. P. Gedda of 23 Dec. 1723 (the original of which is in R. A., Düben collection), is printed by S. E. Bring in *K.F.Å.* 1920, pp. 204–6.

32 First printed by J. A. Lagermark (from the original in Uppsala University Library, Nordin collection) in *H.T.* 1898, pp, 259–60; also available in the edition by S. E. Bring, *K.F.Å.* 1920, pp. 253–5, with, ibid., pp. 238–52, reviews of earlier identification and attempts of his own. For the first tentative identification of Kaulbars as the author see O. Kuylenstierna, *Kring Karl XII:s död* (1912), pp. 259–60; for the definitive one see N. Ahnlund, 'Ögonvittnen', *Sanning och Sägen*, pp. 79–85.

33 See Kaulbars's report: *K.F.Å.* 1920, pp. 224–5 for the position the King adopted and ibid., pp. 225–6, Carlberg's report of the height of the footholds.

34 ibid., pp. 226–7, Carlberg's report.

35 ibid., p. 205, Maigret's letter.

36 ibid., p. 255, Kaulbars's report.

37 ibid., p. 205, Maigret's letter.

38 ibid., p. 230, Carlberg's report; ibid., p. 255, Kaulbars's report.

39 See S. E. Bring, 'Karl XII:s likfärd och begrafning', *K.F.Å.* 1918, pp. 170–275; cp. ibid., 1913, pp. 95–104, Djurberg's article on Neumann.

40 S. Stenström, 'Karl XII:s dödsmask och Simon Josse', *Livrustkammaren* 1967, pp. 107–46; for the 1723 rumours see S. E. Bring, 'Bidrag till frågan om Karl XII: död', *K.F.Å.* 1920, pp. 202 ff.

41 Neumann's report: *H.H.* 4, p. 190.

42 Thanner, op. cit., pp. 63–5, doubts whether the Duke did so; but even in the official report of the council of war, printed by Thanner in *H.H.* 36: 1 (1956),

pp. 10–12, Charles Frederick's stronger emphasis on continuing the late King's campaign is noticeable.

For Frederick's actions and Görtz's arrest see Holst, *Fredrik I*, pp. 102–3; cp. the letters of Frederick of Hesse (to his wife and father) printed in *H.H.* 36: 1. This letter, in R. A. Görtz collection (undated) of Dec. 1718, was presumably written after his arrest, see J. S. Jägerskiöld, *Sverige och Europa 1716–1718*, p. 455. H. Lindeberg, *Görtz. Et offer för enväldet* (1925), p. 68; for Dernath in 1718–19 see G. Lindeberg, 'Greve von Dernath och hans "ostensible" Brev', *K.F.Å.* 1934, pp. 71–101; cp. Jägerskiöld, op. cit., p. 479, for the Holsteiners' realization that their position would become critical if Charles XII died.

C. Paludan-Müller, loc. cit. passim.

S. Jagerskiöld, 'Det hessiska partiet', *Sanning och Sägen*, and the same author's 'Mordskott av misstag?', *Svenska Dagbladet* 1/9, 1953, referring to the letter from Ranck to Frederick of 4 Nov. 1718 which went by courier from Stockholm to Norway.

See Holst, *Ulrika Eleonora*, pp. 158 ff., and the letter from M. Riben of 10 Dec. 1718 cited by Bring, *K.F.Å.* 1918, pp. 182–3. Note, Holst, p. 64, an expression in Ulrika's letter to her husband of 10 Dec. 1718 which is strangely reminiscent of Charles XII in 1709: she finds it difficult to write her late brother's name because of the 'tender hurt I feel when that name is mentioned'.

S. Jagerskiöld, *Sanning och Sägen*, pp. 23–5.

G. Hultkvist, 'Karl XII:s skottskada', *Sanning och Sägen*, pp. 237–52; cp. the same author's 'Skottet vid Frederikshald', *Svensk Tidskrift* 1937. For criticism of the ballistic conclusions of N. Strömbom in *Carl XII:s död*, 283 ff.: Th. Jacobsson, 'Kritisk granskning etc.' in *K.F.Å.* 1941, pp. 148–98 with, ibid., pp. 199–217, T. Schreber von Schreeb, 'Några vapenhistoriska reflexioner'.

H. Seitz stresses this in *Dagens Nyheter* 31/8, 1951, pointing to the mistaken argument of T. Holmquist, 'Dödskottet år 1718. Reflexioner kring skottritt- ningen', *K.F.Å.* 1950, pp. 111–46, and in particular pp. 142–3.

Carlberg's report: *K.F.Å.* 1920; Landsberg's report: Paludan–Müller.

The best topographical examinations are by F. Backer, 'Karl XII:s dödssted', *K.F.Å.* 1936, pp. 219–94 and ibid., 1939, pp. 15–41, C. Bruusgaard, 'Under- søkelser og funn 1936–1937 vedrørende Carl XII:s løpegraver og dødssted ved Frederiksten'; cp. ibid., 1942, pp. 210–31, E. Zeeh, 'Kartmaterialet och frågan om det svenska löpgravssystemet samt Carl XII dödsplats'; and, ibid., 1944, pp. 161–210, T. Holmquist, 'Löpgravarna vid Frederiksten', in which the Backer-Bruusgaard results are upheld against N. Strömbom in *Carl XII:s död* (1940).

See Ahnlund, 'Rapporter och brev från December 1718', *Sanning och Sägen*, pp. 41 ff.; and the letters from Frederick of Hesse and Ulrika Eleonora to the Landgrave of Hesse printed by L. Thanner in *H.H.* 37: 2 (1961).

Axel von Fersen, *Historiska skrifter*, I (1867 ed. by R. M. Klinckowström), 6 ff.; cp. N. Ahnlund, 'Den nyaste tesen och källmaterialet', *Sanning och Sägen*, p. 103.

E. Hornborg, *Finlands hävder*, III, 144, note 1 makes the telling point that since the officers present recorded the sound of the entry of the projectile it could not have come from close by: in that case the sound of the shot would have drowned the sound of the entry.

w

57   Voltaire's report of conversation with Sicre: *Histoire de Charles XII* (173
      p. 169, with a fuller version in the 1748 ed.

EPILOGUE

1   W.Holst, *Fredrik I* (1953), pp. 103–11; L.Thanner, *Revolutionen i Sveri*
     efter Karl XII's död (1953), pp. 20 ff.; R.M.Hatton, *New Cambridge Mode*
     History, VII (1957), pp. 350 ff.

2   This money has sometimes been thought to imply the buying of 'connivan
     in the Hesse murder of Charles XII' and the fact that Cronstedt received fi
     times the amount of the other officers of his rank has been held as specifica
     significant; in reality, as Samuel Åkerhielm testified, Cronstedt was particula
     rewarded because Charles XII had promised him a gratification for his magi
     ficent work with the artillery: see N. Ahnlund, *Sanning och Sägen om Karl XI.*
     död, p. 152.

3   A typical expression of dislike for the 'miserable' Norwegian campaign
     Lieutenant-General Z. Francs's memoirs, printed by H. Brulin in *K.F.*
     1927, pp. 70–1; for the illness of many of the soldiers whose first campaign
     was see G.Petri, *Livgrenadjärregimentets historia*, III, 471–2.

4   For his share in these peace-makings see H.Grönroos, 'England, Sverige o
     Ryssland 1719–1721' (Finnish) *H.T.* 1931; B.Sallnäs, *Samuel Åkerhielm a*
     (1947) and W.Holst, *Ulrika Eleonora* (1956), pp. 196 ff.; B.Lundberg, *K.F.*
     1914, pp. 238 ff.

5   The English need for such advantages, long desired and sought, is explicab
     by the unfavourable trade balance with Sweden: for Sweden's exports betwe
     1691 and 1715 being much larger than her imports (even when genero
     allowance for smuggling is made) see O.Bjurling, *Sweden's Foreign Tra*
     and Shipping around the year 1700 (1961); cp. J.M.Price 'Multilateralis
     and/or Bilateralism', *The Economic History Review*, 1961, for figures of th
     English deficit in trade with Sweden 1697–1700.

6   For details of the peace-making see J.Rosén, *Svensk Historia*, I (1962), 610 f
     and Chance, op. cit., pp. 340 ff.

7   The preliminary peace treaty between Prussia and Sweden was signed on
     July 1719, the final treaty on 21 Jan. 1720. Prussia paid 2 million *riksdaler* f
     the part of Pomerania (which included the islands of Usedom and Wolli
     ceded.

8   The peace between Sweden and Denmark–Norway was signed on 3 July 172
     after an armistice for six months from October 1719: apart from the claus
     mentioned in the text it stipulated a payment of 600,000 *riksdaler* to Denmar
     and Sweden's loss of freedom from the payment of Sound dues. The Slesw
     guarantees by Great Britain and France were signed on 23 July and 20 Oc
     1720 respectively.

9   See W.Holst, *Fredrik I* (1953), pp. 126–30; R.M.Hatton, *New Cambridg*
     Modern History, VII, 351 ff.; L.Thanner op. cit., pp. 144 ff. and the sam
     author's article 'De franska gratifikationerna före tronskiftet 1720', *H.*
     1956, pp. 162–70, for the negotiations by which Ulrika Eleonora laid down th

crown on 24 March 1720 and Frederick became King. His coronation took place on 2 May 1720.

10 E. Carlsson, *Freden i Nystad* I (1932 – no further vol. has appeared), who carried his investigation from May to August 1720 emphasized the Hesse 'dynastic' theme strongly; cp. the same author's 'Frederik I och den hessiska successionen', *H.T.* 1949; for a different point of view see O. Reinius, 'Sveriges utrikespolitiska lage 1720–1721', *K.F.Å.* 1936 and discussions between E. Carlsson and O. Reinius in *H.T.* 1937.

11 For this see J. Rosén, *Den svenska utrikespolitikens historia*, II: 1 (1952), pp. 174 ff.; D. Gerhard, *England und der Aufstieg Russlands* (Munich, 1933) pp. 7 ff.; Nikiforov, op. cit., pp. 166 ff. and Feygina, op. cit., p. 461 ff.; Mediger, op. cit., chapter 8, 'Englische und Hannovershe Ostpolitik 1719–1721', pp. 416–57; M. Braubach, *Prinz Eugen von Savoyen*, IV, 38 ff.

12 Rosén, op. cit., pp. 161–74, has rightly pointed to the element of pressure in Hanoverian and English policy and shown that the older authorities (Chance, Michael, Ballantyne's biography of Carteret and B. Williams's biography of Stanhope) have overemphasized the British commitment in the vital year 1719–20: the uncertainty he points to in respect of Admiral Norris's instructions may be cleared up by research at present in progress by D. D. Aldridge of the University of Newcastle-on-Tyne. The article by H. Seitz, 'Den stora förödelsen år 1719 och striden vid Södra Stäket,' *K.F.Å.* 1960, pp. 149–75, illustrates the problems of Sweden's defence against Russia. Cp. G. Petri, *Försvaret mot öster 1719*, nr. 26 of 'Meddelanden från Föreningen för Stockholm fasta försvar', 1922.

13 Wittram II, 435 ff. has demonstrated how active Peter was in improving his relations with Vienna and how significant was the defection of Prussia.

14 The most recent examination of the South Sea Bubble is by P. G. M. Dickson, *The financial revolution in England* (London, 1967), pp. 90–156; see also J. Sperling, *The South Sea Company* (Boston, Mass., 1962); for the Mississippi bubble in France see H. Lüthy, *La Banque Protestante en France*, I (Paris, 1959), ch. 3.

15 For the consequences of this see – apart from the article of Reinius mentioned above – N. G. Hildeman's 'Ryssarnas härjningar i Gästrikland och Hälsingland år 1721', *K.F.Å.* 1950, pp. 147–216; H. Wrangel, *Kriget i Östersjöen 1719–1721* (1906–7); cp. Wittram, II, 437 ff.

16 For the Suedo-Russian negotiations and the peace of Nystad see C. G. Malmström, *Sveriges politiska historia från konung Karl XII:s död till statshvälfningen 1772*, I (1893), 304 ff.; S. Grauers, 'Till belysningen av Nystad-fredens verkningar', *Historiska Studier tillägnade Sven Tunberg* (1942), pp. 359–70; Rosén, op. cit., pp. 181–6. Wittram, II, 458–62. Peace with Poland was not made till 1731: see H. Ahnlund, 'Sveriges sista fred med Polen', *K.F.Å.* 1915, pp. 269 ff., though a preliminary convention with Augustus had been drafted on Jan. 1719. The Swedes continued to support Stanislaus financially since his estates in Poland had been confiscated.

17 See the historiographical studies by K. G. Hildebrand 'Till Karl XII – uppfattningens historie', in *H.T.* 1954 and 1955; G. Jacobson, 'Carl XII i gotisk historieskrivning', *K.F.Å.* 1941, pp. 120–47; ibid., 1956, pp. 187–244, E. Olsoni, 'Karl XII-gestalten genom tiderna'.

w*

18 See R.M.Hatton, 'Palmerston and Scandinavian Union', *Studies in International History* (ed. A.K.Bourne and D.C.Watt, London, 1967), p. 139, for the political context of this meeting.

19 The pose of the statue commissioned from J.P.Molin in 1866 was based on that by N.Byström made (with companion statues of other Swedish kings of the name of Charles) for Charles XIV's private collection: the gesture may in both cases be traced back to a portrait of Charles by Wedekind which shows him with a hand raised and a finger pointing to Norway, but this is a post-humous portrait. For the fate of the Zhedre statue see S.Bring *K.F.Å.* 1918, p. 159, note 4.

20 For Southey's dream of 16 Aug. 1808, see H.G.Wright, 'Some English writers and Charles XII', *Studia Neophilologia* XV (Uppsala, 1942–3), 128.

21 See the discussions between G.Jonassen and G.Rystad in *H.T.*, e.g. G. Rystad's review of G.Jonasson's book on Charles XII and his advisers in *H.T.* 1961, pp. 445 ff.; ibid., 1962, G.Jonasson, 'Några Omstridde spörsmål från Karl XII:s första regeringsår'; ibid., 1963, pp. 59–68. G.Rystad, 'Karolinska spörsmål' and pp. 69–71, G.Jonasson, 'Genmäle'. In their controversy, while appreciating Jonasson's work on the 'march-tickets' (see text, p. 161), I find myself in sympathy with Rystad's criticism of Jonasson's stark dichotomy between Charles XII (all bad) and his advisers (all good).

22 Such assumptions are, in my opinion, made too readily by Tarle, Nikiforov and Feygina.

23 H.Hantsch has, however, in a significant sentence in *Reichsvizekanzler Friedrich Karl Graf von Schönborn* (Augsburg, 1929), p. 208 called the Great Northern War *'ein später Sprosse'* of the Thirty Years War.

24 P.Sörensson, 'De karolinska krigsfångarnas hemfärd från Ryssland', *K.F.Å.* 1923, pp. 120–200.

25 E.Holmberg, 'Vår flottas fallne och fångna karoliner', *K.F.Å.* 1915, pp. 38–9.

26 E.F.Heckscher, *Sveriges ekonomiska historia*, I: 2, pp. 406–13.

27 The results of S.Schartau in Bring, *Karl XII* (1918), pp. 499 ff. have been supported by some later local investigations but challenged, in part, by G. Olander, *Studier över det inre tillståndet i Sverige under senare delen av Karl XII:s regering med särskild hänsyn till Skaraborgs län* (1946). J.Rosén, *Svensk Historia*, I, 703 ff. summarizes the research done, though in his conclusion he tends to ignore that farms were left derelict for purposes of tax evasion.

28 T.Söderlund, *Stockholms handverkare 1719–1721* (1943), pp. 24 ff.

29 The work of the women is illuminated where their letters to husbands serving abroad have been preserved; one can tell much even from the husband's letters as, e.g. those from Creutz to his wife printed in *K.F.Å.* 1911. Cp. A. Åberg, *Skånska slott och deras herrar* (1960): section on Margareta Barnekov (born Ascheberg) who as a widow completed the recruitment and remained responsible for a dragoon regiment set up by her late husband.

30 Olander, op. cit., pp. 155 ff. with instances which are reminiscent, though in the field of taxation and coinage, of the local disobedience in France uncovered by E.Asher, *The Resistance to the Maritime Classes* (Berkeley and Los Angeles 1960).

31 G.Petri, *Livgrenadjärregementets historia*, III, 458.

32 Thanner, op. cit., pp. 32 ff.

33 See, e.g. Browallius's diary of 22 Jan. 1736 for Reuterholm's opinion.
34 Charles Frederick's letter to the Council of 1 Dec. 1718 is printed in *Norske Samlinger* (ed. Lange II, 1860), 560; cp. his letter to Ulrika Eleonora of the same date in Holst, *Ulrika Eleonora*, pp. 156–7.
35 Rehnskiöld's and Mörner's letter of 1 Dec. 1718 in *Norske Samlinger*, II, 561–2.
36 The phrase a 'sluted levnad', i.e. a life ended at a time when there was no possibility of change or hope, was coined by Geijer; the most typical example of this view in our day is by Munthe, *Karl XII och den ryska sjömakten*, III, 790 ff.
37 Rhyzelius's memoirs, pp. 3, 5, 10, 16, for the division; W. Holst, 'Gustav III:s of Carl G. Tessins Karl XII', *Ord och Bild*, 1937, pp. 510–13 for the elder Tessin's comment.
38 Löwen, *Mémoires*, pp. 38–9.
39 J. Rosenadler, *Personalier vid Karl XII:s begravning* (1721). It may be worth noting that he was the uncle (his name before ennoblement in May 1719 was Upmarck) to whom the student Alstrin wrote the letters from Saxony cited in text, pp. 3, 217–19; for the task given him and the persons he consulted see S. E. Bring, 'Johan Rosenadlers personalier vid Karl XII:s begravning', *K.F.Å.* 1956, pp. 109–20. For the sermon by the Archbishop of Uppsala and for the funeral arrangements (by Tessin) see S. E. Bring, ibid.; and R. Josephson, *Tessin*, I, 199 ff.; for an eyewitness account see 'Ur Eric von Roland litteräre kvarlatenskap', ed. S. Tunberg, *K.F.Å.* 1917, pp. 232 ff.
40 For Cederhielm's remark see his journal of 1705: *K.F.Å.* 1960, p. 136; for Motraye's observation: *Remarques*, (1732), p. 32; for the 1718 negotiations Sörensson, III, *K.F.Å.* 1928, pp. 268 ff.
41 For Frederick II's opinion of Charles XII see his 'Réflexions sur les talents militaires et sur le caractère roi de Suède', in *Œuvres de Frederic le Grand*, VII, (Berlin, 1847), 66–8; cp. R. Nürnberger 'Friedrichs des Grossen Reflexions sur Charles XII' in *Spiegel der Geschichte. Festgabe für Max Braubach* (Münich, 1964), pp. 590–601, edd. K. Repson and S. Skalweit.
42 Maurice de Saxe, *Reveries* (English translation, 1757), pp. 97 ff.
43 I consulted E. Porfiriev's book of 1952 in a Swedish MS. translation in Krigsarkivet, Stockholm; it has since been translated under the title *Peter I, grundläggaren av den ryska arméns och flottans krigskonst* (1957); for S. Hedengren's summary of the article by A. Kotchekov on Peter's tactical and organizational innovations during the war see *K.F.Å.* 1953, pp. 214–24.
44 Bennedich was the editor of the *Generalstaben* volumes; for A. Stille's contribution see P. Sörensson, 'Arthur Stille', *K.F.Å.* 1922, pp. 20–3. For justified criticism of the difference postulated between linear tactics and the Caroline ones see F. Wernstedt's article in *K.F.Å.* 1957, pp. 153–64. For two brief, but valuable, studies of Charles XII as a commander see G. Petri's article, ibid., 1937 and O. Ribbing's article in *Historielärarnes Årskrift* 1945. J. O. Hannula 'La conduite de la Guerre pendant La Grande Guerre du Nord', *Revue Internationale d'Histoire Militaire*, 1939, pp. 26–32, is accessible but of little value.
45 The latest study by Åmark, *Sveriges statsfinanser*, takes issue with the Heckscher thesis of the 'indelingsverk' as a deplorable return to an inflexible primitive economy.

46   For Folard's place among the military writers of the eighteenth century see
      R.S.Quimby, *The background of Napoleonic Warfare* (Columbia Studies in
      Social Sciences, 1957), pp. 16 ff.; for the French during the War of the Spanish
      Succession being inferior to the Allies in the use of *armes blanches* see Löwen,
      Mémoires, p. 68.

47   For Schönström's comment see his memoirs, p. 451; for Posse's letter see *H.T.*
      1882, pp. 166–7; for the comment of the Danish officer (who had served with
      Löwen in the War of the Spanish Succession) and fought the Swedes in the
      post-1709 years see Löwen, *Mémoires*, p. 66.

48   See C.de Folard, *Histoire de Polybe ... avec un commentaire ou un corps de
      science militaire*, III, 61 for the comment; for Folard's naval armaments plans
      see Coynart, *Le Chevalier de Folard 1669–1752*, p. 195; for Folard's corres-
      pondence with Görtz ibid., pp. 180 ff.

49   For his plan for the dedication see his *Nouvelles Decouvertes sur la Guerre*
      (Paris, 1726), p. 83; the quotation in the text is from *Histoire de Polybe etc.*
      (6 vols., Paris, 1727), V, 484.

50   The quotation from ibid., V. pp. 155 ff.; the comment on the river crossings in
      III, ch. VII.

51   ibid., V, 418. A similar thought, but expressed more generally, in Löwen,
      Mémoires, p. 17.

Index*

* The Swedish ä, ö, å (at the end of the alphabet of that country) have been listed, for the convenience of the English reader, as if they were a and o; the Danish and Norwegian ø has been listed as if it were o, the Polish ł as if it were l, and the Russian soft sign t' has been listed as if it were t.